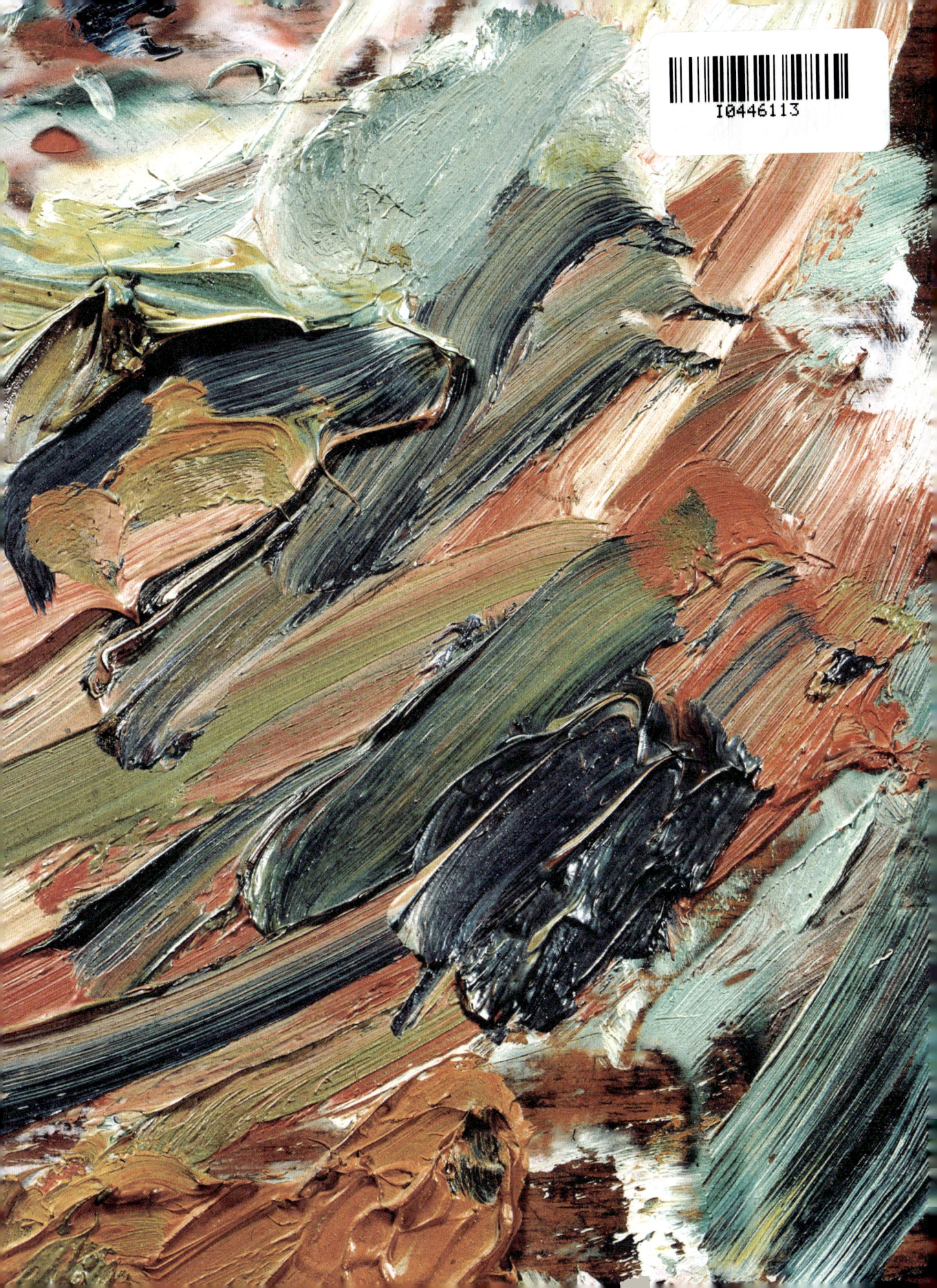

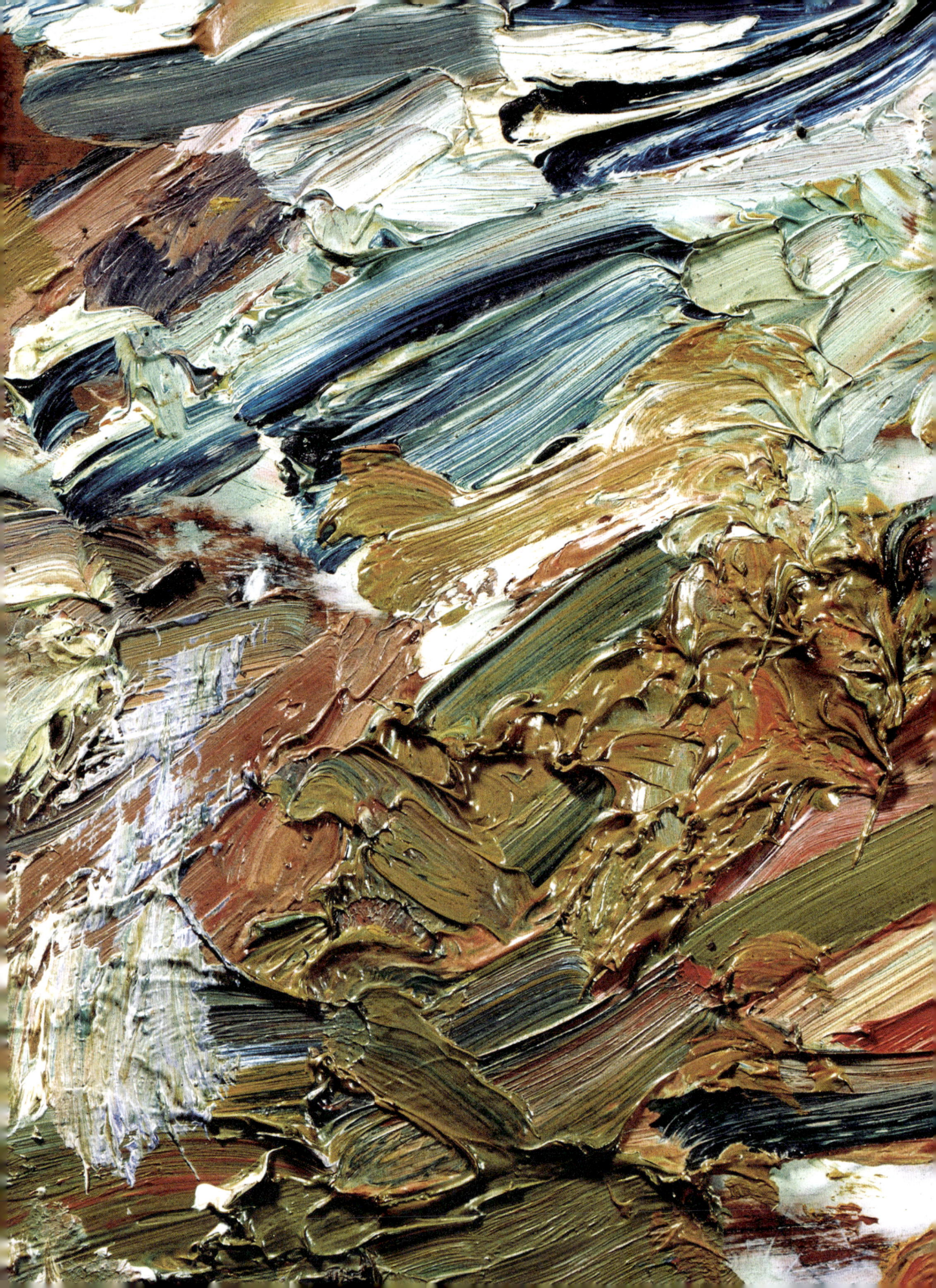

THE ARTIST'S PALETTE

Plate. I.

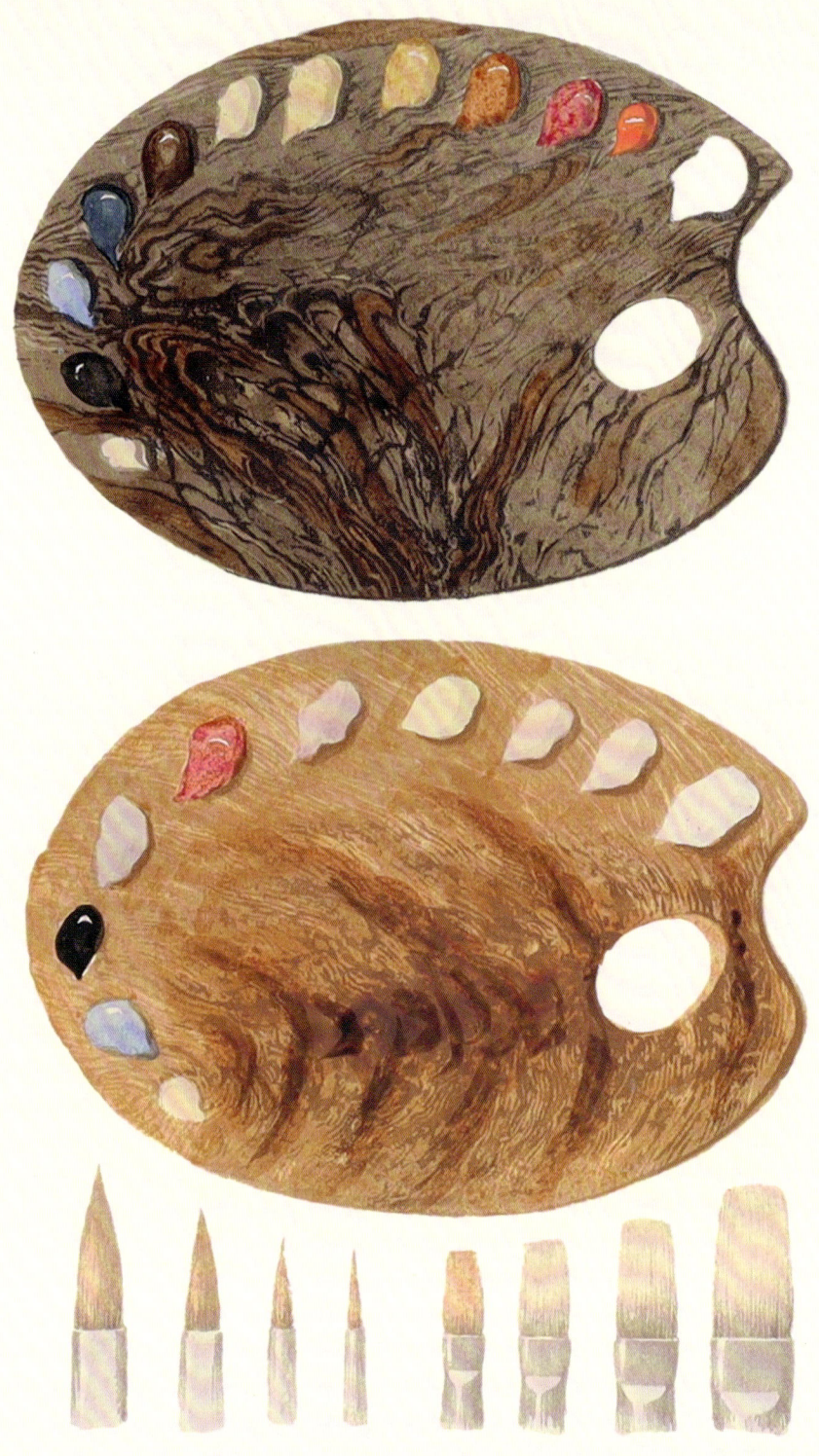

ALEXANDRA LOSKE

THE ARTIST'S PALETTE

The palettes behind the paintings of 50 great artists

Princeton University Press

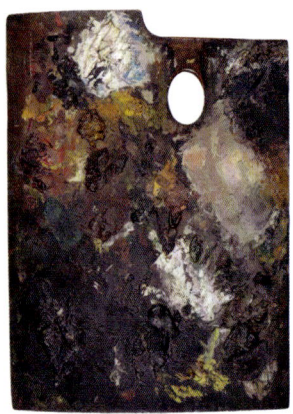

GUSTAVE COURBET
1819–1877

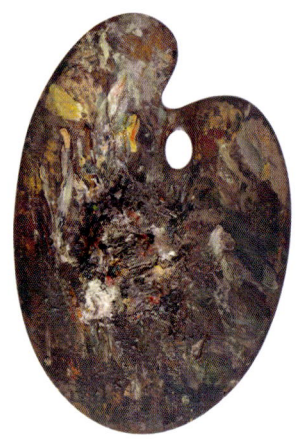

JAMES ABBOTT McNEILL WHISTLER
1834–1903

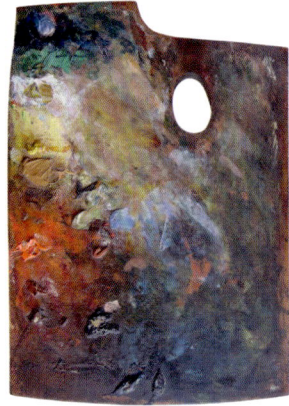

ROSA BONHEUR
1822–1899

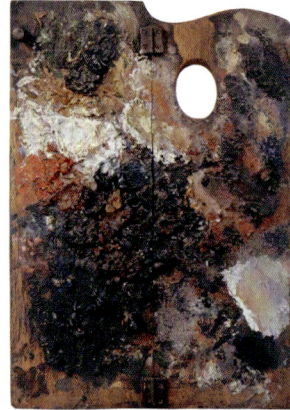

PAUL CÉZANNE
1839–1906

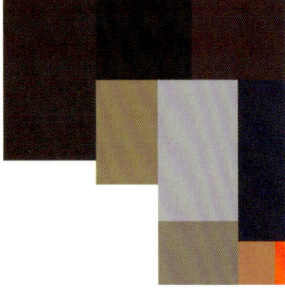

Le Désespéré (The Desperate Man),
1843–45

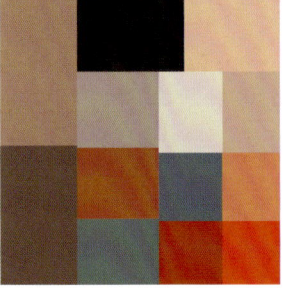

The Princess from the Land of Porcelain
1863–65

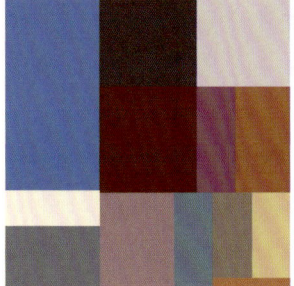

The Wounded Eagle
c. 1870

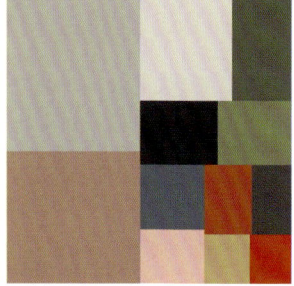

A Modern Olympia
1873–74

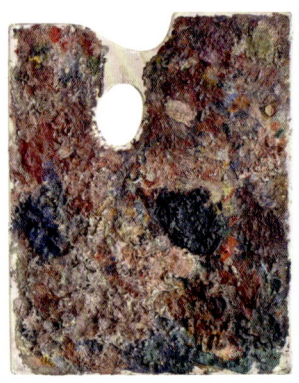

JAMES ENSOR
1860–1949

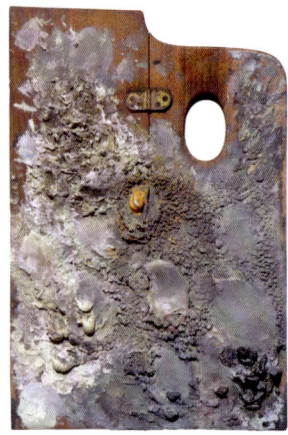

VILHELM HAMMERSHØI
1864–1916

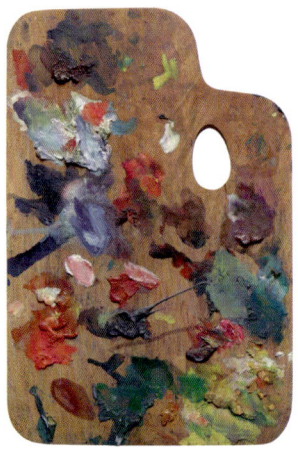

EDVARD MUNCH
1863–1944

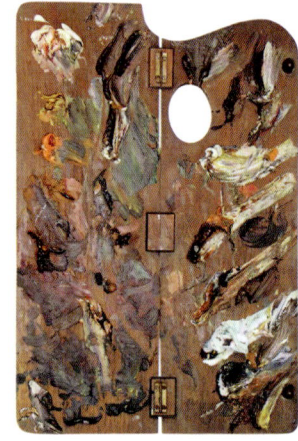

PAULA MODERSOHN-BECKER
1876–1907

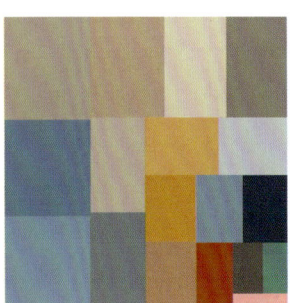

The Skeleton Painter
1896

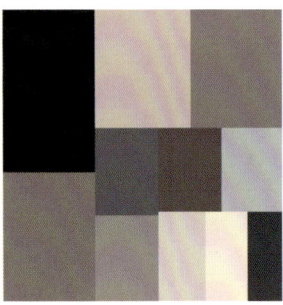

Interior from Strandgade 30
1900

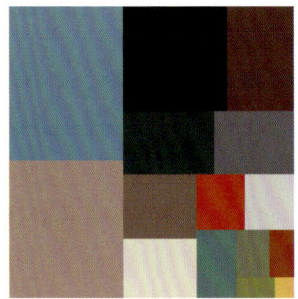

The Girls on the Bridge
1901

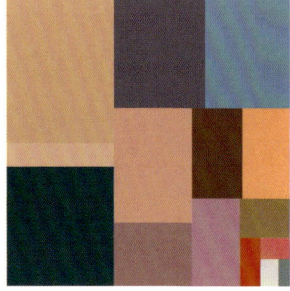

*Self-portrait as a Half-length Nude
with Amber Necklace I*, 1906

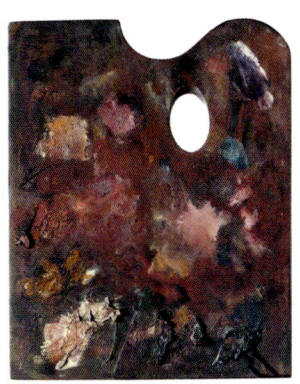

EDGAR DEGAS
1834–1917

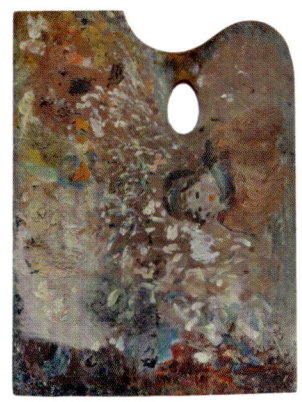

BERTHE MORISOT
1841–1895

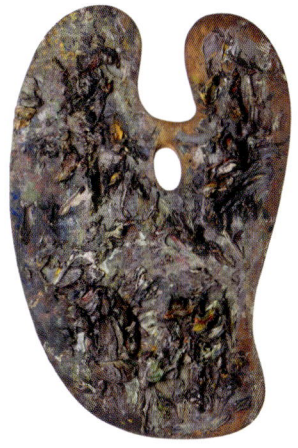

JOHN SINGER SARGENT
1856–1925

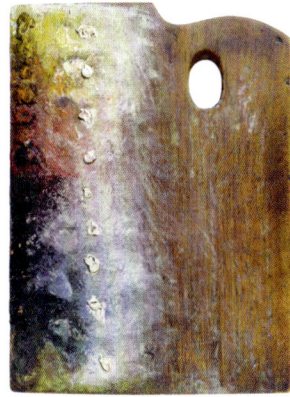

GEORGES SEURAT
1859–1891

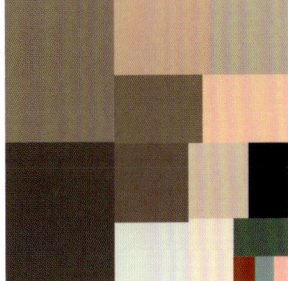

The Rehearsal
c. 1873–78

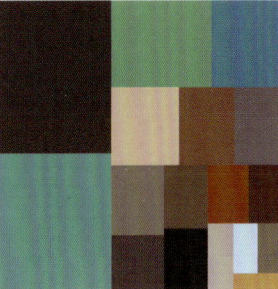

Child Among Hollyhocks
1881

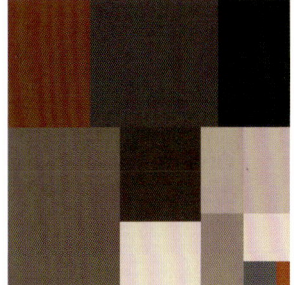

*Madame X (Madame Pierre
Gautreau)*, 1883–84

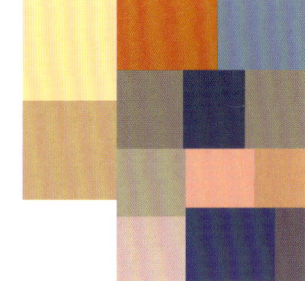

The Circus
1891

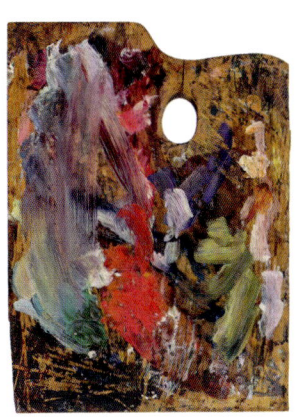

EGON SCHIELE
1890–1918

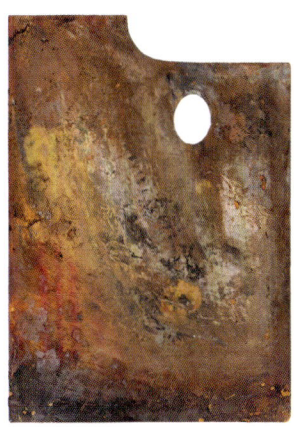

EDWARD HOPPER
1882–1967

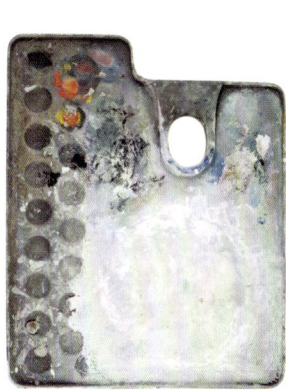

PIET MONDRIAN
1872–1944

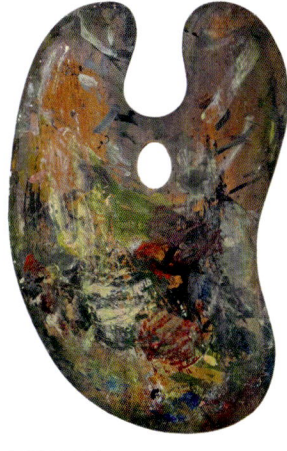

PAULA REGO
1935–2022

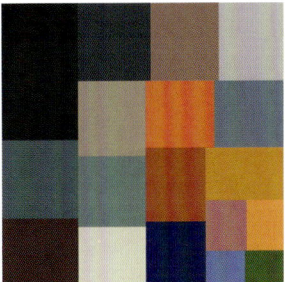

*Edge of Town (Krumau Town
Crescent III)*, 1918

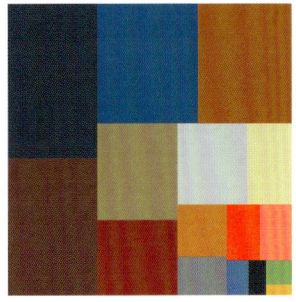

Chop Suey
1929

*Composition with Yellow, Blue
and Red*, 1937–42

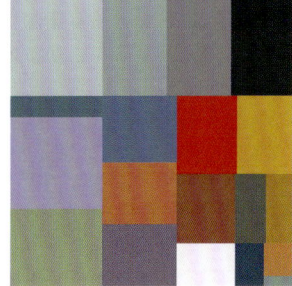

The Artist in Her Studio
1993

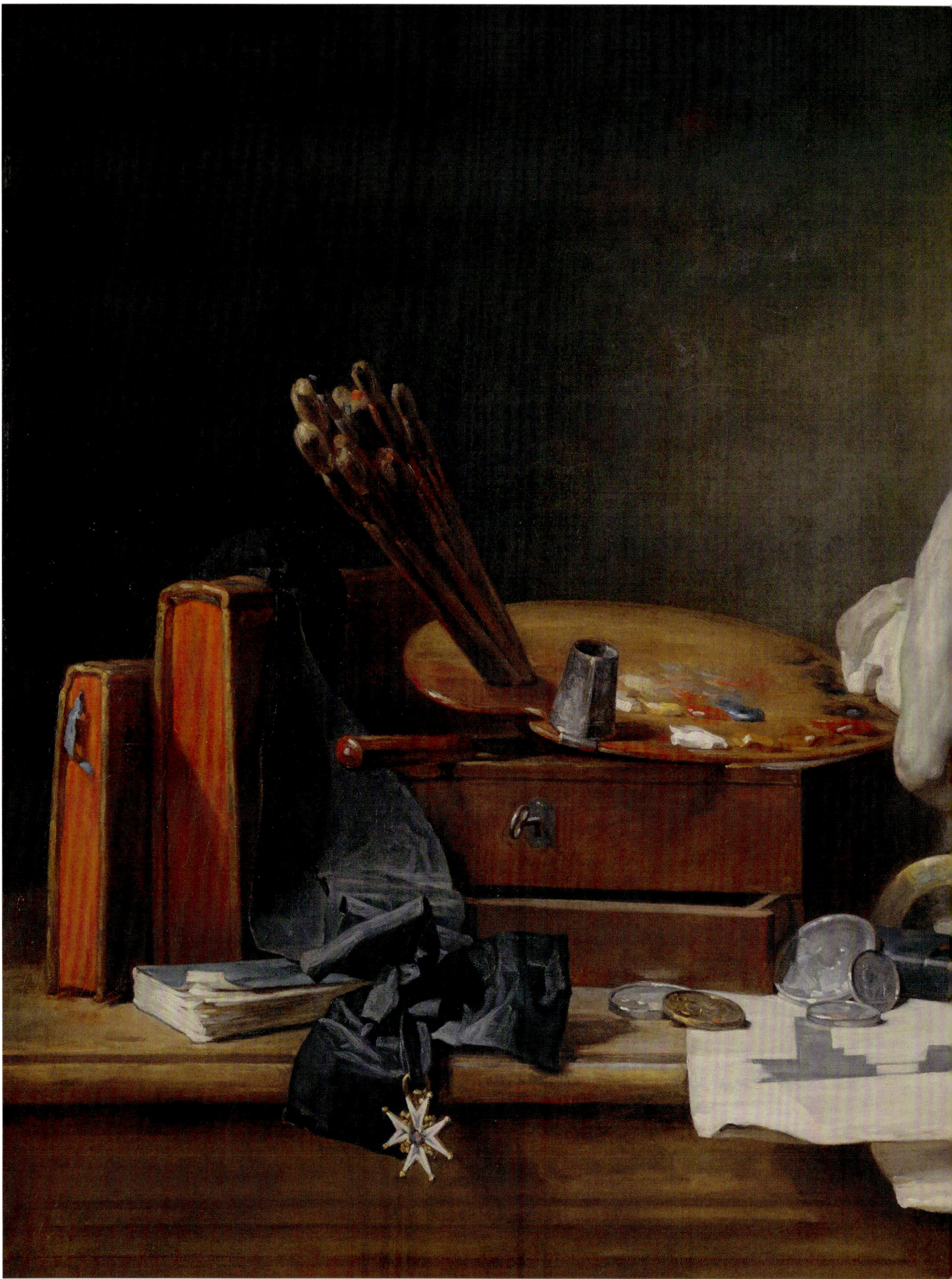

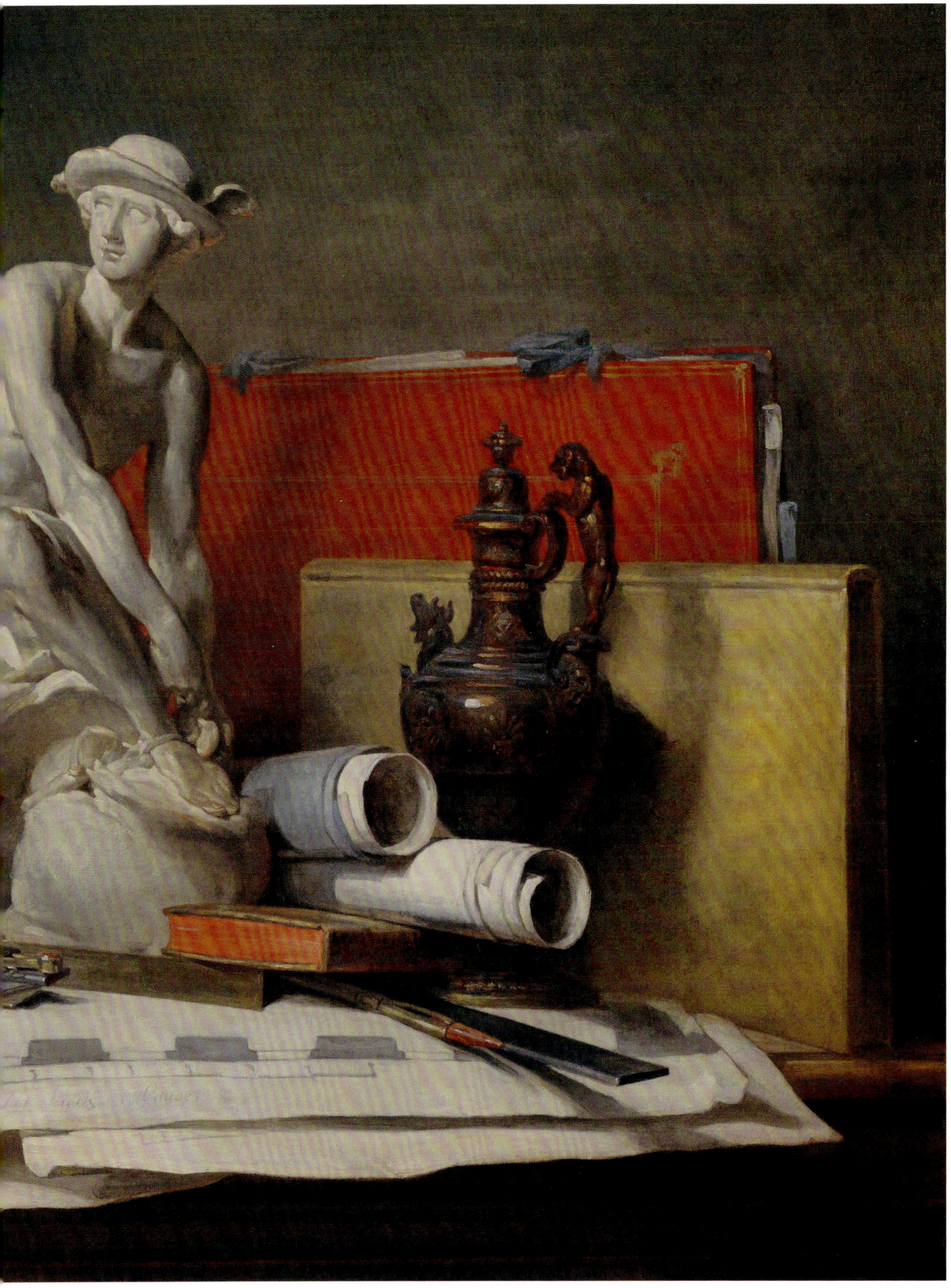

CONTENTS

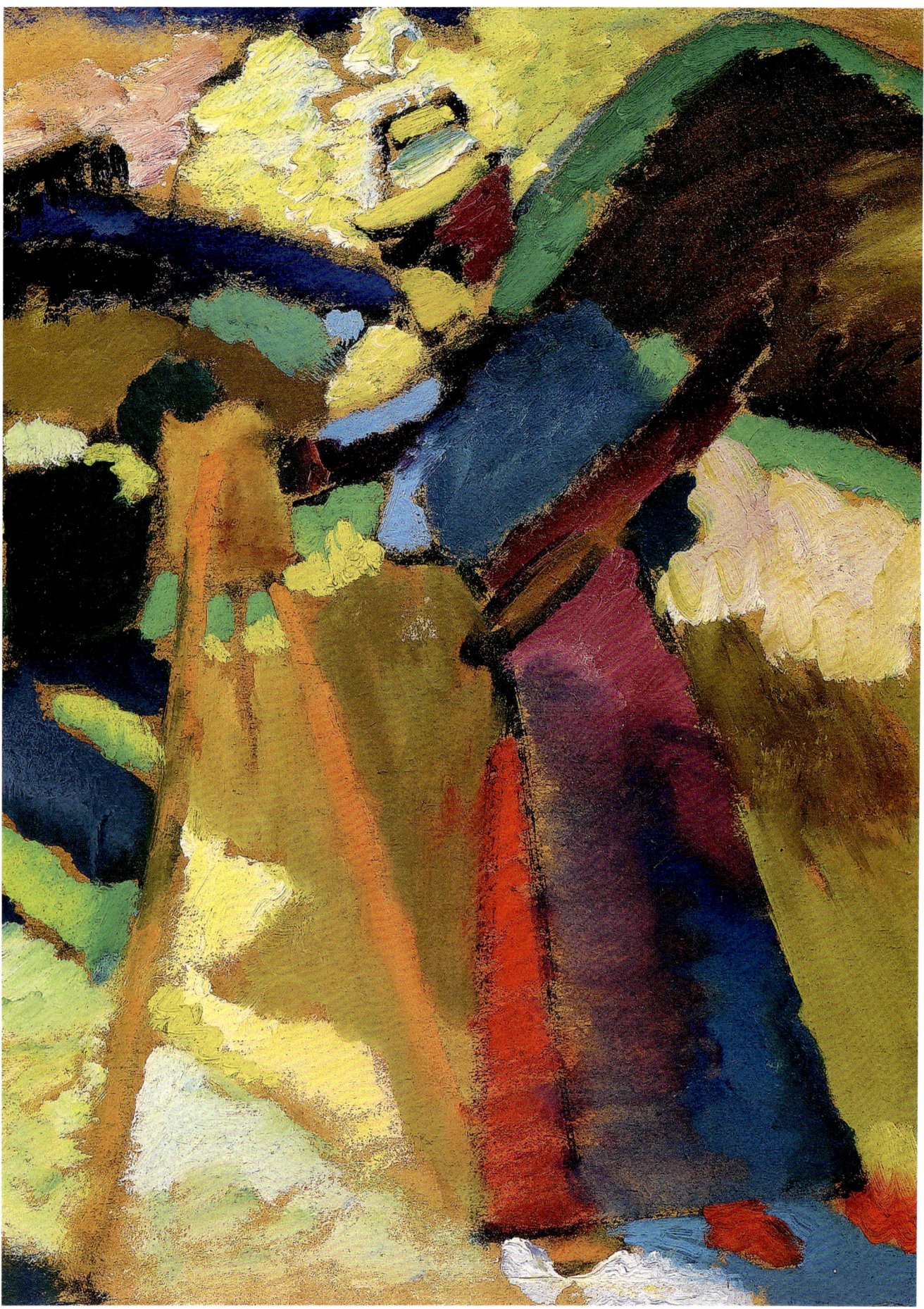

INTRODUCTION

'A drop of water is large enough to contain the image of the sun, why then would a palette not be able to give a notion of our school of painting?'

ANONYMOUS, *ALGEMEEN HANDELSBLAD*, 10 MARCH 1893

In his groundbreaking modernist manifesto *Concerning the Spiritual in Art* (1911) Wassily Kandinsky (see pages 164–69) begins the chapter on painting with a discussion about the effects of colour on the viewer. He suggests imagining looking at an artist's palette: 'When the eye wanders over a palette laid out with colours, two main results occur: 1) a *purely physical effect*, i.e., the eye is enchanted by the beauty and other aspects of colour. The viewer experiences a feeling of satisfaction, pleasure, like a gourmet tasting something delicious.' Kandinsky continues with this synaesthetic analogy of colour and taste, and elaborates on the temperature of colours, their sharpness, brightness and even their volume, all of which he considers superficial and transient. But, he argues, there is a second consequence of looking at the palette: at a higher, spiritual level there is the 'psychological effect of colour. It is at this point that the psychological power of colour becomes apparent and causes a vibration of the soul. This first, elementary physical power creates the path through which colour reaches the soul.'[1]

Kandinsky elevates colour as an expressive rather than imitative tool, drawing on avant-garde artists before him and paving the way for non-representational art of the 20th century. Yet his choice of an artist's palette as an example is significant: it is a fitting symbol of the painter's art, easily imaginable, familiar in shape and concept, and one that links the past with the present. For Kandinsky, there was another reason to choose a palette in his argument. It is perhaps the most neutral starting point, a simple tool and plain surface that can carry both ideas and concepts about art, as well as being a physical platform for material colour. A palette is both a timeless blank canvas and the ultimate abstract work of art: it speaks in colours and traces of movement, and thus triggers emotions, thoughts, associations. Kandinsky's argument would not have worked quite so well had he used a specific painting as an example.

THE POTENT STORYTELLING TOOL

This book is about that deceptively simple but potent tool, the artist's palette. The fifty palettes (and variations or reinterpretations of them) collated here tell stories, pose questions, hide secrets and are often reflections of the life and times of the artist who once held, prepared and used them. Many of these stories are evocative and moving, creating the path to the soul that Kandinsky described. The palette left behind in Paula Modersohn-Becker's studio (see page 148) at a turning point in her artistic career – on the brink of recognition and success as she brimmed with inspiration and ideas – is a painful reminder of what might have been and how her style would have developed. She was never able to pick up this palette again, as she died shortly after giving birth to her daughter, leaving her studio filled with new and unfinished work. A palette left behind by Vincent van Gogh (see page 102), uncleaned, with thick layers of paint left on it, allows us to imagine him painting quickly and feverishly for his client, with his mixture of conviction and anxiety, his brush marks visible, perhaps even a fingerprint left behind in the smeared paint. We can almost see his hands squeezing more paint out of those tubes of manufactured paint that his brother supplied for him.

Palettes are tactile objects. Even though we cannot touch them when they are represented as photographic reproductions, on a screen or displayed in a museum cabinet, we instinctively

Gabriele Münter Painting Outdoors in Front of an Easel (detail)
Wassily Kandinsky
1910
Oil on board
32.5 × 44.5 cm
(12 ¾ × 17 ½ in.)

associate them with the artist's hands and the greater context of the studio. An artist's palette can be an indicator of their preferences, practices and choices of pigments, binders and thinners, some of which can be verified through scientific analysis. Yet, perhaps more importantly, simply by looking at a palette with traces of paint we can become witnesses to an artist's rhythm of brushstrokes, their frantic or precise blending, their studio practice, their inventiveness and sheer individuality. We see signs of palettes being scraped, wiped, made or even broken by the artist. Pablo Picasso (see page 202) cut one out of cardboard when he needed it quickly, but he did so with typical verve, his creative vigour apparent even in this most disposable of tools.

Even the subtler signs left by an artist can be moving and visceral: on several of the palettes included here we can see shadows of the artist's thumb or fingers in the patina of empty areas near thumbholes and edges. More than any other painting tool or material, the palette links the body and hands of the artist with the art itself. It is the most intimate and personal of tools, and perhaps the closest we will ever come to connecting with a long-dead artist. This connection between body, mind, art and viewer is emphasized further by the organic shape of many traditional palettes – a heart- or kidney-shaped smooth object – held by an artist. It may well serve as a visual analogy or symbol of the body, and has been used as a motif to that effect in many self-portraits. For example, in William Hogarth's from *c.* 1757–58, the oval-shaped palette does not tell us much about his ideas on colour and beauty – the paint blots are simplified and without nuance – but as a compositional element, it is not only the focal point of the painting, it also forms a direct visual and symbolic link between the artist's body, heart, hands and the canvas. Similar examples can be seen in the self-portraits of Artemisia Gentileschi (see page 30), Paul Cézanne (see page 89) or James Ensor (see page 132), where palettes follow, continue or fit into the outlines of the artist's body. By contrast, Hogarth's diagram of an orderly set palette in one of the engraved plates of *Analysis of Beauty* (1753) is all about attitudes to colours, tonality, taste and mixing, and by extension 18th-century aesthetics and techniques.

THE DUAL MEANING OF THE PALETTE

The artist's palette has two different meanings: the literal and the figurative. They cannot always be separated, as the stories of the palettes in this book aim to show, but it makes them fascinating objects of observation and study. The literal palette is the object itself, the smooth portable tablet that holds an artist's paint and therefore has to meet certain material requirements, depending on the medium with which it is used. The figurative meaning of a palette is the personal arrangement of colours that a painter uses; the planned, organized or intuitively chosen chromatic layout that often precedes the artwork. We can frequently see this type of palette on a palette, but it may also be purely conceptual and in the mind, or seen and analysed in the finished artwork. A palette can therefore be both an object and an idea, both tactile and conceptual, physical as well as spiritual.

This book looks at both meanings but considers artists' palettes as objects of accidental or constructed beauty first – as symbols of an artist's style, their character, their time, and often as messengers or storytellers. Sometimes these stories can only be told through the painted image of a palette and how it is incorporated into a composition. Where physical palettes do not survive or have not yet been identified, as is the case with some of the greatest artists included here, for example Artemisia (see pages 30–33) and Rembrandt (see pages 34–37), the palettes seen in their self-portraits, allegories or images of studios provide a different but equally fascinating angle on what the palette meant to them, both physically and symbolically.

A. Iaia (or Laia) painting a self-portrait, from Giovanni Boccaccio's *De mulieribus claris*, fol. 101v., 1402–3

B. Thamyris (or Timarete) painting, from Giovanni Boccaccio's *De mulieribus claris*, fol. 86r., 1402–3

C. Eirene (or Irene) painting, from Giovanni Boccaccio's *De mulieribus claris*, fol. 92r., 1402–3

D. Iaia (or Laia) painting a self-portrait, from Giovanni Boccaccio's *De mulieribus claris*, fol. 100v., 1402–3

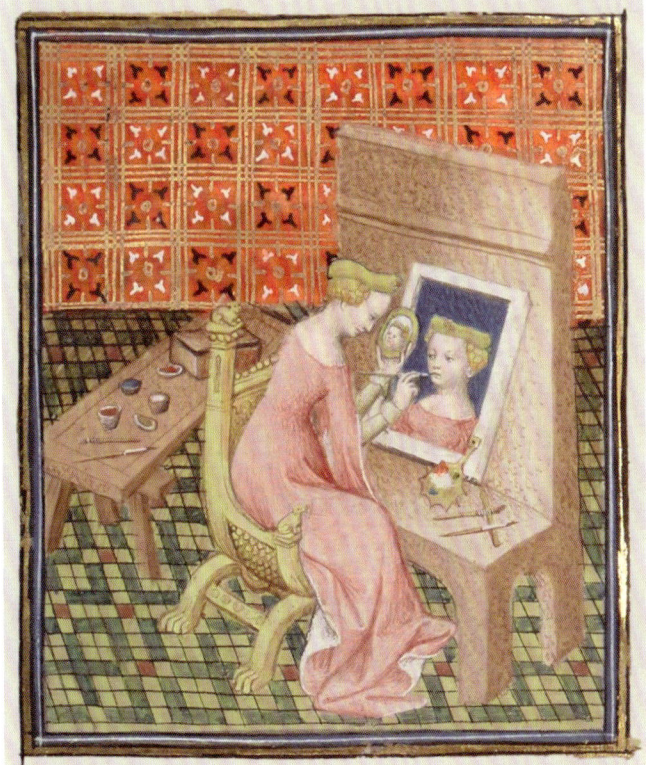

A.

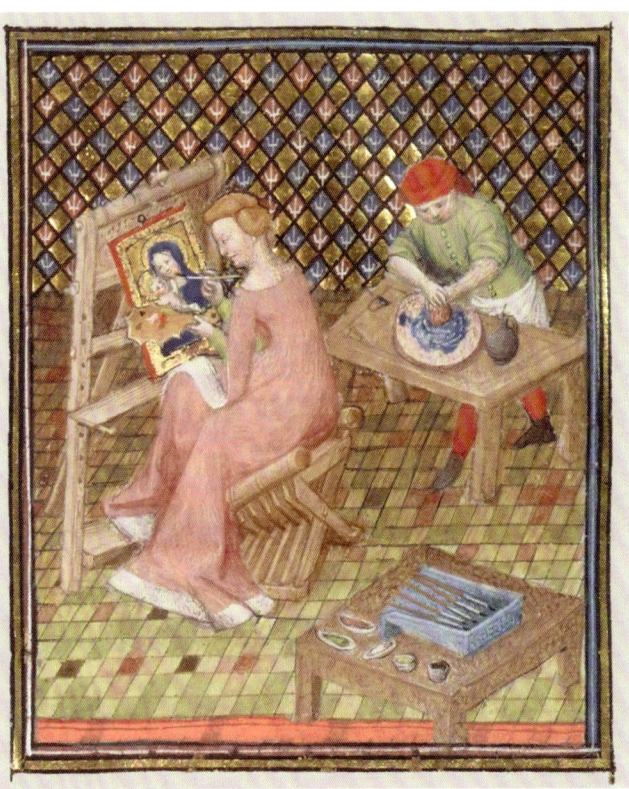

B.

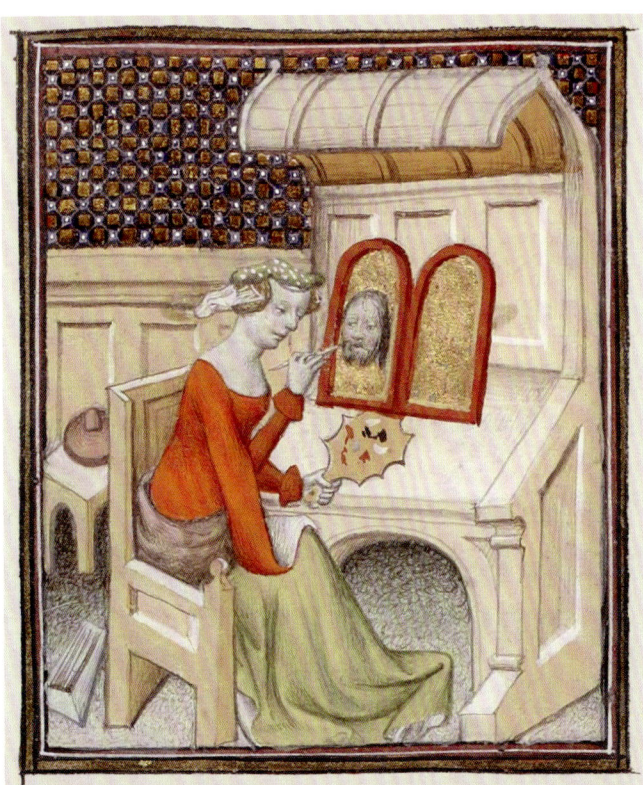

C.

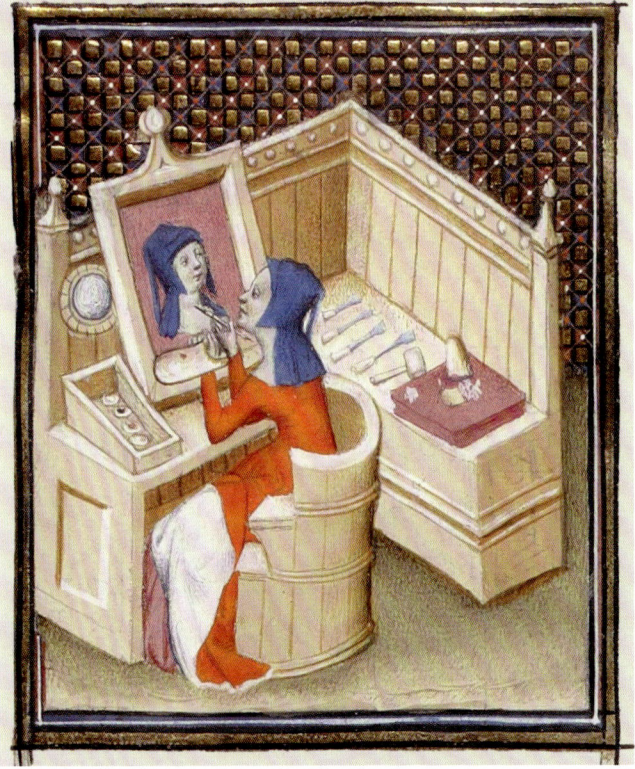

D.

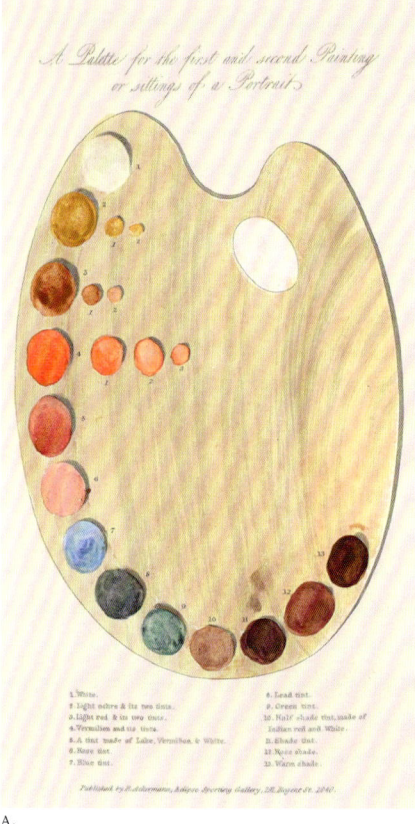

A.

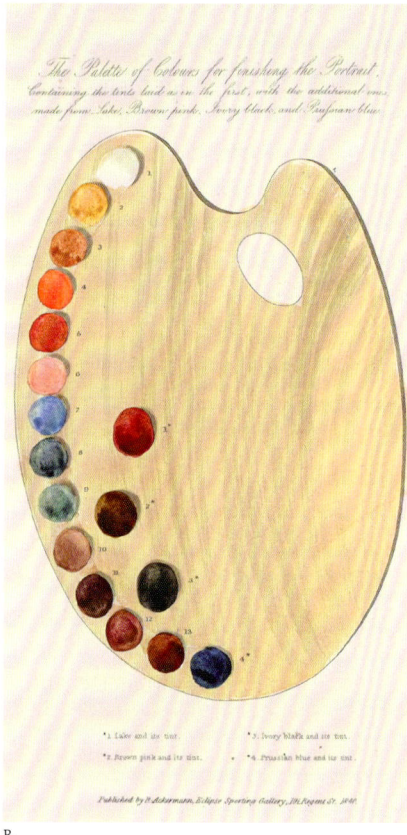

B.

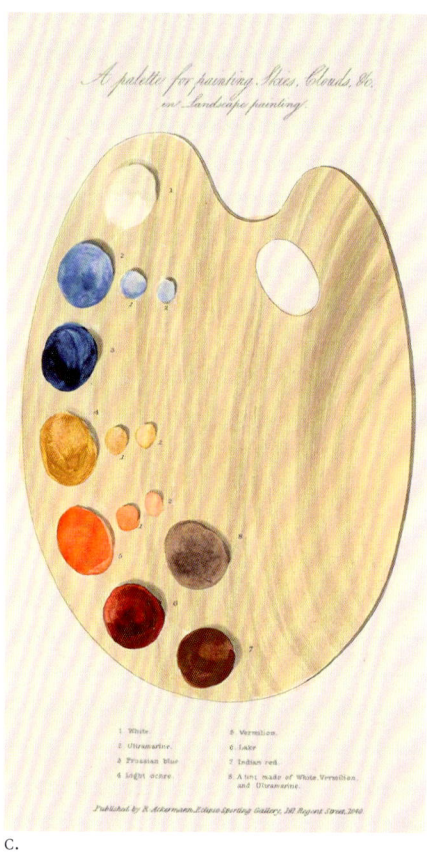

C.

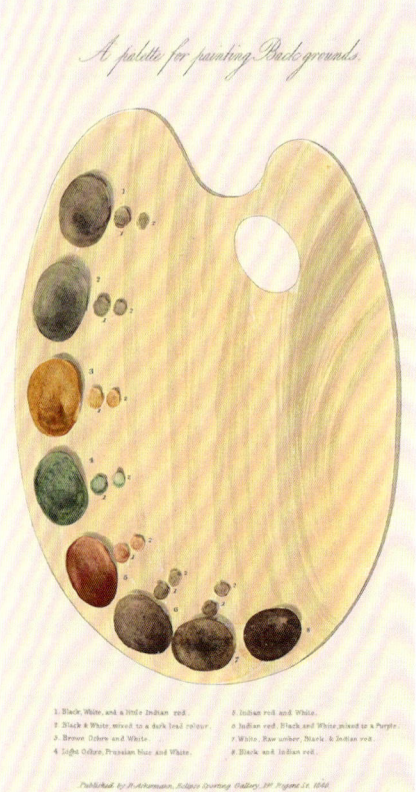

D.

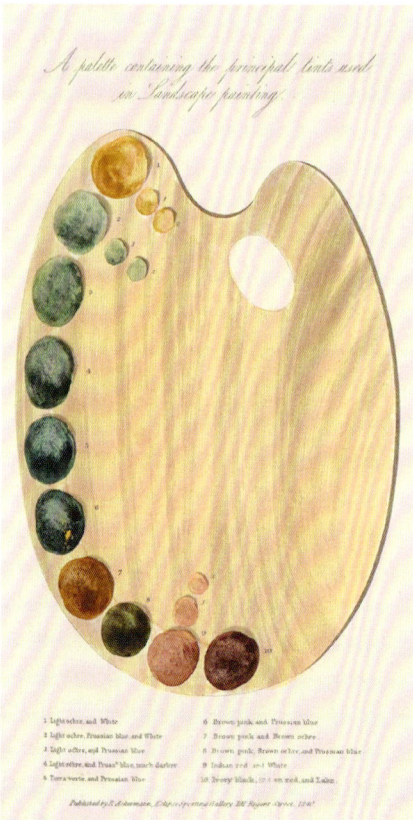

E.

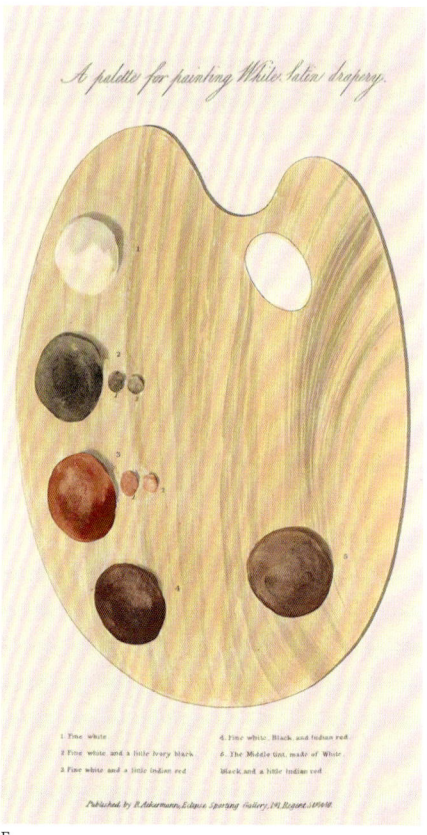

F.

Figurative and literal palettes are mentioned in almost every artist's and painter's handbook of the last few centuries, but the concept of a surface for holding, laying out and mixing colours is, of course, as old as painting itself. In prehistoric art, any slightly hollowed and reasonably smooth material could have been used to mix earth pigments or charred coal with spit, grease, blood or other binder, to create paint. Polished wood, shells, animal bones (scapula) or even simply the palm of a hand were all contenders, and many of these materials are still used today. But is a receptacle a palette? And to what extent is a palette defined by colour order? Ancient Egyptian, classical Greek and Roman paintboxes and containers survive in physical and pictorial form, but it is not always clear whether these were mere storage receptacles or whether they constitute some colour order or arrangement.

At what point does a paintbox become a palette that reflects an artist's preferences? Looking at J. M. W. Turner's home-made travelling paintbox (see page 56) into which he stuck his motley assortment of watercolour cakes from various sources, we could make a case for it being a palette. We could also extend this to Paula Rego (see page 243) arranging her hundreds of pastel sticks on trolleys in her large studio, or Helen Frankenthaler (see pages 218–19) stacking paint buckets on a vertiginous shelf. The definition of a palette is fluid, but we may loosely link it to some kind of colour and paint order, a mirror of an artist's plan for a colour scheme in an artwork, or more generally of their aesthetic chromatic vision. This is, of course, where the concepts of literal and figurative palette overlap. For this reason, some of the palettes in this book transgress the traditional idea of the artist's palette, and artists have been included who discarded palettes altogether, pushed boundaries and found new ways of using, storing, ordering and blending colour, often on a vastly different scale to their predecessors.

THE HISTORY OF PALETTES AND ARTISTS' STUDIOS

Palettes have been mentioned in literature since classical times, but mostly in a figurative context, relaying ideas of colour aesthetics or colour theory and providing evidence of which pigments and paints were available or desired in any one period. Roman authors Marcus Vitruvius Pollio (*fl.* 1st century BCE) and Pliny the Elder (23–79 CE) wrote about natural pigments, whereas in ancient Greece the works of Theophrastus (*c.* 372–*c.* 287 BCE) and Pedanius Dioscorides (*c.* 40–*c.* 90 CE) include passages of pigment recipes and painting techniques. The Middle Ages offered several anonymous documents on illuminating manuscripts and the text on fresco and secco wall and panel painting, *Il Libro dell'Arte* (written around the turn of the 15th century) by Cennino Cennini, contains invaluable information about pigments and their use, but the main principle remained the separation of paints when stored and used, partly out of necessity, partly for aesthetic reasons. A literal palette simply wasn't necessary or physically possible for many water- or egg-based media.

The concept of colour mixing, arranging and blending is intrinsically linked to the widespread adoption of oil-based colours in the 15th century and changes in representational style in painting. This slow-drying medium allowed artists to mix, modulate and interfere with their paints over a longer period of time, creating subtle tonalities, shades, shadows and detail not seen before. Crucially, the consistency of pigment in an oil-based binder meant that colours could be prepared and laid out in advance and kept moist for several days on a suitable non-absorbent surface that could even be flat. This is when the first images of small, handheld palettes appear in art, often oddly shaped and looking like mirrors. Some of the earliest can be seen in a series of 15th-century images of female artists painting self-portraits in an illuminated manuscript of Boccaccio's *De mulieribus claris*, as shown on the preceding page. In the illumination shown in image A. on page 13, we see Iaia (an image inspired by Greek painter Iaia of Cyzicus), also

A. 'A palette for the first and second painting or sittings of a portrait', frontispiece to John Cawse's *The Art of Painting Portraits, Landscapes, Animals, Draperies, Satins, &c. in Oil Colours*, 1840

B. 'The palette of colours for finishing the portrait', from John Cawse's *The Art of Painting Portraits, Landscapes, Animals, Draperies, Satins, &c. in Oil Colours*, 1840

C. 'A palette for painting skies, clouds, etc. in landscape painting', from John Cawse's *The Art of Painting Portraits, Landscapes, Animals, Draperies, Satins, &c. in Oil Colours*, 1840

D. 'A palette for painting backgrounds', from John Cawse's *The Art of Painting Portraits, Landscapes, Animals, Draperies, Satins, &c. in Oil Colours*, 1840

E. 'A palette containing the principal tints used in landscape painting', from John Cawse's *The Art of Painting Portraits, Landscapes, Animals, Draperies, Satins, &c. in Oil Colours*, 1840

F. 'A palette for painting white satin drapery', from John Cawse's *The Art of Painting Portraits, Landscapes, Animals, Draperies, Satins, &c. in Oil Colours*, 1840

known as Marcia, holding a mirror to paint her self-portrait. A small paddle-shaped palette with a star-shaped edge is propped up next to her, showing a very limited arrangement of separate colours – red, white and two dark shades. To her left is a long table on which the colours, which may be egg tempera or oil, have been prepared. This is a very simple palette layout, but the image gives a very early glimpse into painters' studios in the broadest sense, a theme in art and literature that has developed across the centuries, reflecting both the cultural circumstances and the artist's individuality. Several chapters in this book consider the studio space as an extension of the palette and the artist's self. Few early artists' palettes survive, but we can learn much about how they developed from works depicting St Luke in his study painting the Virgin Mary. For example, in Niklaus Manuel Deutsch's St Luke from 1515, the painter holds a square palette similar in layout to Marcia's, but in the background a much more elaborate palette is being laid out by an assistant. From here, we can follow the concept of the artist's studio as motif and informant in art all the way to Frankenthaler (see pages 218–21), Francis Bacon (see pages 222–27), Lucian Freud (see pages 228–31) and Paula Rego (see pages 240–43). We can observe if, how and which palettes and colours they used.

Many artists' guidebooks have elaborated in detail about how colour should be ordered on the palette, for example, John Bate in the third volume of *The Mysteries of Nature and Art* (1635) in a passage that is preceded by a simple woodcut illustration of an empty oval palette: 'For the drawing of a picture, you must first lay out your single colours in order upon your Pallet thus: a little white lead, a little vermilion, a little lake, so tawny colour, or seacoale black, oker, verdigrease, then your bices for your blewes, yellowes, and other colours, at your pleasure, each apart: when you have so disposed them, make your mixtures under them.'[2] The message is simple: pigments are expensive, so economy is key. Prepare well, keep your colours separate and only start mixing once you have neatly 'loaded' your palette. In the frontispiece to Bate's volume, several of these small palettes are seen in the artist's studio, including a prepared one in the artist's hand.

Apart from simple outline engravings of various palette shapes (square, round, oval, paddle, heart or kidney), almost all 17th- and 18th-century guidebooks focus on the palette as a figurative concept, with little detail on the material object itself. Most palettes used for oil- and water-based paint were made of thin pieces of polished hardwood, commonly cherry, walnut or rosewood, although many other materials are also known, such as ceramic or enamelled metal. The choice of material may depend on which medium is used or which colours are preferred. Oil paint is opaque, unless diluted heavily and used as a glaze, so a dark hardwood is suitable for oils, but watercolours and other transparent paints may require a lighter surface, as seen in the example of Turner's ceramic watercolour palette, or in the white enamel or even plastic trays often included in modern watercolour paintboxes. Some artists are known to have used ceramic bowls and shards, while white shells have been used for centuries for holding and mixing paints. Sometimes the artist may choose a palette in accordance with the ground colour they prefer for a painting, as seen in the example of James Ensor (see pages 130–33).

The 19th century saw a great surge in practical literature about painting, both in watercolour and oil, aimed at professional and amateur artists, with a much wider range of pigments available than in previous centuries, including new synthetic pigments. The arrangement of colours on palettes could now also be depicted in more detailed and elaborate illustrations, many of them in colour, often using a combination of mechanical image reproduction with printed colours or hand-colouring. Some magnificent examples of books with figurative palettes that are illustrated with realistic images of literal palettes were published, reflecting the full splendour of the 19th-century colour range and a general excitement about colour. T. H. Fielding's *On Painting in Oil and Water Colours* (1839), for example, tells us almost

A. Trade card for
S. & I. Fuller, London,
England, aquatint
by Thomas and Janart
Sutherland, 1823

B. Sennelier shop, Quai
Voltaire, Paris, France,
early 20th century

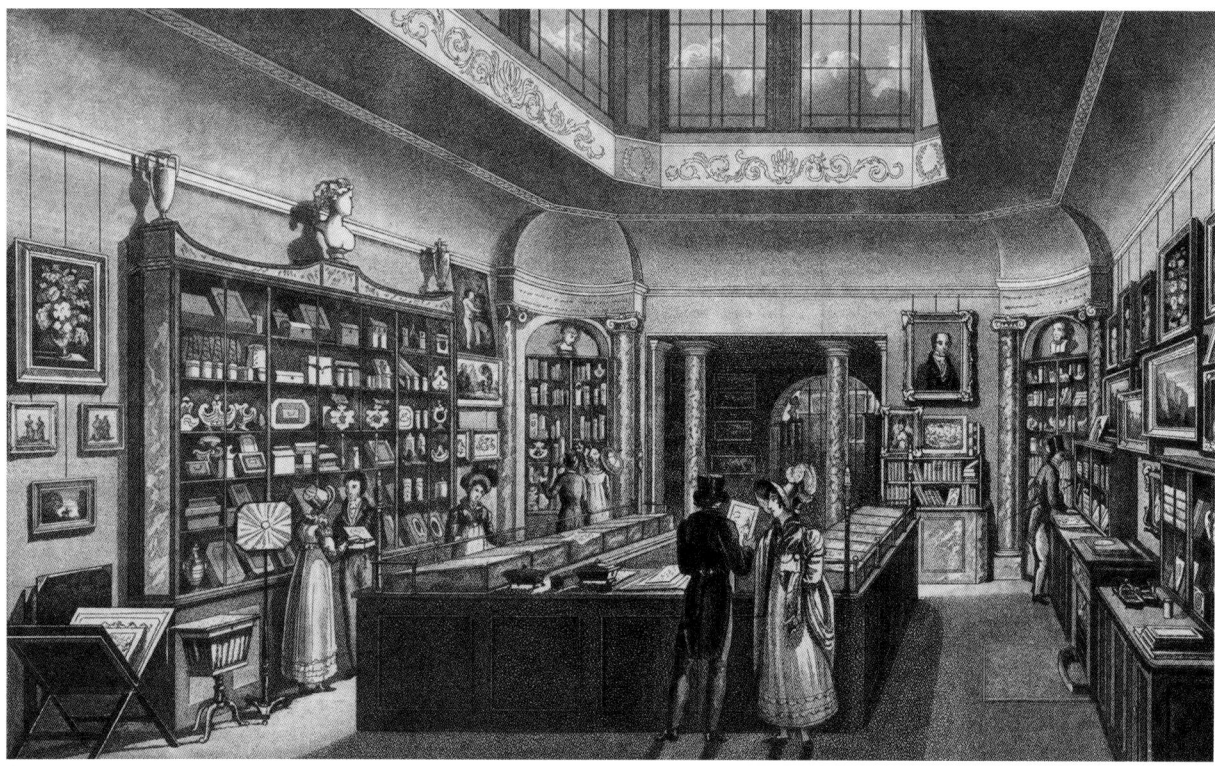

A.

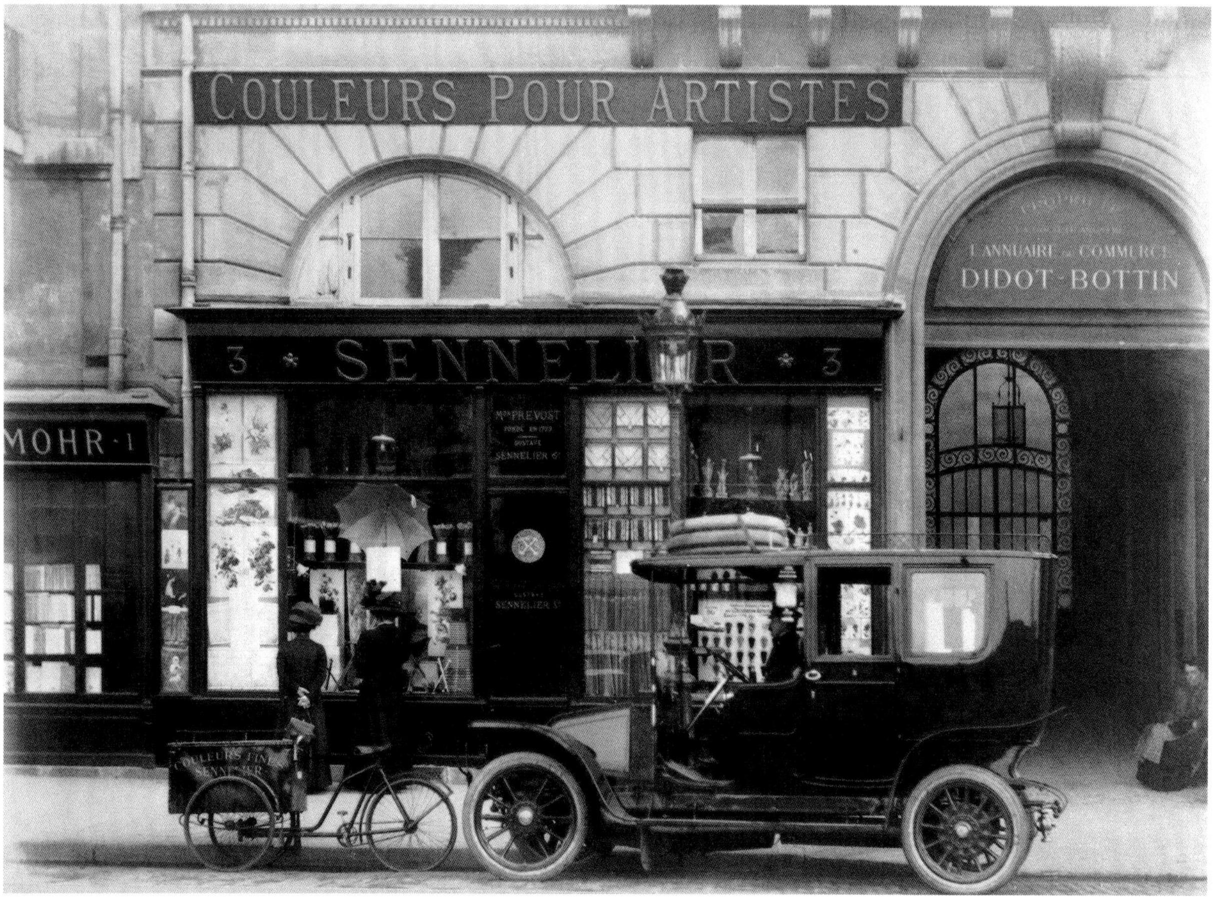

B.

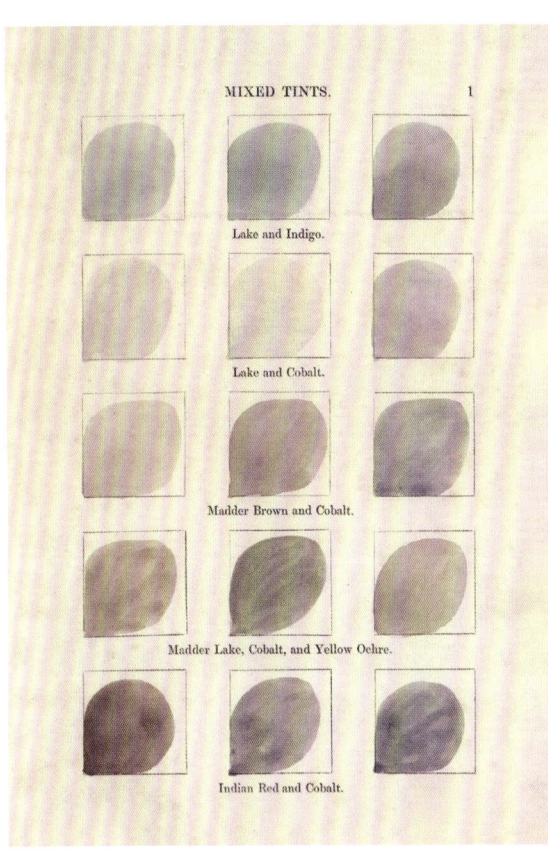

A.

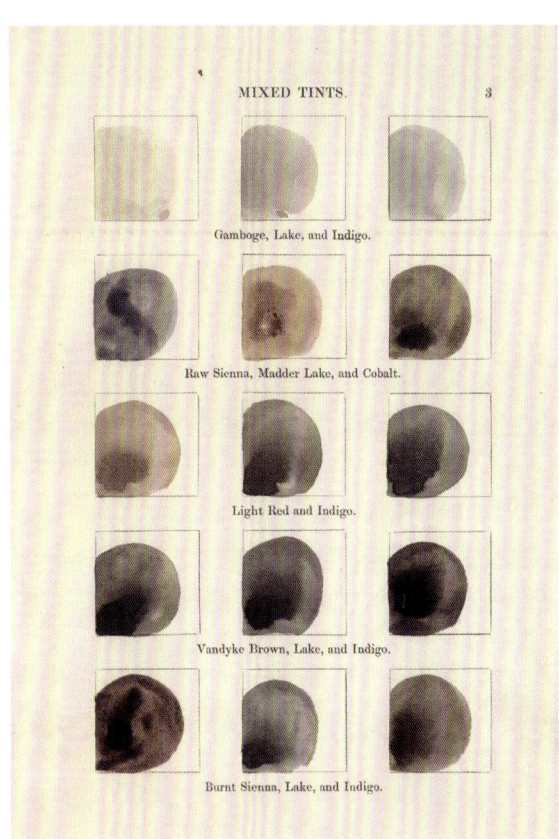

B.

MIXED TINTS. 1

Lake and Indigo.

Lake and Cobalt.

Madder Brown and Cobalt.

Madder Lake, Cobalt, and Yellow Ochre.

Indian Red and Cobalt.

MIXED TINTS. 3

Gamboge, Lake, and Indigo.

Raw Sienna, Madder Lake, and Cobalt.

Light Red and Indigo.

Vandyke Brown, Lake, and Indigo.

Burnt Sienna, Lake, and Indigo.

MIXED TINTS. 4

Gamboge, Light Red, and Indigo.

Gamboge, Burnt Sienna, and Indigo.

Gamboge, Burnt Sienna, and Indigo.

Vandyke Brown, Gamboge, and Indigo.

Italian Pink and Antwerp Blue.

C.

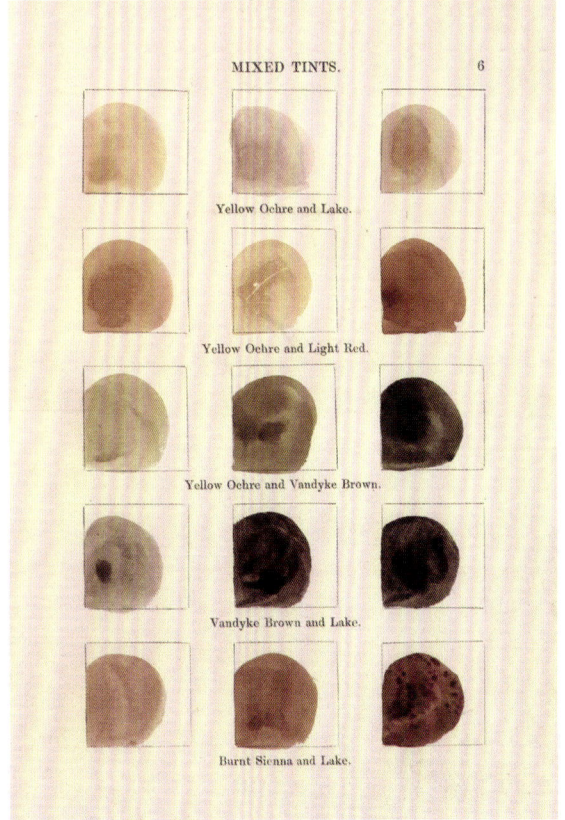

D.

MIXED TINTS. 6

Yellow Ochre and Lake.

Yellow Ochre and Light Red.

Yellow Ochre and Vandyke Brown.

Vandyke Brown and Lake.

Burnt Sienna and Lake.

nothing about the palette as a tool, but includes a lithographed frontispiece showing two oval palettes of different shades, a darker one for landscapes and a lighter one for portraits, as shown on page 2.[3] The woodgrain is realistically rendered and a complex range of twelve and ten colour blots respectively is shown on them, with highlights indicating their shape and volume. An even more sophisticated blending of figurative and literal palettes can be found in John Cawse's *The Art of Painting Portraits, Landscapes, Animals, Draperies, Satins, &c. in Oil Colours* from 1840, which includes no fewer than eleven lithographed plates depicting oval palettes with colour layouts for specific motifs and details in a painting, such as clouds, different coloured satins or portraits, six of which are shown on page 14.[4] While these plates offer predominantly practical advice, the representation of the palettes is extraordinary in its realistic detail: each blot of paint appears to have been added by hand, even showing the shadows thrown by the blobs of the material paint. Glazes have been applied in certain areas to give the impression of wet oil paint having just been laid on the palette. The book, first published in 1822 with slightly simpler images, is perhaps an unintentional homage to the mid-19th-century palette, in both senses of the word.

THE PALETTE AS SYMBOLIC OBJECT

Cawse's palette illustrations were perhaps a precursor to a cult of the palette that developed from the mid 19th century as a strand of the emerging 'cult of the artist'. The ergonomic shape and abstract beauty of loaded and unloaded palettes is undoubtedly appealing, and the humble artist's tool gradually became desirable to collectors and souvenir hunters. We see examples of palettes being sold, chased, bought and even commissioned, both as mementos of a living artist or for their decorative value. In some cases, artists painted pictures directly onto palettes or prepared a colour layout as a representation of their style, then signed them before giving them away or selling them, thereby cementing their elevated status as artworks. We see examples of this in the palettes of Henri Fantin-Latour (see page 74), Rosa Bonheur (see page 81) and Camille Pissarro (see page 122). The palette thus becomes a totemic object, a small physical manifestation of the creative spirit of the artist.

The palette has been a prominent motif and symbol in art, frequently used as a signifier of the artist's profession or as one of the attributes of painting or the arts in general from the Middle Ages onwards. In self-portraits, a palette is often a visual representation of the artist's professionalism, taste and skill, with particularly fine examples being Sofonisba Anguissola's superb self-portrait from 1556, Anna Waser's from 1691 and Élisabeth Louise Vigée Le Brun's from 1782 (see page 42). From the late 19th century onwards, these depictions became more experimental and expressive, and arguably even more personal. In the work of Marc Chagall (see pages 206–9), for example, palettes are often symbolic messengers and tokens of love and desire. In the 20th and 21st centuries we see many examples of artists using the palette as literal extensions or representations of their body, often associated with the heart or with skin and flesh. In her self-portrait in 1917, Swiss avant-garde painter Alice Bailly seems to merge with her large, vertically placed palette, which envelops her body like a colourful cape, whereas in 1934 Dutch artist Charley Toorop painted a close-up of her head dramatically framed by her heart-shaped palette, rendered in the same tone as her bobbed hair with the outline of the painting tool continuing the line of her jaw. In Frida Kahlo's *Self-portrait with the Portrait of Doctor Farill* (1951) a flesh-coloured palette with visible veins lies in the painter's lap, resembling a pulsating heart. Is Kahlo suggesting that she has dipped her brushes into her own blood to paint her surgeon's portrait? It is tempting to refer to these symbolically loaded motifs as 'anatomical palettes'.

A.–D. Hand-coloured mixed tints, from T. H. Fielding's *The Theory and Practice of Painting in Oil and Water Colours for Landscape and Portraits,* 5th edition, 1854

For contemporary sculptor and painter Anselm Kiefer, the palette has developed several complex meanings. A motif in his work since the 1970s (two examples of which can be seen overleaf), Kiefer's simply rendered palettes (usually only the outline of an oval palette with a small thumbhole) were initially symbols of hope: seemingly transparent, sometimes being carried by angels, gently embedding themselves in landscapes, a link between heaven and earth. Later, they turned into darker icons, depicted as winged creatures, floating or fallen, hung up on ropes, threatened or already charred by flames, or approached by snakes – undoubtedly Kiefer's response to the Nazis' sinister appropriation of art. The palette's significant historical symbolism is addressed by the artist in two- and three-dimensional form, and his choice of materials in the latter underlines his message: an earthenware palette trapped in a nest of barbed wire or a sculpture of a winged palette made from lead suggests that the freedom of the arts may have been lost.[5] Whether this is Kiefer's bleak prediction or a look back in anger, one thing is consistent: the use of the palette as a traditional emblem of art by an artist who himself doesn't use palettes.

THE PALETTE OF THIS BOOK OF PALETTES

This anthology of artists' palettes is presented in a roughly chronological order and has been arranged in four sections that highlight themes in the history of art, colour and painting. These themes and time frames are fluid and reflect certain developments or changes in taste, often caused or made possible by the invention of new pigments, tools and techniques. Materiality matters, and the physical palette, whether thickly loaded with paints or left with faint traces of colours, is always the focus, but I discuss them in the context of the artist's individual story, style and work. Sometimes it is possible to link a palette to a specific work of art (for example, in the case of van Gogh, see pages 102–7) or a particular phase in an artist's career. In these instances, I have paired the palette with those works. Where available, scientific analysis of an artist's materials and techniques informed the discussion of the paint on the palette. In most cases, artworks have been the subject of technical analysis, but there has been a recent trend to also investigate artists' painting tools and materials more directly. Where neither was available, I have relied on visual examination and linked colours and paint to pigment history. It should be noted that deterioration and colour change affect palettes with paint traces in the same way that they affect artworks (with the exception of yellowing due to ageing layers of varnish, which were rarely applied to palettes). For example, a red colour for which a fugitive organic red pigment was used will fade on the palette in the same way it fades in the finished painting. In addition, abrasion and other physical damage are even more likely with a working tool compared to an artwork.

In each case the relative proportions of the colours in the key artwork have been analysed digitally to discover the colours that cover the greatest percentages of the painted surface. These are presented in a square grid, with the colour that has the greatest percentage value in the painting covering the largest area in the grid. The breakdown of colour coverage on each grid therefore represents the most prevalent colours that can be seen in the respective painting. Breaking down colour schemes in a grid format has been used by some artists and art teachers for many decades, perhaps most convincingly by the American educator Emily Noyes Vanderpoel in her book *Color Problems* from 1902. Among her inventive illustrations are dozens of so-called 'colour analyses', in which a historic decorative object is broken down into its chromatic components. These are presented in the shape of a colour key on a 10 × 10 square grid, with the proportional distribution of each colour noted below the 100 squares. Her aim was to depict the 'simple proportions of quality and quantity' of colour in complex patterns and decorations, and thus aid the study and understanding of historic artefacts.[6]

A. 'Colour analysis from a panel of the Taj Mahal, India', from Emily Noyes Vanderpoel's *Color Problems*, 1903 edition

B. 'Colour analysis from a Chinese "egg-shell" plate', from Emily Noyes Vanderpoel's *Color Problems*, 1903 edition

C. 'Colour analysis from Arabian illumination', from Emily Noyes Vanderpoel's *Color Problems*, 1903 edition

D. 'Colour analysis from a rose-colored vase', from Emily Noyes Vanderpoel's *Color Problems*, 1903 edition

E. 'Colour analysis from Chinese porcelain', from Emily Noyes Vanderpoel's *Color Problems*, 1903 edition

F. 'Colour analysis from a mummy case', from Emily Noyes Vanderpoel's *Color Problems*, 1903 edition

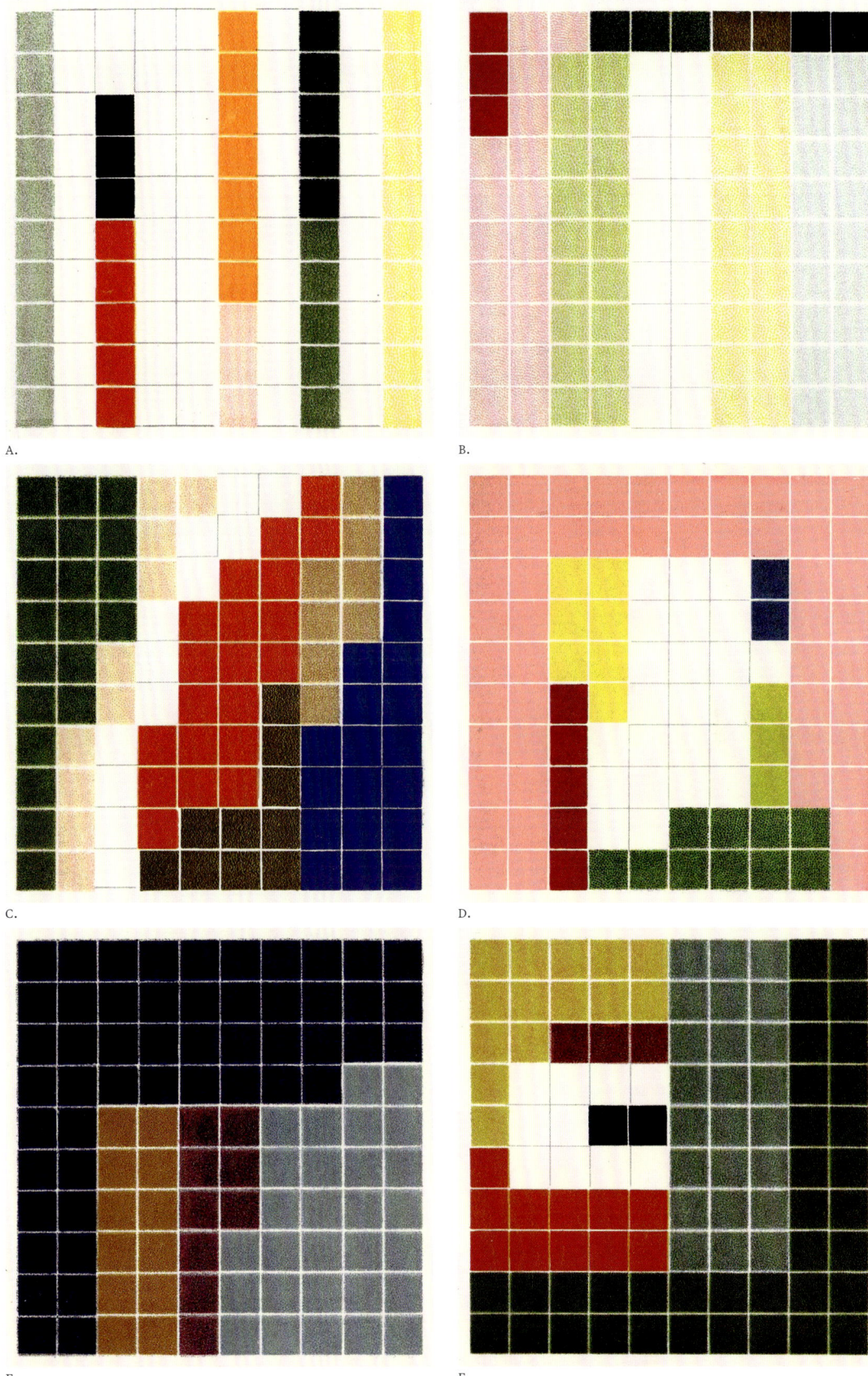

A.

B.

C.

D.

E.

F.

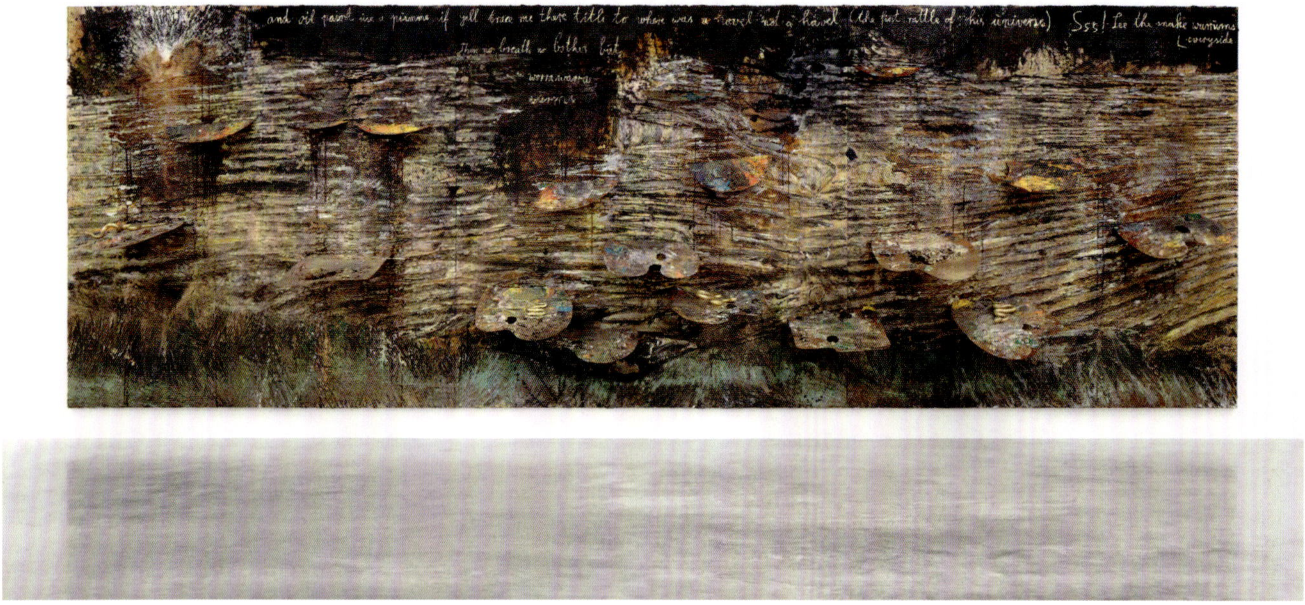

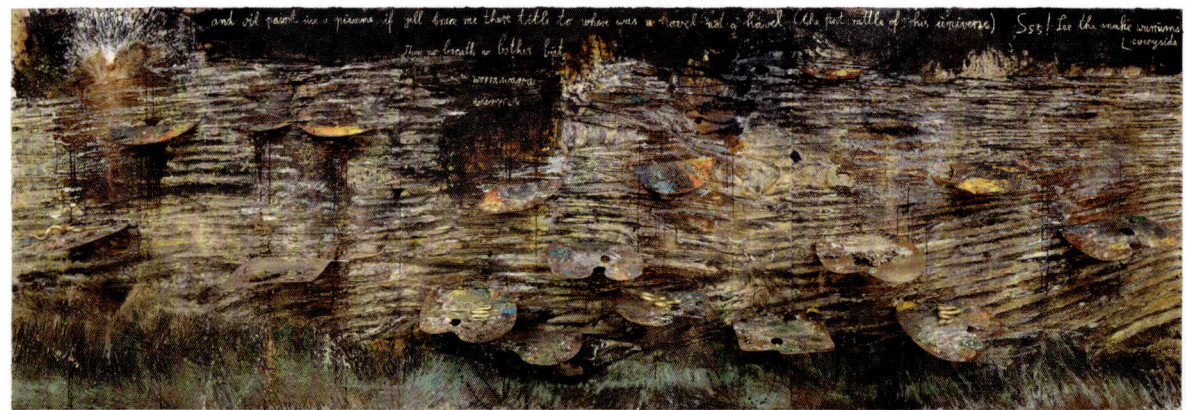

A.

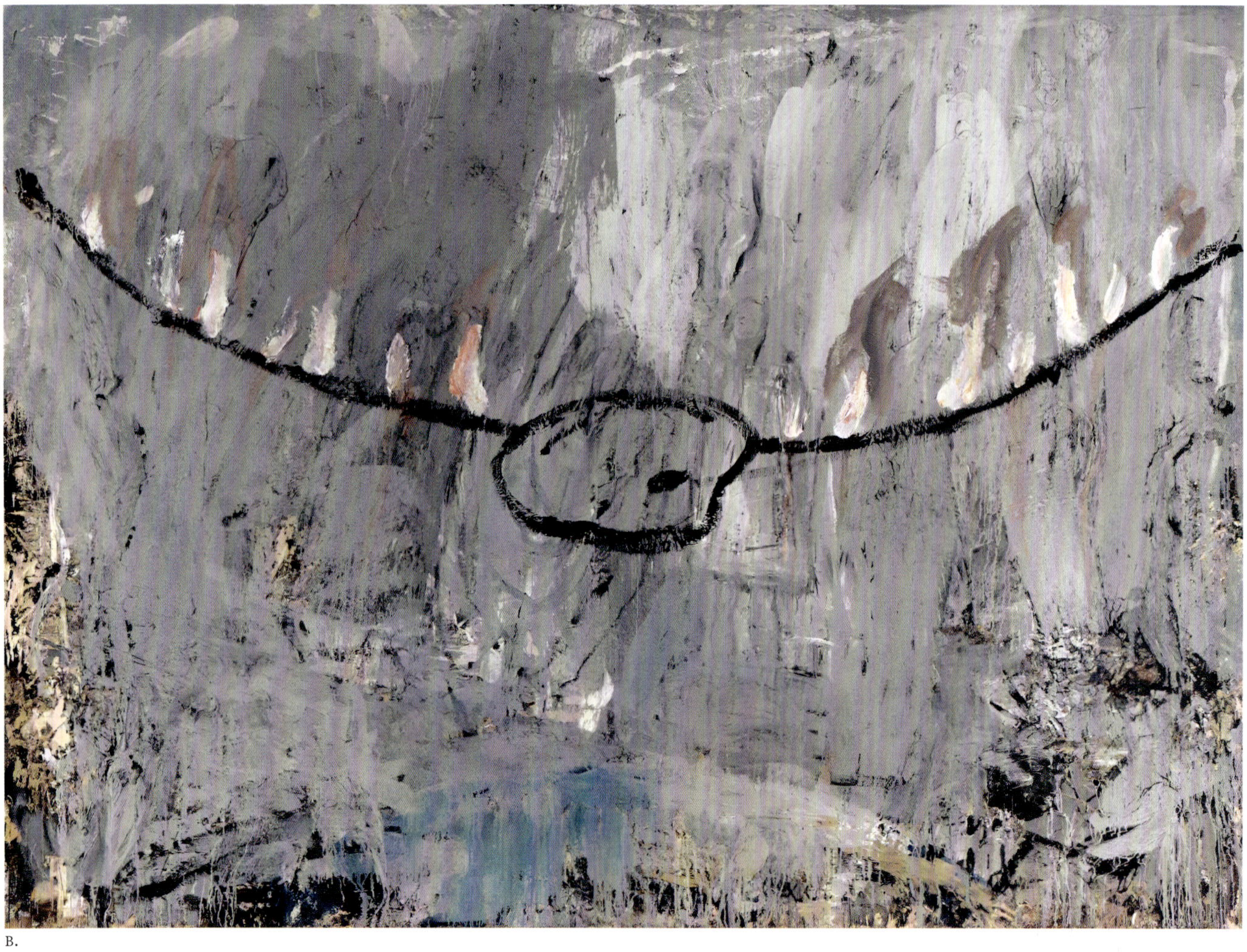

B.

Now, digital apps can help create these simple colour breakdowns. The proportional grids in this book provide a clear, abstract approximation of the colour DNA of a work of art, helping us to understand the creation of a painting a little better. However, they cannot fully convey the power of colour in the context of each composition, and the significance of colour and form. A small blob of a particularly contrasting or carefully placed colour in a painting may not command much space on a digitally produced colour grid but can make a lot of visual noise in the artwork. For example, in Paula Modersohn-Becker's *Self-portrait as a Half-length Nude with Amber Necklace I* (1906) (see page 149), she is holding in each hand a flower with a small pink head, while three of the same flowers are depicted on her head, like a floral crown. Although pink only forms a small part on the colour grid, these flowers structure the portrait visually and symbolically, linking the body of the figure with the background and sky, while their shapes mirror Modersohn-Becker's breasts and the titular necklace. Equally, subtle shading, certain glazes and effects created by the artist's skilful handling of paint are unlikely to be represented fully in the grids, as for example in the case of Vilhelm Hammershøi (see pages 138–41), who painted in very thin layers, working from dark to light, often applying a final transparent grey layer to achieve the gauzy appearance of his paintings.

PALETTES THROUGH TIME: PAST, PRESENT AND POSSIBLE FUTURES

This book is divided into four sections. The first one, 'The Tonal Palette', covers a period from *c*. 1540 to *c*. 1870 and tells the story of the development of the physical palette, from first small and oddly shaped objects to much larger artists' tools that were used not just to carry and mix paint, but also to represent artistic skill and technique, especially in self-portraiture. The second section, 'The Dynamic Palette', includes palettes from the last few decades of the 19th century and focuses on the full rainbow range of bright synthetic or commercially produced natural colours available as ready-to-use paints by that time. Academic and theoretical discussions of colour and palette layouts dominate this period. Section three, 'The Experimental Palette', covers the exciting period of the first few decades of the 20th century, when the entire gamut of affordable, zingy, synthetic paints was available, and artists were expanding the concept of colour as an expressive and powerful tool, moving ever further away from naturalistic depiction. The final section, 'The Liberated Palette', deals with interpretations and developments of the traditional palette from the 1930s onwards. Acrylic paints, spray paints and even more synthetic new pigments influenced where, what and in which style artists could paint, effectively democratizing art and taking it out of the enclosed and restricted space of the studio.

So, where and how will palettes feature in the future? In his book on Anselm Kiefer, published in 2014, Daniel Arasse argued that by the 1970s, the physical painter's palette was an object that 'harks back to painting techniques of the past that are now obsolete'.[7] Yet, you are possibly still holding this book in your hands, turning physical pages, marvelling at the obvious beauty of these palettes and the hidden meaning they may hold. While many artists have moved beyond easel painting and traditional painting methods, many have also returned to them or have included them in a greater, more varied body of work. Although often excluded from artists' and museums' inventories, palettes and other artists' materials and tools have been commanding eye-watering prices at auction sales in recent years, suggesting a similar attitude to that of 19th-century palette collectors. Their significance as items that offer insight into an artist's life and work beyond the chemical analysis of painting materials is being recognized. Perhaps it is the combination of tactility, materiality, abstract visual beauty and association with the artists' hands and bodies that makes them such fascinating objects.

A.   *And oil paint use a pumme*, Anselm Kiefer, 2023, emulsion, oil, acrylic, shellac, gold leaf, sediment of electrolysis, terracotta, plywood, spatula and wire on canvas, 3.8 × 11.4 m (12 ft 5 ⅝ in. × 37 ft 5 in.)

B.   *Palette*, Anselm Kiefer, 1981, oil paint, shellac, emulsion, paper and nails on canvas, 2.9 × 4 m (9 ft 6 ⅜ in. × 13 ft 1 ½ in.)

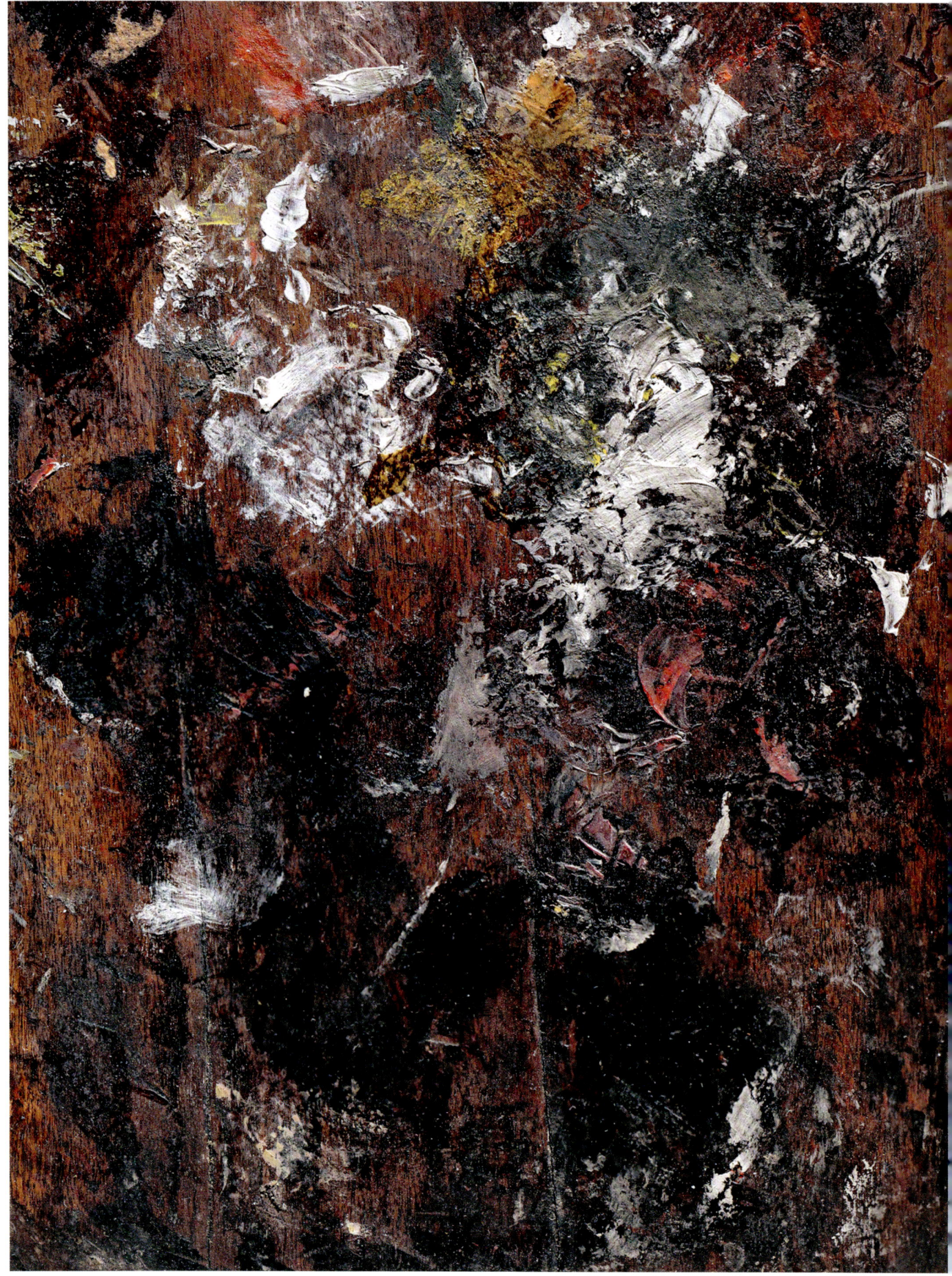

Pre-1870

The Tonal Palette

FEW PHYSICAL PALETTES SURVIVE from the early period of painting in oil, but there is a rich body of palettes in art and literature that provide information about artists who used and prepared them, working with a much more limited range of pigments available than in the 19th century. In the 17th and 18th centuries, with the invention of the first so-called 'modern' pigments and the commercialization of artists' materials, palettes (in the figurative and literal sense) gradually expanded and increased in range. Colours were still predominantly used to imitate nature and create realistically rendered images. Where palettes are shown in self-portraits or allegories of painting, they often represent aesthetic styles and skills. Angelica Kauffman and Élisabeth Louise Vigée Le Brun are particularly good examples of artists who used palettes as signifiers of their profession and professionalism. By the mid 19th century, artists had a much wider range of colours at their disposal that allowed them to capture and record nature with great precision. By the end of this period, we see artists such as J. M. W. Turner beginning to treat colour and paint in more abstract and experimental ways.

CATERINA VAN HEMESSEN 1528–AFTER 1565

A palette like a dagger

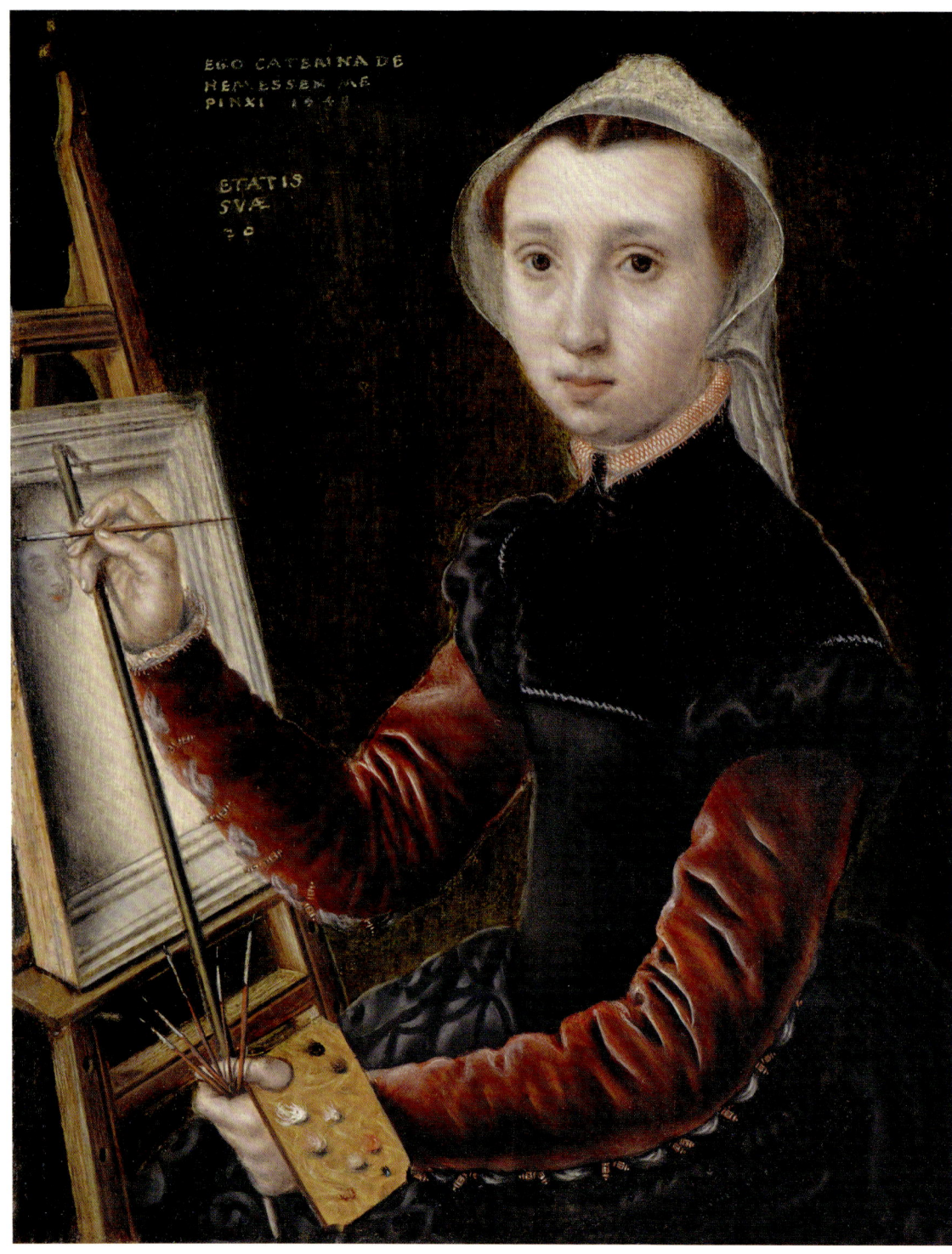

Self-portrait at the Easel
Caterina van
Hemessen
1548
Oil on wood
32 × 25 cm
(12 ⅝ × 9 ⅞ in.)

'I Caterina van Hemessen painted myself 1548 // her age 20.'

SIGNATURE OF CATERINA VAN HEMESSEN'S *SELF-PORTRAIT AT THE EASEL*, 1548

THE PALETTE IN THIS PAINTING from 1548 is small but of immense significance. As explained in the introduction, few physical palettes from before the 1800s survive, but palettes seen in artworks, and especially in portraits of artists, can tell us a great deal about the painting techniques, use of colour and paint, and historical context. Here, we have not only a palette that informs us about the size and style of this tool in mid-16th-century Europe, but one that tells us about an individual artist, a young woman from northern Europe, who added her name in bold letters to the painting: EGO CATERINA DE/ HEMESSEN ME / PINXI 1548 // ETATIS SVAE/ 20 (I Caterina van Hemessen painted myself 1548 // her age 20). It is the first known self-portrait of a painter, male or female, in Western art, and one that includes many of the tools of her profession.

We cannot look at this palette without its pictorial context in the painting. It appears to be made of polished wood (the artist took care to depict some of its graining) and has a thumbhole, which is typical of early palettes used for oil paint. Hemessen embraced this relatively new medium, which makes it possible to arrange paint in ready-to-use creamy blobs on one small surface, rather than working with individual containers necessary for egg tempera paints. The palette is small and rectangular, with slightly indented corners. The size, too, is standard for an early wooden palette, but it also reflects the dimensions of the painting Hemessen is working on, the reduced range of colours she is using, and – in a self-referential way – the small size of the actual painting, which is only slightly larger than an A4 sheet of paper.

The palette appears to be dangling precariously from the artist's hand, in which she is also holding five thin round brushes, spread out like a fan. They were probably made from sable hair. The practical reason for anchoring the palette with her thumb and using the back of her hand to hold it flat is to have quick, easy access, and to be able to get close to the board she is painting on, propped up on an easel. Pictorially though, the artist's hand and palette are tilted towards the viewer in order to showcase one of the key tools of her work. We can clearly see which colours she uses, and unsurprisingly, they correspond with the ghostly face in the upper left corner of the image she is working on. It is the face of a woman, with pale complexion and bright red lips. Some contouring and shading have already been applied, but we will, of course, never see the finished painting-within-a-painting. We will never know whether, at a later stage, Hemessen would have used colours that are noticeably absent on the painted palette, such as an ultramarine, azurite or smalt blue, or a shimmering copper-based green.

What we see instead are nine small blobs of a reduced colour range, comprising a greyish-white (probably lead-based), two dark shades that could be either a burnt umber or sienna, a carbon black, possibly a yellow ochre, and what appear to be some ready-mixed tints of flesh colour.[1] The only strong chromatic colour here is red, likely a vermilion, which she has already used for painting the lips. On the tip of the brush she is holding in her right hand is a tiny amount of one of those achromatic tints, about to be applied to the fictional painting. With these small visual markers, Hemessen is showing us what she is capable of – that she can capture the subtleties of a realistically rendered human face with this limited array of colours, on a surface only slightly larger than the back of her hand.

This is, of course, a pictorial illusion, or a bluff, since the real evidence of her skills is the figure of the artist herself, looking at us and, in the reality of her world in 1548, her own image, as she would have needed a mirror in order to paint this self-portrait. It is a calculated construction of an image of a painter with the tools of her trade, a representation of how she works, what she uses, how she presents herself –

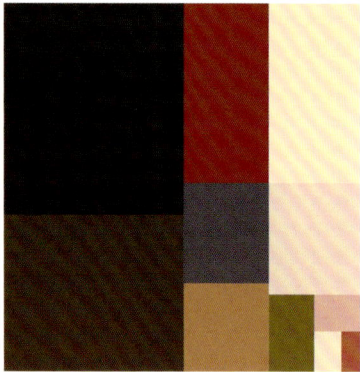

Proportional breakdown of colours used by Caterina van Hemessen in *Self-portrait at the Easel*, 1548, displayed on page 26.

demurely dressed, seated, pale and quiet. Because this is a self-portrait of a woman in mid-16th-century Antwerp presenting herself as a painter and making us look at her looking at herself, the small palette becomes a powerful symbol.

Although she lived in a time of great intellectual progress in Europe, Hemessen was still limited in what she could achieve as a woman. She probably received training and gained access to materials through her father, an established Antwerp painter who had studied in Italy. Yet, here she depicts herself, considering herself worthy of a portrait, and, as art historian Jennifer Higgie observes, 'she holds her palette and a fistful of brushes as tightly as you might hold a dagger in a dark wood.'[2]

A.   Antwerp, unknown artist, *c.* 1520–40, oil on panel, 183 × 108 cm (72 ⅛ × 42 ⅝ in.)
B.   *Portrait of a Child*, attributed to Caterina van Hemessen, 1559, oil on panel, 19.7 × 14.6 cm (7 ¾ × 5 ¾ in.)

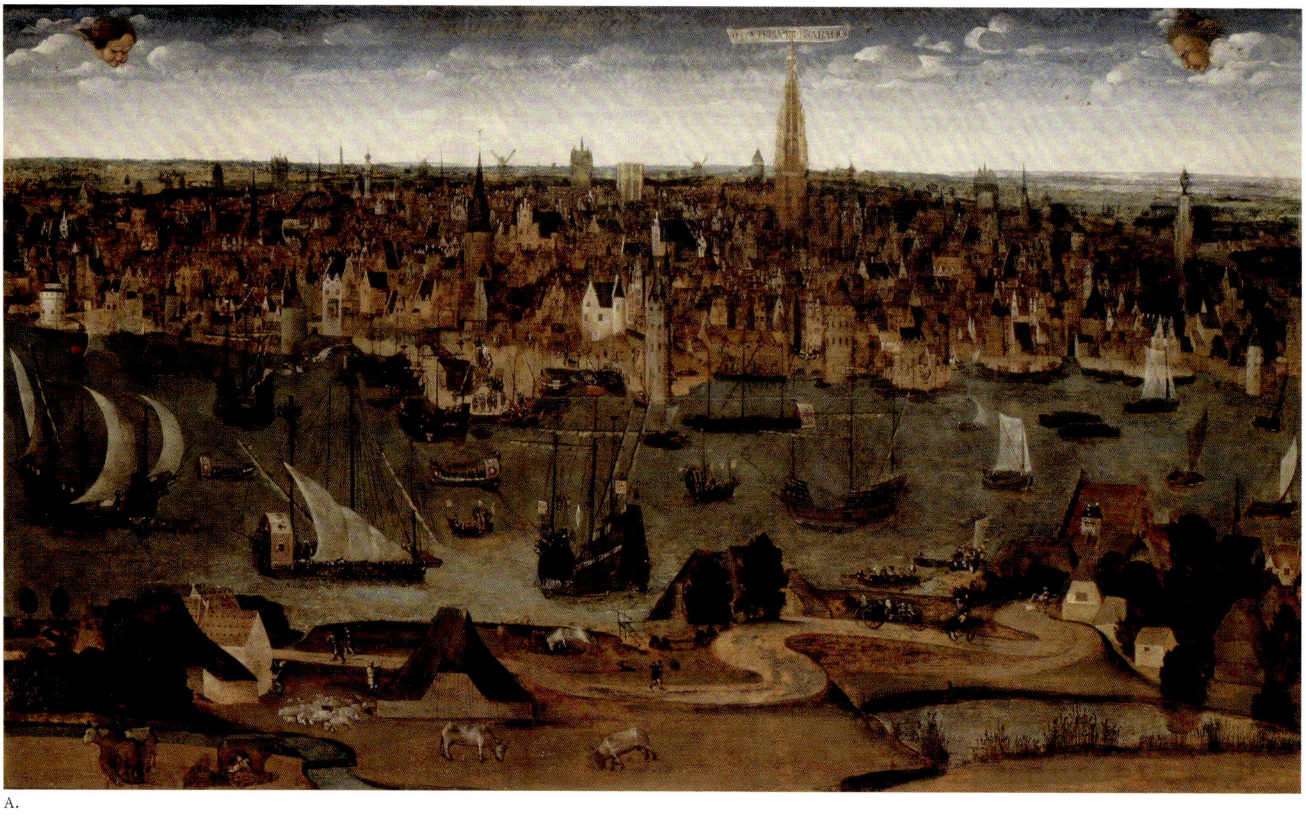

A.

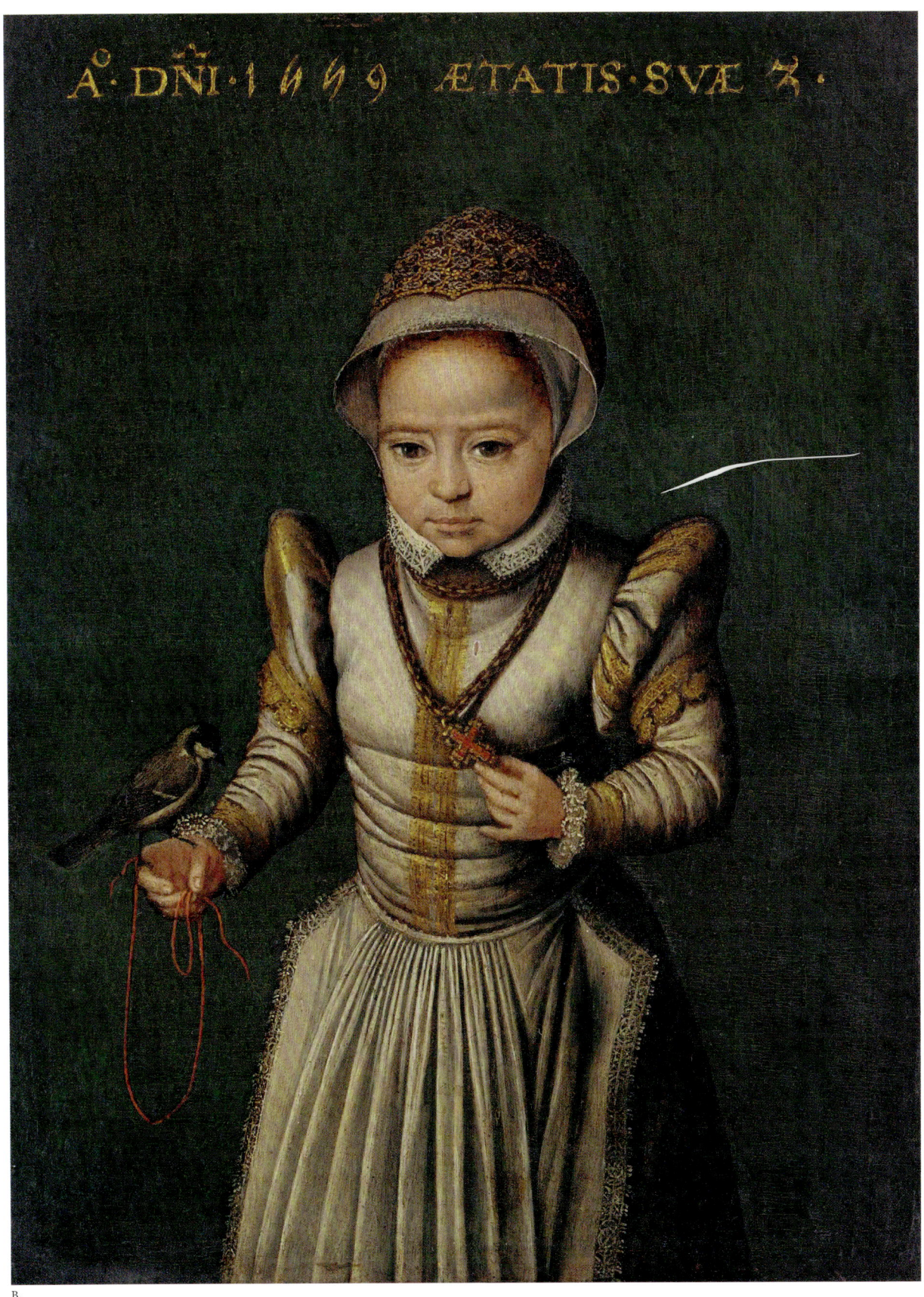

ARTEMISIA GENTILESCHI 1593–*c.* 1656

A palette ripped from the artist's hand, and reclaimed

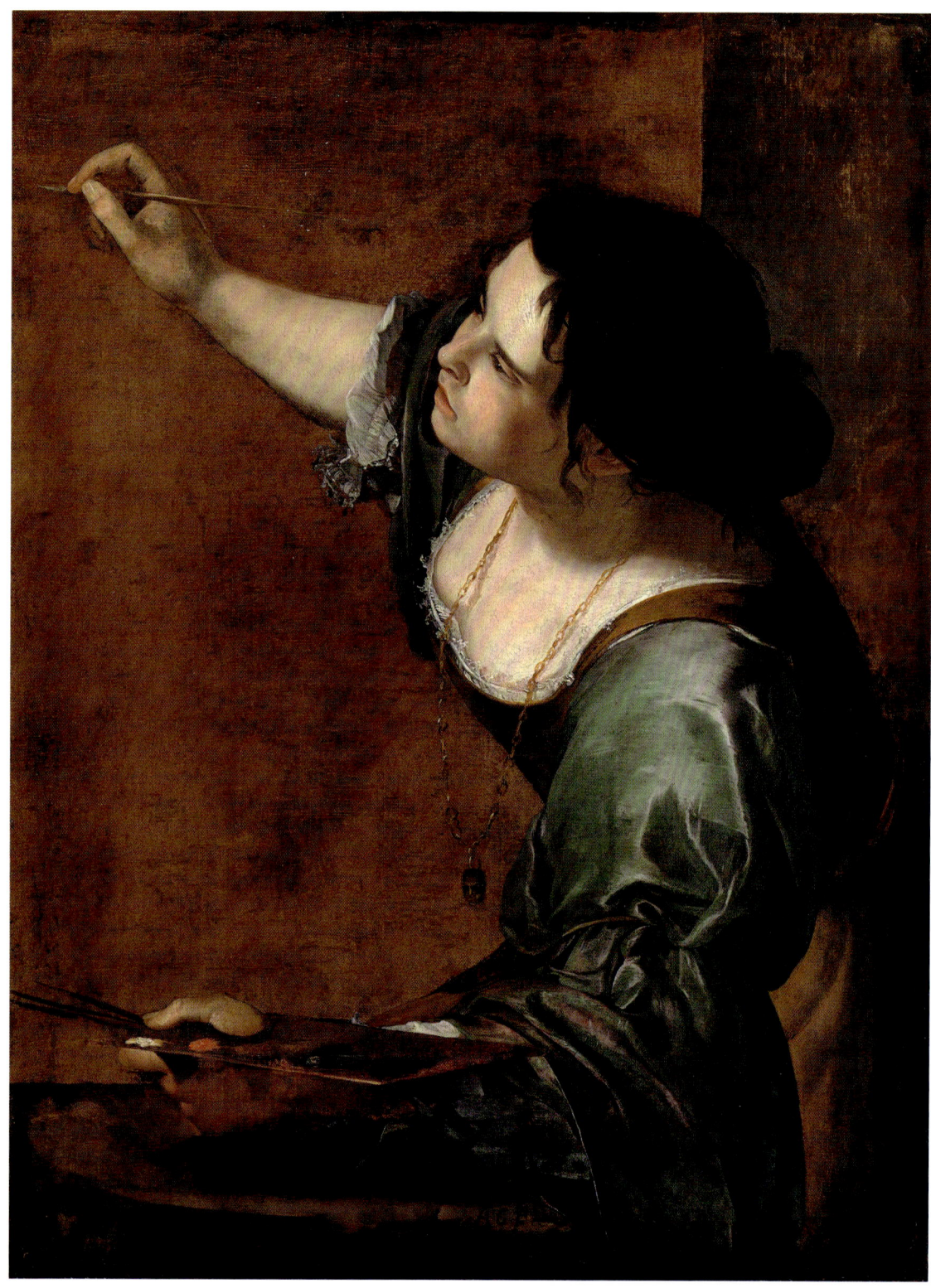

*Self-portrait as the
Allegory of Painting*
(Also known
as *La Pittura*)
Artemisia Gentileschi
c. 1638–39
Oil on canvas
98.6 × 75.2 cm
(38 ⅞ × 29 ⅝ in.)

'I will show Your Illustrious Lordship what a woman can do. ... With me Your Illustrious Lordship will not lose and you will find the spirit of Caesar in the soul of a woman.'

ARTEMISIA GENTILESCHI, LETTER TO HER COLLECTOR DON ANTONIO RUFFO, 7 AUGUST 1649

ARTEMISIA WORKED AT A TIME when a thorough knowledge of pigments and paint preparation was essential. She had learned how to source, grind, mix and store pigments in her father Orazio's studio. The value and scarcity of certain colours would have demanded careful and measured use, in placing within a composition as well as when mixing, as colours can easily become dull or corrupted when combined. A typical 17th-century palette would have included lead white, ivory black, lamp black, red lake, lead-tin yellow, the cheaper earth ochres and umbers, and more expensive pigments like vermilion, azurite and ultramarine. Some of these pigments, including azurite, lead-tin (antimony) yellow (also known as Naples yellow), lead white and ochre, were recently identified in Artemisia's work in studies by the National Gallery, London.[1] Although we don't have an actual palette belonging to her, she painted palettes at least once in her work, including in this painting, *Self-portrait as the Allegory of Painting (La Pittura)*.

Female personifications of Painting were common in 17th-century art and followed the description in Cesare Ripa's *Iconologia* (1593), a book of emblems, in which the figure of Painting is a dark-haired woman with raised eyebrows and in a somewhat dishevelled state (indicative of imagination and creative power). She wears a pendant around her neck on which is written 'imitation', while her mouth is covered with a cloth, alluding to the silence of images. Other attributes are the tools of painting, including palettes, brushes, sometimes a canvas, and her clothes often bear symbolic colours.

Artemisia references many of Ripa's details in her self-portrait and presents an astonishing image of female creative force and confidence. She portrays herself in the act of beginning a painting. In a pose full of movement, with her arms forming a semi-circle, the figure occupies almost the entire pictorial space. Her right arm arches at the upper edge of the painting, her hand holding the brush that is about to fill the large,

empty, earth-coloured background that represents the canvas. Her gaze is firmly fixed on this space. The line of the right edge of the canvas is aligned with the figure's head and body. Her sumptuous green dress is an indicator of the colours she is going to produce, and her skin seems to exude light rather than reflect it. In her left hand, placed at the bottom of the painting, she holds the palette and more brushes. Some blots of paint, as yet unmixed, are just about visible on the palette, including what appears to be lead white and precious vermilion, while her arm rests on a grinding stone for pigments. Yet, what matters more here than identifiable colours is the symbolic placing of the painter's tools. Both the square palette and the grinding stone are horizontal shapes that contrast with the vigour and movement of the figure. They form the visual and metaphorical stage that this artist has claimed and mastered.

Artemisia was born in Rome in 1593. Her mother died early, and she was effectively brought up by her father. Her extraordinary talent and her strong, resilient personality were apparent at a young age, and she would become one of the most celebrated artists of the Baroque era. In her lifetime, she was internationally known, and became the first female member of the Accademia di Arte del Disegno (Academy of the Arts of Drawing) in Florence. At the age of only seventeen, she painted her powerful version of *Susanna and the Elders,* capturing the voyeurism, abuse, invasion of female space, and terror of the story. In typical Baroque manner, her compositions were full of movement and drama, involving claustrophobic framing, realistic detail, strong contrasts of light and dark, and figures depicted in complex, often contorted positions. A gifted colourist, Artemisia excelled visually at telling classical and biblical stories, often involving violence and murder. Through precise modulation of earthy browns, blacks and greys she created shadows and chiaroscuro, out of which illuminated faces, hands, necks, whole bodies – clothed and unclothed – appear in vibrant colours, bodies often about to be violated or already bleeding profusely.

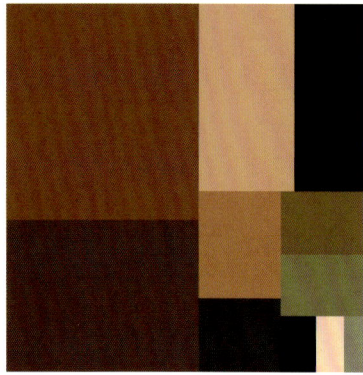

Proportional breakdown of colours used by Artemisia Gentileschi in *Self-portrait as the Allegory of Painting* (also known as *La Pittura*), *c.* 1638–39, displayed on page 30.

It is hard not to link these themes with an event that shaped Artemisia's life. At the age of eighteen, Agostino Tassi, an artist she worked with at the time, entered her studio, violently ripped her palette and brushes from her hands and shouted, 'Not so much painting, not so much painting', before raping her. In the struggle she managed to injure him with a knife. Tassi was taken to court and the trial was documented in a 300-page-long transcript, from which we know that during her interrogation Artemisia's fingers were strapped into a sibille, a device made of metal and rope that was tightened during interrogation to make her speak the truth. She stayed strong and endured the torture, and Tassi was convicted. Artemisia would go on painting many strong women who take action and are in control, who assert their place; women with strong hands that hold tools, weapons or the severed heads of their victims. This self-portrait was created many years after the rape and trial but it remains a potent expression of her confidence as an artist and the reclaiming of the tools of her profession that Tassi had so cruelly torn from her when she was a teenager.

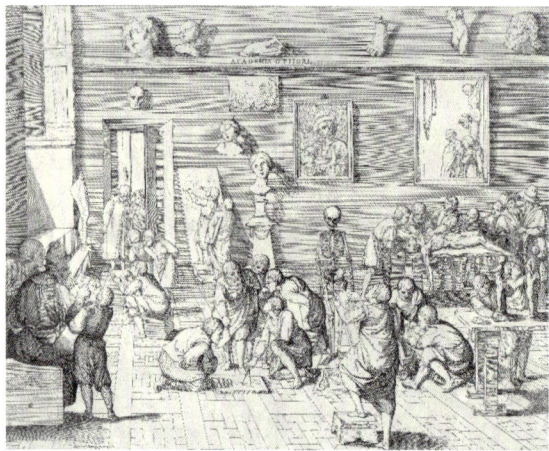

A.

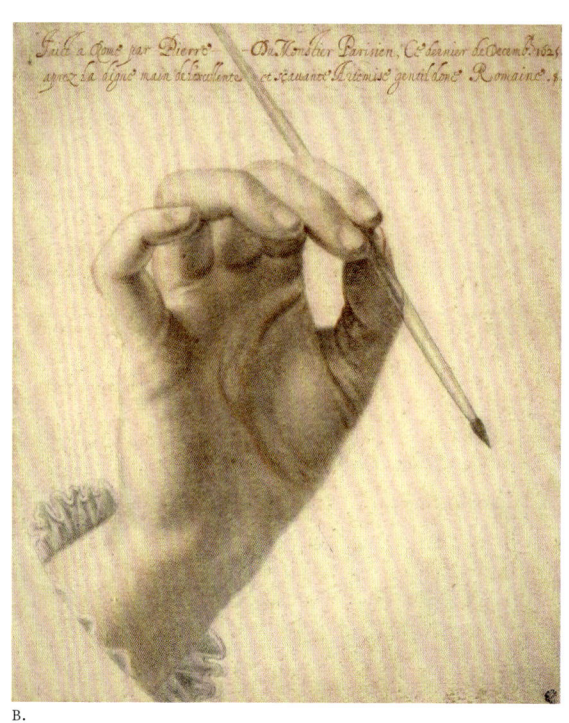

A. *An Academy of Painters*, Pierfrancesco Alberti, 1600–38, etching, 41.2 × 52.2 cm (16 ¼ × 20 ⅝ in.)
B. *Right Hand of Artemisia Gentileschi Holding a Brush*, Pierre Dumonstier II, 1625, black and red chalk on paper, 21.9 × 18 cm (8 ⅝ × 7 ⅛ in.)
C. *Susanna and the Elders*, Artemisia Gentileschi, *c.* 1610, oil on canvas, 170 × 119 cm (67 × 46 ⅞ in.)

B.

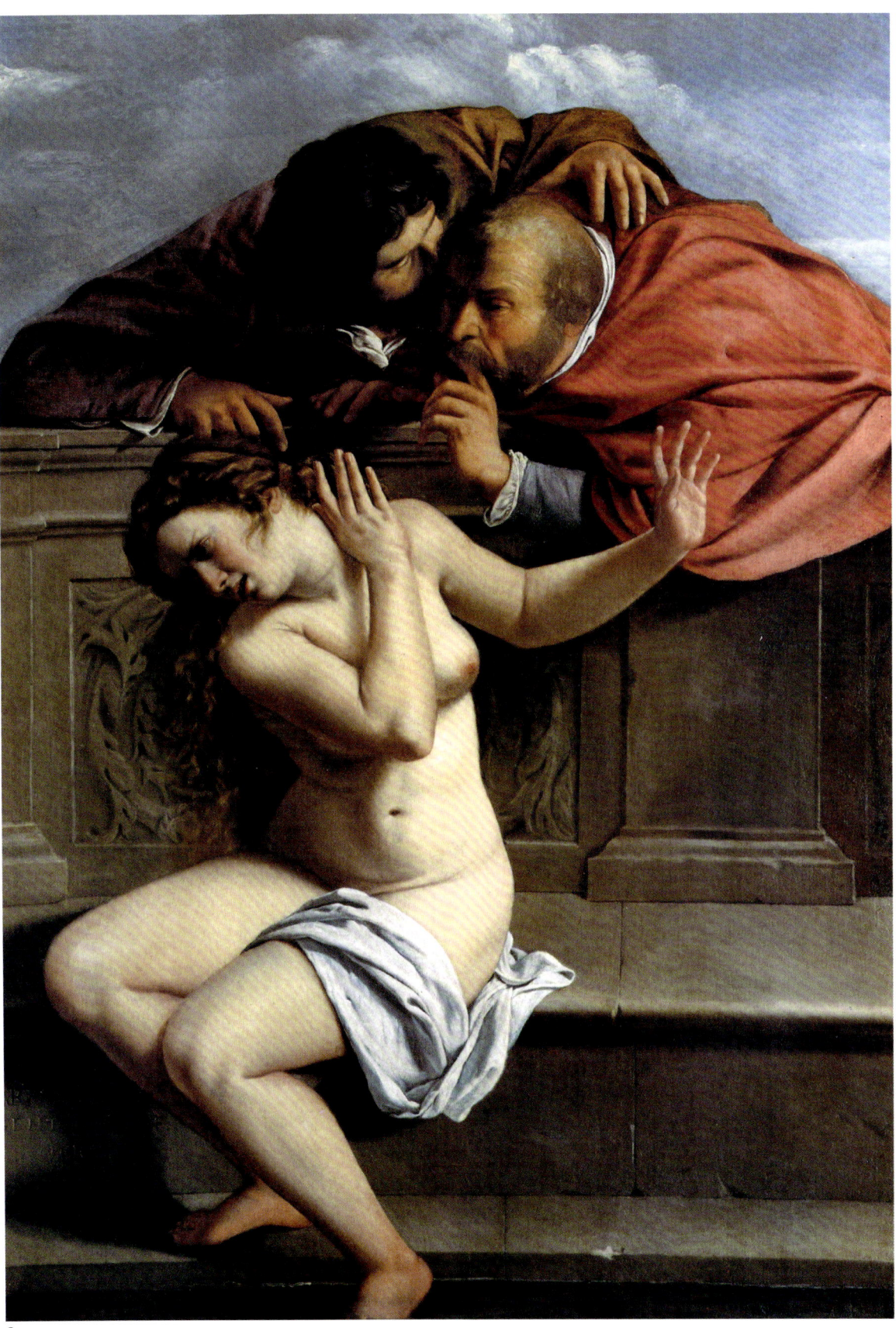

c.

REMBRANDT 1606–1669

A limited palette of liquid shadows

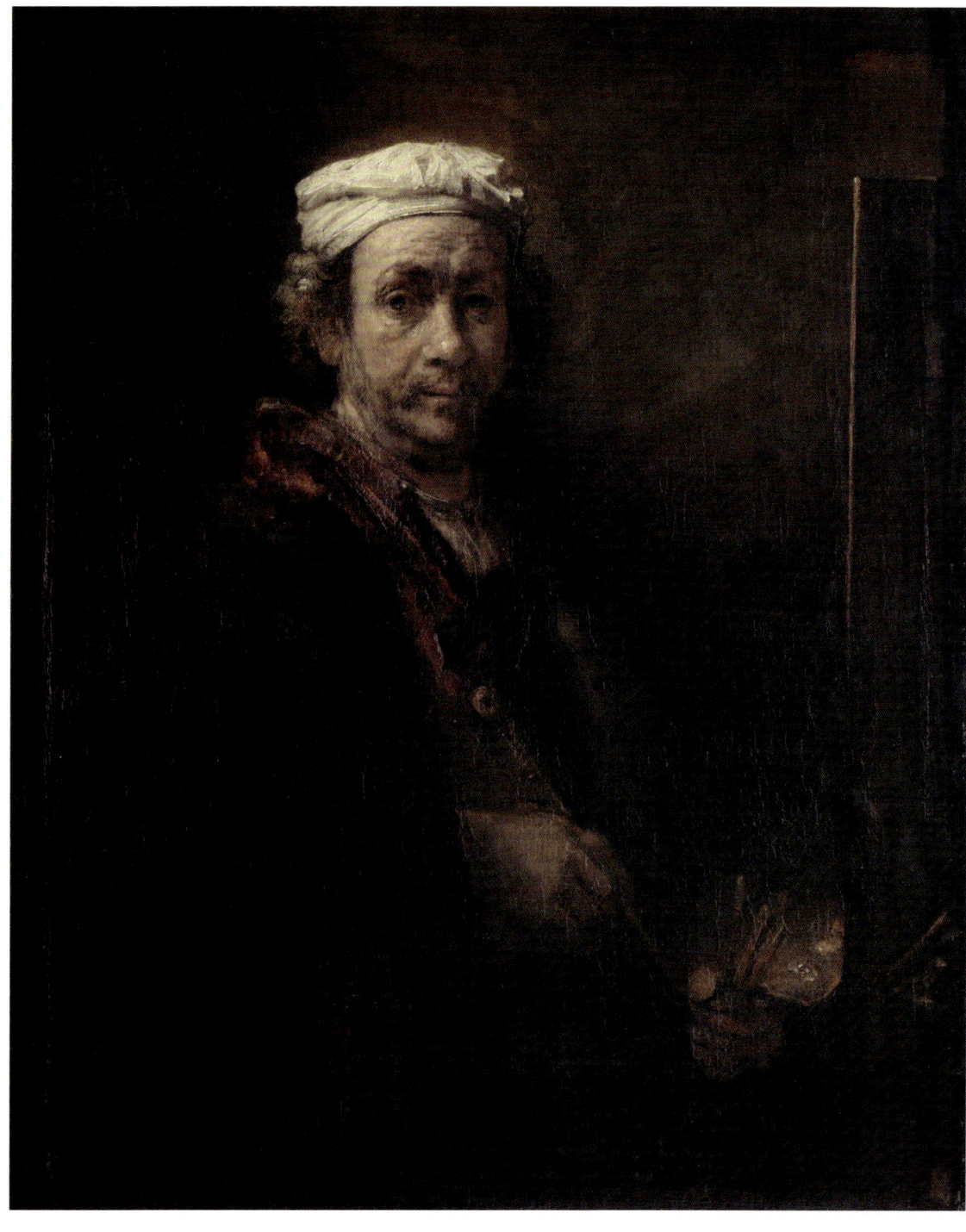

*Self-portrait at
the Easel*
Rembrandt
1660
Oil on canvas
111 × 85 cm
(43 ¾ × 33 ½ in.)

'Roughness should never be confused with casualness. In Rembrandt's case, the rougher he became, the more wondrously elaborate he made his paint layers, giving them a geologically tiered density.'

SIMON SCHAMA, *REMBRANDT'S EYES*, 1999

FEW PAINTERS HAVE RENDERED light and darkness as effectively and with so few colours as Rembrandt. Marcia B. Hall describes Rembrandt's colouring as 'subtly varied tones of brown, ranging through every tint from gold to cinnamon to chestnut and mahogany to chocolate', with only touches of reds and hardly any blues.[1] There is ample information about what pigments and other paint materials were available in 17th-century Holland, how they were prepared and used, which ones Rembrandt preferred, and how studios were laid out and run, including Rembrandt's own in Leiden and Amsterdam. Regrettably, however, we lack an actual physical palette by this master of light, shadow and carefully placed and layered colour. Yet, Rembrandt did paint himself a couple of times with palettes, and depicted painters' studios (including his own) in several other drawings and paintings.

In this late portrait from 1660, Rembrandt even gives us a rare glimpse of his loaded palette. The painting is of conventional composition, with the artist shown in the process of painting, seated very close to the panel or canvas, holding a mahlstick in one hand, several brushes and a small palette in the other, looking at the viewer, or – in his world – at a mirror necessary to create the image we are looking at. It is a typically dark Rembrandt picture, featuring carefully placed areas of illumination, with the main one being the painter's head. Light also falls only on his hands and his small palette, which is tilted in such a way that allows us to see some of the paint on it. The colours are sketchily depicted, but it is clear that the palette is extremely limited: only a few flecks of white, a warm yellow and a small daub of red are visible, and much of the surface is obscured. Yet, this is enough to understand how Rembrandt worked, how he mastered the art of mixing colours and how his painting style had developed over the years. By the late 1650s, he had moved on from his earlier 'fine style' and applied paint in looser, rapid, visible brushstrokes, working in thick impasto, often adding colour to dried or half-dried paint surfaces,

a technique called scumbling. This roughly painted palette is likely a fairly accurate representation of Rembrandt's actual palette at this stage of his career.

In an earlier small painting of a painter's studio, which is possibly his own (image D., overleaf), we can't see what is on the palette the artist is holding, but we are shown the greater context of the studio, in particular the importance of light conditions. It is an idealized, impossibly minimalist studio in which light seems to both fall on and emanate from the easel picture we cannot see. The artist stands a distance from it, perhaps to inspect what he has created so far, or perhaps waiting for inspiration. Between him and the easel is an empty wall, on which hang two clean oval palettes. Rembrandt wasn't a symbolist, but there may well be a symbolic element to these palettes: they are placed, perhaps subconsciously, at the height of the painter's heart, appearing to hover between him and the easel, and may represent the beginning of the creative process.

Several images of prepared palettes appear in paintings by Rembrandt's contemporaries, such as his pupil Gerrit Dou or Arent de Gelder. These tend to look much more orderly, with pigments neatly arranged and untouched, but they all have one thing in common: the colour range is limited to white, small amounts of red and yellow, and a range of darker earth pigments and blacks, with a conspicuous absence of blues and greens. By the 17th century, it had become common practice to mix more than one colour. Medieval and Renaissance artists had largely avoided heavily mixed colour, instead using pure colours where possible, with little modulation. Compared to a modern painter, Rembrandt's colour palette was restricted, but he benefited from a steady supply of good-quality artists' materials, with Holland having become a centre of pigment manufacturing and a trading point for colours imported from Italy.

Which pigments did he use to create his chiaroscuro and shimmering golden browns? He had a few staples, such as lead white, which he used in almost all his

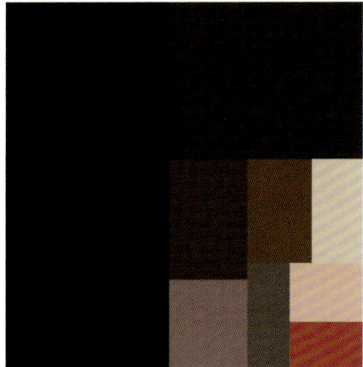

Proportional breakdown of colours used by Rembrandt in *Self-portrait at the Easel*, 1660, displayed on page 34.

paintings, chalk white and a wide range of natural earth pigments (siennas, umbers and ochres, raw and burnt). While these earth pigments lack chromatic vibrancy, they were relatively cheap and stable and mixed well. It is these colours that give Rembrandt's paintings their warm appearance. Where a dark umber was not dark enough for his shadows, he used warm bone black, which is found in his works in great quantities, including as transparent glazes, mixed with lake pigments. The yellow we see on the shadowy palette in the self-portrait may be a light ochre but could also be a lead-tin yellow, or even artificial orpiment. Rembrandt's reds are rich and glowing, an effect achieved partly through complex layering and glazing. He used vermilion sparingly, instead creating his reds predominantly from red ochres mixed with madder or carmine lakes. Blues, as noted, do not feature greatly in his work. In contrast to his contemporary Vermeer, who excelled at using brilliant, expensive, natural ultramarine, the few blues found in his work are usually either azurite or smalt, both of which he also used to create green tones and glazes.[2] Bright blue skies were not for Rembrandt, he preferred to keep his palette in chocolate-coloured, liquid shadows.

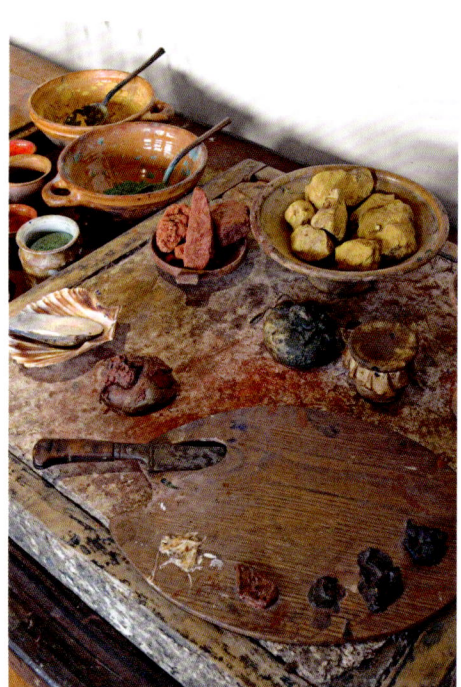

A.

A.   Recreation of the paint pigments Rembrandt would have used, The Rembrandt House Museum, Amsterdam, Netherlands
B.   *The Artist's Studio*, Rembrandt, *c.* 1654–58, pen, brown ink, grey-brown wash and white bodycolour on paper, 20.5 × 18.9 cm (8 ⅛ × 7 ½ in.)
C.   *A Painter in his Studio*, pupil of Rembrandt (previously attributed to Gerrit Dou), panel, *c.* 1630, 53 × 64.5 cm (20 ⅞ × 25 ½ in.)
D.   *The Artist in his Studio*, Rembrandt, *c.* 1628, oil on panel, 24.8 × 31.7 cm (9 ¾ × 12 ½ in.)

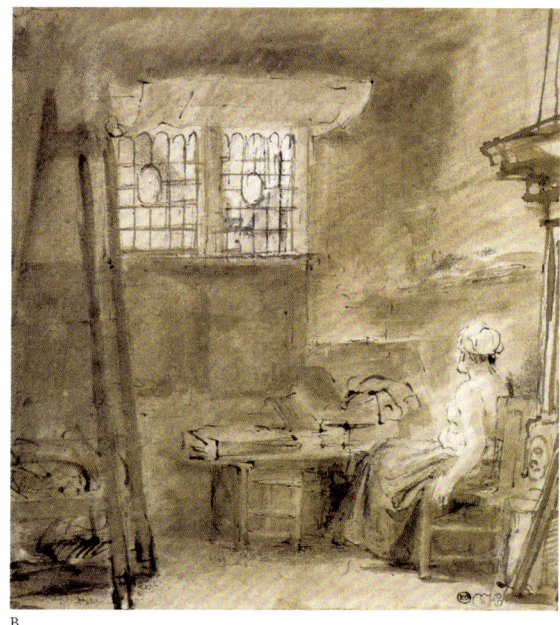

B.

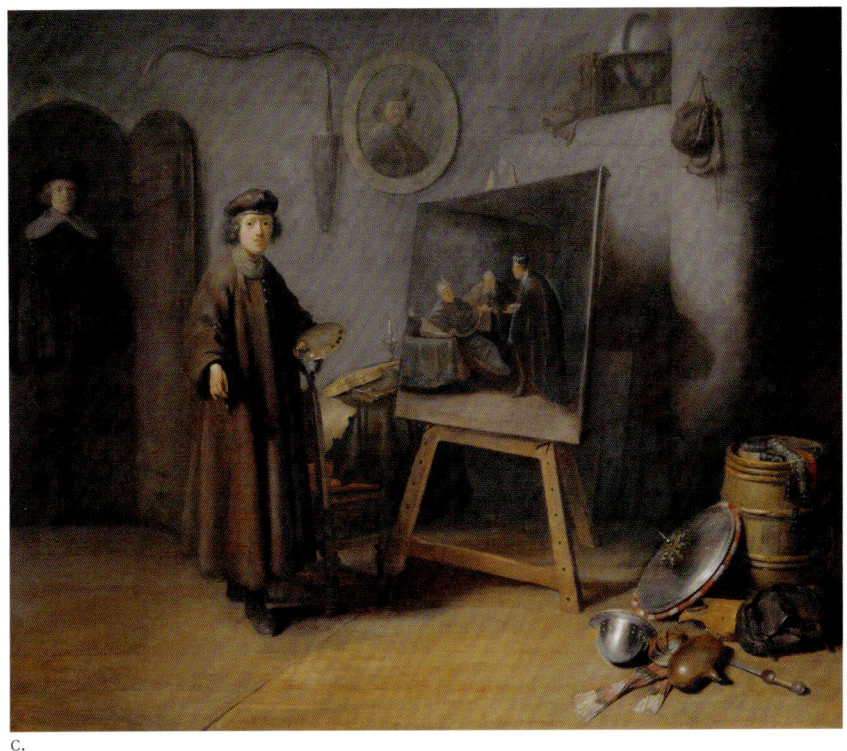

C.

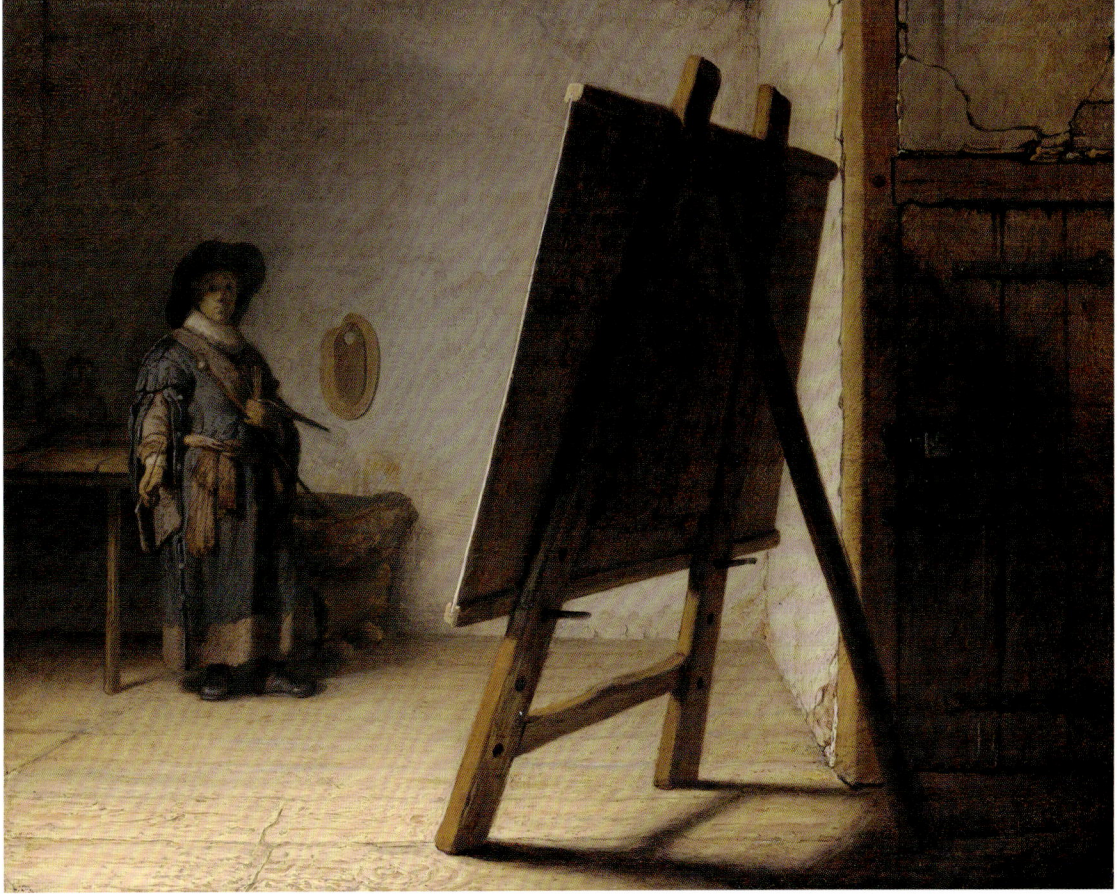

D.

ANGELICA KAUFFMAN 1741–1807

Allegorical and personal palettes

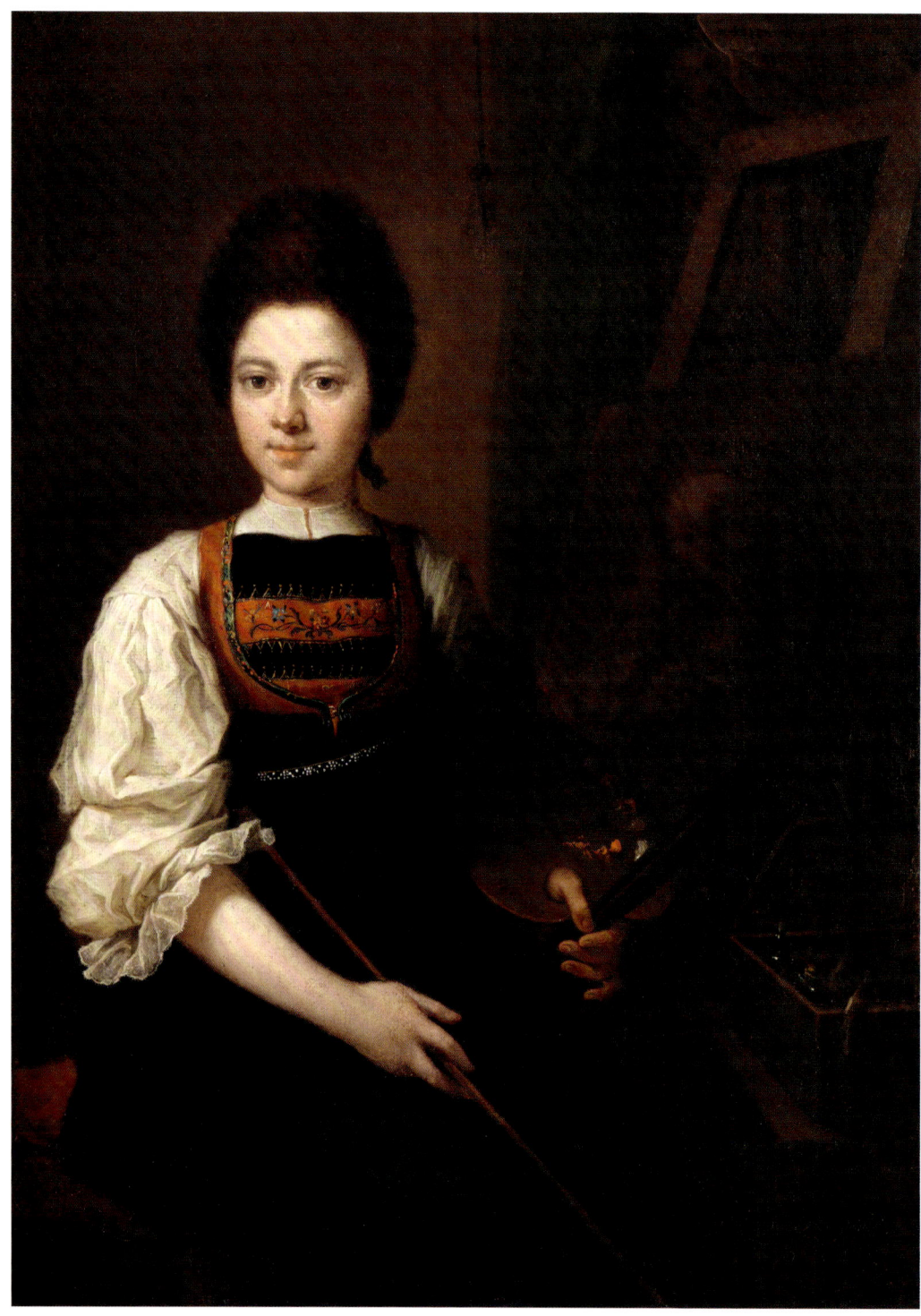

Self-portrait
Angelica Kauffman
1763
Oil on canvas
46 × 33 cm
(18 ⅛ × 13 in.)

'[To achieve] harmony and truth of colour is one of the hardest things.'

ANGELICA KAUFFMAN, LETTER TO JOHANN HEINRICH MEYER, 6 JUNE 1793

SOMETIME BETWEEN 1757 AND 1759, the teenaged Angelica Kauffman painted herself as a painter, seated by an easel and holding a mahlstick, a handful of long brushes and a palette. She chose to wear the traditional costume of her home region, the Bregenz Forest in Austria, comprising a black pleated linen dress and a white silk or cotton blouse. The painting is dark in tone, and nowhere close in style and accomplishment to Kauffman's many later works, but it does show us the young artist, shortly after the death of her mother, as having made the choice to become a painter. Her confident look is a precursor to the fascinating series of self-portraits she would later produce during her astonishing career in 18th-century Europe. She was extraordinarily gifted, not only as a painter; a few years earlier, barely thirteen years old, she had painted herself in shimmering rococo dress as a burgeoning singer and composer.

No actual palettes by Kauffman are known to have survived, but they appear several times in her work, as representations of her profession and her style, and as symbols of the theory and practice of painting, and more specifically, colouring. As such, they reflect changes in attitude towards colour in Kauffman's time. The palette painted by the young Kauffman is both personal and informative. In the context of this self-portrait, she demonstrates that she knows how to make, mix and arrange colours; how to plan a painting and how to use these precious ingredients skilfully and tastefully. A large paintbox with raw pigments and binders stands nearby. She has laid out the colours in the traditional manner from dark to light (a blob of somewhat tarnished white, probably lead-based, is clearly visible), and has placed a saturated red (perhaps vermilion) and a very dark colour slightly apart from the ochres and umbers. Some paint has been moved around on the palette, indicating that she is in the act of painting and not just posing. Those small smudges of paint counteract the stiffness of her pose. In many later self-portraits, she chooses a drawing implement,

such as a crayon-holder, as a symbol of her painting skills instead, often pointing it subtly towards her heart. Where the palettes still appear, she lifts them up to her chest, almost like a musician holds an instrument, and tilts them towards the viewer, the neat colour layout visible.

Kauffman became a hugely accomplished colourist at a time when colour was by some still considered inferior to line and composition. Discussions about the status of colour were rife at London's Royal Academy, of which she was a founding member. In 1778 she was commissioned by the Academy to create pictorial ceiling decorations that depicted personifications of the 'four elements of art' – Design, Invention, Composition and Colour or Colouring. In the image of Colour (image C., overleaf), Kauffman applies attributes of the allegory of Painting from Cesare Ripa's *Iconologia* (1593), exactly as Artemisia Gentileschi (see pages 30–33) had done in her self-portrait 140 years earlier. Yet, Kauffman's image is much lighter in tone and additionally pays homage to Isaac Newton's groundbreaking publication on colour, *Opticks* (1704), which informed all subsequent colour discourse. Her painter, likely a self-portrait in allegorical disguise, holds a near-empty palette in her hand, and dips her paintbrush into a Newtonian rainbow, stealing its light, utilizing science and thus elevating colour. At her foot is a symbolic colour-shifting chameleon. This was a clever yet light-hearted visual commentary on discussions about Newton's immaterial colours of light and the material colours used by artists. Incidentally, Kauffman's application of paint became thinner and more layered as her career progressed, and she probably considered the optical effects of semi-transparent colour, replacing coloured with white grounds in the early 1780s. She often used several variants of one colour family, for example, three different types of blue (Prussian blue, real ultramarine and azurite), to allow for the subtlest modelling of tone.[1]

Coincidentally, Kauffman would later befriend one of the greatest writers on colour of the Romantic

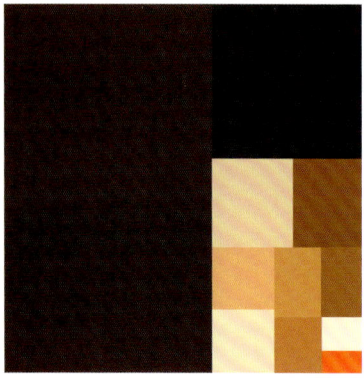

Proportional breakdown of colours used by Angelica Kauffman in *Self-portrait*, 1763, displayed on page 38.

age, Johann Wolfgang von Goethe, who was preparing the anti-Newtonian *Beyträge zur Optik* (1791/92) around that time. It is likely that they discussed colour in art, science and philosophy, perhaps disagreeing about Newton.

Also in the early 1790s, then in her fifties and a celebrated, hugely successful artist, Kauffman revisited her early decision to pursue a career as a painter and painted another symbolic palette. The large-scale *Self-portrait of the Artist Hesitating Between the Arts of Music and Painting* (1794), which exists in two versions, is both allegorical and overtly autobiographical. Referencing Annibale Carraci's painting *The Choice of Hercules* (1596), Kauffman inserts her younger self between the two allegorical figures of Music and Painting. She depicts herself in neoclassical white dress as an active, decisive and assured woman who chooses the harder but more rewarding path of painting. She is offering her hand to the figure of Painting, who is dressed in vibrant blue, red and yellow – the three primary colours of painters – and is holding a palette that contains four small blots of colour: a dark and a lighter red, a yellow, and a white. Kauffman will take that palette and fill it with her colours, and take the rockier path, towards the Newtonian light at the top of the classical hill.

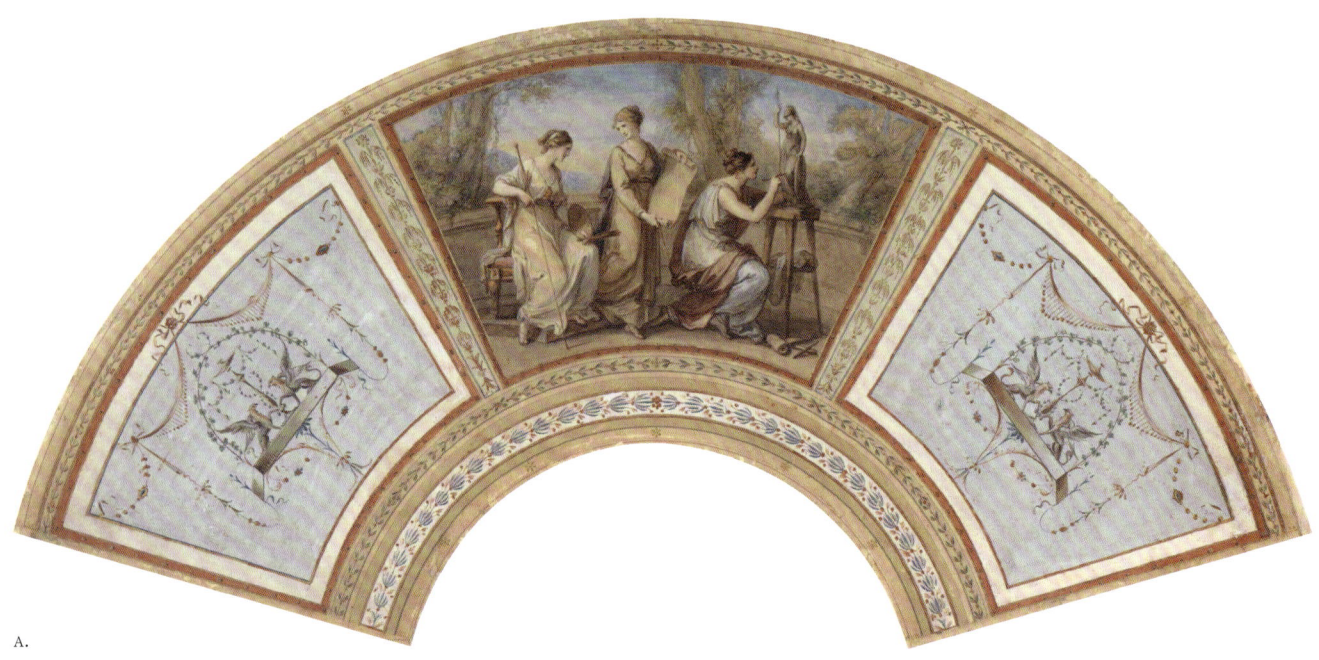

A.

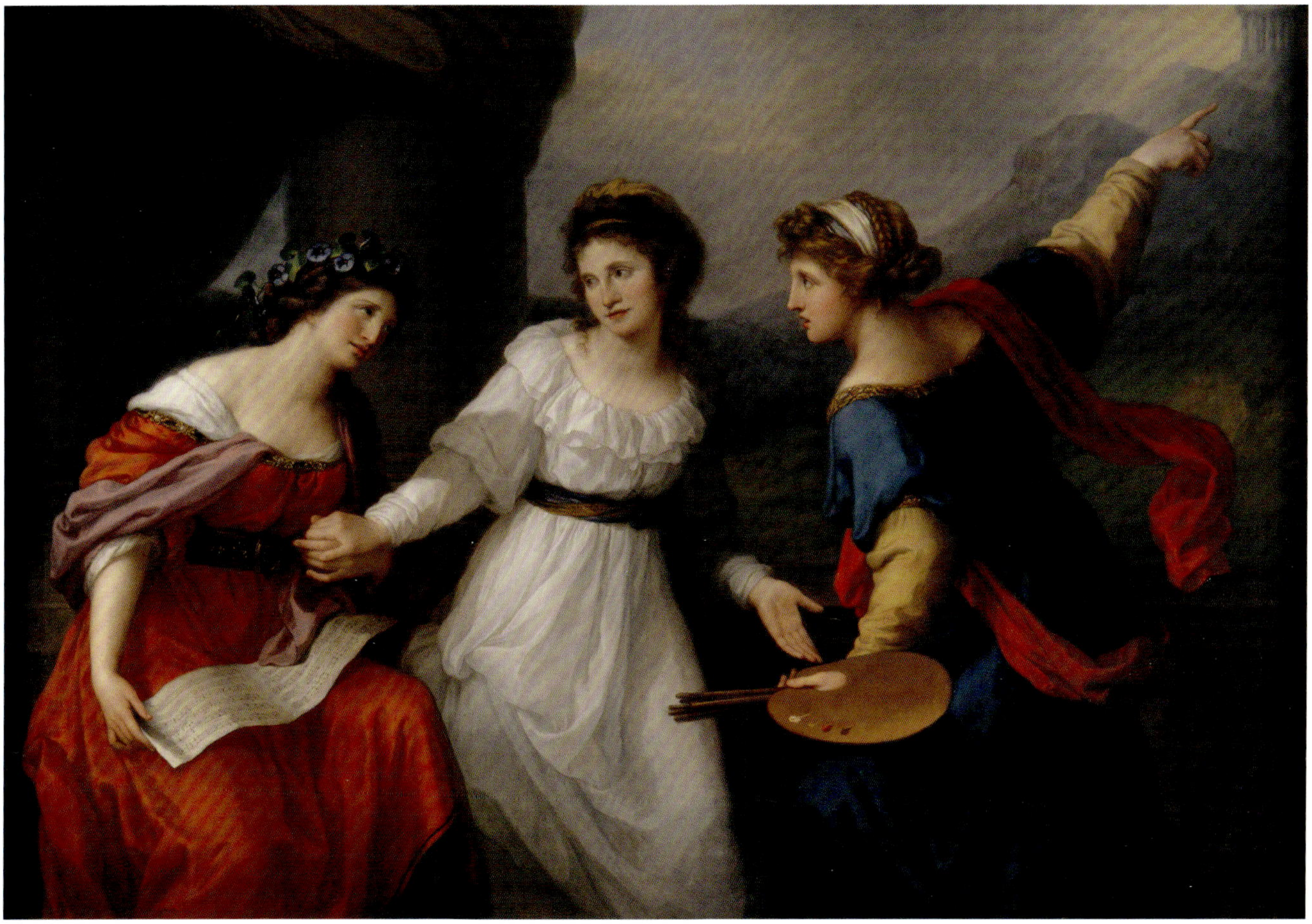

B.

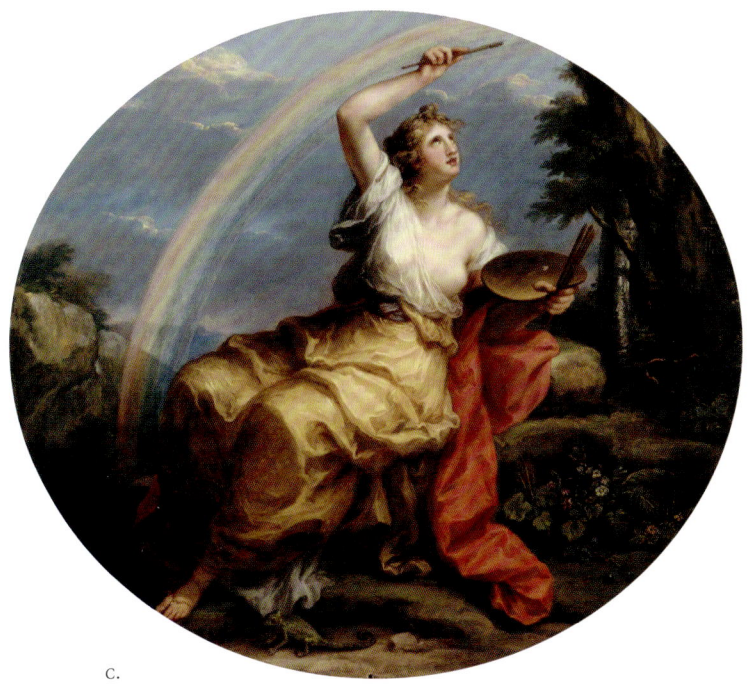

A. *Design for a Fan*, Angelica Kauffman, 1775, watercolour, gouache
    and gold on paper, 17.1 × 53.3 cm (6 ¾ × 21 in.)
B. *Self-portrait of the Artist Hesitating Between the Arts of Music and
    Painting*, Angelica Kauffman, 1794, oil on canvas, 147 × 215 cm
    (57 ⅞ × 84 ¾ in.)
C. *Colouring* (also known as *Colour*), Angelica Kauffman, 1778–80,
    oil on canvas, 126 × 148.5 cm (49 ⅝ × 58 ½ in.)

C.

ÉLISABETH LOUISE VIGÉE LE BRUN 1755–1842

A neat and calculated palette

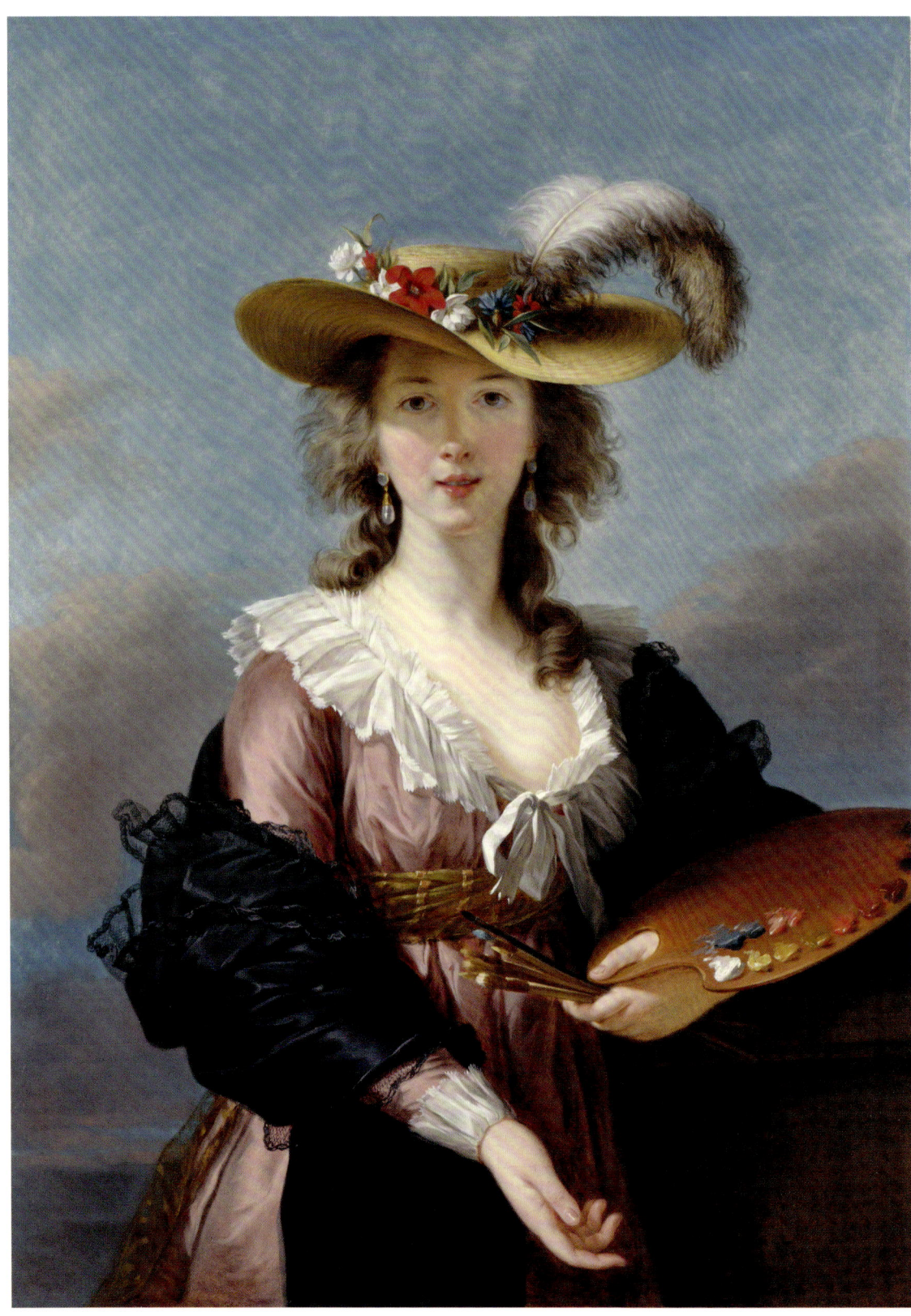

'This painting delights me and inspired me to make my own portrait in Brussels in search of the same effect. I painted myself wearing a straw hat with a feather and a garland of wild flowers, and holding my palette. When the portrait was exhibited at the salon, I dare say it greatly enhanced my reputation.'

ÉLISABETH LOUISE VIGÉE LE BRUN, *THE MEMOIRS OF MADAME VIGÉE LE BRUN*, 1835

IT IS REGRETTABLE THAT so few painting materials survive from the studios of great early women artists such as Élisabeth Louise Vigée Le Brun, but luckily, they frequently portrayed themselves as artists, proudly and assuredly holding the tools of their profession. Vigée Le Brun painted herself with her palette and brushes several times during a long international career that was marked by political upheaval (having worked for the French court, she decided to leave her native France just before the Revolution in 1789). In the one that was included in the Vasari Corridor of artists' self-portraits at the Uffizi in Florence (1790), she withholds a glimpse of her palette's surface, as if to guard her secret of colouring. However, this one, originally painted in Brussels in 1782, includes a realistically depicted palette with colours that reads like a textbook of late-18th-century portrait painting.

Self-portrait in a Straw Hat is a visual reference to a well-known painting by Peter Paul Rubens, *Portrait of Susanna Lunden*, from the 1620s. There are some chromatic and compositional similarities between the two, but Vigée Le Brun's main intention was to associate herself in a light-hearted way with the great painter of colour and light effects. Here is a female artist of the late 18th century, showing us her palette as if it was her business card. The tool pushes itself into the pictorial foreground, with every blob of carefully placed paint clearly visible. Vigée Le Brun leaves us in no doubt about her professionalism and the neatness of her working methods.

She is holding the large arm or studio palette in her left hand, tilting it towards us to allow us to see what is on it. Nine colours are neatly laid out along its top curved edge, arranged from light to dark, with white closest to the thumbhole and two barely visible, very dark shades at the other end. Vigée Le Brun frequently used jet-black shades in her painting, usually for depicting shimmering black fabrics and clothes, such as the shawl she is wearing

in the self-portrait. She often contrasted these blacks with renderings of brilliant white textiles and accessories, such as ruffles, lace collars and feathers.

Between these two sentinels of light and dark we can make out three yellows of different brightness, and three reds, also of varying degrees of intensity. Below this line of colours, she has placed two shades of blue (probably Prussian blue) and a light pink, the latter most likely a mixture of lead white and one of her brilliant reds. Separating the blues from the rest of the colours is somewhat unusual on 18th-century palettes. It is frequently the strongest reds (such as vermilion or lead red) that are placed slightly apart from the rest. Vigée Le Brun was famous for her bold use of reds, especially in her later paintings, and often combined vermilion red with a translucent top layer of cochineal. She used a similar technique of subtle cochineal glazes over skin tones, to give the impression of blood pulsating under the skin.[1]

It is easy for our eyes to follow the chromatic trail of this painted palette: the light blues form the celestial background of the painting, against which her tall, confident figure is silhouetted, and the pink was obviously used for the dress she is wearing in this version (a copy by the artist herself, created soon after the original). The yellows were used for the titular straw hat, while the reds can be seen in her lips and some of the flowers on her hat. The palette looks incredibly neat, and like most women painters who created self-portraits with their tools in the 18th and 19th centuries, she is wearing fine clothes that would not have been suitable for actually working with oil paints and large canvases. This is a clever and meticulously composed image, an example of calculated self-promotion. The palette becomes the main iconographical signifier of Vigée Le Brun's art, craft and taste. In her earlier portrait of the painter Joseph Vernet, who once advised her to strictly paint 'from nature', she used a palette in a similar

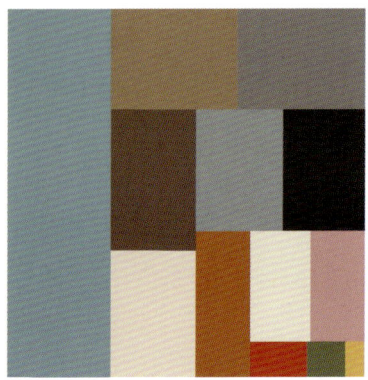

Proportional breakdown of colours used by Élisabeth Louise Vigée Le Brun in *Self-portrait in a Straw Hat*, 1782, displayed on page 42.

representative way. On his palette, some delicate mixing can be seen in the centre of the palette. Although she didn't follow Vernet's advice about realistic representation of nature, she did perhaps follow the general arrangement of his palette.

The paint on Vigée Le Brun's own palette appears untouched, but look closer and you can see that she has dipped some of the brushes she is also holding into the colours. The brushes in turn link the palette and artist's hand with the painting itself, adding to the joyful visual confusion that is inherent in self-portraiture. Has she just added the finishing touch to one of those wildflowers on her hat? Has she now turned towards us to present the finished work? In respect of line and shape, the straw hat with its garland of flowers may even mirror the shape and arrangement of the palette.

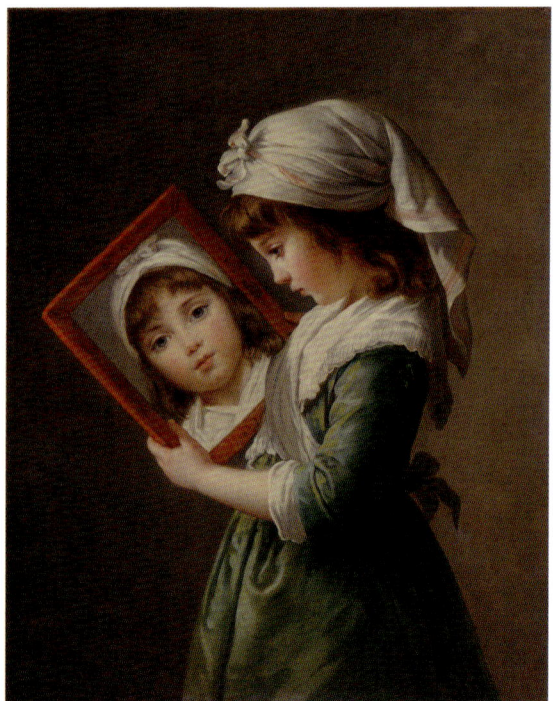

A.

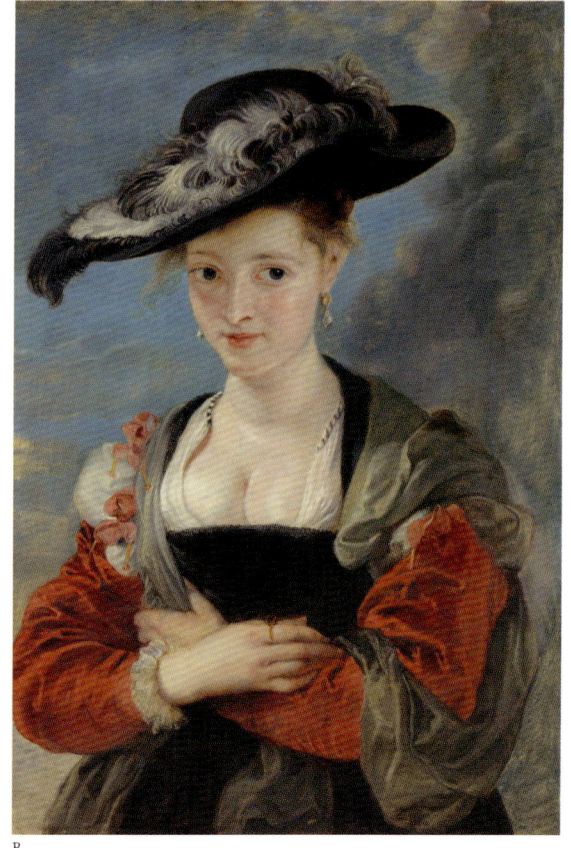

B.

A. *Julie Le Brun Looking in a Mirror*, Élisabeth Louise Vigée Le Brun, 1787, oil on canvas, 73 × 59.4 cm (28 ¾ × 23 ⅜ in.)

B. *Portrait of Susanna Lunden* (also known as *Le Chapeau de Paille*), Peter Paul Rubens, probably 1622–25, oil on oak, 79 × 54.6 cm (31 ⅛ × 21 ½ in.)

C. *Marie Antoinette in a Chemise Dress*, Élisabeth Louise Vigée Le Brun, 1783, oil on canvas, 89.8 × 72 cm (35 ⅜ × 28 ⅜ in.)

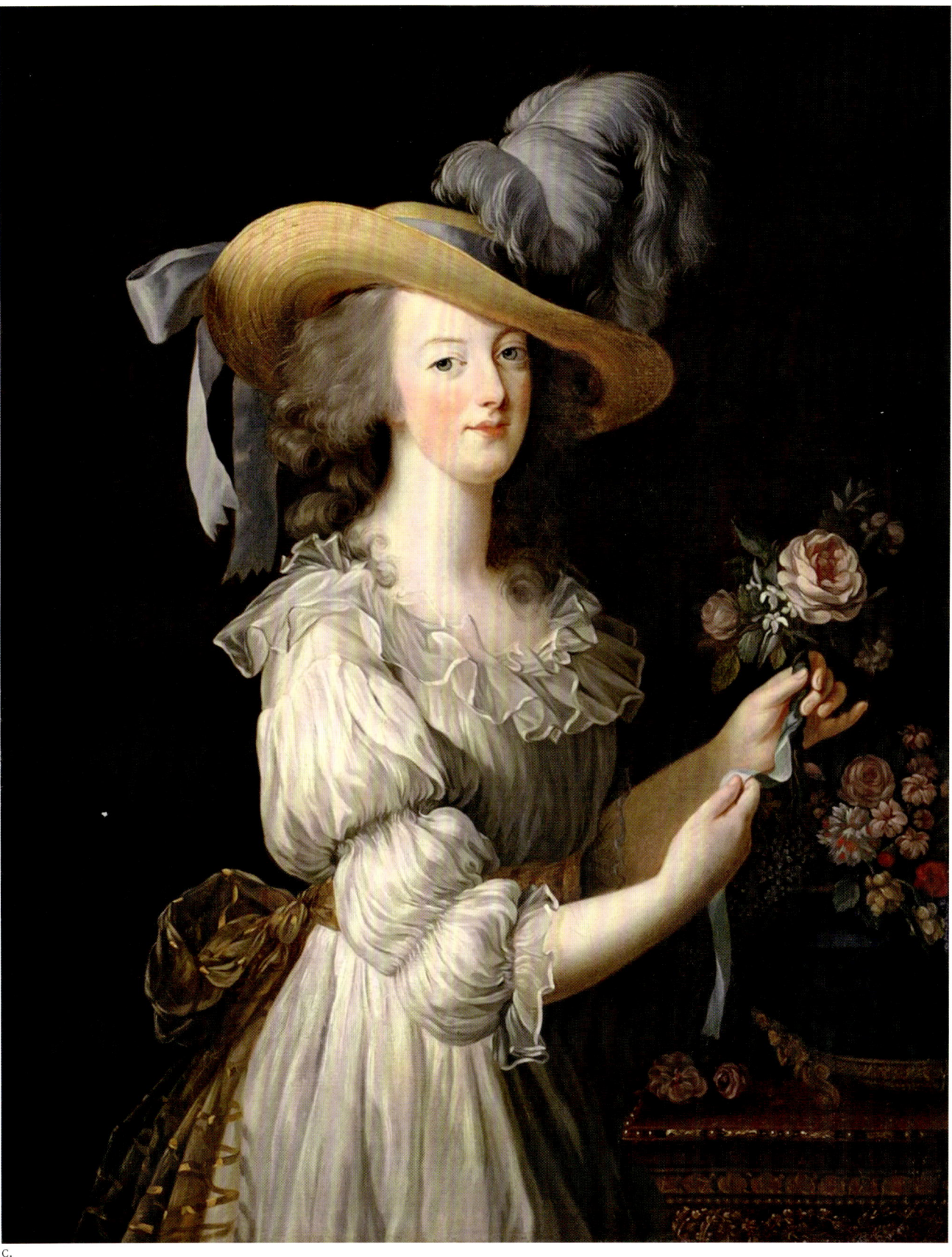

JOHN CONSTABLE 1776–1837

A palette facing the elements

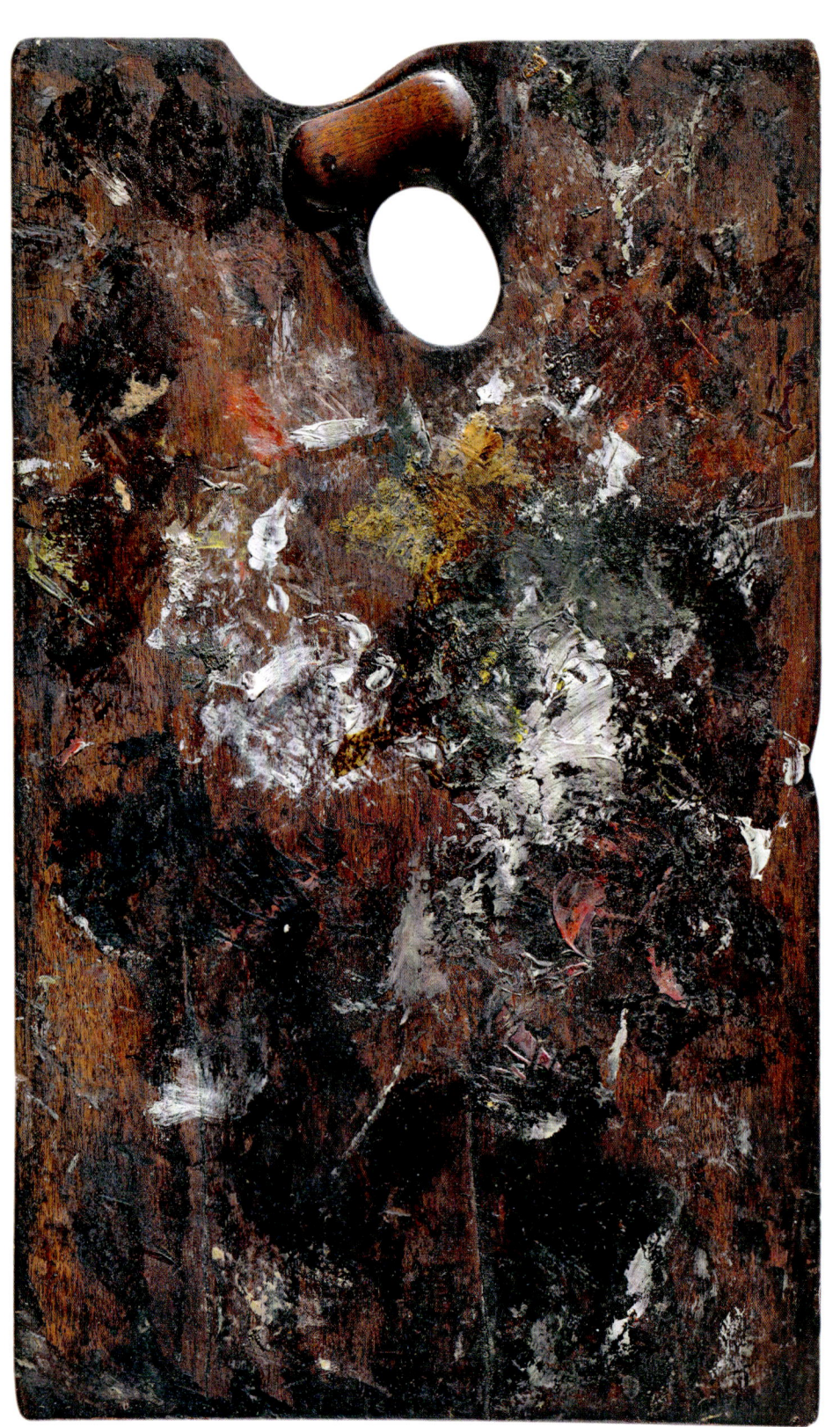

John Constable's palette
Undated
Paint on wood
40.5 × 24.5 cm
(16 × 9 ¾ in.)

Dedham Vale
John Constable
1828
Oil on canvas
144.5 × 122 cm
(57 × 48 ⅛ in.)

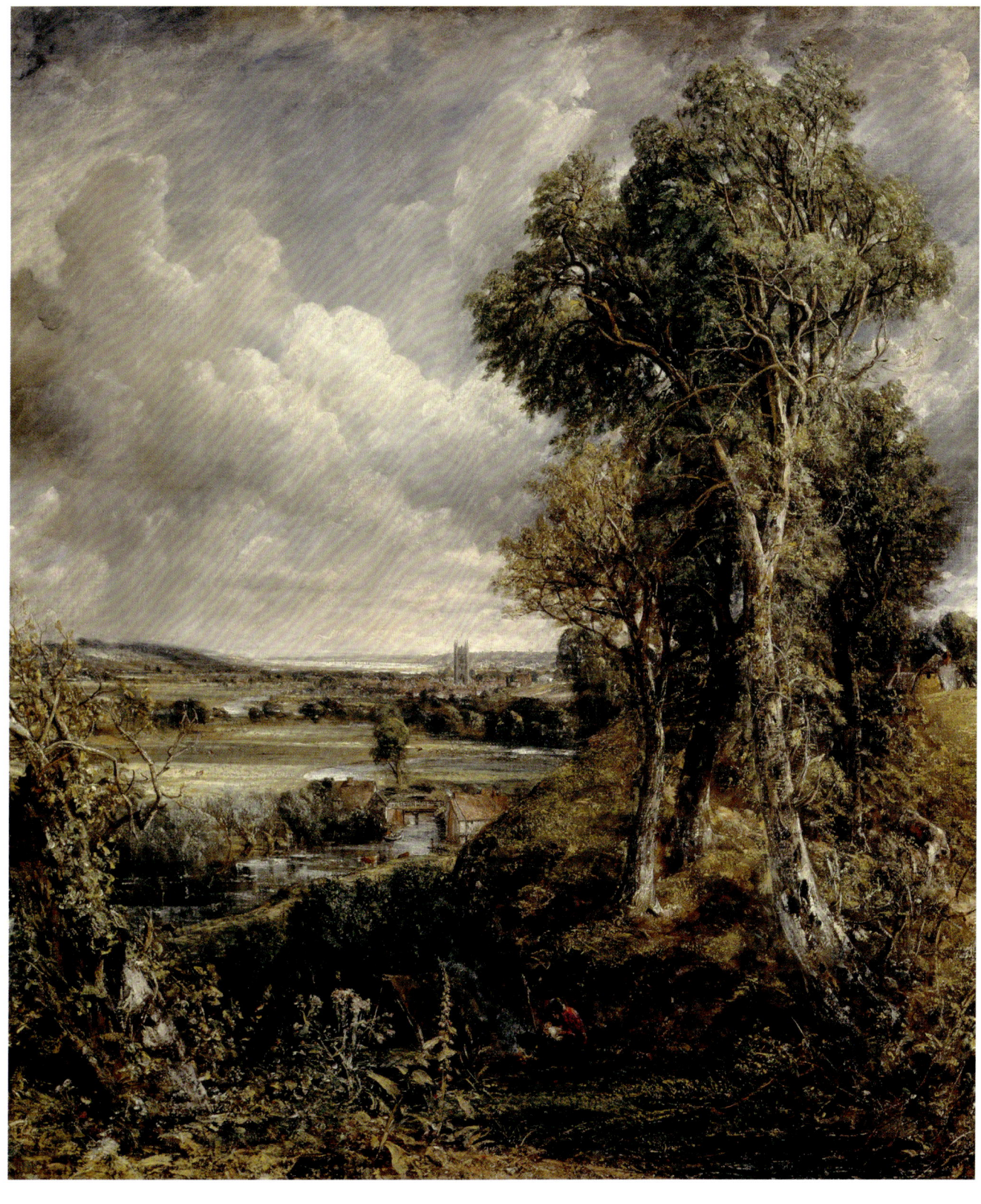

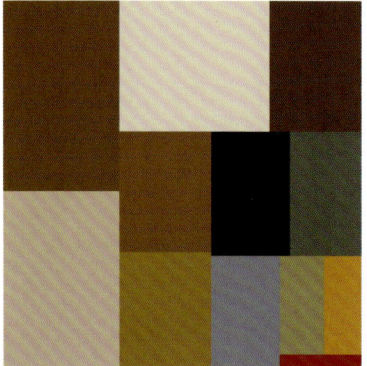

Proportional breakdown of colours used by
John Constable in *Dedham Vale*, 1828, displayed
on the previous page.

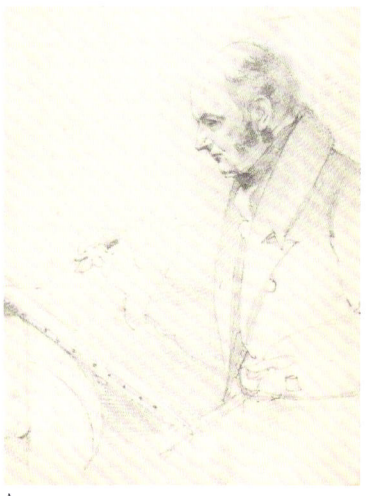

A.

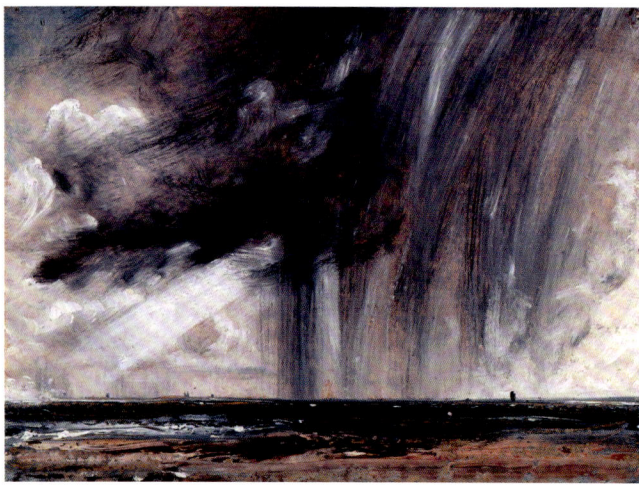

B.

WHEN JOHN CONSTABLE DIED, four palettes, a wooden paintbox and many more painting materials were left in his studio. A metal box containing oil paints in pigs' bladders, gypsum and blue pigment in a small jar also survive. The square palette with a thumbhole and thumb rest shown here is made of hardwood, and shows identifiable traces of some of Constable's preferred pigments, including vermilion (which he used sparingly but to great effect in some compositions, or to add warmth to colour mixtures), emerald green (for foliage and pastures), chrome yellow, cobalt blue, lead white and madder. All of these pigments are present in his late work. He also used large quantities of Prussian blue, which can be found in most of his skies, but he favoured the expensive natural ultramarine blue over the synthesized version that had become available in the late 1820s. Due to its expensiveness, he often used it as a finishing glaze over other blues.

His colouring is largely naturalistic, with close attention to detail of vegetation, accurate proportions and perspective, and his brushwork is vibrant and varied. The large oil paintings intended for display at galleries and exhibitions were precisely worked, but he deliberately avoided a flat finish in order to convey the variety of texture in nature. The painting shown on the previous page, a sweeping view of the Stour Valley in Suffolk with a dramatic sky, is typical of Constable's colour choices and techniques. The landscape and atmospheric conditions are acutely observed and painted in naturalistic colours, a small figure is painted in vermilion red, but each brushstroke is visible, with many carefully placed highlights in lead white that give the textured paint surface a characteristic Constablesque shimmer.

Constable also produced hundreds of small working sketches that were not meant for display. These give us the most illuminating glimpses of the dedicated, skilful and unflinching Constable at work. Landscape was his main passion, and although he produced most of his larger paintings in the studio, they almost all began out in the open. Constable went out in search of motifs in all weather conditions, often chasing storms. He took his painting materials with him, including a range of sheets of paper or cardboard, some prepared with ground colour to save time. These he would stick into the lid of his paintbox and start painting. In a letter to his friend John Fisher in 1825, he describes the physicality of these sketching sessions: 'I have enclosed in the box a dozen of my Brighton oil sketches...they were done in the lid of my [paint] box, on my knees as usual.'[1]

Sketching in oil was messy in Constable's lifetime, as batches of oil paint still came in tied-up pigs' bladders that had to be pricked to release the paint. The pins were tack-shaped and would also be used to seal the

'When we speak of the perfection of art, we must recollect what the materials are with which a painter contends with nature. For the light of the sun he has but patent yellow and white lead – for the darkest shade, umber or soot.'

JOHN CONSTABLE, *THE SECOND LECTURE ON LANDSCAPE PAINTING*, 1836

bladders to slow down the process of the colour drying out. By contrast, watercolour had for several decades been available as easily portable, moist cakes, but Constable opted for the more substantial, malleable and intense medium of oil paint. One reason may have been that he was particularly interested in capturing wet and windy conditions. For his many sky studies, he often used washes of body colour first, then added oil paint, to achieve a more powdery, luminous effect.

Constable was not as overtly interested in using colour experimentally as his contemporary J. M. W. Turner (see pages 54–57), but he was a superb observer and chronicler of the natural world, and more inventive in his use of pigments and paint than some acknowledge. He considered art a science, but he also saw emotion and deeper meaning in landscape. 'Painting,' he told John Fisher 'is but another word for feeling.'[2] The son of a mill owner, he grew up in the flat countryside of Suffolk, which provided him with a profound understanding of changing meteorological conditions and became particularly fascinated by clouds. Unlike Turner, he had no desire to experience the light of Italy, and never left Britain. He spent part of his life in Hampstead Heath, London, and in the 1820s some extended periods in Brighton, on the Sussex coast.

The majority of his small oil sketches appear to have been very quickly painted, with the paint applied in thin layers. He used a variety of sable-hair brushes, and sometimes even the palette knife or his fingers to apply more paint, often combining smooth and rough surfaces. He thus managed to capture fleeting cloud formations, approaching storms, downpours (as in *Rainstorm over the Sea*, image B.), and bright blue skies after rain, but he often got soaked in the process. Many of the sketches in impasto got flattened and smudged on the way home, but they still worked as visual notes for later, larger compositions. Today, they impress us with their expressive visual power and give us a real sense of an energetic Constable at work, trying to capture the textures, colours and light of nature.

C.

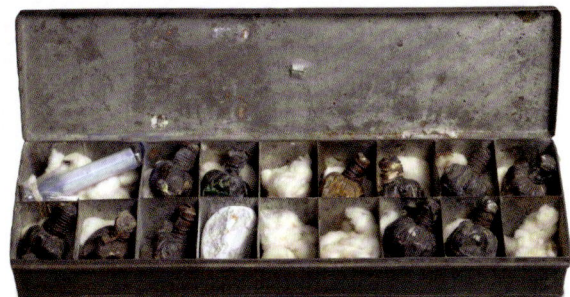

D.

A.   *John Constable*, Daniel Maclise, *c.* 1831, pencil, 14.9 × 11.4 cm (5 ⅞ × 4 ½ in.)

B.   *Rainstorm over the Sea*, John Constable, *c.* 1824–28, oil on paper laid on canvas, 23.5 × 32.6 cm (9 ⅜ × 12 ⅞ in.)

C.   *Landscape with a Double Rainbow*, John Constable, 28 July 1812, oil on paper laid on canvas, 33.7 × 38.4 (13 ⅜ × 15 ⅛ in.)

D.   John Constable's tin box containing oil paints and varnishes, 5.1 × 33 × 8.6 cm (2 × 13 × 3 ⅜ in.)

EUGÈNE DELACROIX 1798–1863

A palette composed of precious stones

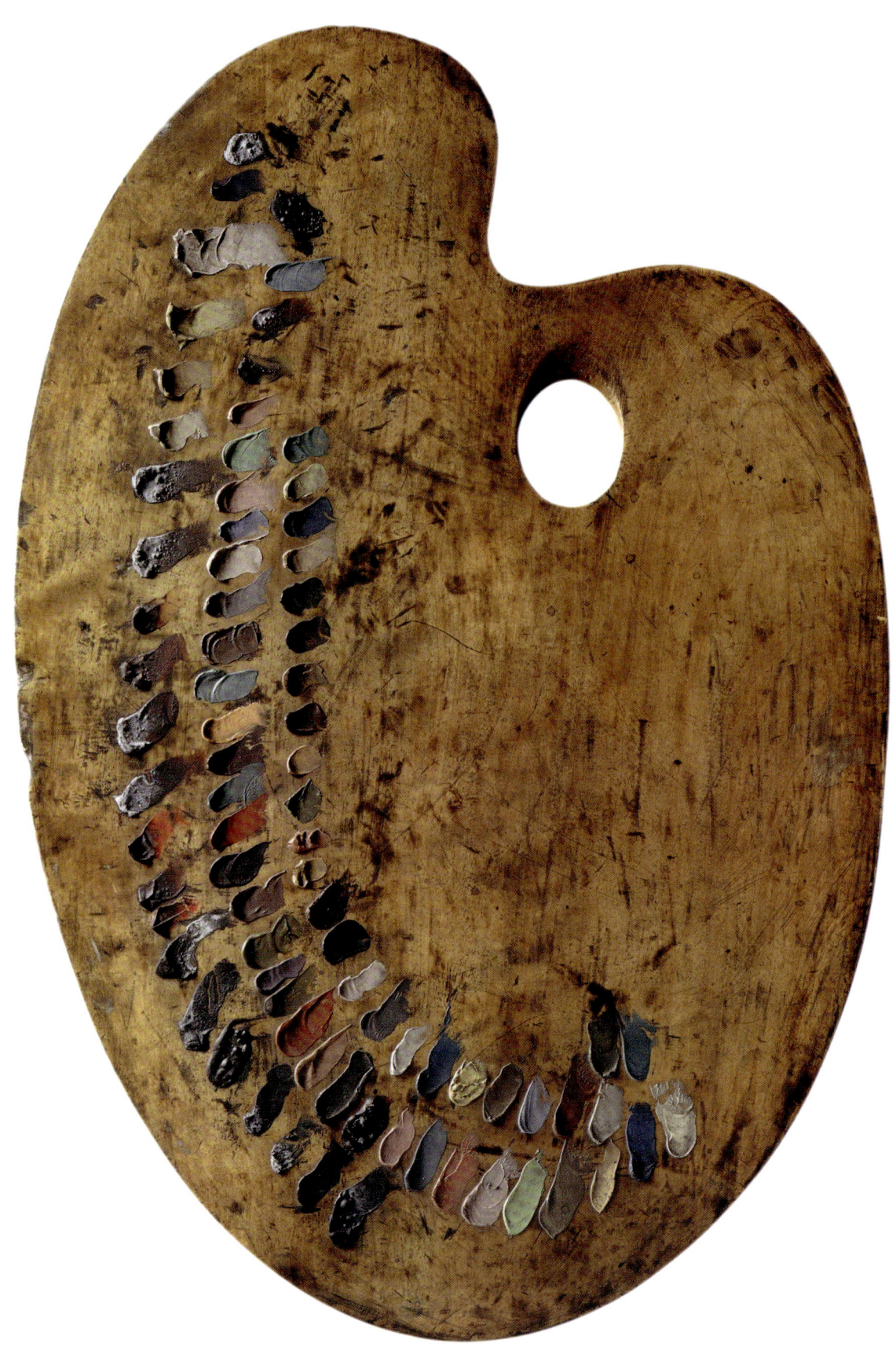

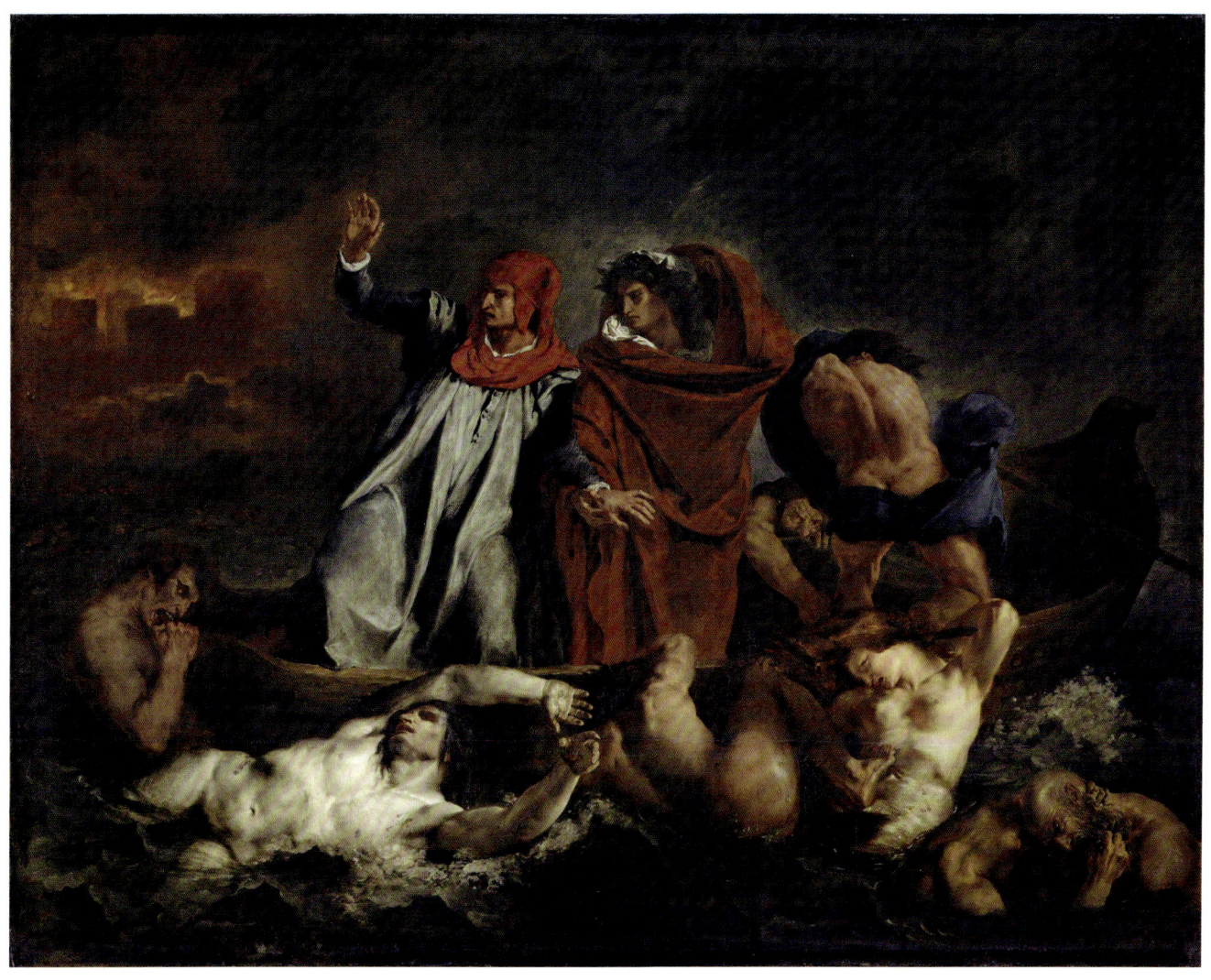

Eugène Delacroix's palette
Before 1863
Pigments on wood (chestnut)
31 × 45.2 cm
(12 ¼ × 17 ⅞ in.)

Dante and Virgil in Hell
(Also known as *The Barque
of Dante*)
Eugène Delacroix
1822
Oil on canvas
189 × 241 cm
(74 ½ × 95 in.)

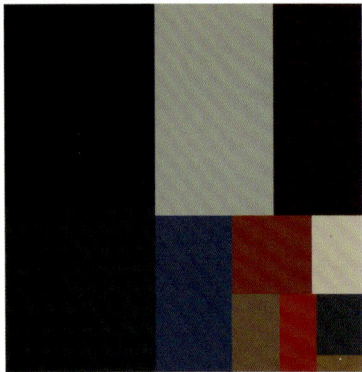

Proportional breakdown of colours used by Eugène Delacroix in *Dante and Virgil in Hell*, 1822, displayed on the previous page.

EUGÈNE DELACROIX'S PALETTES WERE, as the poet Charles Baudelaire noted, the most minutely and carefully prepared ones he ever saw, similar to a tasteful floral arrangement. This one is indeed a meticulously arranged palette, with more than eighty individual strokes of pre-mixed colours neatly arranged in three rows. It does not look like a palette that was actually used for painting, but more like a chromatic plan for the layout of a painting, as the colours remain untouched. It is likely that this palette was created as a gift for another painter, his admirer Henri Fantin-Latour (see pages 74–77), whose sense of colour was comparable to Delacroix's. It may look staged, but other palettes used by Delacroix show a similarly careful layout of dozens of pre-mixed colours, precursors of his often monumental and busy paintings, filled with narrative, pictorial and chromatic detail.

Delacroix had a great interest in colour theory, symbolism, and its material qualities and powers. He filled many sketchbooks with colour notes and pigment lists, and kept a journal in which he elaborated on his relationship with and thoughts on colour. One diary entry from 1856 contains no fewer than twenty-three pigments for the layout of a painting, others comprise long lists of colours requested or received from art suppliers, among them Maison Haro in Paris.

Delacroix's lifetime saw an unprecedented wave of new synthetic pigments, and oil paints became available in convenient collapsible metal tubes. His extensive notes and journal entries reveal that he frequently sought out new pigments as soon as they became available, for example zinc yellow, cadmium yellow, viridian, cobalt green and blue, and zinc white. In addition to the many pigments mentioned by name

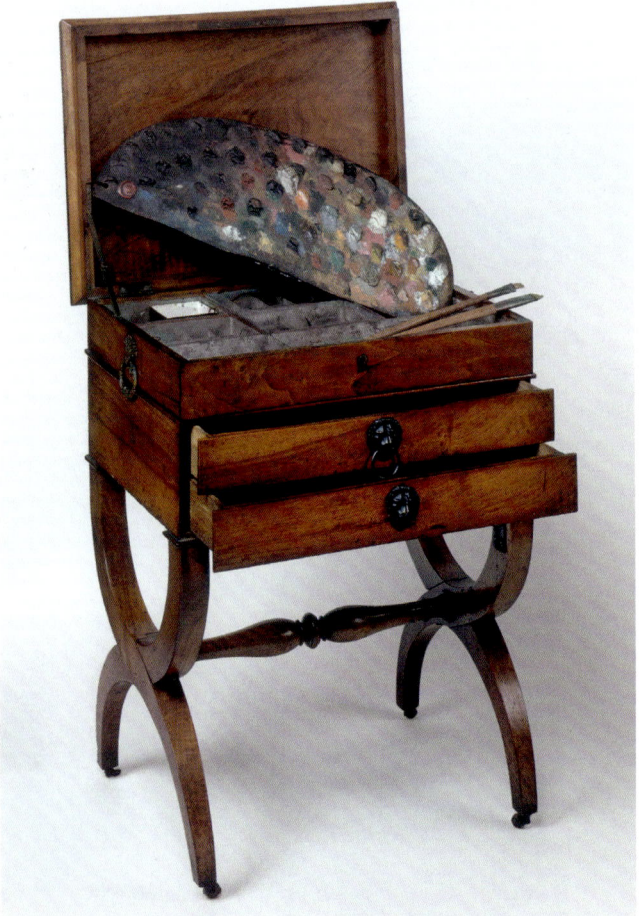

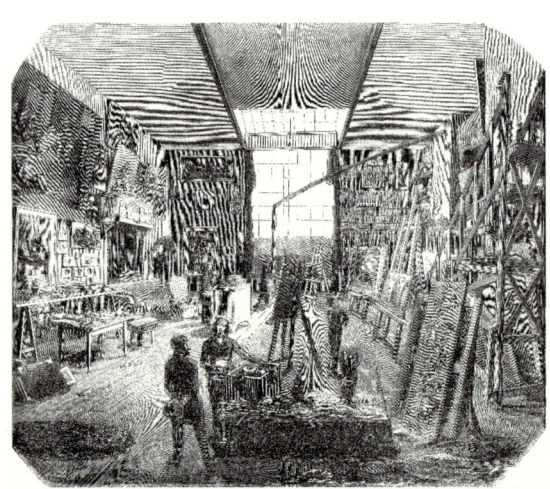

'My freshly arranged palette, brilliant with contrasting colours, is enough to fire my enthusiasm.'

EUGÈNE DELACROIX, JOURNAL ENTRY, 21 JULY 1850

in his journals, others can be identified, such as bone black, chalk white, Naples yellow, carbon black and a mineral black.[1] More was more for Delacroix when it came to colour. He saw energy and power in it, and the palette was the catalyst for each new creative process: 'My freshly arranged palette, brilliant with contrasting colours, is enough to fire my enthusiasm.'

The striking look of Delacroix's physical and conceptual palettes did not go unnoticed. Fantin-Latour must have cherished his material example, Baudelaire repeatedly praised them and a contemporary critic compared them to a 'jewel composed of precious stones'.[2] During Delacroix's lifetime, the artist and teacher Madame Cavé wrote a book about his painting methods, titled *La Couleur* (1863). Several others followed, including one in 1930 by artist Léon Piot on Delacroix's palettes alone, in which he claims that the great Romantic painter, who impressed even Vincent van Gogh with his command of colour, took his palettes to bed when he was ill, mixing colours and laying out his chromatic gemstones.

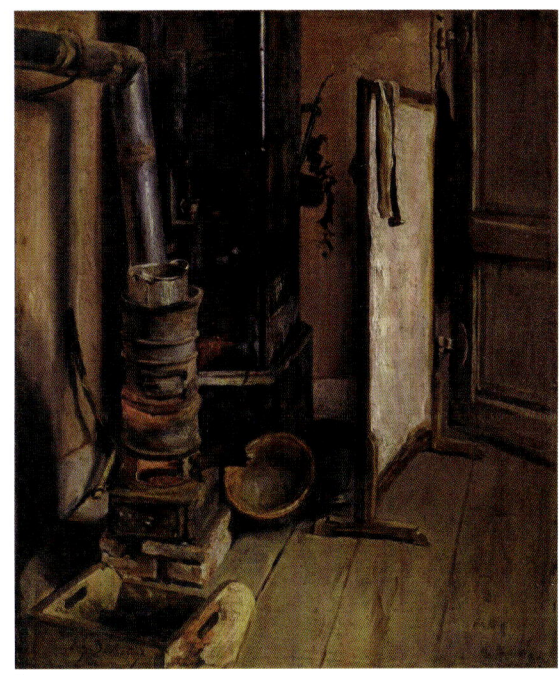

C.

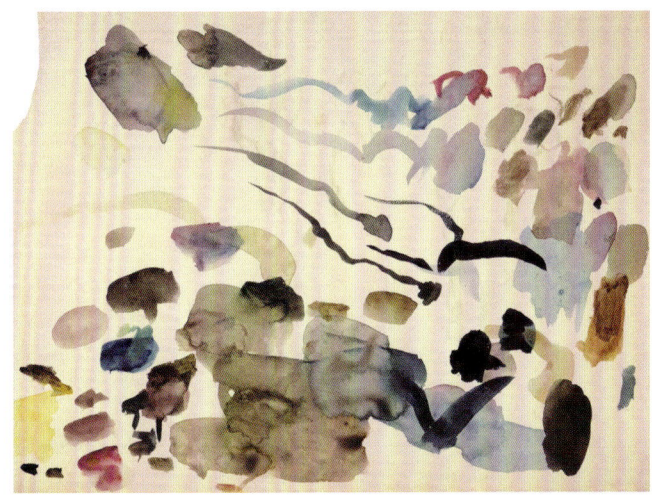

A. Eugène Delacroix's painting table with palette and brushes, 77 × 54.2 × 43 cm (30 ⅜ × 21 ⅜ × 17 in.)
B. 'Eugène Delacroix's studio', Ed. Renard, engraving from *L'Illustration: Journal Universel*, 25 September 1852
C. *A Corner of the Studio*, school of Eugène Delacroix, 1825–50, oil on canvas, 51 × 43.4 cm (20 ⅛ × 17 ⅛ in.)
D. Watercolour trials from album 29, fol. 112v., Eugène Delacroix, 21.2 × 28.4 cm (8 ⅜ × 11 ¼ in.)

D.

J. M. W. TURNER 1775–1851

Painting sea, rain and sky with a watery palette

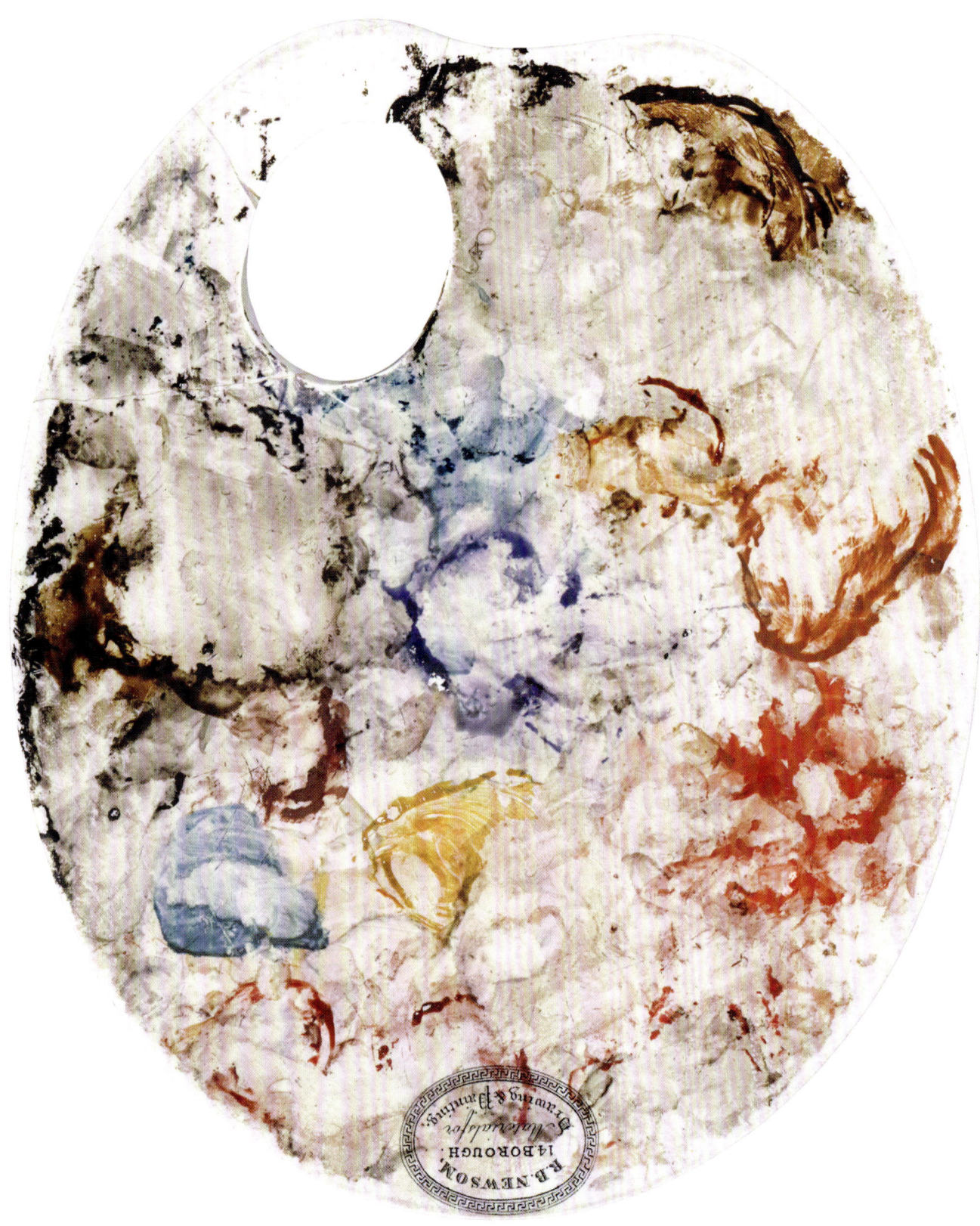

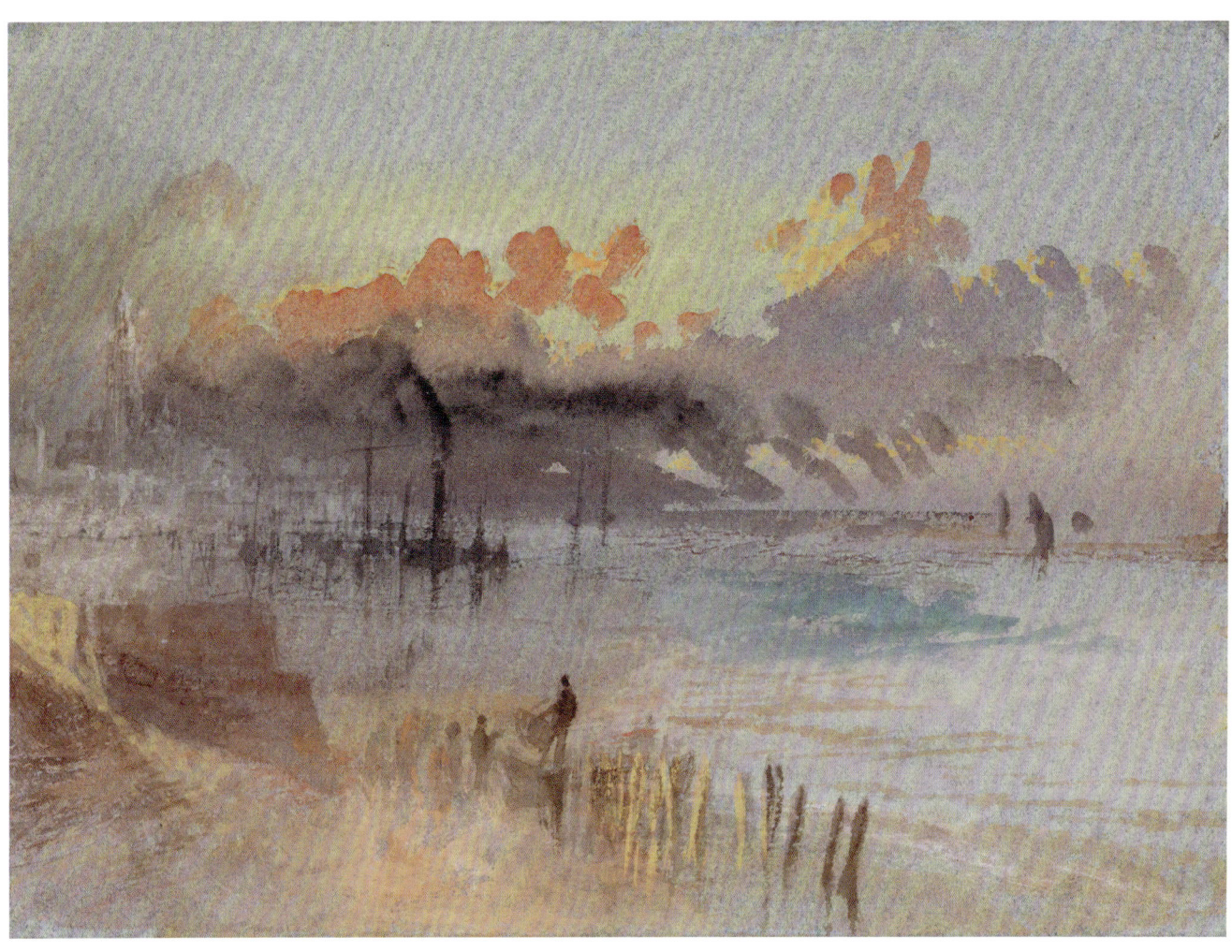

J. M. W. Turner's palette
Undated
Watercolour on ceramic
17.5 × 14.8 cm
(7 × 5 ⅞ in.)

Margate: The Great Beach with
the Pier and Lighthouse and
Jarvis's Landing Place at Sunset
J. M. W. Turner
c. 1829–40
Gouache and watercolour
on blue paper
13.7 × 19 cm
(5 ½ × 7 ½ in.)

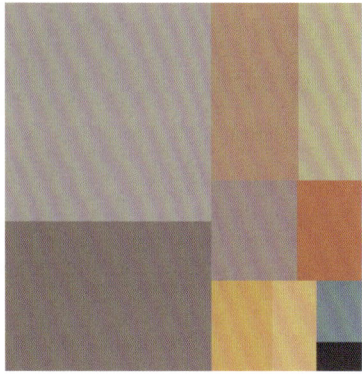

Proportional breakdown of colours used by J. M. W. Turner in *Margate: The Great Beach with the Pier and Lighthouse and Jarvis's Landing Place at Sunset*, c. 1829–40, displayed on the previous page.

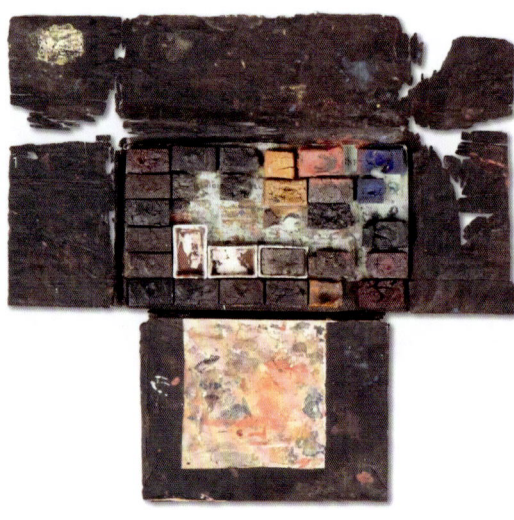

A.

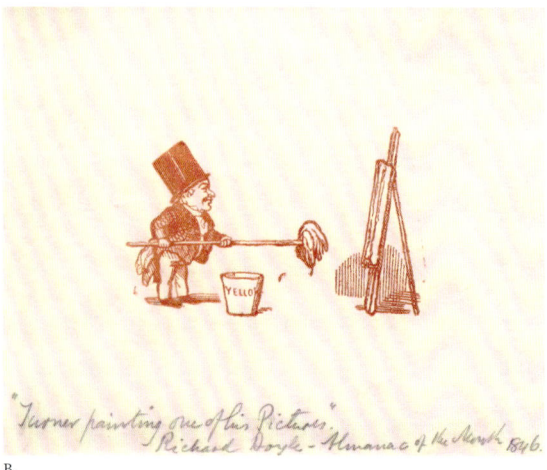

B.

THIS CERAMIC WATERCOLOUR PALETTE is one of two that belonged to J. M. W. Turner. Due to the breakable nature of the material, ceramic palettes survive in far fewer numbers compared to those made from wood or board. Watercolour, by its very nature, is more fleeting and fugitive and less substantial than oil, egg tempera or acrylic paint. A ceramic plate provides a non-absorbent surface suitable for water-based paint and is essentially a larger version of ceramic mixing trays found in many 18th- and 19th-century paintboxes (today largely replaced by plastic). The smoothness of the material also means that it could be easily wiped and cleaned, making the traces of paint on this palette even more remarkable.

The whiteness of the palette emulates white drawing paper and would have given Turner a good indication of how certain paint mixtures and layers would appear on paper (although he used a variety of coloured papers and backgrounds). The palette was supplied by Richard Bowden Newsom, who had a shop at 14 Wellington Street, Borough, London, between 1834 and 1837. The three primaries, red (possibly vermilion or a red lake), yellow (possibly a yellow ochre or a darkened chrome yellow) and blue (likely indigo, cobalt or Prussian blue) are clearly identifiable. He placed these at the centre of the palette, above the thumbhole, from where he began his experimental mixing, radiating outwards. Almost the entire surface of the palette is covered in mixtures, at times creating very dark browns, as well as large areas of very lowly saturated greys, likely the result of adding water to the paints to create more subtle and transparent layers.

Although much better known for his radical use of oil paint, often on large canvases, Turner was also one of the most gifted watercolourists of his time, having exhibited watercolours from 1790 onwards. In the same year, he began filling small notebooks with sketches. He continued to do so until the end of his life, creating tens of thousands of sketches, many of which in watercolour, provided an unparalleled visual record of his art, life and techniques.[1] He also produced larger watercolour sketches of chromatic layouts, some of which he called 'colour beginnings', a term later adopted by art historians. These were precursors to more finished compositions in oil or other media. Some sketches consist of simple trials in the shape of blots or strokes, to see how mixtures would appear on paper, or how certain colour combinations and layering might work. The painting shown here is a watercolour and gouache sketch on blue paper. We cannot link it to the palette, but it displays similarly rich colours with mixed browns seen in the foreground, bright blues for the sea and near-pure reds and yellows used to create the cloud formations in evening sunlight.

'Your business [William] Winsor is to make colours for Artists, mine is to use them.'

J. M. W. TURNER TO WILLIAM WINSOR (OF WINSOR &
NEWTON), QUOTED IN W. E. KILLIK'S *A SHORT HISTORY
OF WINSOR & NEWTON*, 1925

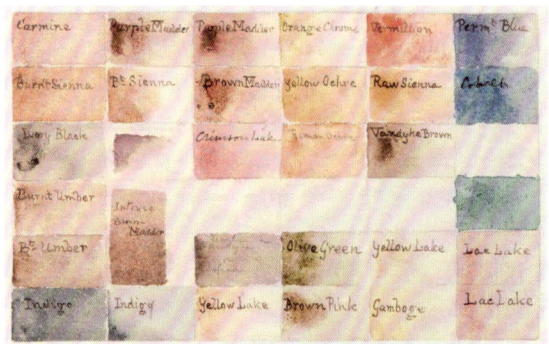

C.

Watercolour as a medium had become increasingly popular in the late 18th century, largely due to its portability and quick drying time, which made it suitable for sketching outdoors and while travelling. The invention of moist watercolour cakes and the rise of watercolour painting as an art form pursued by professionals and amateurs alike further popularized the medium. However, Turner was not simply part of a trend: from an early age his watercolours had a distinctive look and he mastered the medium like few other artists, giving it the same visual power as oil paints. It could be argued that when he painted in oil he would often try to emulate the transparent, luminous quality of watercolour paint.[2] Turner's watercolours range from the faintest colour samples to sketches in combination with outlines in pencil, and highly worked, finished paintings that would frequently be turned into prints. As Joyce H. Townsend has explained, Turner's use of paints was highly experimental and daring, and he would manipulate watercolour further once applied to paper. This could mean removing colour from the wet surface, using blotting paper, cloth or even breadcrumbs, or scratching into it with the end of brushes, palette knives or fingernails.[3] While he bought many paints from William Winsor (founder of Winsor & Newton), he also made watercolour cakes himself, mixing raw pigments with gums or honey. We get a sense of Turner's physical and impulsive use of painting materials when looking at some of his heavily used, travelling watercolour boxes. Other objects and works reflect his more methodical and intellectual side: a neatly inscribed test paper of colours from one of his watercolour boxes (image C.) was probably not made by him, but kept as a useful visual reference. Turner made extensive notes on colour throughout his life and read widely and thoroughly about colour in theory and practice. He was familiar with the work on colour by Moses Harris and used a version of his colour diagrams in his own teaching at the Royal Academy (image D.), and he later painted two important canvases in response to Johann Wolfgang von Goethe's theory of colour and light.

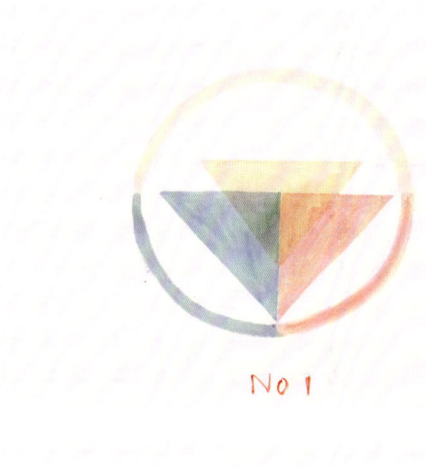

No 1

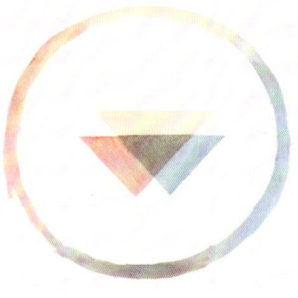

N° 2

D.

A. J. M. W. Turner's travelling watercolour box, *c.* 1842, 29.6 × 31.7 cm
    (11 ¾ × 12 ½ in.)
B. *J. M. W. Turner*, Richard Doyle, 1846, woodcut, 8.5 × 10.5 cm
    (3 ⅜ in. × 4 ⅛ in.)
C. Watercolour test paper taken from J. M. W. Turner's travelling
    watercolour box, 10 × 17 cm (4 × 6 ¾ in.)
D. *Colour Circle No. 1* and *Colour Circle No. 2* (lecture diagrams),
    J. M. W. Turner, *c.* 1824–28, graphite and watercolour on paper, no.
    1: 55.6 × 76.2 cm (22 × 30 in.) and no. 2: 55 × 75.8 cm (21 ¾ × 29 ⅞ in.)

GUSTAVE COURBET 1819–1877

A realist's 'dirty' palette

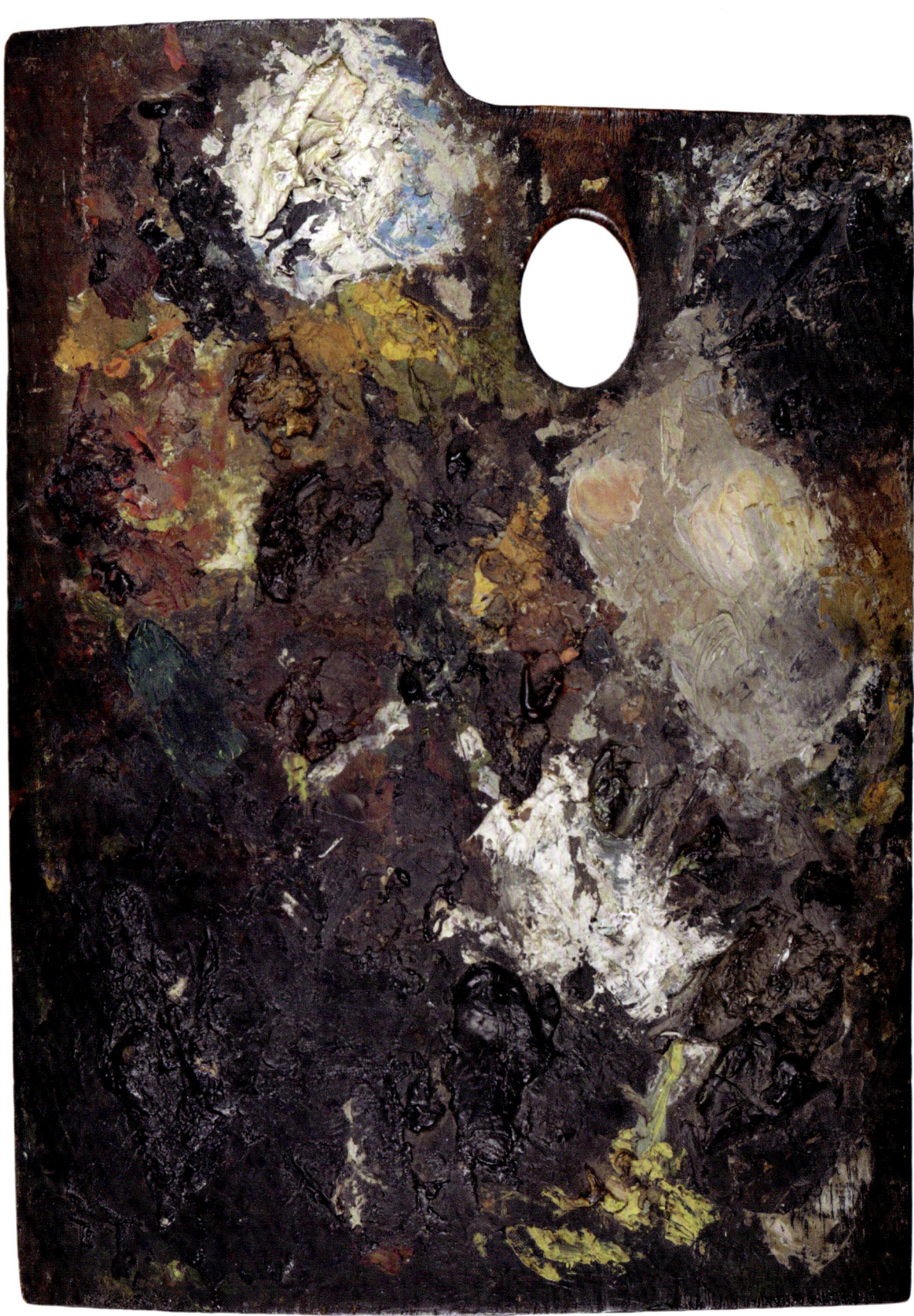

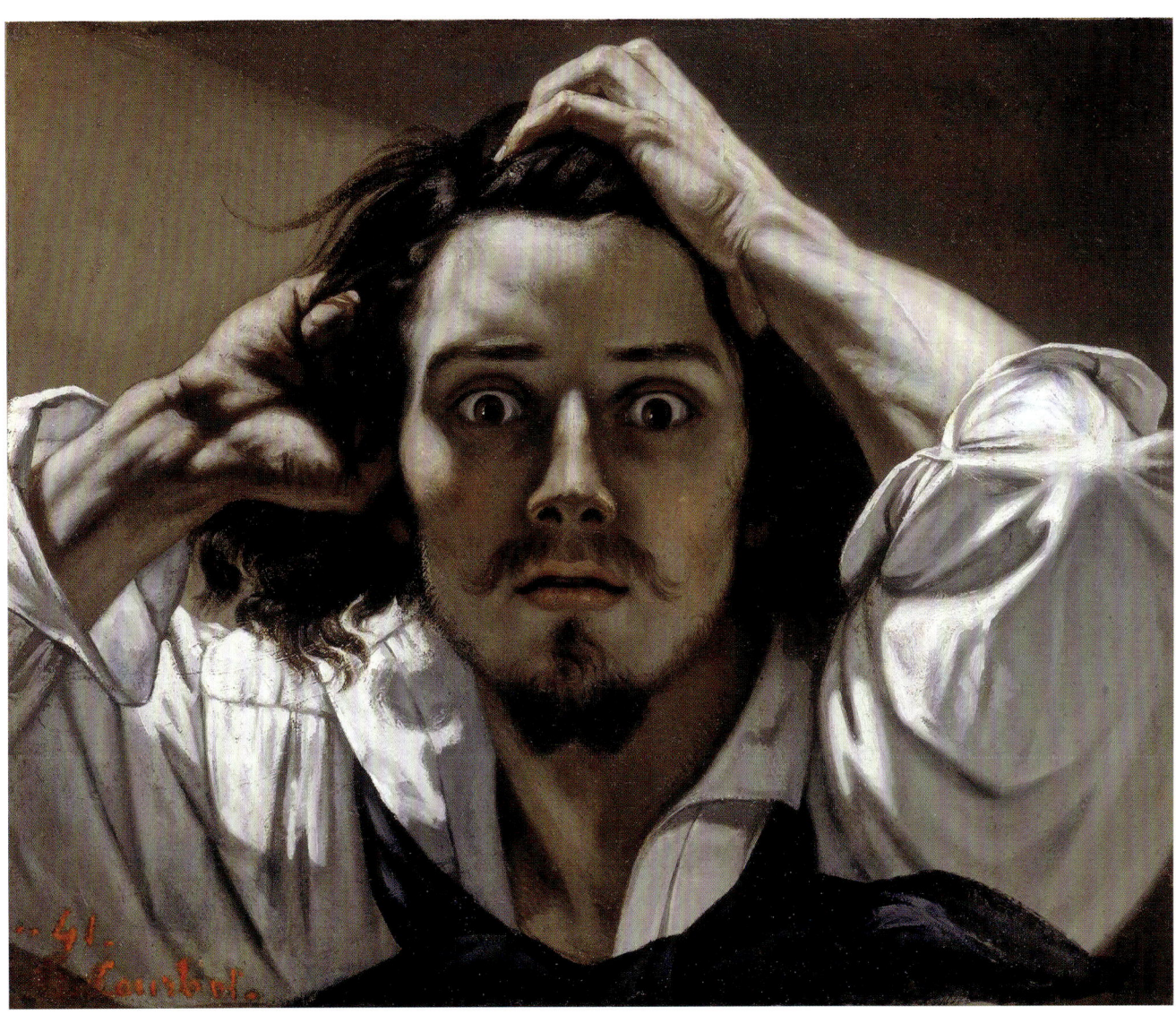

Gustave Courbet's palette
Undated
Paint on wood
24.7 × 34.5 cm
(9 ¾ × 13 ⅝ in.)

Le Désespéré
(The Desperate Man)
Gustave Courbet
1843–45
Oil on canvas
45 × 55 cm
(17 ¾ × 21 ⅝ in.)

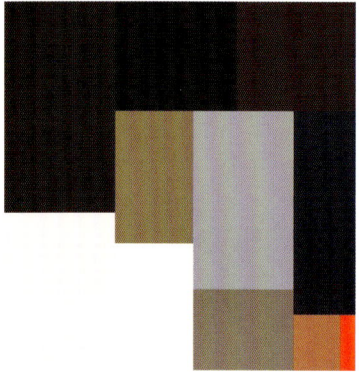

Proportional breakdown of colours used by Gustave Courbet in *Le Désespéré* (The Desperate Man), 1843–45, displayed on the previous page.

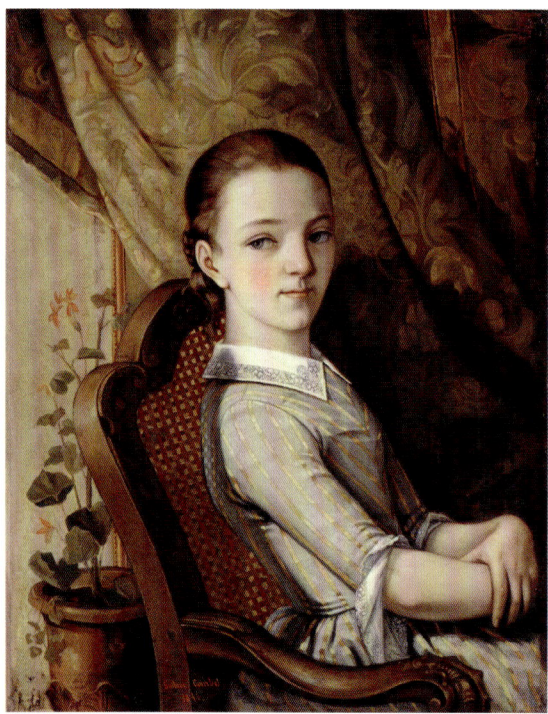

A.

A. *Portrait of Juliette Courbet*, Gustave Courbet, 1844, oil on canvas, 77.5 × 62 cm (30 ⅝ × 24 ½ in.)
B. *The Artist's Studio* (also known as *The Artist's Studio, a Real Allegory Summing Up Seven Years of my Artistic Life*), Gustave Courbet, 1854–55, oil on canvas, 3.6 × 6 m (11 ft 10 ¼ in. × 19 ft 7 ½ in.)
C. Portrait of Gustave Courbet in his studio, before 1870, albumen print, 9.5 × 5.7 cm (3 ¾ × 2 ¼ in.)

GUSTAVE COURBET SAW HIMSELF as a rebel in the art world. He rejected the idealizing aesthetics and smooth finishes of neoclassical and Romantic painting, and used colour as a tool in his quest for realism. It may seem odd to think of Courbet as a 'King of Colour', as contemporary critics called him, as his tonal range seems neutral, dominated by dark umbers and greys, and displaying little contrast. Yet, as art historian Klaus Herding argued in an excellent chapter on Courbet's use of colour, it is the relationship between colour and content, the placing of almost-abstract colour fields in large compositions, and the complex interplay of darkness and light that makes Courbet a master of colour.[1]

The palette shown here is undated but gives a good impression of Courbet's painting and blending techniques: much of the surface is covered in heavily mixed paint, and although now discoloured in large areas, we can still see that he laid out roughly diagonal lines of thick blobs of oil paint, likely squeezed from collapsible tubes. The predominant shades are umber, dark ochres and what looks like dark blues and blacks, with the only lighter tones a yellow, traces of blue within the white paint and a large amount of ubiquitous lead white in two places, some of which he has also transferred to other areas, possibly to create skin colour, as seen in his self-portrait *Le Désespéré* (The Desperate Man) from 1843–45. The white shirt, rendered realistically despite the visible loose brushstrokes, shows a similar combination of blue and white as the one seen on the palette, with blue used for the shadows of the folds of the shirt fabric. The small amounts of a vibrant red that are visible on the palette reflect his sparing use of the colour, but with great piercing effect. In his self-portrait, red not only creates his flushed complexion, it is also used in the emphatic, signal-red signature in the bottom left corner.

The palette shows clear signs of a palette knife and possibly partially dried, flat bristle (or hogs' hair) brushes having been used to mix and blend paint. Courbet was known to paint rapidly and in thick impasto, sometimes manipulating the paint surface further by scraping and wiping, adding more layers of paint in the wet-over-dry technique, or varnishing layers before adding more paint. His methods were experimental, messy and radical. He was breaking up the smooth paint surfaces so prominent in 18th- and 19th-century art and was dubbed by some of his contemporaries as a 'defender of the ugly'.

In respect of darkness and grittiness in depiction and texture, he was greatly influenced by Rembrandt. Although not a painter of light, he explained to his students that in any composition they should begin with the darkest tonal area, then work gradually through

'I cannot teach my art, nor the art of any school whatever, since I repudiate the teaching of art... art is wholly individual.'

GUSTAVE COURBET, *REALIST MANIFESTO: AN OPEN LETTER*, 25 DECEMBER 1861

the intermediate tones and lastly add highlights.[2] Courbet often used a dark reddish-brown underpaint, and true to Rembrandt's chiaroscuro style, frequently applied whites over darker shades. His best works have sumptuous, golden-brown tonal areas, but he favoured bituminous colours, which were cheap but slow-drying and unstable, resulting in the dirty and murky appearance of many of his paintings.

Some of Courbet's works were immense, including *The Artist's Studio* from 1854–55, which measured nearly 6 metres (19 feet) in length. It is a large, self-dramatizing, allegorical image of Courbet in his studio, surrounded by supporters, friends and a motley crew of characters. His use of colour here is significant, as he is using it to denote almost abstract areas in the background that add sharpness to the complex figure groups in the foreground. Perhaps more important is the symbolism he attaches to his painting materials, and how he stages himself as an artist.

Critic James Hall compares the composition of *The Artist's Studio* to a triptych altarpiece, with the Christ-like figure of Courbet in the middle, and 'the thumbhole of Courbet's palette, and his knife, are dead centre, emphasizing his firm grasp, and physical engagement.'[3] Courbet places himself at an almost impossible angle to the large canvas propped on an easel. The nearly finished picture shows a grand landscape, but the presence of a naked model grasping a mass of white drapery alludes to his other subject matter. If he had been true to his ideas of realism, he would have painted himself with his back to us, but this is painting as performance. He is sitting at this angle to show off his profile, his work and his palette. On it, we see a reduced range of colours: a large amount of black or very dark blue, a mixed green (likely a chrome green), a small amount of bright yellow (possibly artificial), a tiny fleck of bright orange, and what looks like earth ochres and reds. Patches of white, with which to create the final highlights, are also visible in several places. With this pictorial image of his palette, Courbet shows us what he can create from a limited range of colours. He loved performing in the studio. According to his friend Castagnary, his studio was often filled with visitors, and he sang, drank, smoked and laughed while painting for his audience. Yet, Castagnary also recalls that he was meticulous and accomplished, and painted 'with marvellous control. I followed the movement of his arms. The hands were long, elegant and of a rare beauty. I took an extreme pleasure in watching him work. [...] I saw how he used the [palette] knife and what marvellous effects he could create with it.'[4]

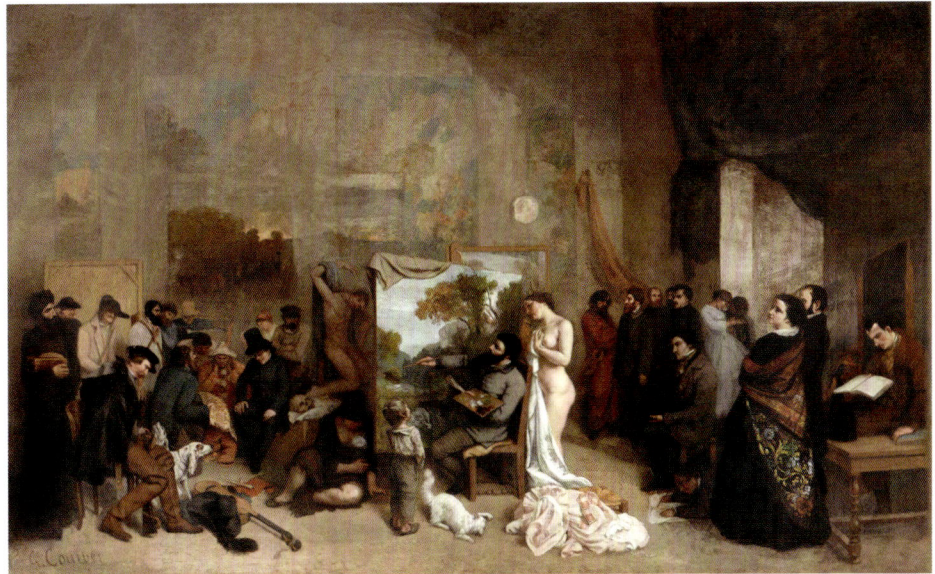

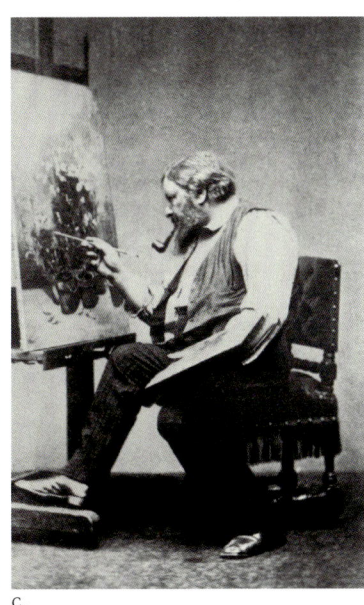

JEAN-AUGUSTE-DOMINIQUE INGRES 1780–1867

A warm, academic palette

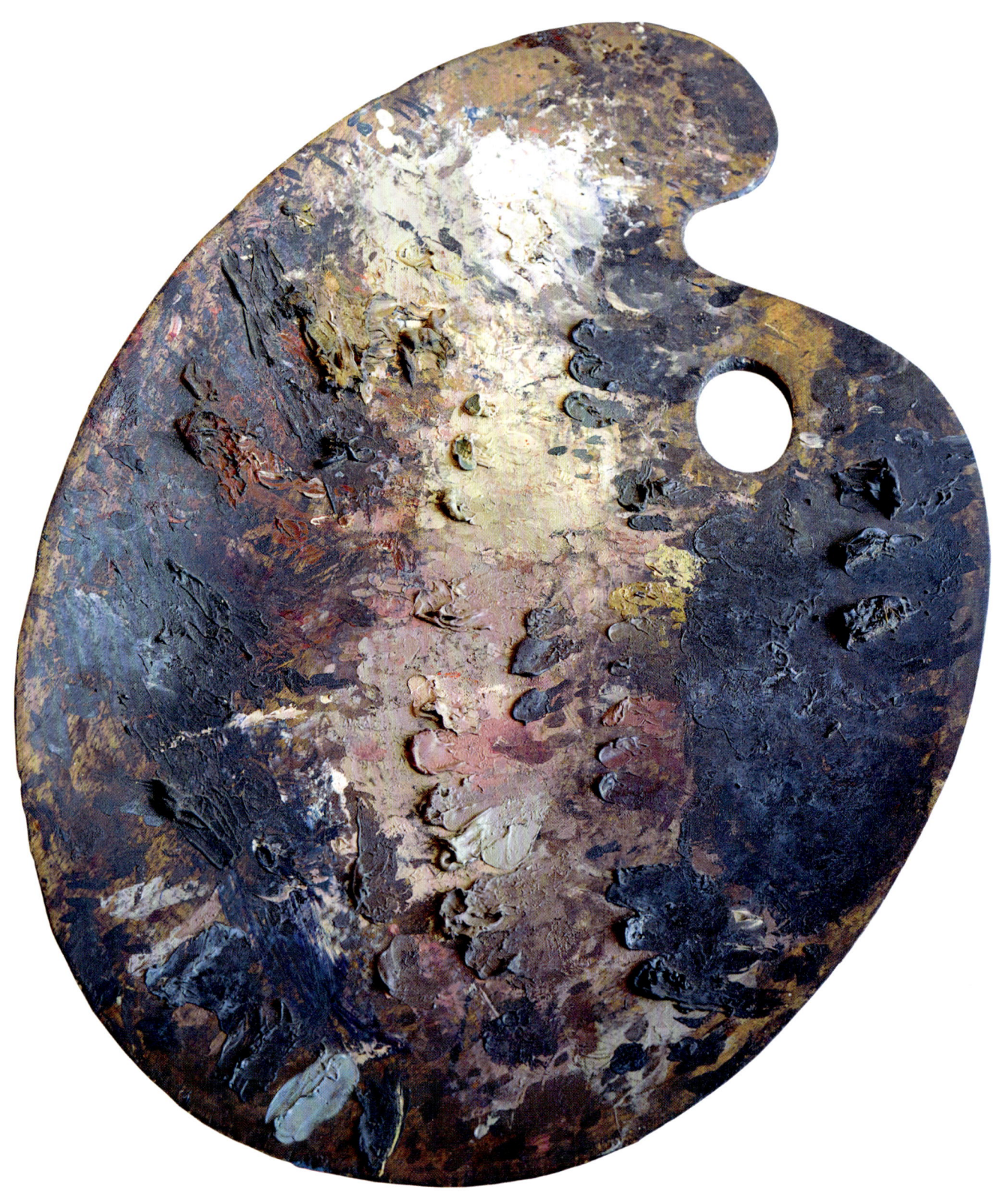

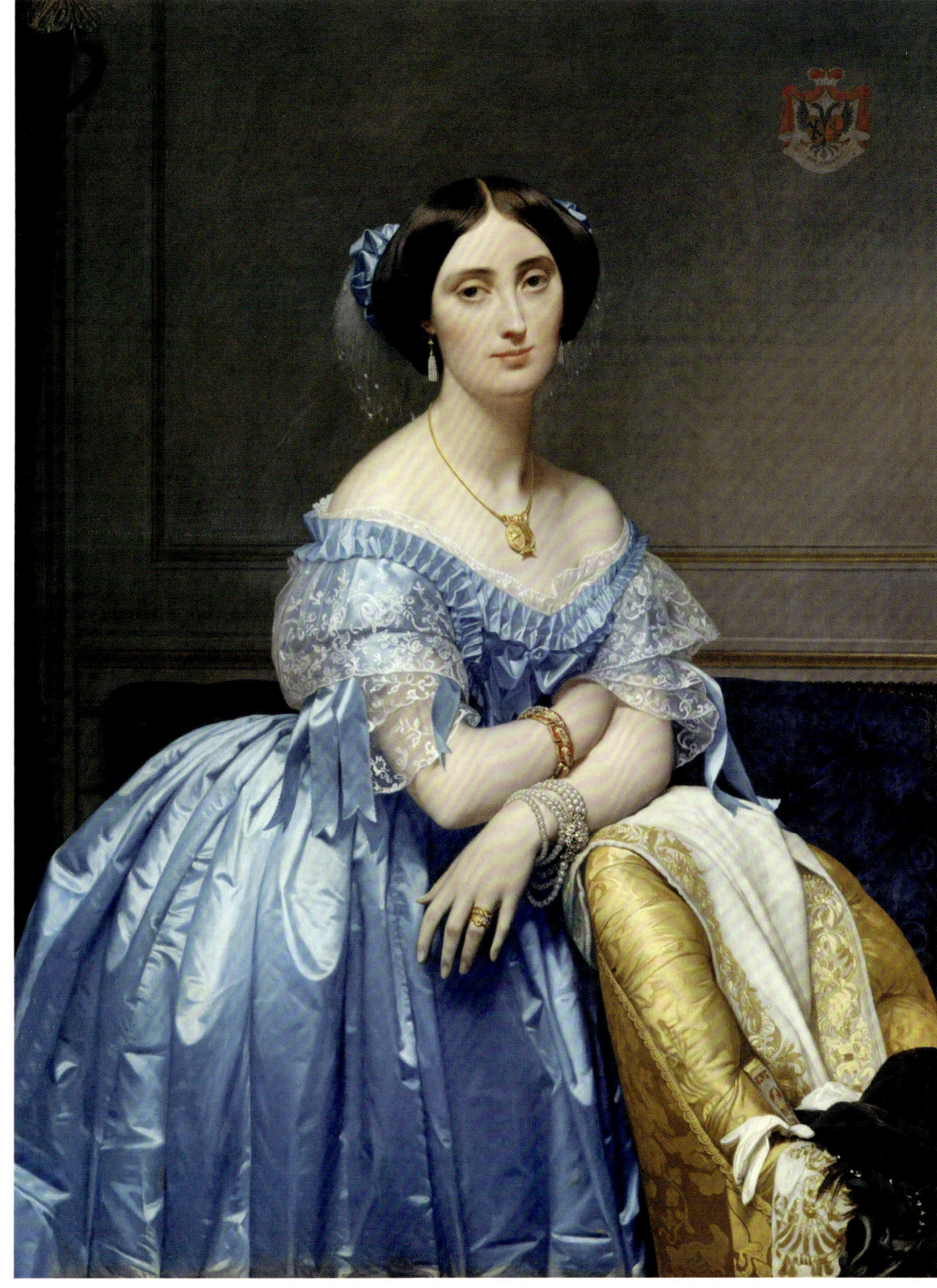

Jean-Auguste-
Dominique Ingres's
palette
Undated
Paint on wood

*Joséphine-Éléonore-
Marie-Pauline de
Galard de Brassac de
Béarn (1825–1860),
Princesse de Broglie*
Jean-Auguste-
Dominique Ingres
1851–53
Oil on canvas
121.3 × 90.8 cm
(47 ¾ × 35 ¾ in.)

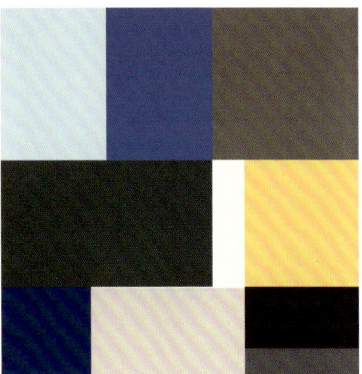

Proportional breakdown of colours used by Jean-Auguste-Dominique Ingres in *Joséphine-Éléonore-Marie-Pauline de Galard de Brassac de Béarn (1825–1860), Princesse de Broglie*, 1851–53, displayed on the previous page.

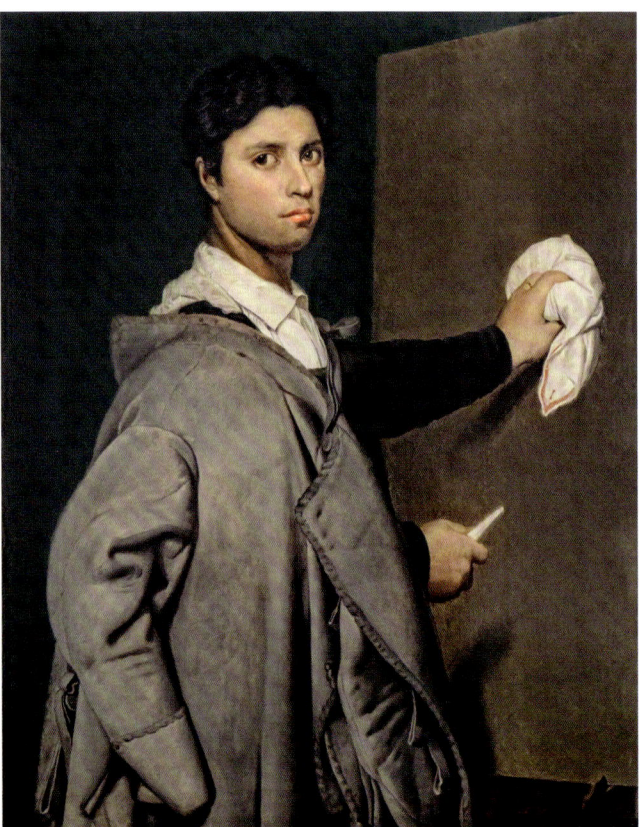

A.

THE PALETTE OF JEAN-AUGUSTE-DOMINIQUE INGRES shows all the signs of meticulous, detailed brushwork and fine mixing of a range of subtle tints and shades. Lengthways along the centre runs a line of blots of subtle variations of flesh tones, ranging from pale warm whites and rosy pinks to slightly darker earthy shades. Below and above this spine of skin colours are more blots of other darker colours, possibly blues, umbers and black. A few yellow ochres make an appearance, as well as a saturated red (possibly vermilion), both of which are also necessary in the creation of skin tones or may have been used by the artist in pure form to make an iconographical statement, such as a colourful piece of clothing or an accessory.

Above the thumbhole is a large amount of white, no doubt used to create the delicate tones of classical shapes and forms, such as the white fabrics of Empire-line dresses or ermine-lined robes. Almost the entire palette's surface has been used for mixing and blending, and it appears as if large areas of blue were created on it, perhaps not dissimilar to the painting shown on the previous page, a relatively late work, *Princesse de Broglie* (1851–53). His earlier famous work *La Grande Odalisque* (1814, overleaf) is rich in oriental imagery and alludes to Venetian colouring, but is surprisingly restrained in tonal range and rests largely on Ingres's typical contrast of sumptuous blues, white skin and warm yellows. For the former painting (and likely this palette, as it probably dates from later in his career) he would have been able to use oil paint straight from tubes, although he would still have pre-mixed a range of colours in batches beforehand. When he painted *La Grande Odalisque,* though, each batch of oil paint would have had to be prepared individually and stored in tied-up animal bladders, and then pricked open to release the required quantity of paint. Indeed, examples of both tubes and bladders can be found among Ingres's surviving artist materials. The clarity and precision of his paintings reveal nothing of the messiness of working in the oil medium in the early 19th century.

Ingres was firmly rooted in neoclassicism and followed the concept of the classical Greek palette of gradations of earth colours limited, if at all possible, to red and yellow ochre, black and white. This was the approach advocated by academies and educators. The artist John Cawse (see pages 14 and 19) was one of several authors of handbooks describing the precise palette layout necessary to produce idealized flesh and skin tones and several types of fine fabrics. Ingres would only have augmented this pared-down, natural palette with other colours where absolutely necessary. While he used strictly warm earth colours only for his underpaint, he would select more vivid pigments, or even synthetic

'Colour adds adornment and renders the tone perfections of art...more amiable.'

JEAN-AUGUSTE-DOMINIQUE INGRES, QUOTED IN D. PAVEY'S
COLOUR CONCEPTS, 2015

paints, such as Prussian blue, Naples yellow and later artificial ultramarine, when he wanted to achieve a dramatic visual effect. Ingres applied paint in thin, even layers, in small brushstrokes that are almost invisible, and often added transparent glazes, resulting in homogenous flat paint surfaces, relying entirely on the artist's modelling and tonal shading to create texture. The effect was one of almost hyper-realistic brilliance and finish.

As a follower of classical ideas of beauty, Ingres would at least theoretically assign the greatest importance to line and contour, and this may be the reason why his images appear static and frozen. Yet, this also allows the flawless beauty of the colours and surfaces to shine brighter, as our eyes can concentrate on the detail of each pictorial element without distraction from movement, emotion and narrative. In *Princesse de Broglie* the metallic-looking blues and yellows of the pyramidal composition are not simply realistic renderings of silks and brocades, but are also masterfully contrasted with the muted soft-grey background, which contains minute quantities of blue to harmonize with the foreground. The large area of brilliant blue, in combination with warm golds, soft greys and white, adds to the impression of composure and calm exuding from the sitter. It is a silent and emotionally empty picture, but its colours sing.

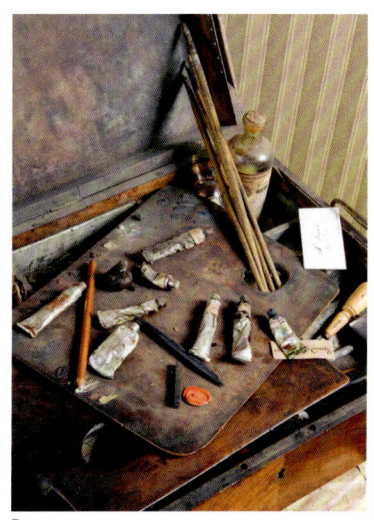

B.

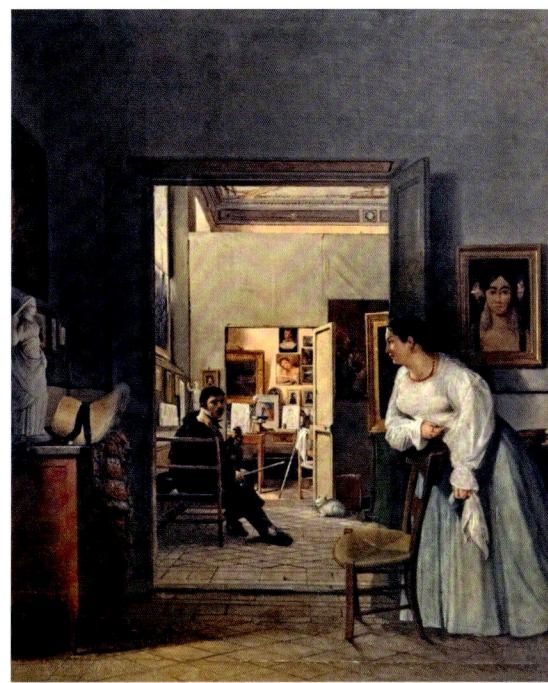

A.   *Portrait of Ingres*, Marie Anne Julie Forestier, 1807, oil on canvas,
      62.5 × 52 cm (24 ⅝ × 20 ½ in.)
B.   Jean-Auguste-Dominique Ingres's palette, paints and brushes
C.   *The Studio of Ingres in Rome in 1818*, Jean Alaux, 1818, oil on canvas,
      55.4 × 46 cm (21 ⅞ × 18 ⅛ in.)
D.   (Overleaf) *La Grande Odalisque*, Jean-Auguste-Dominique Ingres,
      1814, oil on canvas, 91 × 162 cm (35 ⅞ × 63 ⅞ in.)

C.

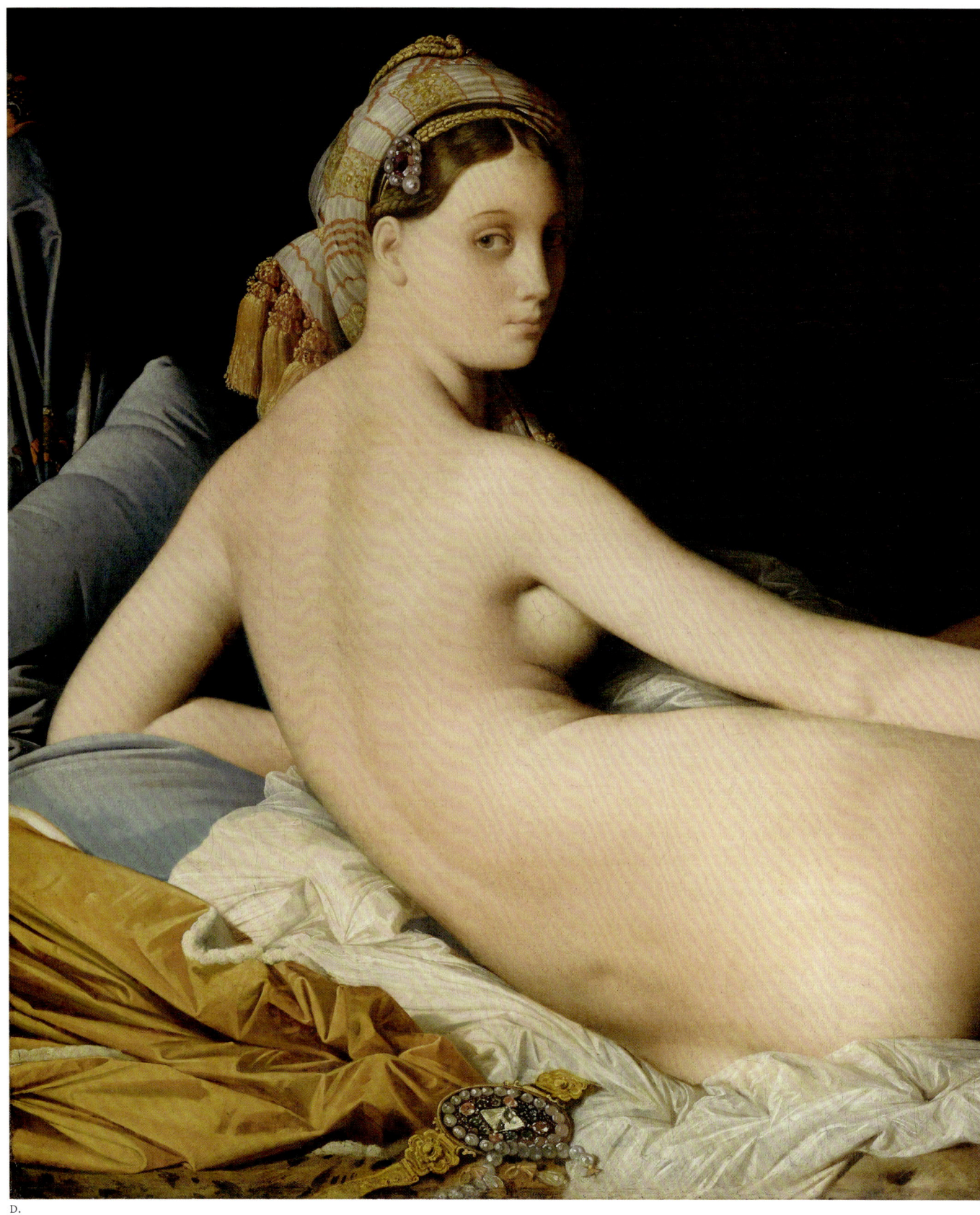

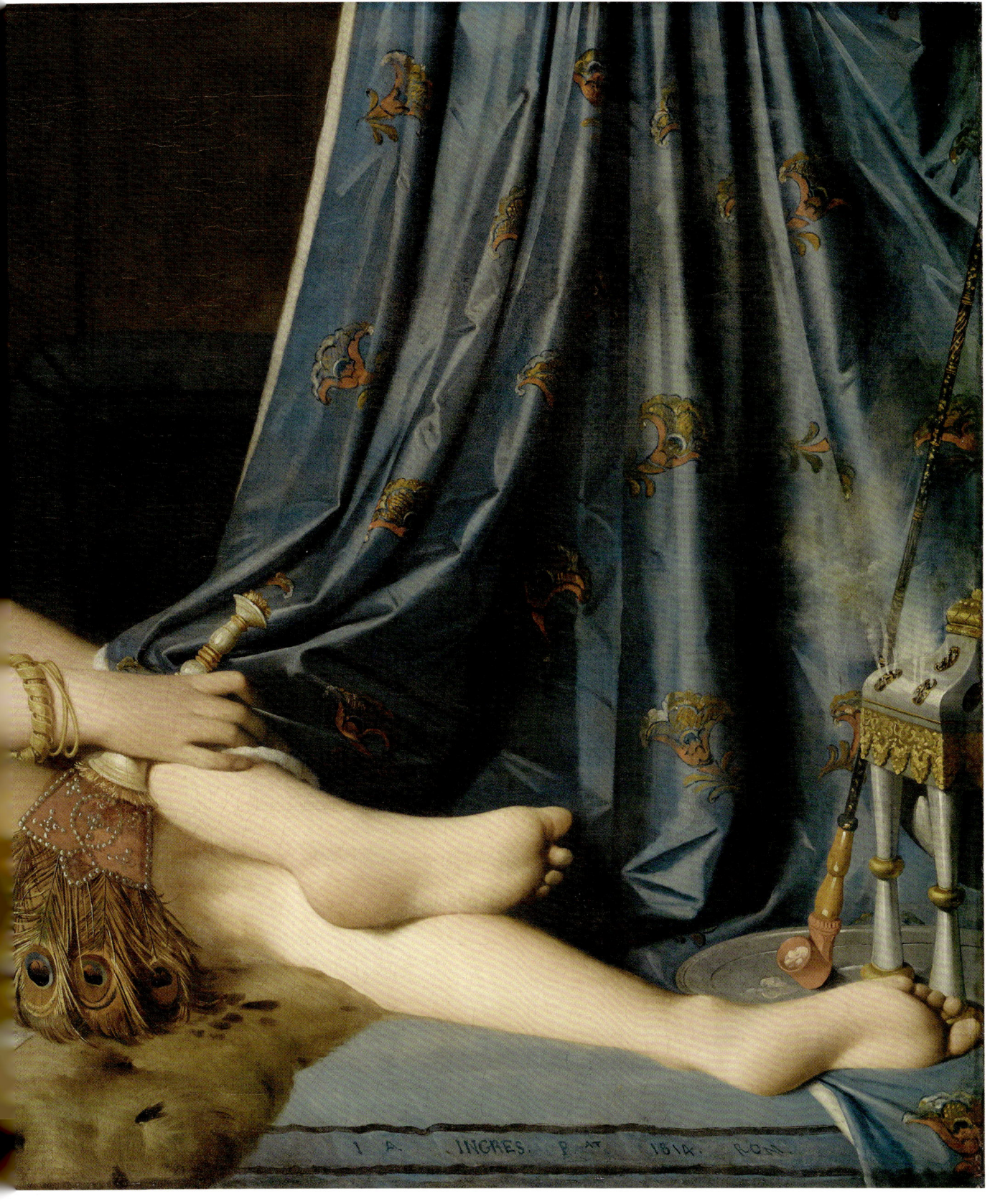

JAMES ABBOTT McNEILL WHISTLER 1834–1903

One gorgeous mass of aesthetic nothingness

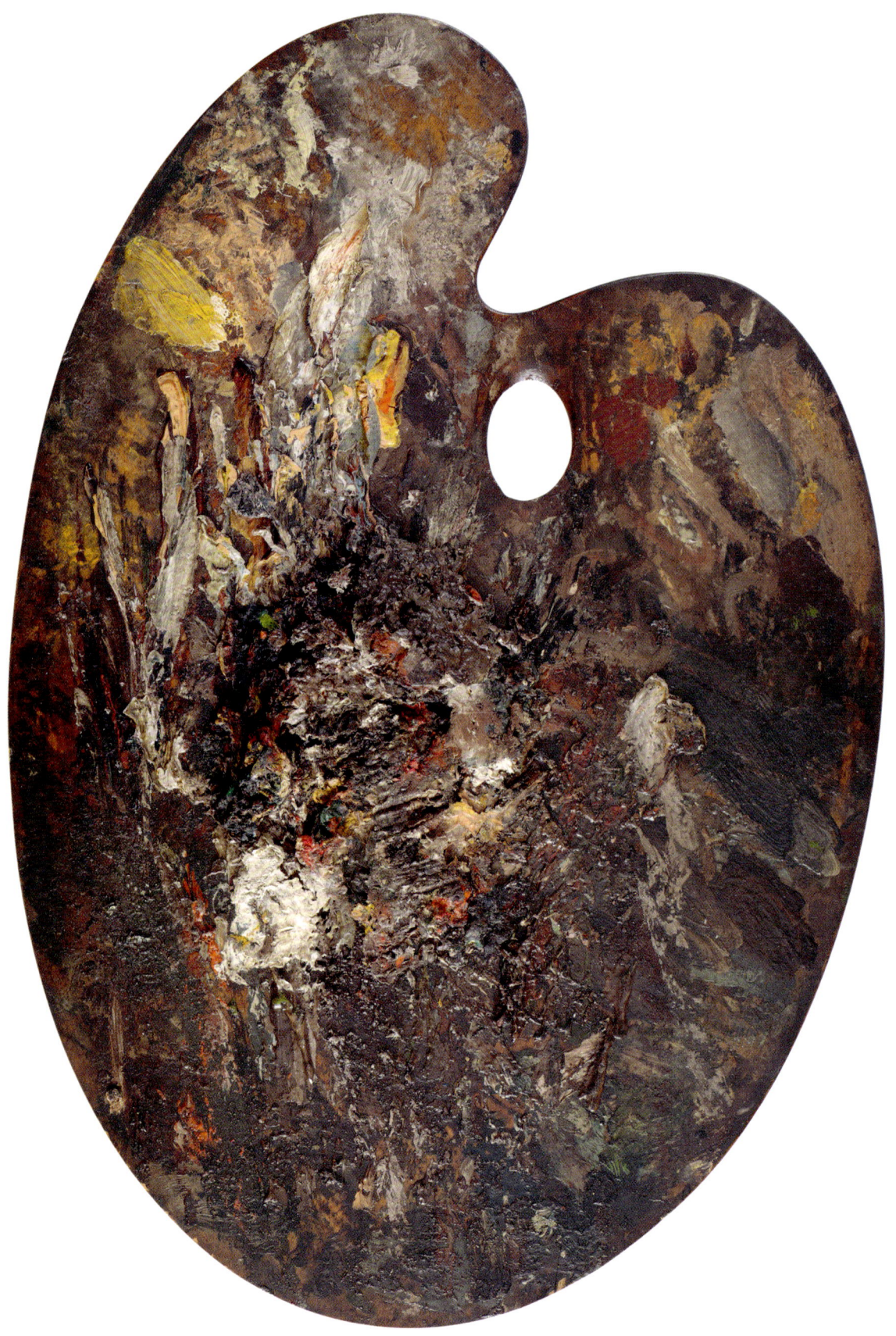

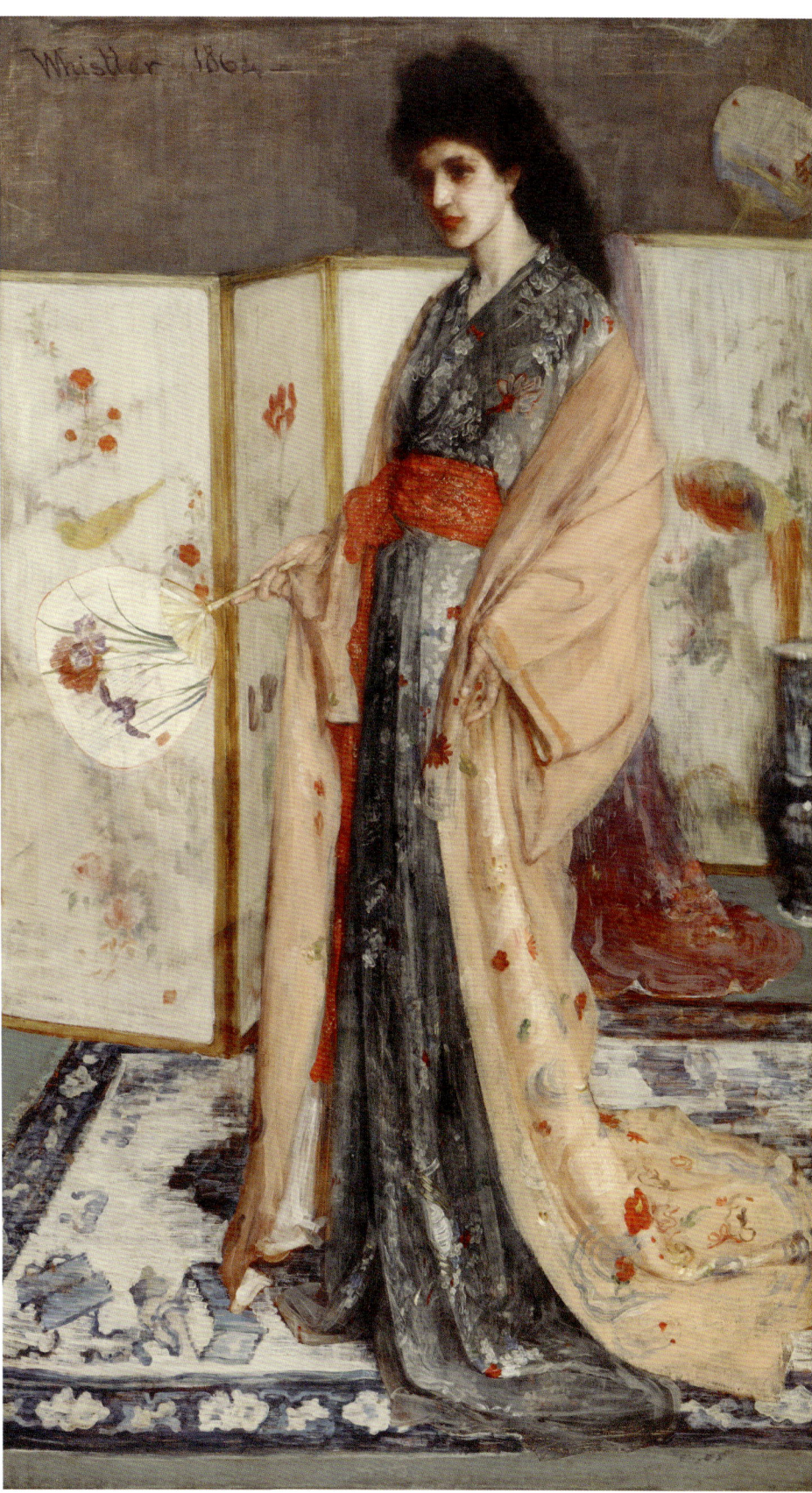

James Abbott McNeill
Whistler's palette
19th century
Paint on wood
51.1 × 35.9 cm
(20 ⅛ × 14 ⅛ in.)

*The Princess from
the Land of Porcelain*
James Abbott McNeill
Whistler
1863–65
Oil on canvas
201.5 × 116.1 cm
(79 ⅜ × 45 ¾ in.)

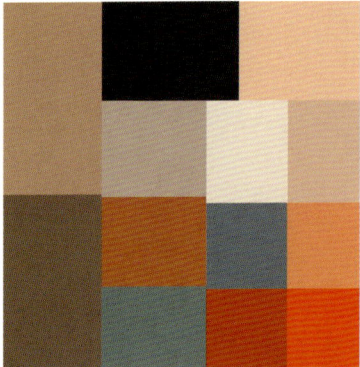

Proportional breakdown of colours used by James
Abbott McNeill Whistler in *The Princess from the Land
of Porcelain*, 1863–65, displayed on the previous page.

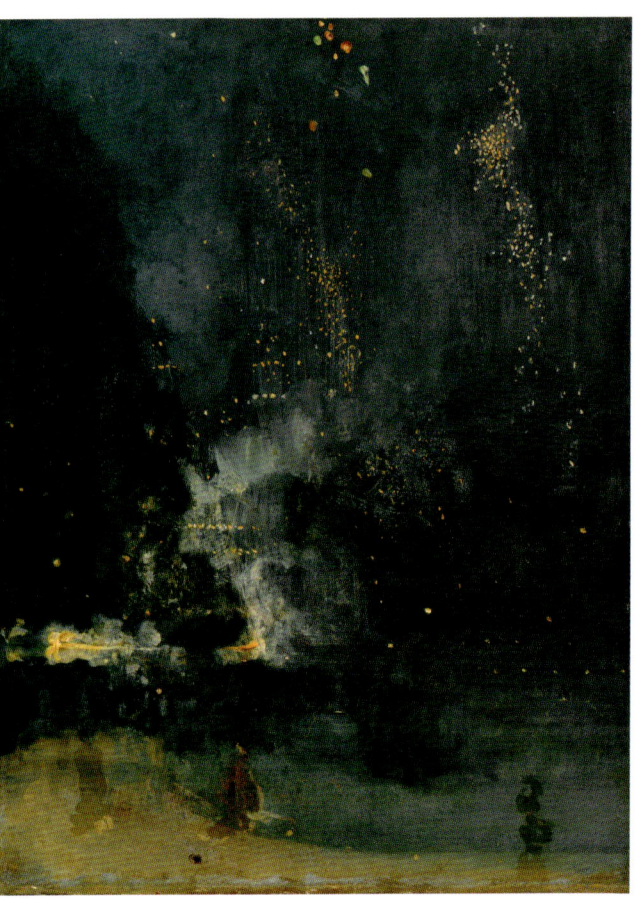

A.

IN HIS TEACHING WHISTLER stressed the importance
of carefully laying out the palette, prescribing a range
of pure colours, a mixture of synthetic and earth
pigments and including black, to be applied neatly,
straight from tubes. Between yellow and red, in the
centre of the palette, a large amount of white should
be placed. This palette, one of many of his artist's
materials that survive, is heavily worked, showing
intense and deliberate mixing. While the precise initial
layout of the colours is no longer visible, there is still a
ubiquitous blob of white (most likely lead white) visible
in the centre, as well as strokes of vibrant oranges and
yellows, probably scooped up with the long brushes he
preferred. Whistler made full use of the vast variety of
pigments available in the late 19th century, and sourced
his materials from many suppliers, including Winsor &
Newton. Among the pigments that have been identified
in his range were cadmium orange, emerald green,
green verditer, crimson lakes, French ultramarine
and several kinds of white.[1]

The prescriptive nature of Whistler's theoretical
palettes seems to contrast with the appearance of much
of his art, which tends towards hazy reduction and the
deliberate blurring of contours, concentrating instead
on tonal harmonies, light effect and impressions.
Figures and forms are often, but not always, hinted
at in sketchy shapes, and paint was applied in very
thin layers and glazes, rubbed and blended further by
Whistler on the canvas. Some highlights were applied
by letting paint drip onto the composition, creating
an overall watery and sparkling effect, while he
incorporated areas of jewel-like colour sparingly, but
to great effect. The few strokes of orange and yellow on
this palette are testimony to his subtle use of colour and
colour contrast. Whistler's precise and ordered initial
palette layout can be considered a solid framework
that allowed him to create his carefully tuned and
often restricted compositions, which he tended to
call 'harmonies' or 'symphonies'.

At times Whistler's art seemed almost abstract
and caused outrage in Victorian Britain. *Nocturne in
Black and Gold: The Falling Rocket* (*c.* 1875, image A.)
a night scene of fireworks at the 18th-century Cremorne
Gardens in London, was heavily criticized by the
eminent art critic John Ruskin, who famously accused
Whistler of 'flinging a pot of paint in the public's
face'.[2] His palette and teaching tell us that quite the
opposite was true. Whistler achieved the impression
of immediacy and fleetingness through careful
planning and application, and duly sued Ruskin for
libel. David Curry has argued that Whistler's art was
not so much a pot of paint flung at a canvas, but 'an
incendiary cocktail tossed by an aesthetic terrorist',

'As music is the poetry of sound, so is painting the poetry of sight, and the subject-matter has nothing to do with harmony of sound or of colour.'

JAMES ABBOTT McNEILL WHISTLER, 'THE RED RAG',
THE WORLD, 22 MAY 1878

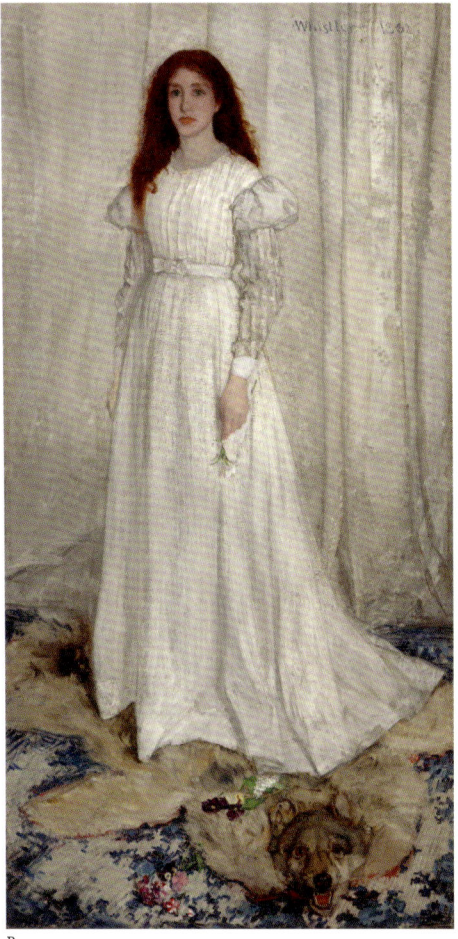

B.

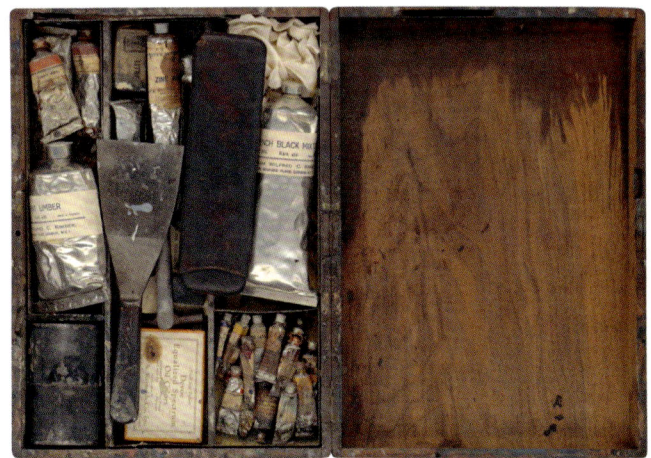

C.

ripping up the orderly textbook of design, colour and beauty.[3] Both Whistler and Ruskin were mercilessly caricatured in popular magazines, with cartoonists often using palettes as symbols of their overly precious aesthetic views and vanities.

Whistler also designed colour schemes for interiors, aiming for light and uncluttered spaces, in a departure from the polychrome and highly ornamented interiors of the time. Artist friend Mortimer Menpes recalled that he would take ready-made distemper housepaint and mix it to create the tone he wanted, and then hand pots to the decorators. His favourite wall colours, Menpes noted, were 'lemon yellow, Antwerp blue and apple green'.[4] The picture shown on the preceding page, *The Princess from the Land of Porcelain* (1863–65), shows a more vibrant palette containing many of the synthetic greens, reds and blues identified in technical analysis and recommended by Whistler himself. It was also part of an interior design scheme, the Peacock Room, designed for Frederick R. Leyland's house in London in 1876–77. It is Whistler's only surviving interior decoration scheme, now preserved at Freer Gallery of Art in Washington.

Whistler is, of course, mostly associated with neutral greys and pure whites, a colour theme he explored in many of his works, most famously in the series of 'Symphonies in White' (1861–63), of which *No. 1: The White Girl* (1872, image B.) is the best known. The public and critics were quite disturbed by its whiteness and speculated about the iconography of the painting, which led to it being rejected by the Royal Academy. Could this be a virginal bride about to lose her innocence? Or was this an illustration of novelist Wilkie Collins's troubled *Woman in White*? Whistler himself described his work as 'one gorgeous mass of brilliant white' (except for the model's auburn hair),[5] but rejected any deeper meaning. For him his 'symphony' was about the superficial beauty of a white composition: 'My painting simply represents a girl dressed in white standing in front of a white curtain.'[6]

A. *Nocturne in Black and Gold: The Falling Rocket*, James Abbott McNeill Whistler, c. 1875, oil on panel, 60.3 × 46.7 cm (23 ¾ × 18 ⅜ in.)
B. *Symphony in White No. 1: The White Girl*, James Abbott McNeill Whistler, 1872, oil on canvas, 213 × 107.9 cm (83 ⅞ × 42 ½ in.)
C. James Abbott McNeill Whistler's paintbox containing paints and tools, c. 1875–1903, closed box: 36 × 27 × 8 cm (14 ¼ × 10 ¾ × 3 ¼ in.)

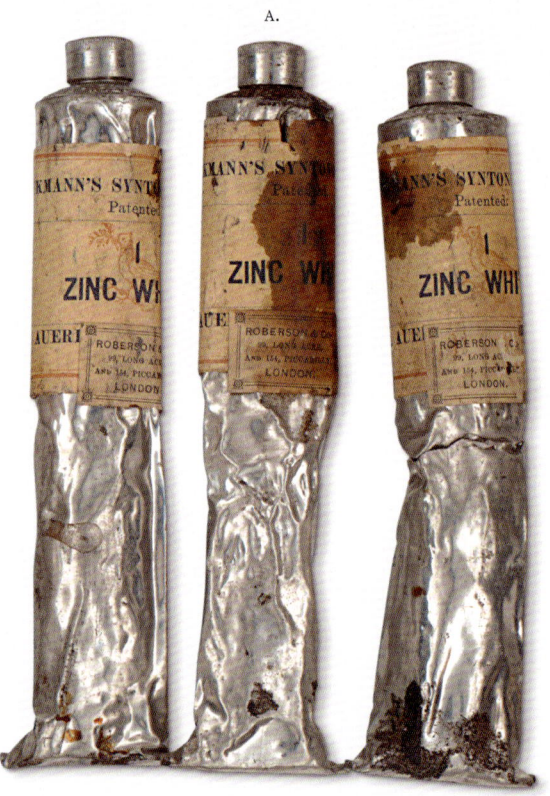

A.

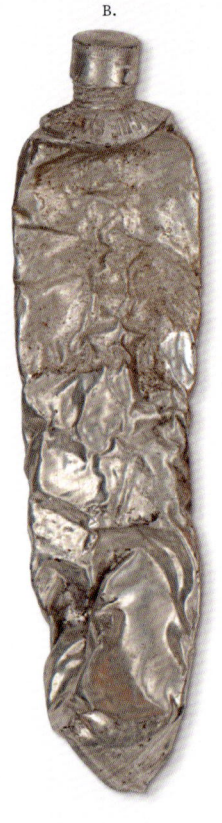

B.

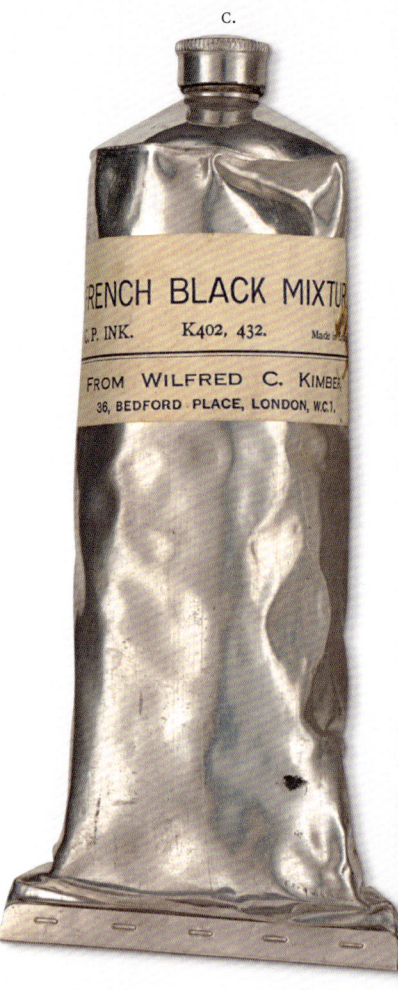

C.

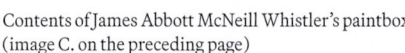

Contents of James Abbott McNeill Whistler's paintbox
(image C. on the preceding page)

A.   Three tubes of zinc white, Beckmann's
       Synotonos-colour, resold by C. Roberson & Co.
B.   Unlabelled paint tube
C.   French black mixture, Wilfred C. Kimber
D.   Burnt umber, Wilfred C. Kimber
E.   Bone brown
F.   Antwerp blue, C. Roberson & Co.
G.   Vermilion, C. Roberson & Co.
H.   Crimson alizarin, C. Roberson & Co.
I.   Vermilion, C. Roberson & Co.
J.–K. Rose madder, Madderton & Co.
L.   Madder orange, Newman's
M.   Cadmium yellow, L. Cornelissen & Son
N.   Neutral tint, Rowney & Co.
O.   Moist cadmium orange, Newman's
P.   Cobalt blue, Dr. Fr. Schoenfeld & Co.
Q.   Raw sienna, Dr. Fr. Schoenfeld & Co.
R.   Moist golden ochre, Newman's
S.   French ultramarine, C. Roberson & Co.
T.   Crimson lake, Geo. Rowney & Co.
U.   Trial size box of Devoe equalized spectrum
       oil colours, Devoe & Raynolds Co.
V.   Light red, C. Roberson & Co.
W.   Burnt sienna, C. Roberson & Co.
X.   Burnt sienna, Newman's
Y.   Emerald green, C. Roberson & Co.
Z.   Indian red, C. Roberson & Co.

D.

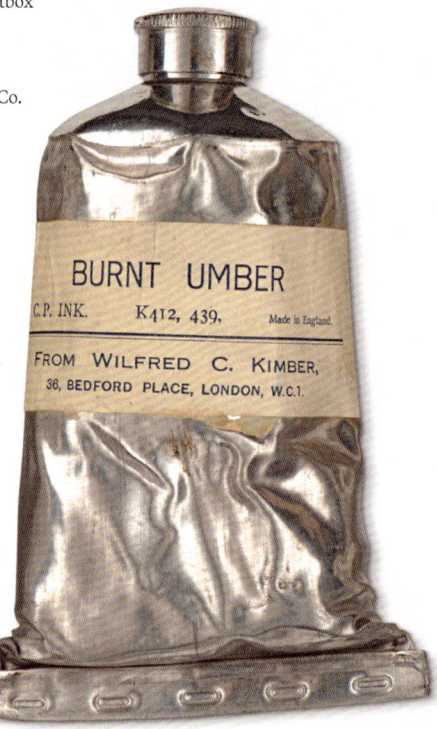

E.   F.

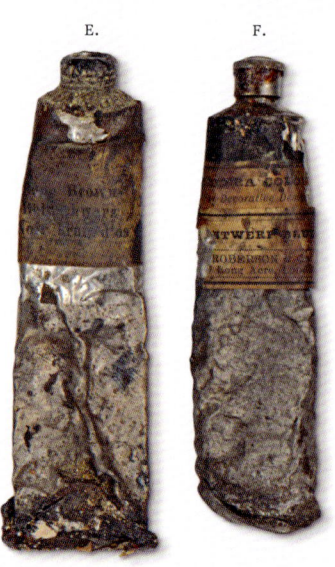

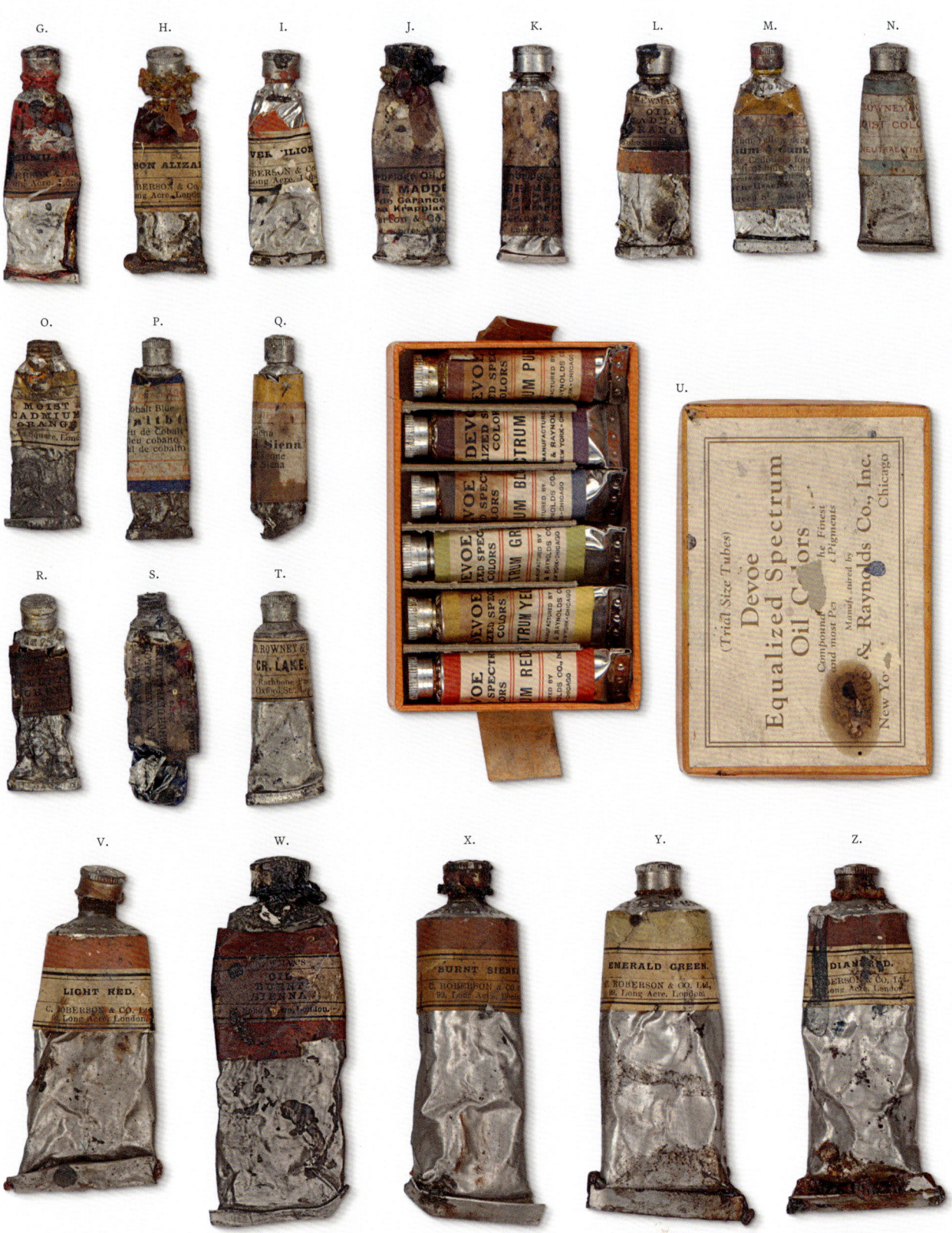

HENRI FANTIN-LATOUR 1836–1904

A palette of vibrating stillness

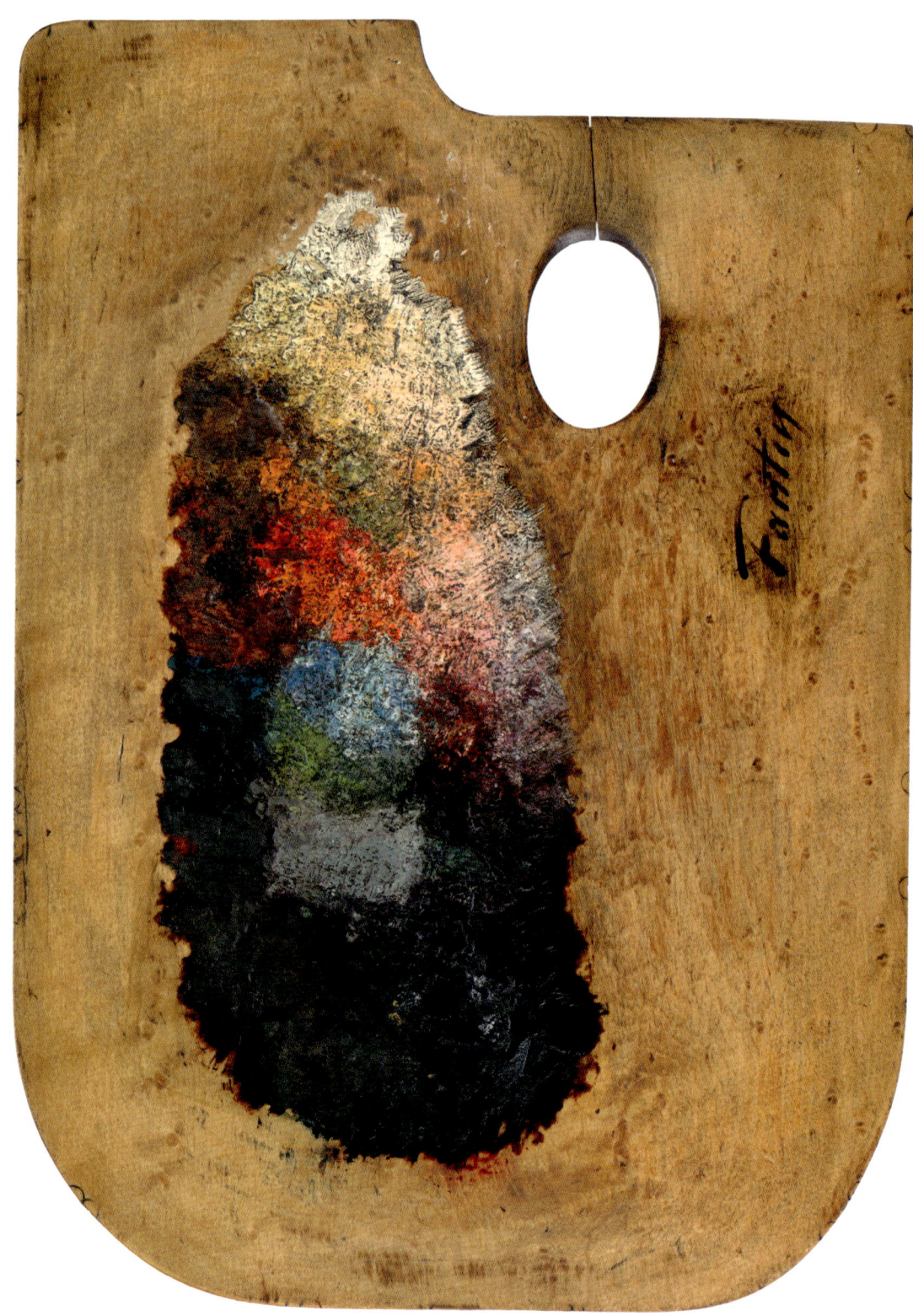

Henri Fantin-Latour's
palette
1887
Oil on wood
36.8 × 26.7 cm
(14 ½ × 10 ½ in.)

*Still Life with Flowers
and Fruit*
Henri Fantin-Latour
1866
Oil on canvas
73 × 60 cm
(28 ¾ × 23 ⅝ in.)

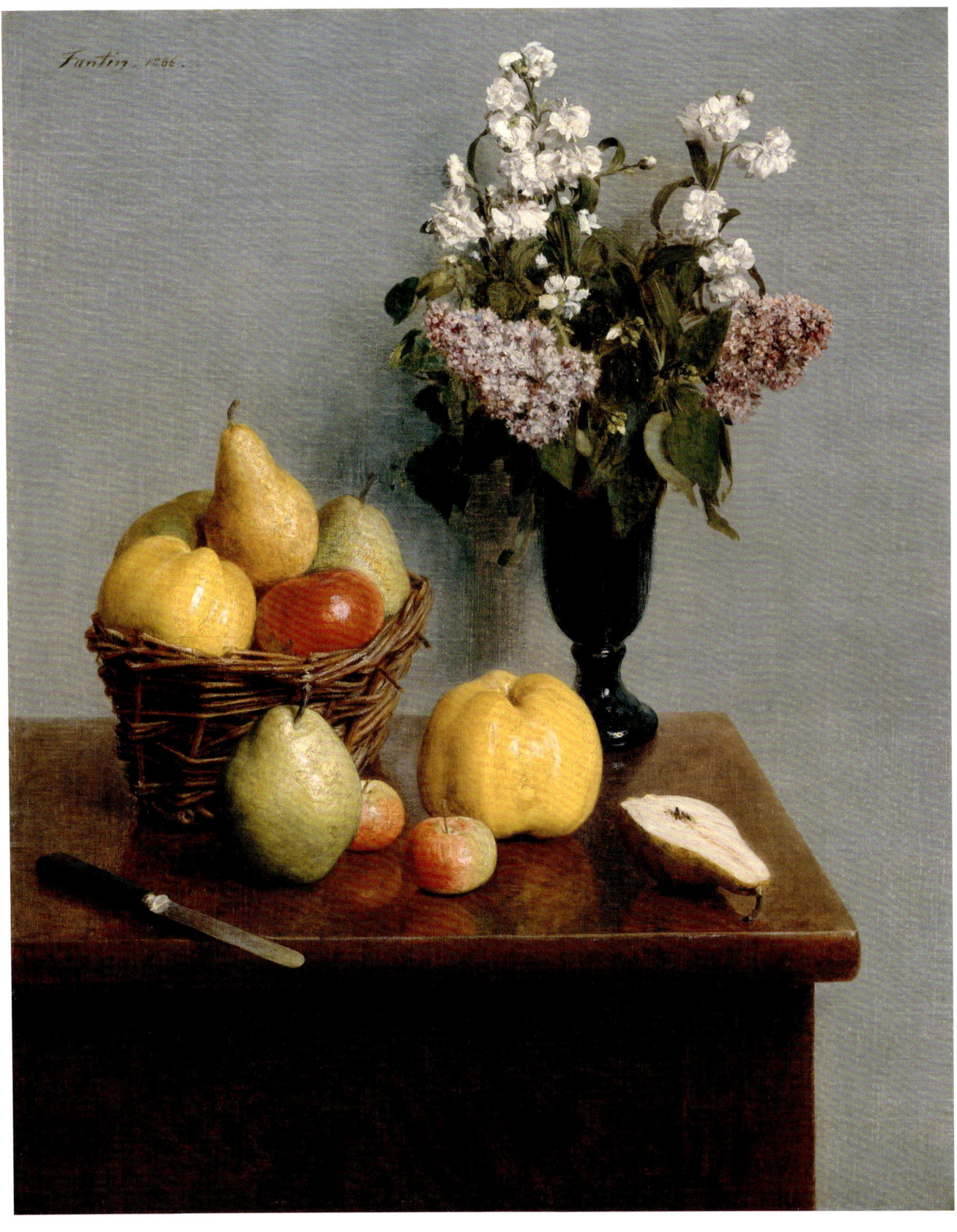

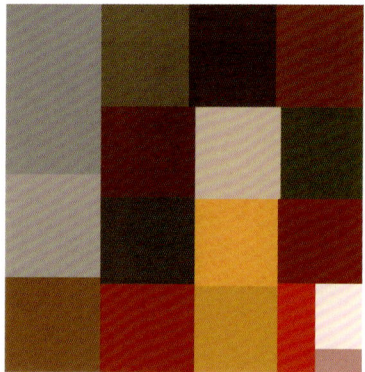

Proportional breakdown of colours used by Henri
Fantin-Latour in *Still Life with Flowers and Fruit*,
1866, displayed on the previous page.

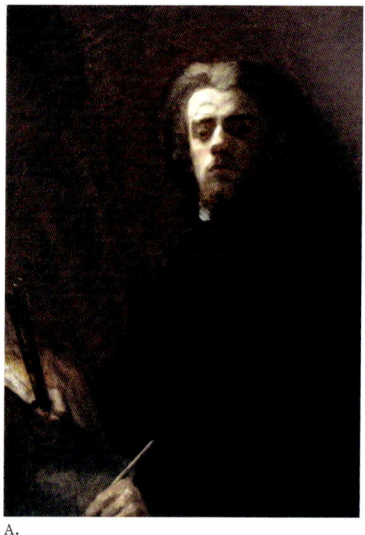

A.

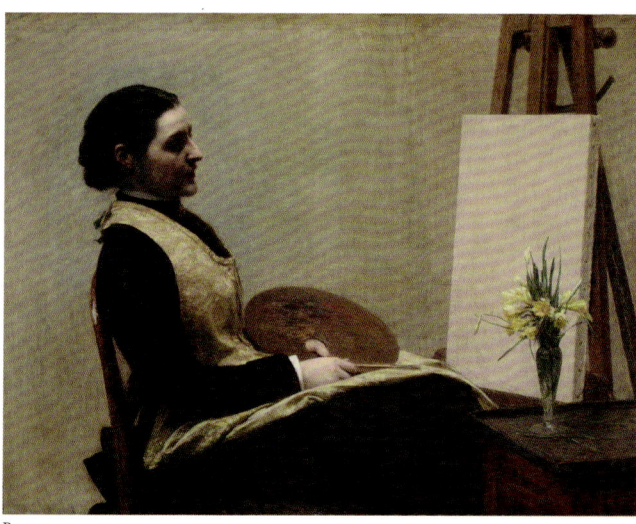

B.

HERE IS A TRADITIONAL WOODEN PALETTE on which
the oil paint is densely arranged, leaving much of the
surface unused. The artist zoomed in rather than out,
limiting himself to a restricted area on the palette,
perhaps to replicate the idea of a framed pictorial space.
He placed pure colours close to each other in the centre
of the upper half of the palette, using the full spectrum,
from brilliant white closest to the thumbhole, via yellow,
red, blue and green, while dark browns and black seem
to underpin everything. We do not know exactly how
this palette was originally laid out, but what is clear
is that much careful mixing happened on its surface,
resulting in additional tones of pink, pale blue and
fiery orange, while the dark shades seem to want to
usurp the brighter colours. The palette is signed by the
artist, Henri Fantin-Latour, perhaps simply to mark
the object as his, but more likely because he considered
it representative of his work and style.

This palette looks highly saturated and full of
contrast, but Fantin-Latour is mostly associated with
paintings that appear dreamy and soft, with colours that
look as if seen through a slight haze. His early biographer
Frank Gibson described his paintings' 'peculiar effects
of irradiating light, which illuminates all parts of the
compositions [and creates] a magical atmosphere and
softens the form and colour into tender harmonies'.
He found it hard to describe Fantin-Latour's painting
technique, but noted that he added 'little vibrating
touches of colour rubbed over masses of tone' resulting
in a 'peculiar webbed or reticulated appearance'.[1]

In the 1980s, a team of conservators analysed
manuscript notes and a similar palette at the Musée de
Grenoble, while some pigment analysis was carried out
by the Philadelphia Museum of Art on one of Fantin-
Latour's flower paintings. The conceptual palette derived
from the archive material showed a great variety of
readily available pigments, both synthetic and natural,
pure and mixed, including emerald green, vermilion,
a number of raw and burnt earth pigments, Prussian
blue, Indian yellow, Naples yellow, lakes, and several
cadmium-based paints.[2] The researchers also found
that Fantin-Latour's palette was almost identical to one
belonging to Eugène Delacroix (see page 50) from the late
1850s. The great Romantic painter's influence on Fantin-
Latour had not gone unnoticed. One of his best-known
works was, after all, *Homage to Delacroix* (1864). Shortly
after his death, another French painter, Jacques-Émile
Blanche, noted that Fantin-Latour would take a very
long time to prepare his palettes, meticulously laying out
small heaps of paint, in a manner similar to Delacroix.

From the man himself, we have only a few comments
on his choice of materials. In a letter from 1880, he
mentions some of his preferred pigments for his fruit

'Little vibrating touches of colour rubbed over masses of tone.'

FRANK GIBSON, *THE ART OF HENRI FANTIN-LATOUR: HIS LIFE AND WORK*, 1924

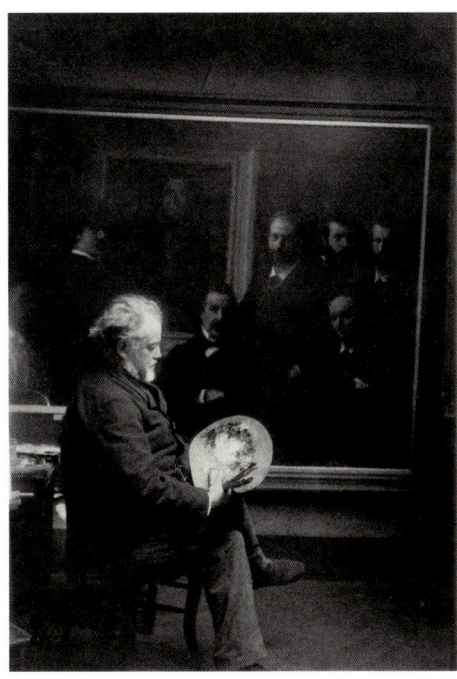

C.

and flower still lifes: chrome yellow, emerald green, malachite, cobalt blue and violet, raw sienna, as well as a range of lakes.[3] He achieved the soft appearance of his paintings by using canvas prepared with a particular ground of calcium white and animal glue, which allowed the oil paint to dry quicker, and he often used slightly tinted grounds, such as pink or pale grey. He combined transparent and opaque colours and glazes, added colour wet-in-wet on the canvas, mixing some shades and tints on the canvas rather than the palette. He would scratch and scrape the paint surface subtly and add small amounts of fresh paint to dried areas. The way he set his palette – chose, mixed, layered and manipulated colours – is a reflection of his sensitive and completely focused character.

Fantin-Latour was a reserved and quiet man, who preferred painting motionless, arranged scenes, such as these still lifes, or exquisite, sensitive portraits. Movement distracted him, and he was not inspired by changing weather conditions, or landscape in general. His only paintings showing figures in motion are mythological scenes and fantasies, imagined and created entirely in his studio. He rarely worked outdoors, and only ever changed his studio once, creating most of his vibrating images of stillness there. One wonders what the artist would have made of the fact that one of his still lifes, *A Basket of Roses* from 1890, became an integral part of the cover art for rock band New Order's album *Power, Corruption & Lies* in 1983. The designer Peter Saville juxtaposed Fantin-Latour's enigmatic painting with sleek minimalist graphics that engaged directly and indirectly with pop art and subsequent strands of postmodernism. The subtle tonality of the still life was fused with blank functional visuals representing contemporary technology and computerization, including overlays of colour coding bands. It was a radical re-contextualization of Fantin-Latour, and, as Michael Bracewell noted, 'a masterclass in postmodern thinking'.[4] Saville himself considered it one of his most significant works.

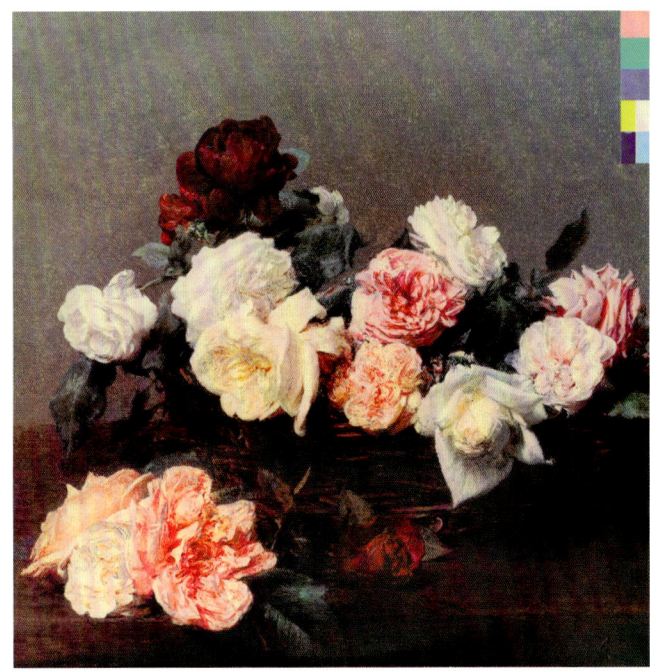

D.

A. *Self-portrait with a Palette*, Henri Fantin-Latour, 1861, oil on canvas, 81 × 65 cm (32 × 25 ⅝ in.)

B. *Portrait Study of Miss Sarah Budget*, 1883, Henri Fantin-Latour, oil on canvas, 100 × 133 cm (39 ⅜ × 52 ⅜ in.)

C. Portrait of Fantin-Latour seated in his studio in front of *Homage to Delacroix* (1864), 1895–1905, aristotype, 17.7 × 12.4 cm (7 × 5 in.)

D. Album cover of New Order's *Power, Corruption & Lies*, 1983, designed by Peter Saville, featuring Henri Fantin-Latour's *A Basket of Roses* (1890)

ROSA BONHEUR _{1822–1899}

The truthful palettes of an extraordinary woman

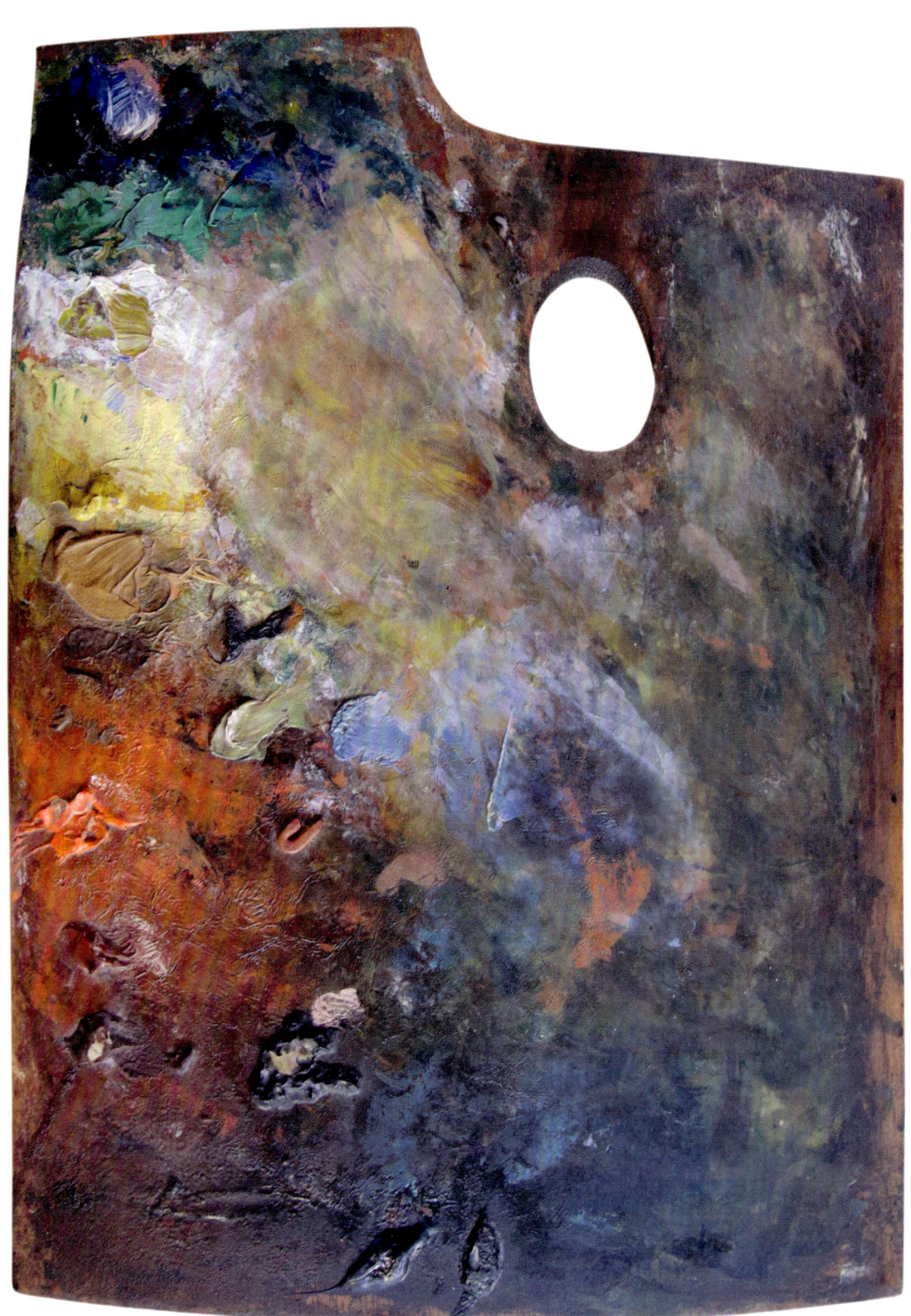

Rosa Bonheur's palette
19th century
Paint on wood

The Wounded Eagle
Rosa Bonheur
c. 1870
Oil on canvas
147.6 × 114.6 cm
(58 ⅛ × 45 ⅛ in.)

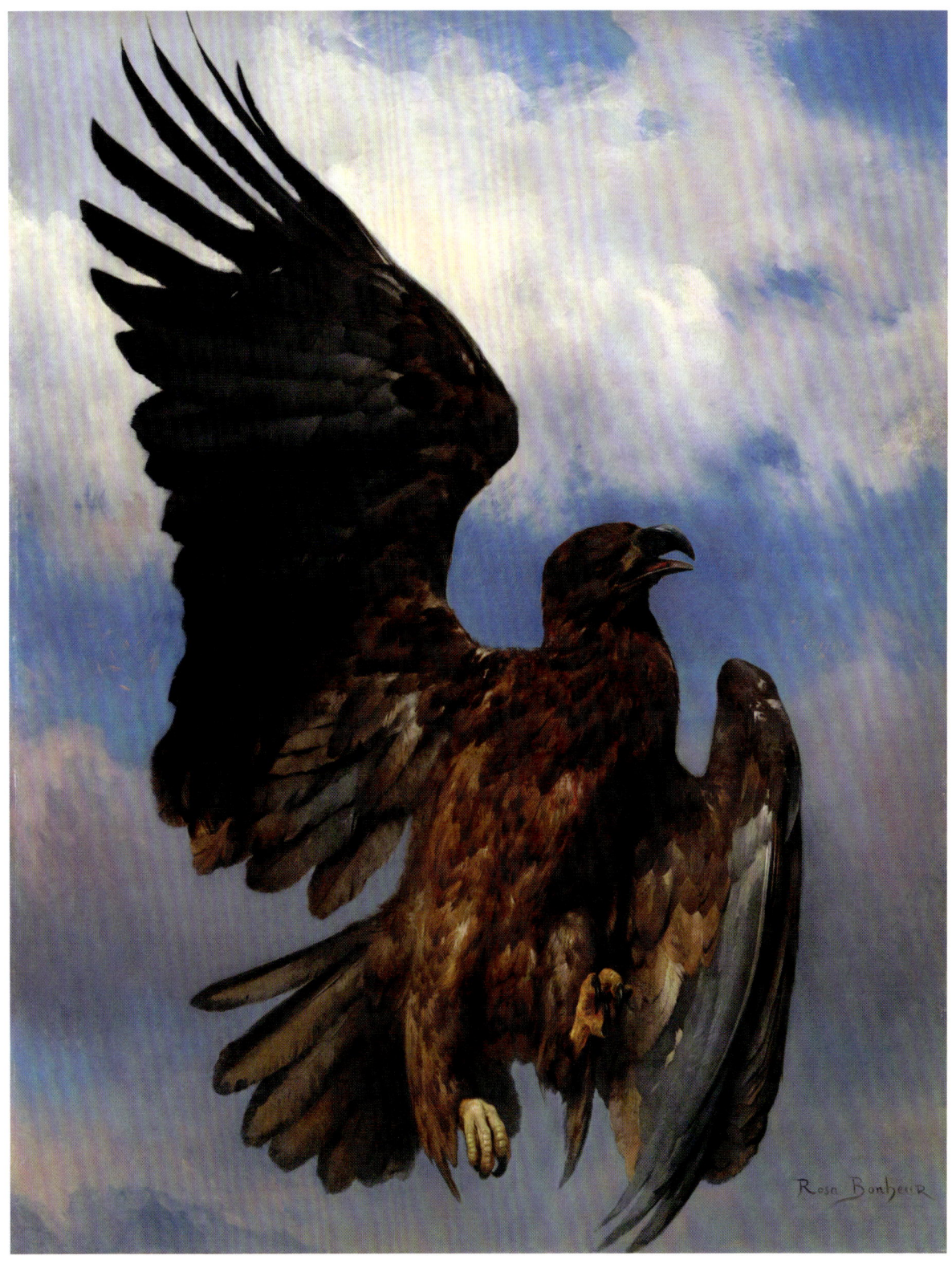

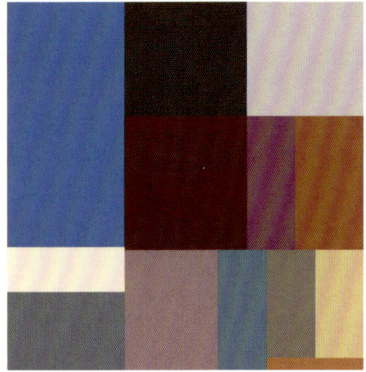

Proportional breakdown of colours used by Rosa Bonheur in *The Wounded Eagle*, *c*. 1870, displayed on the previous page.

SEVERAL OF ROSA BONHEUR'S PALETTES survive with large amounts of paint left on them, giving us a fascinating insight into her painting skills and working methods. Predominantly a painter of animals, Bonheur was unconventional and daring in her lifestyle, but traditional in her methods and motifs. She preferred realistic detail and colouring to impressionist ideals, following in her art the guiding principle of depicting, in her own words, 'a vision of truth'.[1] All her work was based on careful and meticulous study of nature.

It may be surprising that this palette appears to follow a prismatic layout similar to impressionist prescriptions of colour order, with pure colours arranged from light to dark along the top edge, but this is where the similarities end. There is a separate focus on brilliant greens, and extensive blending has been carried out on the lower half of the palette, creating a wide range of mixed greenish yellows and a multitude of shades of green and brown, typically used in Bonheur's realistic depiction of vegetation, wildlife and landscape settings. In the centre of the palette the artist has started creating luminous bright blues, probably intended for painting skies.

Many of her oil and watercolour paints were sourced from the British art supplier Winsor & Newton. Bonheur visited the United Kingdom several times and her work met with great approval there. We owe it to her partner Anna Klumpke that we know more about Bonheur's pigment choices and exact working methods. Klumpke not only painted Bonheur several times with her artist materials, but also wrote and published a biography, *Rosa Bonheur: Sa vie, son oeuvre* (1908), based on their years of living together and their many conversations about art. From it, we learn not only how Bonheur applied colour in a painting, starting with greens, then blues, white, yellow, reds and finally the darker shades of brown and black, but also about an exact layout of one of her palettes: emerald green, Veronese green, cobalt green, chromium oxide green; cobalt blue, ultramarine blue, Prussian blue; silver white; Naples yellow, yellow ochre, gold ochre, burnt gold ochre, raw and burnt sienna; vermilion, Venetian red, Indian red, Van Dyck red, red ochre, burnt lacquer, madder lake, Van Dyck brown; ivory black and peach black. There is a clear preference for combining earth pigments with more vibrant artificial colours, resulting in an overall warm tonal appearance crucial for a realistic depiction of nature. Indeed, Bonheur states that her all-important greens are often created from Prussian blue and yellow ochre (a large blob of the latter is visible on this palette, next to a much brighter yellow).

Displaying great technical knowledge and understanding, she stressed that even more important than choosing the right colours was knowing how to

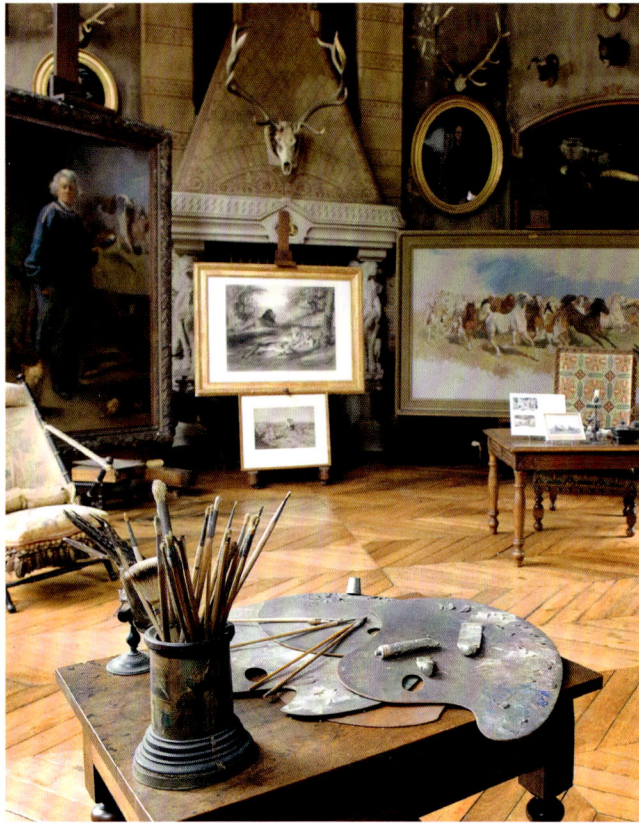

*'The eye is the way to the soul, and the crayon or brush
must simply and faithfully render what you see.'*

ROSA BONHEUR, QUOTED IN ANNA KLUMPKE'S *ROSA BONHEUR:
THE ARTIST'S (AUTO)BIOGRAPHY*, 2003

mix them. This is manifest in her astounding ability
to paint light and shade in her compositions, and her
skies are particularly shimmering and subtle. For
these, she would begin with the lightest shade of a grey
mixed from white and blue as a background, then add
deeper layers of grey and blue. She often silhouetted
animals against fine blue skies, as she has done here in
the life-sized image of a wounded eagle (*c.* 1870), still
majestic and defiant, despite its injuries. For the warm,
naturalistic browns of the creature, Bonheur used
mixed tones similar to those seen on the lower half
of the palette.

For nearly forty years she worked in a large,
converted billiard room with purpose-built, floor-
to-ceiling windows in the Château de By, overlooking
the River Seine in Thomery, near the forest of
Fontainebleau. The studio was filled with boxes,
cabinets, tables and easels overflowing with painting
materials, including several palettes and watercolour
boxes. Stuffed animals hung on the walls, while her
living menagerie of dogs, monkeys, birds, horses and
even lions, shared this artistic house and grounds.
She had bought the château in 1859 with the money she
made from one of her greatest paintings, *The Horse Fair*
(1852–55), a monumental work more than 5 metres
(16 feet) in length, which secured her fame and fortune.
After her death, the house, its contents and her work
were inherited and looked after by Klumpke. In 2018
it opened as the Château de Rosa Bonheur, having
been bought and restored by Katherine Brault. The
studio now appears almost exactly as it did in 1899,
and reflects an extraordinary woman's life and art.

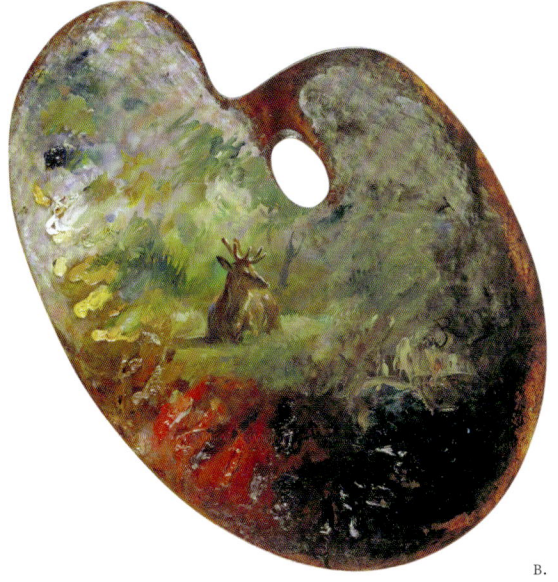

B.

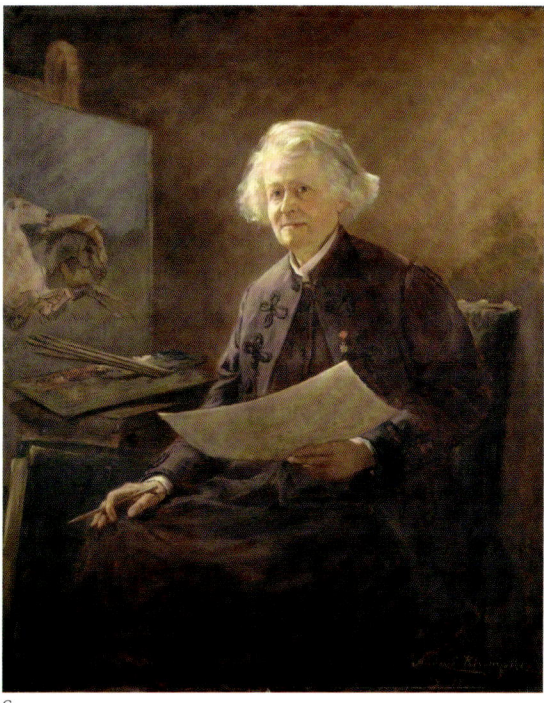

A.   Rosa Bonheur's studio, Château de By (also known as Château
     de Rosa Bonheur), Thomery, France
B.   Palette with a painting of a deer for Bonheur's godson, Rosa Bonheur,
     1850s, oil on wood, framed: 51.3 × 47 cm (20 ¼ × 18 ½ in.)
C.   *Rosa Bonheur*, Anna Klumpke, 1898, oil on canvas, 117.2 × 98.1 cm
     (46 ⅛ × 38 ⅝ in.)
D.   (Overleaf) Rosa Bonheur's paint tubes
E.   (Overleaf) Rosa Bonheur's palette and art materials

C.

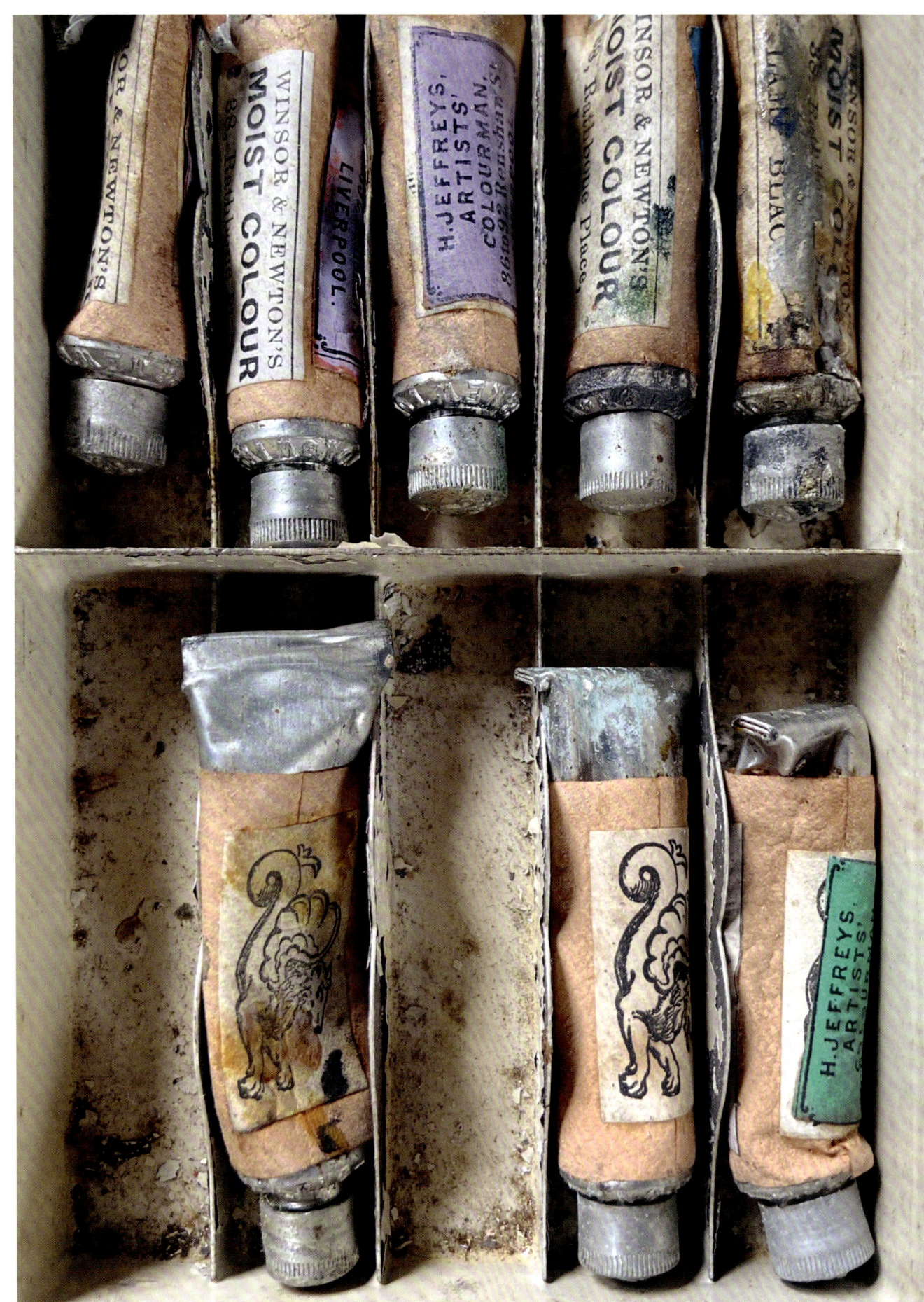

D.

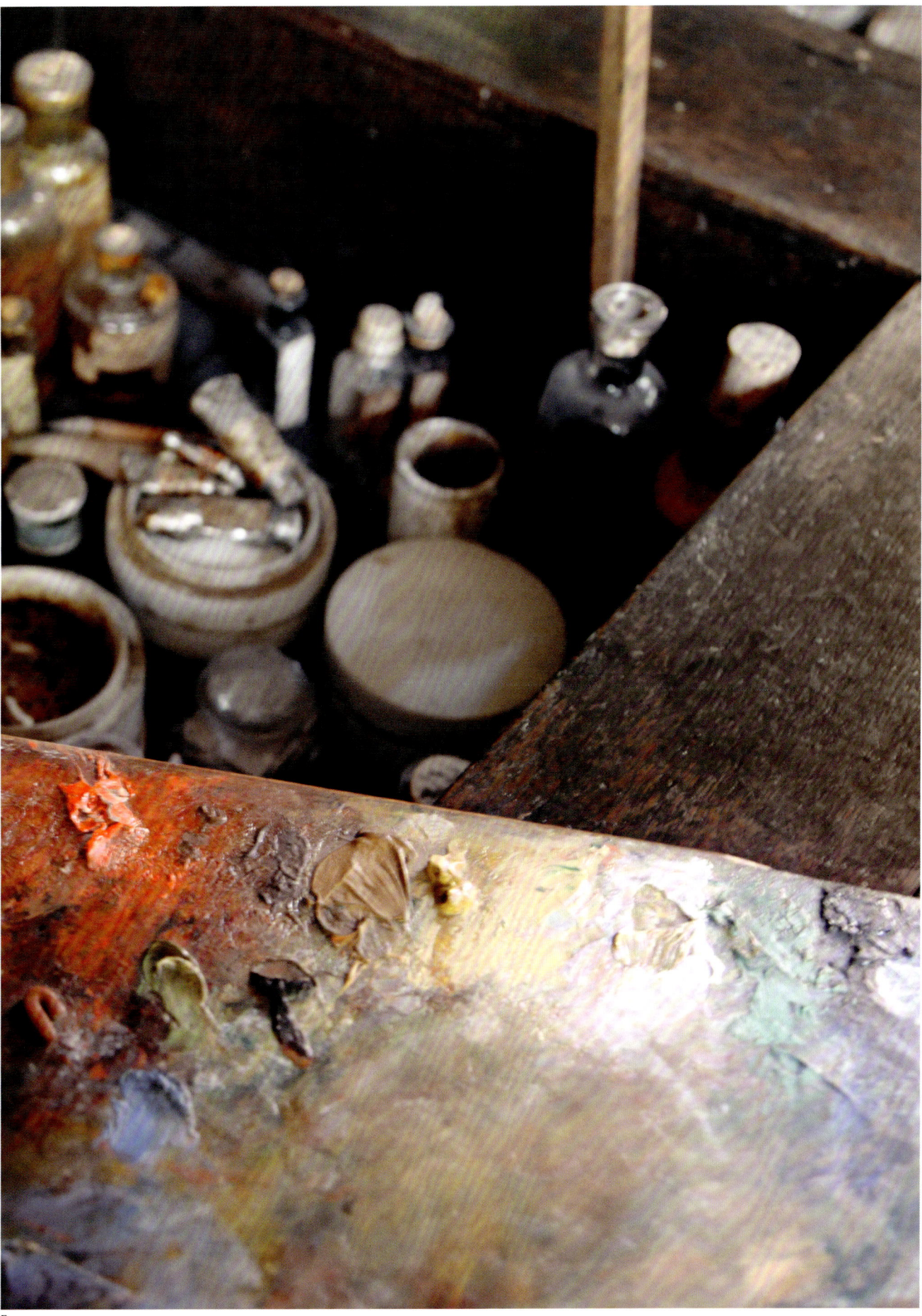

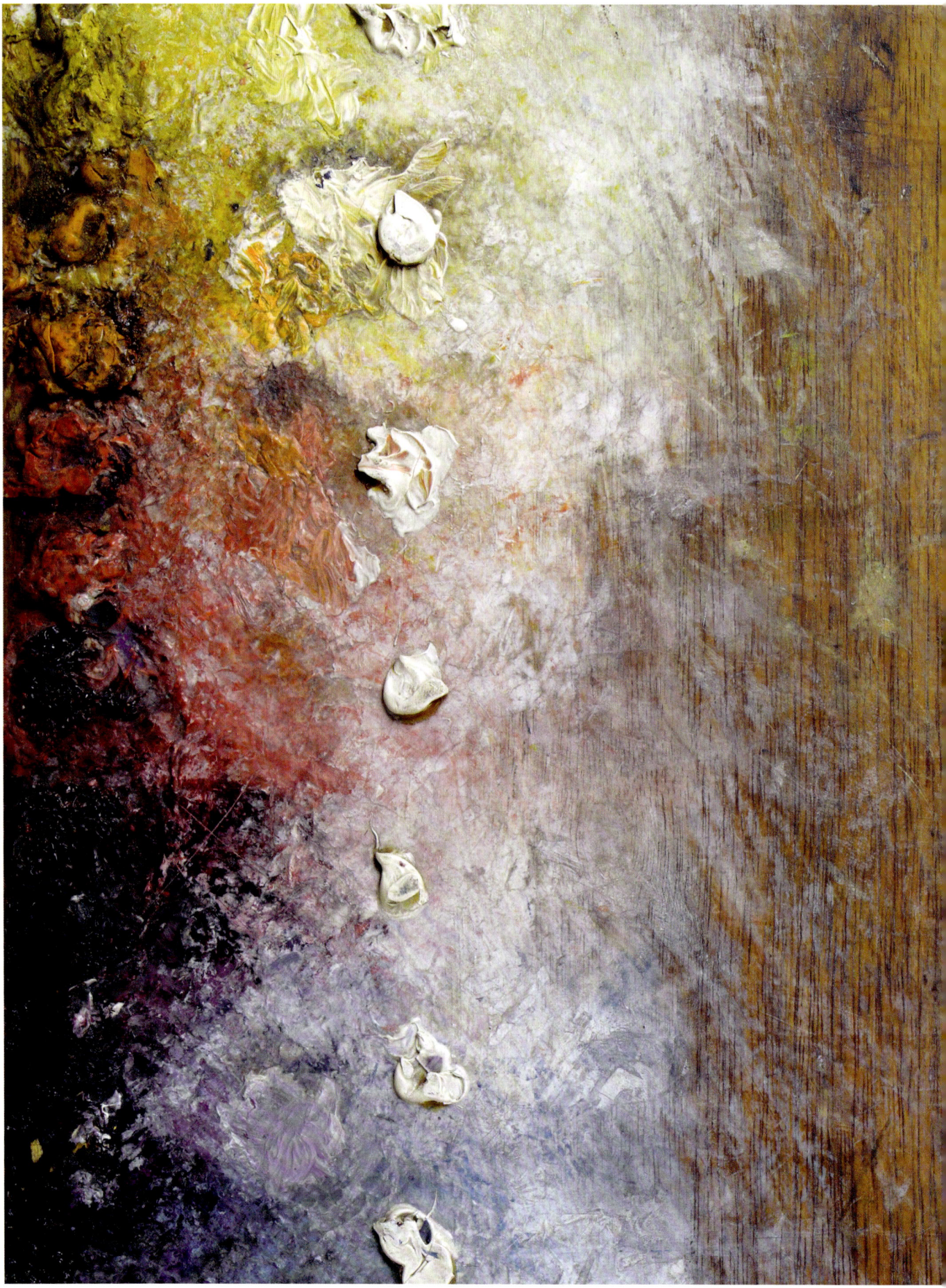

1871–1900

The Dynamic Palette

IN THE FINAL DECADES OF THE 19TH CENTURY the full rainbow range of bright synthetic or commercially produced natural colour had become available as ready-to-use paints. Oil paints were now available in collapsible tubes that could be transported easily and used over a longer period than the freshly made batches kept in pigs' bladders that John Constable had relied on. This coincided with the rise of photography, which made the need for realistic depiction in the fine arts less urgent. A greater awareness of the science behind colour and optics, rooted in the publication of some influential 19th-century texts on colour theory, for example by Michel Eugène Chevreul, Charles Blanc and George Field, was reflected in the painting methods and colour choices of many artists. Across all movements and strands of the visual arts in the later 19th century, the chromatic range became wider, more nuanced and more sophisticated. Impressionists and post-impressionists in particular followed and promoted the concept of a 'prismatic palette', mirroring spectral colour. Most used manufactured oil paints, often squeezed straight from tubes onto their palettes, with many – but not all – artists avoiding harsh blacks, at least for a while.

PAUL CÉZANNE 1839–1906

A singing palette with dark undertones

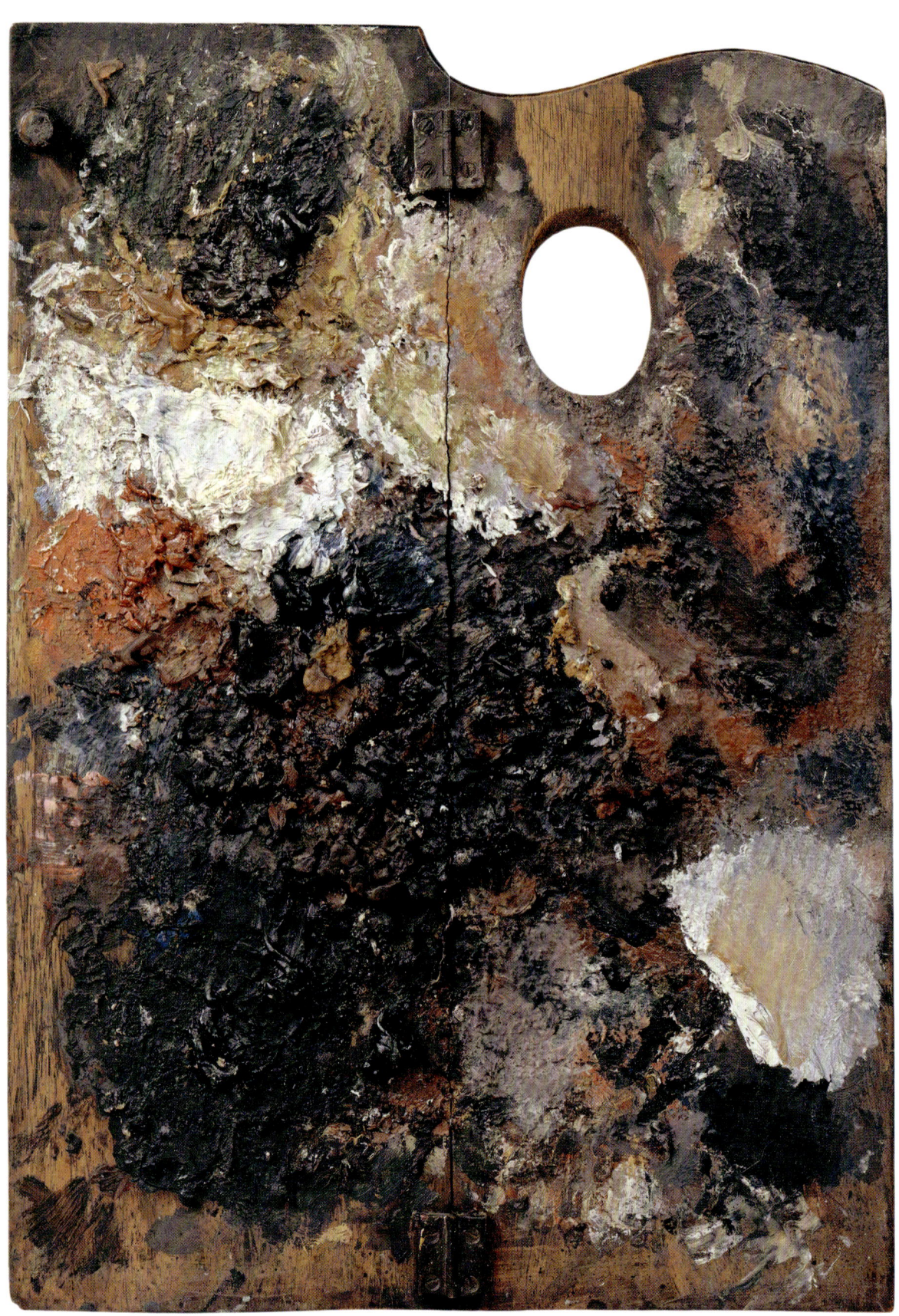

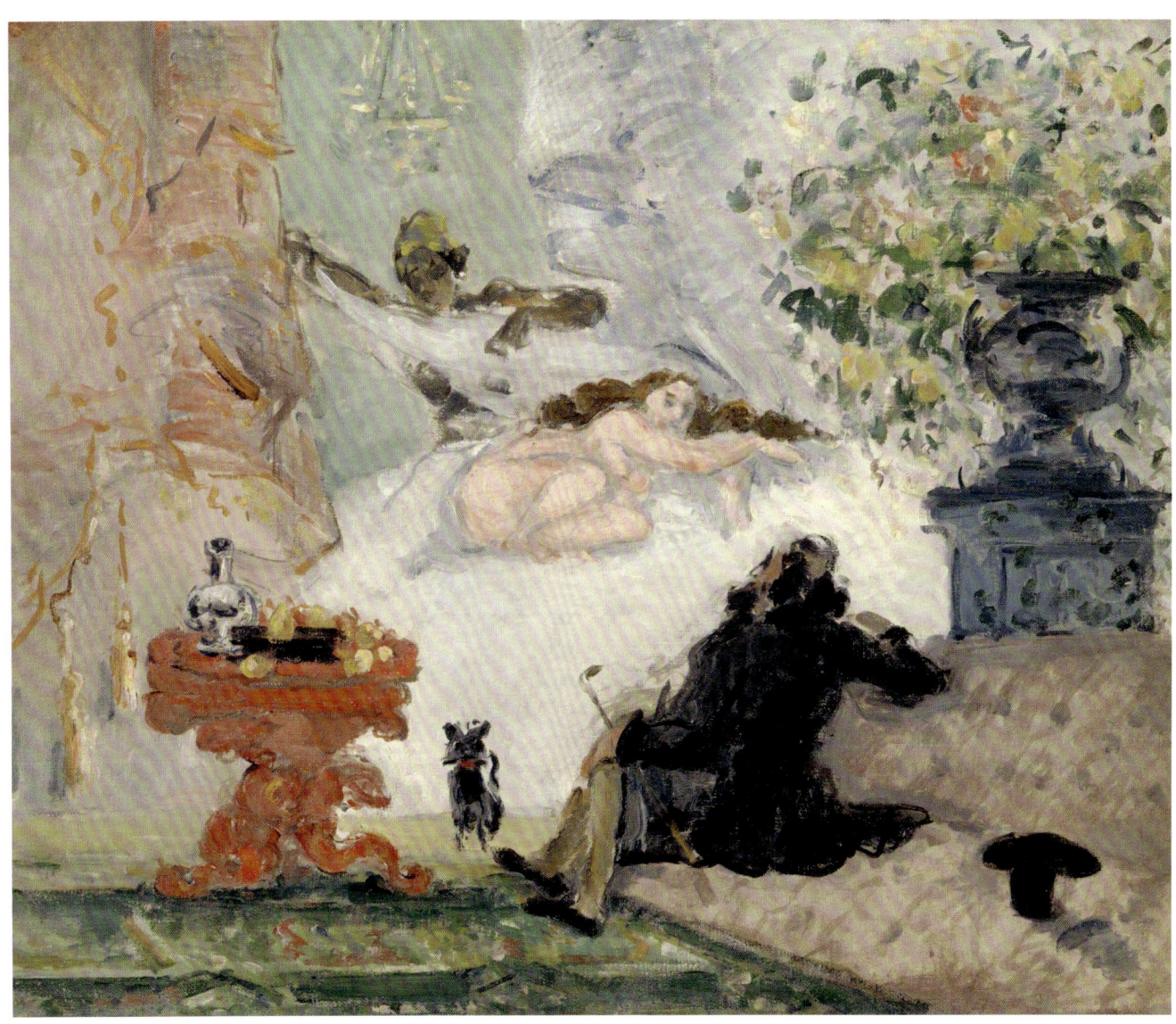

Paul Cézanne's folding palette
c. 1873
Oil on wood and metal
33.5 × 24 cm
(13 ¼ × 9 ½ in.)

A Modern Olympia
Paul Cézanne
1873–74
Oil on canvas
46.2 × 55.5 cm
(18 ¼ × 21 ⅞ in.)

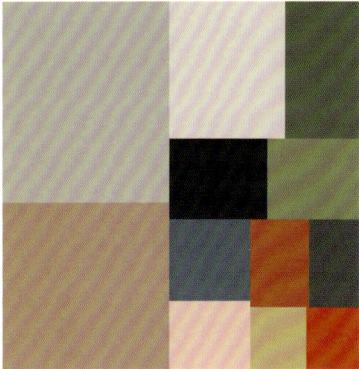

Proportional breakdown of colours used by Paul
Cézanne in *A Modern Olympia*, 1873–74, displayed
on the previous page.

THIS IS A PALETTE that can be precisely dated and
linked to a specific painting, Paul Cézanne's second
version of *A Modern Olympia*, from 1873–74, shown
on the previous page. The simple, folding palette with
metal hinges did not actually belong to Cézanne, but
to another Paul, the physician, amateur artist and art
collector Paul Gachet, who treated Vincent van Gogh
in the last weeks of his life. Cézanne had been staying
at Auvers-sur-Oise near Paris and befriended Gachet,
who was a great supporter of the impressionist movement.
The palette was allegedly lent by Gachet when Cézanne
decided, possibly on the spur of the moment, to paint
this version of *Olympia* for the doctor. The small
painting – perhaps an homage to but just as likely
a parody of Édouard Manet's painting *Olympia* from
1863 – was rapidly executed in loose brushstrokes in
a distinctly brighter, higher colour key than Cézanne's
earlier version from *c.* 1869, although their spatial
composition is similar. The physical palette gives a
clear sense of rapid execution, and the bright whites
and intense reds that are dominant colours in the
painting are clearly visible.

The palette is a fascinating document of Cézanne's
impressionist period (1872–83), which saw him
develop his profound sense of colour, and gradually
move away from the darker compositions of his early
work. Yet, there are still elements of darkness in this
palette, and in the painting. A surprisingly large part
of the palette is covered in dark, heavily mixed shades,
which in the painting are used to depict the Black
servant unveiling the naked figure of Olympia, a few
small objects, the rough outline of a cat and, most
importantly, the dubious figure of the male voyeur,
gazing at the woman presented to him. She is lying
on an indistinct white mass of bedsheets and pillows,
echoing Manet's original contrasting colour schemes.
The painting was included in the first impressionist
exhibition in 1874 and caused a minor scandal, similar
to Manet's *Olympia* at the Salon in 1865. However,
it wasn't just the subject matter of prostitution that
outraged the critics, it was also the painting style, with
one reviewer commenting that 'Mr Cézanne merely
gives the impression of being a sort of madman who
paints in delirium tremens'.[1]

In the 1870s, Cézanne's chromatic palette included
combinations of warm and cool colours, such as lead
and zinc whites, yellow ochre and chrome yellows,
a range of artificial blues and considerable quantities
of black.[2] The vibrant red in the painting and on this
palette was most likely vermilion. Cézanne's style
would change dramatically in the 1880s, when he
replaced tonal modelling and loose brushwork with
using colour in bold, wider strokes, creating solid

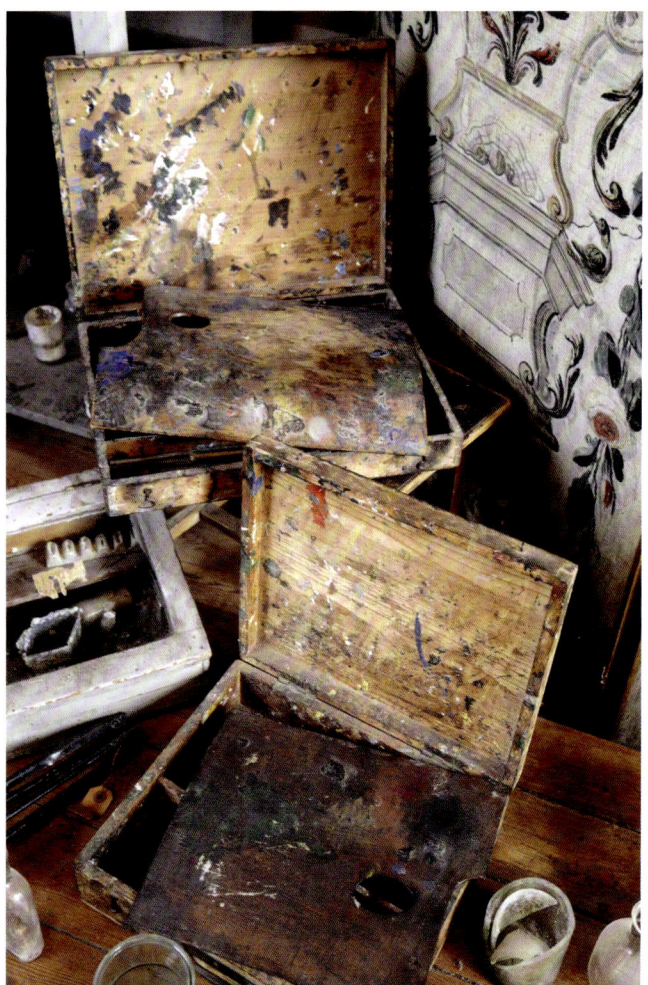

A.

'From all sides, here there and everywhere, I select colours, tones and shades; I set them down, I bring them together... They make lines, they become objects – rocks, trees – without my thinking about them.'

PAUL CÉZANNE, QUOTED IN JOACHIM GASQUET'S *CÉZANNE: A MEMOIR WITH CONVERSATIONS (1897–1906)*, 1991

shapes in composition. He developed a particular skill in combining different shades of green, using emerald, verdigris and possibly viridian green. Throughout his career, he used several art suppliers, including Sennelier, Lefranc et Cie and Bourgeois Aîné. In his self-portrait with a palette from *c.* 1890 (image C.), his fondness for green is apparent, in the green-tinted background against which he is silhouetted and on the painted palette itself, where several areas are covered in green mixtures. He had become, as Roger Fry would later state, a painter who was able to make colours '"sing" with a ravishing intensity and purity',[3] and he would never abandon black. In 1904 his friend Émile Bernard recorded the colours used by Cézanne, noting that they resembled a wide chromatic circle from flake white to black via the prismatic spectrum. Among the yellows Bernard listed were chrome yellow, ochre and sienna; the greens comprised emerald, viridian and green earth; the range of reds is the largest and includes opaque vermilion as well as red lakes, while a peach black is listed as the darkest colour among the blue pigments.[4] Cézanne became a true new master of using colours as structural elements in compositions and was much admired by the German poet Rainer Maria Rilke, who in 1907 sent excited letters to his wife Clara about Cézanne's sense of colour, claiming that 'no one before him has ever shown so clearly how much painting depends on what happens between colours, and that one has to leave them completely alone, so that they can communicate with each other. The interaction of colour: this is the whole of the art of painting.'[5]

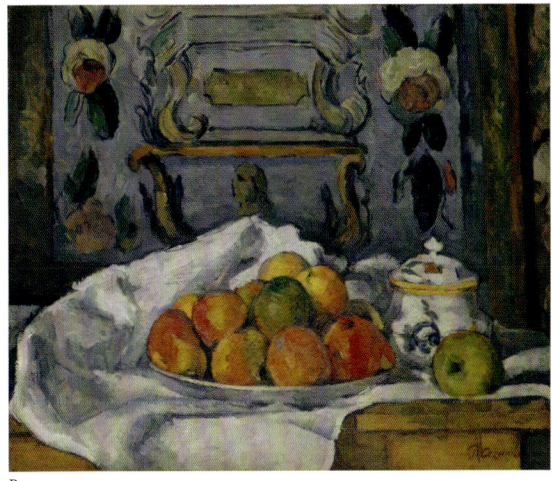

B.

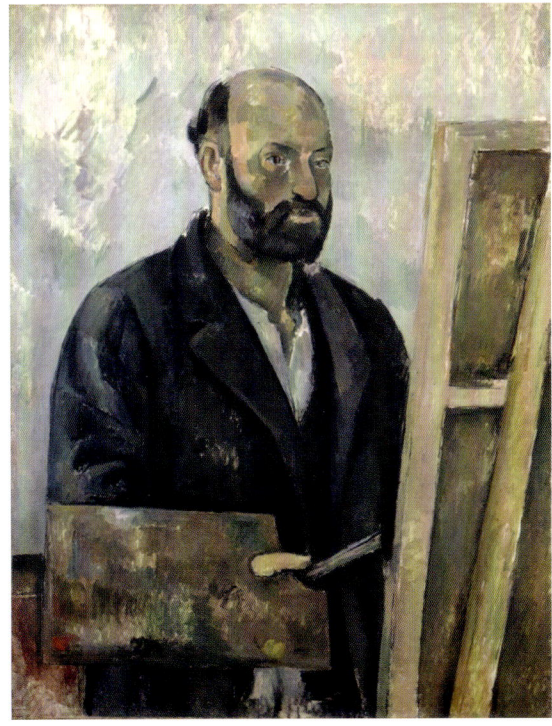

C.

A. Paul Cézanne's studio, Atelier des Lauves, Aix-en-Provence, France
B. *Dish of Apples*, Paul Cézanne, *c.* 1876–77, oil on canvas, 46 × 55.2 cm (18 ⅛ × 21 ¾ in.)
C. *Self-portrait with Palette*, Paul Cézanne, *c.* 1890, oil on canvas, 92 × 73 cm (36 ¼ × 28 ¾ in.)

EDGAR DEGAS 1834–1917

A blurred palette, capturing movement and light

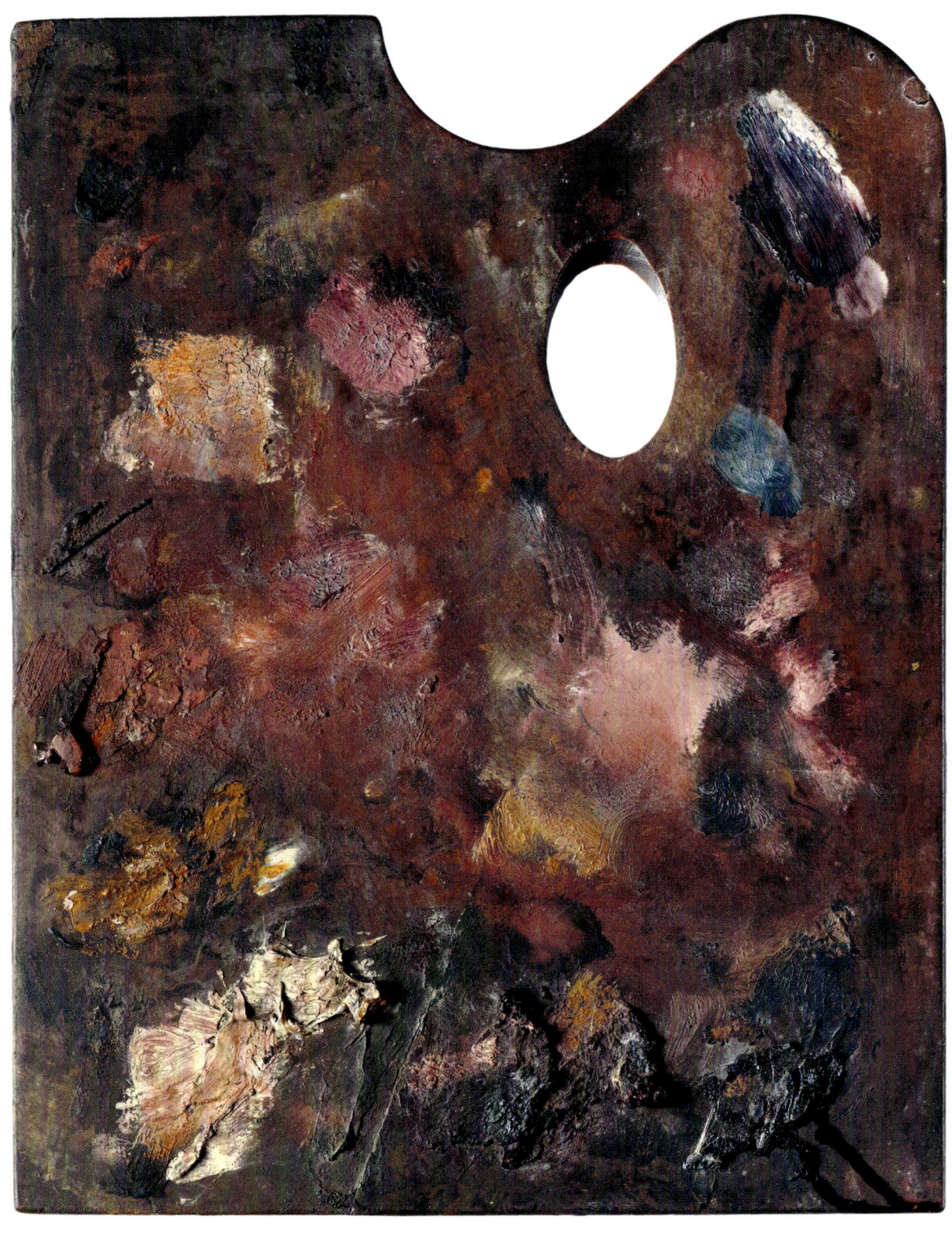

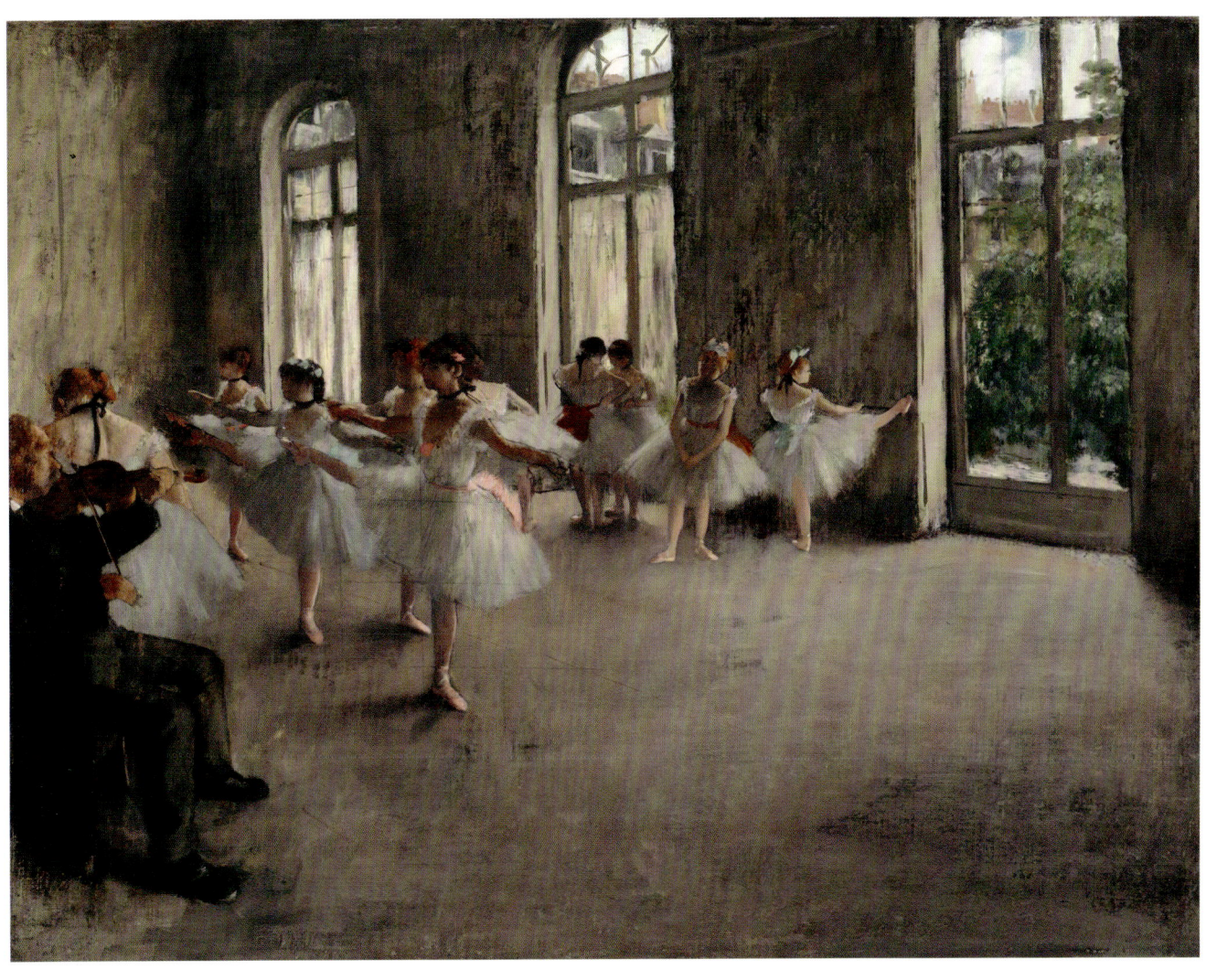

Edgar Degas' palette
1855–1917
Paint on wood
26 × 36.9 cm
(10 ¼ × 14 ⅝ in.)

The Rehearsal
Edgar Degas
c. 1873–78
Oil on canvas
47.2 × 61.5 cm
(18 ⅝ × 24 ¼ in.)

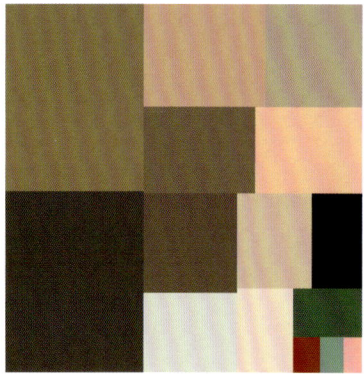

Proportional breakdown of colours used by Edgar Degas in *The Rehearsal*, *c*. 1873–78, displayed on the previous page.

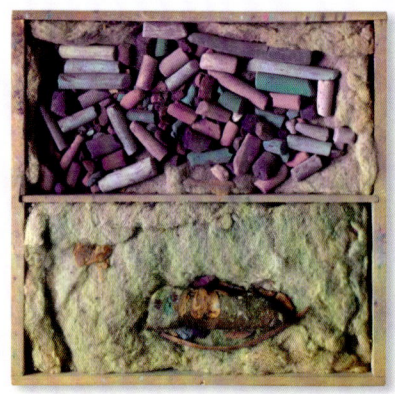

A.

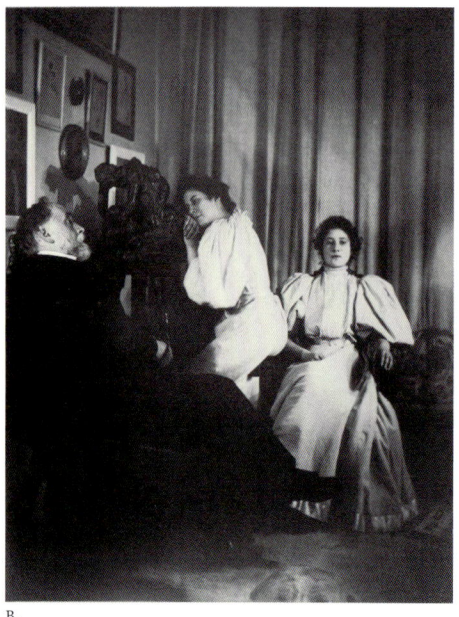

B.

SEVERAL PALETTES BY EDGAR DEGAS survive, of varying sizes and shapes, all made from polished wood. They reveal an artist who was both spontaneous and methodical in equal measures. This palette has been heavily used and looks messier than some of his others, and it is possible that a section of it broke off along the long top edge. For Degas, a disciplined draughtsman and accomplished in several media, this is a rough-looking palette, on which considerable mixing and blending has been carried out. Yet, there is a structure to it, and it vaguely follows the concept of a typical impressionist layout of pure prismatic colours in a line, with large amounts of white – to achieve luminosity and create lighter hues of the pure colours – placed near the thumbhole. In this case, though, Degas needed additional mounds of white, as well as a wider range of neutral colours, possibly to create a light brown or grey background colour as seen in the walls and floor of the painting shown here, *The Rehearsal* (*c*. 1873–78). Several delicate dusty pinks are visible among the mixtures, alongside a surprisingly vivid green, warm reds, yellows, and a powdery blue. The pigments he used likely included zinc and lead white, yellow ochre, cobalt and Prussian blue, vermilion and several chrome colours. He was particularly fond of red and brown earths, to create the warm tones that characterize many of his works.

Although this palette shows thrown-up mounds of colour, Degas usually applied his heavily diluted oil paint thinly, using palette knives and brushes, and often scraped down the paint before it had dried, adding further layers later, sometimes working wet-on-dry, sometimes wet-in-wet. When painting on canvas, this scraping down method would leave a ghostly image of the colours in the fabric.[1] In doing this, he effectively treated oil paint like transparent sheets of paper or watercolour, giving his paintings a dreamlike, gauzy appearance similar to blurred photographs. He was also known to use blotting paper to extract oil from paint layers, a technique referred to as *peinture à l'essence*, to achieve a matte, chalky finish.[2]

This is one of the many images of ballet dancers that he painted from the early 1870s onwards, pictured from unconventional angles backstage or during rehearsals, and infused with a notion of intimacy, unpredictability and voyeurism. In his depictions of frozen movements, such as pirouetting dancers, he was possibly inspired by early photography. The compositions seem natural and spontaneous, but are, in fact, meticulously constructed. Degas often made several preparatory sketches for each figure, concentrating entirely on shape and posture, and disregarding the individuality of the young women. Content, mood and atmosphere

'A painting is a thing which requires as much trickery, malice and vice as the perpetration of a crime; make counterfeits and add a touch from nature.'

EDGAR DEGAS, QUOTED IN ROBERT L. HERBERT'S *IMPRESSIONISM: ART, LEISURE & PARISIAN SOCIETY*, 1988

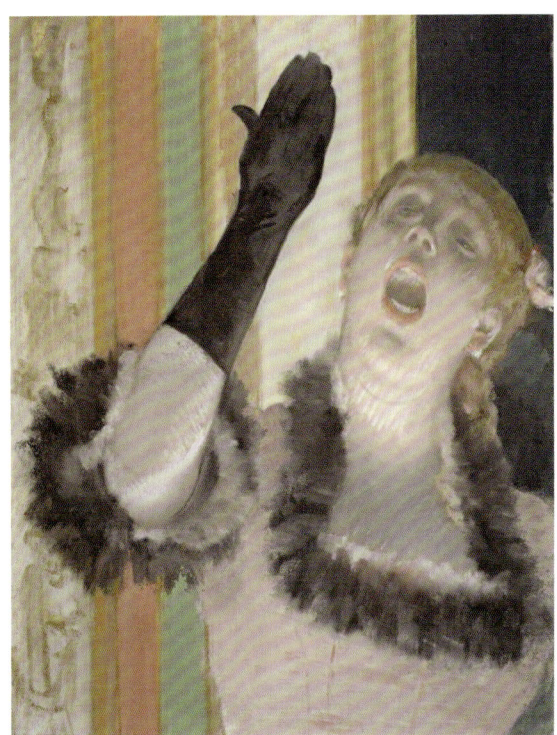

C.

are created entirely through colour, shade and contour. Unlike his impressionist colleagues, Degas rarely focused on landscape and natural light, but preferred contained, complex, artificially lit spaces. Although influenced by Manet, Delacroix (see pages 50–53) and other French contemporaries, he had also carefully studied and copied Dutch and Italian old masters, and learnt much about subtle colouring from them.

Degas was also drawn to another paint medium that would allow him to further achieve his luminous, matte, feathery effects: chalk pastels, which he sometimes combined with distemper. For these, palettes were not necessary as nearly all mixing and blending would take place on the picture, and largely relied on optical mixing. A box of pastels shown here contains a range of mauves, blues and violets, used so extensively by many impressionists as a representation of light and twilight that they were accused of 'violettomania'. The art dealer Ambroise Vollard visited Degas in his studio in Paris in the late 1880s and watched him working on one of his pastel drawings, 'those marvellous things that have been compared to butterflies' wings'. He witnessed him spread out his pastel sticks on the windowsill, leaving them in broad sunlight, to drain the colour out of them. Asked how he was able to achieve the bright colouring of his works despite this treatment, Degas answered, 'Opaque colour, Monsieur'.[3]

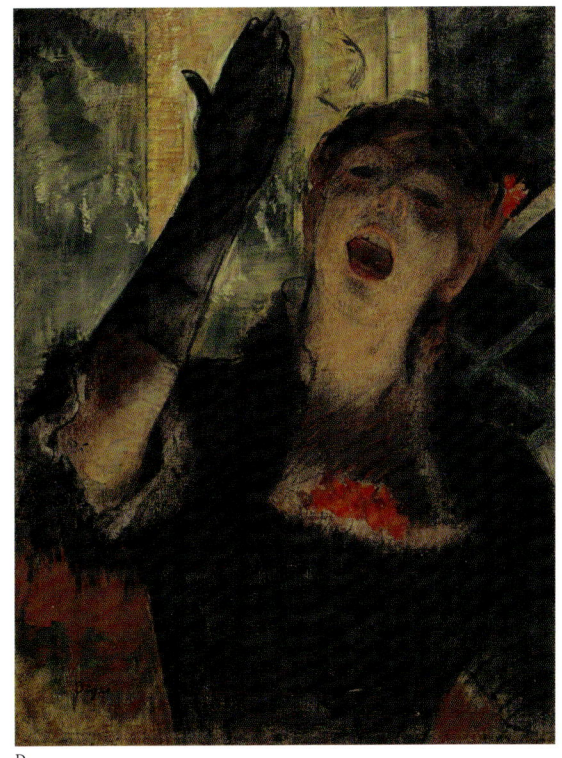

A.   Edgar Degas' box of pastels, 1848–1914
B.   *Self-portrait with Christine and Yvonne Lerolle*, Edgar Degas, probably 1895–96, gelatin silver print, 37.1 × 29.3 cm (14 ⅝ × 11 ⅝ in.)
C.   *Singer with a Glove*, Edgar Degas, *c.* 1878, pastel on canvas, 53.2 × 41 cm (21 × 16 ¼ in.)
D.   *Café Singer*, Edgar Degas, 1879, oil on canvas, 53.5 × 41.8 cm (21 ⅛ × 16 ½ in.)

D.

BERTHE MORISOT 1841–1895

A personal palette, capturing the fleetingness of childhood

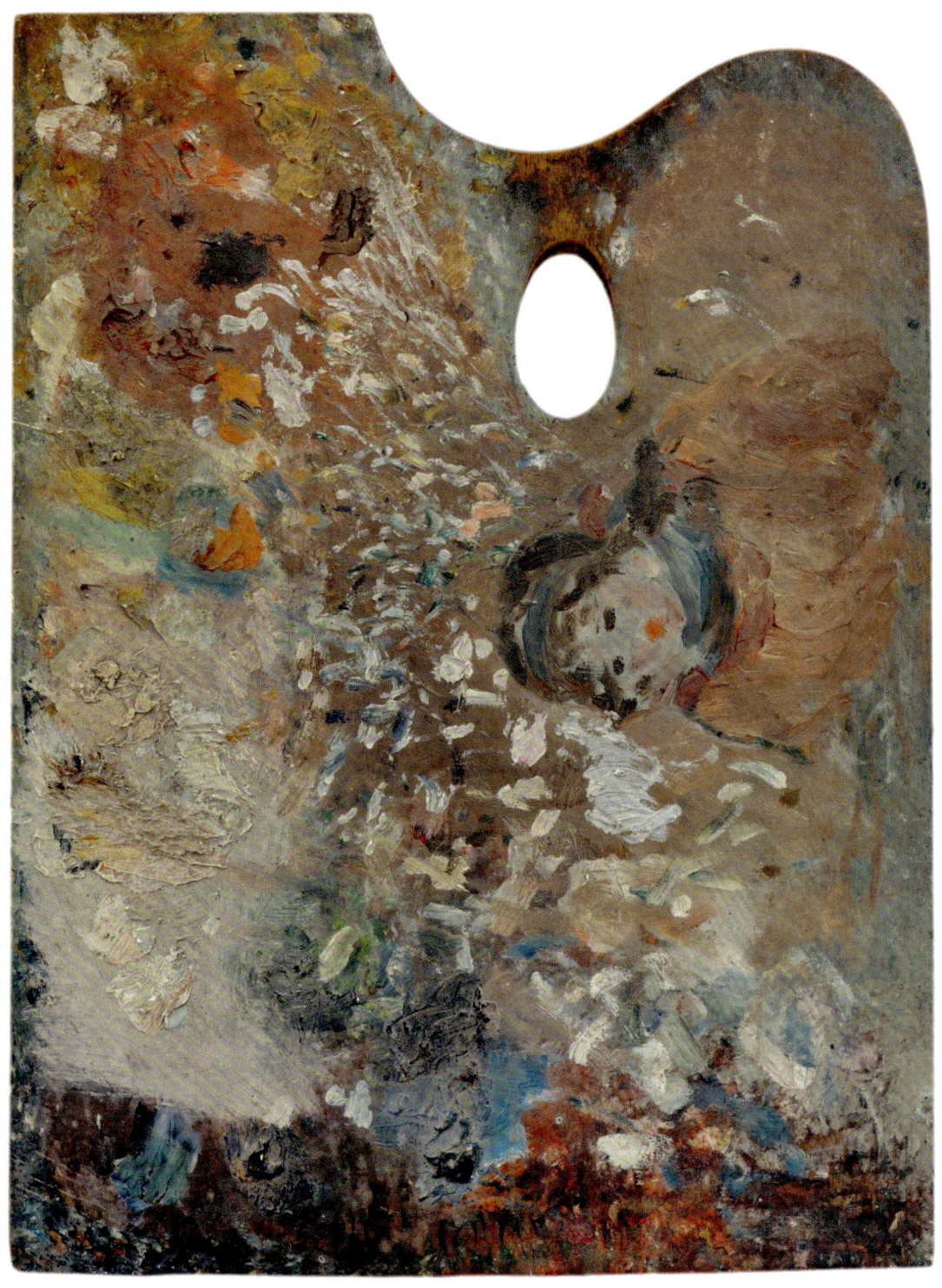

Tête d'enfant (child's head)
Berthe Morisot
c. 1881–82
Oil on wooden palette
31.2 × 41 cm
(12 ¼ × 16 ⅛ in.)

Child Among Hollyhocks
Berthe Morisot
1881
Oil on canvas
50.5 × 42.5 cm
(20 × 16 ¾ in.)

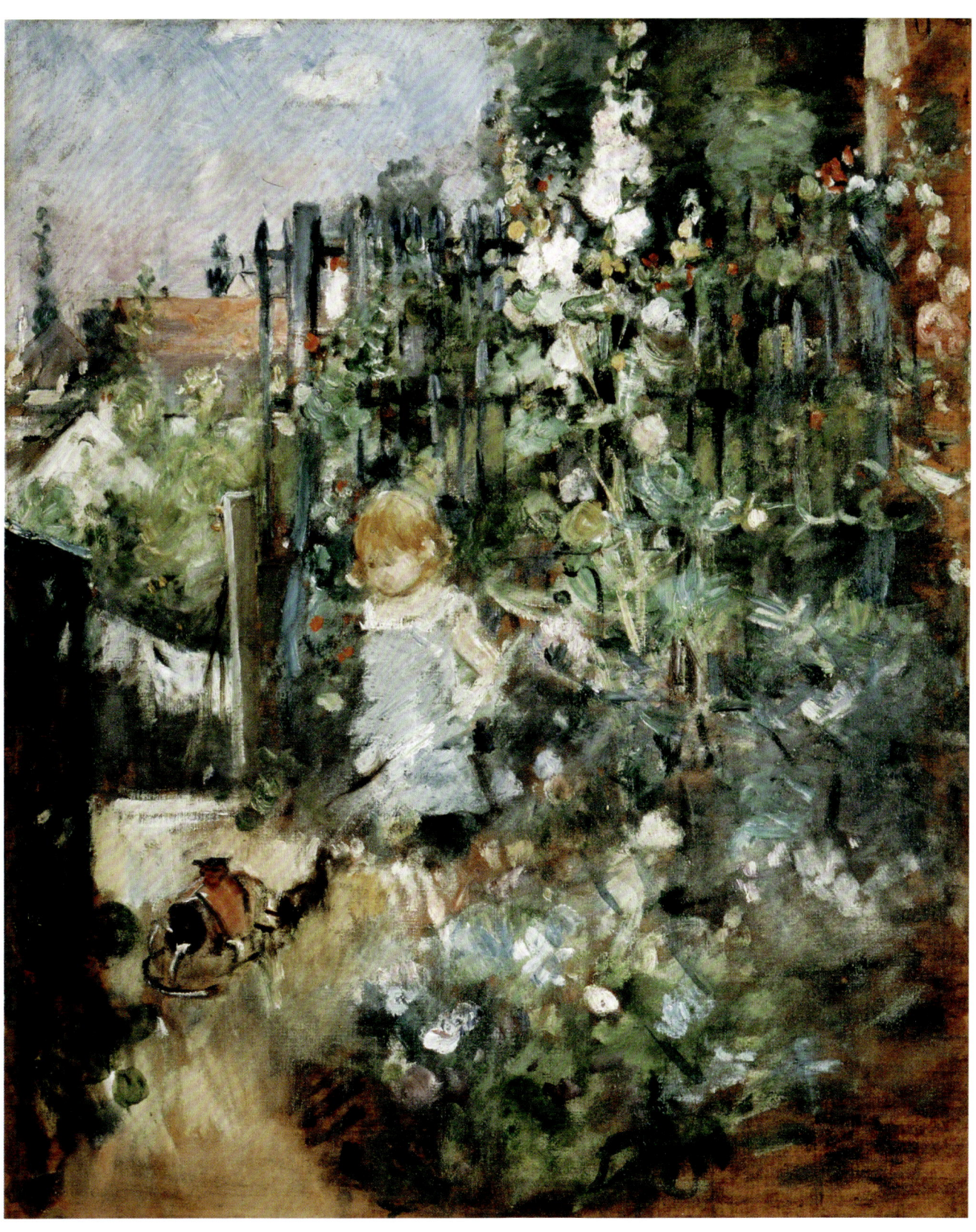

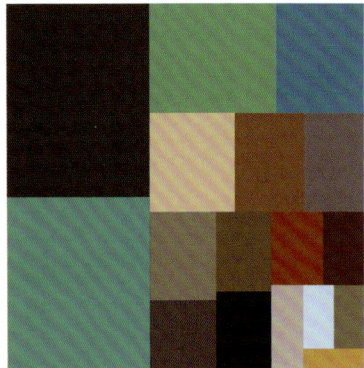

Proportional breakdown of colours used by Berthe Morisot in *Child Among Hollyhocks*, 1881, displayed on the previous page.

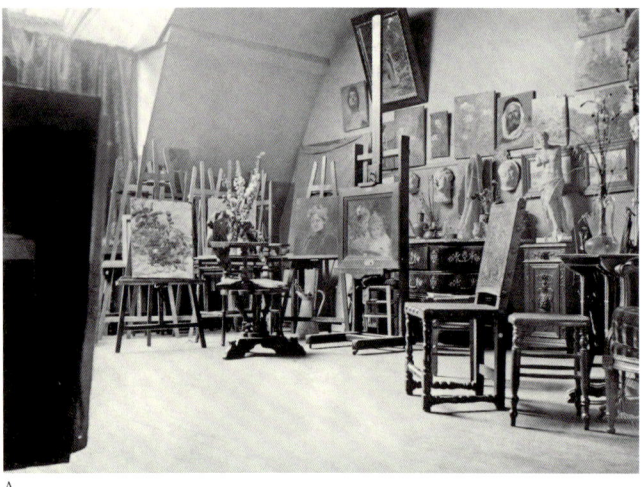

A.

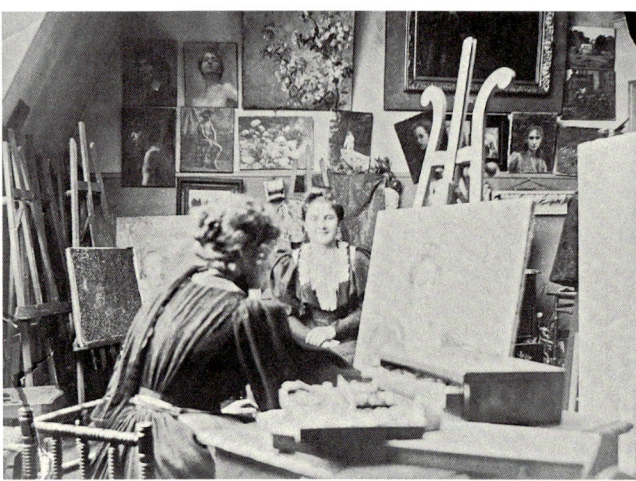

B.

AT FIRST GLANCE this looks like a typical impressionist painter's palette, with conspicuous quantities of white paint for lightening and brightening the few pure colours used to capture the fleeting, ever-changing appearance of the world. Small daubs of oil paint covering the surface of the square wooden palette suggest that the artist painted quickly, impulsively and lightly, and quite possibly outdoors (*en plein air*) with a box of collapsible paint tubes in her lap or on the shelf of a lightweight easel. Look closer, however, and a face emerges: a child's head, with eyes marked out in near-black, single small strokes and bright shining lips that appear to be executed in a single light red daub of paint. A blue collar and perhaps a red dress are hinted at, and auburn hair frames the child's face. This is a fleeting portrait of a girl, painted in *c.* 1881–82, most likely of Morisot's only child Julie with her husband Eugène Manet, who was the younger brother of Édouard Manet.

Once the portrait emerges from the loose mass of colour, this becomes more than simply a working palette. The wooden surface becomes a picture plane that emulates a canvas, the abstract daubs of colour around the child's head could be interpreted as a shower of flowers, a part of the composition, especially to those who are familiar with Morisot's art. Importantly, the palette evokes stories even more personal than those relating to technique and materiality. It becomes a highly intimate, biographical object that can transport us into the life of a 19th-century female artist, one who, although at the heart of the French avant-garde scene, was still more restricted than men in her choice of subjects and places where she could paint.

Did Morisot's daughter (then only three years old) join her mother painting in the garden, or did she come running into her studio in Paris, prompting her to put an image of her child symbolically at the centre of her professional artistic life? Was this perhaps a creative act that perfectly encapsulates the impressionists' idea of capturing a moment? Whether this was an impulsive or more considered act, Morisot turned a working tool into a token of maternal love. A painting of a child in a rose garden from around the same time (shown on the previous page) is similar in colouring to the palette sketch, and likely also shows Julie. The palette remained with Julie until the end of her life.

While impressionism generally purported to portray 'modern life', often in urban environments, Morisot largely had to stay within what was deemed acceptable for a woman to do and paint. She was commercially successful and positively received in her lifetime, but neglected by art critics for much of the 20th century. Her important role in the history of modern French art has only recently been fully

'Real painters only understand with a brush in their hands.'

BERTHE MORISOT, *CARNET DE MÉZY*
(ALSO KNOWN AS *CARNET NOIR*), 1891

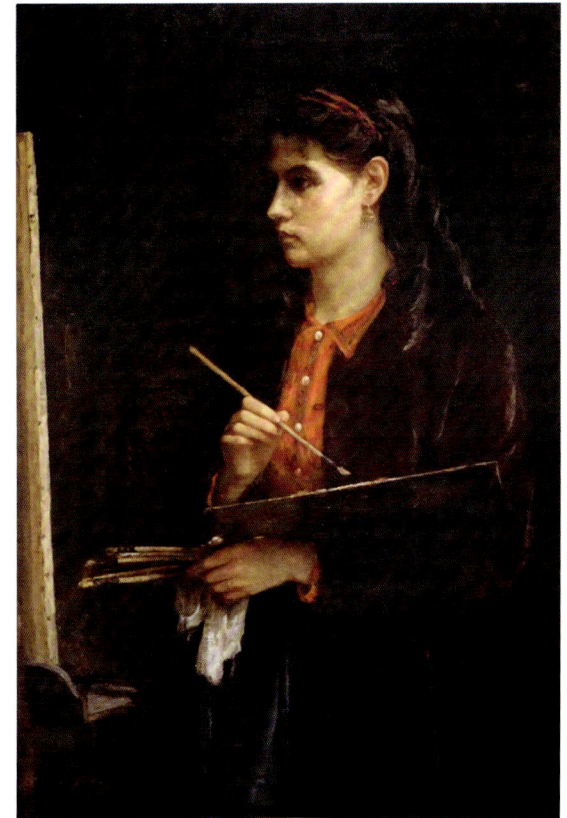

C.

acknowledged. She was the sole woman to be included
in the first impressionist exhibition in Paris in 1874,
and only missed one of the subsequent annual exhibitions,
when recovering after giving birth to her daughter. Her
style, although often strikingly similar to that of her male
colleagues and friends, such as Monet (see pages 152–55),
Degas (see pages 90–93), Pissarro (see pages 122–25),
Renoir (see pages 98–101), Manet and many others,
was in her time often condescendingly and wrongly
described as simply 'feminine'. She did, however,
embrace the subjects, motifs, and models closest to her,
and painted many sensitive portraits of mothers and
children, often against hazy, dissolving backgrounds,
loosely painted using copious amounts of white paint
mixed with a few pure colours, in whichever medium
she was working.

Although we know Morisot well as a figure in some
of the best-known impressionist paintings (she is, for
example, the seated woman in Manet's *Le Balcon* from
1868–69), her male colleagues never portrayed her
as an artist. Her sister Edma painted a serious-looking
young Berthe in *c.* 1865 in front of an easel, holding
a palette and brushes (image C.). In 1885 Morisot
produced a striking self-portrait (image D.) in which
her own palette is painted in only a few assured
brushstrokes, anchoring her figure to the edges of the
canvas. The colouring and technique in this self-portrait
are remarkably similar to the palette with the child's
head, deliberately blurring the boundaries between
sketch and finished painting. In some related sketches
to the self-portrait a child appears in the composition.

A.   Berthe Morisot's studio, Paris, France, *c.* 1892
B.   Berthe Morisot at work in her studio, 10 Rue Weber, Paris,
     France, *c.* 1892
C.   *Portrait of the Artist's Sister Berthe Morisot Painting*, Edma
     Pontillon née Morisot, *c.* 1865, oil on canvas, 100 × 71 cm
     (39 ⅜ × 28 in.)
D.   *Self-portrait*, Berthe Morisot, 1885, oil on canvas, 61 × 50 cm
     (24 ⅛ × 19 ¾ in.)

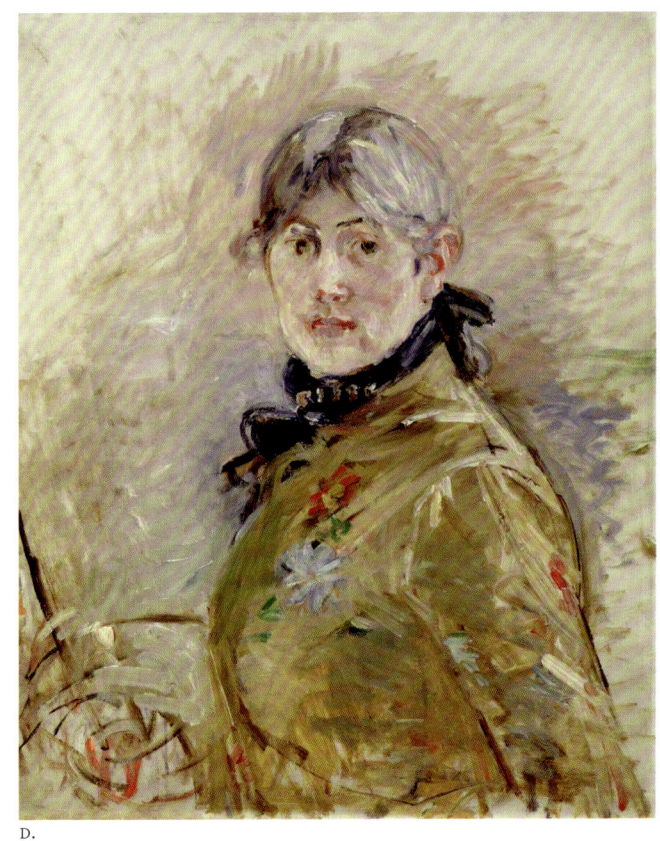

D.

PIERRE-AUGUSTE RENOIR 1841–1919

A palette that reveals all

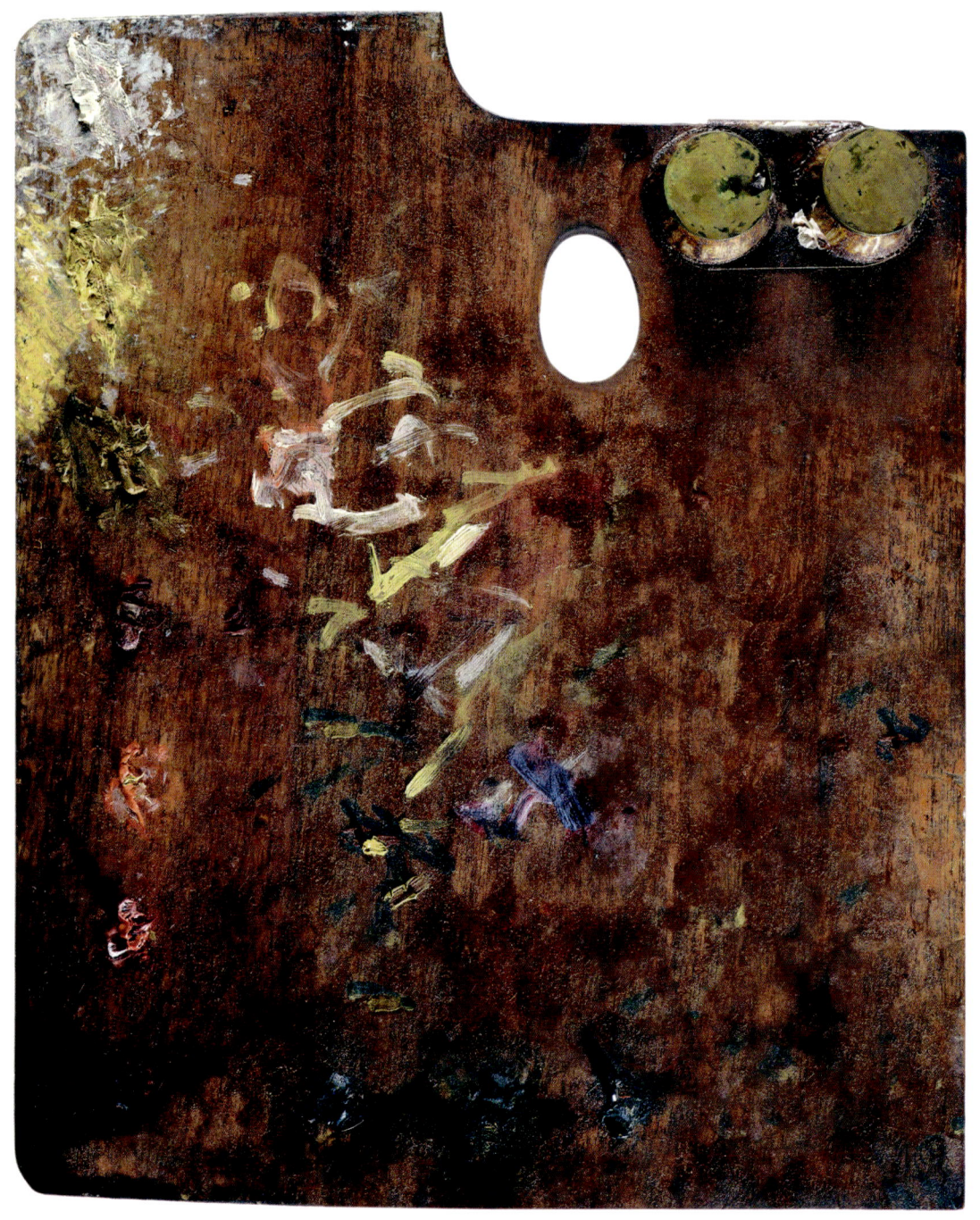

Pierre-Auguste Renoir's
palette
Probably late 19th century
Paint on wood

*Two Sisters
(On the Terrace)*
Pierre-Auguste Renoir
1881
Oil on canvas
100.4 × 80.9 cm
(39 ½ × 31 ⅞ in.)

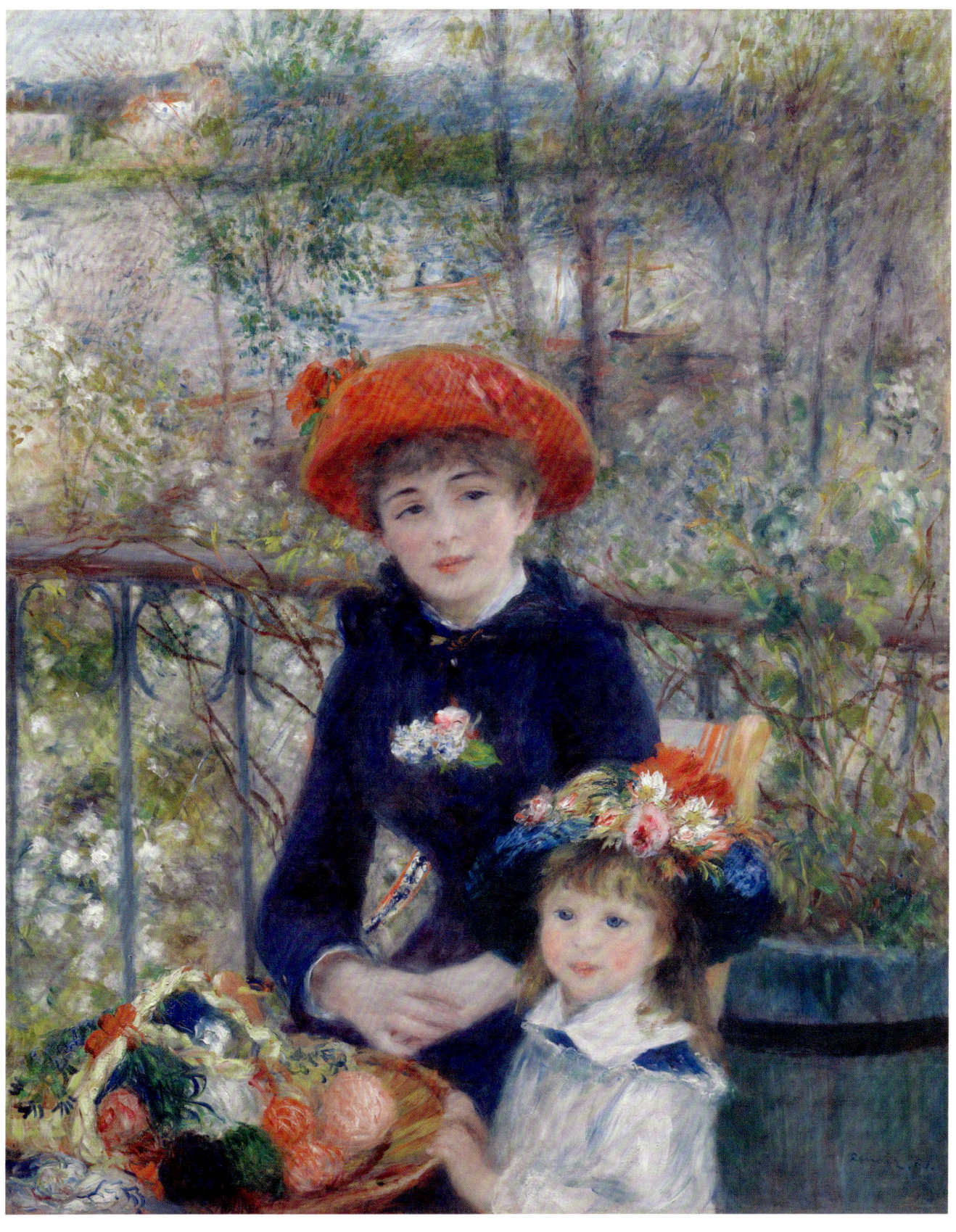

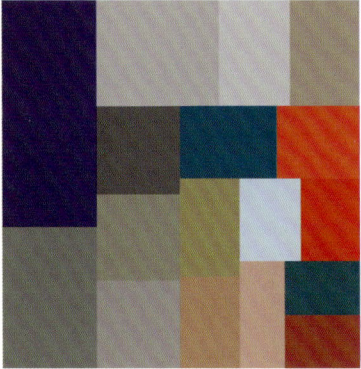

Proportional breakdown of colours used by Pierre-Auguste Renoir in *Two Sisters (On the Terrace)*, 1881, displayed on the previous page.

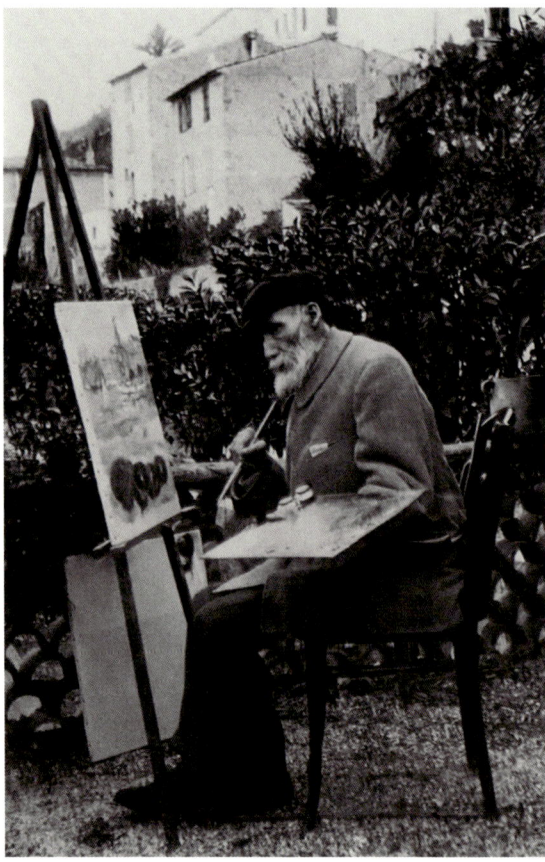

A.

A. Renoir painting in the garden, Cagnes-sur-Mer, France, *c.* 1915–19
B. Pierre-Auguste Renoir's palette and paintbox with brushes, tools and paints
C. *Study of Heads*, Pierre-Auguste Renoir, 1890s, oil on canvas, 46 × 38 cm (18 ⅛ × 15 in.)

THERE IS A JEWEL-LIKE TRANSLUCENCY to Pierre-Auguste Renoir's colouring that may have something to do with the fact that early in his career he was a porcelain painter at the Sèvres manufactory. A pioneer of impressionism, his palette was among the brightest, most luminous and most sugary of the movement. He had a particular fondness for the colour red and, by way of adding zinc or lead white to it, a wide range of pinks that he often used as flesh tints.

Renoir once famously exclaimed that 'The palette of the painter signifies nothing, it is his eye which does everything.'[1] The palette shown here was part of a paintbox and probably originates from the late 19th century. The very small quantities of paint on it may seem surprising. Yet, these faint traces of brushes being wiped in the centre of the palette and the lines of paint blots along two of the edges betray Renoir's technique and attitude to colour. There is a clear and precise chromatic arrangement, including reds, yellows and whites along one edge, and darker colours (most likely blues and greens) along the other, laid out by the artist in a deliberate fashion. Some careful and restrained mixing has taken place on the palette in the yellow and white areas. The thinness of the paint on the palette is indicative of Renoir's technique. In contrast to the thick impasto preferred by some of his contemporaries, he applied paint in several thin layers to the canvas and achieved richness and brilliance through using glazes of transparent colour over opaque layers, especially when modelling faces, bodies and larger areas of solid colour. The two 'dippers' attached to the palette contained liquids such as turpentine or linseed oil, which he used copiously to thin the oil paint, until he could treat it almost like watercolour. All of this tallies with an extensive account given on his painting techniques by his early biographer and fellow artist, Albert André, who noted that 'he scarcely ever mixes the paint on his palette, which is covered with little blobs of almost pure colour.'[2]

The relative emptiness of the palette is also a reflection of his general working methods. According to his son Jean, Renoir was meticulous, tidy and highly organized with his painting tools. His paintbox and table were always in perfect order, brushes were cleaned regularly and discarded after only a few uses, and paint tubes were rolled up neatly from the end. His palette was wiped clean after each use, until it was immaculate, looking 'as clean as a new coin'.[3] It is a minor miracle that this one survives with traces of paint.

While Renoir was organized and tidy with his materials, he claimed that he did not follow any rules in respect of colour arrangement in his compositions:

I arrange my subject as I want it, then go ahead and paint it like a child. I want the red to be sonorous,

'I want the red to be sonorous, to sound like a bell; if it doesn't turn out that way, I put in more reds or other colours till I get it…. I have no rules of methods; anyone can look at my materials and watch how I paint.'

PIERRE-AUGUSTE RENOIR, QUOTED IN WALTER PACH'S 'PIERRE-AUGUSTE RENOIR',
SCRIBNER'S MAGAZINE, MAY 1912

to sound like a bell; if it doesn't turn out that way,
I put in more reds or other colours till I get it…. I have
no rules of methods; anyone can look at my materials
and watch how I paint – he will see I have no secrets.
I look at a nude; there are myriads of tiny tints.
I must find the ones that will make the flesh on
my canvas live and quiver.[4]

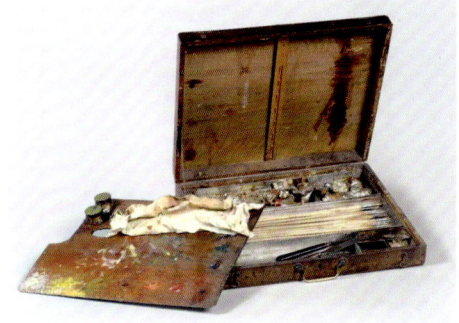

B.

The translucent quality of Renoir's colours can
be seen in some areas of one of his best-known works,
Two Sisters (On the Terrace) from 1881; for example,
in the little girl's dress, the faces and the water in the
background. We also see Renoir's 'sonorous red' here,
piercing through the composition in the form of the red
hat that pulls in our gaze before it wanders off to other
parts in the painting.

Like most of his fellow impressionists, his palette
was arranged roughly following the prismatic spectrum,
usually in pairs of cold and warm pigments of the same
hue. He added copious amounts of white, especially
when painting outdoors, and avoided black. Darker
shades were created by using pure, undiluted paint.
Several lists of paints used by Renoir survive, including
a handwritten note from *c.* 1879 that comprises *blanc
d'argent* (a fine French lead-based white, literally 'silver
white'), chrome yellow, Naples yellow, yellow ochre,
raw sienna, vermilion, madder lake, Veronese and
viridian green, his beloved cobalt blue, and ultramarine
blue (probably artificial). In further notes on the
sheet, he drew a variety of paintbrushes, and dismissed
ochres, Naples yellow and raw sienna as tones that
can be created through mixing other colours. There
is a notable but unsurprising absence of black, although
he occasionally used ivory black. Renoir's penchant
for translucency achieved through thin layers of
glazes resulted in some considerable changes to the
appearance of some of his paintings. The Art Institute
of Chicago recently identified a fugitive red pigment,
carmine lake, in the background of one of his works,
which has faded almost completely, leaving the earlier
layers of green, blue and yellow exposed.[5]

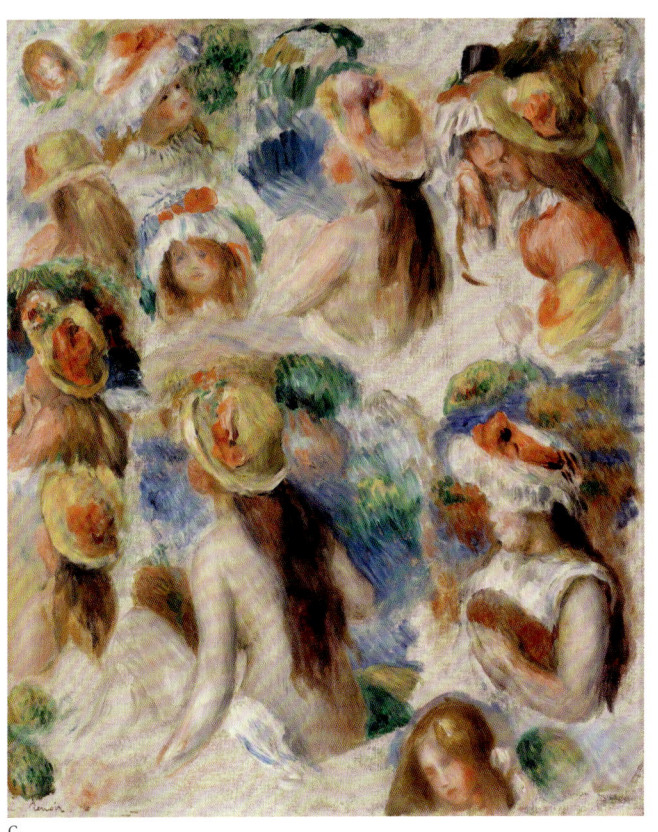

C.

VINCENT VAN GOGH 1853–1890

A visceral palette

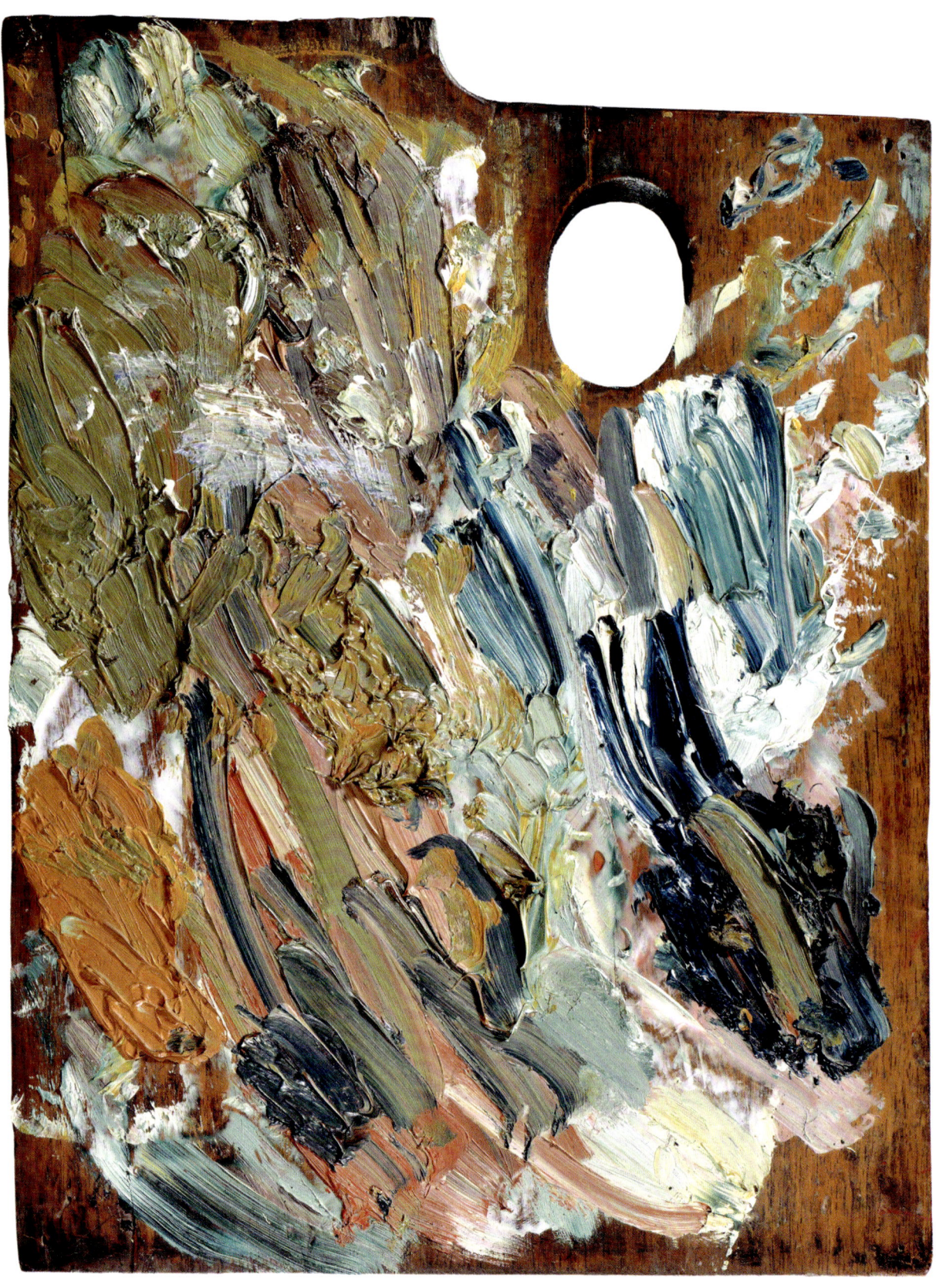

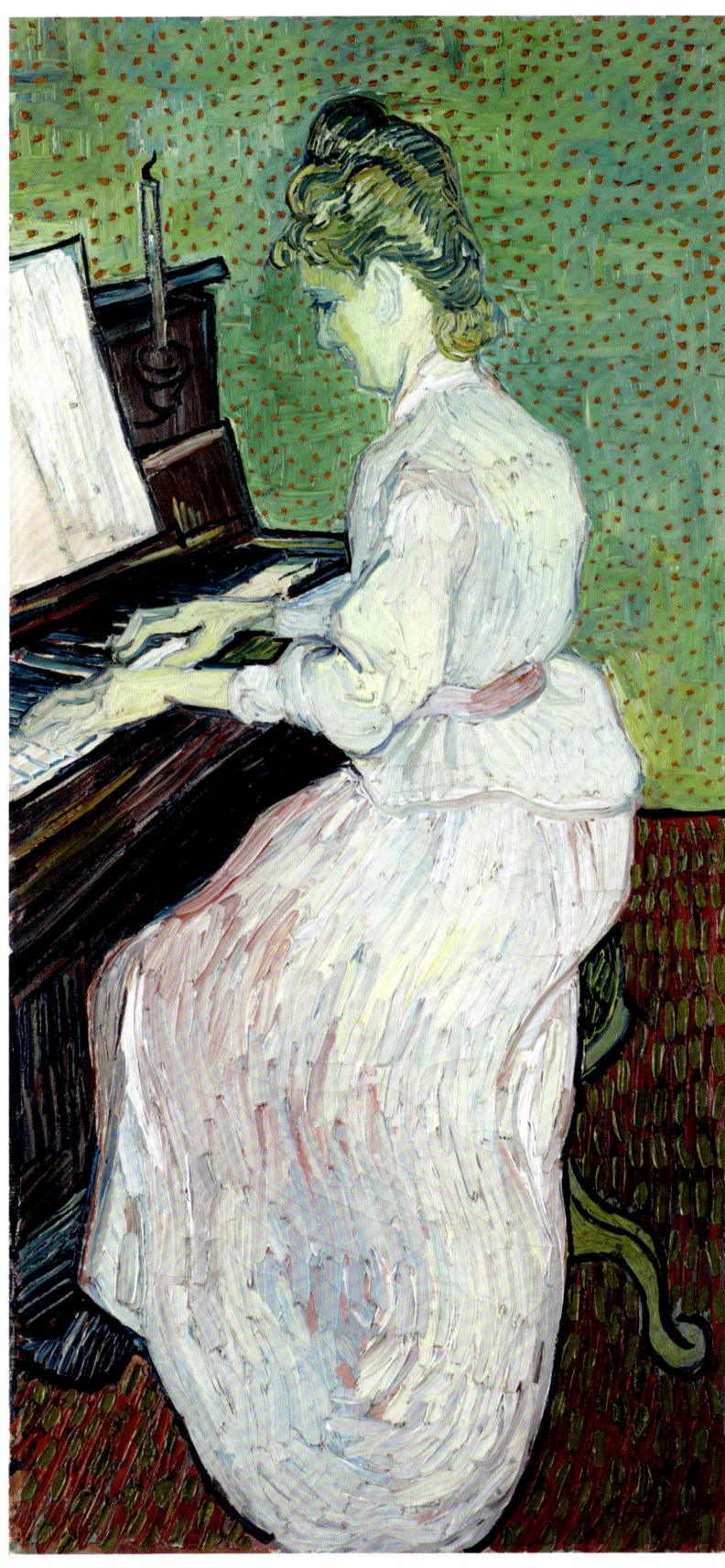

Vincent van Gogh's palette
c. 1890
Paint on wood
35 × 27 cm
(13 ⅞ × 10 ¾ in.)

Marguerite Gachet at the Piano
Vincent van Gogh
1890
Oil on canvas
102.5 × 50 cm
(40 ⅜ × 19 ¾ in.)

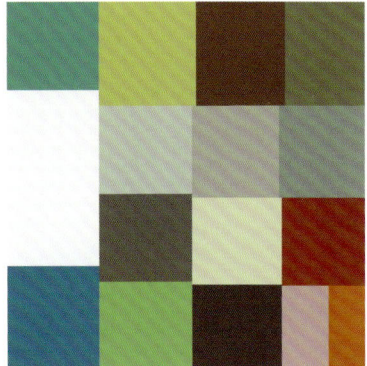

Proportional breakdown of colours used by Vincent van Gogh in *Marguerite Gachet at the Piano*, 1890, displayed on the previous page.

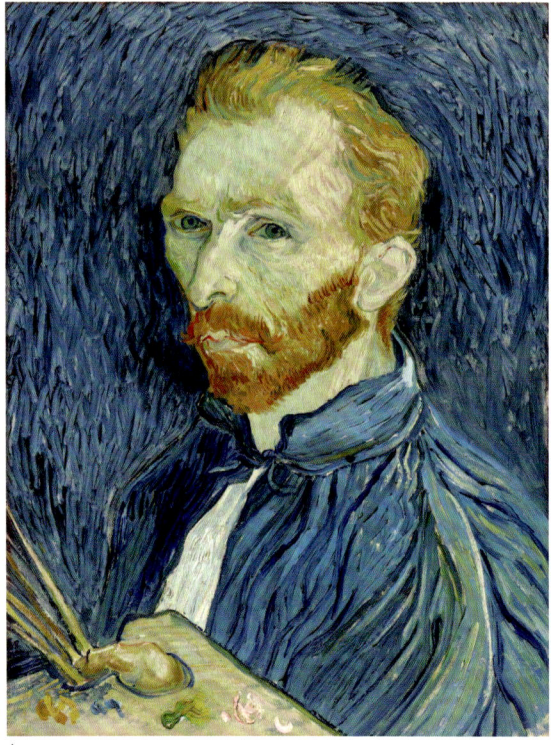

A.

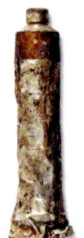 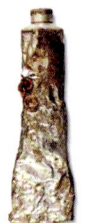 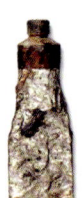 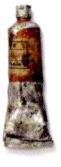

B.

THIS PALETTE IS A VISCERAL and physical link to an artist whose painting habits and techniques were as emotionally charged as his mind. Even if we had no context at all for this object, we could easily imagine an artist painting quickly and impulsively, mixing his colours on the palette's surface with a variety of brushes, possibly a palette knife or even his fingers, and applying them in bold, long strokes and in thick impasto on the canvas, continuing to work wet-in-wet until he considered the work finished. It is hard to tell whether this palette was laid out in a particular order before Vincent van Gogh started painting with it. It is more likely he laid out tubes of ready-made colour, squeezed out two or three large blobs of paint just before starting to paint and then followed his instincts. At times, he would even have bypassed the palette altogether and applied paint directly from the tube onto the canvas, mixing his colours there.

Nonetheless, there was method in his choice of materials, and certainly a heightened awareness of the power of colour. In his many letters, mostly written to his supportive brother Theo, whom he frequently asked for painting materials, van Gogh was very specific about the pigments he desired, and what he wanted to achieve with his colour compositions. Through these letters, we know that the palette shown here probably relates to this portrait of his doctor's daughter, Marguerite Gachet, depicted playing the piano, which van Gogh finished on 29 June 1890. The sittings for it took place at the Gachets' house, and van Gogh had allegedly forgotten his own palette and used one provided by the doctor, which he then left behind. He described the colours planned for the painting in his letters from the days before: 'Yesterday and the day before yesterday I painted Miss Gachet's portrait, which you'll see soon, I hope. The dress is pink. The wall in the background green with orange spots, the carpet red with green spots, the piano dark violet.'[1] The pinks, which he also used in some of his wheatfield compositions around the same time, can be seen clearly in several places on the palette, as can the orange used for the spots on the wallpaper. As for the pigments used, some have been identified on the palette, such as a dark chrome (probably orange), Prussian blue and a geranium lake, but we also get a fuller idea of van Gogh's preferred colours by considering the requests for paint he sent to his brother. A couple of months before painting this, he asked him for the following large tubes: 12 of zinc white, 3 cobalt, 5 Veronese green, 1 ordinary lake, 2 emerald green, 4 chrome 1, 2 chrome 2, 1 orange lead, 2 (artificial) ultramarine, all to be sourced from his colourman Père Tanguy, whom he also painted in bright colours (image C.). He also asked for two smaller tubes of geranium lake to be sourced from Tasset's. The sheer volume of zinc white

'Out of doors…one works as one can, one fills one's canvas regardless. Yet then one catches the true and the essential…. But when one returns to this study again after a time, and orders one's brushstrokes in the direction of the objects – certainly it's more harmonious and agreeable to see.'

VINCENT VAN GOGH, LETTER TO HIS BROTHER THEO VAN GOGH, 10 SEPTEMBER 1889

is astonishing and accounts for much of the brightness of van Gogh's later paintings. Marguerite Gachet's pink dress is most likely a mixture of this white and the geranium lake he asked for in the letter shown.

In a much earlier letter (5 August 1882), written at a time when he was still largely painting in a dark palette dominated by ochres, browns and blacks, van Gogh sketched a small, orderly palette consisting of nine colours laid out in a traditional manner along the upper edge, with each pigment identified (left to right, starting from the thumbhole): white lead, Naples yellow, yellow ochre, red ochre, burnt ochre, raw sienna, cobalt blue, ivory black and vermilion. While this is a conceptual palette and one still dominated by earth pigments, it illustrates van Gogh's intensive engagement with artists' materials, and may have been an indicator of the change that was to come in respect of his chromatic style. In the same letter, he excitedly tells Theo about a paintbox with an integrated palette he had recently purchased, and is convinced that he now has 'all the essentials for proper painting', including colours: '…you will understand that I've limited myself to simple colours in both watercolour and oil: ochre (red, yellow, brown), cobalt and Prussian blue, Naples yellow, terra sienna, black and white, supplemented with some carmine, sepia, vermilion, ultramarine, gamboge'.[2] Van Gogh had not yet been to Paris at this point, he had not yet discovered the full potential of cadmiums, chromes, emerald and viridian, but here is an artist developing a sense for colour that he would later drive to ecstatic, sometimes frightening heights. The palettes he paints in some of his self-portraits are a far cry from the orderly concept of his 1882 drawing. Colour, applied in swirling, sweeping, pulsating strokes, became to him the ultimate expressive artist's tool, something that could convey the full range of emotions, including foreboding, terror and fear. In one of his last paintings, *Wheatfield with Crows* (1890), we see his powerful use of colour contrast, and the painter's soul is laid bare in a few broad strokes of saturated, thickly applied paint.

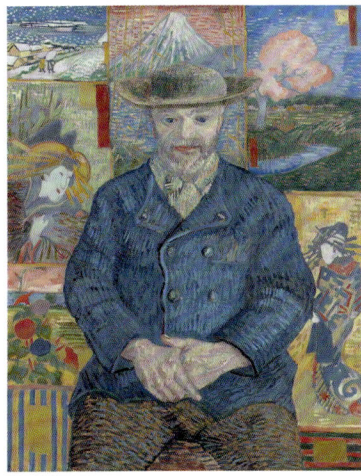

C.

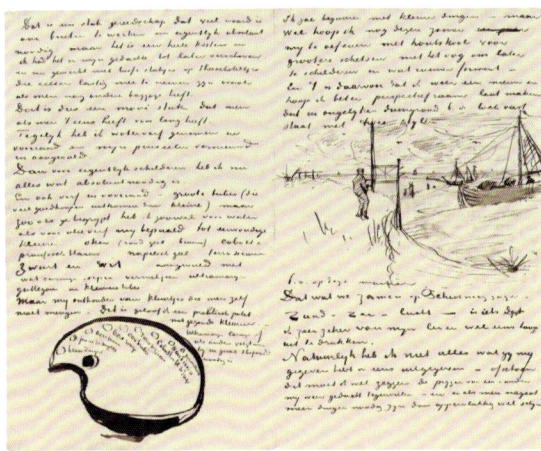

D.

A. *Self-portrait*, Vincent van Gogh, 1889, oil on canvas, 57.8 × 44.5 cm (22 ¾ × 17 ½ in.)
B. Vincent van Gogh's paint tubes, 19th century
C. *Père Tanguy*, Vincent van Gogh, 1887, oil on canvas, 92 × 75 cm (36 ¼ × 29 ⅝ in.)
D. Letter from Vincent van Gogh to Theo van Gogh with sketches of a palette and the beach at Scheveningen, 5 August 1882, pen and ink on paper, 21 × 26.6 cm (8 ⅜ × 10 ½ in.)

Letter from Vincent van Gogh to Theo van Gogh, Arles, France, on or about 5 April 1888.

Colours cited in this letter, with corresponding colour swatches:

A. *Blanc d'argent* (silver white)
B. *Blanc de zinc* (zinc white)
C. *Vert Veronèse* (Veronese green)
D. *Jaune de chrôme citron* (lemon chrome yellow)
E. *Jaune de chrôme no. 2* (chrome yellow no. 2)
F. *Vermillon* (vermilion)
G. *Jaune de chrôme no. 3* (chrome yellow no. 3)
H. *Laque géranium* (geranium lake)
I. *Laque ordinaire* (ordinary lake)
J. *Carmin* (carmine)
K. *Bleu de Prusse* (Prussian blue)
L. *Cinabre vert très clair* (very light cinnabar green)
M. *Mine orange* (orange lead)
N. *Vert émeraude* (emerald green)

A.
B.
C.
D.
E.
F.
G.
H.
I.
J.
K.
L.
M.
N.

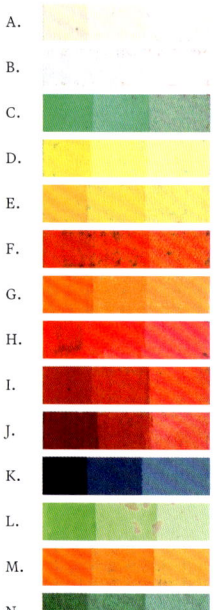

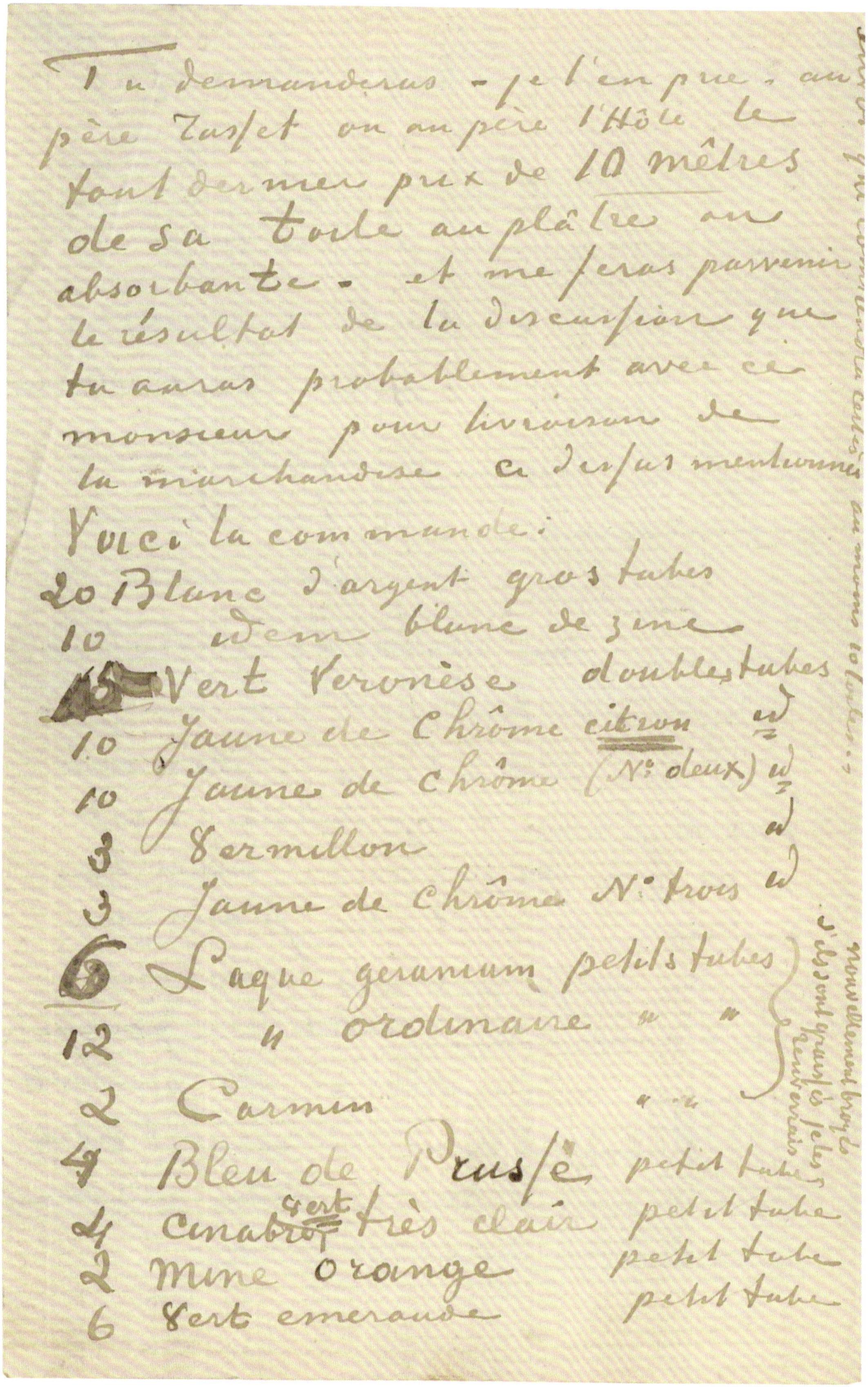

Cette commande est assez grave / cependant Sans compter la différence entre la remise que j'ose espérer et les frais de transport / nous y gagnerons encore ce que je payerais en plus pour frais de transport Sans compter que je n'ai ici aucune remise ——,——

C'ajoute pour que cela ne te presse pas outre mesure une commande *plus petite et don* à détacher de la première laquelle dernière nommée n'est pressée qu'en tant que quant à la réduction ci dessous mentionnée

Pressé

10 Blanc D'argent gros tubes
6 Vert véronèse doubles tubes
    Jaune de chrome citron
                No 2 } doubles tubes
                No 3 }
                            double tube
    Vermillon
    Laques géranium petits tubes
    Laque ordinaire « «
    Bleu de prusse
    Vert émeraude

In the section of the letter pictured opposite, van Gogh requests 10 m (32 ft 9 ¾ in.) of primed or absorbent canvas and for several tubes of paint from Tasset & Lhôte, Rue Fontaine, Paris, France. He notes that geranium lake, ordinary lake and carmine should be 'freshly ground, if they're greasy I'll send them back.' In the section of the letter pictured to the left, van Gogh includes a shorter, extracted list, which he marks as being 'urgent'.

Colours cited in this letter, with corresponding colour swatches:

A. *Blanc d'argent* (silver white)
B. *Vert Veronèse* (Veronese green)
C. *Jaune de chrôme citron* (lemon chrome yellow)
D. *Jaune de chrôme no. 2* (chrome yellow no. 2)
E. *Jaune de chrôme no. 3* (chrome yellow no. 3)
F. *Vermillon* (vermilion)
G. *Laque géranium* (geranium lake)
H. *Laque ordinaire* (ordinary lake)
I. *Bleu de Prusse* (Prussian blue)
J. *Vert émeraude* (emerald green)

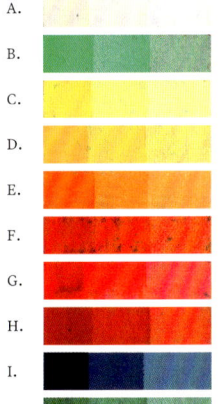

A.
B.
C.
D.
E.
F.
G.
H.
I.
J.

GUSTAVE MOREAU 1826–1898

Thinking imaginatively through colour

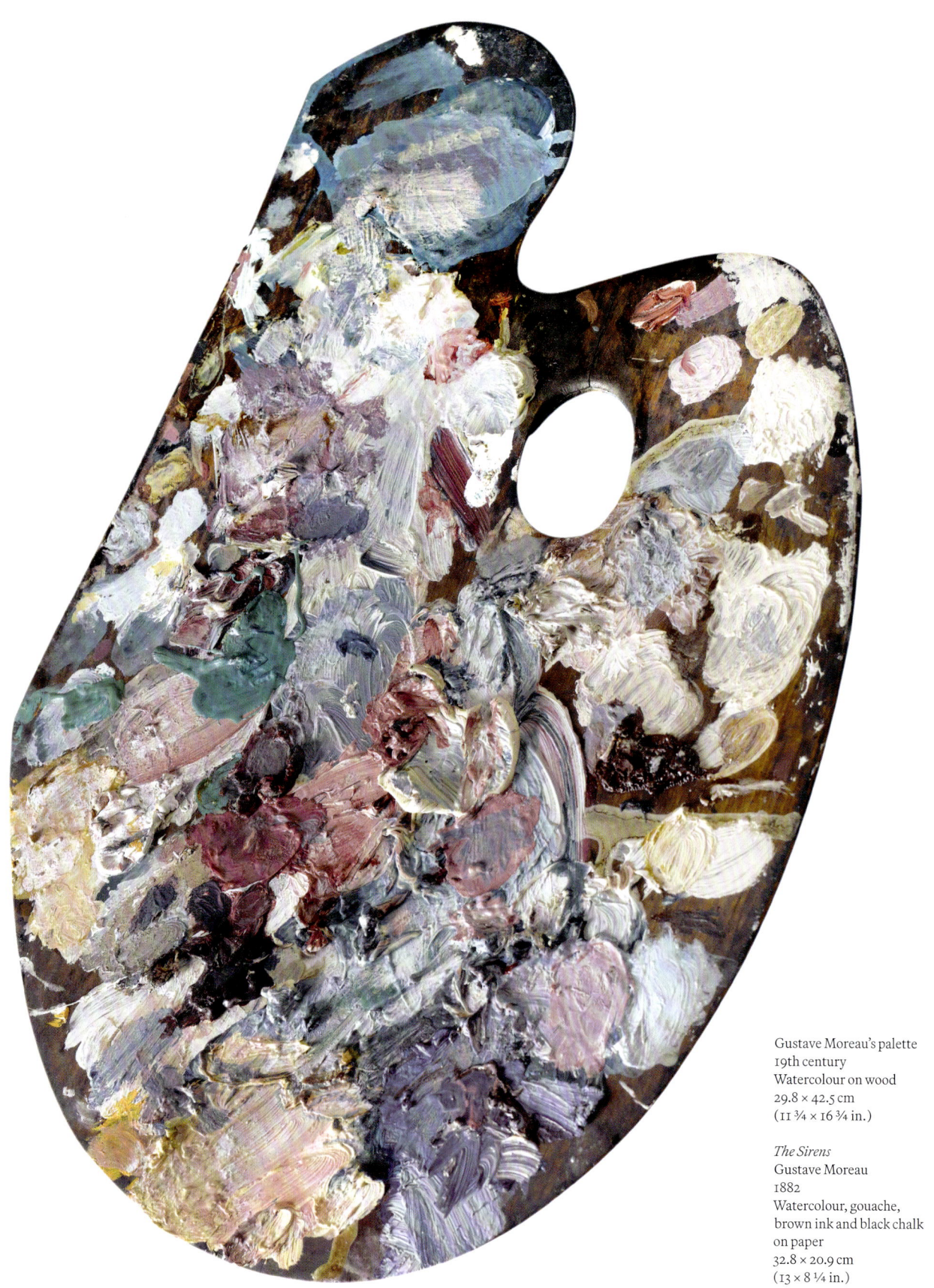

Gustave Moreau's palette
19th century
Watercolour on wood
29.8 × 42.5 cm
(11 ¾ × 16 ¾ in.)

The Sirens
Gustave Moreau
1882
Watercolour, gouache,
brown ink and black chalk
on paper
32.8 × 20.9 cm
(13 × 8 ¼ in.)

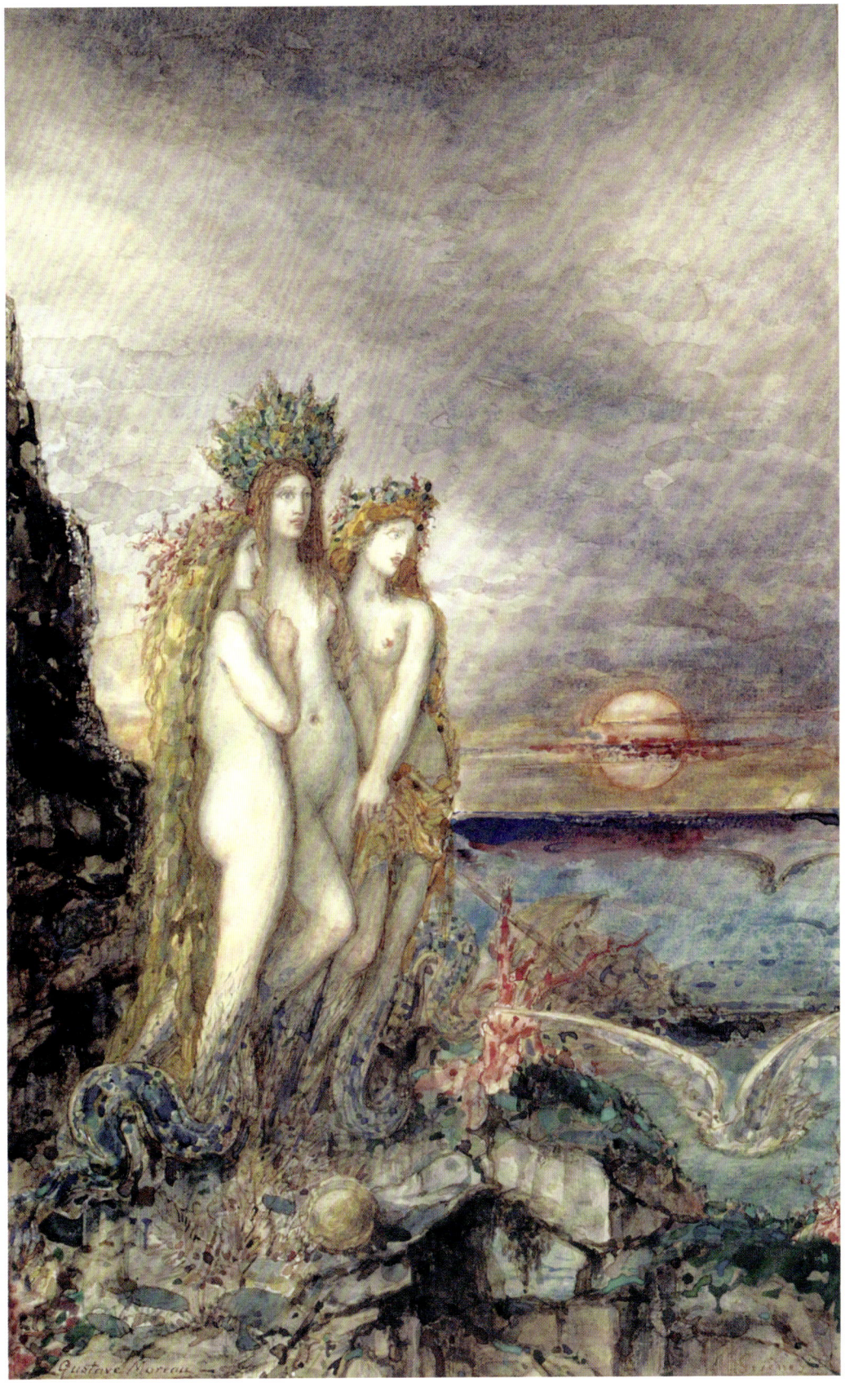

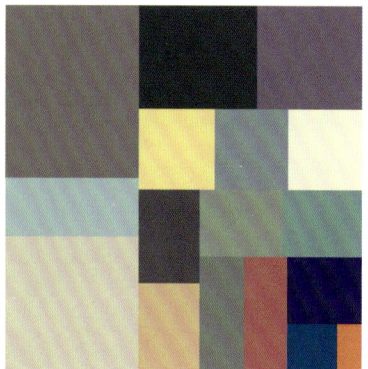

Proportional breakdown of colours used by Gustave Moreau in *The Sirens*, 1882, displayed on the previous page.

THE FRENCH SYMBOLIST painter Gustave Moreau worked predominantly in oil but was also a hugely accomplished painter in watercolour and other media. Many of his materials survive in the collection of the Musée Gustave Moreau, his former home, studio and art gallery in Paris, which he bequeathed to the nation. Among them are portable watercolour paintboxes in many shapes and sizes, watercolour palettes, studies and paint trials on paper, as well as this wooden palette. Almost every inch of the palette is covered in water-based paint that has been mixed rapidly on the wood to create a varied range of blues, purples, lilacs and dusty pinks. Some creamy white and yellow hues can also be seen, punctuated by small blotches of bright green and what might be a very dark blue or a black. Only the area where his thumb was anchored remains free of paint. The colour mixtures have a luminosity that is typical of many of Moreau's works, and it is interesting to see that some of the colours may have been created spontaneously on the palette. We notice his loose brushwork, resembling the texture and effect of watercolour, and a hint of the bright blues that often formed the background of his paintings.

The painting shown here, *The Sirens* from 1882, shows this range of luminous blues, greys, lilacs and pinks that is so typical of Moreau's work, in particular in the depiction of the sea and sky that form the background to the three sirens standing on the rocks. Their nude bodies are painted in that opaque white seen also on the palette. Moreau was known to have used many traditional earth pigments, such as raw and burnt umber and sienna, but happily combined them with new synthetic pigments, including zinc or 'Chinese' white, shimmering viridian green, cerulean blue (alongside French ultramarine and Prussian blue) and cool, bright lemon yellow. The large number of individual paints surviving in the museum's collection show that he used both moist watercolour in tubes as well as watercolour cakes, and sourced them from several manufacturers, including the British companies Rowney & Co., Roberson & Co. and Newman's. In some of his work he also used metallic pigments to increase the otherworldly, shimmering look of his art.

Despite receiving traditional training, Moreau's style was experimental and progressive. While his subjects and motifs remained largely classical and biblical, he moved further and further away from the darker palette of Eugène Delacroix (see pages 50–53) that had informed him in his younger years, towards pearlescent, jewel-like and contrasting colours and a looser brush style, which some early critics found disturbing. He developed a visionary style that perhaps forms a link between the romanticism of the early

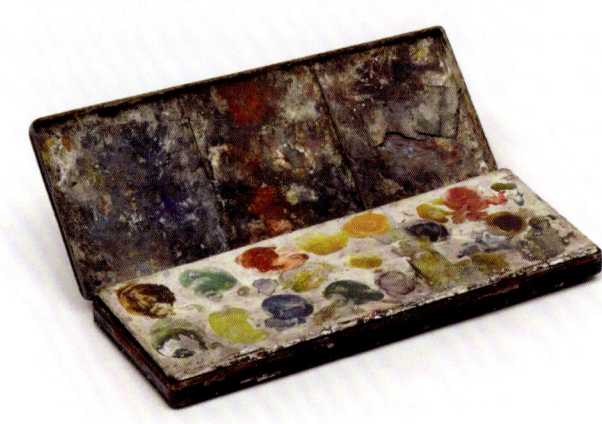

A.

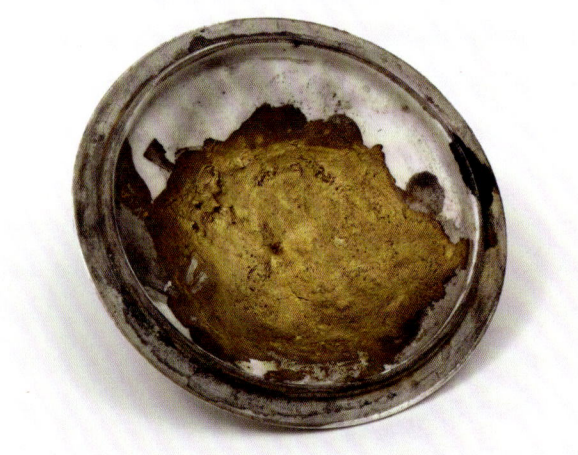

B.

*'I have never looked for dream in reality or reality
in dream. I have allowed my imagination free play,
and I have not been led astray by it.'*

GUSTAVE MOREAU, QUOTED IN BENNETT SCHIFF'S 'THE MANY FACES
OF GUSTAVE MOREAU', *SMITHSONIAN MAGAZINE*, JULY 1999

19th century and the avant-garde groups that emerged
in the later decades of the century. As both teacher
and artist he was influential on several of the artists
who later comprised the so-called *Les Fauves* group,
who were using bright and pure colours in an expressive
manner. He would frequently give his students the
advice to 'think imaginatively through colour'.

Moreau had a long, successful career, and inspired
several poets and writers to immortalize him in their
work. Among them was his admirer Marcel Proust,
who mentioned Moreau's heady ominous fantasies
in his magnum opus *À la recherche du temps perdu*
(*Remembrance of Things Past*, 1922–31). Although
he believed in the powerful symbolism of colour,
he remained true to his subject matter of detailed
mythological and historical scenes and figures, usually
set against grand imaginary architectural spaces or
landscape, and never abandoned realism. Perhaps this
palette and his colour studies inadvertently give us a
sense of what Moreau's art would have looked like had
he lived even longer and experimented with abstraction.

Moreau enjoyed a thorough formal training in
the arts, first at the studio of the neoclassical painter
François-Édouard Picot, and then at the École des
Beaux-Arts in Paris, where he later became a teacher.
Much of his academy training involved studying and
copying old masters in the Louvre and other museums.
Steeped in neoclassicism, he was keen to spend time
in Rome and other Italian cities of high culture, in
the manner of the Grand Tour travellers of the 18th
century. He eventually embarked on the first of several
Italian journeys in the late 1850s. There, he immersed
himself in the masterpieces of Classical antiquity, but
his interest in colour also drew him to Raphael, Titian,
Correggio, Carpaccio and other Renaissance artists.
A gifted draughtsman, he also studied Leonardo da
Vinci's drawings meticulously. While in Italy, he
became a friend and mentor to several younger French
artists, among them Edgar Degas (see pages 90–93),
Jules-Élie Delaunay and Léon Bonnat.

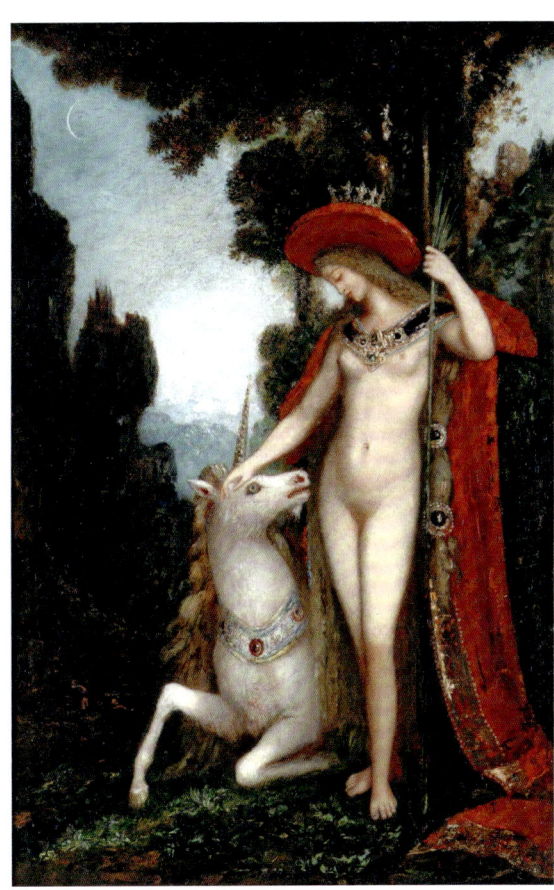

C.

A.   Gustave Moreau's watercolour palette-box, 19th century
B.   Gustave Moreau's earthenware pot lid containing golden pigment,
     19th century
C.   *The Unicorn*, Gustave Moreau, *c.* 1885, oil on canvas, 50 × 34.5 cm
     (19 ¾ × 13 ½ in.)

A. Yellow ochre, moist colour, G. Rowney & Co.

B. Red lead, moist colour, G. Rowney & Co.

C. Indian yellow, moist watercolour, Roberson & Co.

D. Light red, moist colour, G. Rowney & Co.

E. Blue Verditer, moist colour, W. Derby & Co.

F.–G. Watercolour blocks, La Maison Chenal

H. Chrome yellow, watercolour block, J. Newman

I. Nap green, watercolour block, J. Newman

J. Verditer, watercolour block

K. Neutral tint, watercolour block, J. Newman

L. Watercolour block, La Maison Chenal

M. Watercolour block, Parisian manufacturer

N. *Terre de sienne brûlée* (burnt sienna earth), watercolour block, Parisian manufacturer

O. *Terre de sienne* (sienna earth), watercolour block

P. *Jaune brilliant* (bright yellow), watercolour block

Q. *Rouge de saturne* (saturn red), watercolour block

R. *Noir d'ivoire* (ivory black), watercolour block, Maison Ange Ottoz

S. Watercolour block, J. M. Paillard and J. Panier

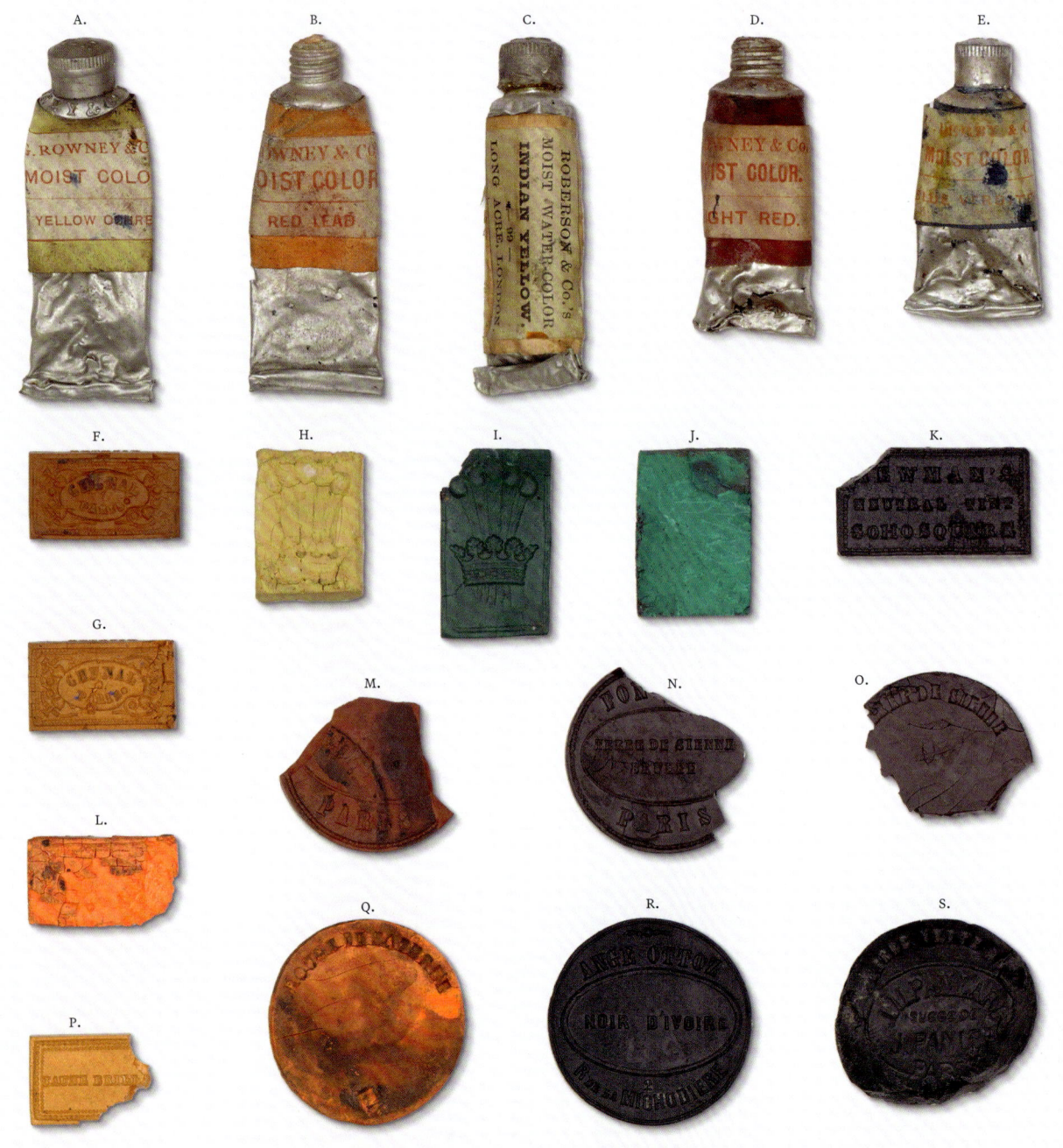

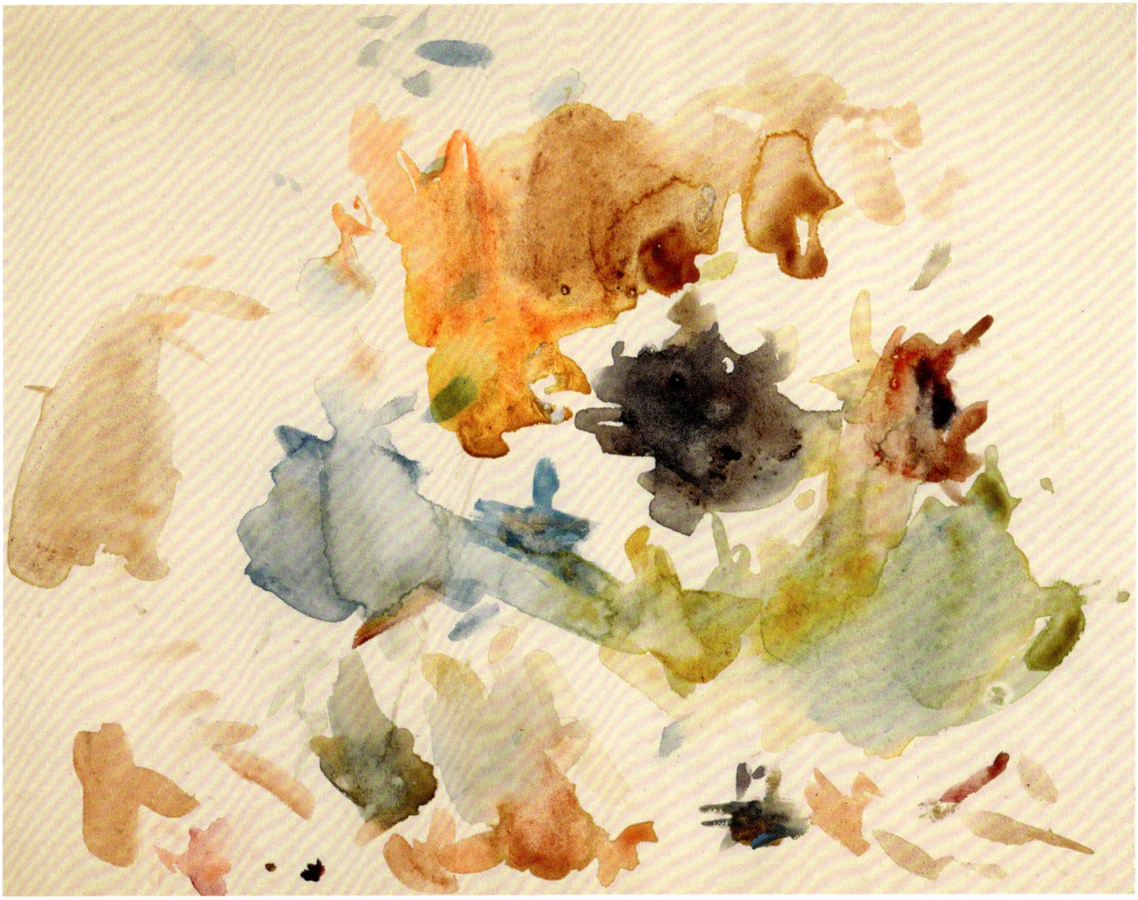

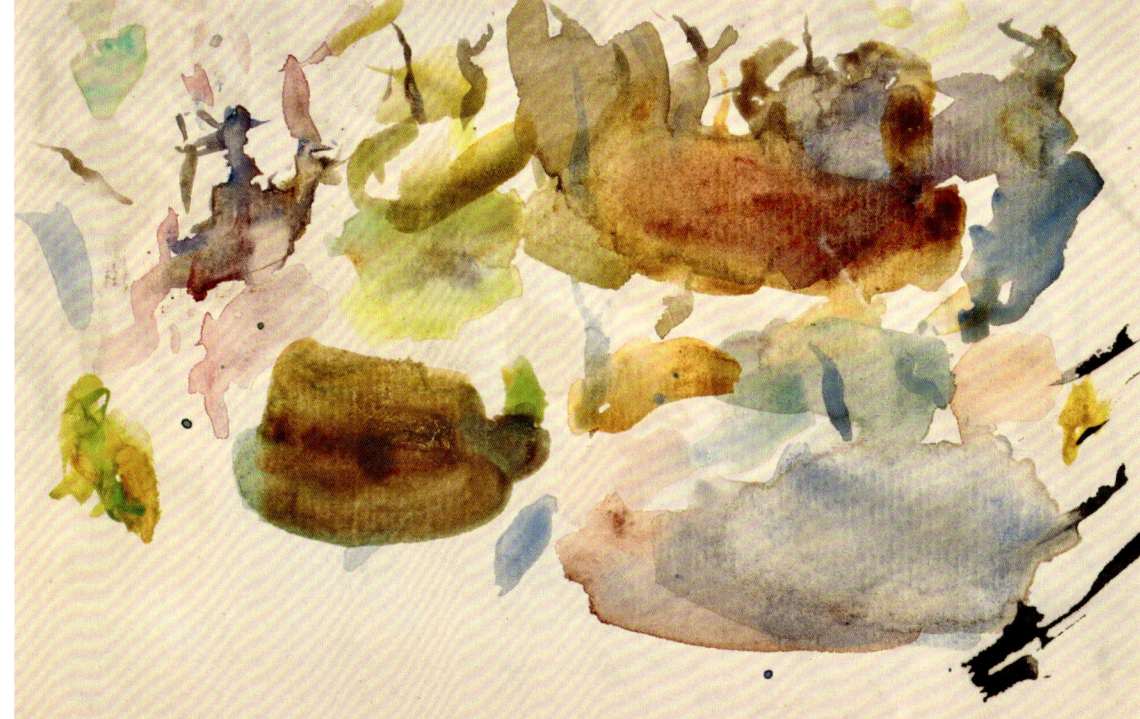

Gustave Moreau's
watercolour
paint tubes
and paint blocks
19th century

Watercolour trials
Gustave Moreau
19th century

JOHN SINGER SARGENT 1856–1925

Mounds of colour on a baffling palette

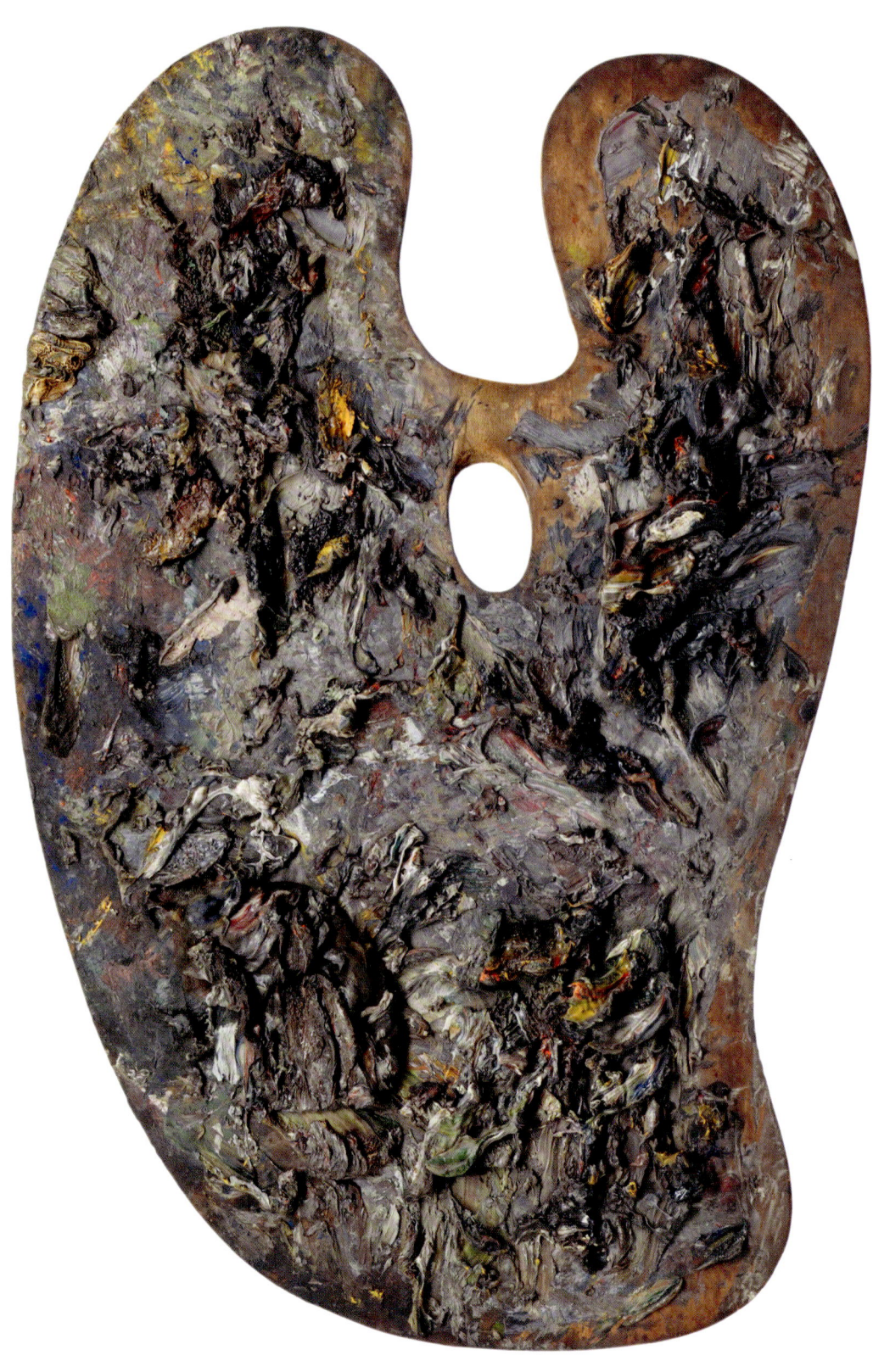

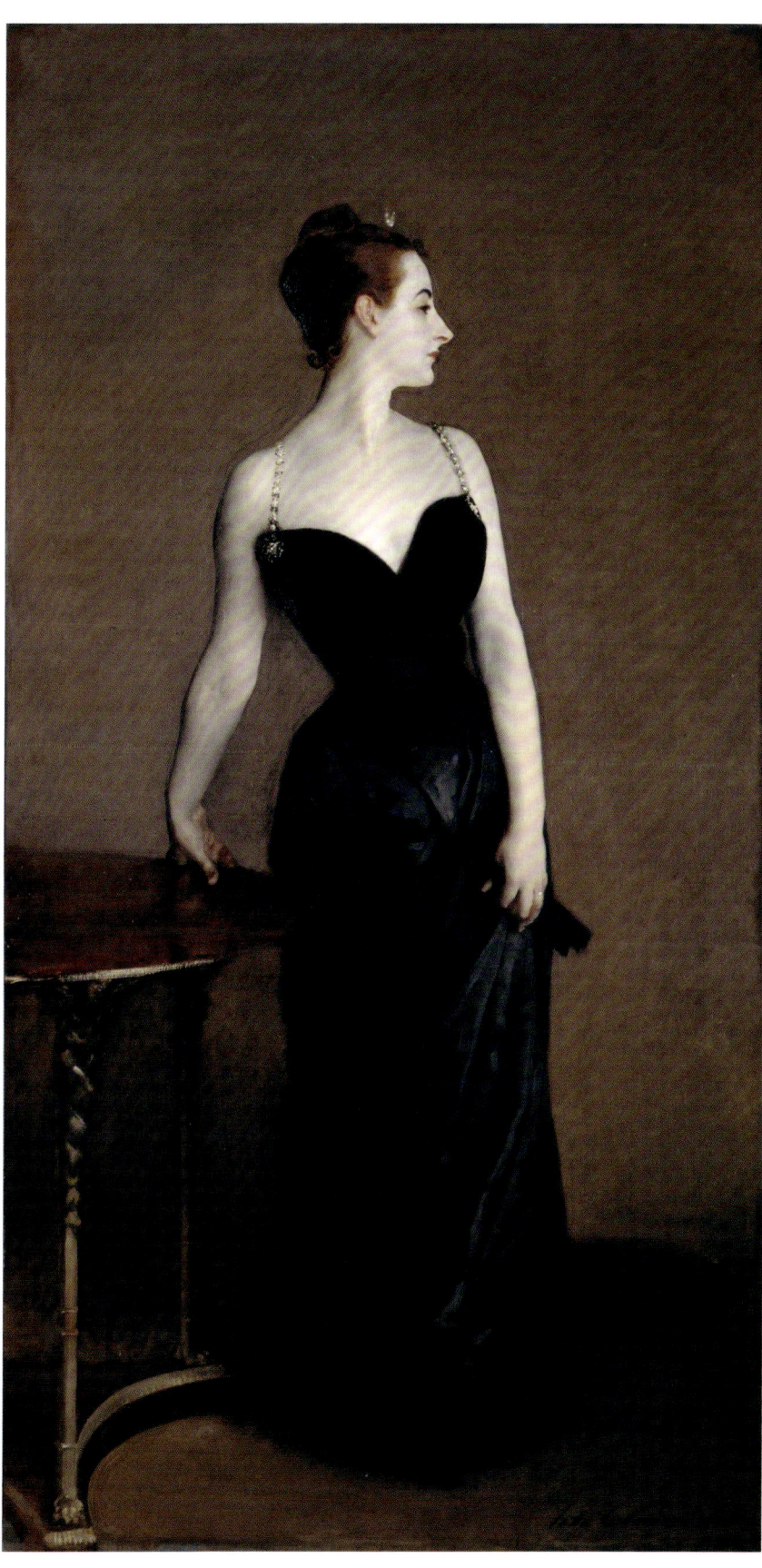

John Singer Sargent's
palette
Undated
Oil on wood
56.5 × 38 cm
(22 ¼ × 15 in.)

*Madame X (Madame
Pierre Gautreau)*
John Singer Sargent
1883–84
Oil on canvas
208.6 × 109.9 cm
(82 ⅛ × 43 ¼ in.)

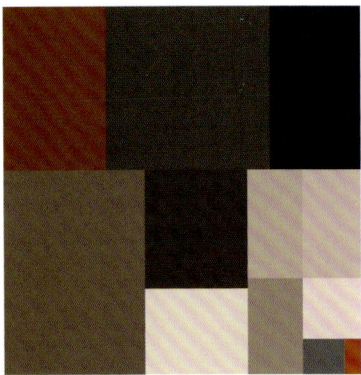

Proportional breakdown of colours used by John Singer Sargent in *Madame X (Madame Pierre Gautreau)*, 1883–84, displayed on the previous page.

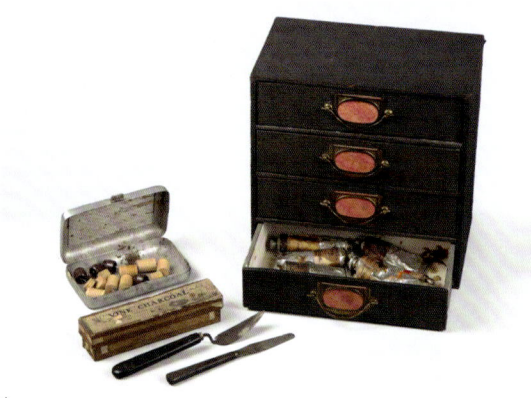

A.

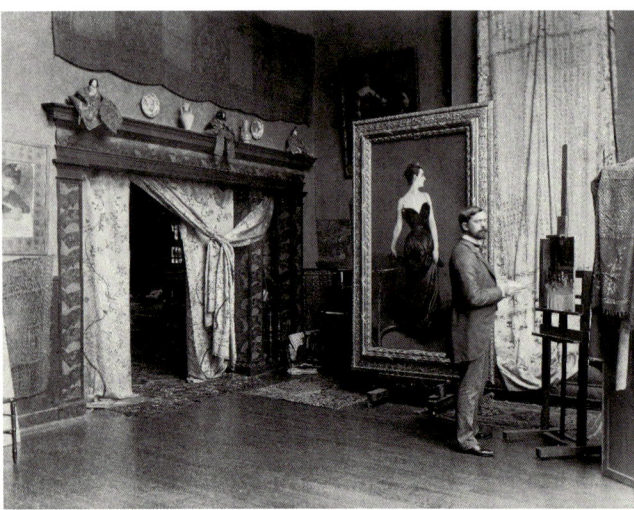

B.

MANY OF JOHN SINGER SARGENT'S artist materials survive in several collections in Europe and the United States. A particularly large collection is at the Harvard Art Museums, including this kidney-shaped arm palette. It is almost entirely covered in paint that appears to be randomly applied, mixed and manipulated with palette knives and brushes. At first, it gives the impression of an almost exclusively grey-scale range of colours, a neutral palette that Sargent applied often in his work, as in the portrait that caused such a scandal in the art world, *Madame X* (1883–84), partly because of the amount of skin visible, its sexual undertones and the social background of the sitter.

A closer look reveals a multitude of chromatic pigments all over the surface, mostly in small quantities and interspersed with other colours. This is somewhat curious, as most other palettes that belonged to Sargent with traces of paint on them show a traditional order and separation of colours, such as a large amount of white near the thumbhole and a line of prismatic colours along the top edge. The central areas were typically used to mix particular tones in thin layers. Not so here. There seems to be no order to this palette, and the thickness of the paint is unusual for Sargent, which led to the assumption that it may have been used for paint scrapes. However, there are clear signs of deliberate mixing and a piece of fabric is embedded in the paint, suggesting that the palette was at some stage covered up to keep the paint moist. Some of the pigments on it have been identified, including lead white, some zinc white, vermilion, cadmium and chrome yellows, a chromium-containing green, cobalt blue, ultramarine and ochres.[1]

Sargent worked fast, applying paint quickly and thinly. At the height of his career he created many large, flattering society portraits that brought him huge success in Europe and America. Despite this studio-focused work, he never lost his passion for painting outdoors, using movable equipment, smaller palettes and canvases, umbrellas and a multitude of small paint tubes. He created a most affecting image of Monet (see page 155) painting *en plein air*, sitting in the grass, his palette and identifiable canvas visible. Defying academy tradition, he would often forego outline drawings and paint directly with brushes onto the canvas. Critic Edmund Gosse once noted that Sargent's daily plan was 'to cover the whole canvas with a thin coat of colour, so as to make a complete sketch which would dry so rapidly that next morning he might paint another study over it. I often could have wept to see these brilliantly fresh and sparkling sketches ruthlessly sacrificed'.[2] Perhaps this palette is a physical manifestation of one of those rapid first sketches or an extended outdoor session.

'[He] thought that the artist ought to know nothing whatever about the nature of the object before him…but should concentrate all his powers on a representation of its appearance. The picture was to be a consistent vision, a reproduction of the area filled by the eye.'

EDMUND GOSSE, QUOTED IN EVAN CHARTERIS'S *JOHN SINGER SARGENT*, 1927

One of his best-known works, *Carnation, Lily, Lily, Rose* (1885–86), was painted outdoors at Broadway, Worcestershire, England, in several sessions. Here, Sargent shows his true mastery of colour, as well as the methodology behind his work: his paintings may capture fleeting moments, movements and light conditions, but they were mostly carefully choreographed. For this image, he meticulously prepared the positioning of the flowers, timed the painting sessions to capture the evening light and had specific outfits made for the children.

Research carried out on other palettes reveals that Sargent made full use of the wide range of natural and synthetic colours available in the late 19th century, among them Indian red, yellow aureolin, chrome and cadmium yellows, mars yellow, orange earth, ultramarine, cerulean blue, several red lakes, viridian, cobalt blue, Prussian blue, indigo, bone and ivory black, often mixed with a green-fluorescing paint medium. The paint tubes were sourced from a range of manufacturers, including Reeves, Winsor & Newton, Rowney, Roberson, Parker, Ewens and others. Occasionally, he would label individual tubes himself. The list continues and is evidence of Sargent's keen interest in new pigments and dyestuffs, such as fugitive aniline colours. In this, and to a certain extent in his methods and style, he was an impressionist at heart, but he never fully aligned with any movement, instead combining the aesthetics of impressionism, Aestheticism and late Pre-Raphaelitism, with a smattering of modernism.

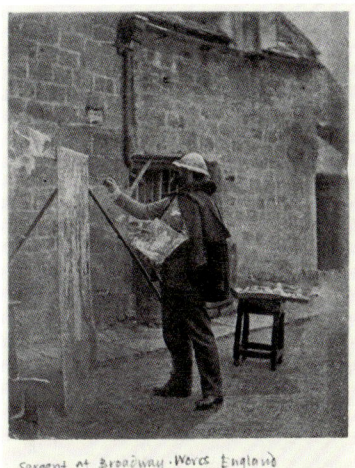

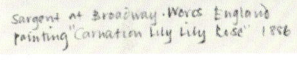

C.

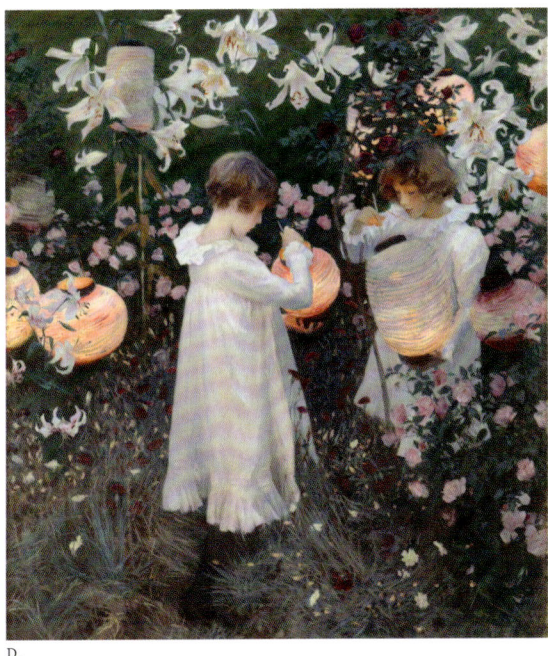

A.   John Singer Sargent's paintbox containing paints and tools
B.   John Singer Sargent in his studio in Paris, France with *Madame X*, 1883–84
C.   John Singer Sargent painting *Carnation, Lily, Lily, Rose*, Broadway, Worcestershire, England, 1885–86, gelatin silver print, 11.2 × 9.4 cm (4 ½ × 3 ¾ in.)
D.   *Carnation, Lily, Lily, Rose*, John Singer Sargent, 1885–86, oil on canvas, 174 × 153.7 cm (68 ⅝ × 60 ⅝ in.)

D.

PAUL GAUGUIN 1848–1903

A voyeuristic palette of symbolist colour

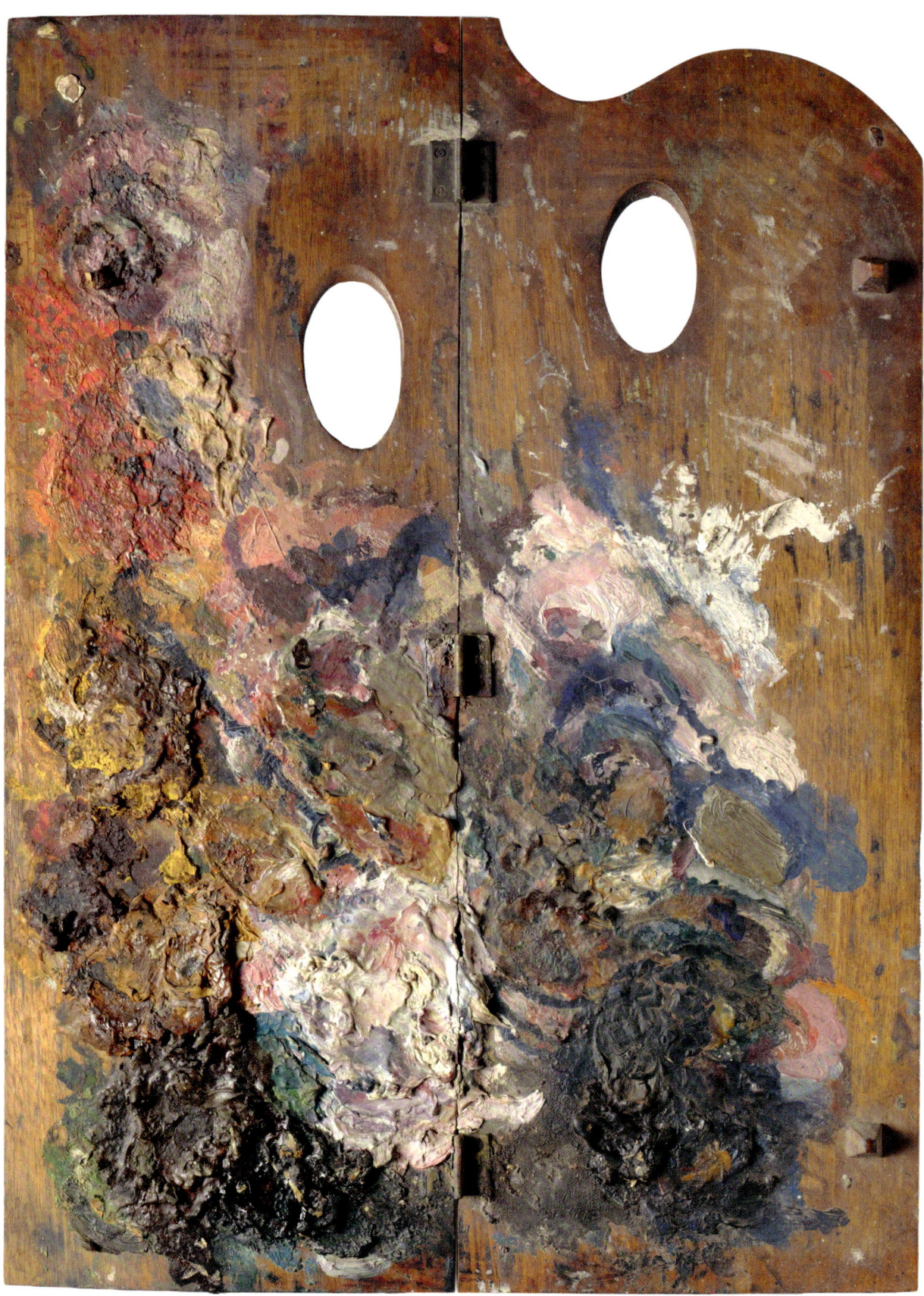

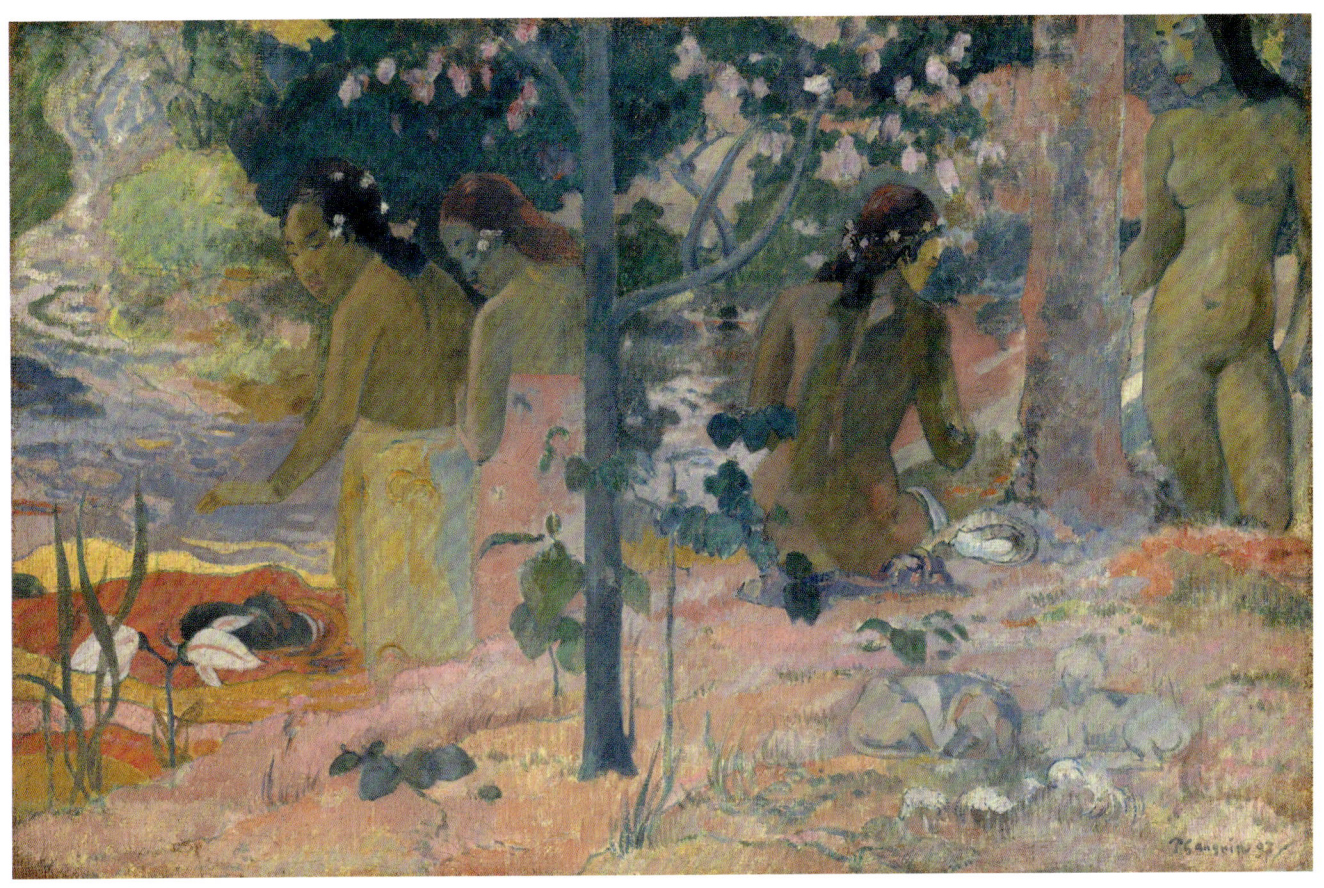

Paul Gauguin's palette
Paint on wood
32.5 × 43.8 cm
(12 ⅞ × 17 ¼ in.)

The Bathers
Paul Gauguin
1897
Oil on canvas
60.4 × 93.4 cm
(23 ¾ × 36 ¾ in.)

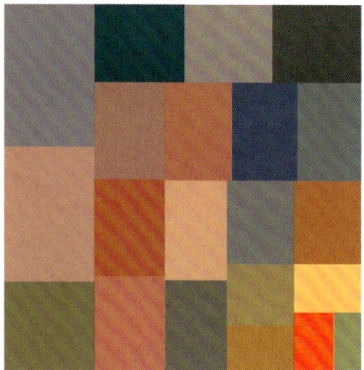

Proportional breakdown of colours used by Paul Gauguin in *The Bathers*, 1897, displayed on the previous page.

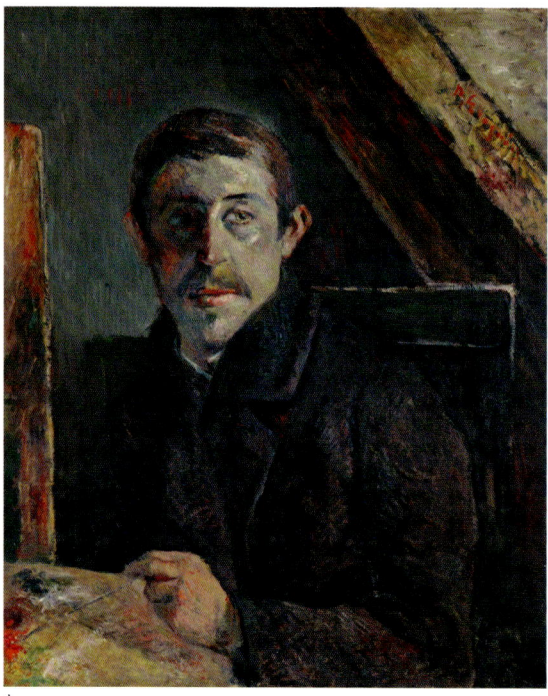

A.

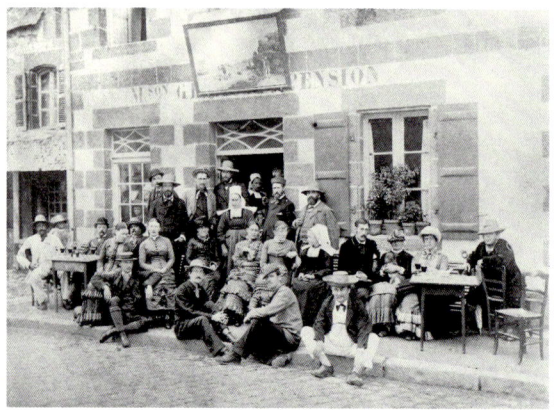

B.

PAUL GAUGUIN'S PALETTE is undated, but probably derives from a later phase in his career, when he had left the systematic brushwork of the impressionists and neo-impressionists behind. It is a hinged palette that was likely part of a portable paintbox and used outdoors. It has heavily mixed heaps of oil paint on it, suggesting rapid, intuitive blending and painting. Yet, some order is detectable in this sumptuous mess of colour, similar to one of Degas's palettes (see page 90): under the mounds of now dirty mixtures, we can just about see that Gauguin probably started this palette with a simple layout of green, yellow, red and blue across the top edge, roughly following academic style. Although Gauguin's pictorial style and attitude to colour composition changed dramatically during his career, his application, choice of materials and brushwork were relatively consistent. When working with oil paint on canvas, his aim was to achieve a flat, matte finish, with texture created through delicate layering and the incorporation of the canvas structure. He would often paint on chalk grounds that absorbed oil, leaving his high-key colours to remain on the surface, emulating mural or fresco painting. He also avoided using varnish. In his technique he differed greatly from his once-friend and colleague Vincent van Gogh (see pages 102–5), who preferred thick impasto and heavily textured paint surfaces. Both were inspired by Japanese aesthetics, folk art and so-called 'primitive' cultures, especially in respect of colour composition.

Gauguin rejected realistic colour and quickly abandoned impressionist ideals of painting naturalistic, atmospheric light conditions. For him, colour became a symbolic and expressive tool, even before he abandoned his wife and children for extended stints on the Polynesian island of Tahiti, then a French colony, in search of silence, isolation, soul-cleansing and career revival. His life and artistic practices there were questionable, as they involved the exploitation of several Tahitian women and girls, but he undoubtedly created his most sophisticated pictures in respect of colour harmony during his stays there. One of these is shown here, *The Bathers* (1897), and although it cannot be directly linked to this palette, it features some of the colours on it, including the saturated primaries yellow and red, a blue brightened with white, a range of greens, as well as powdery pinks that dominate the foreground. By the time he painted this, he had long since abandoned the impressionist style of vertical dabs applied with small brushes. Here, he places large, flat areas of bold, unvariegated colour, almost collage-like, in deliberate juxtaposition, maximizing the effects of colour contrast, using both pure and mixed colours.

'Colour! What a deep and mysterious language, the language of dreams.'

PAUL GAUGUIN, 'NOTES FROM 1896–98',
PUBLISHED IN *THE WRITINGS OF A SAVAGE*, 1978

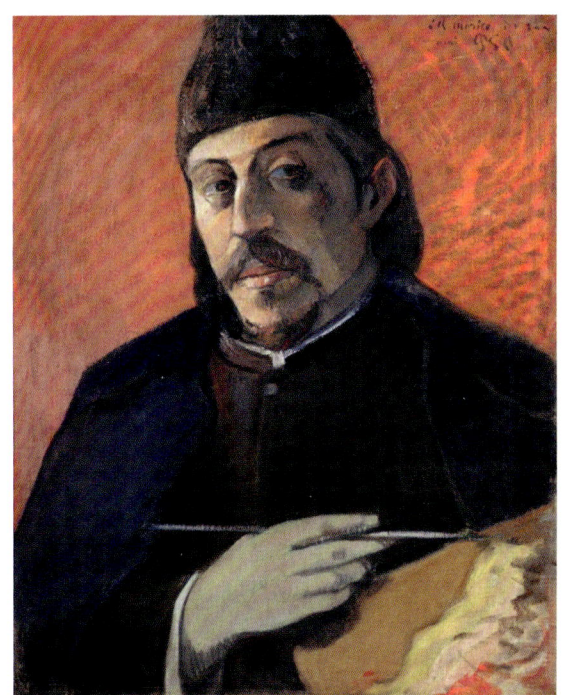

C.

His choice of pigments was typical for the period, and he fully exploited the dizzy heights of an unprecedented number of paints and other artists' materials that were available ready-made. A list of his orders of paint and other materials compiled by Vojtech Jirat-Wasiutynski includes familiar names of French art suppliers, such as Julien Tanguy (who came recommended by Camille Pissarro, see pages 122–25), Maison Edouard, Madame Latouche and Lefranc et Cie. The paints he ordered in the late 1880s included lead white, fine carmine lake, cobalt and ultramarine blue, vermilion, chrome yellow and disproportionately large amounts of copper-based emerald green. After 1893, he also ordered yellow and brown ochres, as well as Prussian blue, cadmium yellow, and copious amounts of emerald and viridian green.[1]

While his command of colour was revolutionary and resulted in some breathtakingly vibrant and beautiful images, Gauguin's story, creative practices and artistic output remain deeply problematic. He was effectively an interloper, a 'Western voyeur' in Tahiti, who used colour to express and live out his 'colonial and misogynist fantasy', as the art critic Chloë Ashby put it.[2] Back in France, his work caused mixed reactions. Having visited an exhibition at Durand-Ruel's gallery in Paris, Félix Fénéon described the colours in Gauguin's Tahitian canvases as 'barbarous, opulent and taciturn in character.'[3]

A. *Self-portrait*, Paul Gauguin, 1885, oil on canvas, 65.2 × 54.3 cm
    (25 ¾ × 21 ½ in.)
B. Pension Gloanec in Pont-Aven, France (Paul Gauguin sitting in the
    first row, second from left), photograph by Albert Harlingue, *c.* 1888
C. *Self-portrait with Palette*, Paul Gauguin, *c.* 1894, oil on canvas,
    92 × 73 cm (36 ¼ × 28 ¾ in.)
D. *Breton Girls Dancing, Pont-Aven*, Paul Gauguin, 1888, oil on canvas,
    73 × 92.7 cm (28 ¾ × 36 ½ in.)

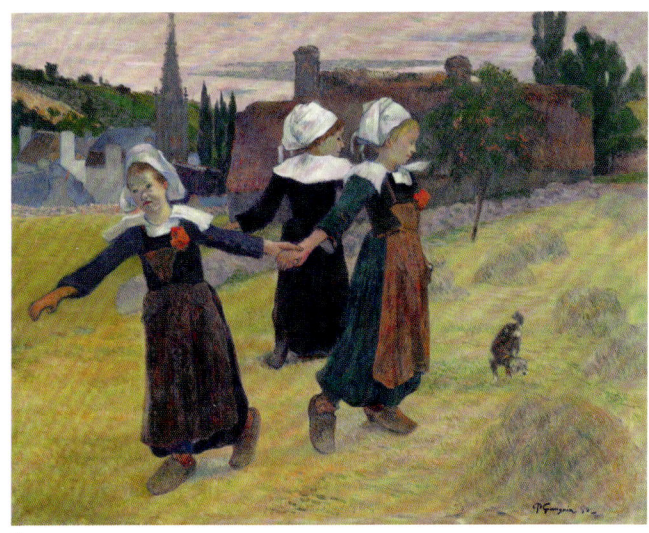

D.

CAMILLE PISSARRO 1830–1903

The palette as a work of art

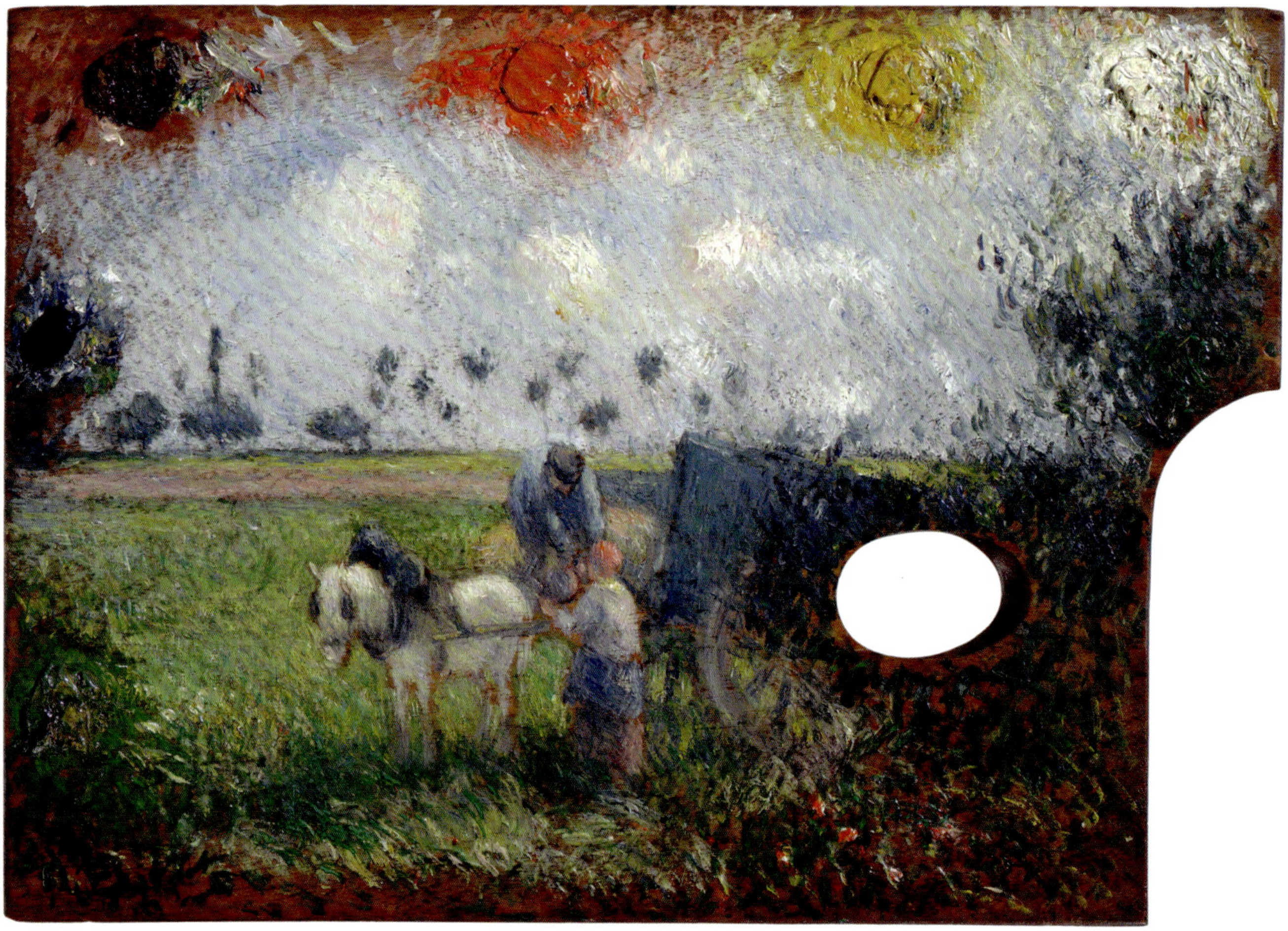

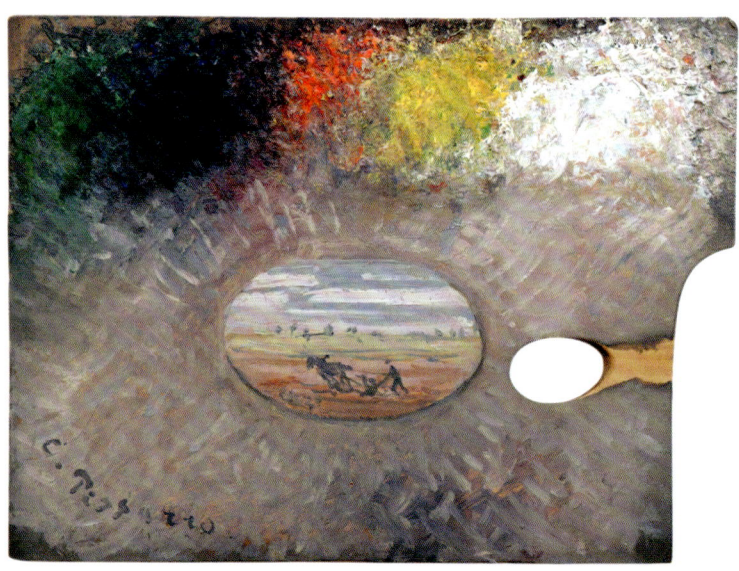

*The Artist's Palette with
a Landscape* (above)
Camille Pissarro
c. 1878–80
Oil on wood
24.3 × 34.7 cm
(9 ⅝ × 13 ¾ in.)

Palette with a painting
of a plough (left)
Camille Pissarro
Undated
Paint on wood

*The Gardener,
Afternoon Sun,
Eragny* (right)
Camille Pissarro
1899
Oil on canvas
92.5 × 65 cm
(36 ½ × 25 ⅝ in.)

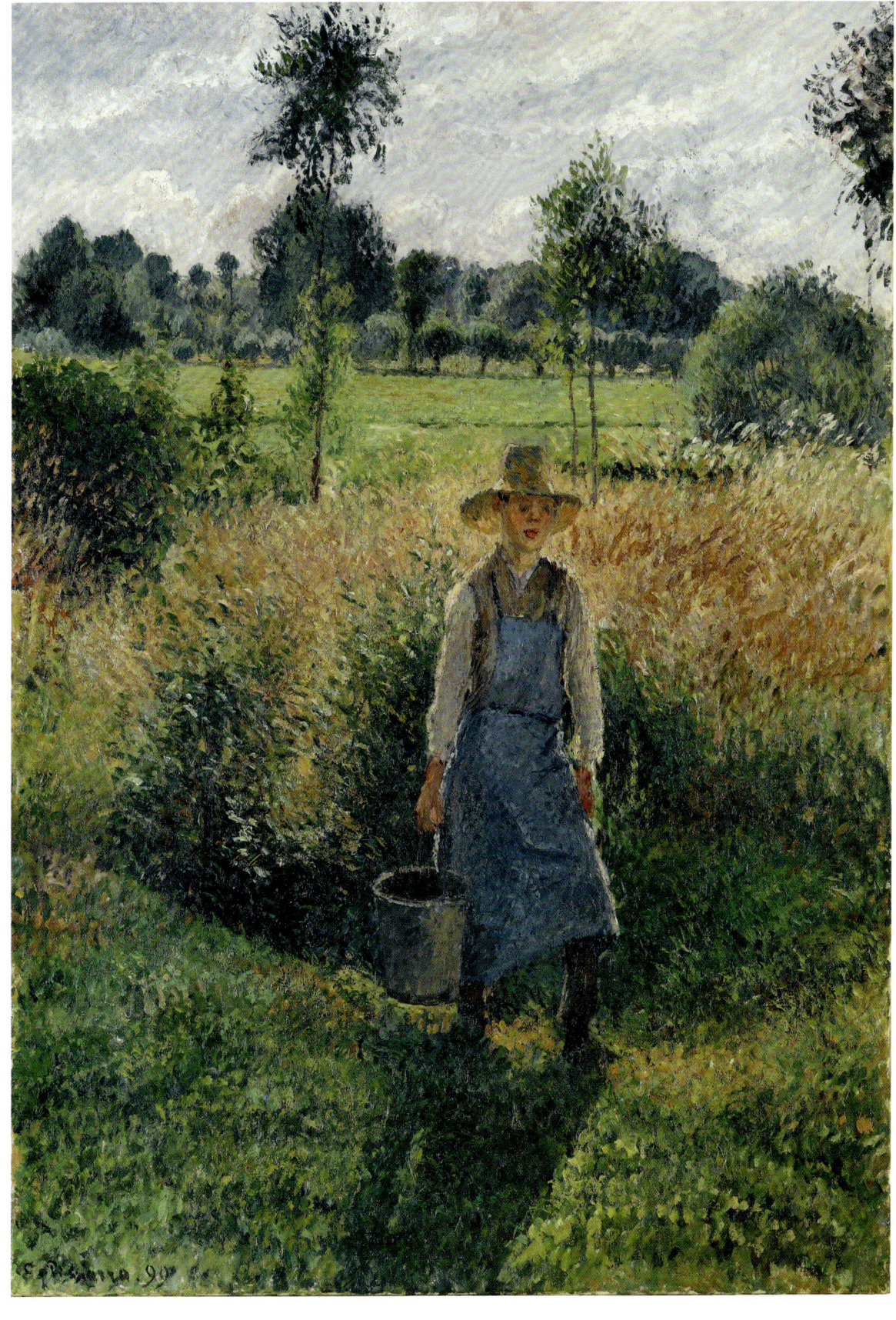

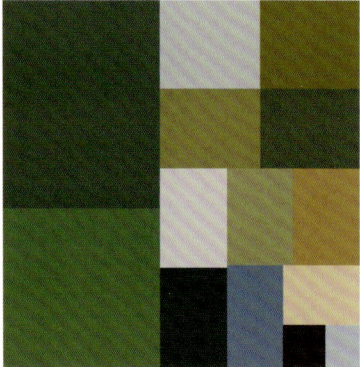

Proportional breakdown of colours used by Camille Pissarro in *The Gardener, Afternoon Sun, Eragny*, 1899, displayed on the previous page.

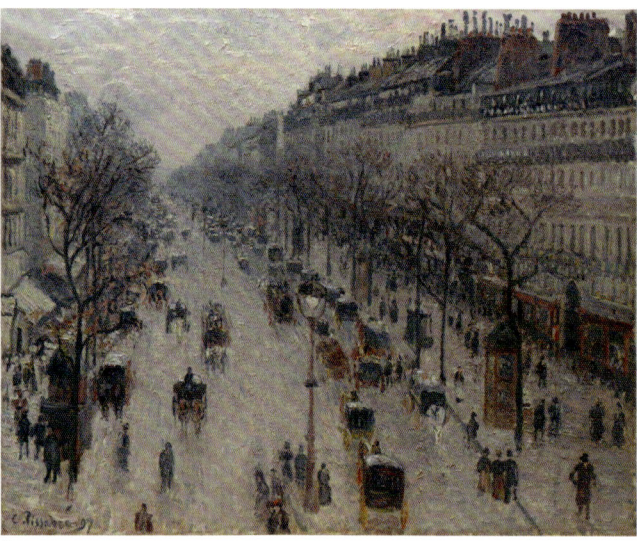

A.

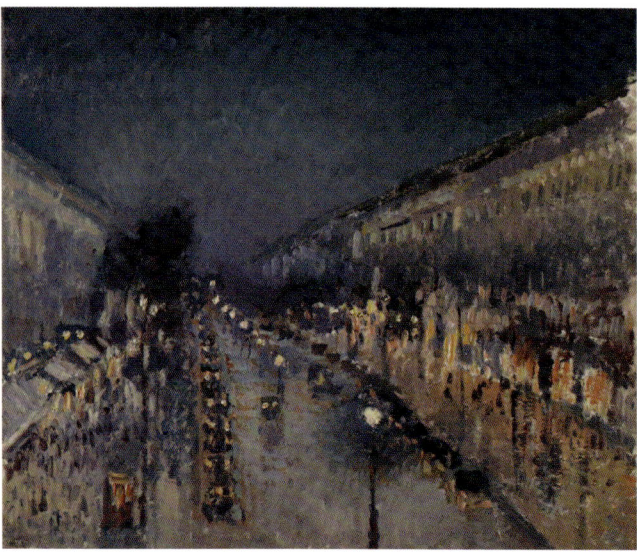

B.

CAMILLE PISSARRO'S PALETTES were tidy. He usually arranged a band of colour along the top edge following a prismatic order from dark to light, using predominantly manufactured paint squeezed from tubes. Pissarro not only signed some of his used palettes, he also specially created several, with integrated pictorial images, as souvenirs (see also Rosa Bonheur, page 81). This may seem whimsical, but in the later 19th century, palettes had started to become collectibles or were given as gifts from one artist to another. The first palette shown here was painted by Pissarro in the late 1870s for the Paris restaurateur Monsieur M. Laplace, who paid him fifty francs for it, possibly with the intention of displaying it in a brasserie. It depicts an entire rural landscape complete with farmers and a cart in a field. However, Pissarro also incorporated visual references to impressionist prismatic colour order: thick blobs of pure colour are placed around the upper and left edges of the palette, giving a sense of a practical colour layout on the palette, from which the pictorial scene developed. Pissarro excitedly wrote about Laplace's interest in painted artists' palettes to Claude Monet (see pages 152–55), clearly seeing financial potential in the field.

Although known as one of the main figures of impressionism, Pissarro actually experimented with different styles and techniques in his long career, and his palette changed considerably over the decades, especially after having worked with Monet and Cézanne (see pages 86–89) in the 1870s. Pissarro's palettes generally followed some basic principles of impressionism, such as a prismatic range of colours and copious amounts of bright white, which were used to create lighter tones of the pure colours. However, in some of his later work we also notice that he embraced darker colours and shades, and the palette may even contain pure blacks or very deep blues, as needed for shadows and outlines. In *The Gardener, Afternoon Sun, Eragny* (1899), we clearly see Pissarro's fascination with the effect of changing light conditions, his preference for outdoor scenes and the juxtaposition of prismatic colours. The gardener's blue apron is complementary to his face, hands and the grasses behind him, illuminated in orange by the rays of the almost-setting sun. Bright green tints used for trees and other foliage complete the prismatic colour range, while some darker shades surrounding the figure, provide depth, shadow and contrast.

Pissarro's pigments have been analysed extensively, but he also left a personal note in a letter to his son Lucien in 1887, in which he lists some of the paints he wants to order from the Paris art supplier Père Tanguy (who was painted by Vincent van Gogh, see page 105, the same year). Among them are no fewer than ten tubes of white (almost certainly lead white), two of

'Painting, art in general, enchants me. It is my life. What else matters? When you put all your soul into a work, all that is noble in you, you cannot fail to find a kindred soul who understands you, and you do not need a host of such spirits. Is not that all an artist should wish for?'

CAMILLE PISSARRO, LETTER TO HIS SON LUCIEN, 20 NOVEMBER 1883

chrome yellow, one red (probably vermilion), one ultramarine (probably artificial), the ubiquitous cobalt blue and five tubes of emerald green.[1] These are the brilliant artificial colours you would expect to see on a late-19th-century impressionist palette, chosen as the best match for each spectral colour. The only neutral colour he requested on this occasion was a brown lake. The large quantities of white are typical of artists in the wider circle of the impressionists, but Pissarro at one point stated caution about using too many 'intermediary whites', i.e., mixtures of the pure colours with white. It seems he was always more interested in darker shades, contours and complex spatial geometry than many of his fellow impressionists. He was also critical of overly mechanical painting techniques, such as the pointillist style of neo-impressionism, which he embraced for a brief period, before reverting to flatter, larger, comma-like brushstrokes that allowed him to work more quickly and freely. He did, however, follow the principle of a limited palette from which to create all other tones in a painting, and shared an interest in 19th-century colour science and theory, and was familiar with the work of Michel Eugène Chevreul and Ogden Rood.

In a late self-portrait from *c.* 1898 (image C.) in which he is holding a palette, he shows us a vastly simplified layout of his palette, with three flecks of yellow, red and a very dark blue peeking over the edge. White is also visible near the thumbhole, but there is a notably large area of earthy browns in the painting itself, in the form of his painting smock, here combined with the deep blues of which he was so fond.

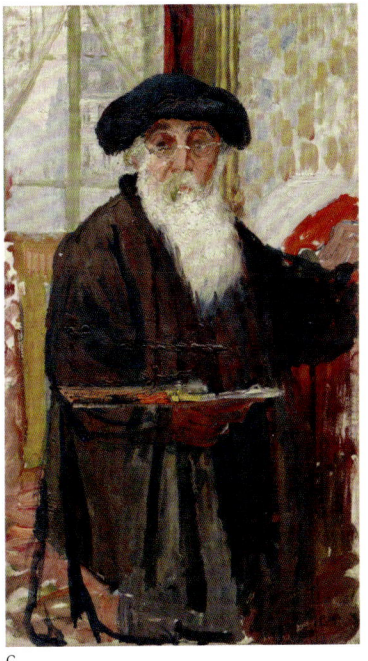

C.

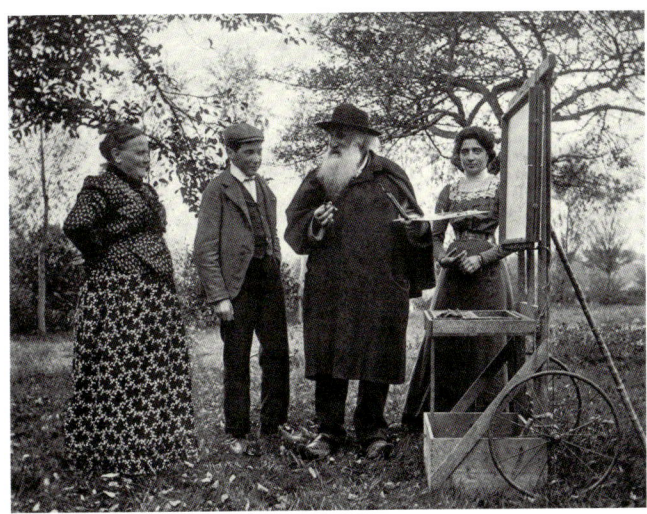

D.

A. *The Boulevard Montmartre on a Winter Morning*, Camille Pissarro, 1897, oil on canvas, 64.8 × 81.3 cm (25 ½ × 32 in.)
B. *The Boulevard Montmartre at Night*, Camille Pissarro, 1897, oil on canvas, 53.3 × 64.8 cm (21 × 25 ⅝ in.)
C. *Self-portrait*, Camille Pissarro, *c.* 1898, oil on canvas, 53 × 30.5 cm (20 ⅞ × 12 in.)
D. (Left to right) Julie, Ludovic-Rodo, Camille and Jeanne Pissarro at an easel in an orchard, *c.* 1890s

GEORGES SEURAT 1859–1891

A palette of light and lustre

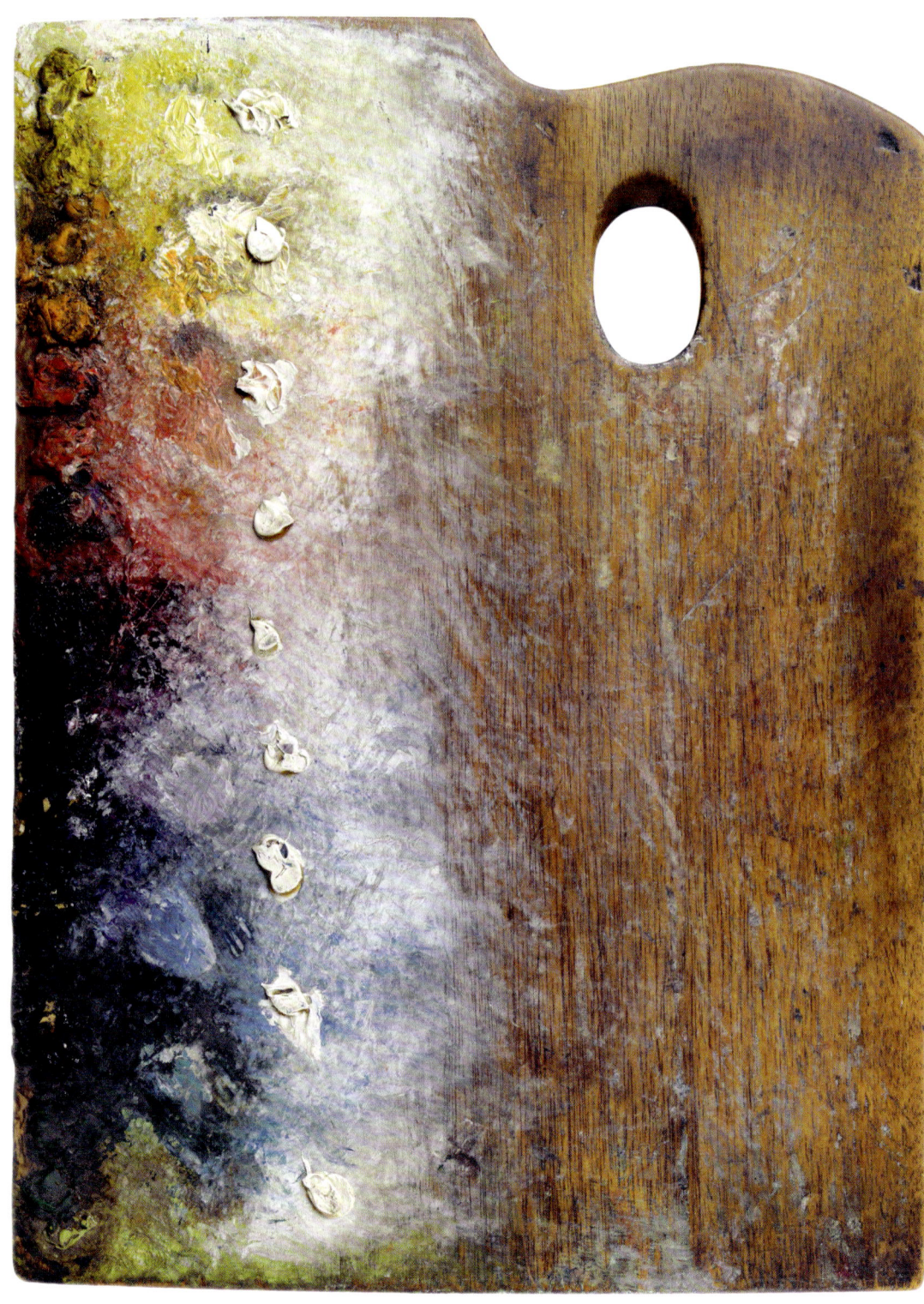

Georges Seurat's
palette
Oil on wood
27 × 36 cm
(10 ¾ × 14 ¼ in.)

The Circus
Georges Seurat
1891
Oil on canvas
186 × 152 cm
(73 ¼ × 59 ⅞ in.)

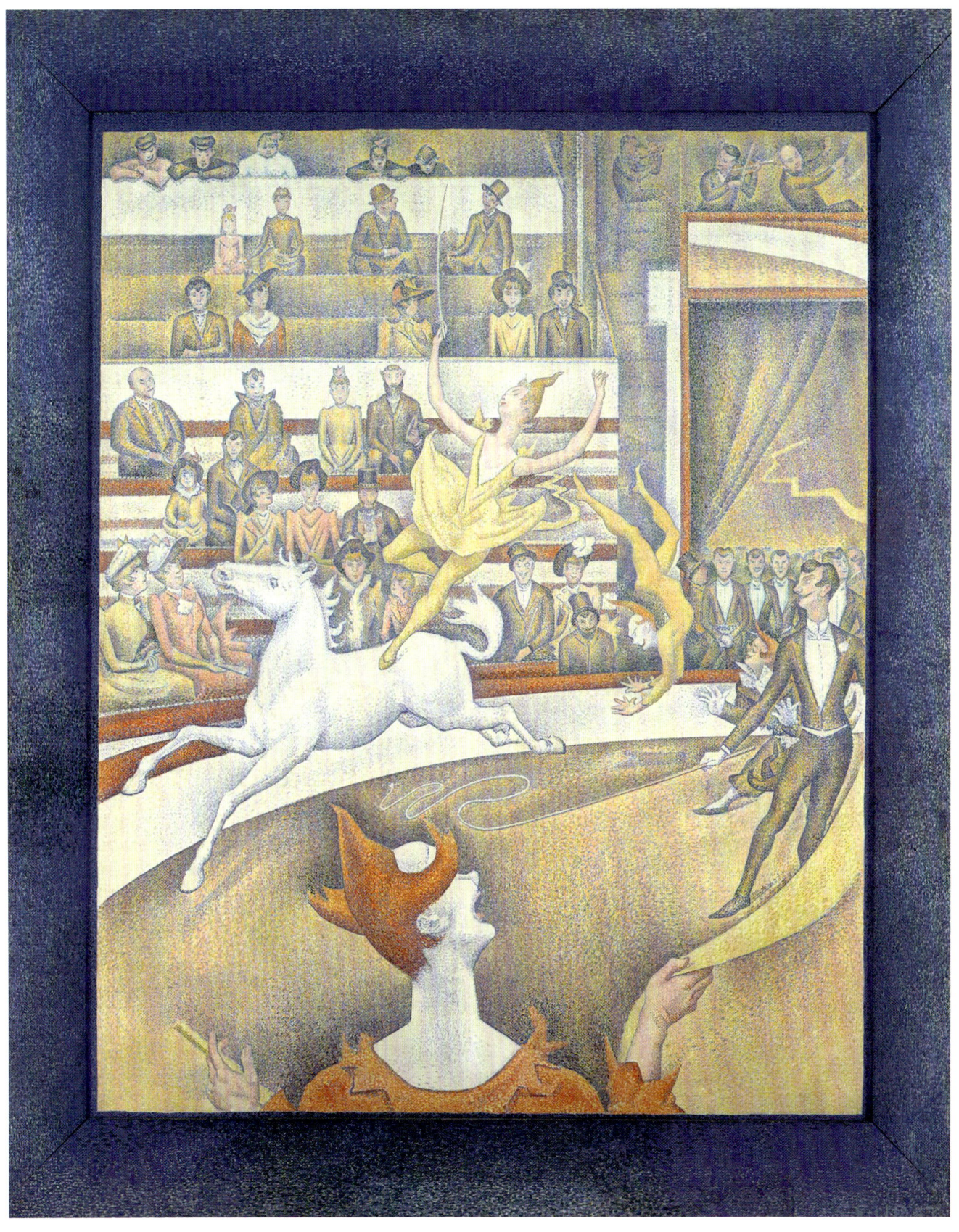

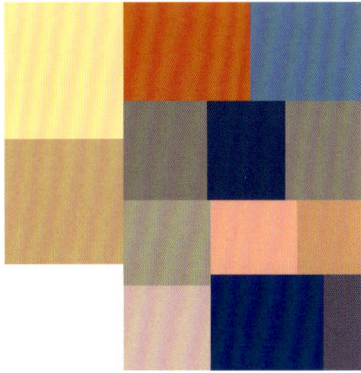

Proportional breakdown of colours used by Georges
Seurat in *The Circus*, 1891, displayed on the previous page.

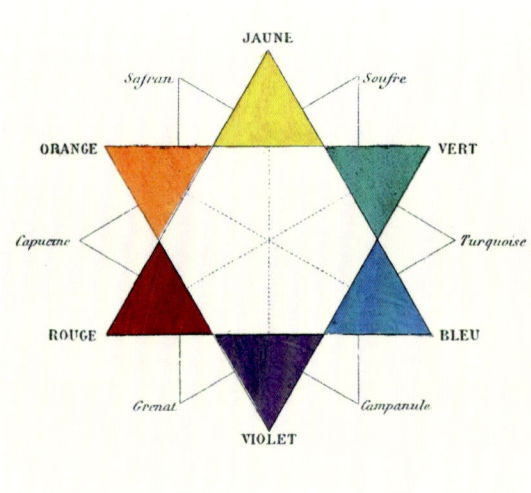

A.

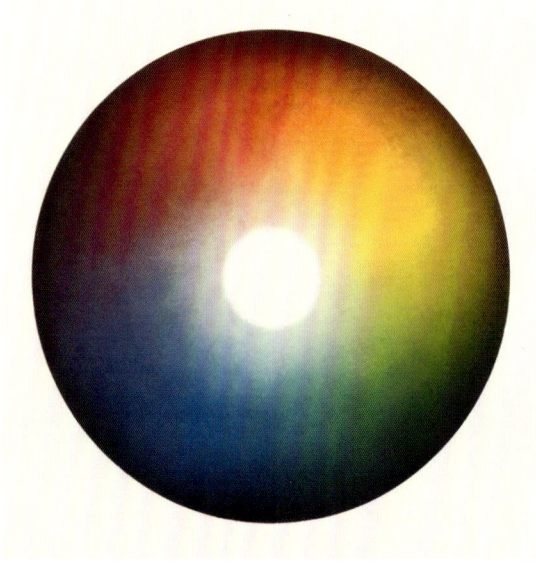

B.

THIS ORDERLY PALETTE belonged to an artist who
wanted to find and perfect a new way of painting both
light and shade, a method he called *peinture optique*
or 'chromoluminarism'. Georges Seurat laid out his
square wooden palette in three neat rows of oil paint,
occupying only the upper horizontal half of the surface.
Along the top edge of the palette are nine smudged blots
of pure colour, following the prismatic range, from
yellow to green. They are most likely (starting from
nearest the thumbhole) cadmium yellow, two oranges
(possibly chrome), vermilion, cobalt violet, artificial
ultramarine, cobalt or cerulean blue, emerald (viridian)
green and chrome green.[1] The lower of the three rows
comprise nine blots of pure white paint, still largely
intact, as if just squeezed out of a tube of lead white, but
it is clear from the areas surrounding them that this is
a new line of white and that there have been white blots
before on this palette. White is omnipresent and clearly
the defining element here. Between these two rows is
a third, and this is the real playground of the artist. It is
where Seurat mixed and blended his pure colours with
white, and nothing but white. There is no black on this
palette and few dark tones. The pigments themselves
are notably bright and almost all artificial, and there is
a conspicuous absence of earth pigments (although they
have been identified in some of his most famous works,
including *Bathers at Asnières*, 1884). This suggests
that Seurat's intention, in line with the impressionist
painters of his generation, was to paint light. However,
it is not as simple as that, and his elaborate, disciplined
palette illuminates his more complex ideas concerning
colour and painting techniques.

Seurat wanted to base the painting of light on a
more methodical, partly scientific basis. His interest in
optical studies and colour theory is well-documented,
and at times overestimated, but he was equally
concerned with colour harmony, line and symbolism.
Indeed, how colours relate to and respond to each other,
and therefore how a painting could convey atmosphere,
emotion and even trigger certain synaesthetic
experiences, is one of the most important aspects
of his work. He became the leading figure of neo-
impressionism, a loose group of Paris artists concerned
with a more structured approach to colour, light and
form in contemporary art. Their technical approach
was to isolate colour on the palette as well as on the
canvas, and apply small dots or strokes of pure colour
to create their compositions. These techniques were
called pointillism and divisionism respectively. Seurat
remains the name most commonly associated with
them, and this palette is an example of his commitment
to the style that is based largely, but not exclusively, on
optical mixing. This means that the blending of colours

'Art is Harmony. Harmony is the analogy of opposites, the analogy of similarities of tone, of tint, of line taking account of a dominant and under the influence of the lighting, in combinations that are gay calm or sad.'

GEORGES SEURAT, LETTER TO MAURICE BEAUBOURG, 28 AUGUST 1890

takes place not on the palette but in the eyes of the viewer (including the artist himself), and is dependent on the distance between the eyes and the paint surface. Crucially, pointillism was not only about creating more brilliance through additive colour mixture (as opposed to subtractive mixing of material colour), but also about lustre and subjective experience. The changing appearance of the paint surface, depending on the distance and angle from which it is viewed, creates a certain movement and a lustrous, shimmering effect.

Almost every one of Seurat's finished works in oil follows the idea of divisionism and optical mixing, including the late work on page 127, *The Circus*, from 1891. He would often continue the principles of pointillism to the picture frame, incorporating it into the composition and covering it in more blots and strokes, as was the case with this work. *The Circus* is also an example of Seurat's interest in line, perspective and structure, something that is inadvertently also obvious in the palette layout.

Seurat had familiarized himself with some of the most important 19th-century European writings on colour theory, among them Michel Eugène Chevreul, Charles Blanc, Charles Henry and Ogden Rood, although it is unclear how deeply he studied each of them. His palette layout and the principles of his methods are clearly informed by colour order and diagrams as proposed by Blanc, Chevreul and Henry, and he was influenced by Rood in particular in respect of identifying material equivalents for spectral colour. Yet Seurat was also a man of black and shade: for many of his great luminous works in colour he produced sketches and studies in monochrome black. He would begin each composition in clear outlines, then build up layers of oil paint, followed by thousands of minute strokes and dabs. He did indeed paint light and luminosity in a methodical way but he also embraced the symbolism of spectral colour, as can be seen in a study for *Bathers at Asnières*, where a rainbow is placed in a non-realistic manner, a luminous symbol of light.

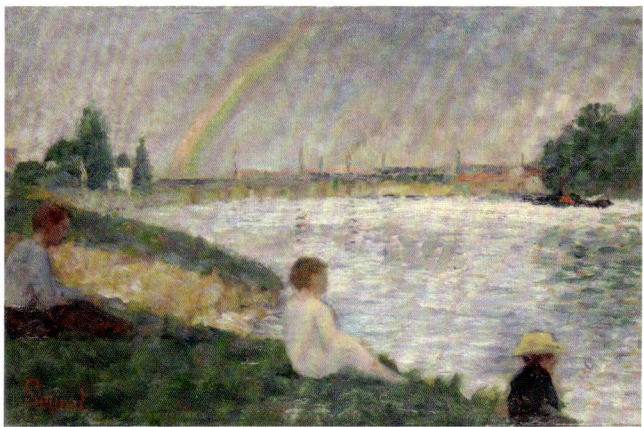
C.

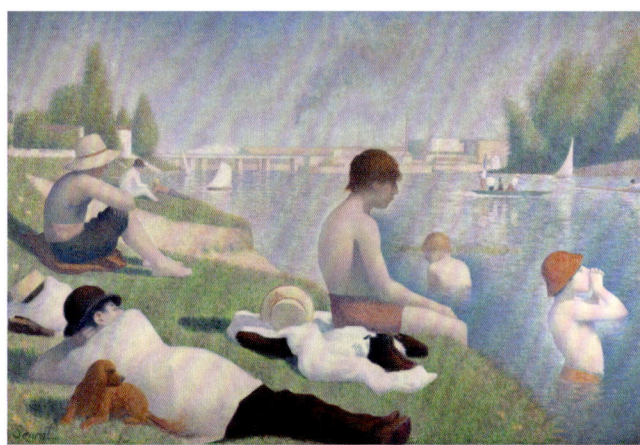
D.

A. Colour circle made from triangles, from Charles Blanc's *Grammaire des arts du dessin*, 1867 (first published in English translation as *The Grammar of Painting and Engraving*, 1874)
B. *Cercle Chromatique* (colour circle), Charles Henry, 1888–89
C. *The Rainbow* (study for *Bathers at Asnières*), Georges Seurat, 1883, oil on wood, 15.5 × 24.5 cm (6 ⅛ × 9 ¾ in.)
D. *Bathers at Asnières*, Georges Seurat, 1884, oil on canvas, 2 × 3 m (6 ft 7 ¼ in. × 9 ft 10 ⅛ in.)

JAMES ENSOR 1860–1949

A carnivalesque palette

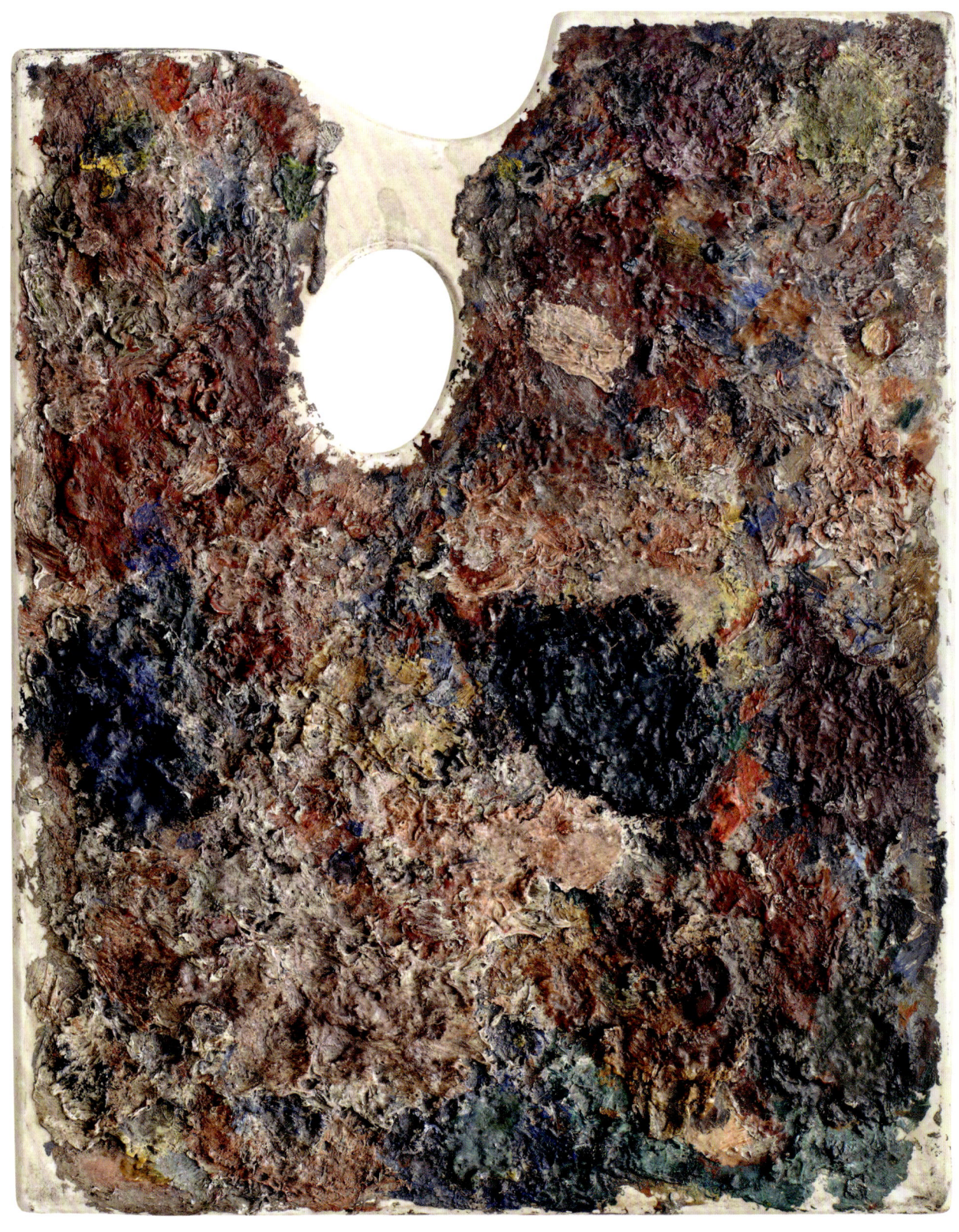

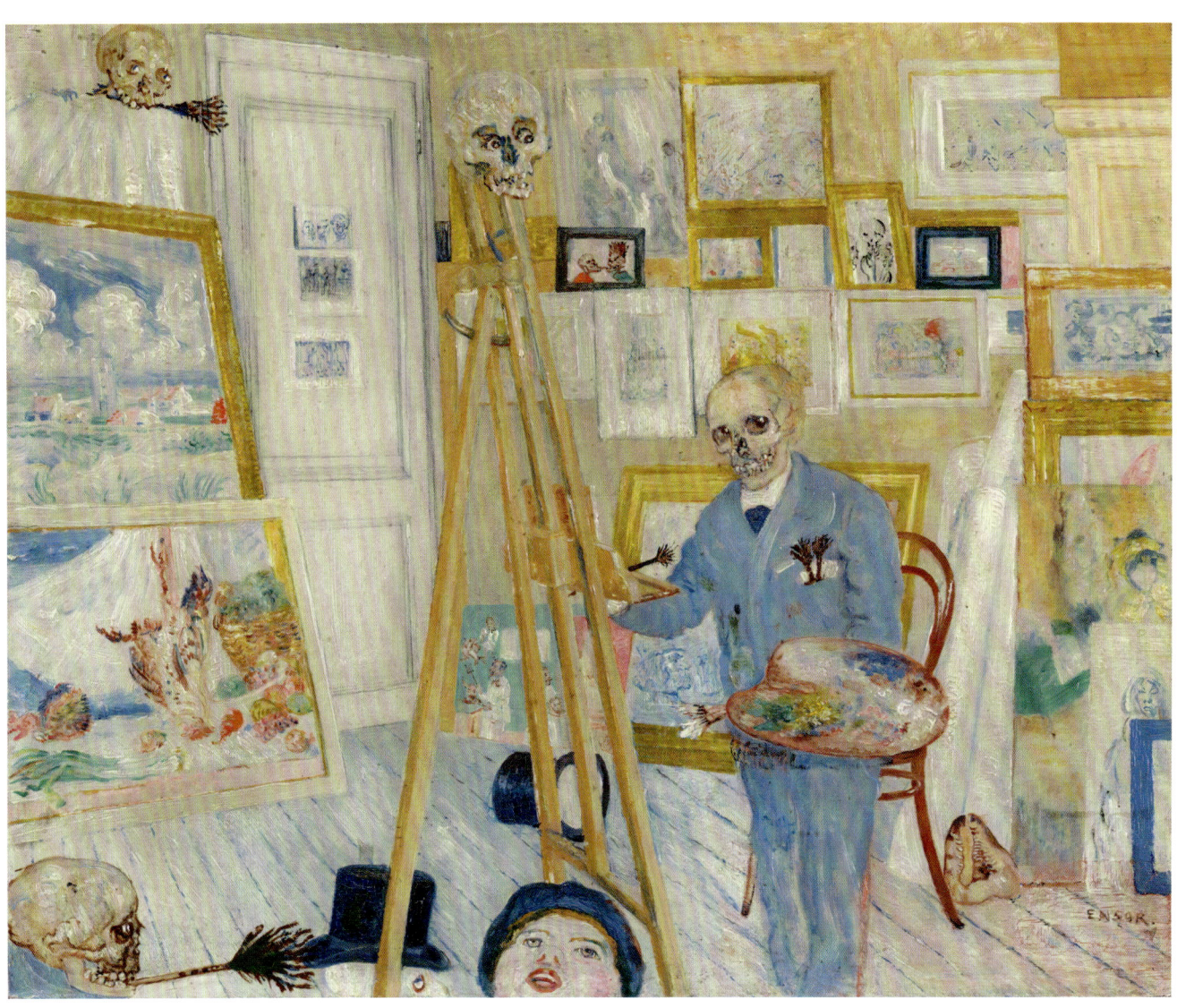

James Ensor's palette
Undated
Paint on ceramic

The Skeleton Painter
James Ensor
1896
Oil on panel
37.3 × 45.3 cm
(14 ¾ × 18 ⅝ in.)

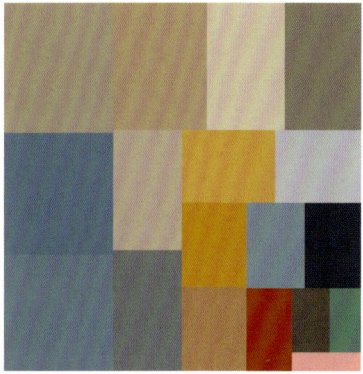

Proportional breakdown of colours used by James
Ensor in *The Skeleton Painter*, 1896, displayed on
the previous page.

JAMES ENSOR'S SURVIVING PALETTES are as
unpredictable, idiosyncratic and wild as his art and
personality. He used a great variety of palettes of all
sizes, shapes and materials. The one shown here is
a more unusual ceramic palette, often used by artists
when painting in watercolour to emulate white paper,
but here used with oil paints. White is a ubiquitous
element in Ensor's art, and especially in his later work
he appears to have worked on white grounds. Indeed it
is likely that Ensor chose his palettes according to which
ground colour and support he was working with. The
palette is caked in heavily mixed and manipulated paint,
looking like a cratered, surreal landscape of colour.

An element of the untamed, and at times violent,
characterizes Ensor's use of paint, colour and motifs.
Among the latter, the palette is a dominant feature.
The apparent messiness of this and other palettes is
a stark contrast to Ensor's aptitude as an engraver and
printmaker. He was a gifted draughtsman, and despite
the anarchic appearance of many of his paintings, he
had a solid understanding of line and composition.

He often used colours in deliberately jarring contrasts,
making abrupt colour changes in compositions and
combining subtle pale tone with heavy harmonies
of saturated tints. His garish use of colour suited his
subject matter. Although initially inspired by the sea as
a motif (he grew up and remained rooted in the coastal
town of Ostend, Belgium), he created many grotesque,
sometimes disturbing, paintings of masked figures,
demonic creatures, occult images and skeletons or
skeletal figures that populate Kafkaesque surroundings.
Much of it was inspired by Belgian carnival and other
folk traditions, as well as literal skeletons that regularly
washed up on the coast in his home town, remnants
of a 17th-century siege that resulted in 130,000 deaths.

Ensor skeletonized himself in several images, either
overtly or through the emblematic use of a palette.
In *Skeletons Warming Themselves* (1889, image C.),
a palette lies in the foreground, at the feet of a collapsed
skeleton wrapped in a painter's smock. It carries the
typical colours of one of Ensor's palettes. *The Skeleton
Painter* (1896), shown on the previous page, is perhaps
the most overt expression of Ensor's morbid fascination
with mortality and the grotesque, but also shows his
humorous side. It is marked by a brightness and positivity
of tone that makes the skeleton look ludicrous: dressed
in sky blue, the skeleton painter looks decidedly fleshy
under his suit and tie, and sports glistening eyes. The
studio is filled with ridiculously bright, sunny pictures
with other goggle-eyed skulls looking on. Like the
paintings in the studio, the palette is filled with
prismatic colour. There is no darkness here, only light,
bright hues, including the self-referential sky blue

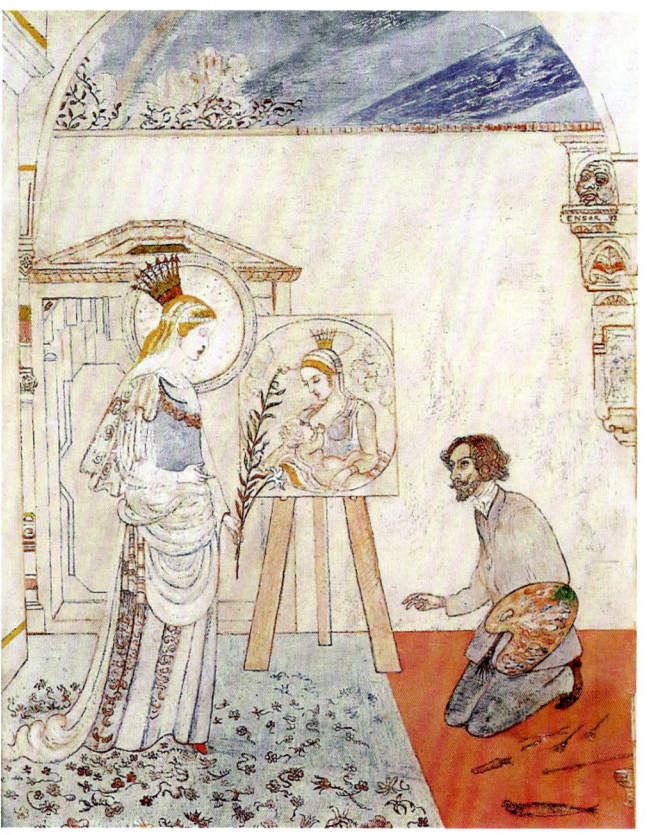

A.

'*The vulgar vision recognizes nothing but chaos, disorder and incorrectness…. Art has evolved from the Gothic line and has traversed the colour and the movement of the Renaissance, in order to attain modern light.*'

JAMES ENSOR, QUOTED IN ERIC PROTTER'S *PAINTERS ON PAINTING*

and copious amounts of white. *The Skeleton Painter* forms a stark contrast to Ensor's earlier, more traditional and realistic *Portrait of the Artist at the Easel* (1879) in which the palette forms a literal symbol of his art, occupying the centre of the composition, simply showing us his colour preferences and working methods.

Ensor's philosophy of painting was markedly different to that of his contemporaries, and he abhorred the laboured techniques of the pointillists – and by extension the impressionists – accusing them of lifelessness: 'They coldly and methodically apply [paint] without sentiment, their dotting between correct and cold lines, only arriving at one aspect of light, its vibration, without coming to give its form.'[1] It is likely that the studio space depicted in *The Skeleton Painter* is a humorous criticism of impressionist painting. To him, painting was a multi-sensory act and experience: 'All the senses take part in the secret pleasure; first the eye, then the taste, then the touch; finally, the mind, whose essence is humbler.'[2]

Ensor's use of the palette motif has also been interpreted in respect of his complex sexuality and Christian faith. In *The Virgin of Consolation* (1892, image A.) the kneeling figure of Ensor represents the Virgin in an annunciation scene. He is in love with the goddess of Painting, represented by the actual Virgin, and his palette and paintbrush may well have phallic meaning in this composition. The paint of the palette reflects, as usual, his joyful and experimental relationship with colour.

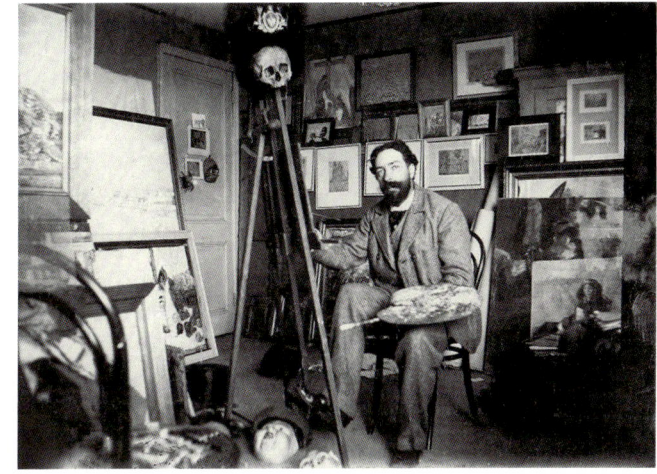
B.

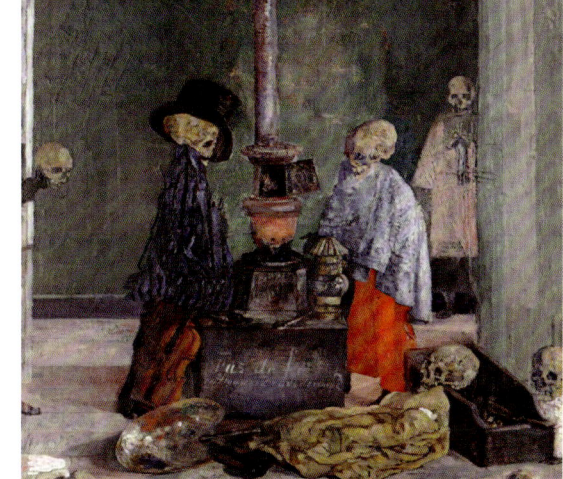
C.

A. *The Virgin of Consolation*, James Ensor, 1892, oil on panel, 48 × 38 cm (19 × 15 in.)
B. James Ensor painting in his studio, *c.* 1896–97
C. *Skeletons Warming Themselves*, James Ensor, 1889, oil on canvas, 74.8 × 60 cm (29 ½ × 23 ⅝ in.)

WINSLOW HOMER 1836–1910

An elemental palette

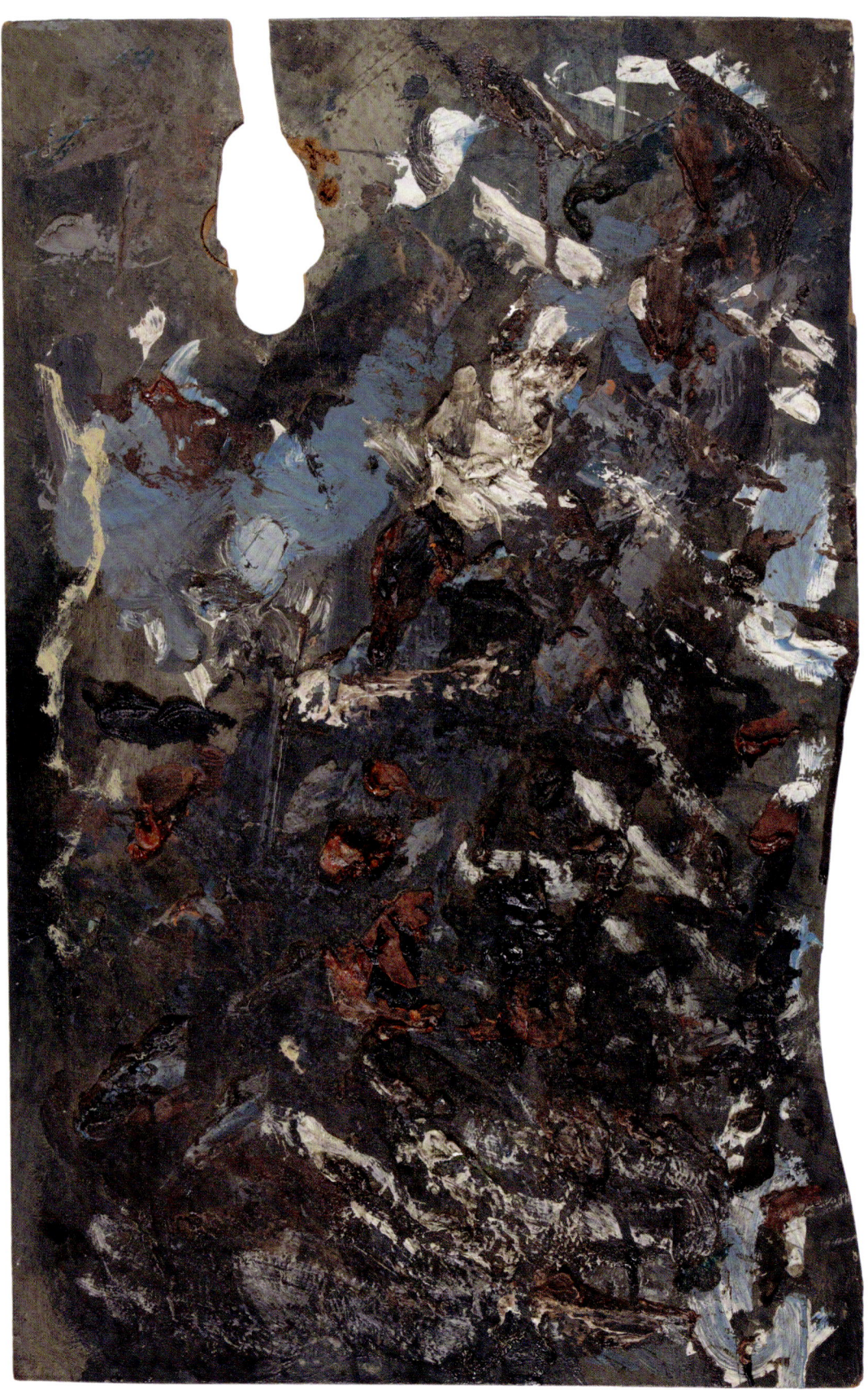

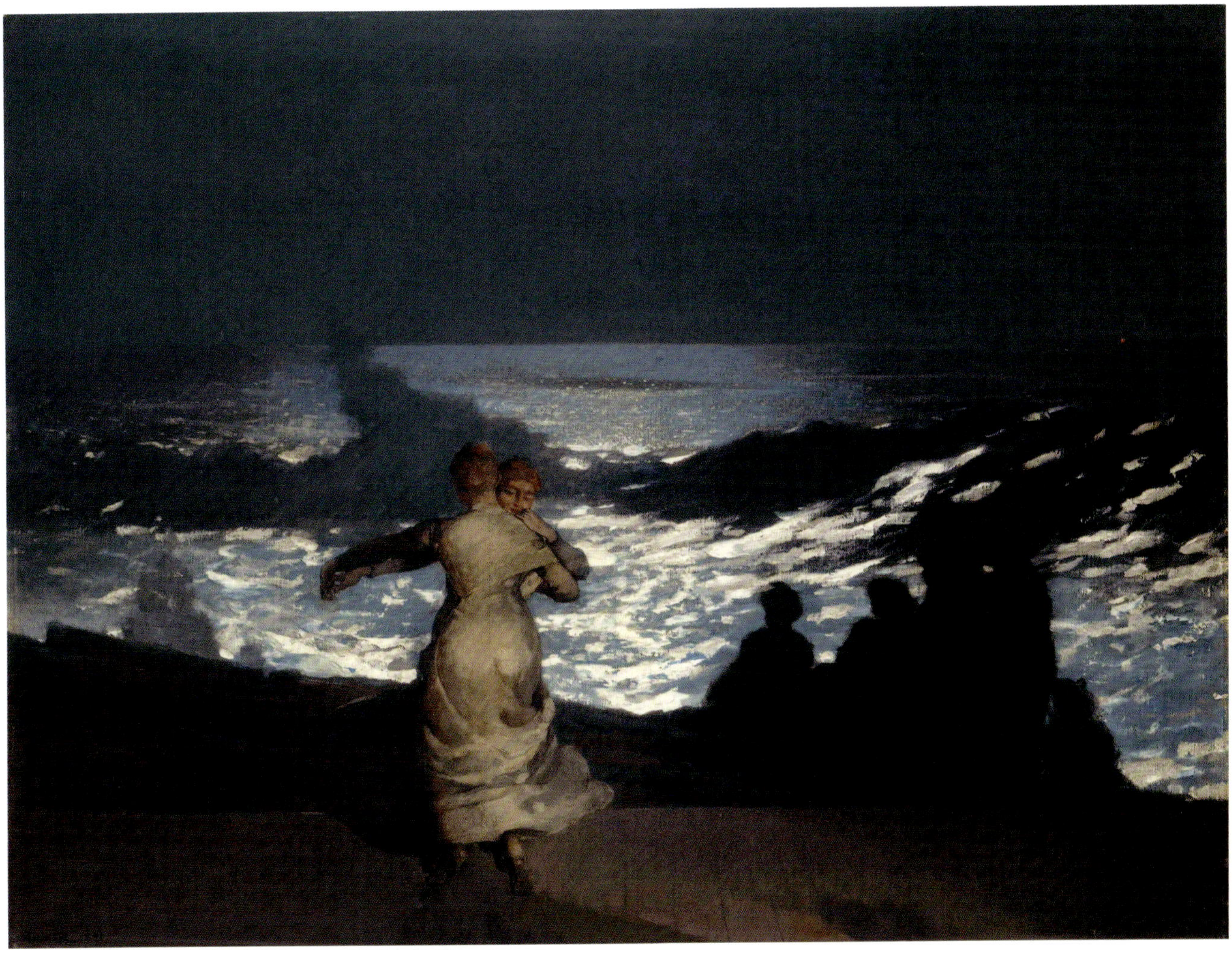

Winslow Homer's palette
(opposite)
1890–1910
Paint on wood
27.9 × 45.7 cm
(11 × 18 in.)

Summer Night (above)
Winslow Homer
1890
Oil on canvas
76.5 × 102 cm
(30 ⅛ × 40 ¼ in.)

*Early Morning After
a Storm at Sea* (right)
Winslow Homer
1900–3
Oil on canvas
76.8 × 127 cm
(30 ¼ × 50 in.)

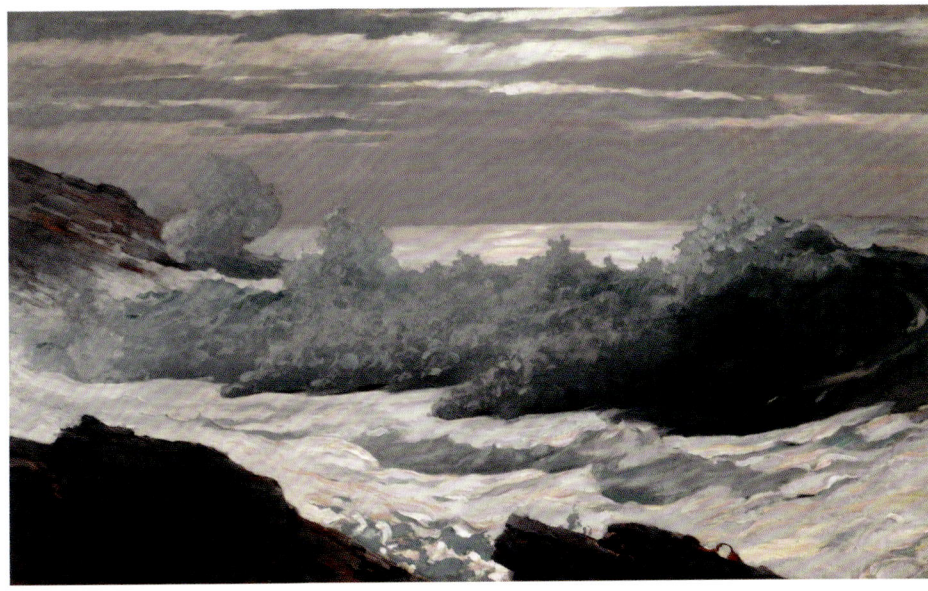

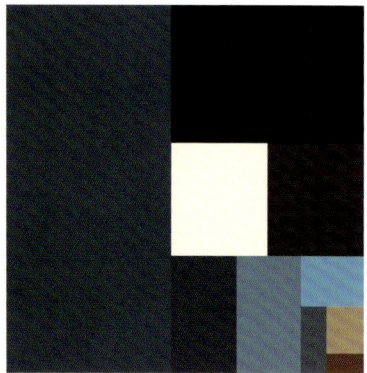

Proportional breakdown of colours used by Winslow Homer in *Summer Night*, 1890, displayed on the previous page.

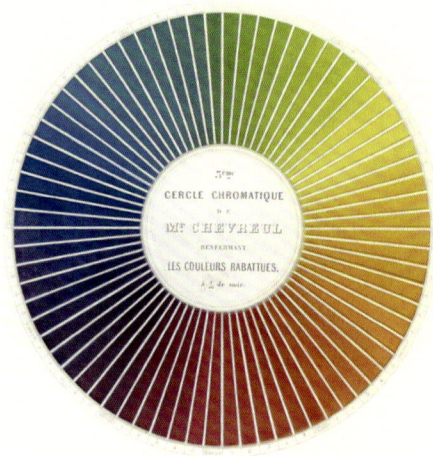

A.

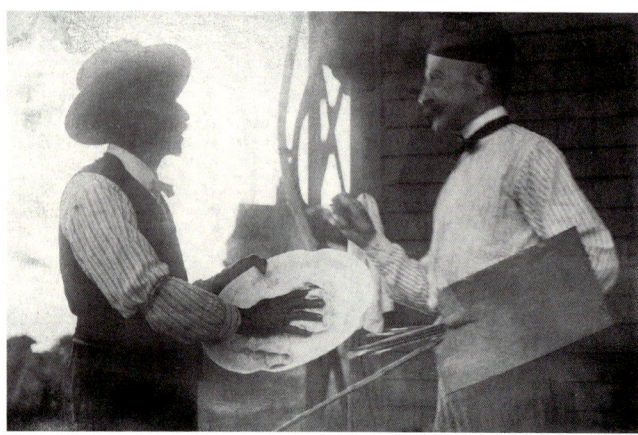

B.

WINSLOW HOMER'S PALETTE looks battered, chipped and weather-beaten, as if its remaining paint has been splattered onto it by an ocean wave. Palettes are often inadvertently mirrors of a painter's character and style, but rarely do they resemble the subject matter of the artist in the way that this palette does. The sea was the main motif and inspiration in Homer's life. Despite having spent many years in New York, he was drawn to coastal landscapes and became best known for capturing the dramatic atmospheric conditions of the rocky coast of Prouts Neck, Maine, overlooking the vast expanse of the Atlantic Ocean.

This palette cannot be dated exactly, but its colour traces show one of Homer's typically focused, strictly limited colour choices for each painting, guided by nature with the aim to produce pure, realistic depictions of the world around him. Extensive mixing has taken place on the palette, the format of which suggests it may have been part of a paintbox. Homer has created a range of silvery whites and greys, muted blues and many darker shades that are no longer distinguishable. Among these are traces of an earthy yellow, probably ochre, and deep reds, the only pure prismatic colours that appear to have been used.

The paint marks suggest he has used brushes and palette knives for blending and painting. He often placed the most saturated colours in the foreground of a painting as chromatic markers, and applied paint in thick daubs and broad brushstrokes, making full use of colour contrast, thus creating dynamic, textured images that would reflect the power and movement of the sea and the elements. Homer had an intellectual interest in colour theory and contrast and had read an early English translation of Michel-Eugène Chevreul's *The Laws of Contrast of Colour* (first published in French in 1839), which would become a key text for avant-garde artists in the late 19th century.

Early Morning After a Storm at Sea (1900–3) – one of Homer's late seascapes, showing high waves crashing onto the shore at Prouts Neck – is an example of tonal and textural composition, where the dark rocks contrast dramatically with white sea spray, and flecks of red and yellow are visible in the foreground. Cool, muted blues dominate the earlier peopled *Summer Night* (1890), in which the sea is calmer, but still a powerful presence. If this palette looks windswept, it quite possibly was. Bruce Robertson notes that while Homer liked to observe and sketch the Atlantic from a purpose-built balcony at his house, for his oil paintings he preferred to stand as close to the water as possible, 'as though he could only paint with his feet planted on the rock'.[1] Another surviving palette by Homer (image C.) has snapped in half and looks similarly ravaged from outdoor painting sessions on the Atlantic coast.

'When I have selected the thing carefully, I paint it exactly as it appears...with reference solely to its simple and absolute truth.'

WINSLOW HOMER, QUOTED IN WILLIAM R. CROSS'S *WINSLOW HOMER: AMERICAN PASSAGE*, 2022

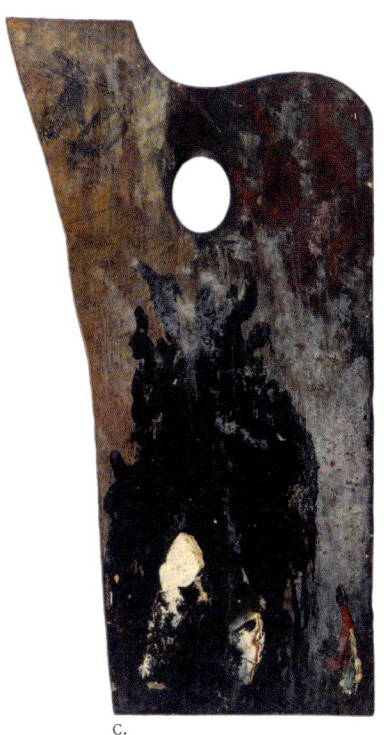

C.

Homer was a true advocate of realism in the style of his French contemporary Gustave Courbet (see pages 58–61) with whom he shared a passion for the sea. Both reduced their palettes and compositions to such a degree that they conveyed a distinct sense of abstraction, as if wanting to create landscape paintings that could serve as blank canvases for emotional responses.

Given the physical, textured nature of Homer's best-known seascapes, it is perhaps surprising that many of these had their beginnings in watercolour. In some cases, he would spend years trialling a composition in watercolour before transferring it to canvas. When working in watercolour, Homer preferred to use Winsor & Newton moist watercolours. A couple of his Winsor & Newton watercolour tin boxes survive at the Art Institute of Chicago, one with his name and 'Scarboro Beach, Maine' inscribed on the inside wing (image D.). Its twenty pans correspond with the typical range of colours available from art suppliers at the time, among them green earth, Prussian blue, Indian yellow, Hooker's green (Prussian blue mixed with gamboge), several types of vermilion (to create various shades of orange and red), and several organic and earth browns. Homer is not known to have painted a self-portrait holding a palette, but he did leave a neat ink drawing of a palette and some brushes, elegantly incorporated into his signature (image E.).

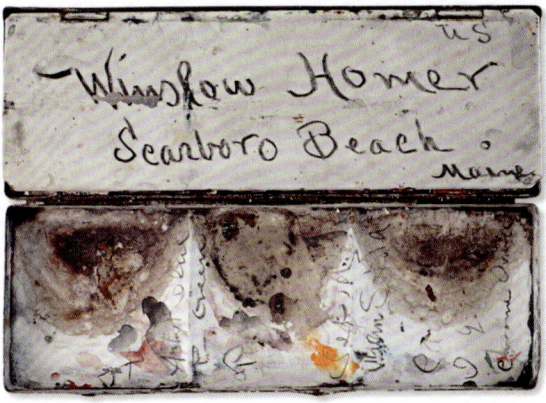

D.

A. Third chromatic circle, from Michel Eugène Chevreul's *Des couleurs et de leurs applications aux arts industriels à l'aide des cercles chromatiques* (Of colours and of their applications in the industrial arts with the help of chromatic circles), 1864
B. Winslow Homer and his servant Lewis Wright, 1883–1910
C. Palette owned by Winslow Homer, 1890–1910, paint on wood, 21 × 38.1 cm (8 ¼ × 15 in.)
D. Winslow Homer's Winsor & Newton metal watercolour box, 1900–10, 20.6 × 20.9 cm (8 ⅛ in × 8 ¼ in.)
E. Signature of Winslow Homer, pen and brown ink on paper, 6.4 × 12 cm (2 ½ × 4 ¾ in.)

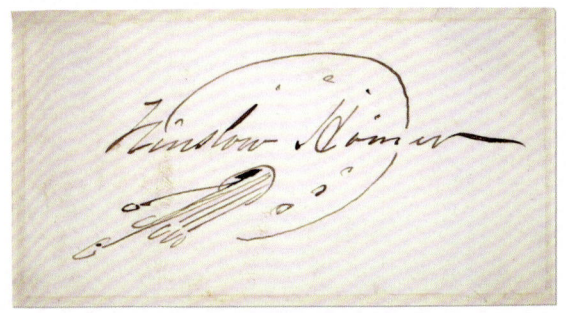

E.

VILHELM HAMMERSHØI 1864–1916

A silent palette in many shades of grey

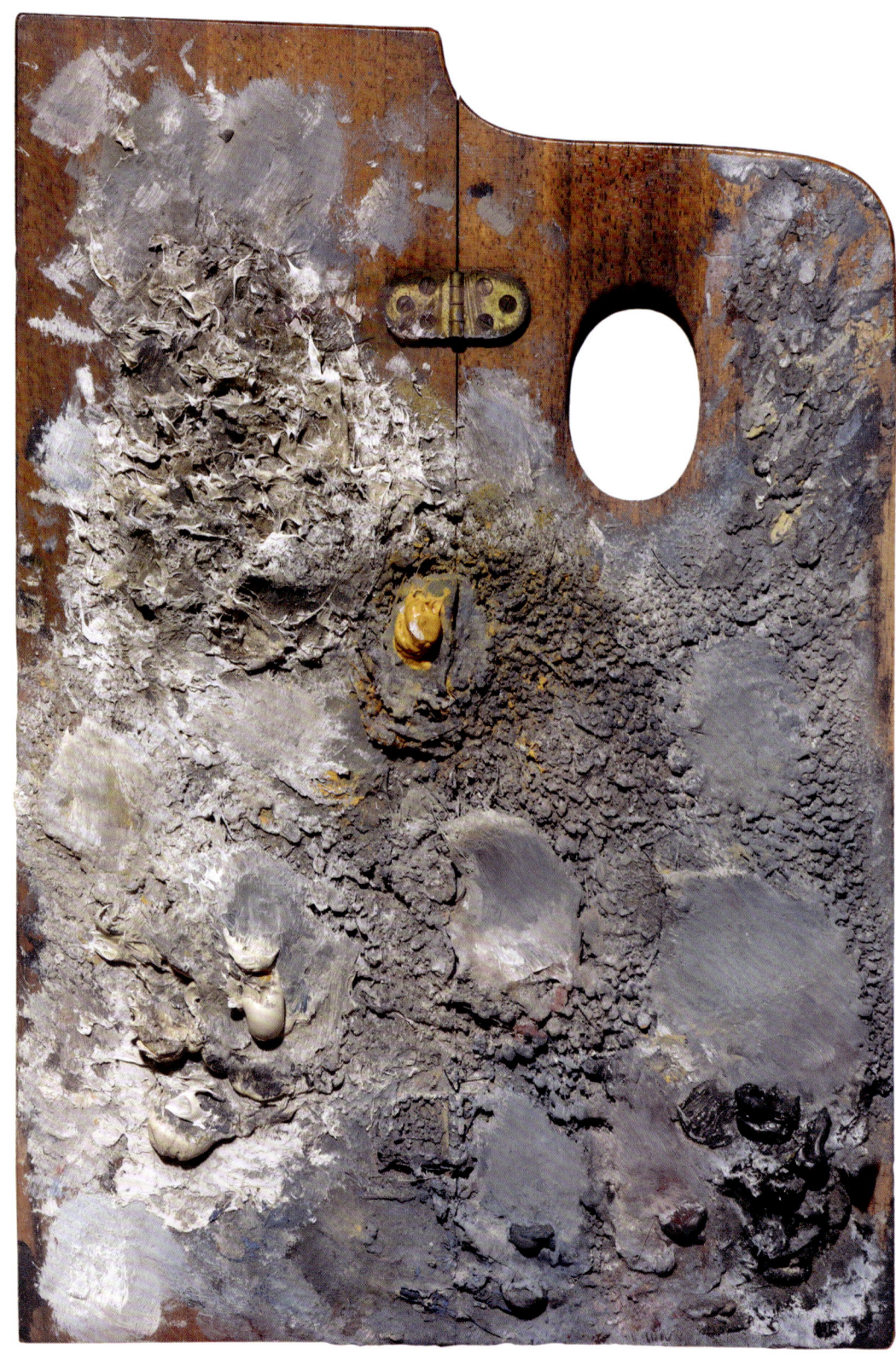

Vilhelm Hammershøi's
palette
Undated
Paint on wood

Interior from Strandgade 30
Vilhelm Hammershøi
1900
Oil on canvas
52 × 45 cm
(20 ½ × 17 ¾ in.)

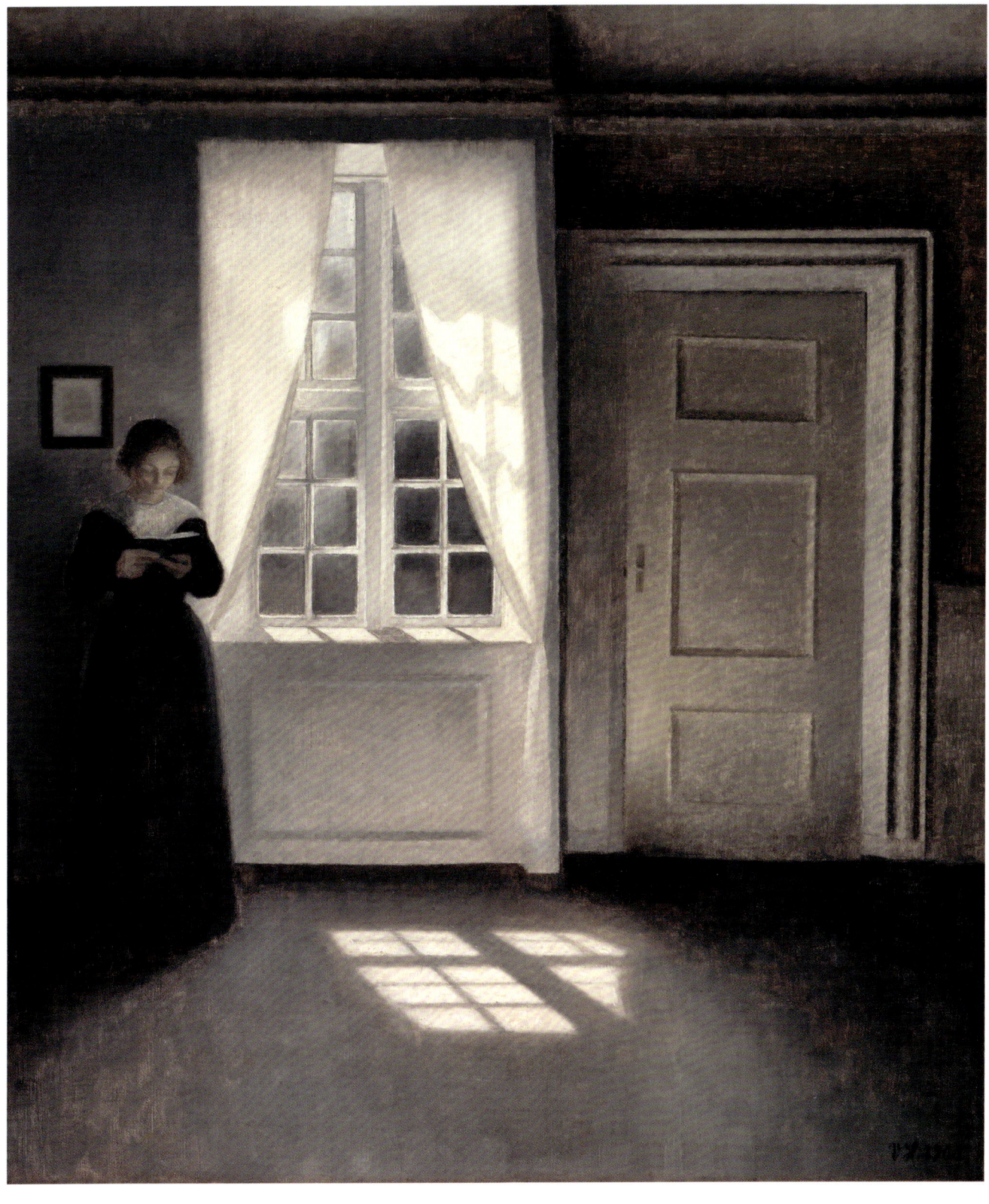

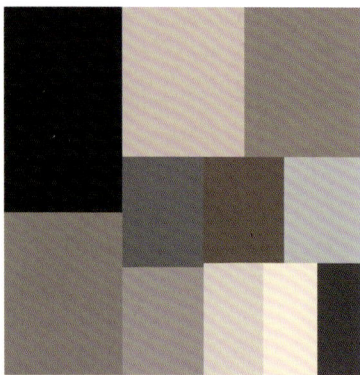

Proportional breakdown of colours used by Vilhelm Hammershøi in *Interior from Strandgade 30*, 1900, displayed on the previous page.

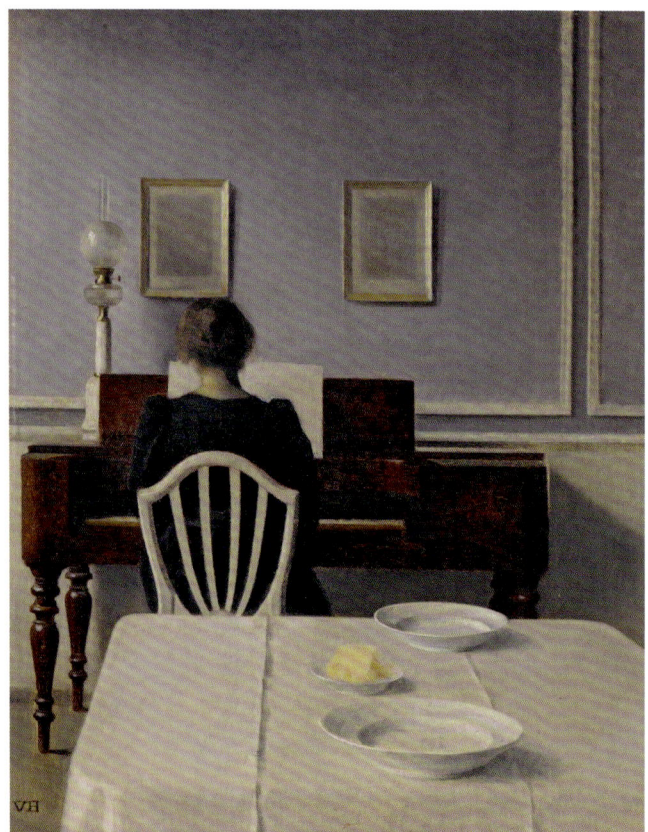

A.

THE PALETTE OF DANISH ARTIST Vilhelm Hammershøi is as discreet and mysterious as the man himself. A folding palette from his late period, it is almost entirely covered in subtle, cool, mixed tones of what appears to be white in one half and grey in the other. It is an almost achromatic palette, were it not for the warm yellow blot of paint that commands the centre of the plane. As with Hammershøi's art, this palette requires closer examination, through which the colours and mixtures used by the artist will come into focus. Once our eyes adjust, the abundance of greys left on the palette reveal themselves as infused with blue, comprising a wide range of grey-blue shades and tints, while the whites are not simply white but show the faintest traces of yellow and black, added to achieve the subtle tonality so typical of Hammershøi. A contemporary artist once described another of Hammershøi's palettes as resembling the layers of an oyster shell. This painstakingly worked palette surprises with its heaps and peaks of mixed paint. By contrast, Hammershøi applied paint on his canvases in thin, almost transparent layers with the structure of the canvas frequently visible. He tended to work from dark to light, starting with dark grounds and adding brighter tones with each layer.

The painting shown on page 139 one of more than sixty that Hammershøi painted of the interiors of his apartment in Strandgade 30, a house in Copenhagen, where he lived with his wife Ida from 1898 to 1909. The ceilings and walls of their apartment were painted white and grey with floorboards in a contrasting dark brown. The apartment – its windows with restricted views of outside spaces, its curiously arranged, old-fashioned furniture and ghostly white doors – became the main subject for his art. Ida, often portrayed from behind as a silent sculptural figure, was one of his few models. All these elements served as carriers of subtle colour, tonality and contrast, as exemplified on the physical palette.

What Hammershøi was really painting was the effects of light and shadow on surfaces, architectural spaces, fabric, even dust. Yet, he treated illumination and local colour in a very different way to many of his contemporaries, and was more interested in line, structure and geometry than vibrant colour schemes. Consequently, his range of colours is minimalist, something he commented on in an interview in 1907:

> Why do I use such a reduced, delicate palette?
> I really do not know. It is really rather impossible
> for me to say anything on the subject. It comes quite
> naturally to me, but I cannot say why. In any case,
> it has been that way since I first started exhibiting.
> The colours can probably best be described as neutral
> and reduced colours. I am utterly convinced that
> a painting achieves its best effect in a colouristic
> sense the fewer colours it has.[1]

> '*Colour is naturally not without importance.... I work hard to make it look harmonious. But when I choose a motif I'm thinking first and foremost of the lines.*'

VILHELM HAMMERSHØI IN 1907, QUOTED IN FELIX KRÄMER'S 'VILHELM HAMMERSHØI: THE POETRY OF SILENCE', *HAMMERSHØI* EXHIBITION CATALOGUE, 2008

Unlike many impressionists, he embraced pure black as a colour in his art and thus created images of cool northern light, without shimmer or prismatic oscillation. If his paintings look as if they are covered with a gauzy veil, it is because often, in the last stages of a painting, he would apply a thin layer of transparent grey over the canvas,[2] as if muffling all sound, pausing a moving picture or stopping a clock. His is a palette that seems to whisper rather than shout. His colour harmonies evoke a sense of serenity, tranquillity and solitude, sometimes bordering on the uncanny.

Within his highly individual, reduced world of greys, whites and blues, Hammershøi masterfully played with contrasts of light and dark, and was likely influenced by James Abbott McNeill Whistler (see pages 68–71), an artist he admired. We know he tended to work on each canvas for a long time, with small, even brushstrokes. Like Monet (see pages 152–55), he preferred to use relatively dry paint, adding to the powdery and hazy appearance of his work.

The Vilhelm Hammershøi Digital Archive (ViHDA) project at the National Gallery of Denmark (SMK) is currently examining around eighty of his paintings. First results show that Hammershøi's palette was more versatile that it appears. He made use of modern pigments, such as cobalt blue and cadmium yellow. It is possible that the yellow blob of paint in the middle of this palette is cadmium yellow and was perhaps used alongside yellow ochre or Naples yellow to paint the sunlight falling into Strandgade 30, the brass door handles or the empty gilt picture frames in his compositions. Cobalt was used to create the delicate ranges of powdery blues and greys seen on the palette, and very small quantities of ultramarine and indigo have also been identified. As for his whites, he preferred lead white for ground layers and mixing, while cool zinc white was used where more brightness was needed, such as for the curtains and doors. At the other end of his mysterious, milky greyscale was bone black, which in his early work he used almost unmixed, but later softened by mixing it with browns.[3]

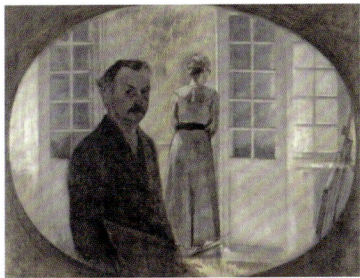

B.

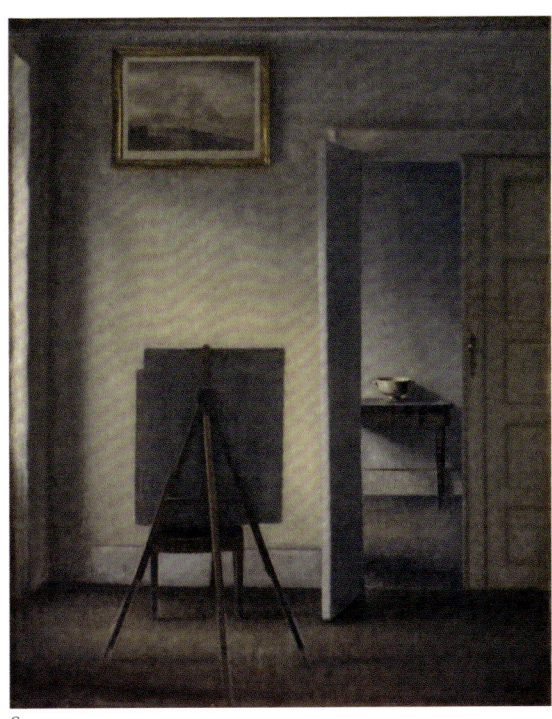

C.

A. *Interior with Woman at Piano, Strandgade 30*, Vilhelm Hammershøi, 1901, oil on canvas, 55.9 × 44.8 cm (22 × 17 ⅝ in.)

B. *Double Portrait of the Artist and his Wife*, Vilhelm Hammershøi, summer 1911, oil on canvas, 55.2 × 76 cm (21 ¾ × 29 ¾ in.)

C. *Interior with the Artist's Easel*, Vilhelm Hammershøi, oil on canvas, 84 × 69 cm (33 ⅛ × 27 ¼ in.)

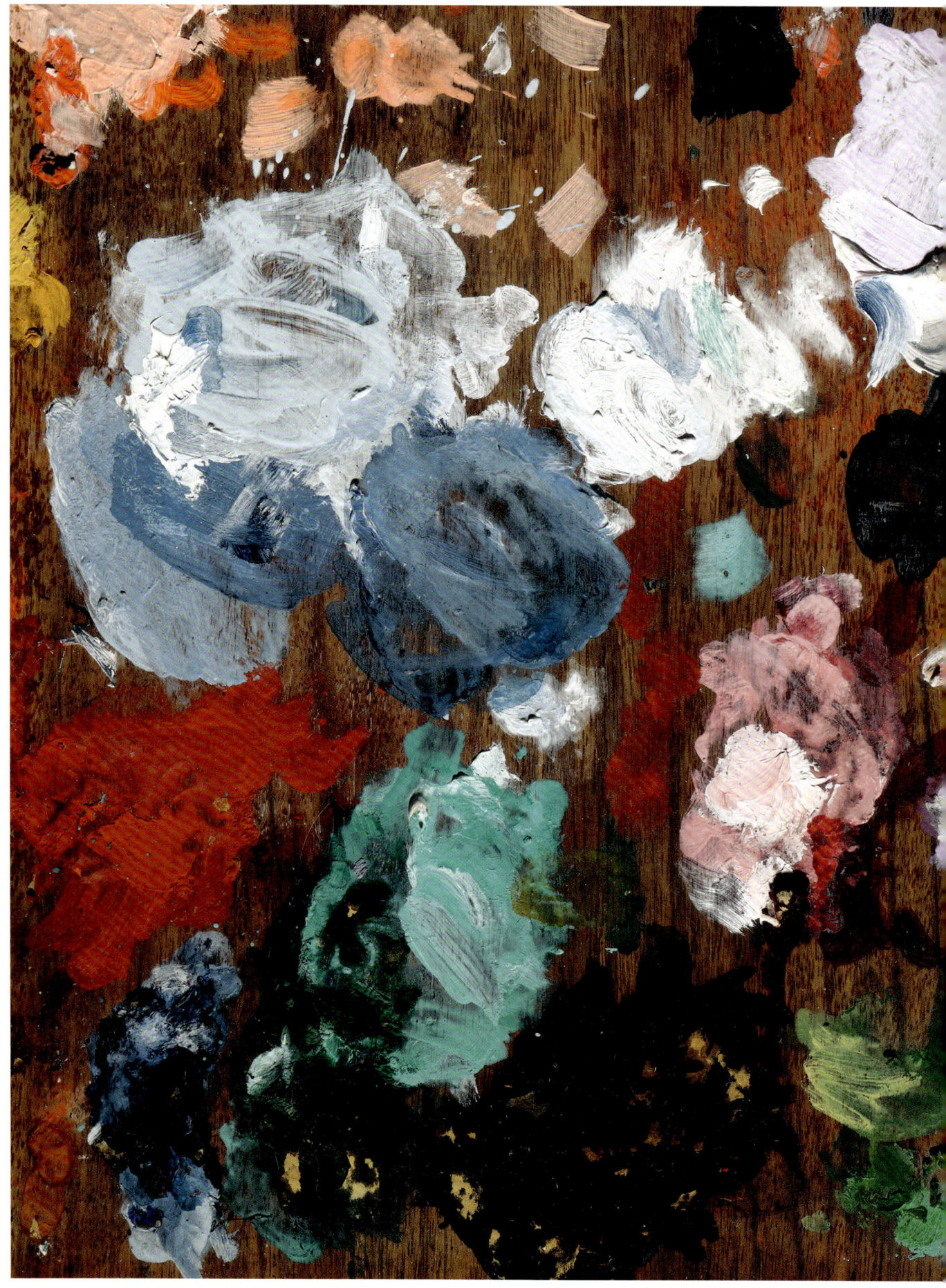

1901– 1930

The Experimental Palette

IN THIS EXCITING PERIOD IN THE VISUAL ARTS, we see many artists experimenting with colour as an expressive tool, moving gradually away from realistic detail and colouring. Yet, as their predecessors had done, they still largely relied on the traditional format and style of easel painting, using palettes, brushes and palette knives when painting in oil, and adjusting their tools when using watercolour paints. It is fascinating to see how their palettes reflect and deal with the move towards abstraction, abandoning classical and traditional composition and depiction. Academic rule books of taste and style were largely ripped up in this age of pure modernism, and some of the palettes we see in this section are wild, raw and wonderful, including that of Monet, used in his late period. We can clearly see him moving beyond the prismatic palette of the impressionists to a modern, almost abstract style.

EDVARD MUNCH 1863–1944

Symbolic, screaming colours

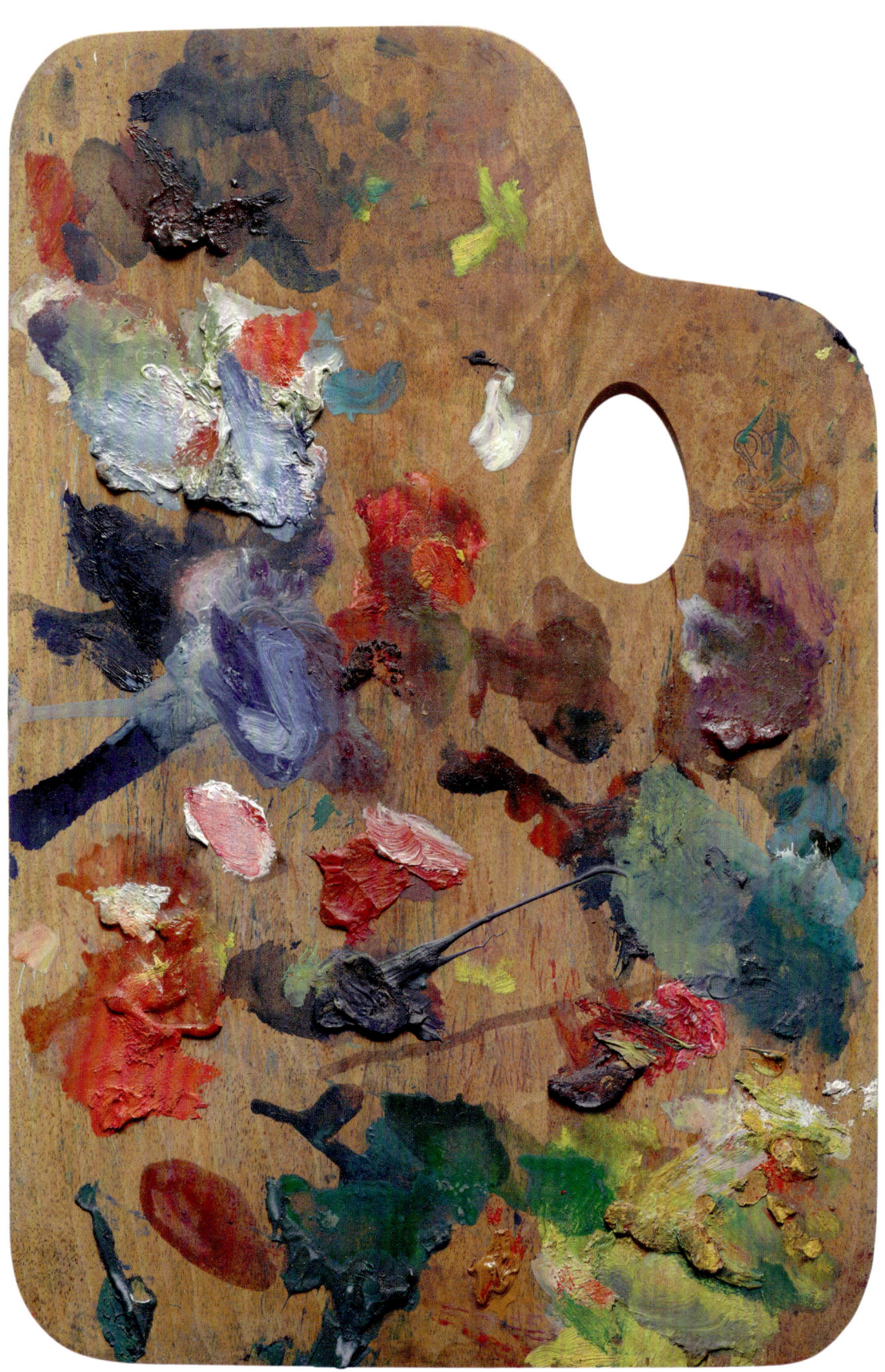

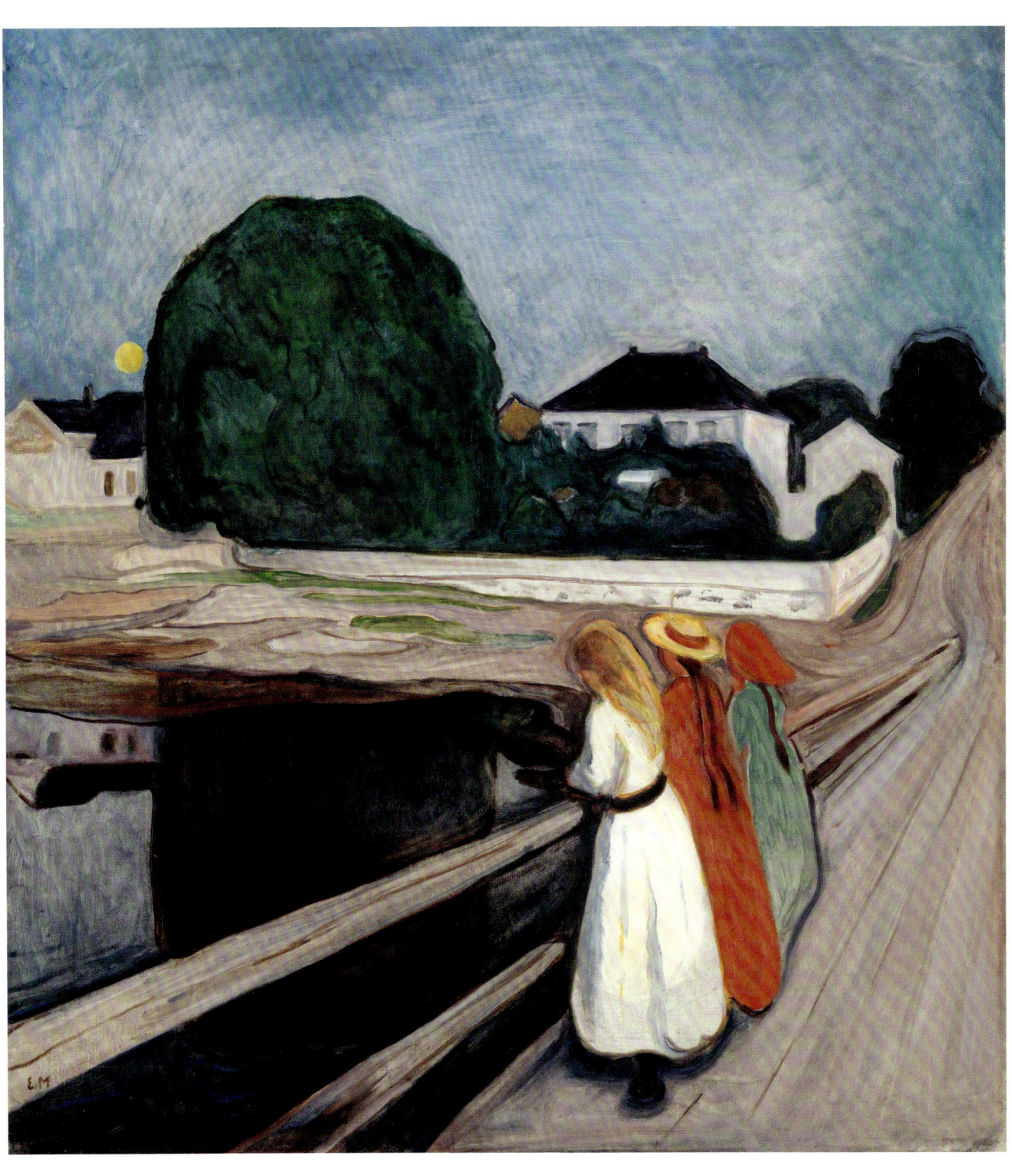

Edvard Munch's
palette
Undated
Paint on wood
43 × 29 cm
(17 × 11 ½ in.)

The Girls on the Bridge
Edvard Munch
1901
Oil on canvas
136 × 125 cm
(53 ⅝ × 49 ¼ in.)

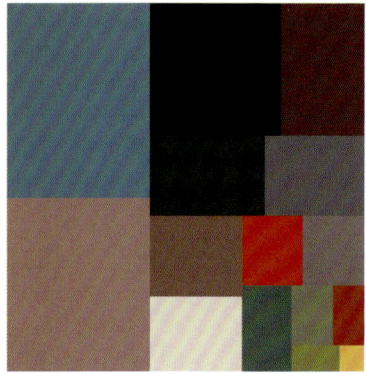

Proportional breakdown of colours used by Edvard
Munch in *The Girls on the Bridge*, 1901, displayed on
the previous page.

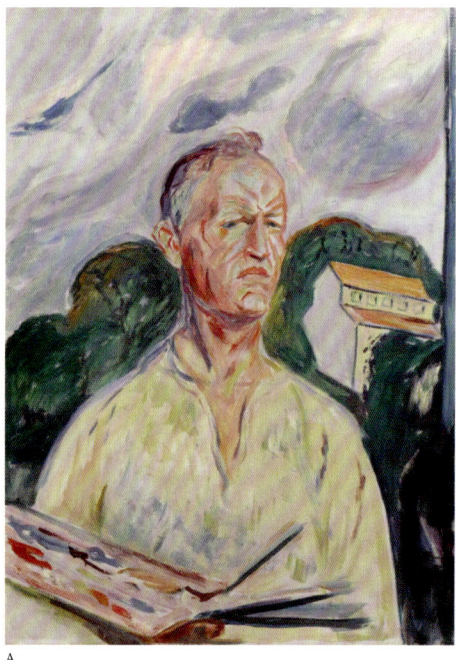

A.

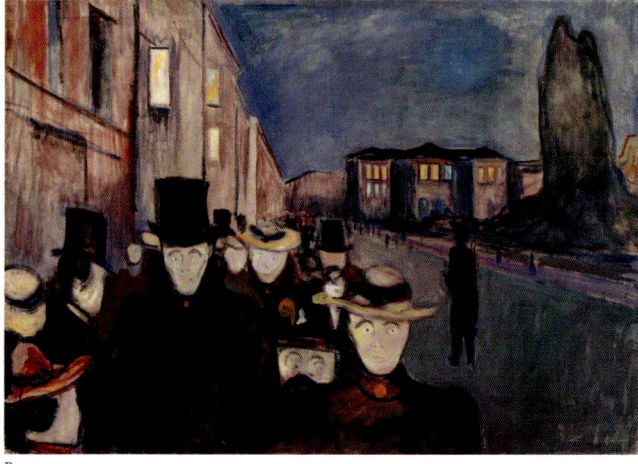

B.

THE NORWEGIAN PAINTER Edvard Munch was a
troubled and melancholy figure. In his art, he expressed
love, anxiety, fear and loneliness in exaggerated colours
and lines. He was famous for painting darkness and
shadows, both metaphorical and real, but he was also
a gifted painter of light, often including cosmic motifs
and atmospheric conditions in his compositions.
Several of his palettes survive and give us a sense
of Munch's intuitive use of colour as a symbolic tool,
a carrier of emotional meaning.

On this mid-size wooden palette, we see how
Munch applied thick blobs of oil paint seemingly
randomly on the surface, separated at first and in
no particular order. We get a sense that, rather than
thinking carefully about mixing certain shades and
tints, he may have thought more about the layout of
the composition of the painting he was working on,
and where to place and juxtapose colours. There is no
structure or strict methodology here, nor on his other
palettes. For Munch, the palette was a simple, practical
surface on which he could experiment with colour in
a completely abstract manner. In a self-portrait from
1926, he depicts his palette in much the same way, with
bold blobs of pure primaries thickly put on, ready to
be transferred to the canvas with broad brushes.

We don't know exactly which painting this palette
was used for, but the colours of this version of *The Girls
on the Bridge* from 1901 show similarities to it. Some
mixing has clearly taken place, and we see, for example,
that although in his lifetime plenty of ready-made
greens were available, he appears to have created his
own complex shades of green through mixture. Munch
opted for a limited range of pure colours, which he
applied in his paintings in an expressionist manner,
with little taste for subtle blending.

There is very little white involved (although Munch
did paint many surprisingly luminous pictures), but
where he uses white, for example in the dress of one
of the young women, it is a powerful visual contrast to
the darkness she is looking into, the murky shadow of
a large tree in the dark blue water of the river they are
crossing. There is a hint of the wide range of melancholy
blues Munch used in his work (perhaps the colour
he understood best) on the palette. There is further
chromatic brightness in the colours of the other two
girls, including intense reds, a bright yellow hat, and
a light green dress, all of which are also present on the
palette. Here, as in most of his works, colour is imbued
with symbolism and carries meaning. This is perhaps
most apparent in all four versions of his most famous
work, *The Scream* (1893), in which the jarring colours
seem to swirl and undulate and take on a synaesthetic
quality (as implied in the title of the work).

'*One must paint precisely the fleeting moment of significance – one must capture the exact experience separating that significant moment from the next – the exact moment when the motif struck one.*'

EDVARD MUNCH IN 1890, QUOTED IN SUE PRIDEAUX'S *EDVARD MUNCH: BEHIND THE SCREAM*, 2007

Although expressionist in his intentions, Munch was never really part of a particular group or -ism in the art world. His work reflected new developments and ideas of his time: he had a great interest in new inventions and technologies, such as radiation and artificial lighting, and was intrigued by psychoanalysis, spiritualism and theosophy. Around the time Munch was painting some of his most famous works, Annie Besant and Charles Webster Leadbeater published several books on their theosophical theories. *Man Visible and Invisible* (1902) and *Thought-Forms* (1905) included abstract or semi-abstract images of spiritual forms, expressed predominantly in cloud-like shapes or rays of colour, which bear a striking similarity to some of Munch's compositions. Both books included a frontispiece with a grid, or 'key', of colours, each one assigned a specific emotion or character trait. It almost reads like a key to Munch's work. We do not know for certain whether Munch read Besant and Leadbeater's books, but he was most certainly aware of the various spiritual movements and ideas emerging in Europe and America.[1]

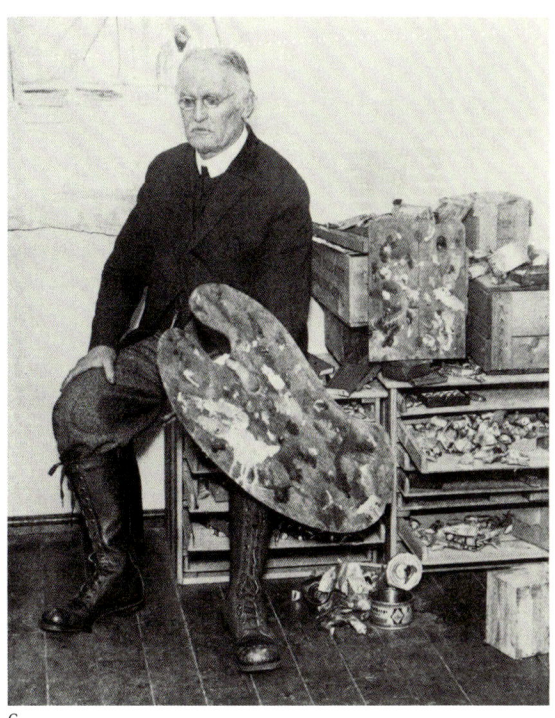

C.

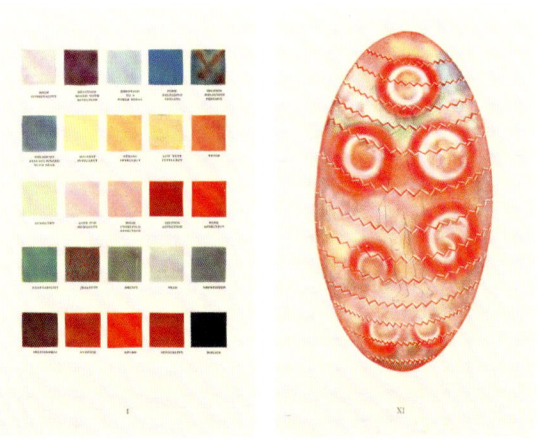

A. *Self-portrait with Palette*, Edvard Munch, 1926, oil on canvas, 90 × 68 cm (35 ½ × 26 ⅞ in.)

B. *Evening on Karl Johan*, Edvard Munch, 1892, oil on canvas, 84.5 × 121 cm (33 ¼ × 47 ⅝ in.)

C. Edvard Munch holding a palette, originally published in *Der Querschnitt* (The Cross Section), 1931

D. Plates I (frontispiece) and XI, from C. W. Leadbeater's *Man Visible and Invisible*, 1903 edition

D.

PAULA MODERSOHN-BECKER 1876–1907

A palette carrying the depth of colour

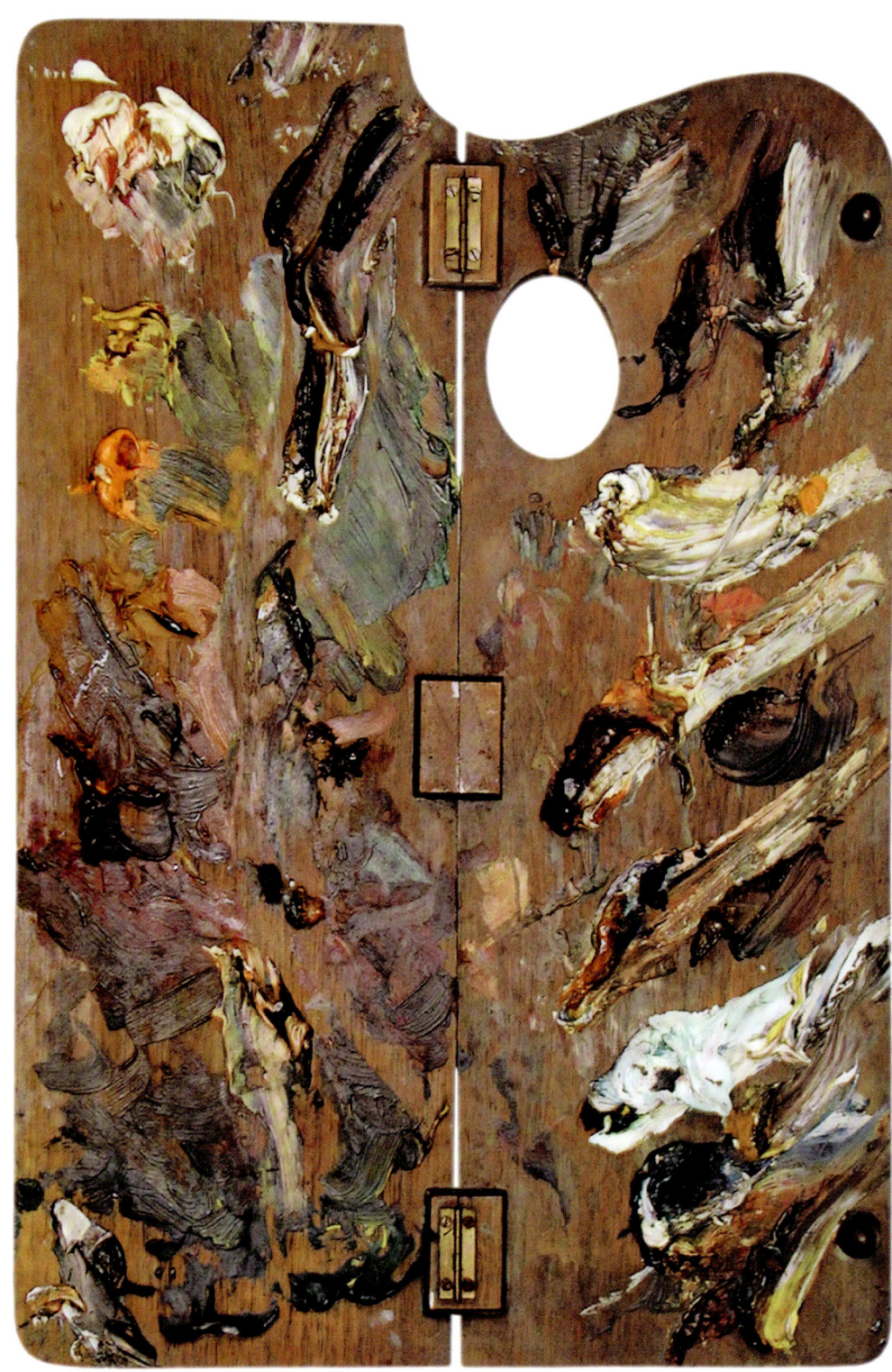

Paula Modersohn-Becker's
last palette
1907
Paint on wood and metal

*Self-portrait as a Half-length
Nude with Amber Necklace I*
Paula Modersohn-Becker
Summer 1906
Oil tempera on cardboard
62.2 × 48.2 cm
(24 ½ × 19 in.)

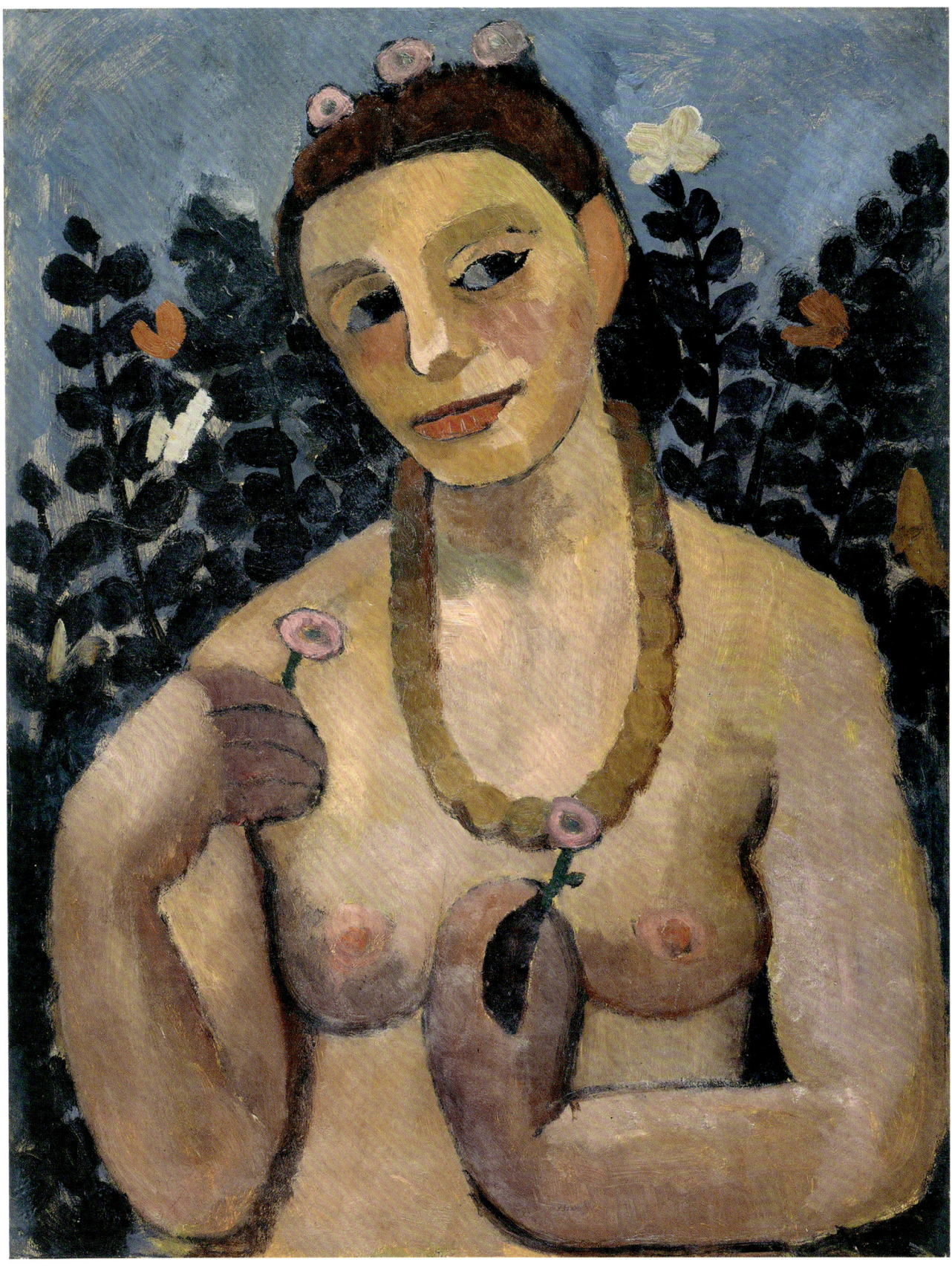

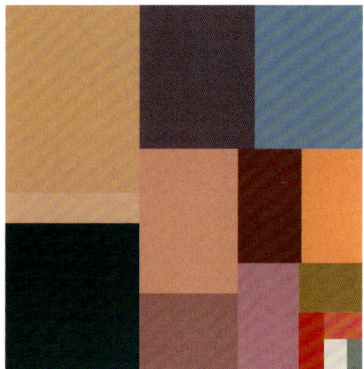

Proportional breakdown of colours used by Paula Modersohn-Becker in *Self-portrait as a Half-length Nude with Amber Necklace I*, summer 1906, displayed on the previous page.

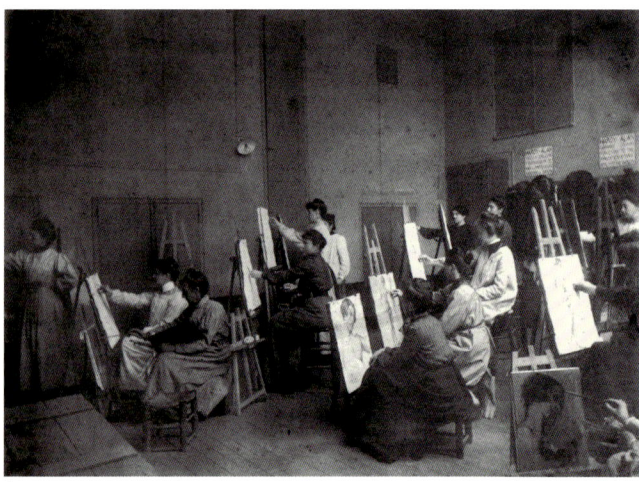

A.

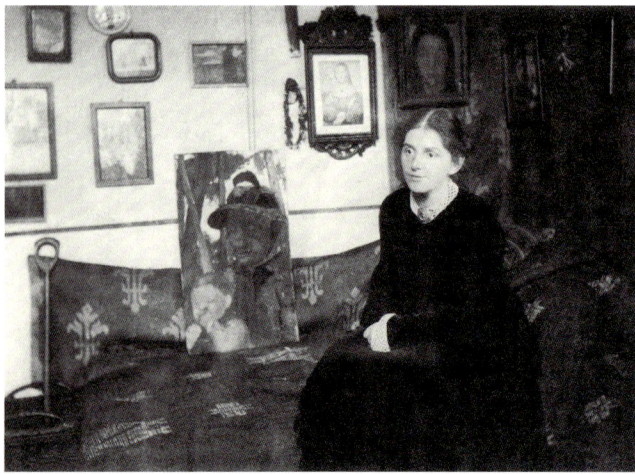

B.

THIS PALETTE IS A POIGNANT SYMBOL of an astonishing artist's life cut short. It belonged to Paula Modersohn-Becker, who lived her brief life with great intensity, sensitivity and devotion to her art. Her sudden death at the age of thirty-one meant that her studio provides an insight into the work of a radical, modernist artist at an early high point in her career. This folding palette was among the items left in her studio, and it is highly likely she used it for her last works. The paintings shown here date from the last three years of her life when she was becoming even more confident and experimental in her distinctive style of painting solid, sometimes monumental figures and shapes in saturated, warm colours, often scratching and modelling the paint surface on the canvas to give it more texture. The small still life with a jug and a bunch of flowers (image D.) may be the last painting she ever worked on.

Many aspects of her technique and colour preferences are present on the palette: thick, assured brushstrokes; rich, muted browns and ochres combined with vibrant zinc white, cadmium yellow and hints of viridian and French ultramarine. In *Self-portrait as a Half-length Nude with Amber Necklace I*, she employs these warm earth pigments to paint her naked body and the titular necklace, while the foliage and sky in the background are deep mixed greens and dusky blues. The pictorial space is dotted with expressively painted, abstract flowers in pink, white, red and orange. Brushstrokes resembling these shapes can be seen on the lower half of the canvas. There is a matte appearance to Modersohn-Becker's work and the paint left on the palette. She predominantly worked in oil, for which she developed a fondness early on during her training. In 1897 she noted: 'I love oil paints. They are so juicy and strong, and so lovely to work with, after the timid pastels.'[1] Yet, she also combined oil with tempera, perhaps to achieve the matte finish.

Modersohn-Becker lived at a time when few institutions offered professional training to women. The great academies of the arts were still not allowing women to enrol as students. She took private lessons in Bremen, and in 1892 spent some months at the St John's Wood Art School in London. Later, she attended the Verein der Berliner Künstlerinnen (Berlin Women Artists' Association). She is most associated with the artist colony in Worpswede in rural northern Germany, which she joined in 1895, and where she met her future husband, Otto Modersohn. Paris beckoned, and at the start of the new century she went to the Académie Colarossi, spent time with Rainer Maria Rilke and Auguste Rodin, and revelled in seeing the art collections of the Louvre and the work of French avant-garde groups.

'I love the depth of colour like my life.'

PAULA MODERSOHN-BECKER, LETTER
TO OTTO MODERSOHN, 16 FEBRUARY 1901

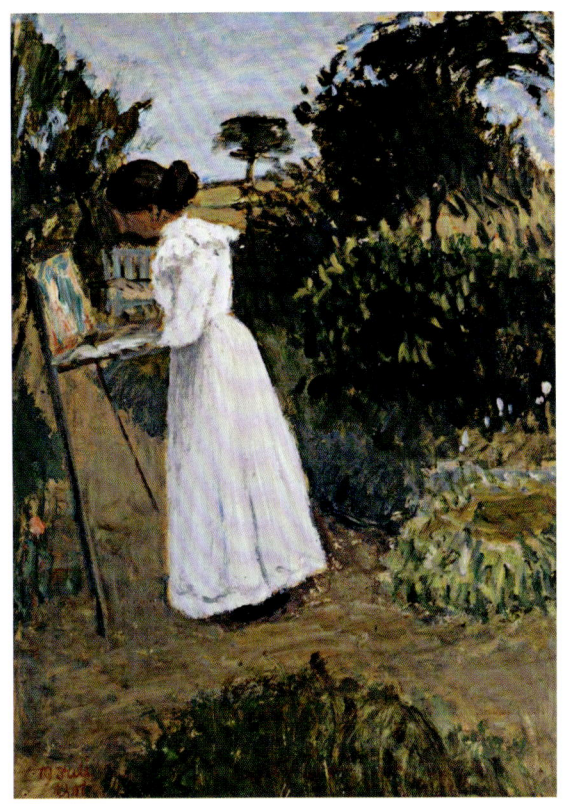

C.

She struggled to combine marital life with her desire to be an artist. In 1906 she left her husband and spent more time in Paris, but returned to him shortly after. She died from an embolism after giving birth to their daughter Mathilde, leaving behind a large body of work, and is now rightly acknowledged as a pioneering figure of expressionism. She produced many images of nude women in a bold, non-erotic, sculptural manner, and may have been the first woman artist to paint a portrait of herself naked and pregnant.

Colour excited her greatly. In her many letters and diary entries she often described the colours and shades of landscapes, cities and people, and how colours create mood. She also recorded her own responses to colour. Frequently, this is in the context of flowers and scents, suggesting synaesthetic sensations. On her first visit to Paris, she described her devotion to her identity as an artist: 'I love colour. It must yield to me. And I love art. I serve it on my knees, and it must become mine.' But she was equally sensitive to the 'beautiful…exquisite brown' of the moors near Worpswede.[2] The symbolic and emotional power of colour was a theme running through her life and art. When in 1901 she wrote to her husband from Berlin about loving 'the depth of colour' and needing it in her life, she uses colour as a metaphor for her thirst for life, but there are just as many comments by the artist where she revels in the materiality of paint. After her death, Rilke wrote a requiem for his friend, in which he touches on her highly developed sense of colour: 'Because this you understood: ripe fruits. / You placed them in bowls in front of you / and found the colours that resembled their weight.'[3]

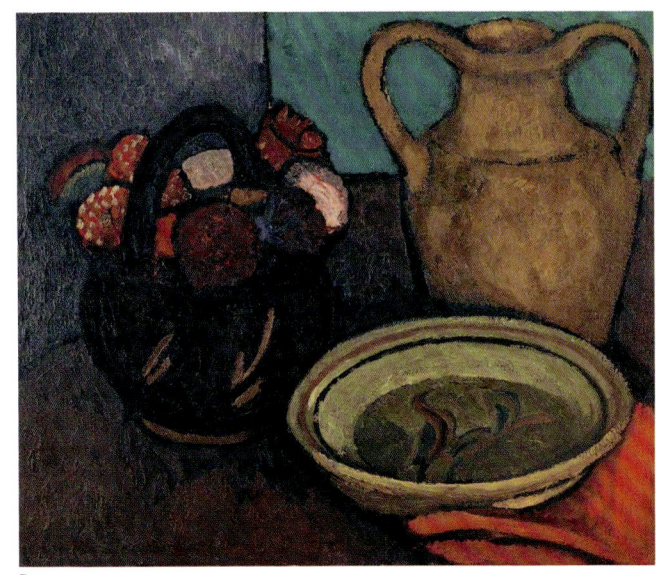

A.   Women's art class at the Académie Colarossi, Paris, France, *c.* 1900
B.   Paula Modersohn-Becker in her studio, Brünjes, Germany, *c.* 1905
C.   *Paula Modersohn-Becker Painting in the Garden*, Otto Modersohn, 1901, oil on cardboard, 58 × 41 cm (22 ⅞ × 16 ¼ in.)
D.   *Still Life with Clay Jug and Dahlias*, Paula Modersohn-Becker, 1907, oil tempera on canvas, 46.5 × 55.4 cm (18 ⅜ × 21 ⅞ in.)

D.

CLAUDE MONET 1840–1926

Turning oil into shimmering images of water

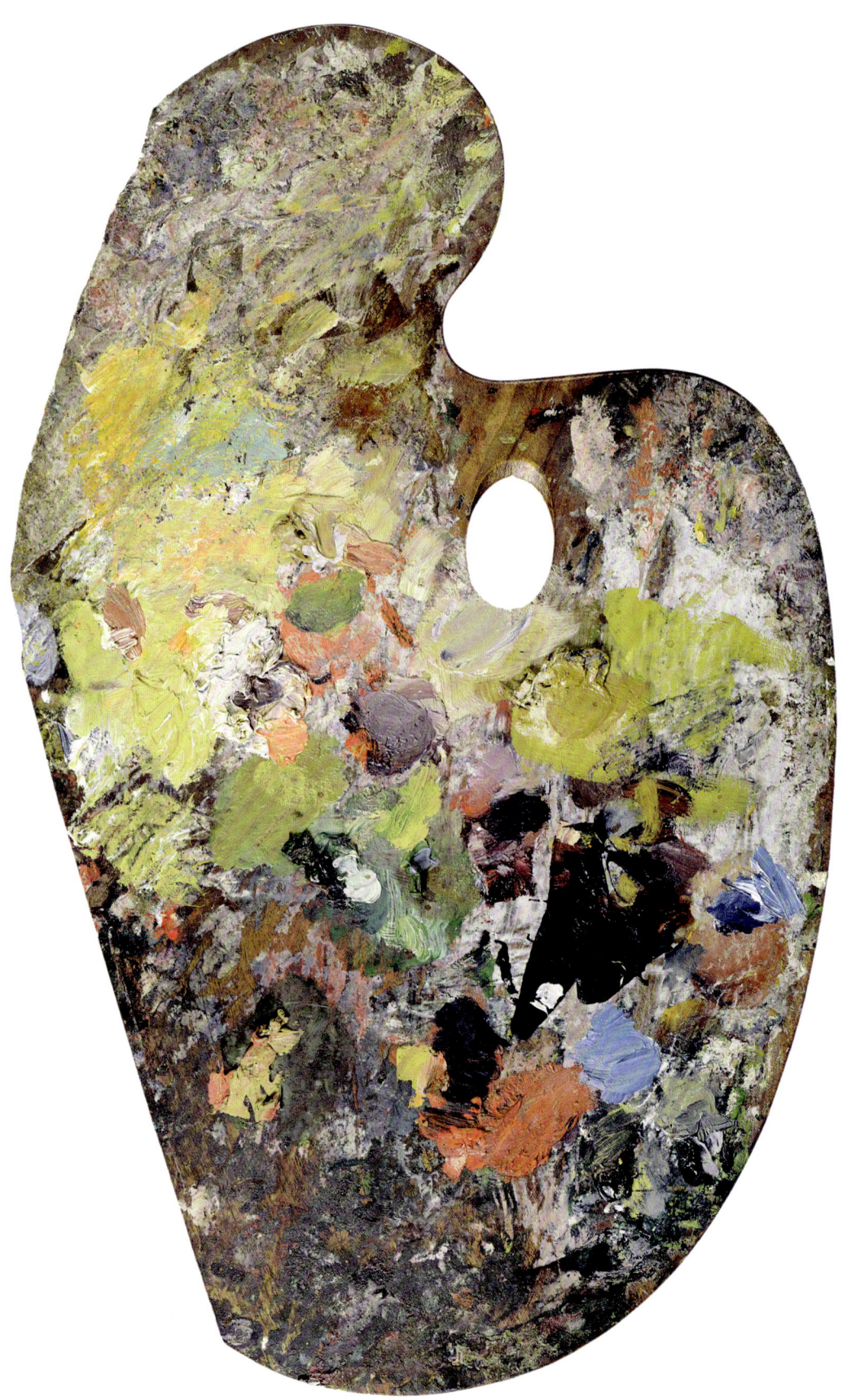

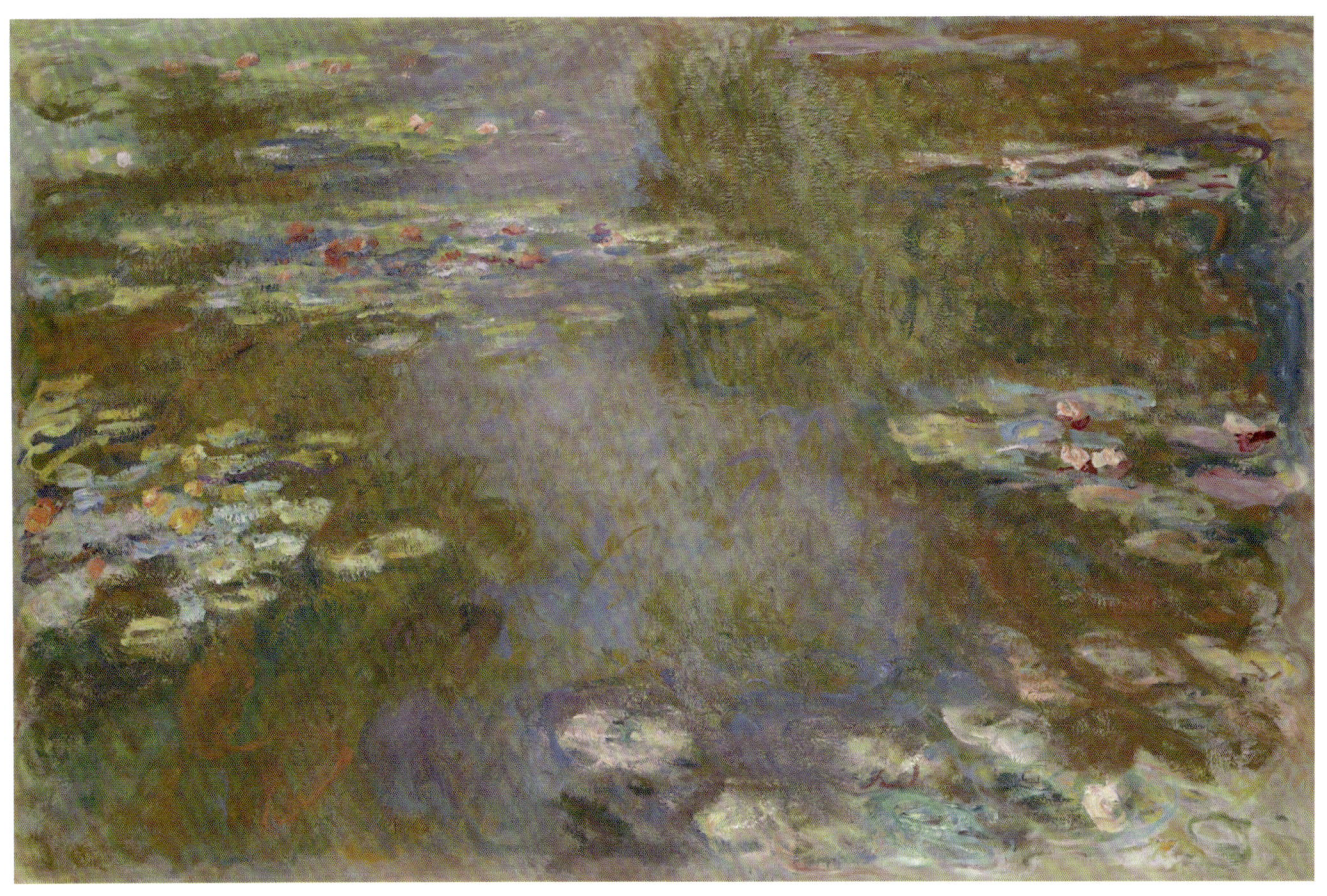

Claude Monet's
palette
Undated
Paint on wood
32.5 × 51 cm
(12 ⅞ × 20 ⅛ in.)

Water Lily Pond
Claude Monet
1917–19
Oil on canvas
130.2 × 201.9 cm
(51 ½ × 79 ½ in.)

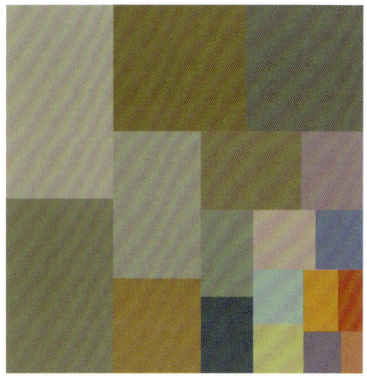

Proportional breakdown of colours used by Claude Monet in *Water Lily Pond*, 1917–19, displayed on the previous page.

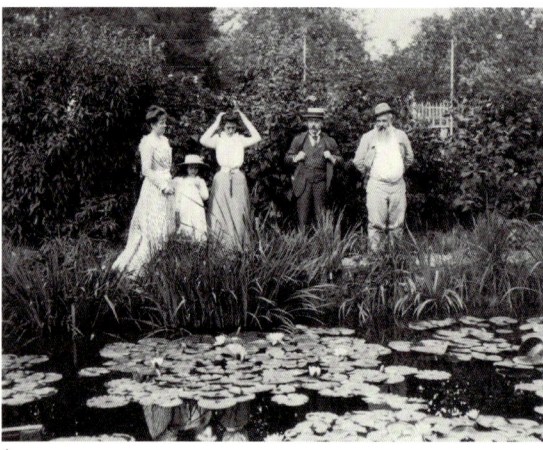

A.

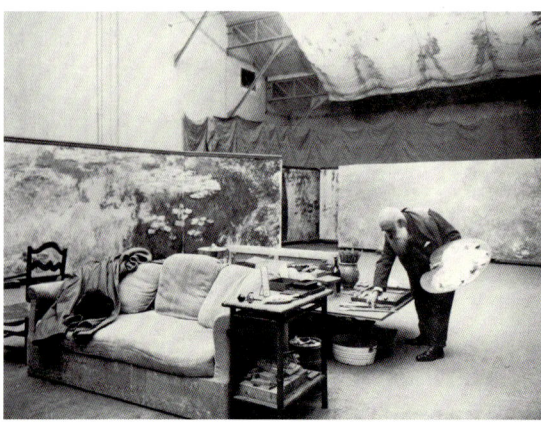

B.

FROM 1883 UNTIL THE END OF HIS LIFE, Claude Monet lived at Giverny, France, where he cultivated his famous flower garden and water lily pond. Marcel Proust once described the garden as a living painting, resembling a ready-made palette with complete colour harmonies.[1] He imagined the artist strolling, working and living in this palette of carefully tamed and designed nature. Although we mostly associate Monet with painting *en plein air*, his tools, motifs and working methods varied greatly during his long career.

This palette, although undated, was likely used by Monet at Giverny in the last few years of his life. During this time, despite his advancing age and problems with his eyesight, he embarked on several painting projects of epic proportions, including the *Nymphéas* (*Water Lilies*) series. The palette, when compared closely to some of his late work, shows how Monet's style and conceptual use of colour had developed over the decades. He had moved further and further away from realistic depiction and naturalistic colouring in favour of almost abstract compositions that made full use of the inherent power of colour. In many of the water lily paintings, he abandoned visual anchors such as a horizon, solid forms such as trees or figures, and even the idea of a vista. Instead, he used a variety of modern pigments and paints available to create multi-layered visions of the effects of light and shadow on barely moving, shimmering water, punctuated by cloud-like shapes of water lilies.

Monet played down the number of colours he used. He claimed more than once that his palette was deliberately limited, comprising only lead white, cadmium yellow, vermilion, deep madder lake, cobalt blue and emerald green (*vert émeraude*).[2] However, surviving lists of pigments bought and used by him over the years present a different picture,[3] as does pigment analysis carried out on some of the water lily paintings by Ashok Roy at the National Gallery, London, in 2007,[4] and more recently by Kim Muir and Ken Sutherland at the Art Institute of Chicago.[5] This research confirmed that Monet made full use of the pigments and paints available at the beginning of the 20th century, including artificial ultramarine, a wider range of cadmium colours than he had stated, several ochres, lake pigments, as well as vermilion and synthesized malachite. The artificial malachite was mixed with viridian to create the subtle shades of lily leaves on the water's surface, as well as green reflections of overhanging trees. These different types of green can clearly be seen in the centre of this palette and around its lower part. Monet's colour lists and the pigment analysis contain several types of cadmium yellow, which were used to create lighter shades of green for sunlit areas and occupy a large part of the palette above the thumbhole.

'I'd prefer to be blind and keep my memories of the beauties I've always seen.'

CLAUDE MONET, LETTER TO GEORGE CLEMENCEAU,
30 AUGUST 1923

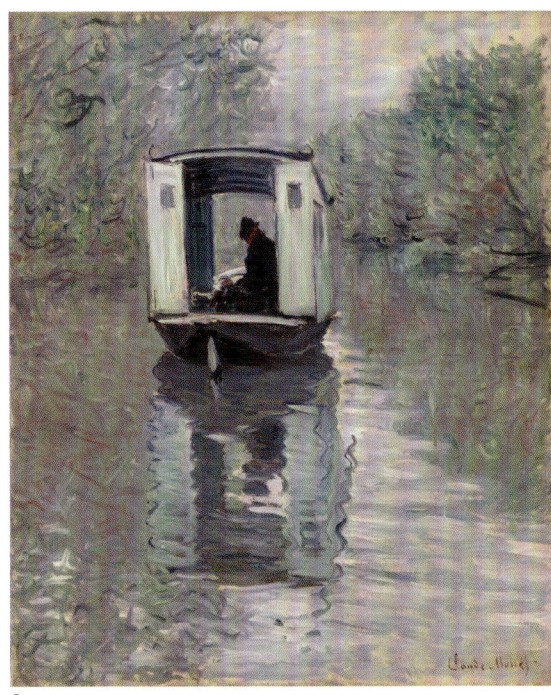

C.

Apart from the brilliant viridian, one of the most expensive pigments used by Monet was a light cadmium violet, essential to create the subtle shades of blue and purple in his late work. On this palette, there may be some evidence of it in the centre near his partially mixed greens. Two types of blue are also visible, likely French ultramarine and cobalt blue. Monet also added texture, shimmer and depth to his late paintings by combining warm and cold colours, for example, by mixing cool and transparent red lakes with warm, opaque vermilion. These reds can be seen both on the palette and as red lilies in the painting shown here. As a white pigment, he preferred a luminous, warm, lead-based, silvery white (*blanc d'argent*), once described by a visitor to his studio in 1918 as 'mountains of white snowy peaks' on his palette.[6]

The paint on this palette, which resembles the almost-abstract water lily paintings, also shows that not all of the mixing took place on the palette. Monet would scoop up the paint, place it on the canvas, where he had already placed layers of dried or half-dried paint, and then drag, swirl and move it around, creating his liquid visions of deep blue and green water.

Monet was not particularly interested in colour theory or science, nor in the meticulous planning of a palette, but he was fully aware of the optical qualities of colours and colour harmonies. He never varnished any of his paintings to avoid the tonal interference caused by the varnish and to retain the pure chromatic effect of his compositions. By the time he used this palette, he had not only replaced naturalistic modelling with colour and texture as the main motif, he had also changed the scale of his work dramatically, creating huge, almost immersive paintings. In 1916 he had built a new top-lit studio in Giverny that could accommodate canvases that were up to 3.6 metres (11 feet 9 ¾ in.) high and 8 metres (26 feet) wide. He had come a long way since he worked in a small floating studio boat on the Epte and Seine. Late in life, he was commanding a huge indoor space to turn his passion for water, colour and nature into monumental, shimmering visions in oil.

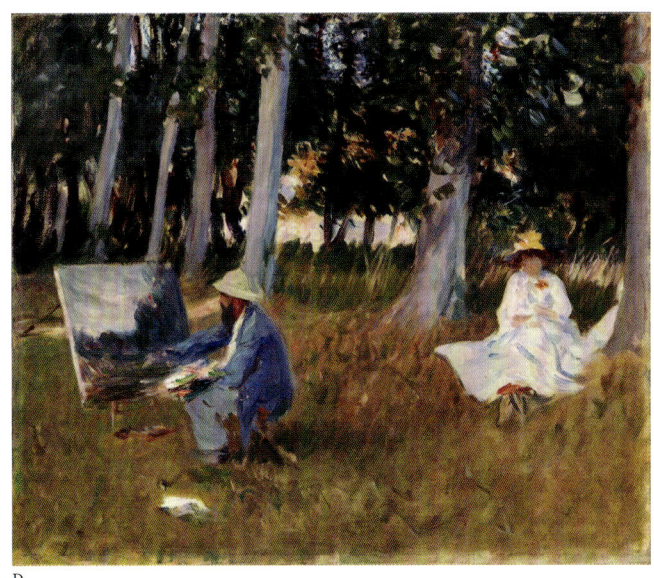

D.

A. (Left to right) Germaine Hoschedé, Lili Butler, Mme Joseph Durand-Ruel, Georges Durand-Ruel and Claude Monet, Giverny, Normandy, France, 1900

B. Claude Monet in his studio, Giverny, Normandy, France, photograph by Henri Manuel, *c.* 1920, gelatin silver print

C. *The Studio Boat*, Claude Monet, 1876, oil on canvas, 72.7 × 60 cm (28 ⅝ × 23 ⅝ in.)

D. *Claude Monet Painting by the Edge of a Wood*, John Singer Sargent, *c.* 1885, oil on canvas, 54 × 64.8 cm (21 ⅜ × 25 ⅝ in.)

PIERRE BONNARD 1867–1947

The colours of memories

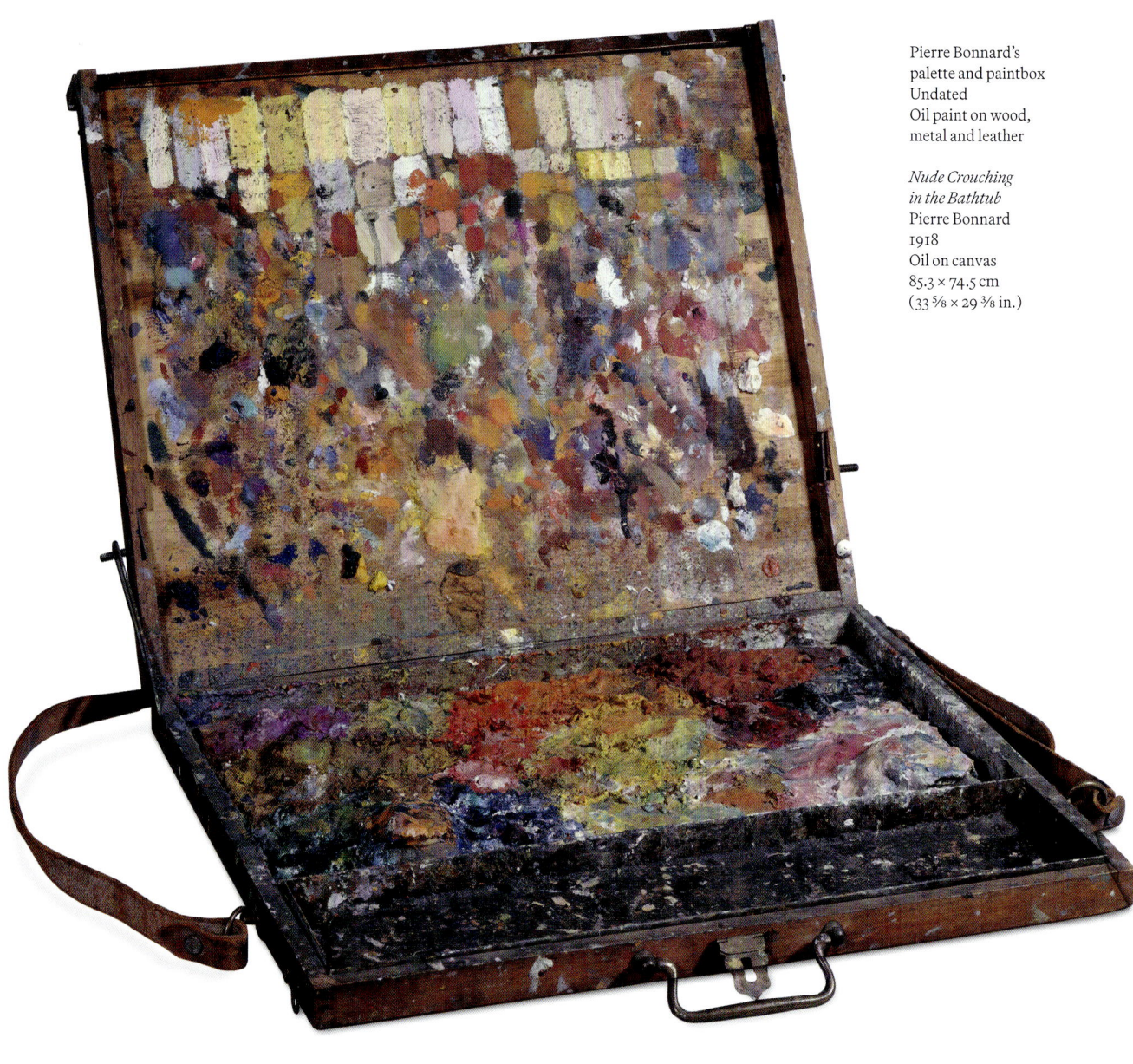

Pierre Bonnard's
palette and paintbox
Undated
Oil paint on wood,
metal and leather

*Nude Crouching
in the Bathtub*
Pierre Bonnard
1918
Oil on canvas
85.3 × 74.5 cm
(33 ⅝ × 29 ⅜ in.)

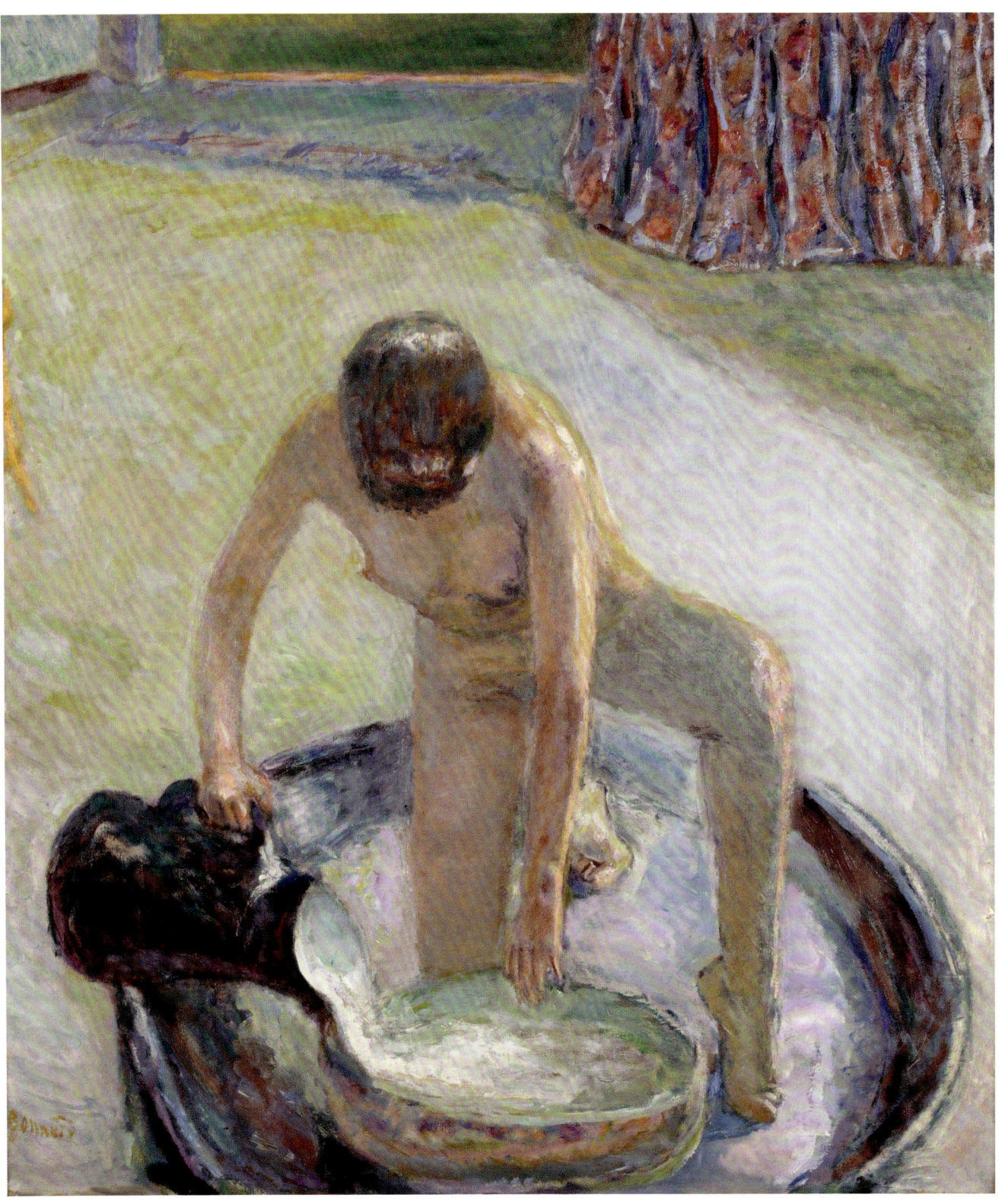

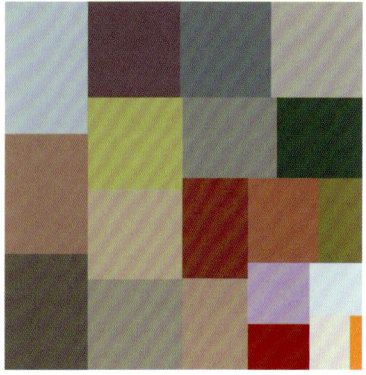

Proportional breakdown of colours used by Pierre Bonnard in *Nude Crouching in the Bathtub*, 1918, displayed on the previous page.

PIERRE BONNARD'S STYLE was often tentative, but there is ample evidence that in spite of what Picasso (see pages 202–5) once so dismissively referred to as 'a potpourri of indecision',[1] his pictorial visions were in fact subtly and deliberately structured. In an exchange with Henri Matisse (see pages 160–63), Bonnard discussed the importance of laying down the colours on a palette, considering this tool the starting point of a work of art, unadulterated by interpretation, mixing and iconographical context: 'The painter's only solid ground is the palette and colours, but as soon as the colours achieve an illusion, they are no longer judged and the stupidities begin'.[2]

Although the palette shown here, which is essentially a paintbox, the interior surfaces of which have been used as palettes, is shown after heavy use, it still provides some information about how Bonnard laid out his colours. In the lid of the box, there are rows of neat paint samples of mostly very light shades of yellow and lilac, with an interfering dark ochre that may have been the intended tonal range for the painting. After three rows, the layout dissolves into what looks like trial mixtures and combinations of broken colour. Here, darker shades of blue make an appearance, perhaps used to create some of his ubiquitous foreground shadows.

The actual palette in the main compartment is completely covered in oil paint, providing evidence of Bonnard's dynamic and intuitive painting style, as well as his strong belief that there should be no gaps in a composition. A closer look at what appears to be messy mixing reveals that there is method here: Bonnard's initial arrangement of paints seems to have followed that of a standard colour wheel. The primaries are located in the centre with mixtures and lighter or darker shades radiating from it. Although it is not known which works he created with this particular palette, there are some colour mixtures visible that appear frequently in his paintings. In the top right corner is a darker shade of red, similar to the one seen in the top right corner of the painting of his wife Marthe in a bathtub. It also closely resembles the shadowy water jug Marthe is holding. Most prominent, though, are the various shades of violet, pink and purple, some achieved by adding large amounts of white, to create shimmering effects. In this painting we see a luminous pinkish violet that represents the metal inside of the tub and the water in which Marthe washes herself. Similar colours are visible in the bottom right corner of the paintbox. They were likely created with some of Bonnard's favoured pigments, such as cobalt violet, alizarin crimson, Prussian blue and lead white.

Often discussed in relation to the impressionists and their legacy, Bonnard drew no direct influence from them and criticized their style later, although he valued the work of Gauguin and his early radical use of colour.

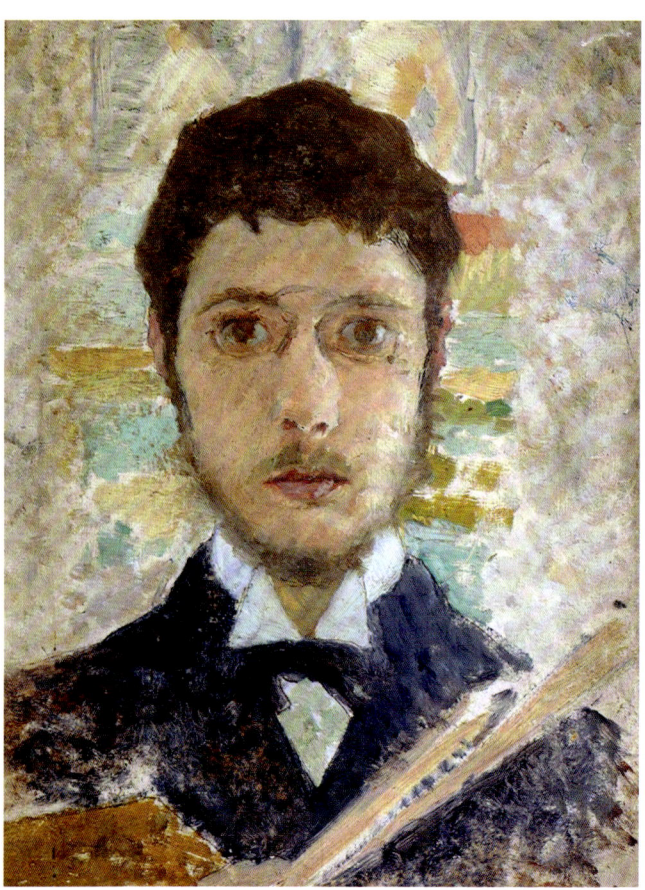

A.

'The painter's only solid ground is the palette and colours.'

PIERRE BONNARD, LETTER TO HENRI MATISSE,
1 FEBUARY 1935

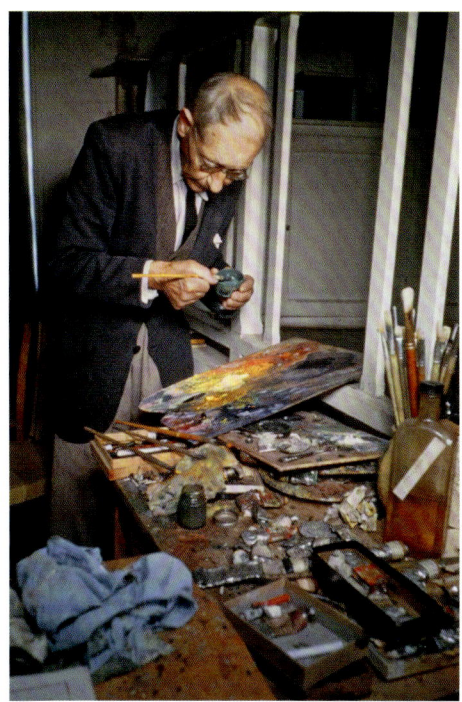

B.

Despite being a member of the loosely structured Nabis group, which advocated the value of decorative painting, Bonnard was an artist without appetite for formal theory or strict schools. He defied definition and pursued his own idiosyncratic path in painting. Yet, he also reflects the times he lived in, especially in respect of artists' materials. Beginning his career in the 1890s, he made full use of the numerous bright, stable, ready-made pigments and paints that had been developed in the 19th century, such as artificial ultramarine, chrome yellows, oranges and greens, and cobalt and cadmium colours.

Bonnard drew inspiration from old masters and travels to North Africa and Germany, but also to print culture, in particular Japanese woodblock prints and colour lithography. This is reflected in his use of colour patterns and a strange but effective flatness in many of his works. Visiting an exhibition of Japanese prints and books in 1890, he realized that 'colour could express everything...with no need for relief or texture'.[3] Colour and shape, rather than naturalistic detail, became the visual building blocks of his paintings, which seem to be glowing with light. Unlike the impressionists, he also embraced darkness, and the eeriness of the colouring of some of his works derives from shadowy figures or objects in the foreground of a composition, created by liberal use of blacks, greys, dark blues and browns.

Perhaps surprisingly, Bonnard rarely painted *en plain air* or directly onto a stretched canvas. Instead, he produced many preparatory sketches and photographs that paved the way to a finished painting. A fellow painter who once accompanied him on a painting excursion recalled Bonnard remaining in the car, not sketching at all and commenting that he was only observing. When he made sketches, they were almost exclusively in pencil. He occasionally recorded colour notes but mostly Bonnard painted his colours from memory. His was a highly subjective colour vision. Over his long career, he developed his own assured language and structure of colour, and was one of the first artists to truly use colour as an expressive and symbolic tool.

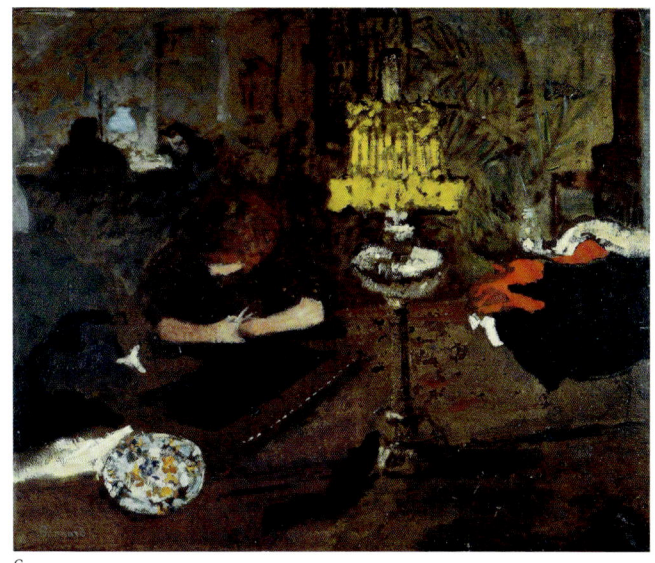

C.

A. *Self-portrait*, Pierre Bonnard, 1889, oil on cardboard, 21 × 17 cm (8 ⅜ × 6 ¾ in.)
B. Pierre Bonnard painting in the studio at his home in Le Cannet, France, photograph by Gisèle Freund, 1946
C. *Young Woman by Lamplight*, Pierre Bonnard, *c.* 1898, oil on canvas, 61.5 × 75 cm (24 ¼ × 29 ⅝ in.)

HENRI MATISSE <small>1869–1954</small>

A pure, emotional palette

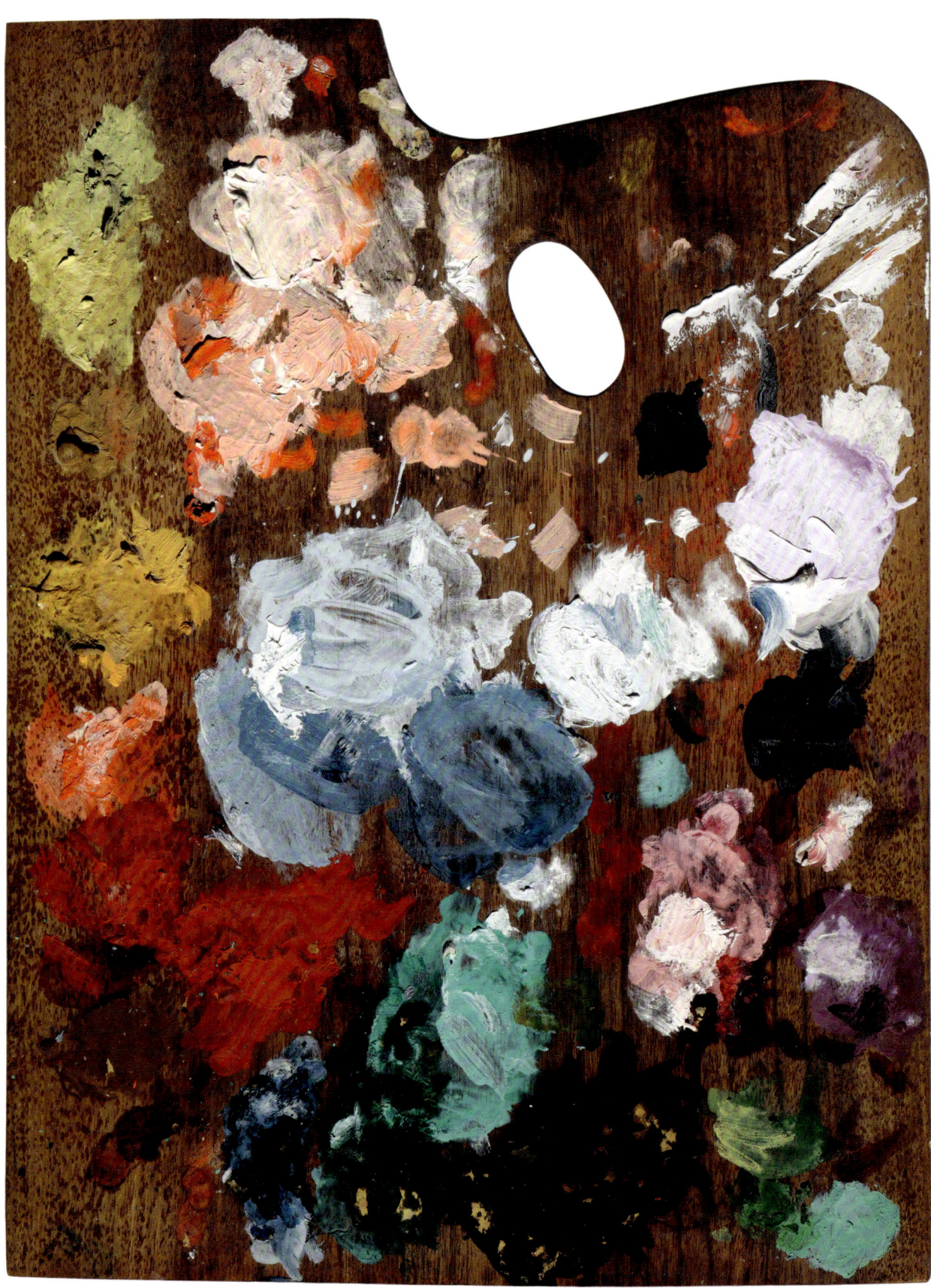

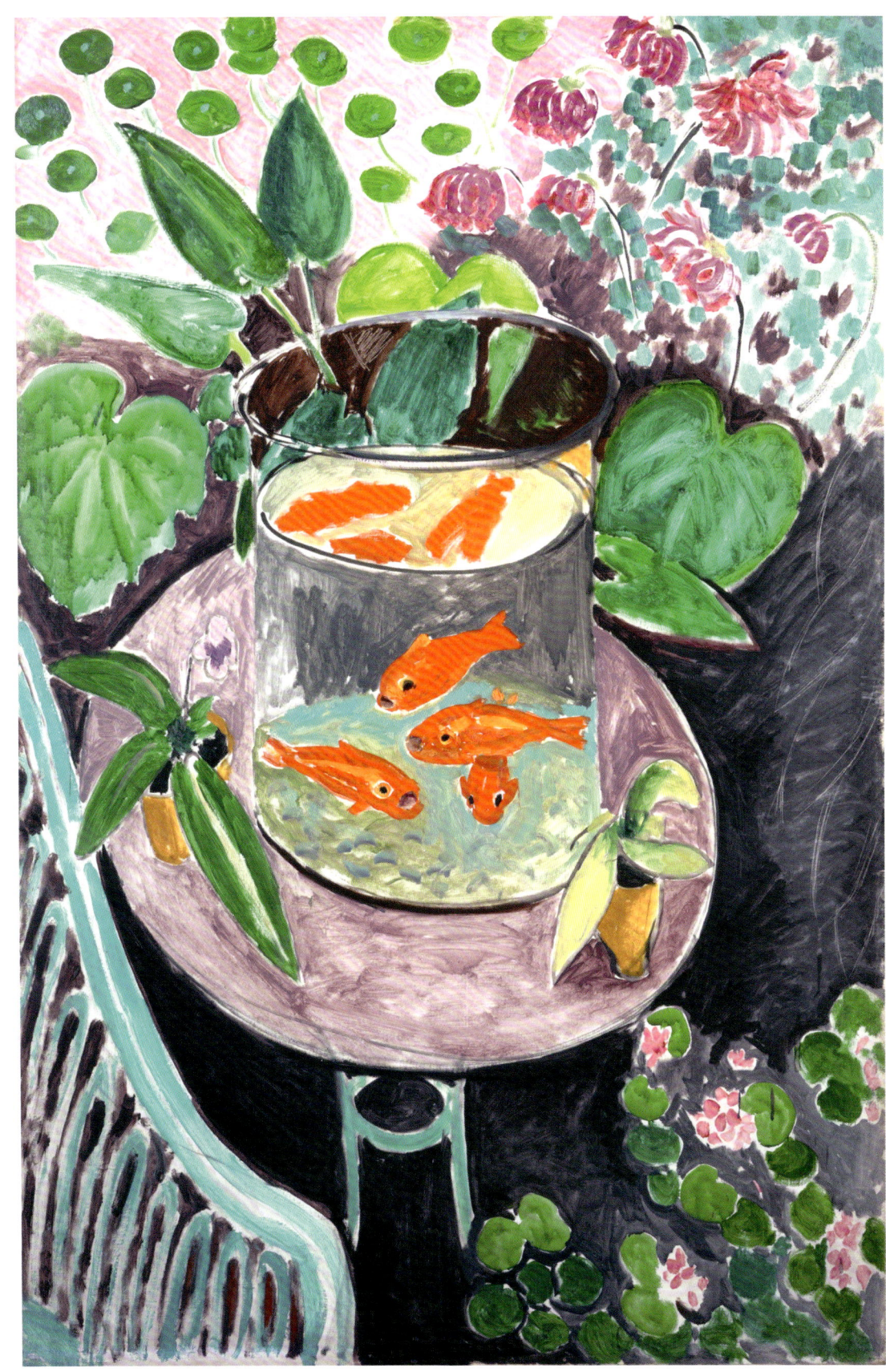

Henri Matisse's palette
Undated
Oil on wood (walnut)
48.5 × 38 cm
(19 ⅛ × 15 in.)

Goldfish
Henri Matisse
1912
Oil on canvas
140 × 98 cm
(55 ⅛ × 38 ⅝ in.)

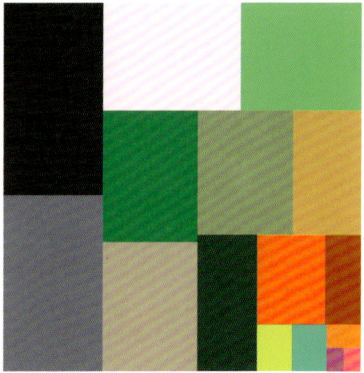

Proportional breakdown of colours used by Henri Matisse in *Goldfish*, 1912, displayed on the previous page.

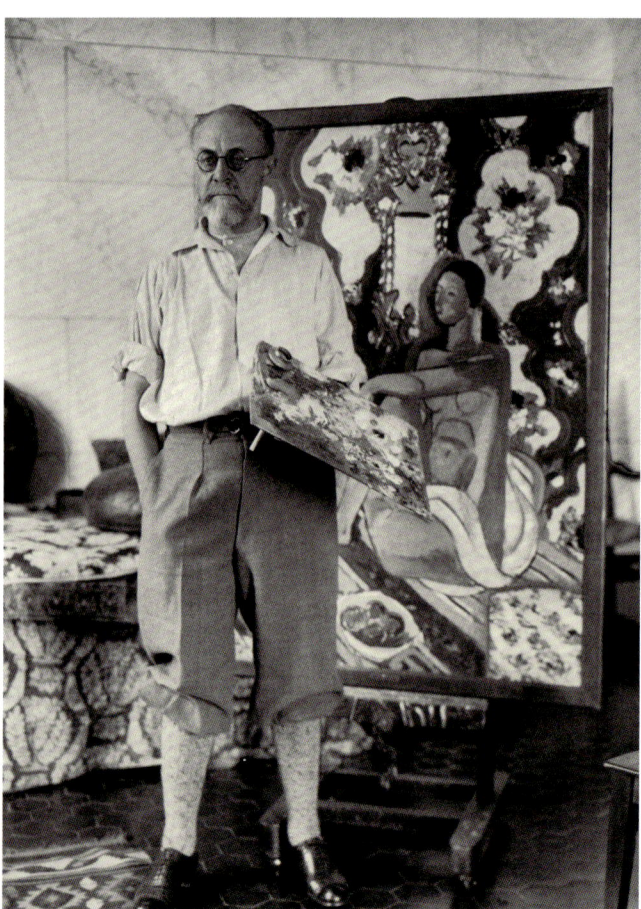

IN 1960, A FEW YEARS AFTER Henri Matisse's death, his heirs donated several artists' palettes and other painting materials to the Matisse Museum in Nice. The dates for these are not known and cannot be linked to any specific paintings, but they are moving examples of his attitude to colour and composition. Although he had famously turned to 'drawing with scissors' in his last years, creating large collages with shapes cut out of coloured paper and card, he never lost interest in the physical act of painting, and – more importantly – the emotional power of colour and paint. It is also possible that he kept these palettes for their pictorial value, among the large collection of objects he kept in his studios for use in some compositions. Two very similar palettes are seen propped up like works of art in photographs taken in 1949 and 1951 by Alexander Liberman, who visited and interviewed Matisse several times in his last years.[1]

The palettes in the collection of the Matisse Museum are made of walnut wood and contain patches of bright colours. Some are covered almost completely, with the swirly movements of the brush blending the colours and lifting them from the palette still visible. Others have only small patches of paint, as if the artist was only trying out colour combinations. At first glance, there does not appear to be a particular order to the colour layout on the palette shown here. It looks intuitive and spontaneous, comprising some vibrant pigments you would expect from a modernist painter with a passion for colour, for example what appears to be a viridian green and a cobalt blue. Yet, there was a method to Matisse's colours. He laid out his palettes thoughtfully and carefully, with a deep understanding for colour harmony, combining modern synthetic colours with warm earth pigments. The relationship between colours mattered greatly to him, and – like Delacroix (see pages 50–53), Kandinsky (see pages 164–69) and many others – he frequently drew on the analogy of music and colour: 'Each relationship of tone, I have found, should produce a chord of living colours, as harmony like that of a musical composition.'[2] At the same time, he was adamant that colour was intrinsically linked to shape, and therefore to the art of drawing and measured design. 'Colour,' he explained in 1945, when this palette may have been used, 'attains its full expression only when it is organized, when it corresponds to the emotional intensity of the artist.'[3]

The prominence of white on Matisse's surviving palettes is perhaps surprising, as we associate him so strongly with bold, flat, pure block colour, saturated colour fields as backgrounds, sumptuous reds placed next to juicy oranges and Mediterranean blues. However, large areas of white paint are also visible

A.

'Colour is never a question of quantity, but of choice.'

HENRI MATISSE, 'THE ROLE AND MODALITIES
OF COLOUR', 1945

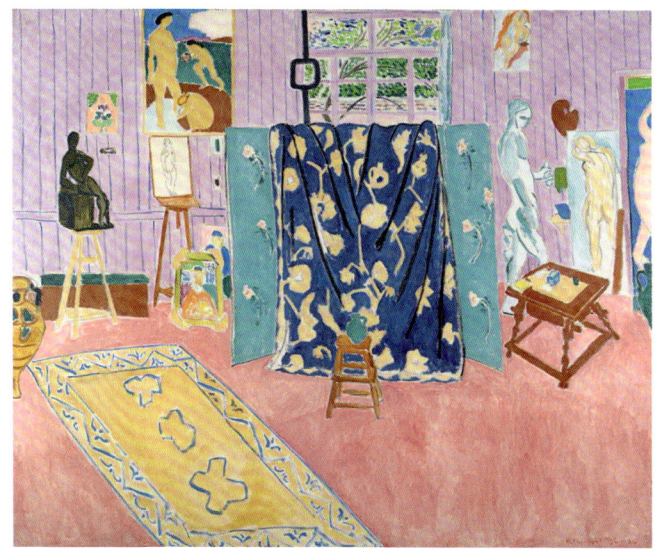

B.

in several photographs of the artist posing with
traditional palettes in his studio (as can be seen
in image A.). In a self-portrait from 1918, he offers
the spectator a muted, almost achromatic palette,
in which whites, blacks and ochres dominate,
as indeed they do in the picture itself.

A drawing of a palette layout from 1937 is another
example: while a range of bright chromatic colours
are arranged around the edge, including several
vibrant cadmium reds and yellows, cobalt blues and
violets, and an emerald green (with some additional
earth colours), the centre part of the palette is reserved
for three large blobs of *blanc d'argent* (a lead-based
silvery white).[4] Matisse also used white tin-glazed
earthenware plates as charts of oil colour samples,
probably to record colours in the most brilliant form
possible, on a white ground. The centre of Matisse's
colour universe appears to have been white, and was
instrumental for him in creating radiant compositions.

Colour was pure sensation to Matisse. Eventually,
when bereft of good health but not of creative spirit,
he took to using scissors and painted sheets of paper
to create monumental collages of block colour and
wondrous colour shapes that dominated whole interiors.
He also embraced new technologies, such as electronics
and colour film, and saw the future of art in light.
When Liberman visited him in his Paris studio on the
sixth floor of a modern apartment block, he entered
an intensely lit studio with glass doors and metal
shutters, filled with objects that he found interesting,
the walls and floors covered in drawings, canvases
and his late *papiers découpés*. Matisse's undiminished
artistic force was on full display, and he had perhaps
more than any other modernist painter truly liberated
colour and allowed it to speak for itself. His studio
space had become a three-dimensional palette.
Liberman concluded that Matisse 'attempted to
advance beyond painting, by imprinting on the senses
of the spectator colours that did not exist in reality
but only in the mind'.[5]

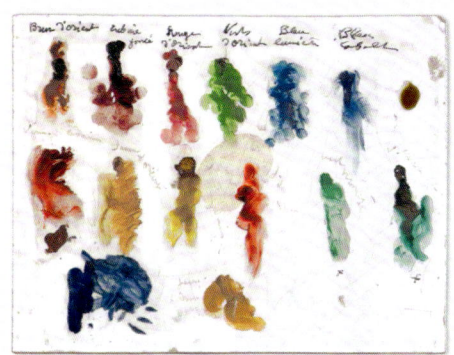

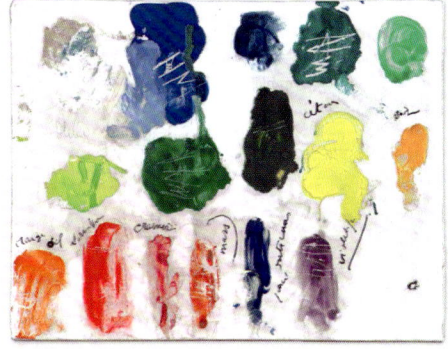

C.

A. Henri Matisse in his studio in Nice, France, in 1926, in front
of *Decorative Figure on an Ornamental Ground* (1925–26)

B. *Atelier d'artiste: Atelier rose* (Artist's studio: pink studio),
Henri Matisse, 1911, oil on canvas, 182 × 222 cm (71 ¾ × 87 ½ in.)

C. Oil paint colour trials, Henri Matisse, oil paint and Indian ink
on glazed terracotta, 23.7 × 31.7 cm (9 ⅜ × 12 ½ in.)

WASSILY KANDINSKY 1866–1944

A palette for colour's sake

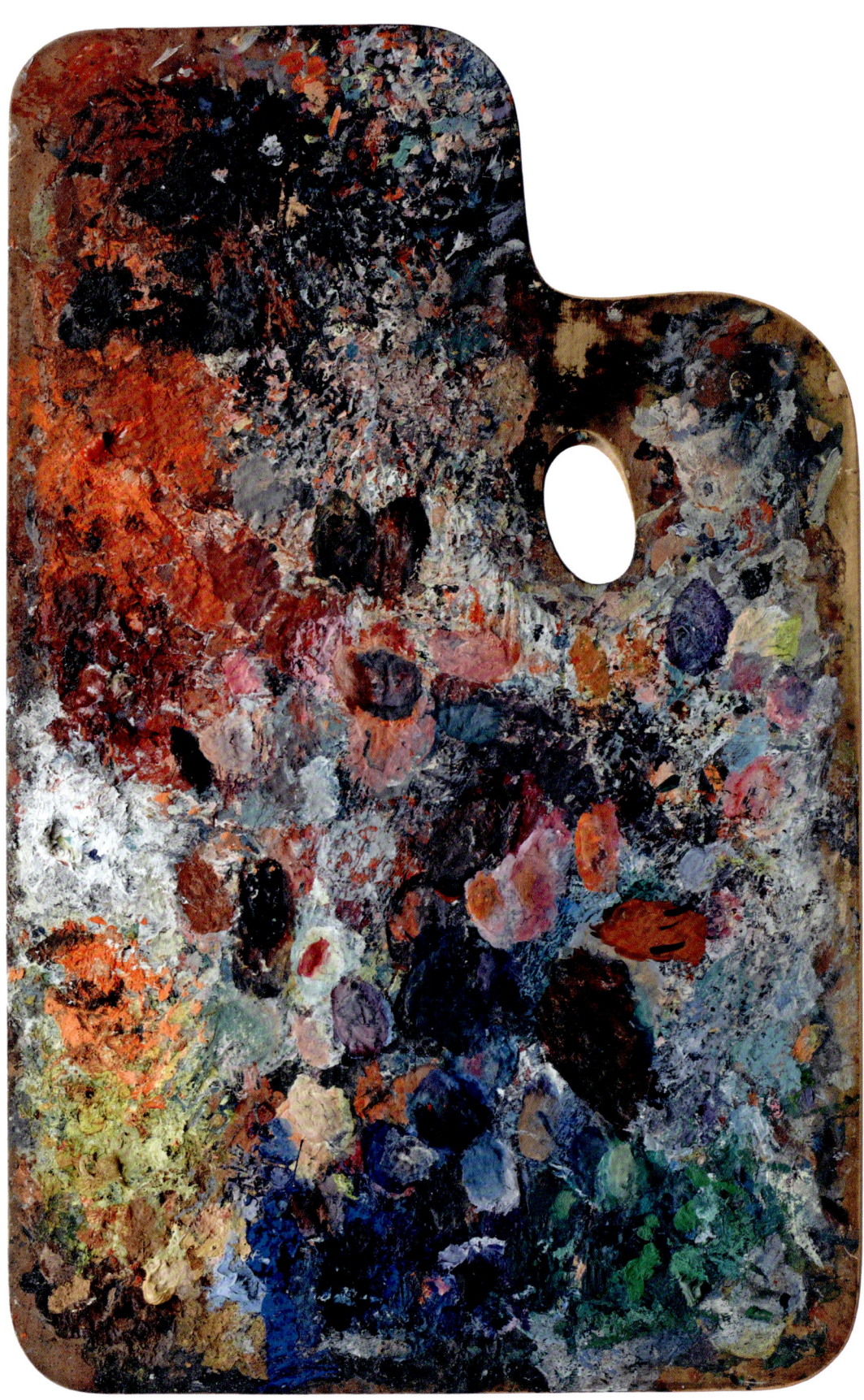

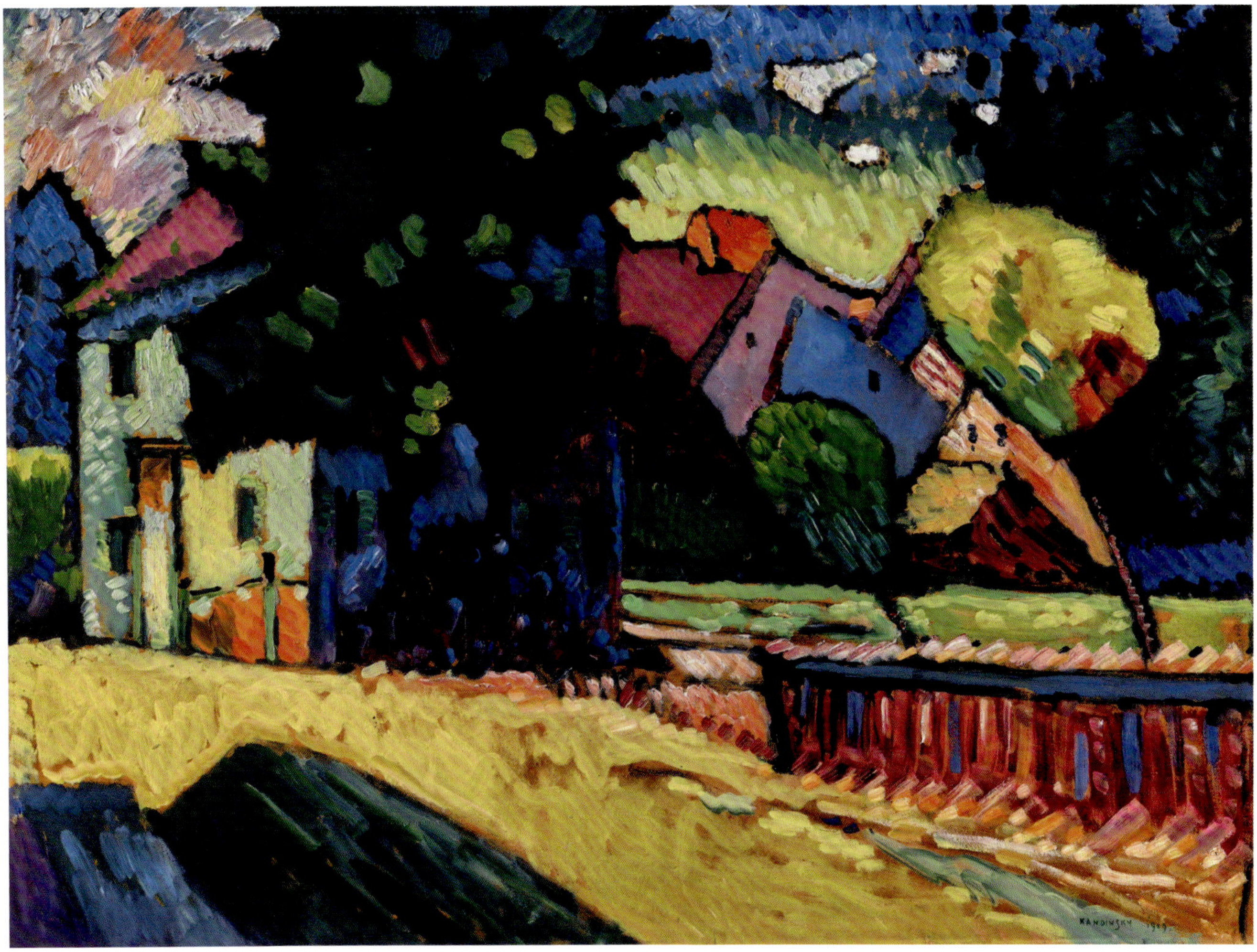

Wassily Kandinsky's
palette (opposite)
1933–44
Paint on wood

*Murnau – Landscape
with Green House* (above)
Wassily Kandinsky
1909
Oil on board
70 × 96 cm
(27 ⅝ × 37 ⅞ in.)

*Colour Study – Squares with
Concentric Rings* (right)
Wassily Kandinsky
1913
Watercolour, gouache
and crayon on paper
23.8 × 31.5 cm
(9 ½ × 12 ½ in.)

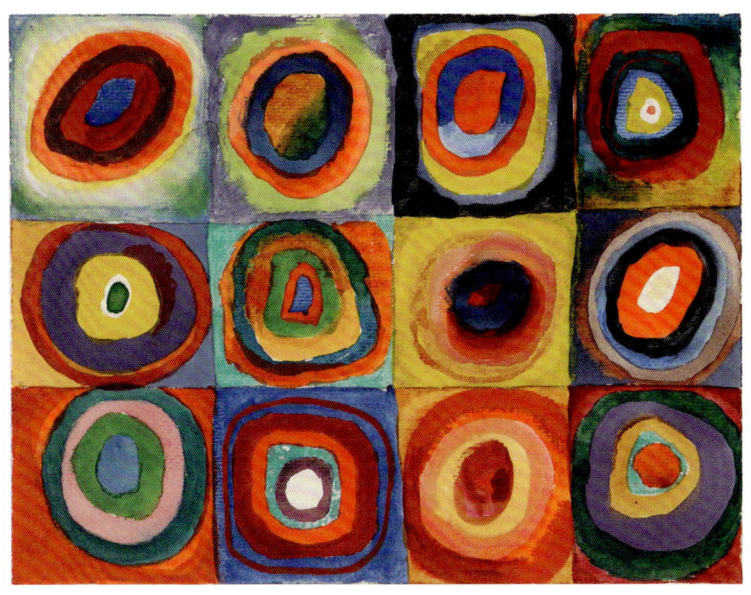

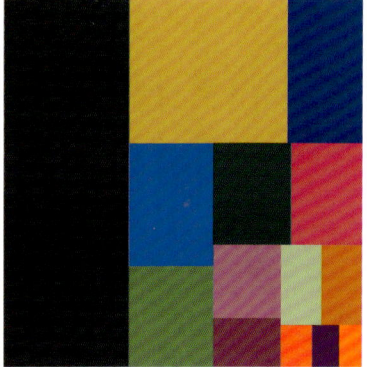

Proportional breakdown of colours used by Wassily
Kandinsky in *Murnau – Landscape with Green House*,
1909, displayed on the previous page.

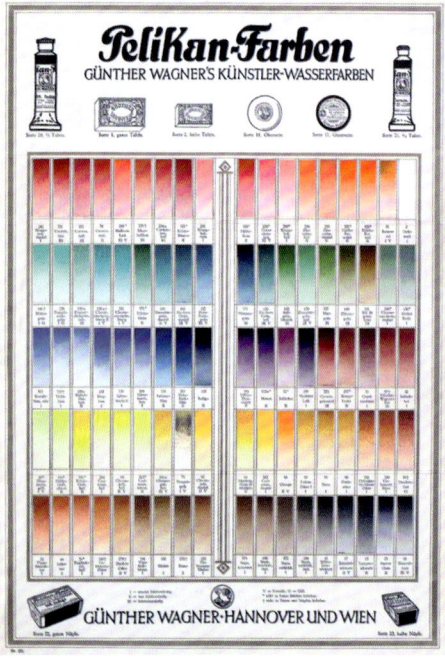

A.

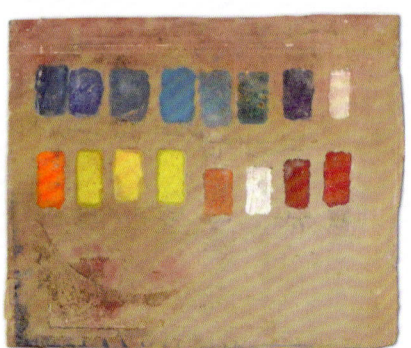

B.

THIS PALETTE DATES FROM between 1933 and 1944,
almost two decades after the disbanding of *Der Blaue
Reiter* (The Blue Rider), the short-lived but radical
expressionist group Wassily Kandinsky co-founded
in Germany in 1911. The palette surprises with its
wild, blooming appearance that seems to jar with the
geometric sharpness of the artist's work in the 1930s. It
conveys the sheer joy Kandinsky had in using colour for
colour's sake and as a powerful visual tool, an attitude
that does not seem to have changed since the early
1900s when he began moving towards abstraction.

An initial layout of red, yellow, green and blue is
still discernible on the palette, but this is broken up
by experimental mixing. A large area is occupied by
blue, the 'heavenly' colour to which Kandinsky and
his *Blaue Reiter* friends assigned such significance and
power. A blob of intense red not yet combined with
other colours gives the impression that he abandoned
the palette suddenly, switching perhaps to a new,
clean one. His blues were created from Prussian blue,
French ultramarine (both with high tinting power
and relatively cheap) and cobalt violet. He used both
traditional lead white and the cooler, cleaner zinc white,
at least four different types of yellow pigments and
an even wider range of reds, freely combining natural
earth and synthetic pigments.

In the two paintings shown here, despite being
earlier in date than the palette, we see how Kandinsky
used saturated, non-naturalistic, complementary
colours intended to create maximum contrast and
brilliance. In *Murnau – Landscape with Green House*
(painted in Murnau, Bavaria), realistic detail has
been replaced with flat, expressive areas of colour,
the brushstrokes visible, but with some features still
identifiable, such as trees, houses, a fence, a path. Only
a few years later, he painted *Colour Study – Squares with
Concentric Circles*, a completely abstract work that is all
about colour and form. Again, we see the cobalt violet
and artificial blues that are so prominent on the palette
and represent houses, the sky and other features in the
landscape painting. Here, however, what matters solely
is how these colours interact with other colours and
how shape influences their appearance.

Kandinsky is often regarded as one of the greatest
pioneers of abstraction, not only on the grounds of his art
but also his writings on art. His small book *Concerning
the Spiritual in Art*, first published in German in 1911
and quickly translated into English, became one of the
most influential texts on modernism and a new, intuitive
and spiritual approach to art. In it, he articulated the
role of colour in the artistic process of painting, drawing
an analogy with music: 'Colour is the keyboard, the eyes
are the hammers, the soul is the piano with many strings.

'Colour is the keyboard, the eyes are the hammers, the soul is the piano with many strings. The artist is the hand that plays, touching one key or another, with the intent to cause vibrations in the soul.'

WASSILY KANDINSKY, *CONCERNING THE SPIRITUAL IN ART*, 1911

The artist is the hand that plays, touching one key or another with the intent to cause vibrations in the soul.' Around the time this palette was used, Kandinsky was photographed by Boris Lipnitzki in his studio in Paris (image D.) where he spent the last decade of his life. These carefully staged, elegant black-and-white pictures show Kandinsky dramatically lit and posing with the tools of his profession. He is immaculately dressed, and in his paint cabinet the pigment jars are methodically arranged by colour, size and classification. An early visitor to the studio noted the contrast between the Russian icons hanging on the walls and the 'stark orderliness' of the space with pencils and brushes laid out in neat alignment. Kandinsky prepared his paints with a chemist's precision and avoided using ready-made paints in tubes. He used manufacturers' colour charts (like the one shown in image A.) and also created his own sample charts. Among the raw pigments that were found in his studio after his death were cadmium orange and yellow, Turkish red (madder), raw and burnt sienna, yellow ochre, ivory black and Indian red from unidentified suppliers. There were also cardboard boxes with pigments by the renowned Parisian paint manufacturer Lefranc (now Lefranc Bourgeois): a particularly vibrant carmine red, Indian yellow and cobalt violet. Kandinsky was known for preparing his paintings with great care, often creating dozens of preparatory sketches before drawing the composition's outline in pencil and working in thin layers of paint. It seems that the only place where Kandinsky allowed himself to be free, messy and spontaneous was on the palette itself.

A. Pelikan-Farben commercial colour scales found in Kandinsky's studio, 42 × 29.7 cm (16 ⅝ × 11 ¾ in.)
B. Gouache colour trials, Wassily Kandinsky, 1922–33, graphite and gouache on paper, 37.5 × 46.2 cm (14 ⅞ × 18 ¼ in.)
C. Cover of Wassily Kandinsky's *Über das Geistige in der Kunst*, 1911 (first published in English translation as *Concerning the Spiritual in Art*, 1914)
D. Wassily Kandinsky in his studio, Neuilly-sur-Seine, Île-de-France, France, photograph by Boris Lipnitsky, December 1936

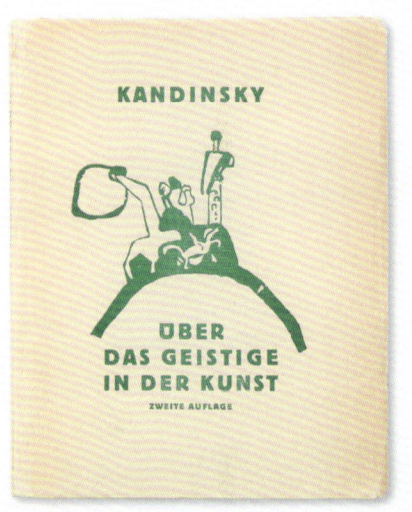

C.

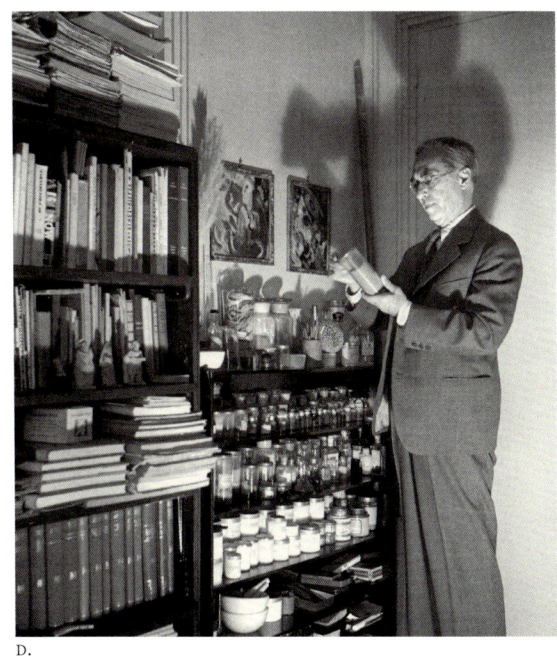

D.

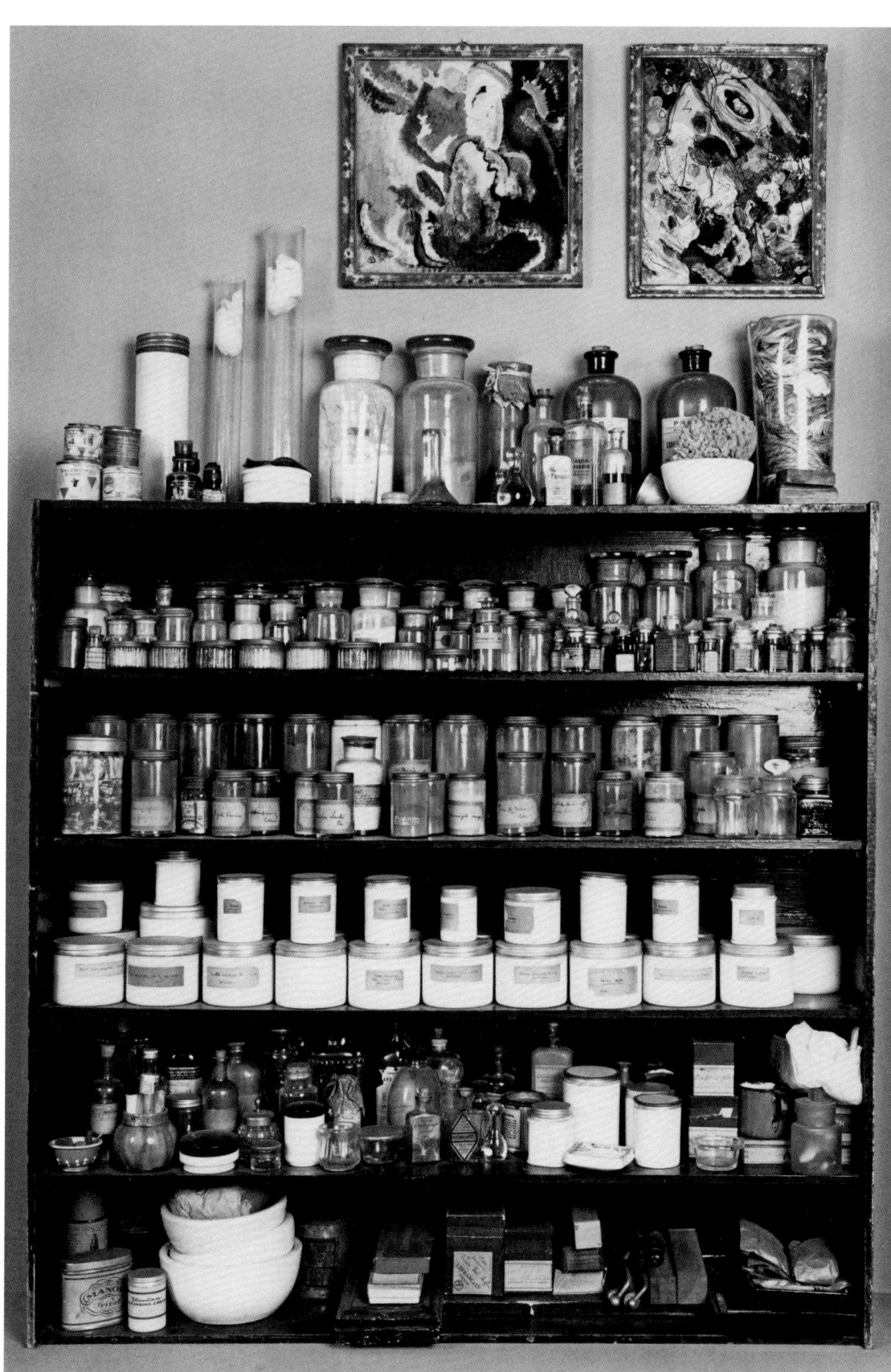

Shelf with pigments
in Wassily Kandinsky's
studio in Neuilly-sur-
Seine, Île-de-France,
France
1933–44

Pigments from
Wassily Kandinsky's
studio in Neuilly-sur-
Seine, Île-de-France,
France

A. *Türkischroth*
    (Turkish red)

B. *Cadmium ächt*
    orange N3 (cadmium
    orange no. 3)

C. *Terra di siena natur*
    (sienna natural
    earth)

D. Unlabelled:
    light yellow ochre

E. Unlabelled:
    red ochre

F. Unlabelled:
    red ochre

G. *Cadmium ächt*
    dunkel N2 (dark
    cadmium No. 2)

H. Unlabelled:
    yellow ochre

I. *Rußschwarz*
    (soot black)

J. Mars yellow

K. *Hell Indischroth*
    (light Indian red)

L. *Gebr. terra di siena*
    (burnt sienna)

M. *Lichter ocker I*
    (yellow ochre I)

N. *Terra di siena*
    (raw sienna)

O. *Violet de cobalt*
    (cobalt violet),
    Lefranc & Co.

P. Ivory black,
    Lefranc & Co.

Q. *Jaune Indian*
    (Indian yellow),
    Lefranc & Co.

R. *Lacquer carmine*
    (carmine lake)

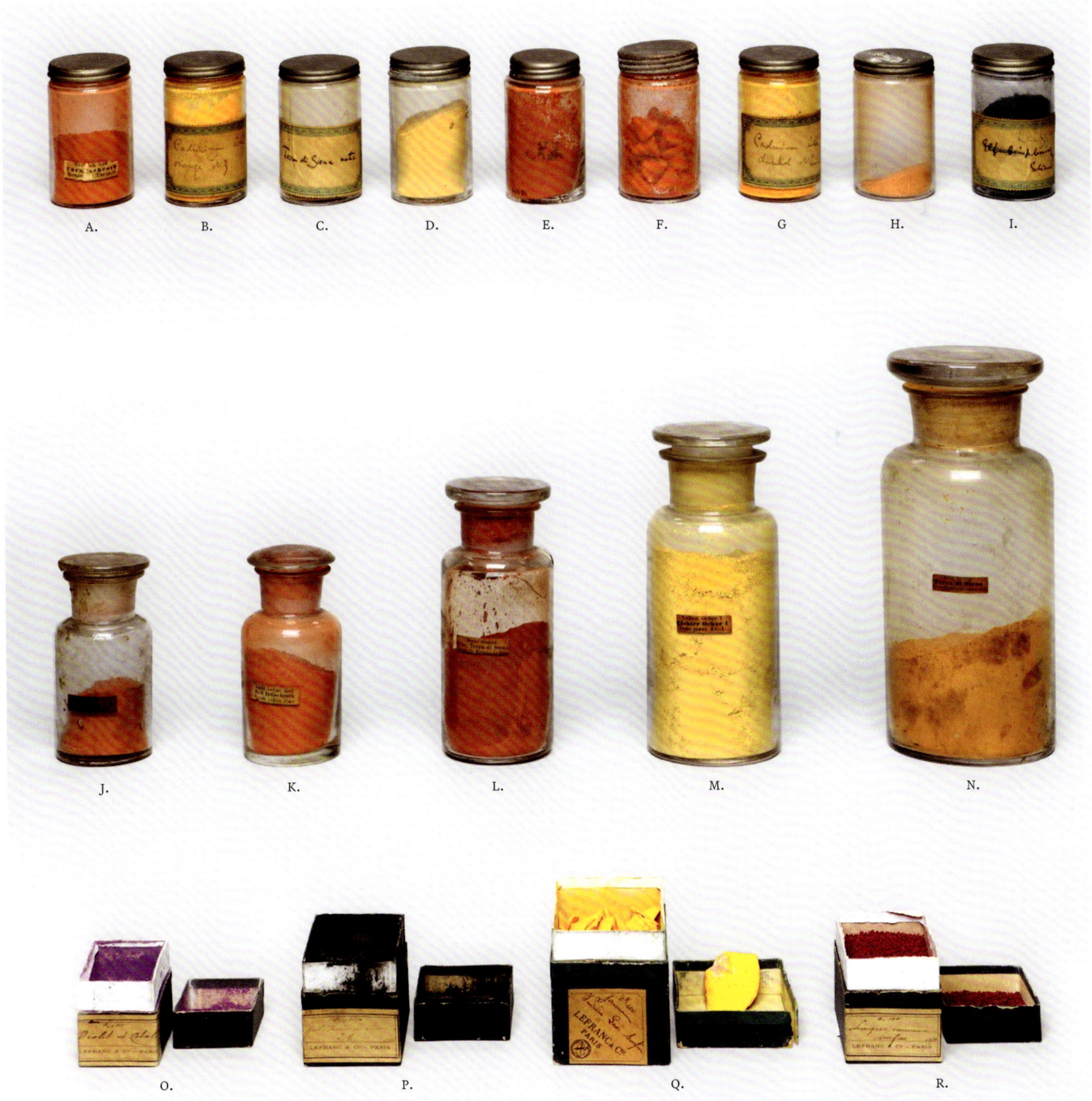

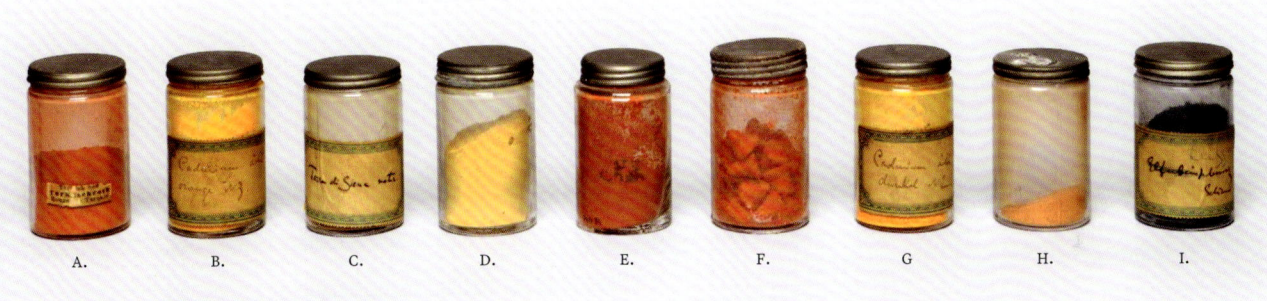

A.   B.   C.   D.   E.   F.   G.   H.   I.

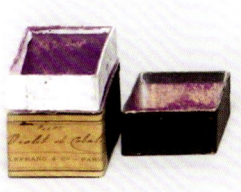

J.   K.   L.   M.   N.

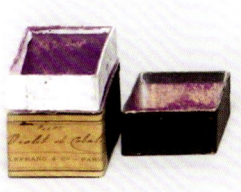
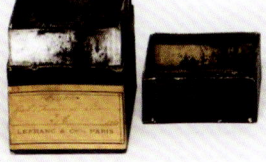
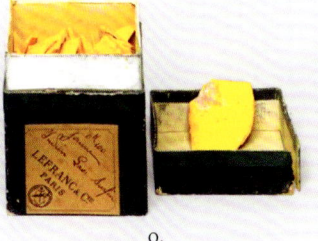
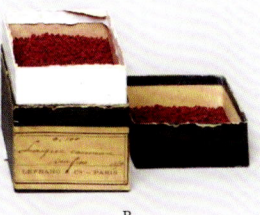

O.   P.   Q.   R.

GABRIELE MÜNTER 1877–1962

A palette like birdsong

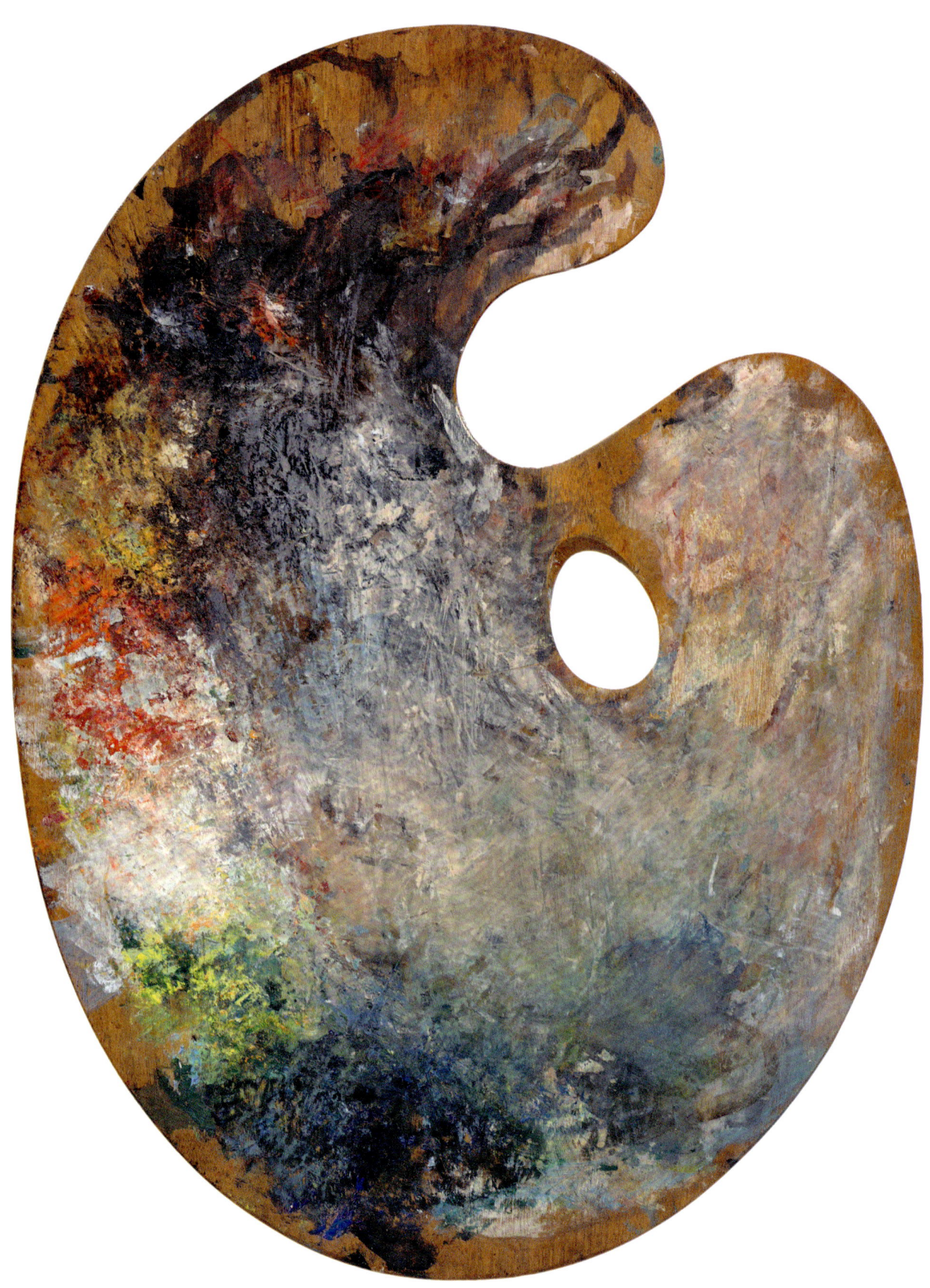

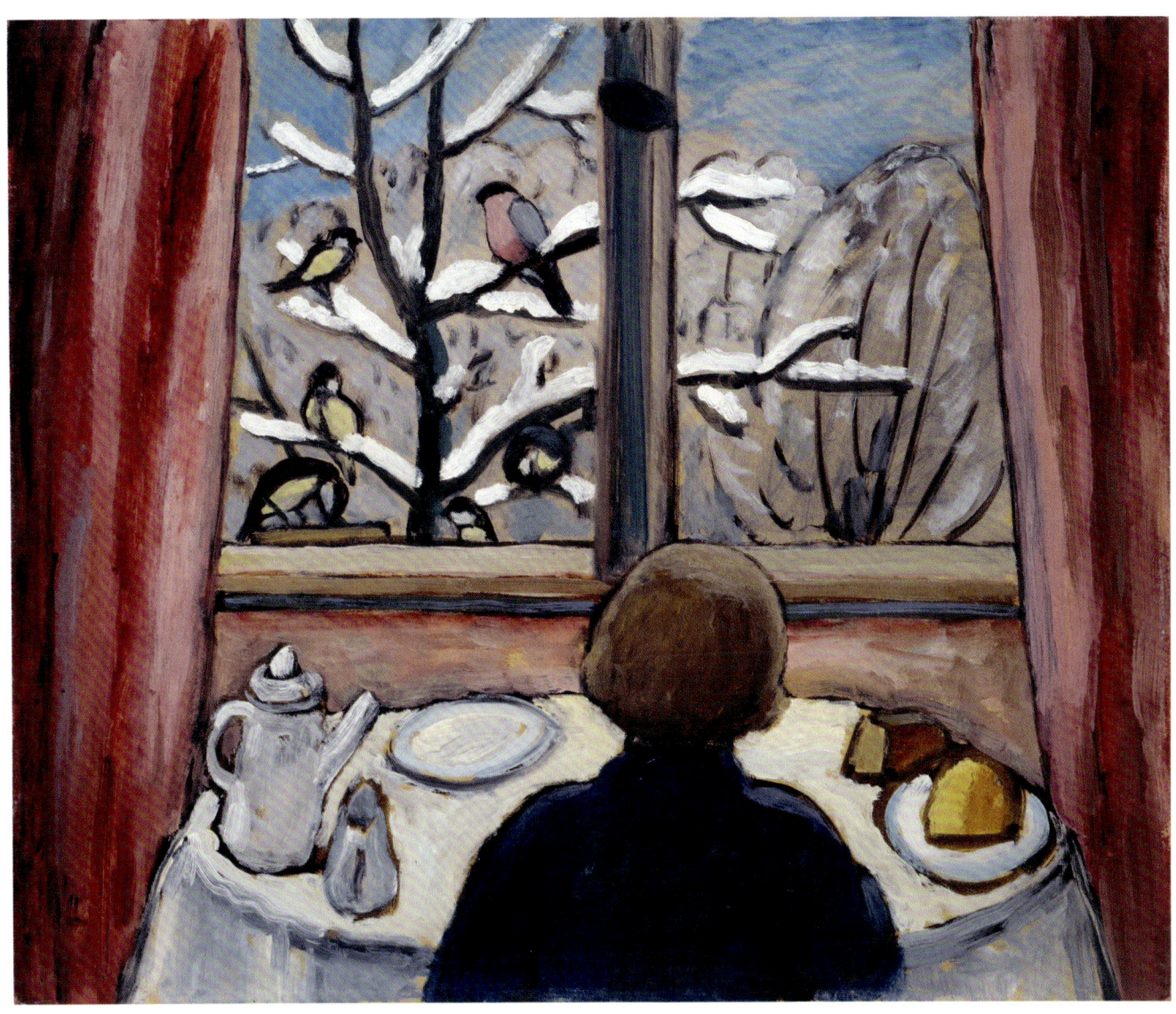

Gabriele Münter's
palette
Undated
Paint on wood
43 × 33 cm
(17 × 13 in.)

Breakfast of the Birds
Gabriele Münter
1934
Oil on board
45.7 × 55.2 cm
(18 × 21 ¾ in.)

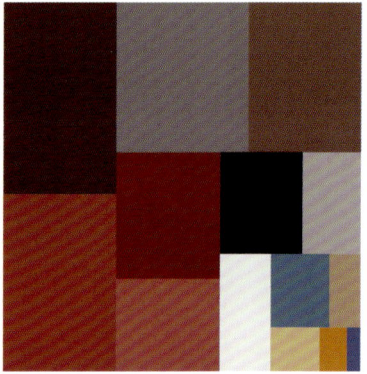

Proportional breakdown of colours used by Gabriele Münter in *Breakfast of the Birds*, 1934, displayed on the previous page.

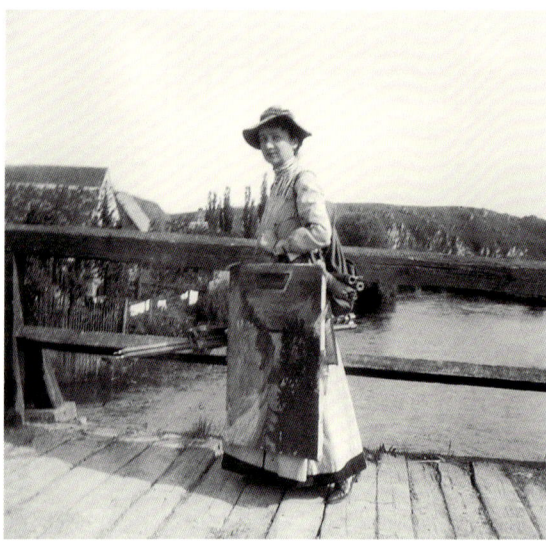

A.

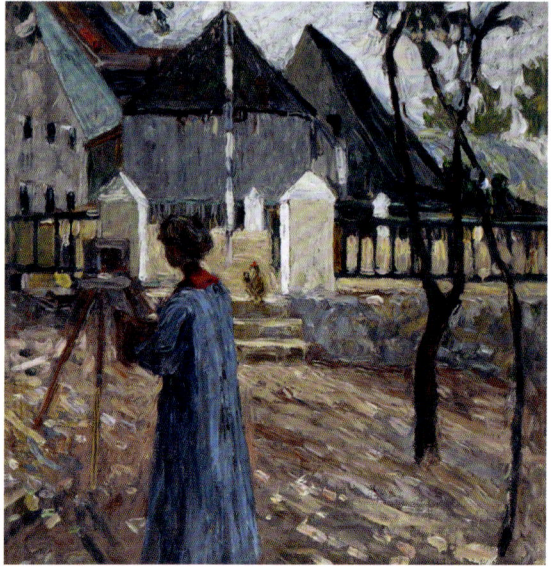

B.

THIS WOODEN ARM PALETTE with its preponderance of white paint mixed liberally with primary colours could be mistaken for a late-19th-century impressionist's palette. Yet, it is in fact by one of the most radical and experimental German expressionist artists, Gabriele Münter, who is best known for her use of highly saturated colours, often in complementary arrangements. It most likely dates from her later period, when she travelled less than she had done in her younger years but was still experimenting with different styles and techniques. Look closer, and you can see how the palette was originally laid out in a vaguely prismatic order but with an added area of very dark colour, possibly black, at one end. Münter had the full range of commercially produced colours of the 20th century available to her. In colour notes in one of her sketchbooks, she mentions ultramarine (probably artificial), madder lake (probably synthetic alizarin) and *émeraude* (emerald green).[1]

Extensive mixing has been carried out on this palette, likely with a variety of brushes, giving it a hazy appearance, but there are also visible scratches on the relatively thin paint layer, which may indicate that a palette knife was also used. Münter had first learned the technique of painting directly with the palette knife from her former teacher Wassily Kandinsky (see pages 164–69), with whom she had a long and complex relationship. Her compositions, although typical of expressionism in respect of the intensity of colours and strong contrasts, often had a darkness to them, partly created by her colour choices, and partly through compressed compositions and stark visual contrasts and contours. This can be seen in *Breakfast of the Birds* (1934), where the close-cropped scene is literally and visually framed by the lines of a window, curtains and a round table. The silhouetted figure, seen from behind, is looking out at a winter scene, most likely in Murnau in the Bavarian Alps, where Münter had lived on and off in a picturesque white house since 1909, and where she spent the last decades of her life.

White colour is an important, if sometimes overlooked, element in Münter's art. If this palette looks like a snowy landscape, it may be because it was used to paint snow, as in *Breakfast of the Birds*. Münter loved painting outdoors, especially in the lush surroundings of the Alps. She had first done this with Kandinsky in the early years of the 20th century, when she was still painting in a thick, broken impasto style, compared with her later flatter and more fluid application. She was known to paint outdoors in all weather conditions, including in thick mountain snow, standing by her portable easel and wearing gloves.

*'I depicted the World as it appeared to me in its essence,
as it moved me.... I still paint as my brush guides me.
Compared to my younger years I am less brazen now
and I paint lighter and more measured pictures.'*

GABRIELE MÜNTER, QUOTED IN GUDRUN SCHURY'S *ICH WELTKIND: GABRIELE MÜNTER*
(I AM A CHILD OF THE WORLD: GABRIELE MÜNTER), 2012

Münter masterfully mixed whites and blues to
depict the subtle shades and shadows of snow, but
also used it as a compositional and sometimes symbolic
element in her paintings, as can be seen in many of
her portraits, still lifes and group portraits. We can
see copious amounts of white on a palette included in
a small, semi-abstract self-portrait in her studio from
c. 1911. There are bright reds, yellows and a dark blue,
just like on her real palette, but white is everywhere,
to give structure and contour. She would also have
developed an understanding for white through creating
woodcut and linocut prints, where the absence of colour
is as important as the coloured areas. The dark contours
of many of her paintings were partly inspired by reverse
glass painting in the Bavarian folk style.

After Münter's death in 1962, an unknown writer
compared her painting style to birds singing.[2] Münter
herself was less poetic about her own work, explaining
that her command of bold, expressive colour was
always based on a solid framework of lines and outlines,
usually sketched out in pencil first in her sketchbooks,
sometimes with added colour notes, then executed
in fluid black brushstrokes on canvas or board: 'If
you look carefully at my paintings, you will find the
draughtswoman in them. Despite all the colours.'[3]

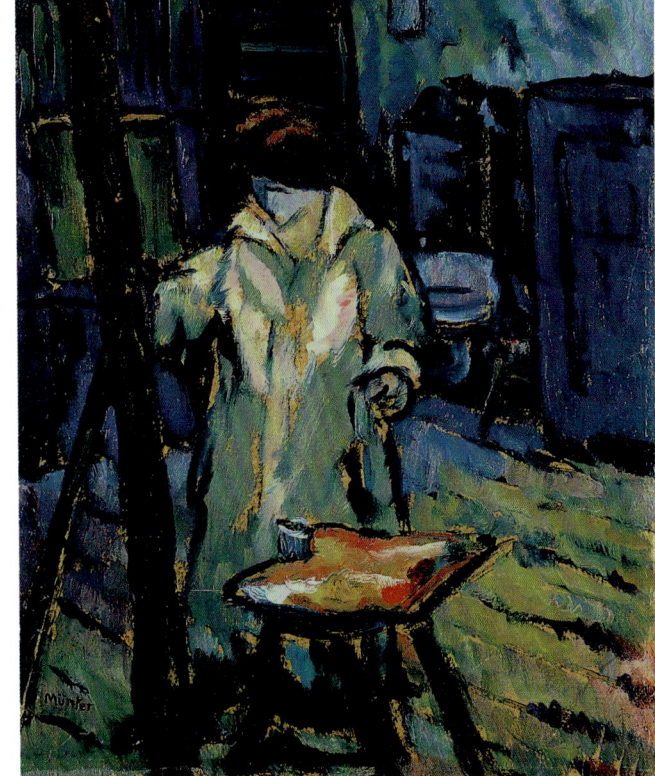

A. Gabriele Münter with painting utensils, Kallmünz Bridge,
    Bavaria, Germany, 1903
B. *Kallmünz – Gabriele Münter painting II*, Wassily Kandinsky, 1903,
    oil on canvas, 58.2 × 58.5 cm (23 × 23 ⅛ in.)
C. *Self-portrait at the Easel*, Gabriele Münter, *c.* 1911, oil on cardboard,
    37.5 × 30 cm (14 ⅞ × 11 ⅞ in.)

C.

EGON SCHIELE 1890–1918

A painful palette, glowing bright as jewels and flowers

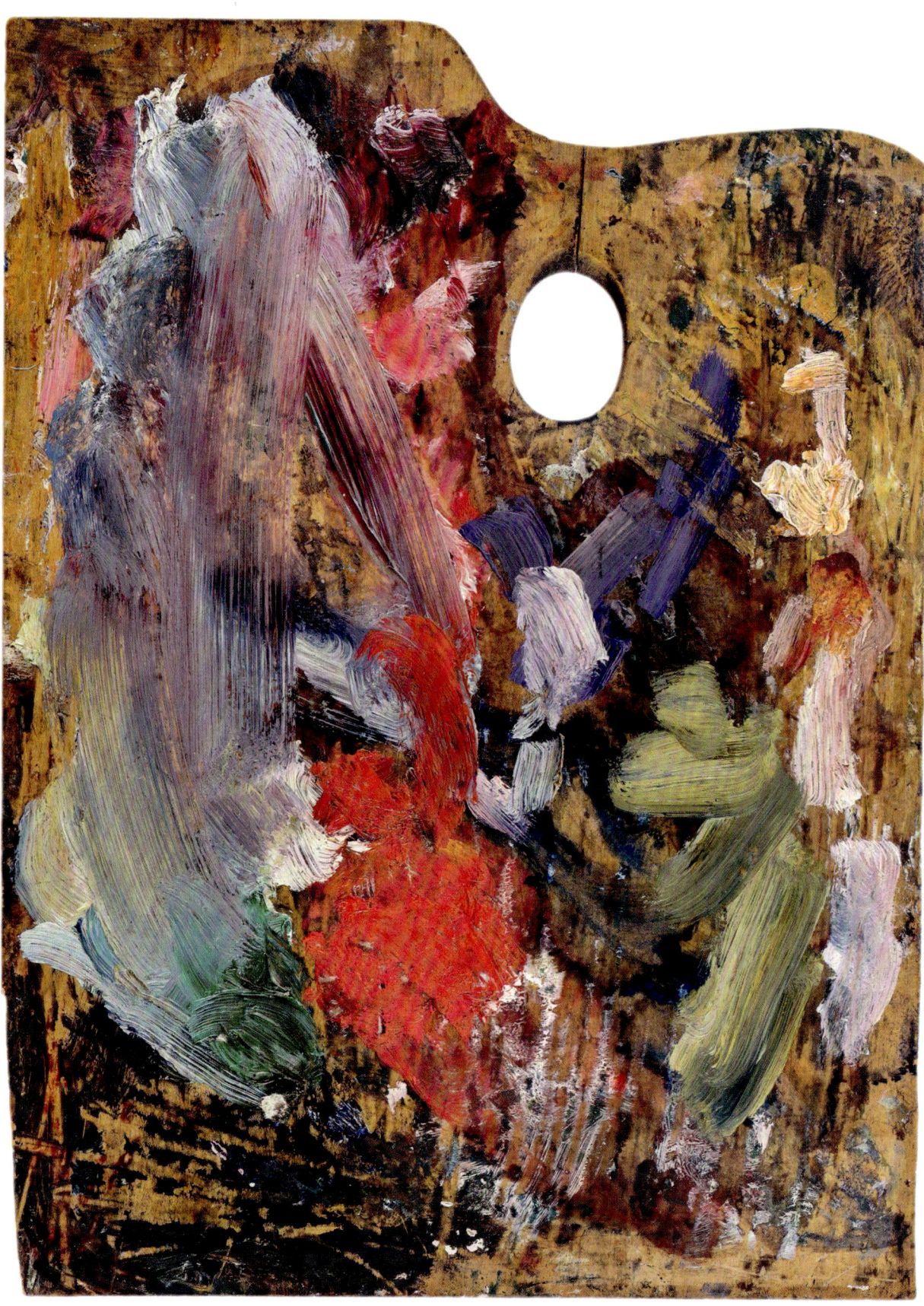

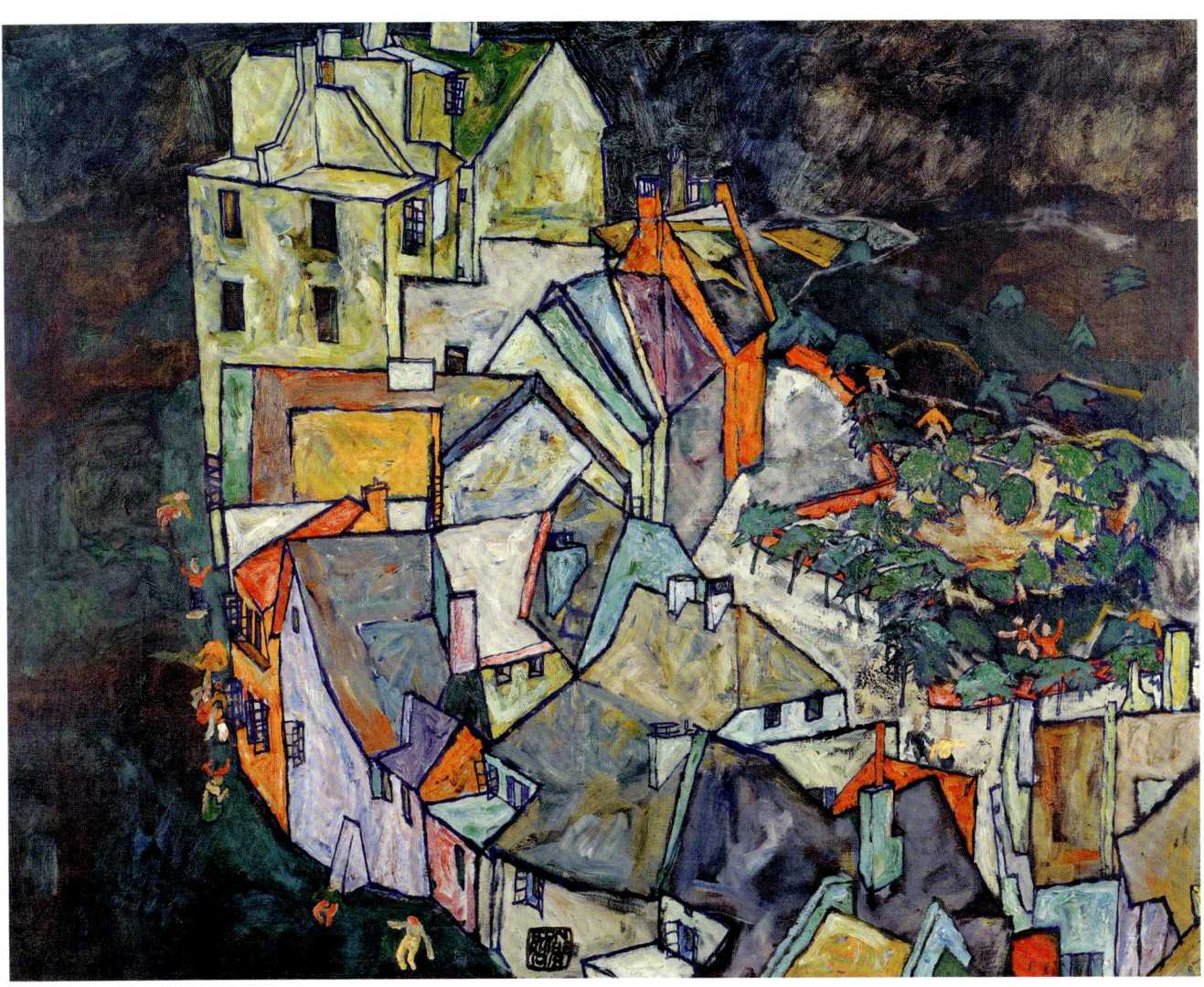

Egon Schiele's last palette
1918
Paint on wood
36.5 × 27 cm
(14 ⅜ × 10 ¾ in.)

*Edge of Town (Krumau
Town Crescent III)*
Egon Schiele
1918
Oil on canvas
109.5 × 139.5 cm
(43 ⅛ × 55 in.)

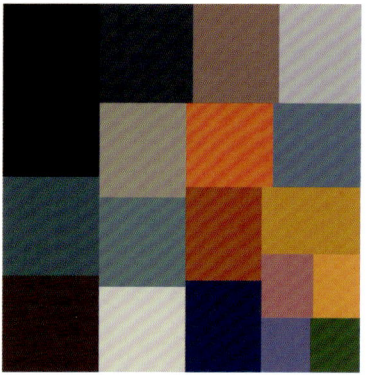

Proportional breakdown of colours used by Egon Schiele in *Edge of Town (Krumau Town Crescent III)*, 1918, displayed on the previous page.

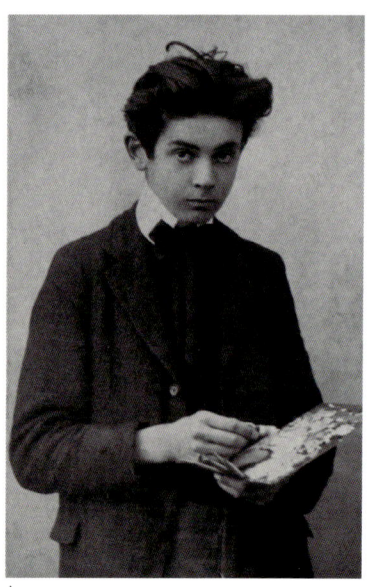

A.

B.

EGON SCHIELE DIED aged only twenty-eight in October 1918 in Vienna, a victim of the influenza pandemic that had also killed his wife Edith and their unborn child a few days earlier. This palette is allegedly the last one he ever used, saved by his brother-in-law Anton Peschka. A note was kept with it, in Peschka's handwriting, possibly recording some of Schiele's last words: 'Dying is sad and difficult. But my death does not seem more painful than my life, which has hurt so many people.' As with the palette of Paula Modersohn-Becker (see page 148), this simple wooden object is a symbol of a life and career cut tragically short, and we instinctively try to read even more of a narrative into the traces of paint, imagining the last creative acts carried out by the doomed artist.

It is a moving object that evokes Schiele at a shifting point in his career when he was on the verge of greater success and developing a richer, more mature style. The palette has been heavily used and shows signs of repeated scraping and cleaning, with traces of previous work left in the woodgrain, and it appears to have split near the thumbhole. The colours are bright and vibrant, and the few brushstrokes are very broad, suggesting the use of a flat brush and fast, assured working.

Among the colours we see here are several that Schiele used in many of his oil paintings, in particular a saturated red, an olive green, a more intense green (possibly viridian) and an almost electric blue. There are no signs of measured mixing or a planned layout on this palette, although some colours have been blended in the process of scooping up the paint. Some of the streaks of paint give the impression of having been placed there to see how they would work together. Schiele sometimes manipulated paint that had already been applied to canvas with a dry brush to give the paint surface texture.[1] He may have used this palette to scrape off paint left on the brush in the process, so what we possibly see here is a palette in reverse, with colour taken from a painting. This is a wild, experimental, intuitive palette, perhaps a desperate one, driven by the looming shadow of death.

It is not known which of Schiele's oil paintings was his last. There are several candidates, some of which may have been completed by other hands – for example, the background of the unfinished *Portrait of Albert Paris von Gütersloh* (1918) – but the palette reflects Schiele's later technique of a thicker application of paint, creating richer and more textured surfaces, compared to his earlier style of working with thin layers and glazes. By 1918, Schiele's once emaciated, contorted figures had become fleshier, his erotic images had lost some of their sexual urgency and his subject matter was broadening, while still combining superior drawing skills with an

'I want to…see light and sun, enjoy wet, green-blue valleys in the evening, sense goldfish glinting, see white clouds building up in the sky, to speak to flowers.'

EGON SCHIELE, LETTER/POEM TO ANTON PESCHKA, 1910

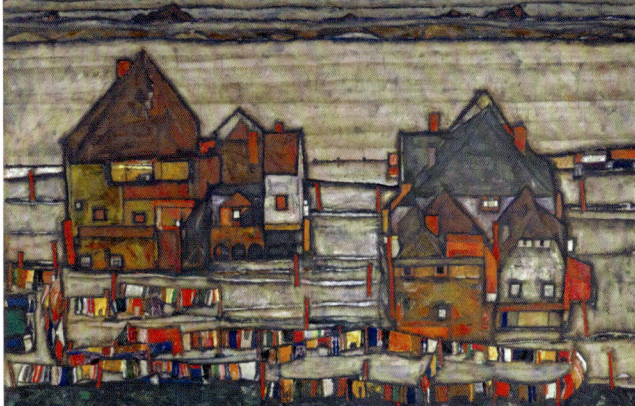

C.

expressive use of sensual colour. Many of his paintings are, in fact, coloured drawings.

He had always combined vibrant, saturated colour with muddy tones or achromatic greys, blacks and whites. In his earlier nudes and pornographic images, including his self-portraits, he often used fiery reds and oranges (possibly vermilion or cadmium-based) for genitals, mouths and other erotic zones in an exaggerated contrast to earth colours, but his almost cubist *Edge of Town* (*Krumau Town Crescent III*) from 1918 and the late landscape *Four Trees* (1917) show a less aggressive, more glowing use of red and orange, combined with vibrant blues and his signature tones, which frame the richer colours.

Arthur Roessler, Schiele's friend, mentor and first editor of his writings,[2] once visited his studio, and described his fiery, feverish colours lighting up the achromatic space:

> You found yourself surrounded by chalk white walls and [countless] black objects. […] In the midst of polyphonic blacks the young artist stood before a black easel in a white painter's smock which looked like a monk's habit. On the easel was a large, stretched canvas on which he was painting a picture which glowed, fierily, in all the colours of the spectrum, bright as jewels and flowers.[3]

D.

A. Egon Schiele at age sixteen with a palette, Vienna, Austria, 1906
B. *The Embrace (Lovers II)*, Egon Schiele, 1917, oil on canvas, 100 × 170 cm (39 ⅜ × 67 in.)
C. *Self-portrait with Lowered Head*, Egon Schiele, 1912, oil on wood, 42.2 × 33.7 cm (16 ⅝ × 13 ⅜ in.)
D. *Houses with Laundry (Suburb II)*, Egon Schiele, 1914, oil on canvas, 99 × 119 cm (39 × 46 ⅞ in.)
E. *Four Trees*, Egon Schiele, 1917, oil on canvas, 110.5 × 141 cm (43 ½ × 55 ½ in.)

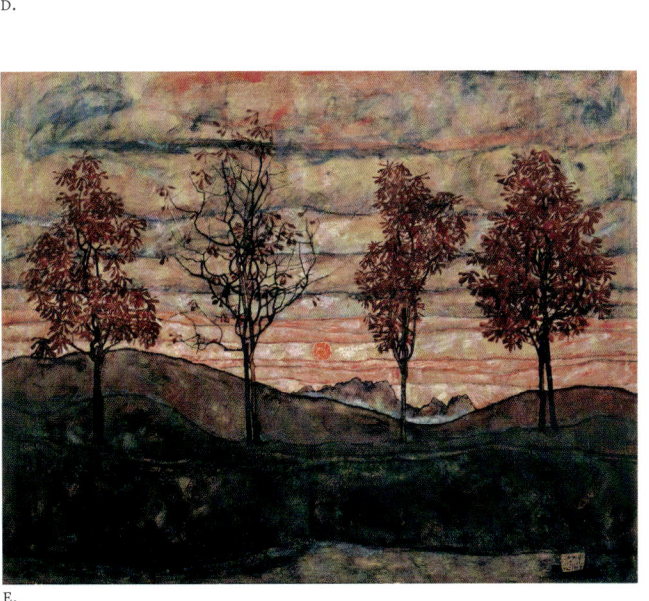

E.

GEORGIA O'KEEFFE 1887–1986

A liquid abstract world in a tin box

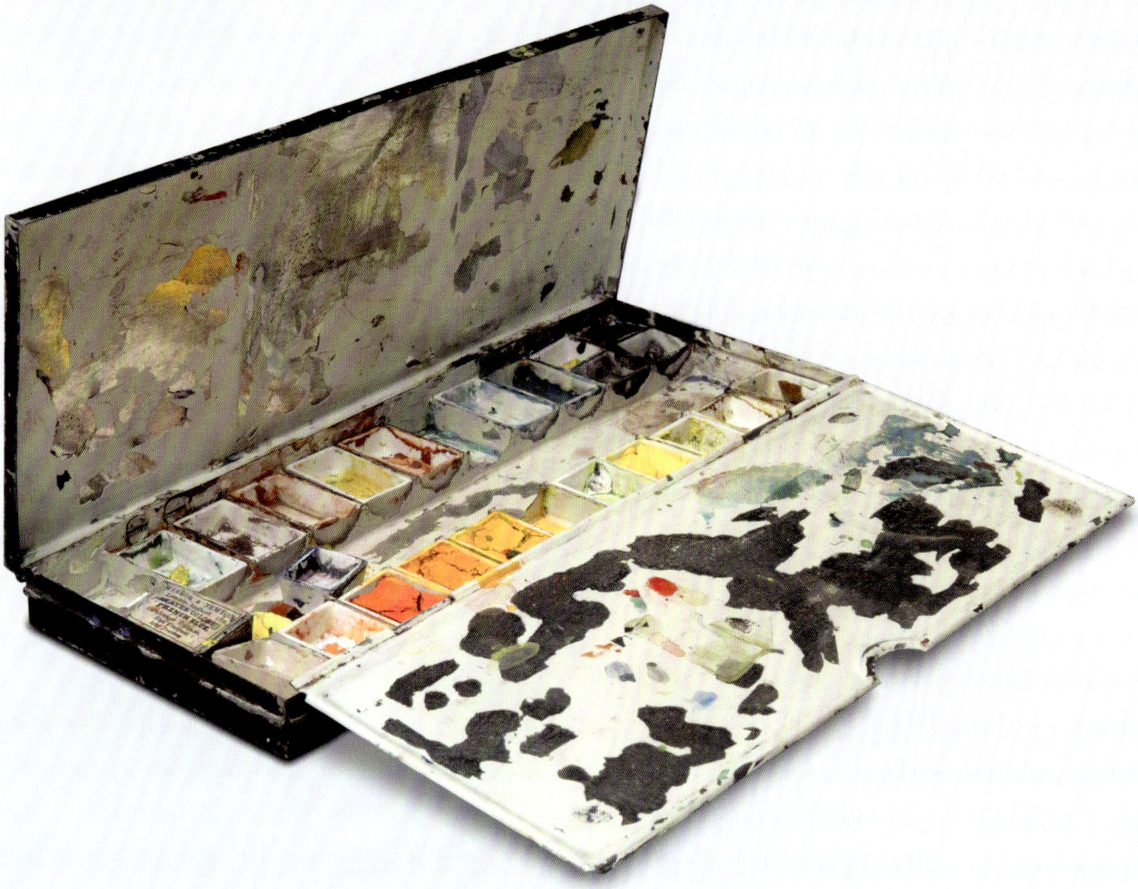

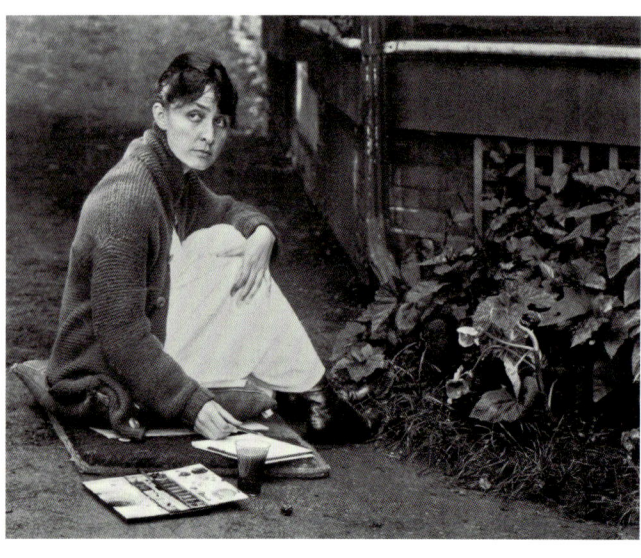

Georgia O'Keeffe's Winsor &
Newton watercolour box (above)
20th century
Watercolour, plastic and metal
23.5 × 9.5 cm
(9 ¼ × 3 ¾ in.)

Georgia O'Keeffe, Lake George,
New York, USA (left)
Photograph by Alfred Stieglitz
1918
Gelatin silver print
9 × 11.5 cm
(3 ⅝ × 4 ½ in.)

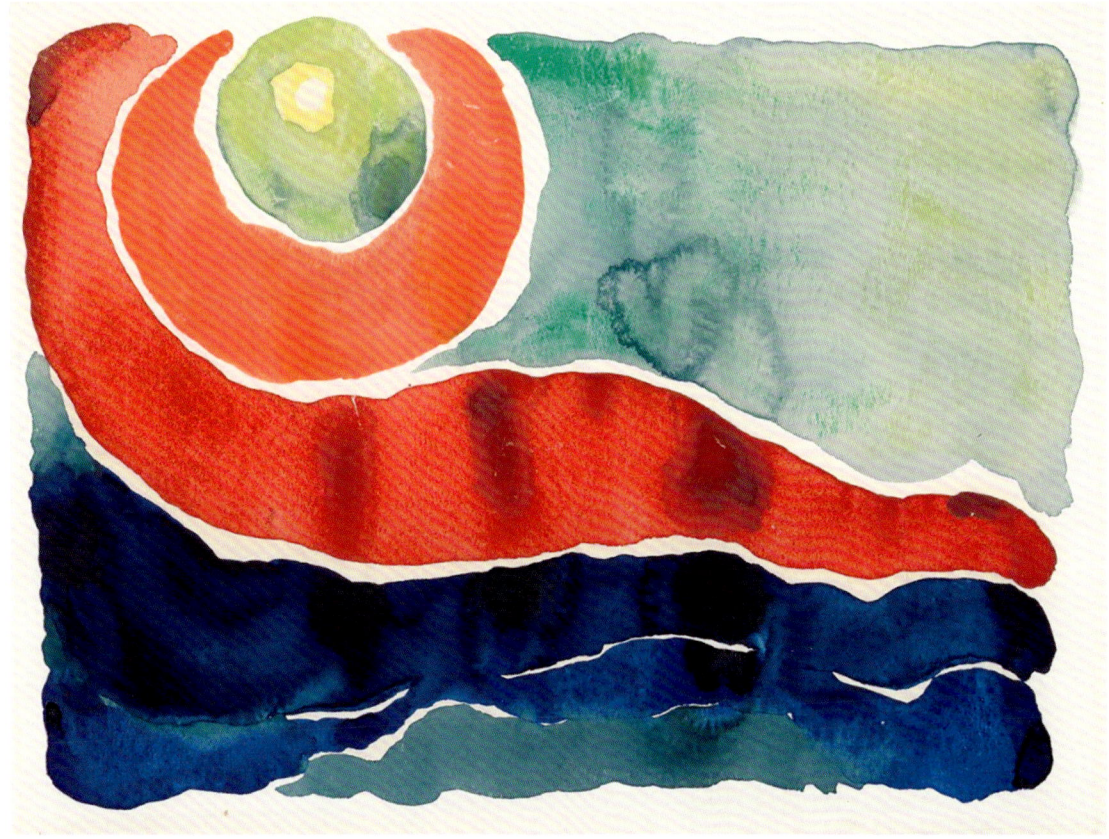

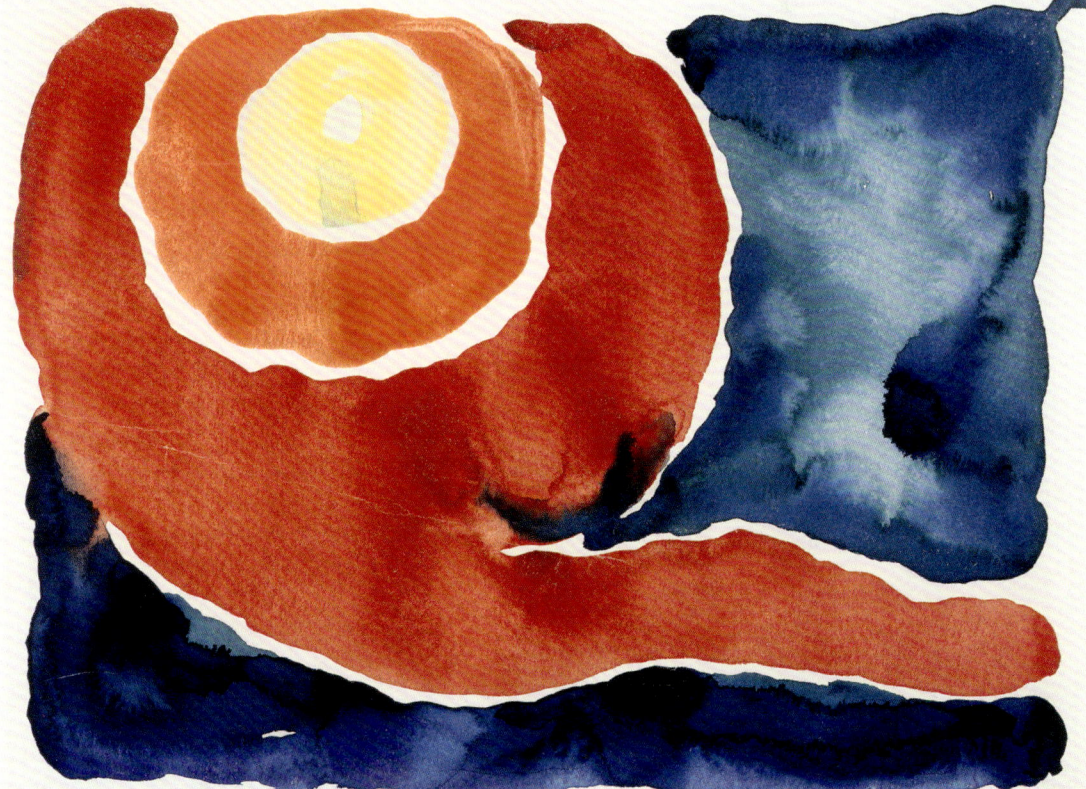

Evening Star No. IV
(top)
Georgia O'Keeffe
1917
Watercolour on paper
22.5 × 30.5 cm
(8 ⅞ × 12 in.)

Evening Star No. V
(bottom)
Georgia O'Keeffe
1917
Watercolour on paper
21.9 × 29.5 cm
(8 ⅝ × 11 ⅝ in.)

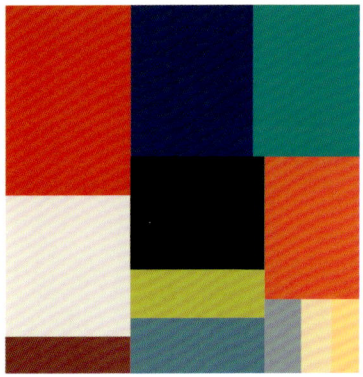

Proportional breakdown of colours used by Georgia O'Keeffe in *Evening Star No. IV*, 1917, displayed on the previous page.

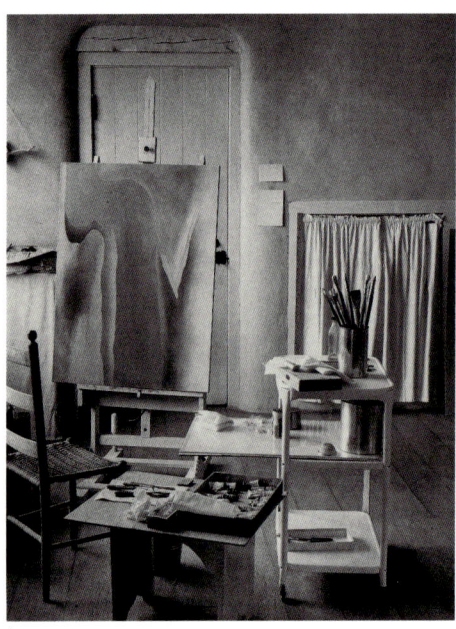

A.

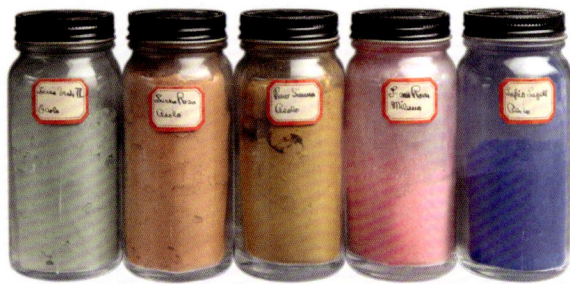

B.

COLOUR, AS GEORGIA O'KEEFFE ONCE EXPLAINED, was a way of expressing things that could not be said in other ways. It became an alternative language to her, when words failed. She first explored colour through the medium of watercolour, after having experimented extensively with charcoal and paper, following her study of Japanese prints and brush paintings. She soon developed a yearning for blue, which would remain a significant colour throughout her artistic life.

With a paintbox like the one shown here, between 1916 and 1918 she created around fifty vibrant watercolours, including the two on the preceding page from a series titled *Evening Star*. Deceptively simple, they amalgamate several influences, including swirling motifs reminiscent of art nouveau, cosmic themes prevalent in her partner's photographic work and spiritualist publications of the era, and strong allusions to the work and writings of Wassily Kandinsky (see pages 164–69). Yet, their most distinctive aspects are abstraction and the use of colour: the nocturnal sky is reduced to bold areas of watercolour in the saturated primaries yellow, red and blue, with some tentative greens. At this stage, O'Keeffe gave each colour its own space in the composition, with white lines separating each area. Only occasionally has her brush veered off and the liquid nature of watercolour makes the colours flow into each other. It is a radical and assured use of the medium.

In one of a large series of portraits taken by her partner Alfred Stieglitz over a period of thirty years,[1] we see the young O'Keeffe sitting on the ground in front of a flower bed at Lake George, New York, in 1918. She is equipped not with the enormous canvases and bleached animal skulls with which she would later become associated, but with a humble tin box of watercolours, as she examines the anatomy of the flowers in front of her. It is likely that the paintbox was sourced from the British art supplier Winsor & Newton, which became one of O'Keeffe's favourite brands. To create her luminous blues, she opted for cerulean, cobalt and real and artificial ultramarine, but she also used Winsor & Newton's flake white, viridian green, cadmium yellow and red, alizarin crimson and iron reds. She made detailed notes of their permanence, drying times and other qualities on colour cards, which she used to plan compositions.

Stieglitz's photograph shows an artist at a turning point in her career, as she is experiencing a slow artistic awakening to a world of colour. Later that year she produced her first paintings in oil. She would become one of the greatest abstract colourists of the 20th century. Her critics praised her mastery of colour, at times referring to her work as 'colour music' and herself as a 'composer', able to create 'deft, subtle, intricate chords' of colour like no other.[2]

'I paint because colour is a significant language to me.'

GEORGIA O'KEEFFE, LETTER TO *MSS* MAGAZINE,
DECEMBER 1922

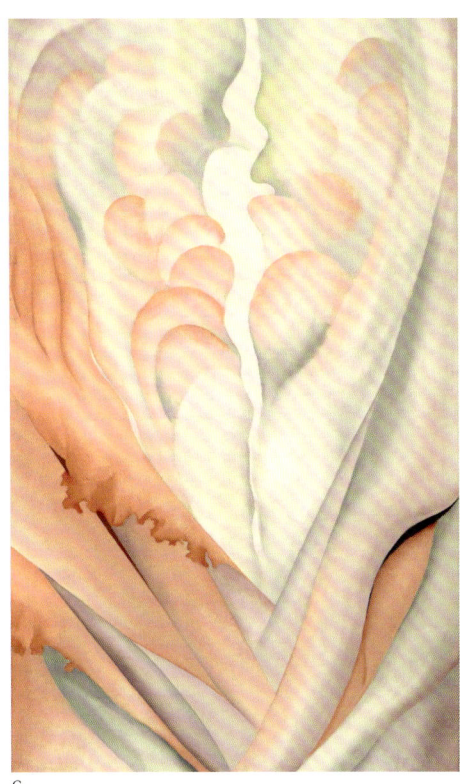

C.

O'Keeffe is perhaps best known for her large fiery-coloured American land- or cityscapes and suggestive semi-abstract close-ups of flowers and bleached animal bones, but she developed her poetic, highly personal style over many years, working with a variety of formats and media. She edged towards her intense polychrome style via the medium of watercolour and mastered it beautifully, making full use of its fluidity and luminosity. Many of her later, large abstract compositions in oil have embryonic predecessors in watercolour.

Her drive towards abstraction was apparent from an early stage, and she considered realism the death of art. Instead, she believed in the purity and power of minimalist compositions in which line and colour were the driving elements. She would begin almost all of her paintings with an outline drawing, adding colours at the next stages. Progressive and modernist in her approach and with a great interest in international art movements and theory, it is perhaps surprising that she did not leave the USA until she was sixty-five years old. The wild expansive landscapes of New Mexico and Texas and the glitter of the newly electrified and upward-surging city of New York offered her more than enough inspiration. When she wanted to find out about European avant-garde movements, she simply sourced the relevant literature. She read, for example, Kandinsky's seminal work *Concerning the Spiritual in Art* as soon as it became available in English translation in 1914 (then titled *The Art of Spiritual Harmony*), as well as Clive Bell's *Art* (1913) in 1916.

In 1905 and 1906 O'Keeffe studied at the Art Institute of Chicago and produced early realistic works. In the early 1910s, she attended art courses by Arthur Wesley Dow and Alon Bement at the University of Virginia,[3] during which she began contemplating more radical approaches and techniques. Dow promoted a synthesis of Eastern and Western culture and had particular views on the teaching of colour. O'Keeffe was clearly inspired by him, but also broke free from his rather rigid methodology to develop her own language of colour.

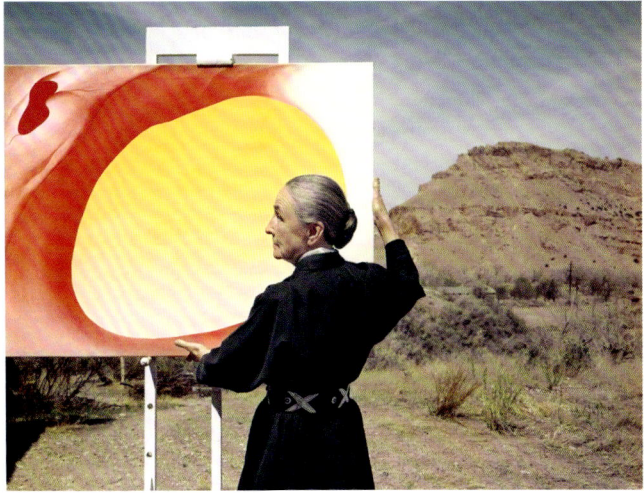

D.

A.   Georgia O'Keeffe's studio at the Ghost Ranch, New Mexico, USA, photograph by Todd Webb, 1962, gelatin silver print
B.   Georgia O'Keeffe's glass jars of pigments (terra verde II, terra rosa, raw sienna, lacca rosa and lapis lazuli)
C.   *Flower Abstraction*, Georgia O'Keeffe, 1924, oil on canvas, 122.2 × 76.2 cm (48 ⅛ × 30 in.)
D.   Georgia O'Keeffe standing outside her studio with *Pelvis Series: Red with Yellow*, 1945, Albuquerque, New Mexico, USA, photograph by Tony Vaccaro, 1960

EDWARD HOPPER 1882–1967

A thin palette of haunted emptiness

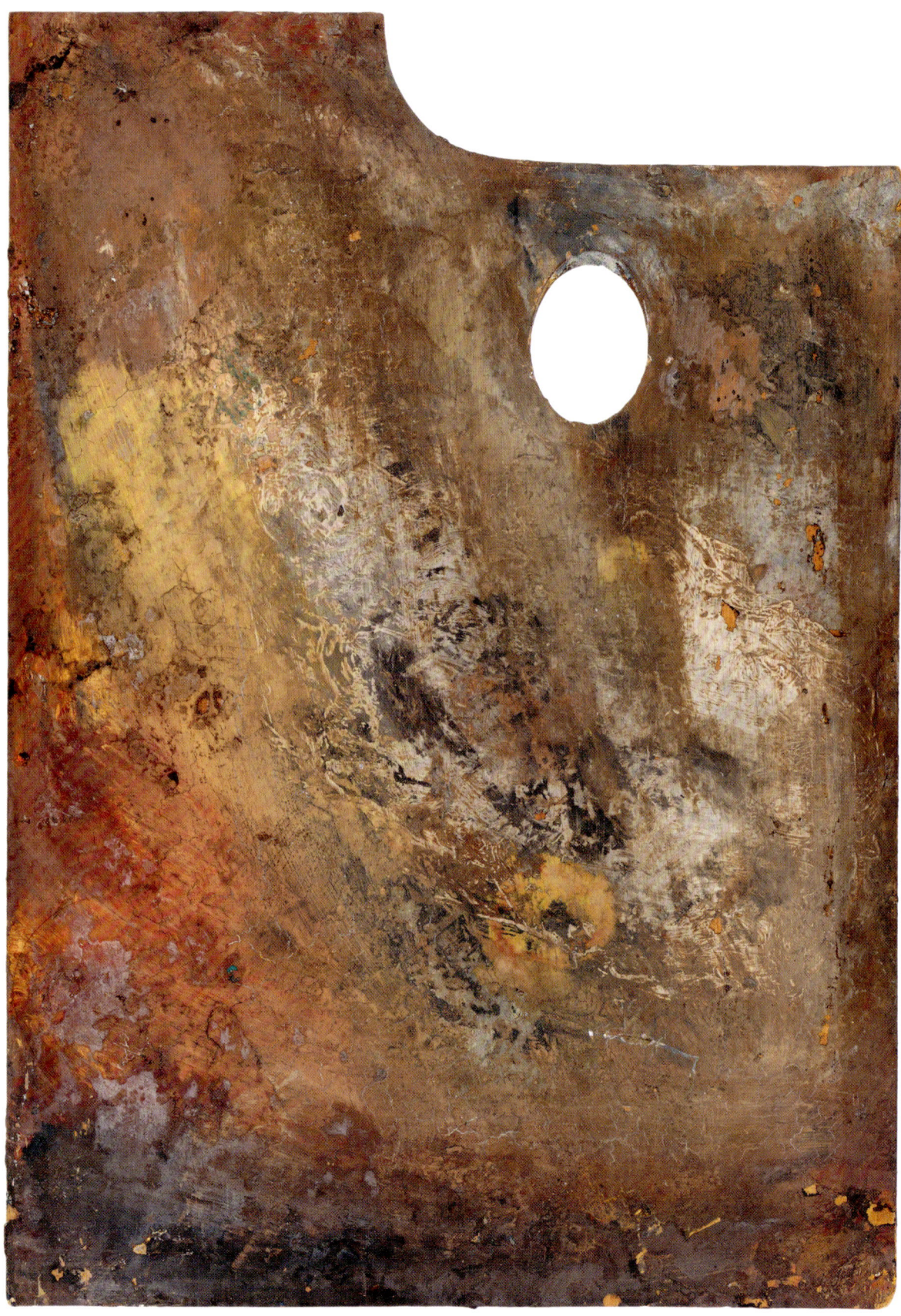

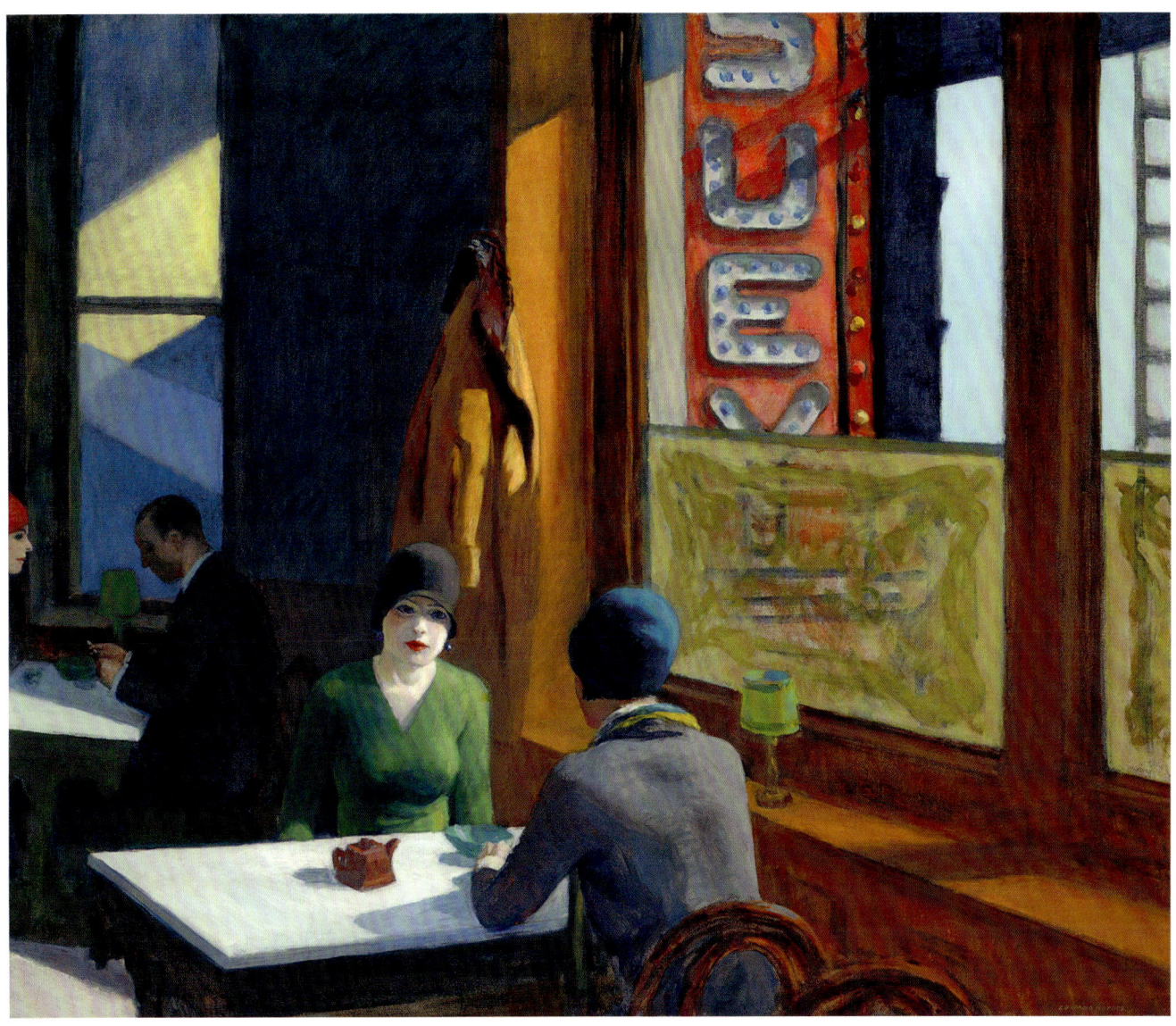

Edward Hopper's palette
Undated
Oil on wood
35.4 × 25.2 cm
(14 × 10 in.)

Chop Suey
Edward Hopper
1929
Oil on canvas
81.3 × 96.5 cm
(32 × 38 in.)

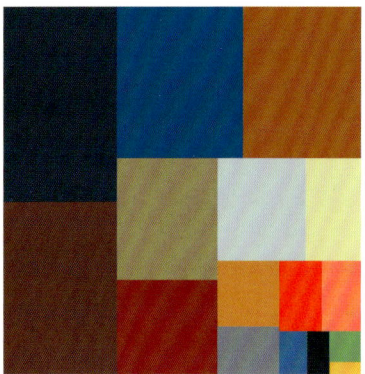

Proportional breakdown of colours used by Edward Hopper in *Chop Suey*, 1929, displayed on the previous page.

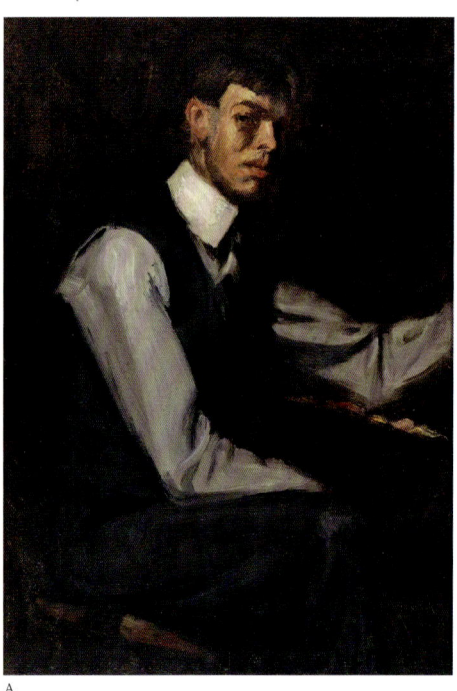

A.

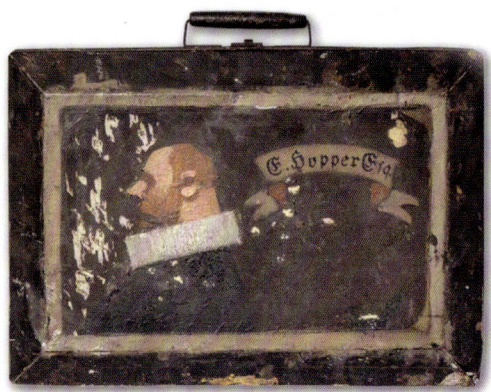

B.

EDWARD HOPPER REMAINS almost as inscrutable as his paintings. Inspired and influenced by several European and American styles and movements, he never fully followed any of them, and did not talk much about his work, preferring quietly to develop his distinctive use of colour, line, light and shadow. Much of his life and work is defined by absence, silence and a sense of mystery. This palette is equally elusive and reluctant to give up its secrets.[1] Rectangular in shape and probably made from mahogany or a similar hardwood, it is the only known palette by the great American painter of eeriness and emptiness. It possibly originates from his earlier period, although it cannot be dated exactly. However, he didn't fully embrace oil paint as a medium until the mid 1920s. It was possibly manufactured by New York- and Chicago-based supplier and manufacturer F. W. Devoe & C. T. Raynolds Co. Hopper owned a personalized tin paintbox made by the supplier, which also traded in European paints, including an extensive range of Winsor & Newton's Prepared Oil Colours for Artists in collapsible tubes. Palettes of this shape were often included in paintboxes, inserted into the lid and held in place with clips, but this one is larger than Hopper's metal box.

The palette has been scraped or wiped down in order to be used again, although not completely. The oil paint left on it is extremely thin yet still glows warmly, giving a sense of Hopper's preferred choice of rich and saturated colours, often in combination with gleaming whites and very dark shades. Hopper had cut his teeth as an etcher and knew exactly where to place shadows and light, taking some inspiration from black-and-white photography. The thinness of the paint may be a result of cleaning the palette, but Hopper did also paint in thin layers, diluting the paint with turpentine and adding oil as he went along, moving swiftly away from his early impasto work in paler colours. Line mattered much more to him than texture, which means that his compositions have a physical flatness that creates depth through a masterful assemblage of colour planes and severe, measured angularity.

He was aware of the colour theory that informed the works of impressionists and post-impressionists: he often used complementary colours, resulting in a glowing, sometimes garish, tonality, especially in his urban and night scenes. In *Chop Suey* (1929) warm, saturated oranges and reds, similar to those seen on the palette, form the central axis of the composition. They contrast with the blues of one of the women's hats, the interior walls and external shadows. To complete the colour wheel, the other woman's top is of a rich green. A bright yellow shaft of sunlight cuts diagonally through the background. Hopper softens this arrangement with ochres, umbers, muted mauves, and the alabaster white

> '*My aim in painting has always been the most exact transcription possible of my most intimate impressions of nature. If this end is unattainable, so, it can be said, is perfection in any other ideal of painting or in any other of man's activities.*'

EDWARD HOPPER, 'NOTES ON PAINTING', 1933

of the table and main figure's face. White can also be seen on the palette.

No one ever seems to speak, look at one another or even move in Hopper's paintings, and the artist himself was not verbose either. He made few comments on his techniques and was not especially talkative when interviewed on the topic in 1959. However, he explained that he switched from brittle zinc white to more powdery lead white in the 1940s, and indicated his trust in Winsor & Newton paints and prepared grounds.[2] He also read from his 'Notes on Painting' on the occasion, a short text he had written in 1933 for his first retrospective, in which he touched on the limiting materiality of paint, while admitting that he saw human emotion as the driving force of art: 'I believe that the great painters with their intellect as master have attempted to force this unwilling medium of paint and canvas into a record of their emotions. I find any digression from this large aim leads me to boredom.'[3]

Hopper's notes on his masterpiece *Nighthawks* (1942) – where he conveys urban alienation through placing figures like statues in geometric lines and shadows, and through his use of a limited palette of contrasting colours – are brusque in their shortness, but they confirm his preference for European materials: 'Finished Jan 21, 1942. [*Belgian*] Blockx and [*English*] Winsor & Newton colours, W & N Zinc white, poppy oil. English linen, domestic priming.'[4] Lines added by his wife Jo manage to capture the strange chromatic map of the *Nighthawks* scene and the spirit of Hopper's palette of the mind:

> Night + brilliant interior of cheap restaurant. Bright items: cherry wood counter…brilliant streak of jade green tiles…. Light walls, dull yellow ocre [*sic*] door into kitchen right. Very good looking blond boy in white (coat, cap) inside counter. Girl in red dress, brown hair eating sandwich. Man night hawk (beak) in dark suit, steel grey hat, black band, blue shirt (clean) holding cigarette. Other figure dark sinister back – at left. Light sidewalk outside pale greenish. Darkish, old red brick houses opposite…. Outside of shop dark green.[5]

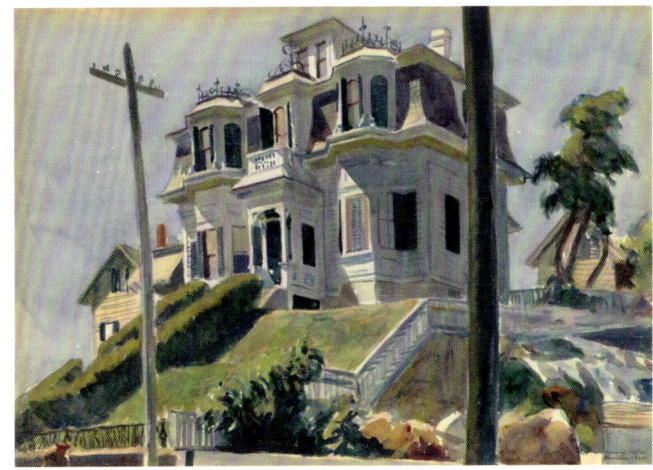

C.

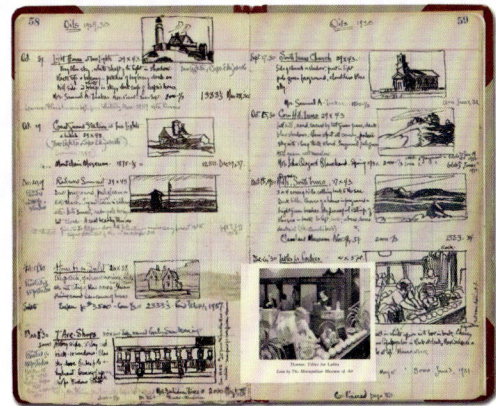

D.

A. *Self-portrait*, Edward Hopper, 1903, oil on canvas, 35.9 × 25.9 cm (14 ⅛ × 10 ¼ in.)
B. Edward Hopper's F. W. Devoe paintbox, *c.* 1892–95, hand-painted metal, 24.1 × 34.3 × 59.1 cm (9 ½ × 13 ½ × 23 ¼ in.)
C. *Haskell's House*, Edward Hopper, 1924, watercolour and graphite on paperboard, 34.3 × 49.5 cm (13 ½ × 19 ½ in.)
D. Edward Hopper's ledger, book I, fol. 58–59, 1913–63, pen, ink and graphite pencil on paper, 31.1 × 19.1 cm (12 ¼ × 7 ½ in.)
E. (Overleaf) *Nighthawks*, Edward Hopper, 1942, oil on canvas, 84.1 × 152.4 cm (33 ⅛ × 60 in.)

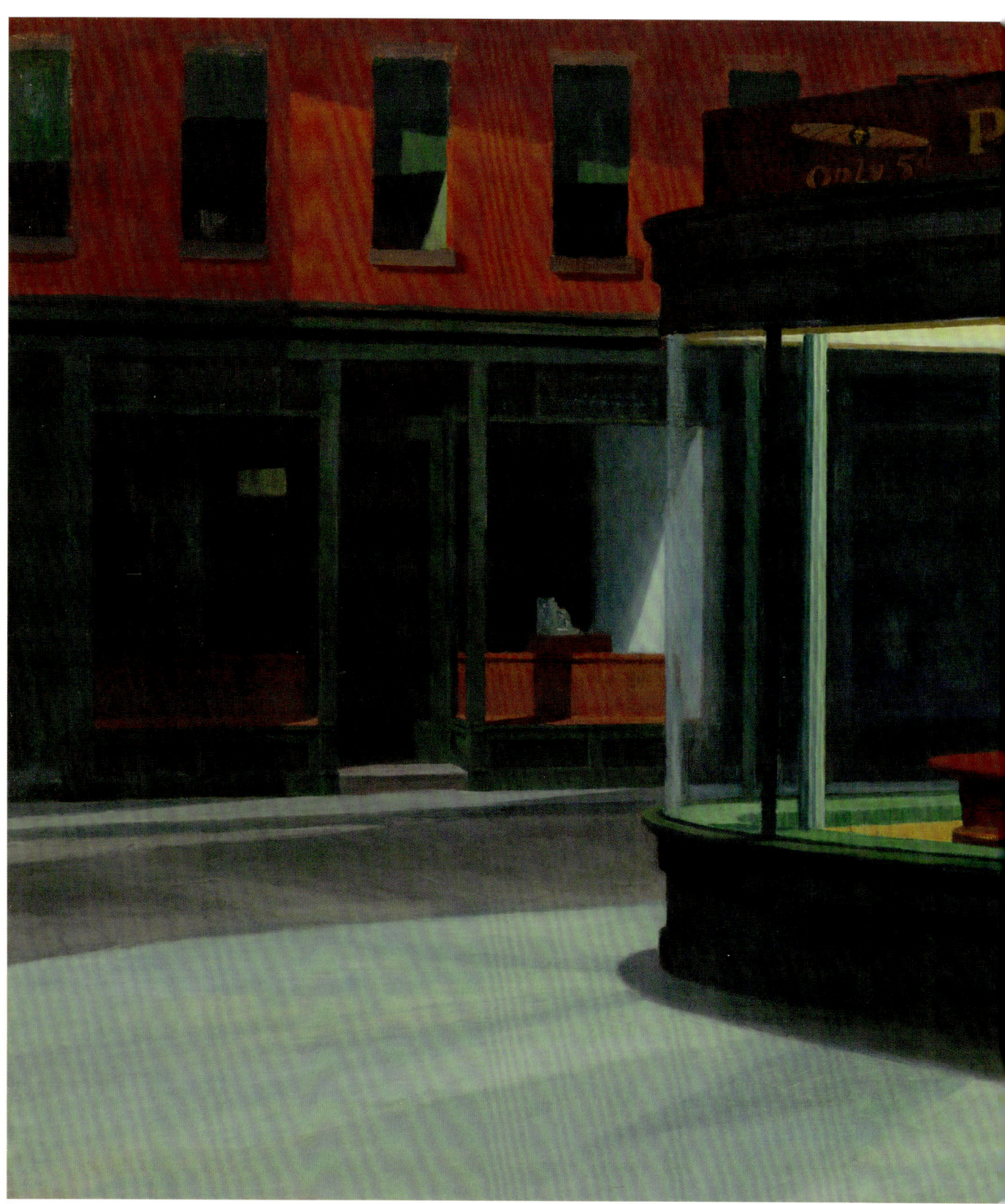

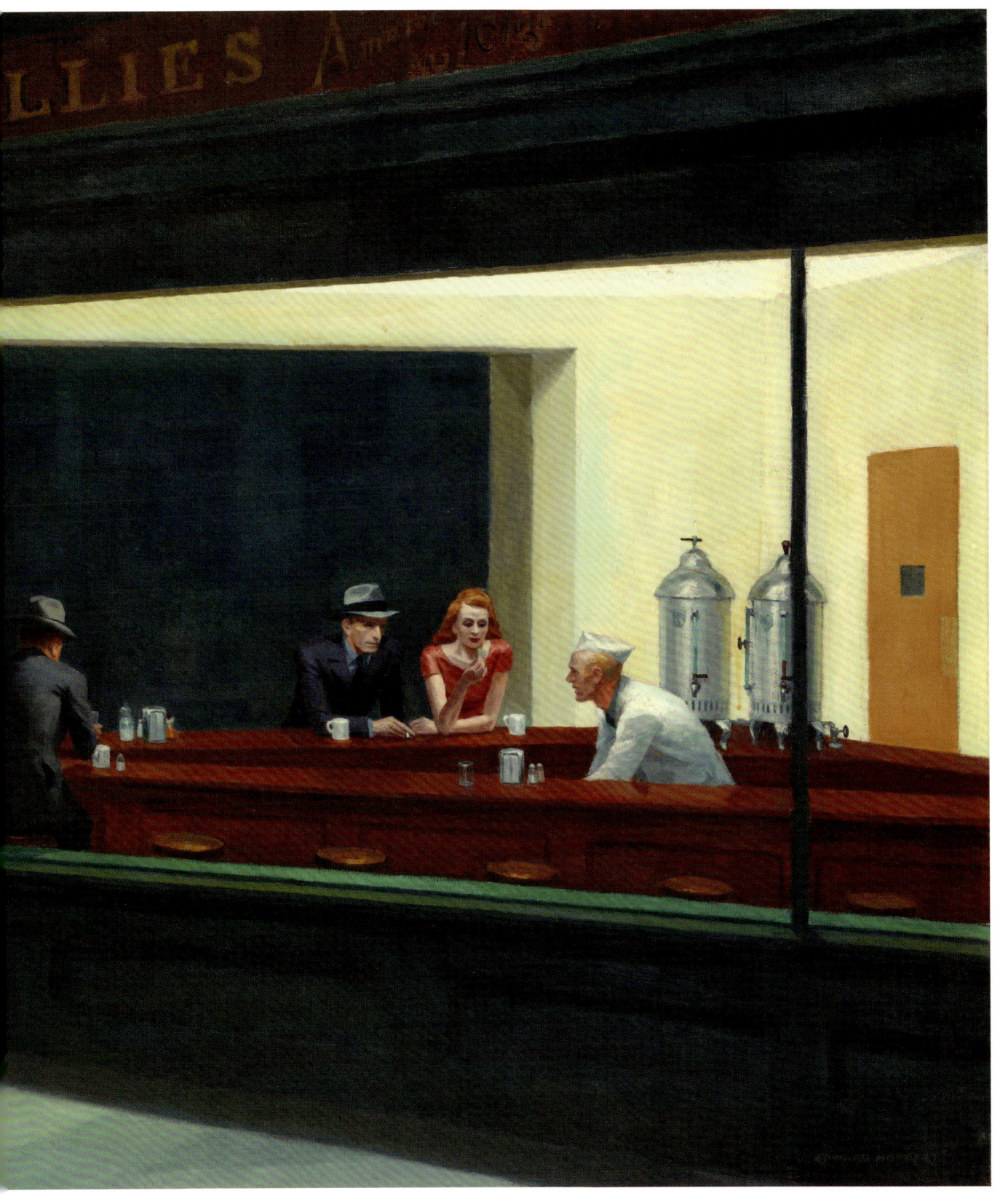

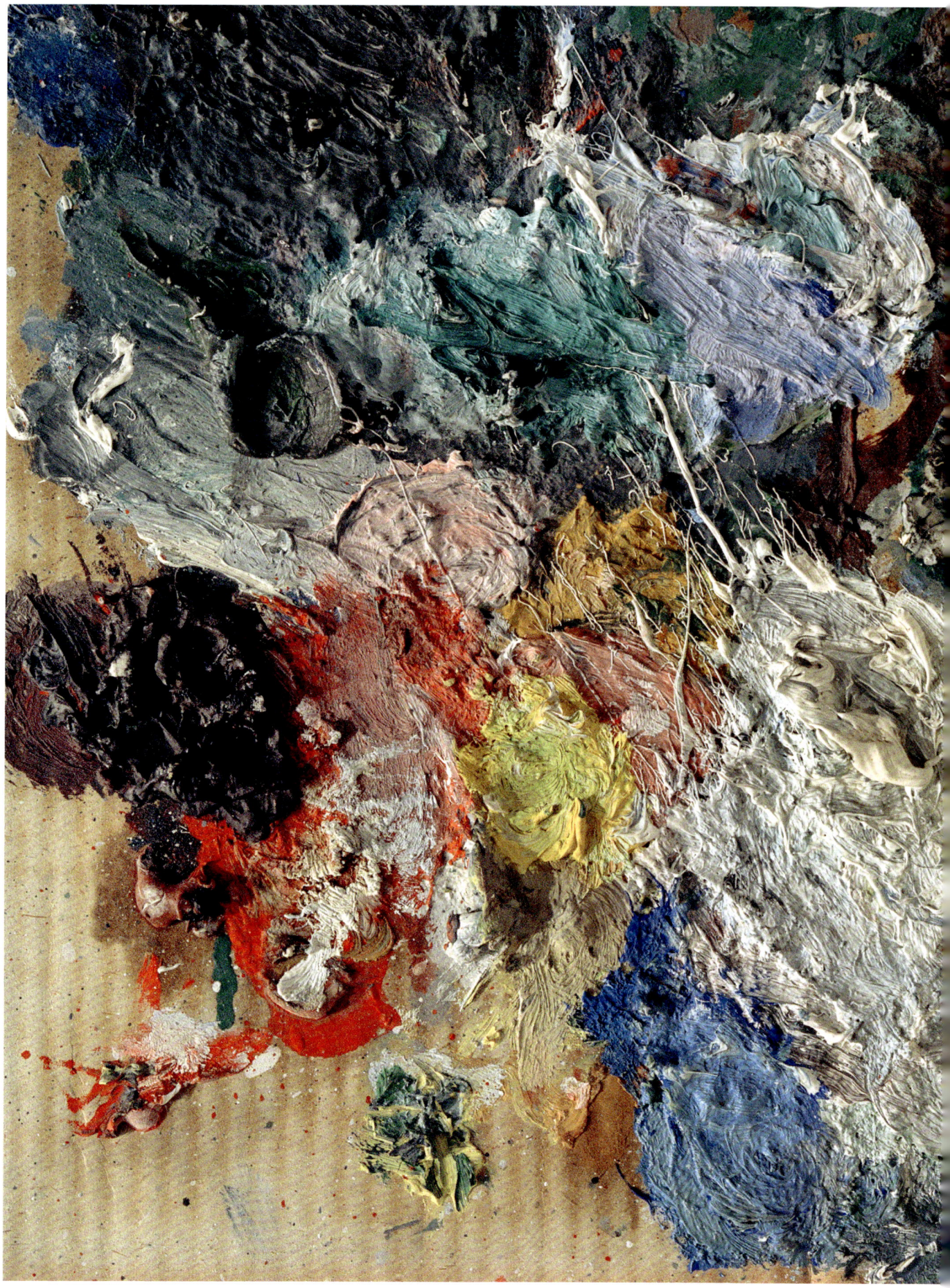

1931– Present

The Liberated Palette

IN THIS FINAL SECTION, covering a period when political events and social changes encouraged breaking with certain traditions and took the visual arts out of the greater academic context, we see examples of artists reinterpreting, refashioning or even relinquishing the traditional palette. Privileged artists such as Helen Frankenthaler were able to experiment with large studios and scales, abandoning the confinement of the historical studio space. The later 20th century also gave rise to artists who used streets, buildings or unused advertising spaces as palettes and paint surfaces. Keith Haring is one of the most experimental figures in this respect. He painted ephemeral works in public spaces, accepting the transience of his art, embracing the commercialization and digitization of art, while also displaying an understanding of historic traditions. This section comprises the full panoply of palettes: from small creative platforms in the traditional sense and irreverent, joyful, transgressive formats to subversive concepts of what constitutes a palette, finishing with Kerry James Marshall's profound exploration of the symbolic power of colour and palettes.

JOAN MIRÓ 1893–1983

A starman's cosmic palette

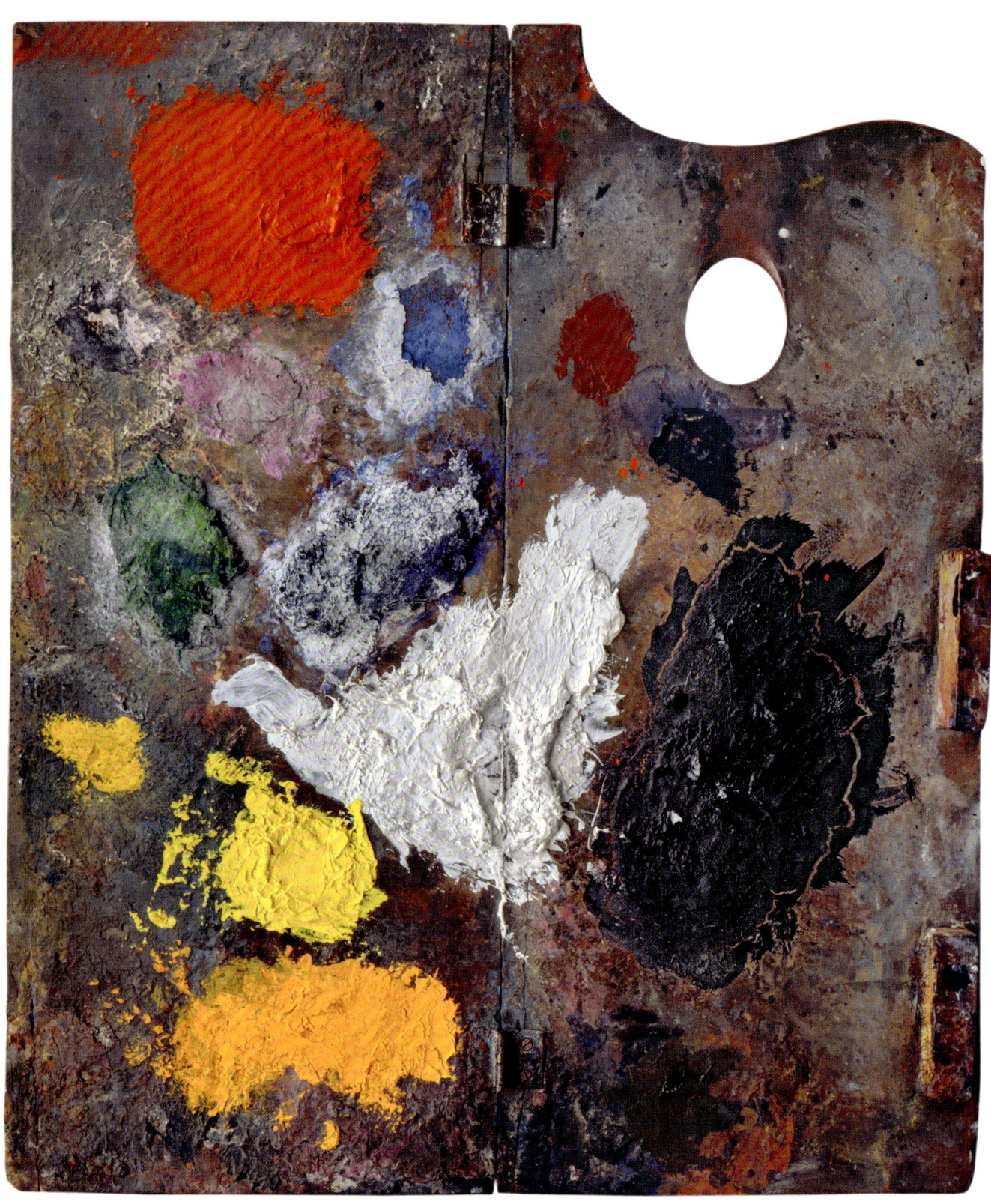

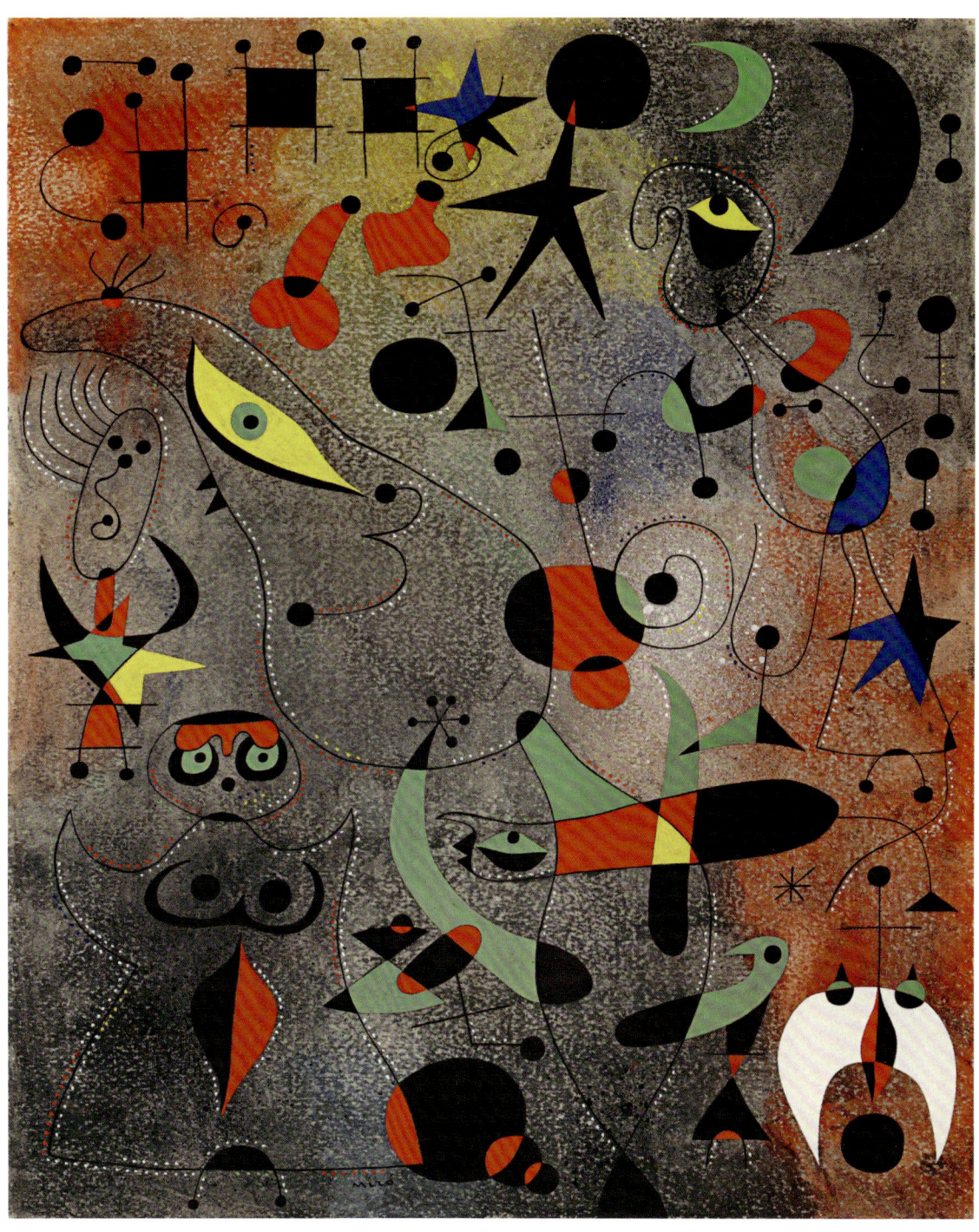

Joan Miró's palette
Undated
Paint on wood

Awakening in the Early Morning
Plate 14 from *Constellations*
Joan Miró
1941
Gouache and oil wash on paper
46 × 38 cm
(18 ⅛ × 15 in.)

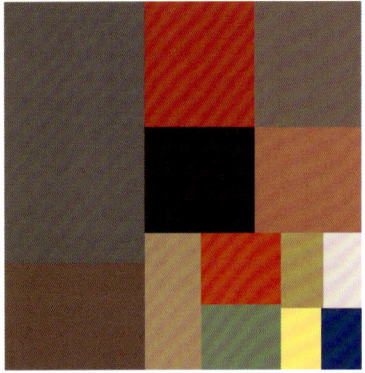

Proportional breakdown of colours used by Joan Miró in *Awakening in the Early Morning*, 1941, displayed on the previous page.

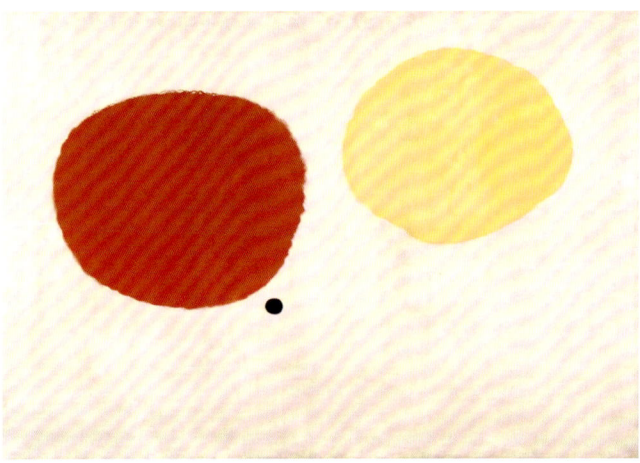

A.

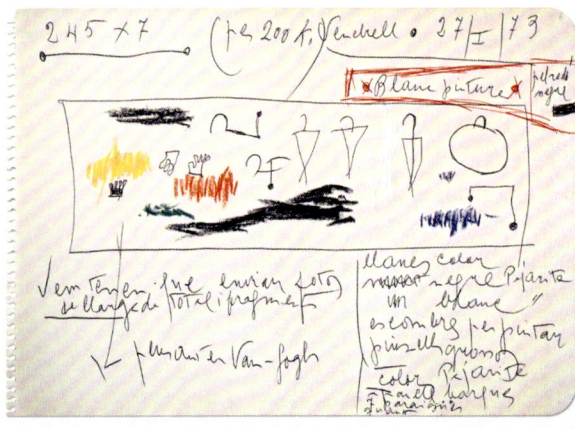

B.

IN JOAN MIRÓ'S WORK we see splattering as well as fine brushwork, black skies as well as pure saturated colours, wild starburst patterns as well as sensitive and precise lines. Underpinning it all lie warmth, humour and the artist's outstanding sense for composition and the relationship of colour, form and poetry.

This undated palette is foldable and made of wood. We don't know which painting he used it for, but it carries colours that are typical of Miró during several periods of his career. The paint is most likely gouache or oil, or possibly both. Black, white and a brilliant red take up most of the space, while a zingy orange and yellow also make an appearance, although there is no discernible order to this layout, nor are there any neutral earth or skin tones. The artist has mixed some greens and a pinkish violet, and has added a small patch of a darker shade of red.

Awakening in the Early Morning, from the *Constellations* series (1940–41), shows some of these typical Miró colours, including the vibrant red. The series was painted in gouache and thinned oil paint on paper, in small formats, but Miró creates the illusion of a vast cosmic space. A multitude of precisely outlined figures – some resembling stars, planets and sickle moons, others more organic, human or birdlike in shape – float free on a homogenous flat background. In his quest for purity and abstraction he gradually tilted his surreal world into a brilliant tapestry of line, colour and contrast.

Miró had been steadily working towards simplification and economy in his work, developing his own version of the dreamlike, lyrical style of abstraction. 'My desire,' he stated, 'is to attain a maximum intensity with a minimum of means. That is why my painting has gradually become more sparse.'[1] This simplification concerned not only representational figures but also colour. From around the late 1930s, he had eliminated any sense of shading, and predominantly used black, white and the primary colours in painting.

Miró once jotted down notes for a proposed series of paintings. He planned to begin with a 'linear motif in sienna or a muted colour', then proceed to 'quickly drawing with a brush and dribbling grey oil paint' on the canvas, after which a green ground would be applied, onto which a final drawing in charcoal would be added. He mentions fine brushes, very liquid paint and 'very pale colours', and considers using Titian pale green, Titian brown and burnt sienna for the preparation. Where then, in these notes, are Miró's brilliant colours and deep blacks? We find them at the very end of the list, like non-negotiable chromatic exclamation marks: 'black, primary colours, black outline.'[2]

By the mid 20th century Miró had a huge range of brilliant synthetic colours at his disposal, as well as

'You already know the pictorial process: 1. Pure line. 2. Pure colours. 3. Nuances, the charm and music of colour.'

JOAN MIRÓ, LETTER TO MICHEL LEIRIS, 10 AUGUST 1924

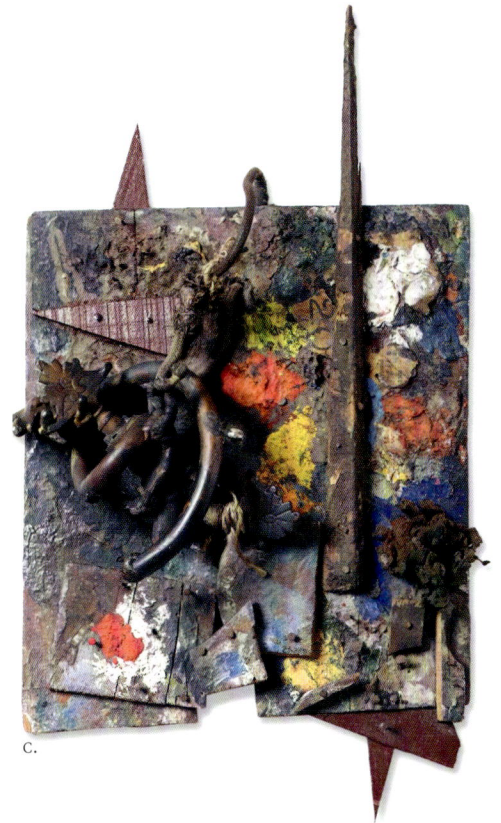

C.

a new type of paint, quick-drying acrylics, which he tried out but did not like. We know that he used emerald green, Prussian blue and cool zinc white. He preferred cadmium-based yellows and oranges to chrome-based paints, which he considered too dull. A recent study has revealed that he paid a price for this choice, as some of his thinly applied cadmium yellows have deteriorated and become almost transparent:[3] Some of Miró's suns, moons and stars don't shine as brightly any more. The artist, it appears, was not worried about this. In a 1959 interview he exclaimed that, like his surrealist friends and colleagues, he did not consider painting as an end in itself: 'One must not worry about whether a painting will last, but whether a painting has planted seeds that give birth to other things.'[4]

It is tempting to look for palette-like outlines in Miró's exquisite catalogue of visual metaphors, but they are surprisingly rare. In 1917, he included a palette in the background of a portrait of the artist Enric Cristòfol Ricart. It hangs on the wall like an abstract work of art, painted in bold outlines, with a random sequence of colour blots that look like boiled sweets. Miró's irreverent attitude to palettes found another expression in 1952, when he turned one into a roughly honed, three-dimensional collage that he called *Barbarian Object* (image C.). The wooden palette, encrusted with remains of oil paint in Miró's typical colours, has broken bits of metal, wood, paper and string attached to its surface in a seemingly random crude manner. Is this perhaps a collage version of a *Constellation* picture, in which the artist's palette forms the cosmic background?

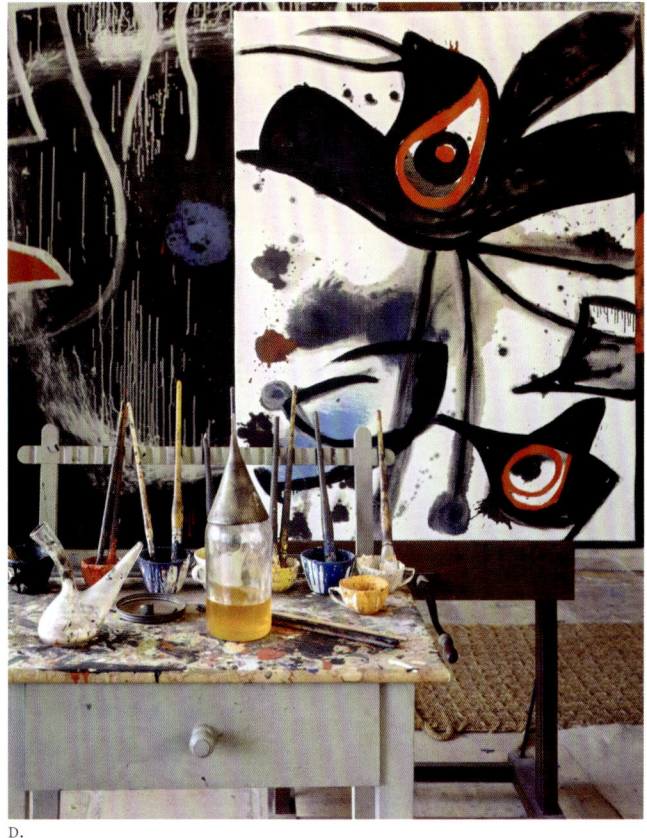

A.   *Painting (The Magic of Colour)*, Joan Miró, 1930, oil on canvas, 150.2 × 225.1 cm (59 ⅛ × 88 ⅝ in.)
B.   Page from Joan Miró's sketchbook, 1987
C.   *Barbarian Object*, Joan Miró, 1952, oil, paper, string, sponge and metal on wood (artist's palette and wedges), 35.5 × 22 × 5.8 cm (14 × 8 ¾ × 2 ⅜ in.)
D.   Joan Miró's studio, photograph by Evelyn Hofer, 1987

D.

GEORGES BRAQUE 1882–1963

A sinuous, intuitive palette

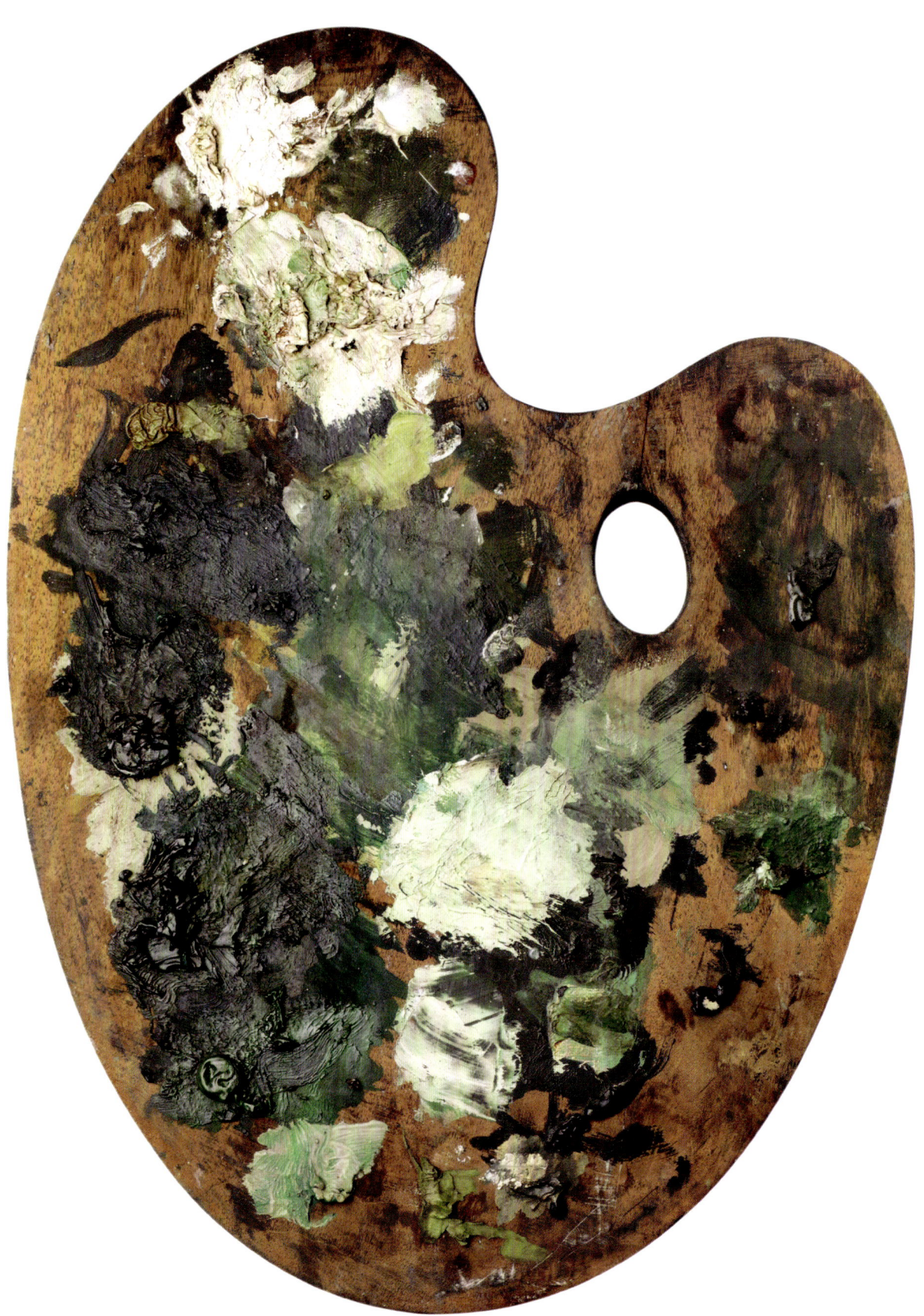

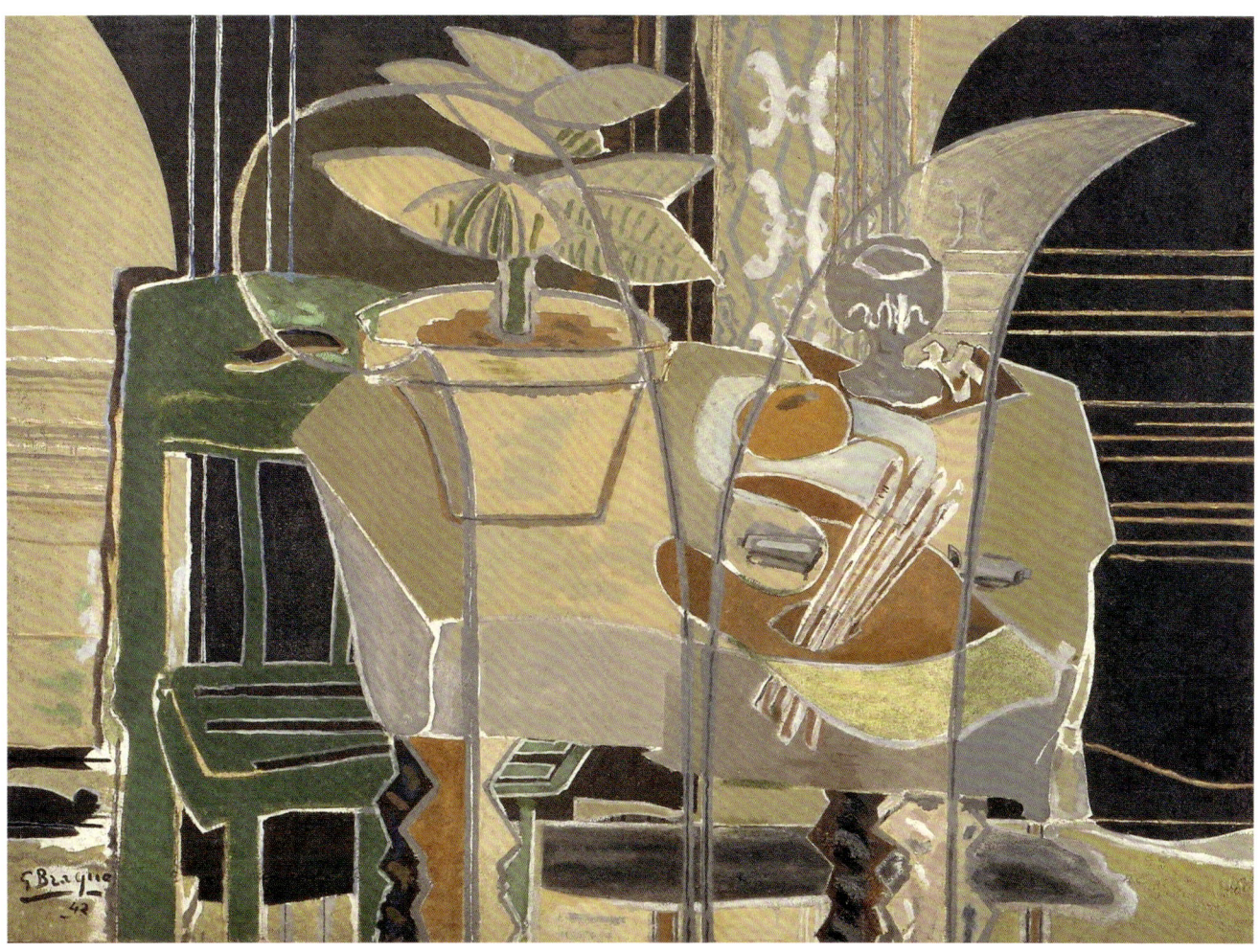

Georges Braque's palette
1948
Oil on wood

Large Interior with Palette
Georges Braque
1942
Oil and sand on canvas
141.3 × 195.6 cm
(55 ⅝ × 77 in.)

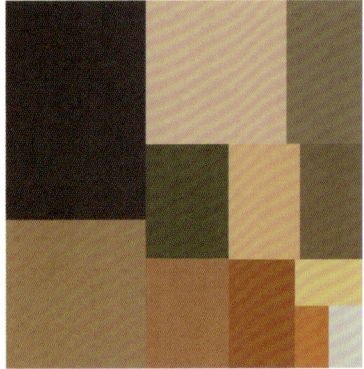

Proportional breakdown of colours used by Georges Braque in *Large Interior with Palette*, 1942, displayed on the previous page.

THIS PALETTE BY THE GREAT cubist artist Georges Braque is loosely covered in a muted, sombre range of soft greens, warm whites and yellows, and blacks, mostly mixed on the surface. It is impossible to detect a pattern or initial layout of paints. This looks like an incidental, intuitive palette, languidly and calmly created with predominantly earth pigments; a painter's tool reduced to a wooden surface for holding and blending paint, instead of a conceptual space for a painting. The warm tonal range and the soft handling of the paint are typical of Braque's style, and although we cannot link the palette to a specific painting, it is close to the work shown on the preceding page, *Large Interior with Palette* (1942), which includes the sinuous outline of a two-toned wooden palette that appears to balance on the edge of a table, complete with a bunch of long brushes. In one of his more vibrantly coloured works, *Studio with Black Vase* (1938, image C.), another heart-shaped, stylized palette makes an appearance, this time with a hint of a colour layout in the form of four squiggly blots of paint: a dusky blue, a black with a grey highlight, a fiery warm orange and a luminous purple, all of which also appear in the painting.

Braque was almost predominantly a painter of still lifes, and some of these are composed in an oval shape or include vaguely oval objects, such as plates, jugs or indeed palettes, giving the appearance of a nucleus, or an ovoid cell. He took immense pleasure in creating elongated shapes and flowing lines, and avoided hard angles. He overlapped these gentle but bold contours with more angular, cubic shapes, creating geometric, yet fluid and layered patterns that he filled with sensitive colour harmonies. The flatness of his compositions betrays the fact that he was also a collagist and printmaker.

Braque's fluidity of line and the collage-style of his paintings was reflected in the arrangement of his studio and his working methods. In the late 1940s he received

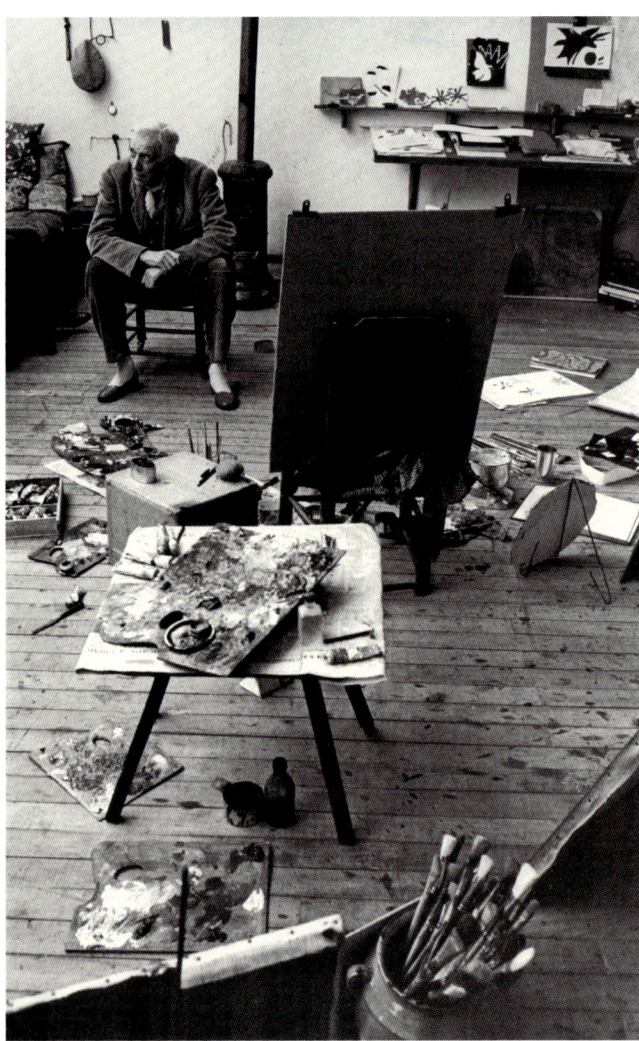

A.

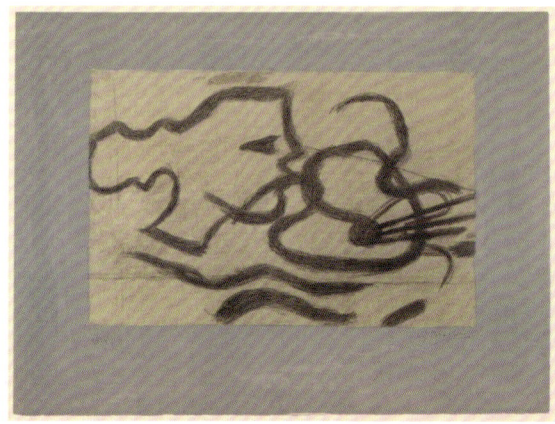

B.

'The Painter thinks in forms and colours. The object is his poetic aim.'

GEORGES BRAQUE, QUOTED IN HENRY R. HOPE'S *GEORGES BRAQUE*
EXHIBITION CATALOGUE, 1949

several visitors in his studio, including the historian Henry Radford Hope, who described it as a space filled with potted plants and flowers – ready to be arranged for the next painting, collage or print. He usually worked on many paintings at the same time, all sitting on easels, with the artist drifting within this forest of unfinished works, moving them around to work nearer the light while leaving others to dry.

Was there method and planning to his colours, his palette layout, his art? He explained that he never planned a picture, and thus it is unlikely that he set palettes in any methodical or academic way, but the ones that survive are a mirror of his creative process:

> I could not do otherwise than I do. The picture makes itself under the brush. I insist on this point. There must be no preconceived idea. A picture is an adventure each time. When I tackle the white canvas, I never know what will come out. This is the risk you must take. I never visualize a picture in my mind before starting to paint.[1]

Hope once watched Braque paint a still life and recalls that he indeed started with a white-ground canvas, drawing rough outlines of his motifs in colour, then filling in the areas around them in a different colour, before adding a broad strip of black across the top. He occasionally added colour notes, presumably in pencil, to half-finished paintings, and was experimental in his treatment of pigments and paint. He was known to add sand to his paints, perhaps to give them more texture, or underline the earthiness of colour schemes. Watching Braque at work, Hope noted that it was 'like watching a virtuoso violinist to see him apply paint.'[2]

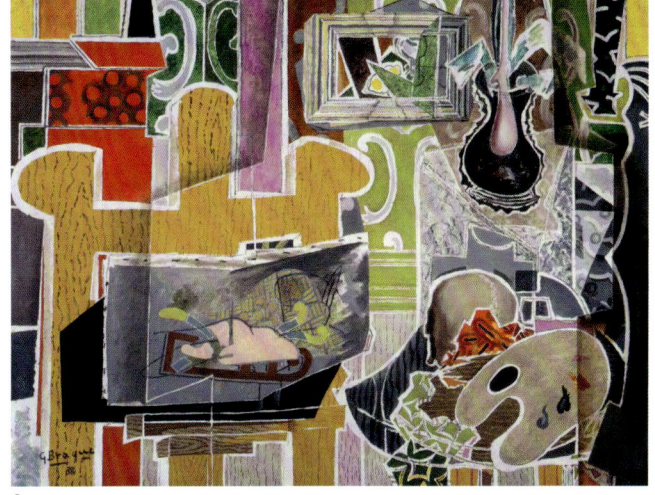

C.

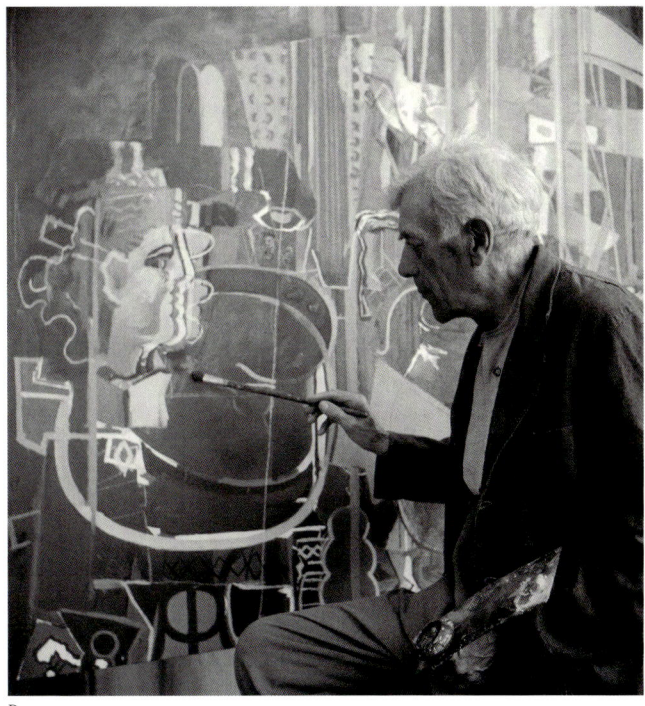

A.   Georges Braque in his studio, Paris, France, *c*. 1963
B.   *Profile with Palette*, Georges Braque, 1953, lithograph on paper, 52 × 71.2 cm (20 ½ × 28 in.)
C.   *Studio with Black Vase*, Georges Braque, 1938, oil and sand on canvas, 97.2 × 129.5 cm (38 ¼ × 51 in.)
D.   Georges Braque, France, photograph by Boris Lipnitzki, 1949

D.

PIET MONDRIAN 1872–1944

An 'abstract-real' palette in search of purity

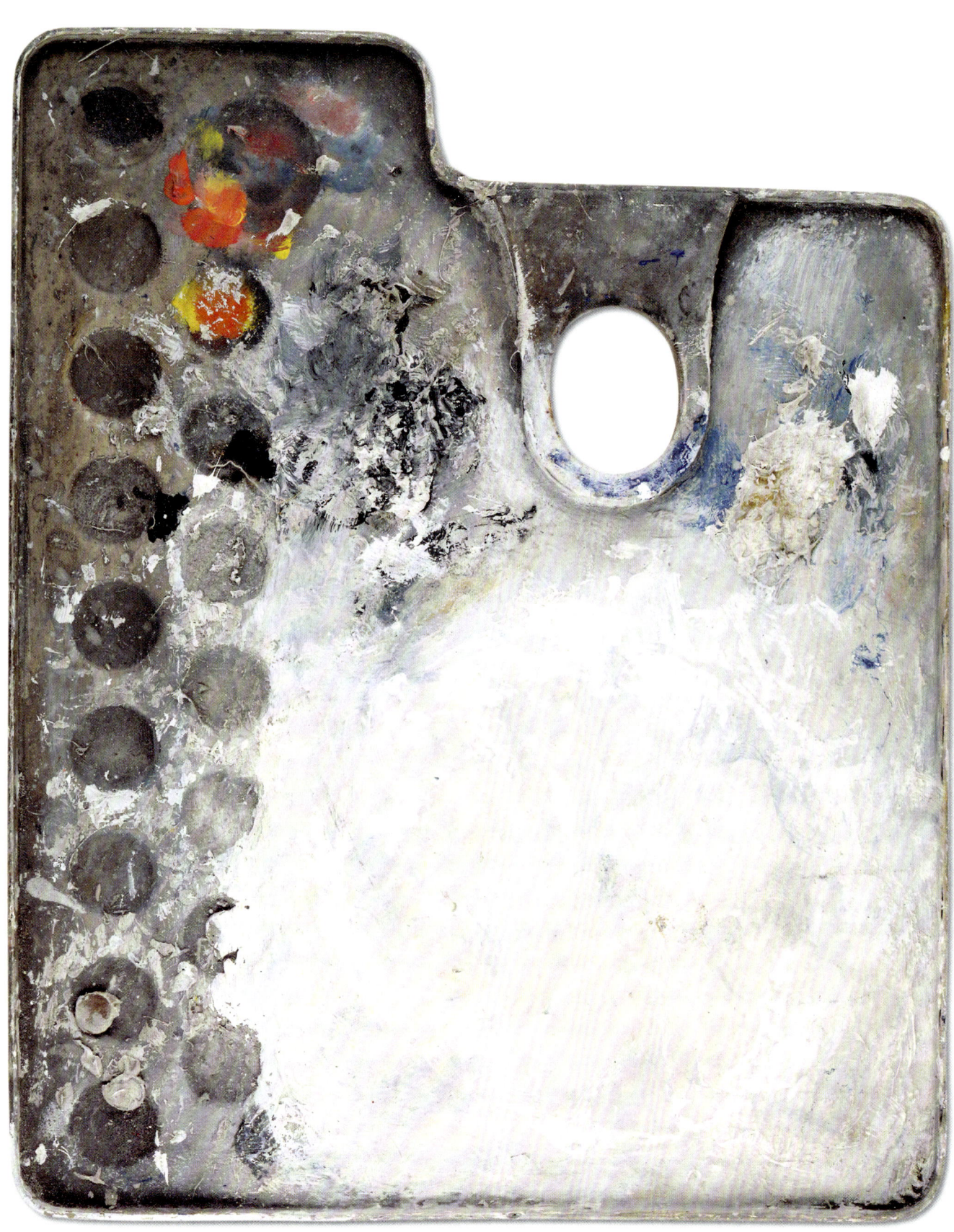

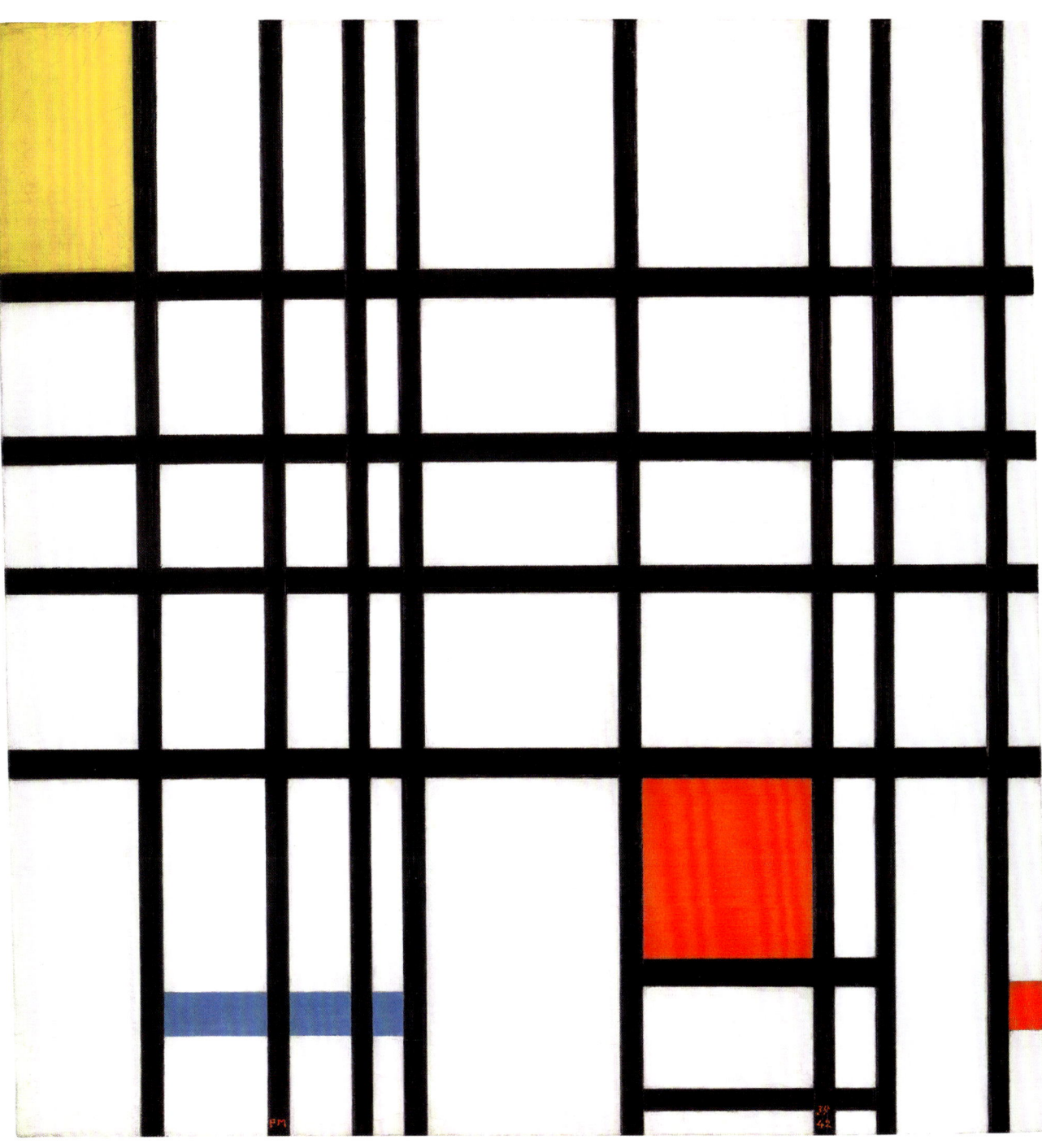

Piet Mondrian's   *Composition with*
palette   *Yellow, Blue and Red*
Undated   Piet Mondrian
Paint on metal   1937–42
                           Oil on canvas
                           72.7 × 69.2 cm
                           (28 ⅝ × 27 ¼ in.)

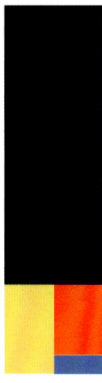

Proportional breakdown of colours used by Piet
Mondrian in *Composition with Yellow, Blue and Red*,
1937–42, displayed on the previous page.

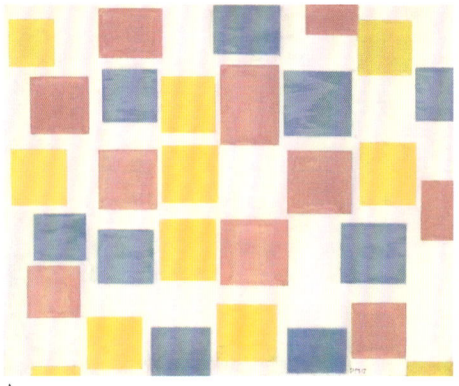

A.

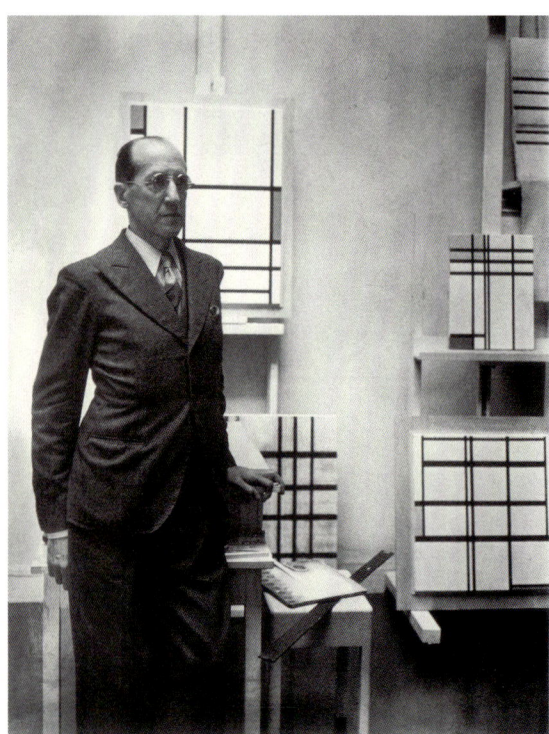

B.

WOULD YOU EXPECT anything other than a square
palette from Piet Mondrian? The shape may or may
not be a coincidence, but the remains of colour left on
it further enhance the resemblance this tool bears to
Mondrian's square, abstract grid paintings of primary
colours on white backgrounds. It is an undated metal
palette with a thumbhole, lipped edges and seventeen
circular indentations to hold small pools or blobs of paint.
The lipped edge and cavities make this a palette suitable
for water-based colour and allow for the thinning of
oil paint. Mondrian's use of the palette almost negates
its purpose, given the sheer amount of white paint left
on it, with only miniscule traces of chromatic colour
in and around two of the indentations, and what looks
like accidental smudges of blue near the thumbhole.
Almost the entire flat mixing area is covered in a thin
layer of white gouache or oil paint, with two mounds
of white above and below the thumbhole. The traces
of pure colour include small flat blots of red, blue,
yellow and green, which appear pure and unmixed,
while a warm orange and a pale pink have been created
through blending.

The proportion of chromatic colour to neutral
white bears a striking resemblance to Mondrian's grid
compositions on white ground from the late 1910s
onwards. These were part of his quest for simple,
abstract, pure order and beauty in art and design, or
'Abstract-Real Painting', as he referred to it in his first
published essay in 1917 ('The New Plastic in Painting'),
the same year he founded the *De Stijl* or neo-plasticist
movement. To achieve this level of purity, naturalism
was sacrificed for a deeper universal realism. One of the
key elements of this was colour, which, in Mondrian's
view, needed to be governed, flattened, reduced and
regulated: 'To determine colour involves, first, the
reduction of naturalistic colour to primary colour;
second, the reduction of colour to plane; third, the
delimitation of colour, so that it appears as a unity
of rectangular colour.'[1]

His own path to abstraction and the purity of his
late square, grid and line compositions was long: for
a couple of decades, he painted figurative pictures
and landscapes, many in muted colours, which in
the early 1900s evolved into more intensely coloured,
theosophical paintings with abstract elements. Slowly
but surely his shadows and horizons disappeared, to
be replaced with solid lines and contours; flowers
became colour planes, trees turned first into silhouetted
skeletons, then grids. Mondrian eventually arrived at
pure abstraction and used almost exclusively primary
colours. In 1941 he reflected on this journey: 'In my
early pictures, space was still a background. I began
to determine forms: verticals and horizontals became

'The first thing to change in my painting was the colour. I forsook natural colour for pure colour.'

PIET MONDRIAN, 'TOWARD THE TRUE VISION OF REALITY', 1941

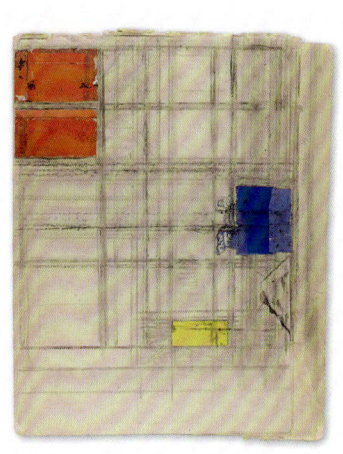

C.

rectangles [but] their colour was still impure. Feeling that lack of unity, I brought the rectangles together: space became white, black or grey; form became red, blue or yellow.'[2] For the sake of unity and purity, Mondrian often painted his frame in the same colour as the background of the composition.

It is tempting to think that this square palette is a material symbol of Mondrian's aesthetics and that it may have been used to create one of these late square paintings, but some aspects of it are puzzling. First, the absence of black. Did he use a separate palette for it or no palette at all? Second, the traces of green, pink and orange paint. In his abstract *Composition* paintings from the 1920s and 1930s, he almost exclusively used secondary or intermediate colours. However, in an earlier series from 1917–18, squares of bright yellows, light blues and dusty pinks without black outlines float on a white background (as can be seen in image A.). In a few paintings in this series, he experimented with gouache (in a departure from oil paint). This choice of medium may have been linked to his aim to create pastel tints, although he achieved similar pastel effects with oil paint.[3]

The black rectangular lines and right angles that define the pictorial space of the *Compositions* later developed into double or treble lines, and even acquired colour. In several versions painted in New York in the early 1940s, Mondrian even replaced paint with coloured tape, abandoning the concept of paint and palette altogether. He extended this concept of abstract purity to architecture and interiors, literally living his aesthetical ideal: his later studios in Paris and New York were designed and decorated according to the same principles, and resembled a three-dimensional version of one of his white-ground *Compositions*. A visitor described his Paris studio in the 1920s as 'a severe, businesslike room flooded with limpid, cool light, where [Mondrian] grapples with his material in monk-like solitude in his quest for his lofty, highly controversial ideal'.[4]

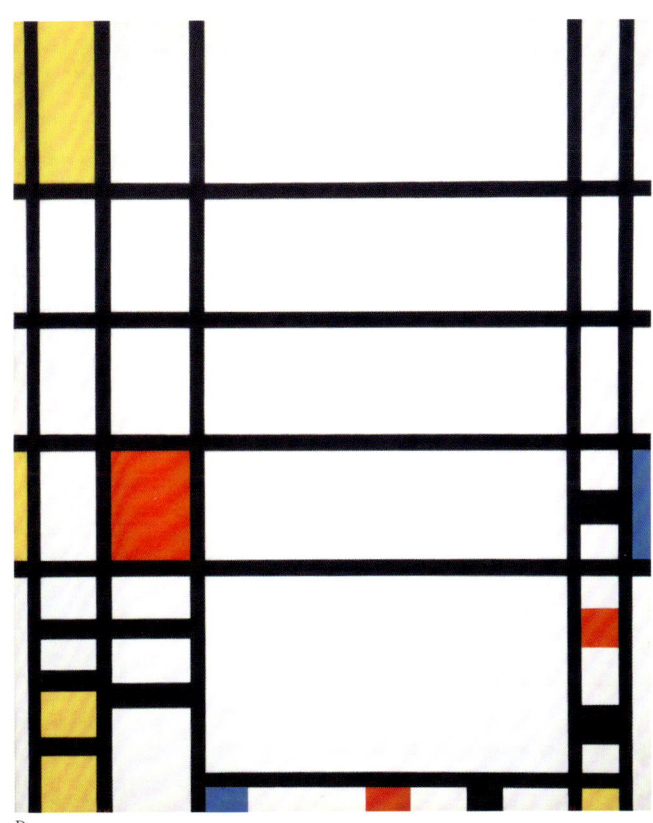

D.

A. *Composition with Colour Fields*, Piet Mondrian, 1917, oil on canvas, 48 × 60.5 cm (19 × 23 ⅞ in.)
B. Piet Mondrian in his studio, 278 Boulevard Raspail, Paris, France, photograph by Rogi André, 1937, gelatin silver print, 51 × 41 cm (20 ⅛ × 16 ¼ in.)
C. *Study for a Composition*, Piet Mondrian, 1940–41, collage of papers, with gouache and charcoal on newsprint in three parts, 33 × 27 cm (13 × 10 ¾ in.)
D. *Trafalgar Square*, Piet Mondrian, 1939–43, oil on canvas, 145.2 × 120 cm (57 ¼ × 47 ¼ in.)

PABLO PICASSO 1881–1973

A palette and some beasts

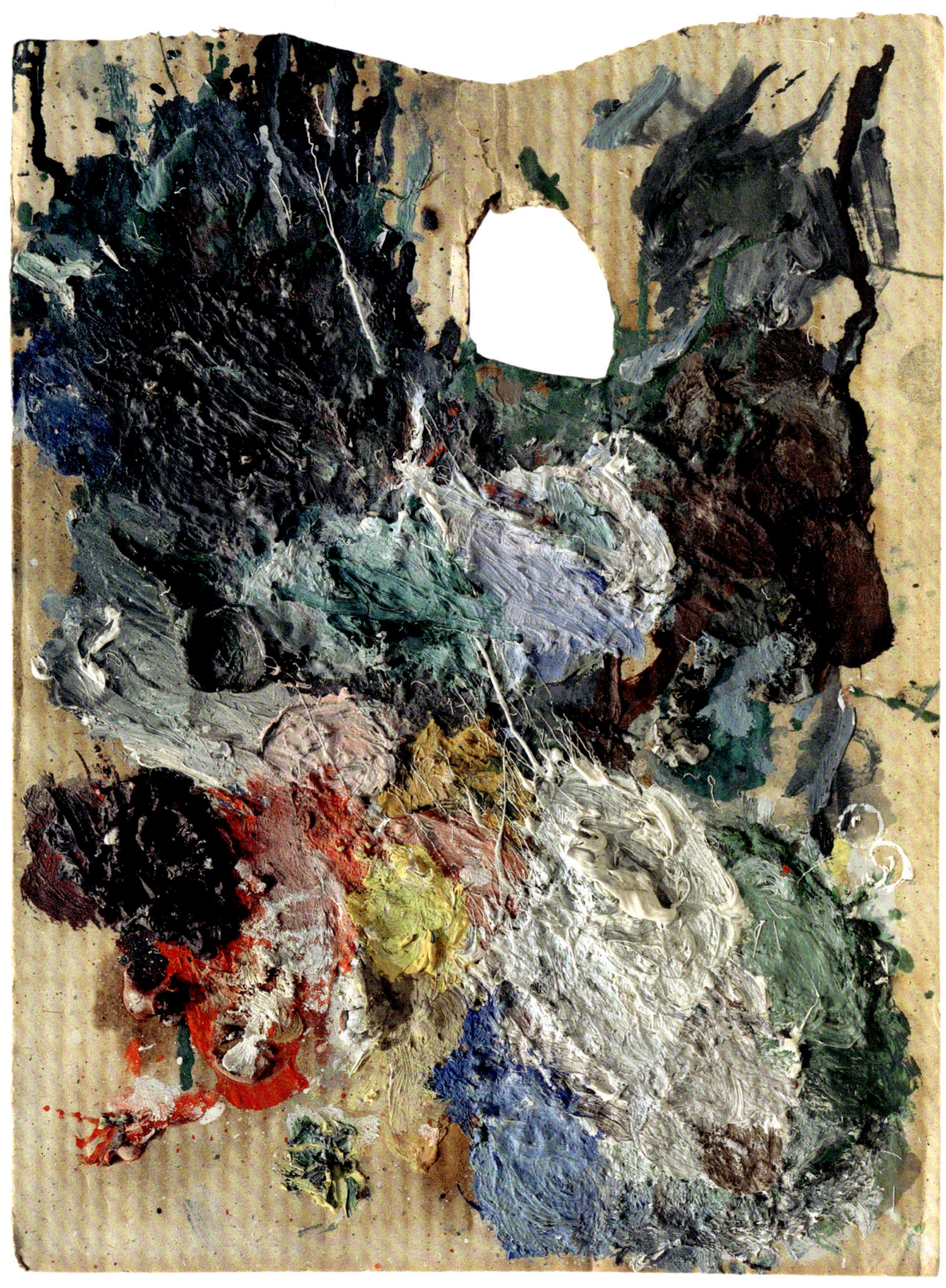

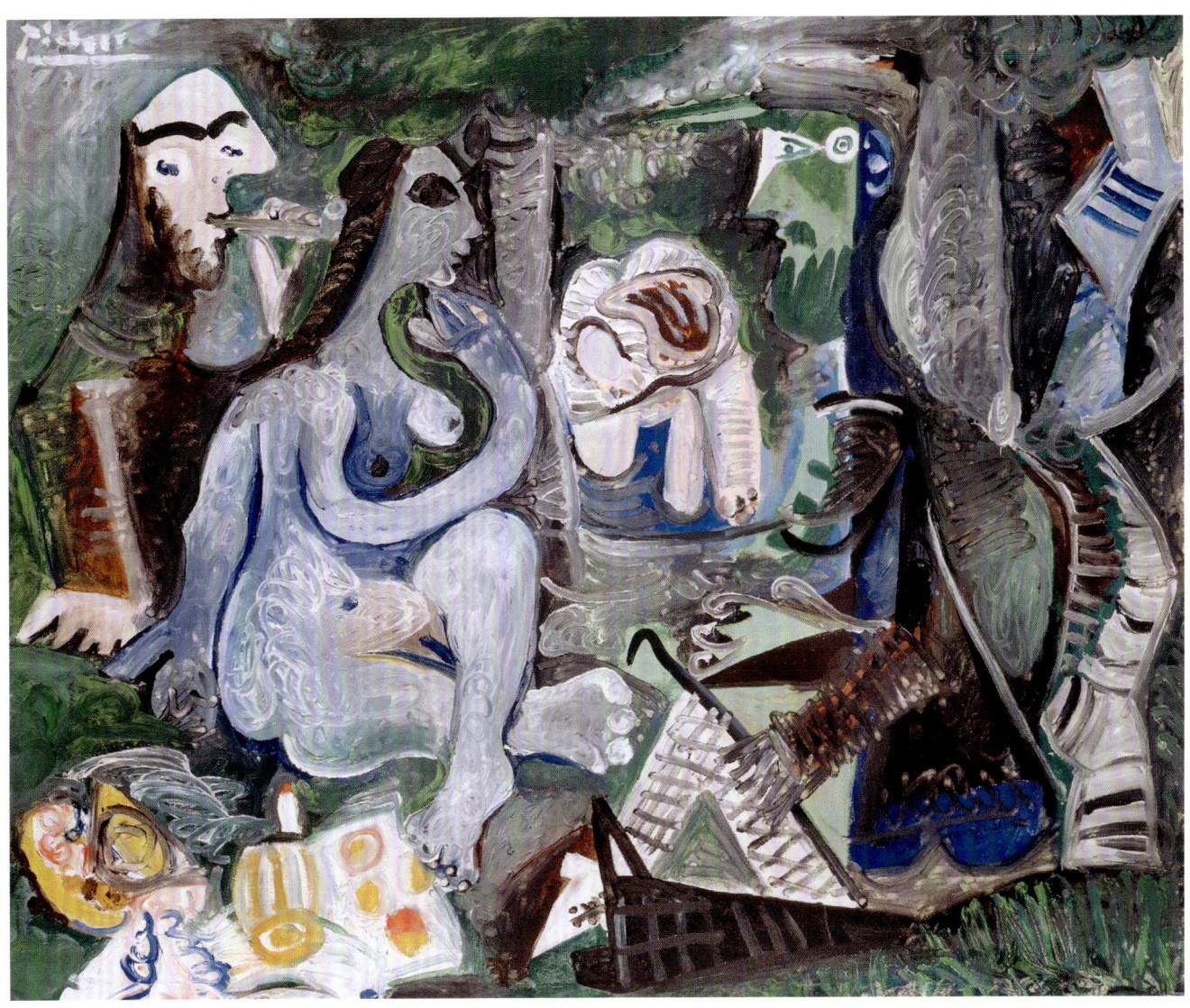

Pablo Picasso's palette
17 June 1961
Oil on card
29 × 37.8 cm
(11 ½ × 15 in.)

Le Déjeuner sur l'herbe
(The Luncheon on
the Grass)
Pablo Picasso
1961
Oil on canvas
60 × 73 cm
(23 ⅝ × 28 ¾ in.)

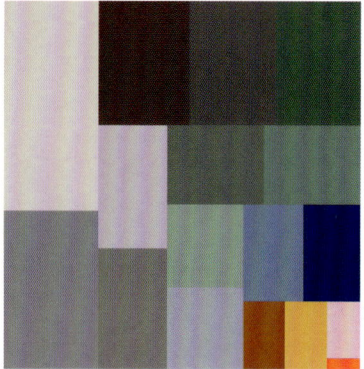

Proportional breakdown of colours used by Pablo Picasso in *Le Déjeuner sur l'herbe* (The Luncheon on the Grass), 1961, displayed on the previous page.

THIS PALETTE IS ONE OF THREE used by Pablo Picasso towards the end of his life that were sold at auction in 2020 for thousands of pounds. This confirms not only Picasso's status as one of the most important and intriguing artists of the 20th century, but also the emblematic, emotional and therefore monetary value attached to artists' palettes. Of these palettes (all dating from the 1960s and 1970s), this one is the most unusual since it was not only used by Picasso, but quite probably also made by him. Unlike the other two traditional wooden palettes, it is made from cardboard, cut out in the shape of a standard rectangular palette with a simple thumbhole. Paper and card were used by Picasso throughout his career in many ways, from experimental trials and sketchbooks to large-scale collages and even sculpture.[1] The idea of the hypercreative Picasso, in urgent need of a new palette, cutting one out of a piece of ordinary, ephemeral cardboard from his studio is as captivating as the remains of paint on it. There is evidence that he utilized other materials and objects as makeshift palettes, such as random pieces of wood and ceramic dinner plates.

The palette is dated precisely on the back, 17 June 1961, and can therefore be cautiously linked to some of his late paintings, among them a 1961 version of *Le Déjeuner sur l'herbe* (The Luncheon on the Grass), an homage to Edouard Manet's large oil painting of the same title painted roughly a century earlier. Manet's painting had inspired Picasso greatly, and he created more than 140 drawings, some linocuts and nearly thirty paintings in response to it, many of them between 1959 and 1961. The paint left on this palette is oil-based (the oil has seeped through the material and appears as large blotches on the back) and follows no particular layout, but certain vibrant colours used by Picasso in this period stand out: pure primaries red, blue

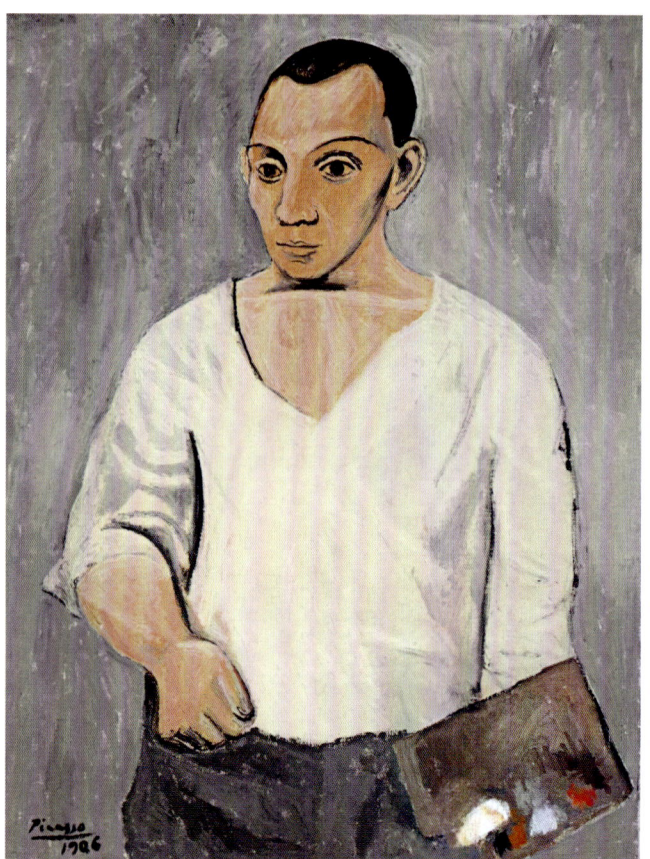

A.

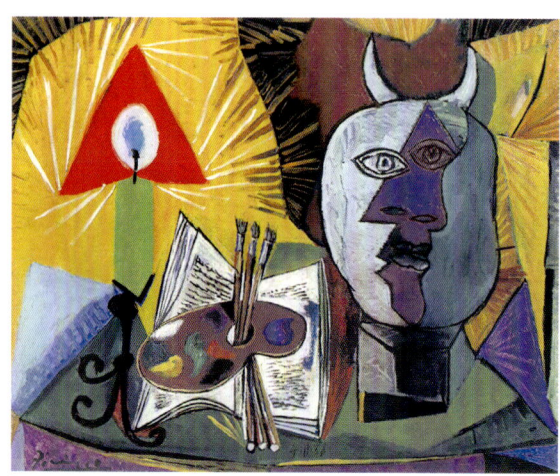

B.

'Actually, you work with few colours. But they seem like a lot more when each is in the right place.'

PABLO PICASSO IN AN INTERVIEW WITH CHRISTIAN ZERVOD, 1935

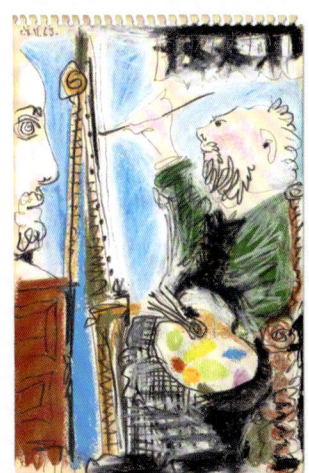

C.

and yellow, mixed in places with white and overlaid with darker colours, and greens that could well have been pre-mixed but to which white has been added. In the centre of the palette, Picasso has combined blue and green, while an ochre-looking yellow peeks through. Some pinks have been mixed from red and white, and there are large areas of dark shades, with green spilling out from under them, typical of the bold contours of many of his paintings.

Palettes also feature prominently as symbols and motifs in Picasso's work, for example, in several self-portraits, such as the early one he painted for Gertrude Stein in 1906 (image A.). Here, he presents the palette in a traditional manner, as an emblem of his art and an extension of himself. Palettes can also be seen in the iconography of his many images of artists' studios, and in a specific group of still lifes he produced in the late 1930s, comprising bulls' heads, candles, palettes and paintbrushes. The minotaur or bull motif is closely related to his monumental *Guernica* (1937), and in this pictorial context the artist's tools represent creativity and sensitivity as contrasted with violence, darkness and destruction.[2] For Picasso, palettes were creative weapons that carried light, colour and joy, whether they were cut out of cardboard for practical use or painted as potent symbols in his compositions.

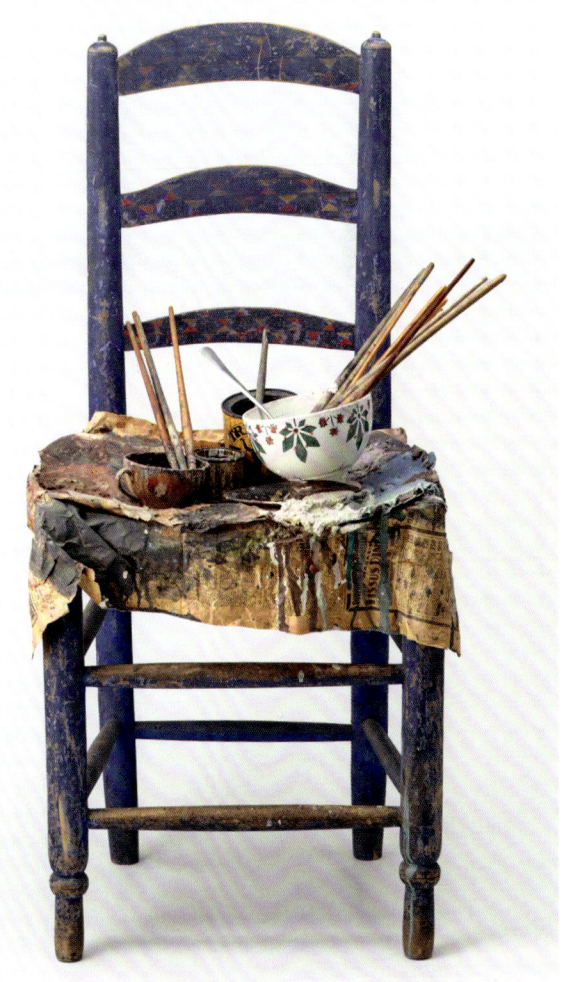

A. *Self-portrait with Palette*, Pablo Picasso, 1906, oil on canvas, 91.9 × 73.3 cm (36 ¼ × 28 ⅞ in.)
B. *Still Life with Palette, Candlestick and Head of Minotaur*, Pablo Picasso, 4 November 1938, oil on canvas, 73.7 × 90.2 cm (29 ⅛ × 35 ⅝ in.)
C. *The Painter in the Studio*, from notebook no. 57, fol. 26r., Pablo Picasso, 1963, coloured pencil, graphite and wax chalk on paper, 21.5 × 13.5 cm (8 ½ × 5 ⅜ in.)
D. Pablo Picasso's 'palette-chair', brushes, bowls, paint pots and newspaper on wooden chair with straw seat, 20th century

MARC CHAGALL 1887–1985

Painted palettes as symbols of love

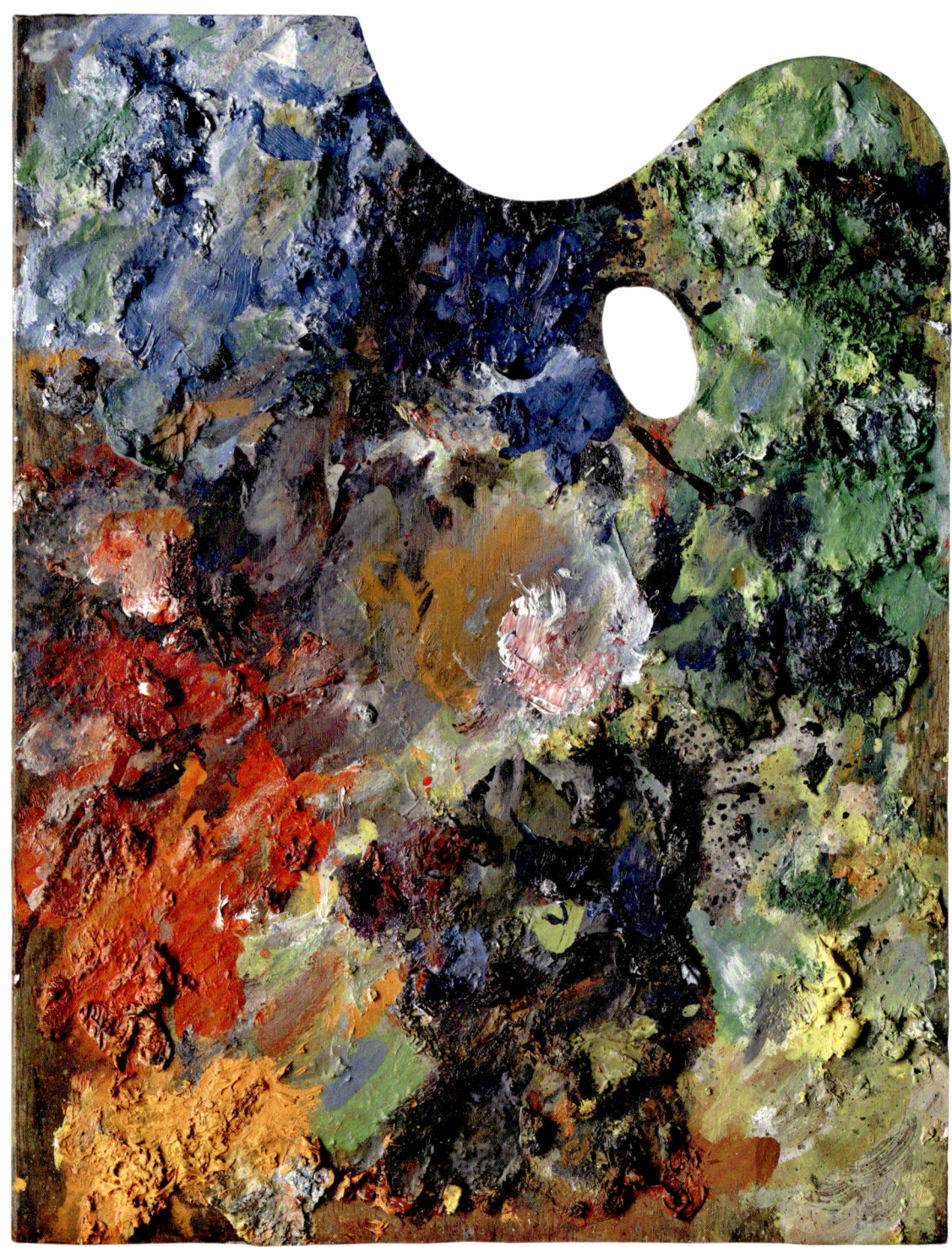

Marc Chagall's
palette
1974
Paint on wood
37.5 × 48 cm
(14 ¾ × 18 ⅞ in.)

The Black Glove
Marc Chagall
1923–48
Oil, tempera, and
coloured Indian ink
on canvas
111 × 81.5 cm
(43 ¾ × 32 ⅛ in.)

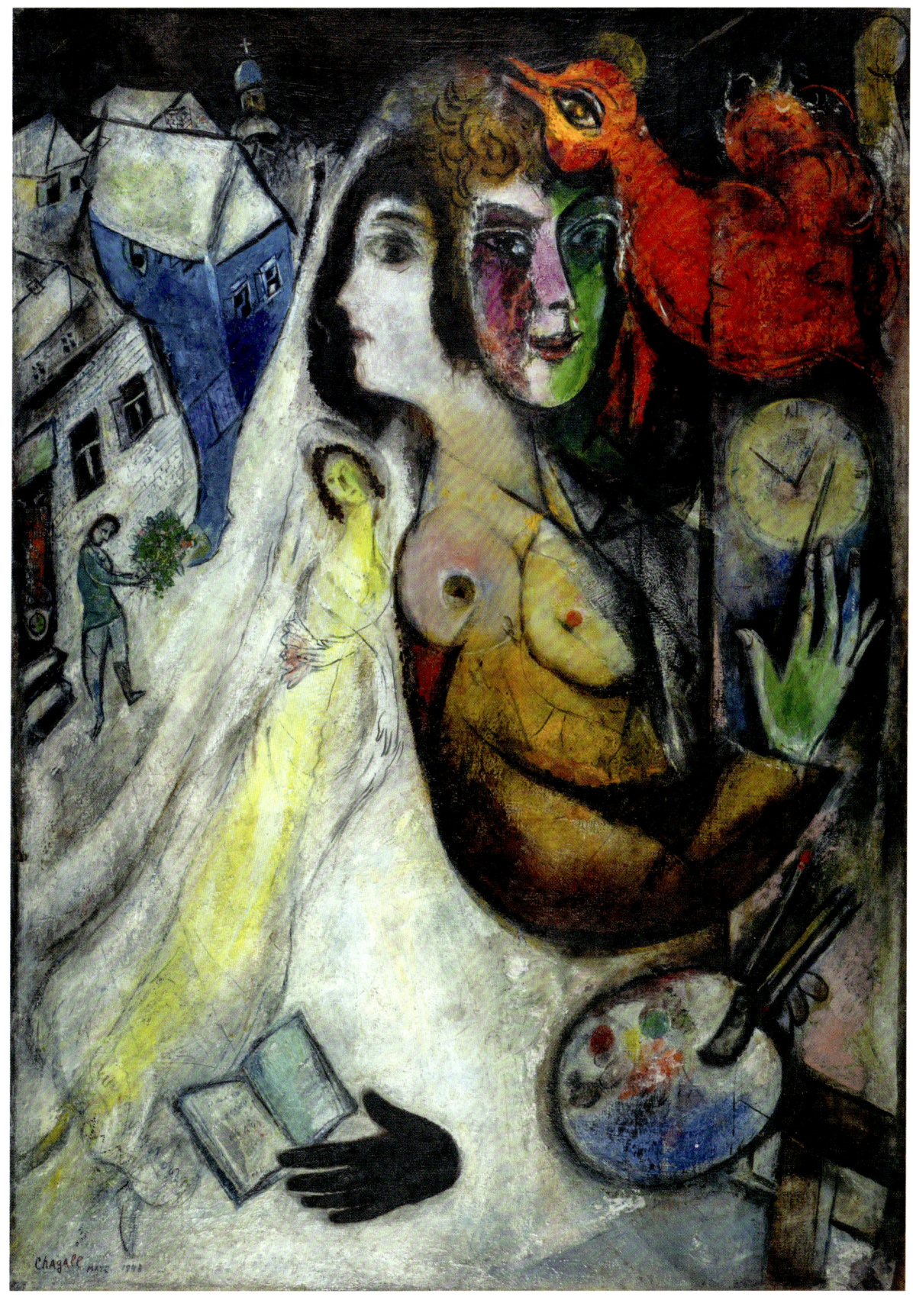

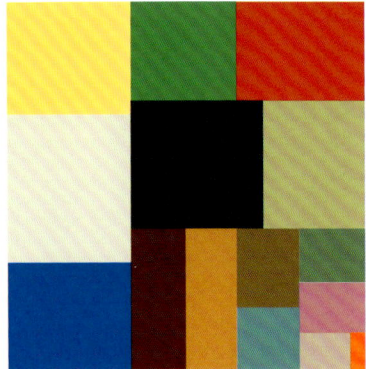

Proportional breakdown of colours used by Marc
Chagall in *The Black Glove*, 1923–48, displayed on
the previous page.

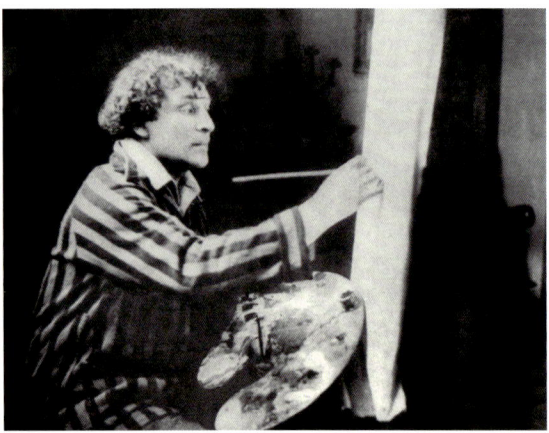

A.

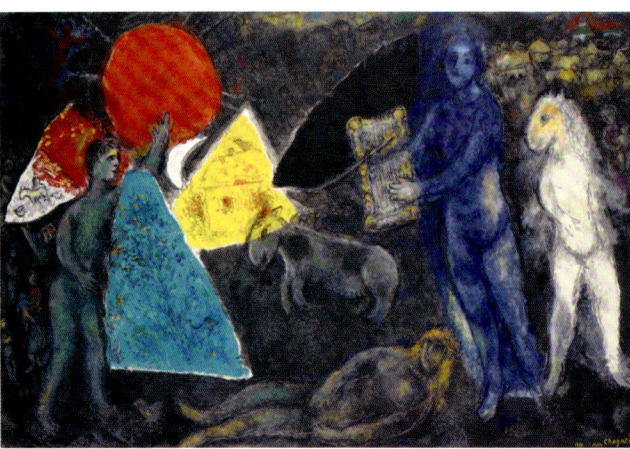

B.

RUSSIAN-BORN ARTIST Marc Chagall preferred
saturated, vivid colours in whichever medium he
worked. In contrast to the exuberance of his motifs and
iconography, he was remarkably organized in his use
of materials, limiting himself to a select few pigments
over a long period of time, and often mixing his own
egg tempera paint.

This palette dates from the late stage of Chagall's
long career. He was nearly eighty years old when he
used it, and it reflects his style, technique and colour
preferences. Every inch is filled with paint, even the
thumbhole area is covered, suggesting that the artist did
not mind getting messy, or that he put the palette down
rather than holding it. The paint is thrown into heaps
of impasto, creating a landscape of colour that allows
us to imagine Chagall's vigorous mixing techniques
and brushwork. Surprisingly, he preferred using tiny
brushes, even for large works. The full joyful range of
pure colours that we associate with him is here, with
some addition of white. There are darker aspects to this
palette and Chagall's work, too, but he largely avoided
using black paint. Instead, he created darker shades
through mixing, as is evident in the middle section
to the left of the pink blot.

While his work was always colourful, in the 1970s,
the decade this palette dates from, he produced several
paintings in which the prismatic colour order becomes
almost the dominant theme of the composition, with
even some hints of abstraction (for example, *Rest*
from 1975 or *The Myth of Orpheus* from 1977). Around
the same time, he also designed many stained-glass
windows for churches, indicative of a heightened
awareness of optical colour. Chagall is perhaps best
known for his intense midnight blues (often using
cobalt blue pigment) and it appears that when setting
out this palette, he had placed blue in prime position,
just above the thumbhole. Brightened with white and
intermixed with small quantities of yellow, his blues
occupy a large portion of the palette, with orange, reds
and purples along the top edge, and yellows and greens
along the lower half.

Palettes also feature prominently as motifs in
Chagall's work and clearly held a special symbolic place
in his life. In self-portraits they function as an emblem
of his profession but are also presented as elaborate
miniature works of art, thereby inserting true abstract
elements into his work. In one self-portrait (image D.),
the palette bears his signature, as if it were a stamp
or a seal. In other paintings palettes with prismatic
colour layouts, and often copious amounts of blue paint,
become tokens of love, perhaps even desire, as in the
one shown on the previous page. A pair of entwined
newlyweds are surrounded by, or are emerging from,

'Despite all the troubles of our world, I have kept the love of the inner life in which I was raised and man's hope in love. In our life there is a single colour, as on an artist's palette, which provides the meaning of life and art. It is the colour of love.'

MARC CHAGALL, *CHAGALL BY CHAGALL*, 1979

symbols of their future together. A painter's palette, on which red, green, brown and pink blots fill half of the surface, while the other half is entirely covered by Chagall's familiar midnight blue, is floating beneath them. This palette may be an offering to the artist's bride, or the tool with which they will paint their lives together, but its colouring and shape also allude to the exposed breasts of the woman. When Alexander Liberman visited Chagall in his studio in the late 1950s, he told the fellow artist about his association of colour with love: 'I now speak of colour-love, and no longer colour-light. Colour-love without theories – it does not deceive.'[1]

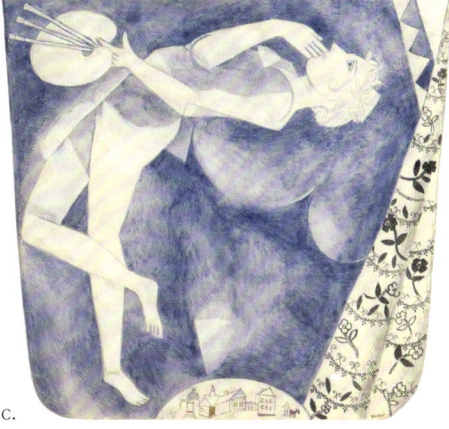

C.

In *The Painter to the Moon* (image C.) a rare blank palette features, held loosely, as if by magnetic force, by a contorted artist who is floating in blue space. The palette echoes the shape and tone of the moon, suggested in faint outlines in the background. Here, Chagall taps into notions of the moon as a blank canvas, a pure space and a source of inspiration.

Chagall spent much of his life in Paris, where he eventually moved permanently in 1947. Throughout his long life he was influenced and loosely associated with many 20th-century art movements, yet never properly belonged to one in particular. Instead, he blended many aspects of several modern art movements, while also referencing his Belarussian and Jewish background. He was a visual storyteller who created compositions in which lovers, fiddlers, painters and goats defy gravity, floating through kaleidoscopic seas and skies of colour.

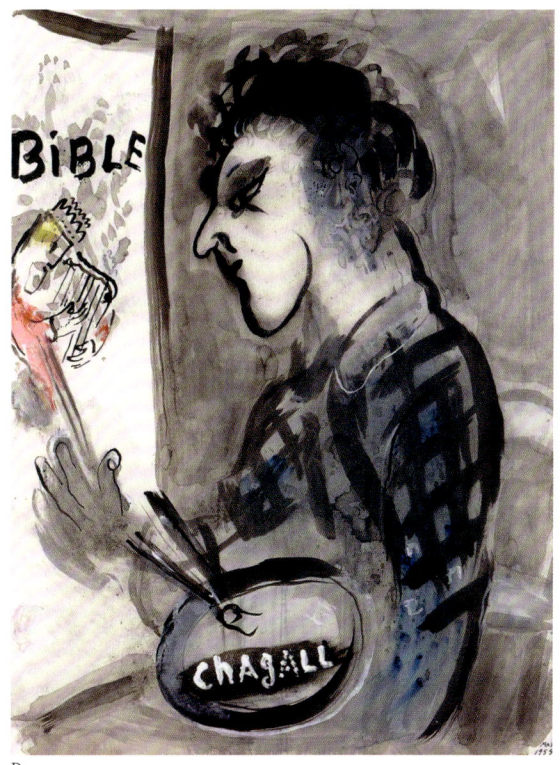

A.   Marc Chagall at the easel, photograph by Abraham Pisarek, *c.* 1920
B.   *The Myth of Orpheus*, Marc Chagall, 1977, oil and tempera on canvas, 97 × 145 cm (38 ¼ × 57 in.)
C.   *The Painter to the Moon*, Marc Chagall, 1917, gouache, watercolour, ink and pencil on paper, 32 × 30 cm (12 ⅝ × 11 ⅞ in.)
D.   *The Artist: Self-portrait with a Palette*, Marc Chagall, 1955, watercolour, gouache and black ink on paper, 65 × 50 cm (25 ⅝ × 19 ¾ in.)

D.

WINIFRED NICHOLSON 1893–1981

A palette of known and unknown colours

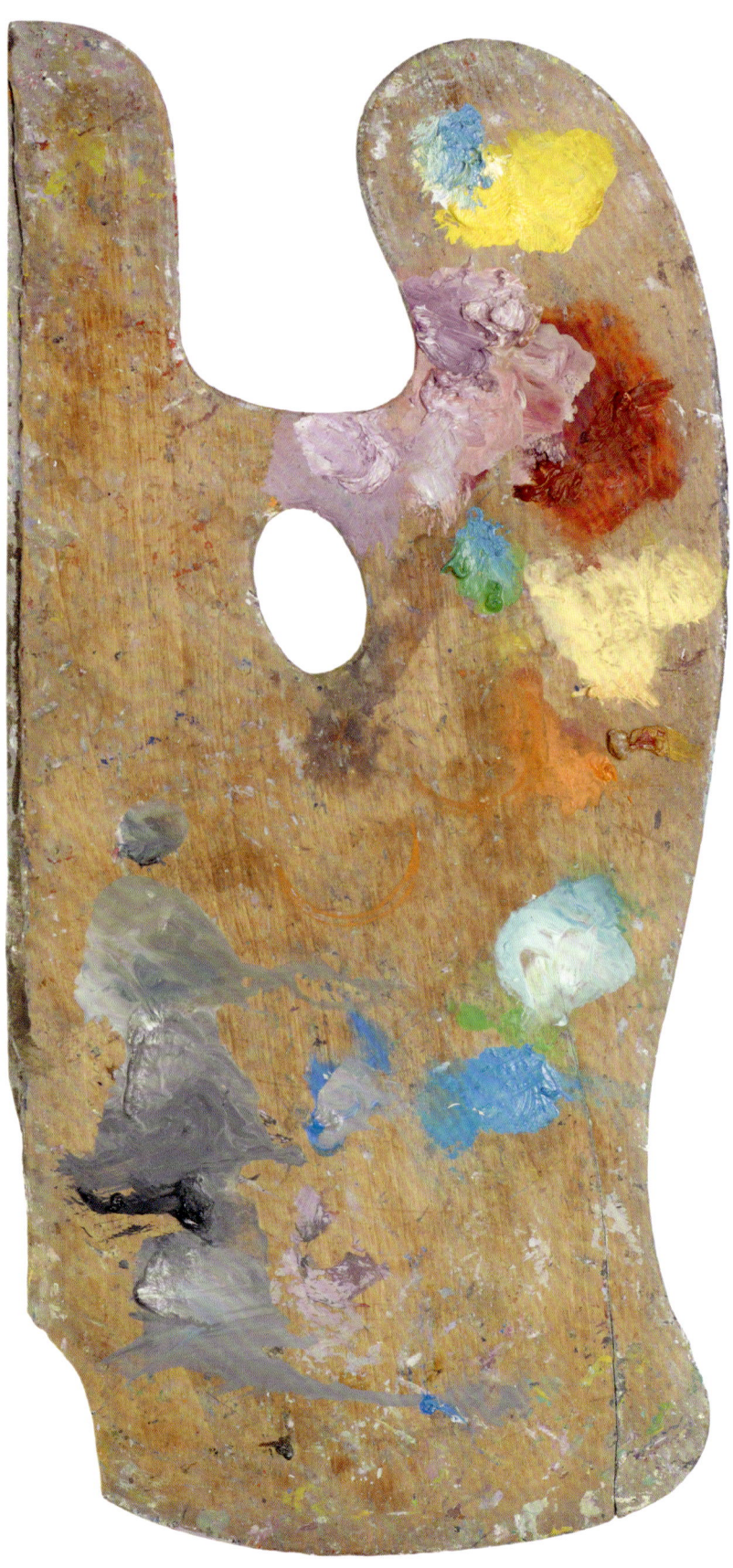

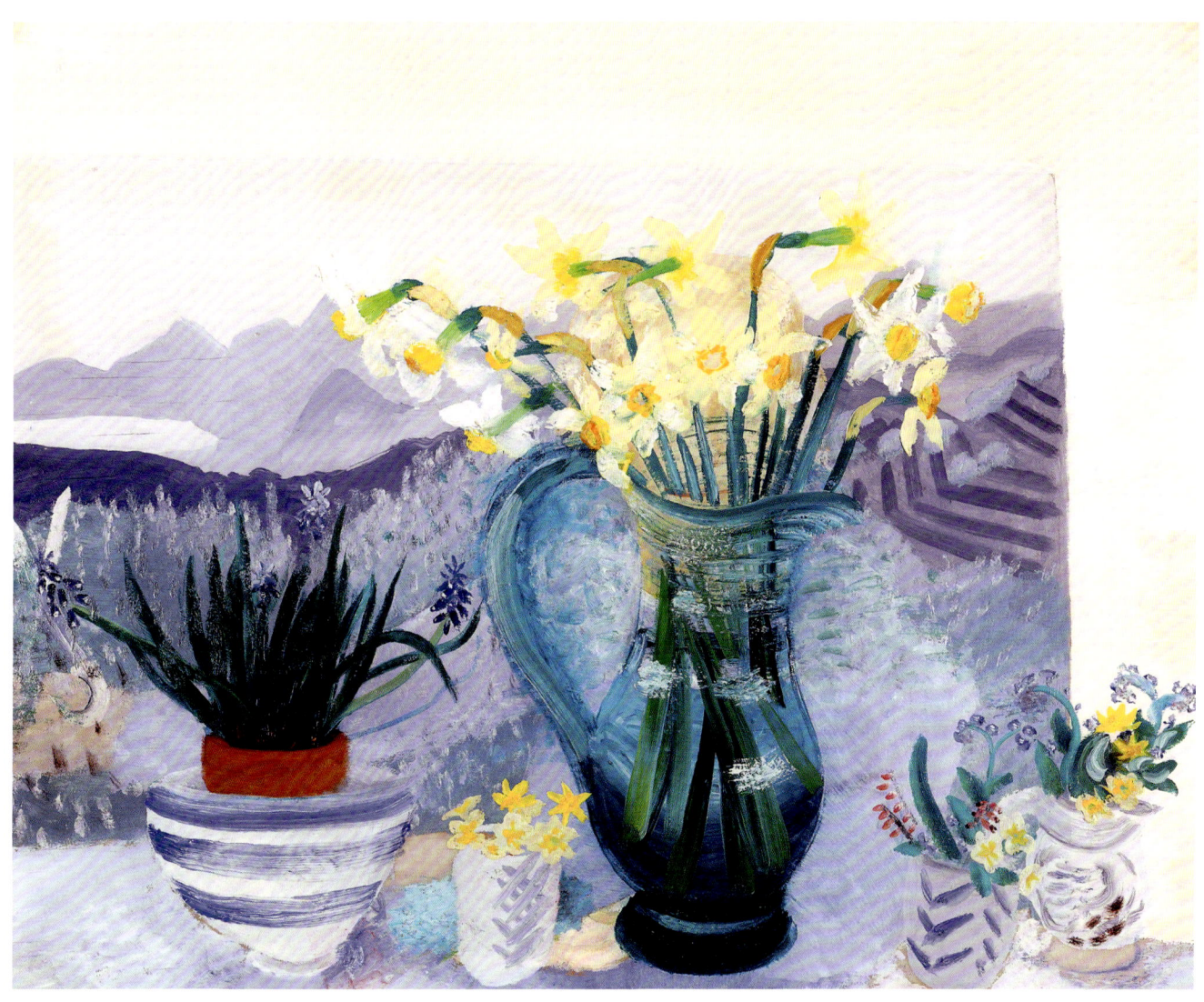

Winifred Nicholson's
palette
Undated
Oil on wood

Recollections
Winifred Nicholson
1940s
Oil on panel
64.8 × 81.4 cm
(25 ⅝ × 32 ⅛ in.)

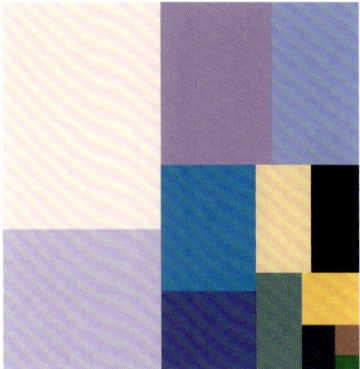

Proportional breakdown of colours used by Winifred Nicholson in *Recollections*, 1940s, displayed on the previous page.

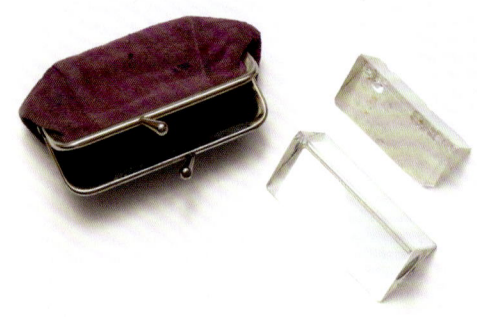

A.

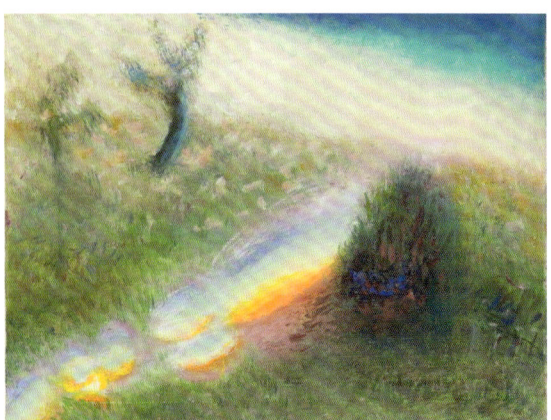

B.

WINIFRED NICHOLSON WAS A PAINTER of light and luminosity. This wooden arm palette probably dates from the last few years of her life, when she painted mostly sitting down in her 'sunroom' in Bankshead, Cumbria, without an easel, her painting surface propped up slightly on a table. The palette looks heavily used and has been wiped and scraped many times. It has chipped edges and a piece of its upper section has broken off. The paint left on it is oil paint, but she was also known to use different media, such as oil pastel crayons, which she used to sketch out compositions. On the palette we see two blots of very bright yellow, a warm orange that appears pure and unmixed, a large blot of highly saturated red, small quantities of a pure green, a light blue, and most importantly, a mixed and blended area of violets and lilacs near the thumbhole, even where her thumb would have been, suggesting that at some point this palette was lying flat on the table or even on the artist's lap. There is also an area of darker, less chromatic shades – greys with a bluish tint and even a small amount of what could be a black pigment.

Nicholson had a passionate, if spiritually tinged, interest in optical science and colour theory. Flowers carried special meaning for her, and her best-known works portray bunches of them set against illuminated landscapes or framed by windows, demonstrating her interest in the interaction of light and colour. In a foreword to her last exhibition catalogue, she explained: 'I found out what flowers know, how to divide the colours as prisms do, into longer and shorter wavelengths, and in so doing giving the luminosity and brilliance of pure colour – in the ordered sequence of the octave of colour.'[1]

Her interest in prismatic colour found a new lease of creativity when, in the mid 1970s and in her eighties, Nicholson was given two glass prisms by the Canadian physicist Glen Schaefer, with whom she shared excited exchanges about the qualities of light and colour. She then created a fascinating series of so-called 'prismatic paintings' based on playful experiments with these prisms, which she carried with her in a small pouch and referred to as 'very little pots of gold'. Occasionally, she would embrace pure abstraction, but mostly she embedded her prismatic visions into landscapes and flower still lifes. With these late paintings, she was trying to paint colour in its purest form, perhaps to liberate it, as she had discussed in her two short essays on the broader subject of colour theory, 'Unknown Colour' (1937)[2] and 'Liberation of Colour' (1944),[3] both published under the pseudonym Winifred Dacre. In these she stated her belief that colour was not tied down to form, but instead floated free. In the latter she included a highly individual colour chart (image C.),[4] relating prismatic colour sequence to musical scales. The prisms allowed her to instantly create rainbow

'A bad painter paints the colour of the surface, a painter whose eyes see light paints the inside that is not exposed to the light of material seeing.'

WINIFRED NICHOLSON, LETTER TO GLENN SCHAEFER, AUGUST 1980

RED	ORANGE	YELLOW	GREEN	BLUE	INDIGO	VIOLET
clay	mud	dust	earth	shadow	slate	lead
terra cotta	dun	putty	khaki	mist	pewter	prune
brick	fawn	beige	faded oak leaf	sea grey	steel	mulberry
roan	bistre	hay	sage	air force blue	blue grey	vieux rose
rust	ochre	straw	willow	fell blue	knife blue	musk rose
coral	sand	amber	crab apple	turquoise	royal	wine
ruby	flame	topaz	emerald	azure	sapphire	amethyst
RED	**ORANGE**	**YELLOW**	**GREEN**	**BLUE**	**INDIGO**	**VIOLET**
sugar pink	alabaster	sulphur	duck's egg	baby ribbon blue	ice blue	pale lilac
scarlet	apricot	lemon	pea green	sky	french blue	lavender
vermilion	fire	canary	grass green	forget-me-not	hyacinth	heliotrope
tomato	fox	brass	cabbage	larkspur	ultramarine	purple
dragon's blood	copper	daffodil	forest green	lapis-lazuli	electric blue	maroon
mahogany	tobacco	mustard	laurel	horizon	midnight	damson
RAVEN	**BLACK COFFEE**	**TIGER SKIN**	**BLACK VELVET**	**ZENITH**	**PITCH**	**CHOCOLATE**

C.

colours, finding those liminal 'unknown' colours she had discussed in her essays and letters. A key colour range in her work was pinks, violets, purples and magenta, which she had in common with many impressionists, often in juxtaposition to yellows, creating vibrating, glowing effects. Nicholson wanted to explore the full potential of violets: 'Those artists,' she noted in 'Unknown Colour', 'who have been interested in the potency of colour have always investigated violet – though they have rarely used more than a little of its suspicious magic.'[5]

She was keen to discuss her interest in colour with many visitors, among them her grandson David Nicholson. David remembers her neatness when painting, even in old age, her pure joy of scumbling oil paint with Chinese ink brushes until they were frayed, and looking at flowers through prisms. She bought most of her paints from a local art shop, which only stocked Rowney and Winsor & Newton materials, but craved other high-quality, pigment-dense oil colours, asking the manager to source them for her. David recalls:

> I brought back some Rembrandt colours from Amsterdam. She was particularly pleased with the light and dark shades of cobalt violet, which other makers only supplied in one mid-shade. Violet was a particularly important colour for Winifred, with its mystical and feminine qualities, always at the edge of things, always hinting of more. [...] From a trip to Paris the following year, I brought back a selection of paints by Sennelier, including a particular *Blue de Sèvres* so packed with pigment that it defied dilution!*[6]

David noticed a slight darkening of her palette in a few paintings at the end of her life. Perhaps the small patches of anthracite grey on the palette are examples of Nicholson letting a little bit of darkness sneak into her prismatic compositions, which have been described by Richard Gilbert, another artist who visited Nicholson in Cumbria, as: 'bathed in a kind of sacramental light, an emanation that preserves the forms in a silvery lustrousness, a colour key that time after time locks what is precious in a state of grace. This is a world without shadows.'[7]

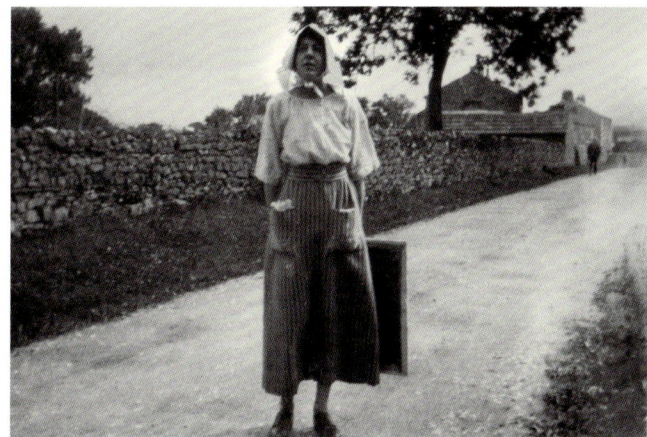

D.

A.   Winifred Nicholson's purse and two prisms
B.   *Rainbow Path in the Grass*, Winifred Nicholson, 1979, oil on canvas, 34 × 44 cm (13 ⅜ × 17 ⅜ in.)
C.   Winifred Nicholson's colour chart
D.   Winifred Nicholson in Westmorland, England, c. 1923

SALVADOR DALÍ 1904–1989

A perfectionist's subconscious palette

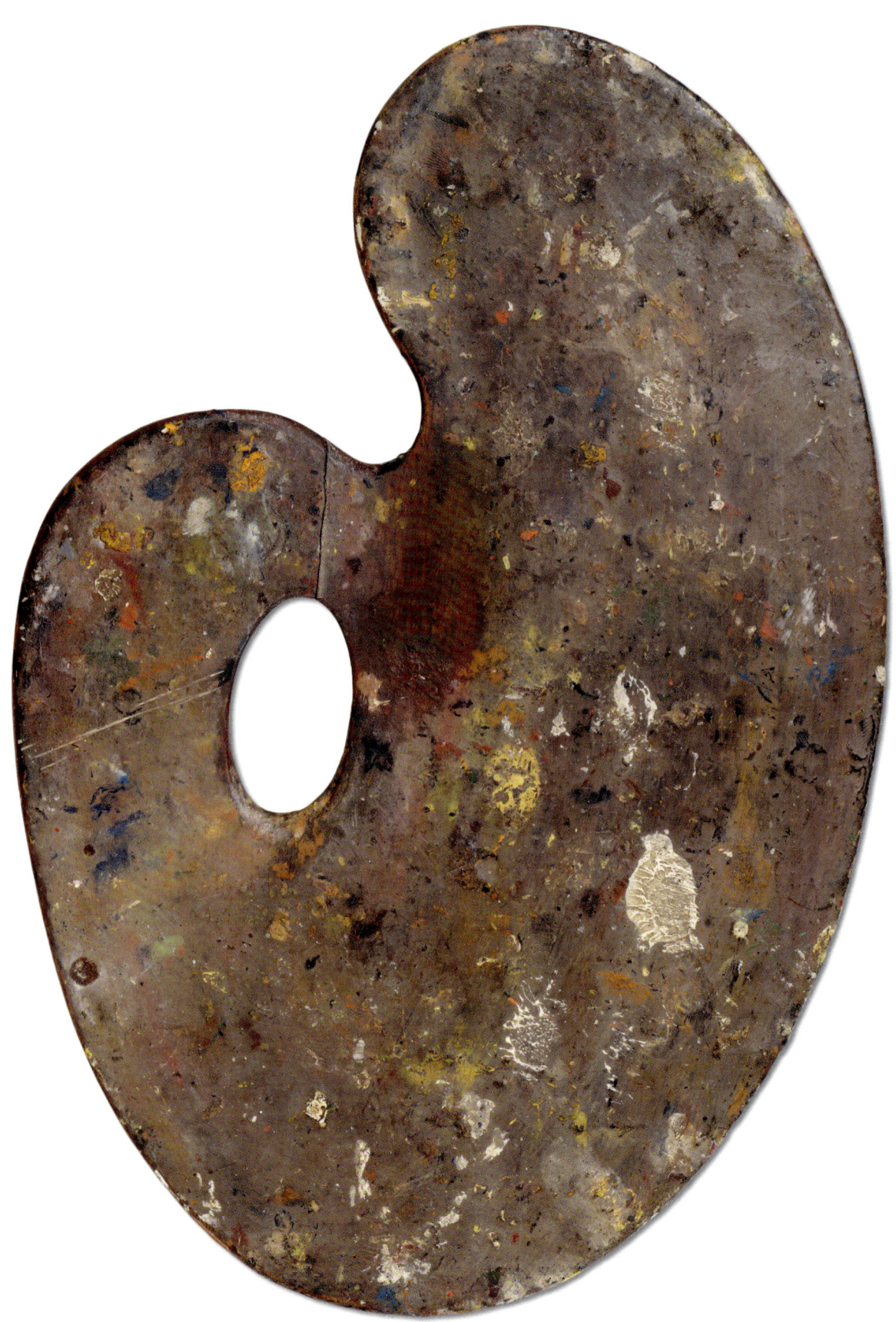

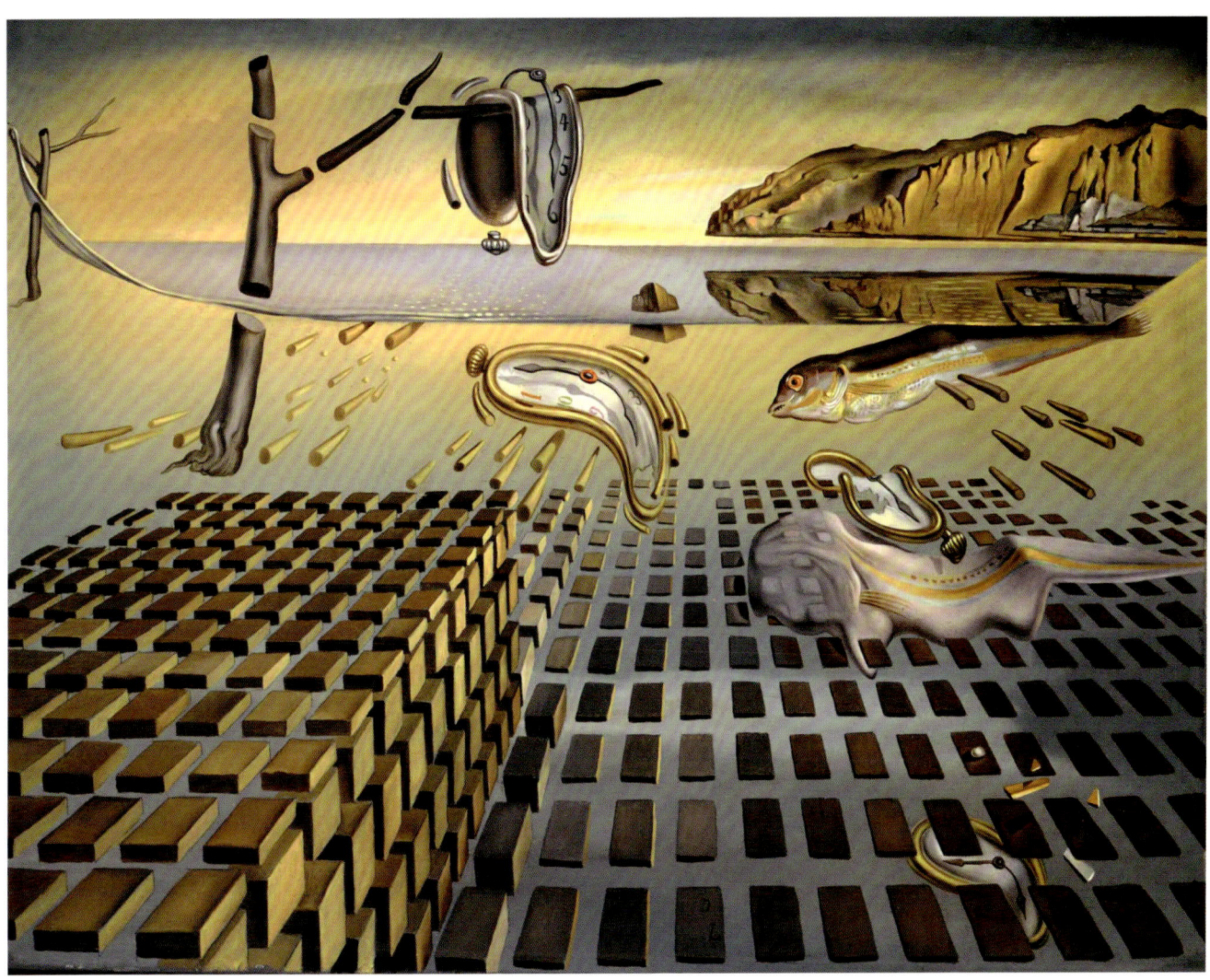

Palette used by Salvador
Dalí in his Portlligat
studio, Catalonia, Spain
c. 1930s/1940s
Paint on wood
(probably beech)
30 × 21 cm
(11 ⅞ × 8 ⅜ in.)

*The Disintegration of
the Persistence of Memory*
Salvador Dalí
1952–54
Oil on canvas
25.4 × 33 cm
(10 × 13 in.)

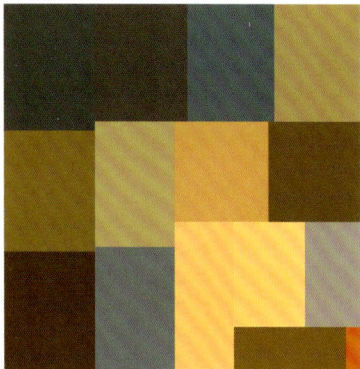

Proportional breakdown of colours used by Salvador Dalí in *The Disintegration of the Persistence of Memory*, 1952–54, displayed on the previous page.

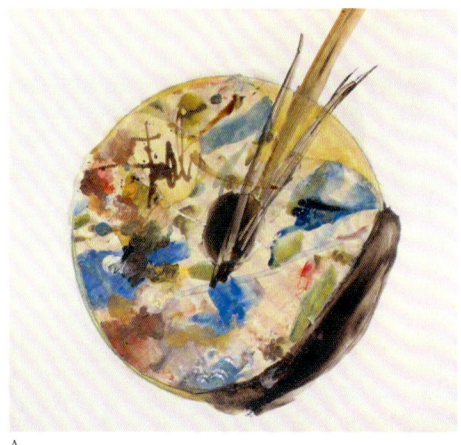

A.

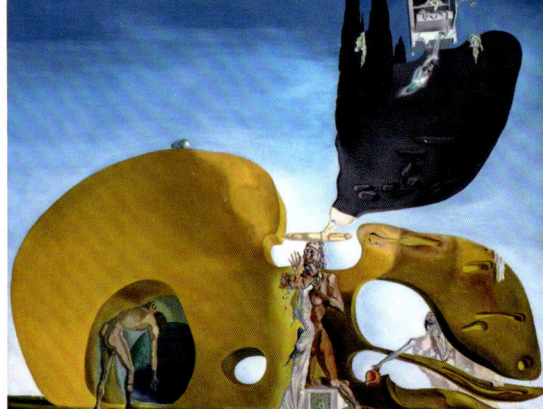

B.

FOR SALVADOR DALÍ, a self-declared 'total genius', more was always more. In his hallucinatory, shape-shifting pictorial worlds he combined the real and the unreal (or, arguably, the surreal). Painting realistically, in meticulous detail and with naturalistic colours, enabled Dalí to create his trademark illusions of impossible spaces, overlapping perspectives and morphing objects.

This traditional kidney-shaped, wooden palette is covered in a gently cratered layer of subtle mixtures and minute flecks of paint. Dalí appears to have used tiny brushes or the tip of a palette knife. A thin layer of muddy grey covers much of the surface, perhaps left over after wiping the palette gently several times or deliberately created to provide a neutral ground. Among the brightly coloured flecks, some saturated blues and reds stand out, while minuscule areas of an emerald green are also visible. The large blots are predominantly white and yellow. Look closely and you can make out a fingerprint in white on the bottom right edge of the palette. With these colours, Dalí could turn his surreal dreams, nightmares and subconscious visions into hyper-realistic images. Clocks and faces in his paintings can melt and morph because they are painted with tiny brushstrokes in believable colours.

Dalí would usually prime his canvas or board with a white ground on which he outlined his complex figures and structures in ink, pencil or diluted black paint, establishing a solid framework on which to hang his soft morphing shapes. He used extremely liquid layers of oil paint, thinned with different types of resin or linseed oil. As researchers at Tate discovered while examining one of his paintings from the 1930s, despite the fluid quality and appearance of Dalí's paints, his precise brushwork is visible through magnification and he seems to have had a remarkably steady hand: every minute stroke and dot is perfectly placed, and nothing is left to chance.[1]

Among the colours Dalí used was the evocatively named dragon's blood, a garnet-coloured resin from the *Dracaena* genus of plants, often used for varnishing furniture. He used this in combination with zinc white to produce shimmering pinks. His pigments were ground finely, sometimes to the detriment of vibrancy, but this ensured a smooth finish. Dawn Ades suggested that Dalí painted effectively in enamel colours, in the style on a miniaturist, and may also have been emulating the smooth flatness of chromolithography.[2] It seems odd, then, that at times he created texture in his works by adding sand, grit and even stones to the paint surface,[3] but Dalí liked to confuse, disorientate and infuriate.

Despite having experimented with cubism before he became a figurehead of the surrealist movement, Dalí was dismissive about the use of colour as an expressive tool and, by implication, abstract art in general. He

'I have always claimed that the ideas of surrealism will work only when they are painted to perfection and in a traditional manner.'

SALVADOR DALÍ IN AN INTERVIEW WITH ALAIN BOSQUET, *CONVERSATIONS WITH DALÍ*, 1969

entertained the thought of destroying all works by Turner, Cézanne and Gauguin, and regarded Chagall as the most inept painter of his time.[4] His guiding lights were old masters who successfully created illusions of three-dimensionality, depth and detail in painting. In particular, he admired and claimed to have renewed Vermeer's methods: 'Vermeer's technique was to superimpose successive and very fine layers of paint to create an illusion of atmospheric space. His miracle was using products of the earth and a simple brush to obtain the illusion of space. Structures almost invisible to the naked eye produced special images.'[5]

Dalí was undoubtedly a technical maverick as well as an insufferable egotist, with thorough knowledge of the science underpinning colour and paint. When asked in the 1960s what his favourite colour was, and why, he answered 'Naples yellow', displaying a profound understanding of it as a pigment: 'because it's the colour of proteins as well as the dominant colour in certain chemical mixtures of cardinal importance for painting. After Naples yellow, I'm most strongly drawn to the colour of oxygen, that is to say blue.'[6] In this context, too, he refers to Vermeer, noting that these two colours are the most ubiquitous in his work. We see pairings of a range of yellows and distinctive blues in many of Dalí's surreal dreamscapes, including in both versions of the 'Camembert watches' paintings (*The Persistence of Memory*, 1931, and *The Disintegration of the Persistence of Memory,* 1952–54, which is shown on the preceding page). It is quite possible that a similar colour scheme was created with this palette, as a consciously subconscious extension of Vermeer's mind and style.

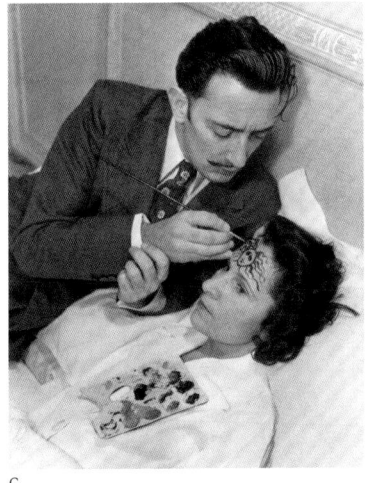

C.

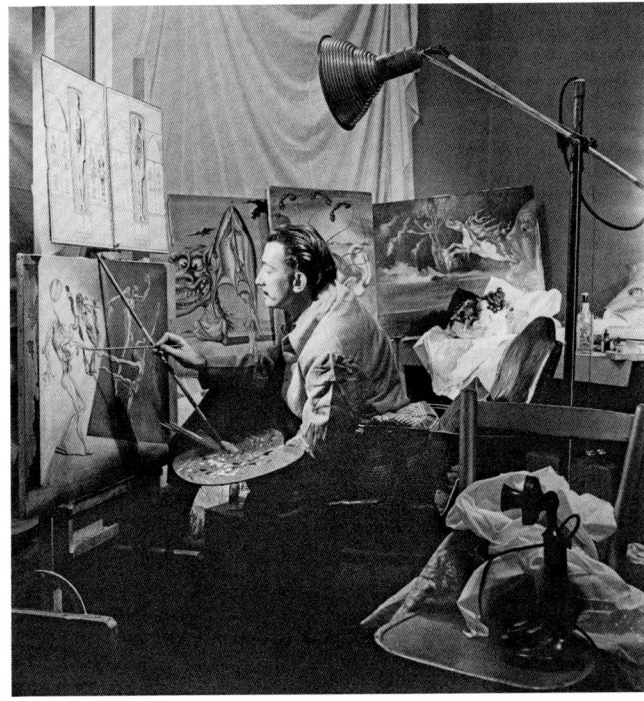

A. *Palette* (project for an enamel mirror), Salvador Dalí, 1961, watercolour on paper, 36.5 × 36.5 cm (14 ⅜ × 14 ⅜ in.)

B. *Birth of Liquid Desires*, Salvador Dalí, 1931–32, oil and collage on canvas, 6.1 × 112.3 cm (37 ⅞ × 44 ¼ in.)

C. Salvador Dalí paints the head of Medusa on his wife Gala's forehead, photograph by Philippe Halsman, 1942

D. Salvador Dalí in his studio on the 8th floor of the Ziegfeld Theatre, New York, USA, photograph by Michael Ochs, 1943

D.

HELEN FRANKENTHALER 1928–2011

The studio as palette, the artist as paintbrush

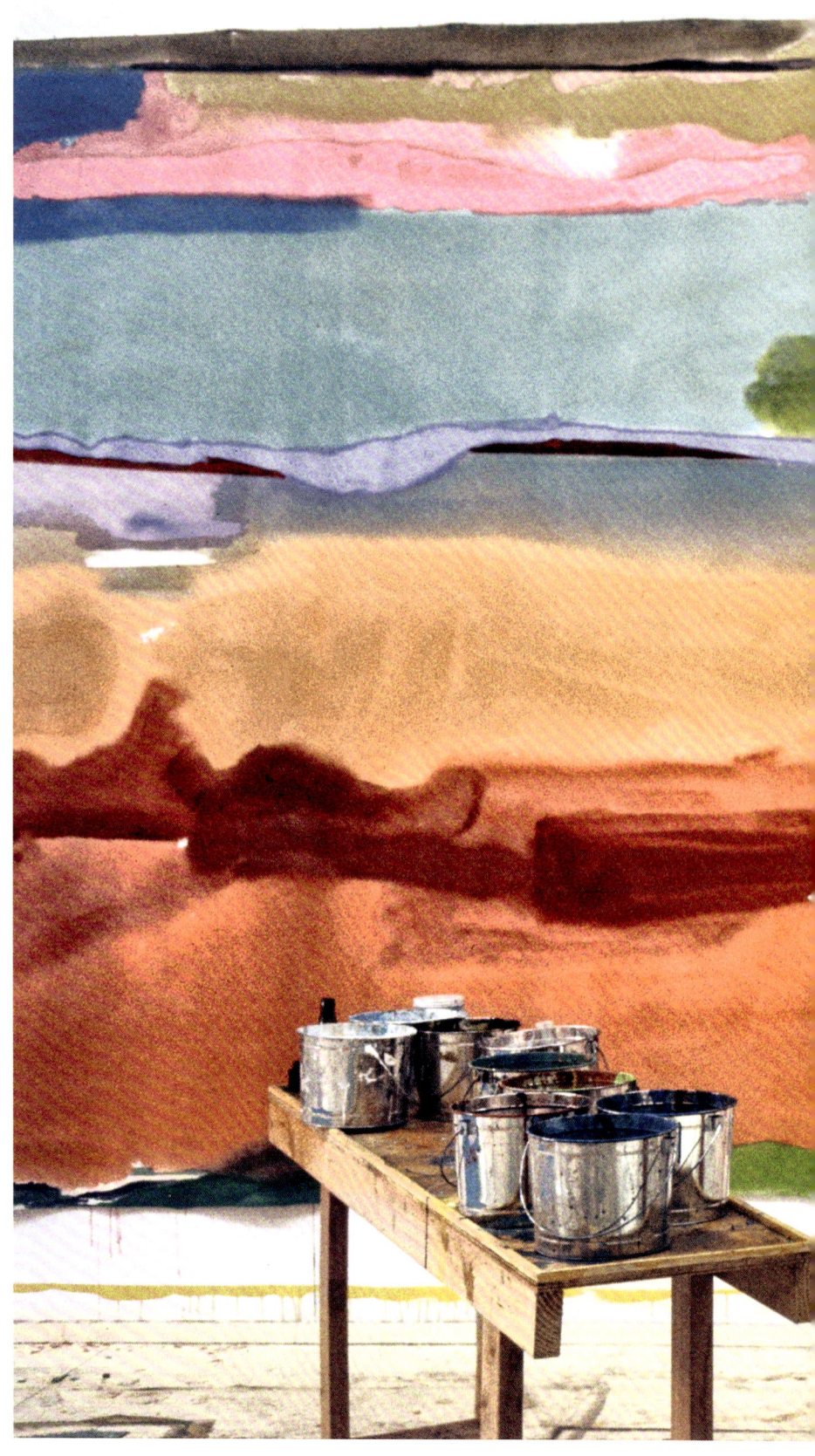

Helen Frankenthaler in
her East 83rd Street studio,
New York, USA, in front of
April Mood and *Under April
Mood* (works in progress)
Photograph by Alexander
Liberman
1974

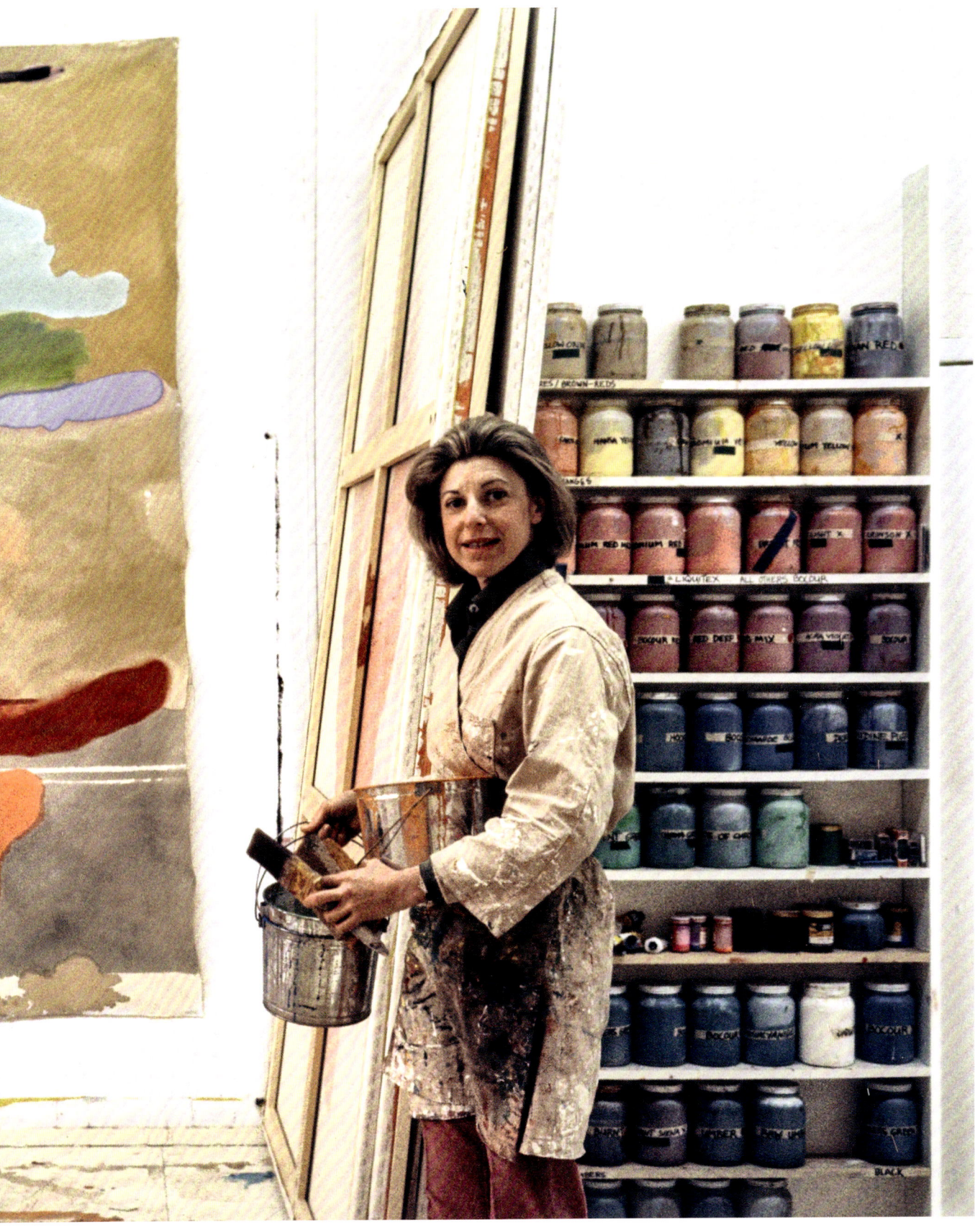

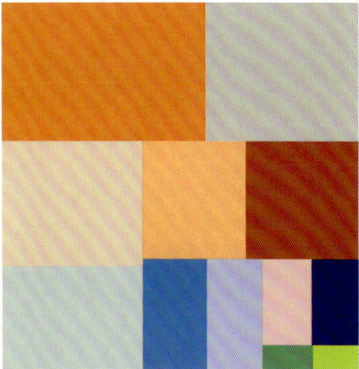

Proportional breakdown of colours used by Helen Frankenthaler in *April Mood*, 1974, and *Under April Mood*, 1974, displayed as a single, work in progress canvas on the previous page.

INSTEAD OF PALETTES or paintboxes, Helen Frankenthaler had a tall cabinet of colours in a vast studio space that gave her the opportunity to create works of very large dimensions, and to abandon traditional forms and techniques of painting. Like other artists of her generation in the United States, she rejected the idea of palettes and frames, of inward-looking art restricted by small formats. Speaking in Emile de Antonio's film *Painters Painting* (1972), which documents the New York art scene from the 1940s to 1970s, Frankenthaler (the only woman featured) talks about how she wanted to break free from easel painting and small sable-hair brushes, and her desire to cast everything on the floor and 'throw the paint around'. She was not interested in small gestures: art had to be radical and on a scale not seen before.

Materiality matters greatly when you produce art on a large scale. Just over a hundred years earlier, an artist had to messily prepare small quantities of oil paint and tie each batch up in a pig's bladder. In the mid 20th century, Frankenthaler was able to work with ready-made pigments and paints, creating buckets of mixed Magna, a solvent-born acrylic resin paint, which is thinner than oil paint, diluting it even further with turpentine to increase fluidity. This allowed her to invent a new form of painting, one in which the traditional paintbrush was an optional afterthought at best.

In 1952, having returned from a sketching trip to Nova Scotia, Frankenthaler had the urge to 'let rip', to tear up the rule book of traditional painting and drawing. Two years earlier, she had seen the first exhibition of works by Jackson Pollock. Like Pollock, she put a roll of unstretched and unprimed canvas on the floor of her studio. She then poured paint directly onto it, with the pools of colour sinking into the fabric, a technique she referred to as 'soak-staining'. This resulted in a flat paint surface, a shallow space in which each colour area had the same importance and weight. The monumental canvas on the preceding page with its saturated, glowing acrylic colours was later divided horizontally in two, *April Mood* (1974) and *Under April Mood* (1974), which emphasized the expansive composition further. Eventually, she abandoned any sense of perspective, with rich colour flooding the entire pictorial space. The act of pouring rather than splattering, with only minimal additional intervention using brushes or palette knives, gave her pictures a lyrical, fluid appearance, in contrast to Pollock's textured compositions. There are strong elements of chance, immediacy and spontaneity in her work. Indeed, one of her aims was to make a painting appear as if it had been created in an instant.

Frankenthaler preferred to work in private but was open to being photographed in her studios. These

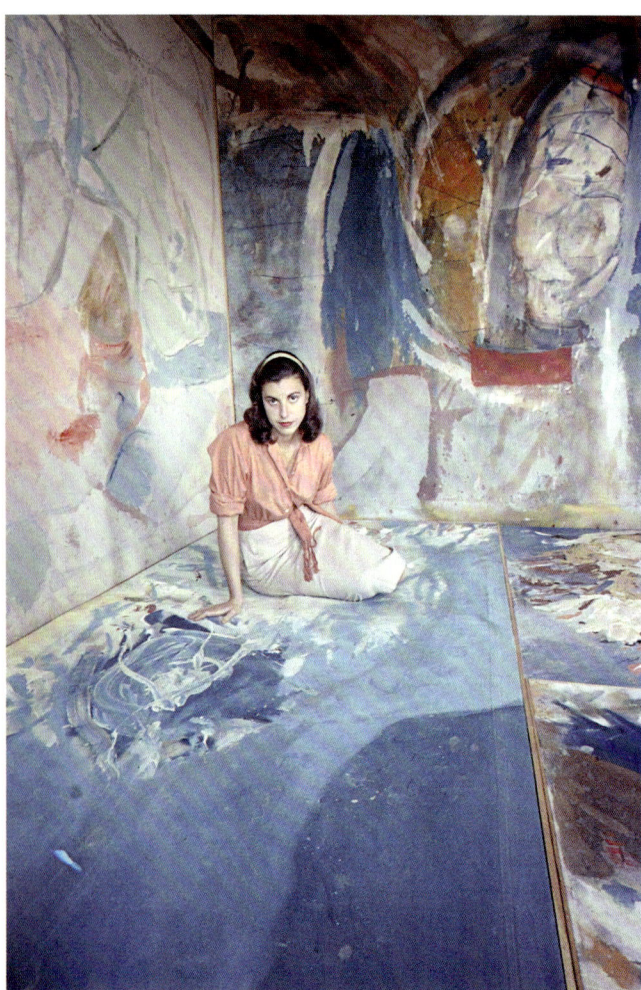

A.

'I think when you're really painting, involved in a painting, what goes on in the art world doesn't matter. When you're making what you have to you're totally involved in the act.'

HELEN FRANKENTHALER IN AN INTERVIEW WITH HENRY GELDZAHLER,
ARTFORUM, OCTOBER 1965

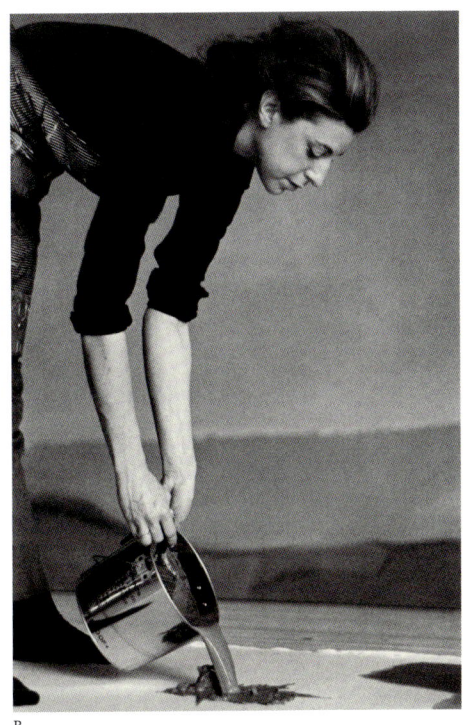

B.

photographs give a sense of the scale of her work and methods, and illustrate how she was pushing the boundaries of painting and how art was displayed. In colour photographs by Gordon Parks from *c.* 1957, her painted canvases cover every inch of wall and floor space, and there is little sense of the architectural design of the room. The artwork has taken over the entire space and boundaries have become blurred. Frankenthaler, dressed in a colour scheme that resembles her work, sits on one of the paintings, visually blending in with her art. Later black-and-white photographs by Ernst Haas convey the physical aspects of creating her soak-stain paintings, including the dramatic, sensual act of pouring the liquid paint straight from the can or bucket onto the canvas. The concept of the traditional artist's palette has disappeared, the entire studio space has become a palette, and the artist has become the paintbrush.

In the wake of World War II and the Great Depression, US artists wanted to break free from the constraints of realist representation and European (especially French) traditional formats and style. They were looking for new ways of expression, radical changes in subject matter and material, and a different scale and scope of the visual arts. Focusing on colour and shape, and largely abandoning representational detail, perspective and narrative content, abstract expressionism and colour field painting emerged in the late 1940s with the aim of creating a new, true and emphatically American art.

Being from a wealthy, educated New York family, Frankenthaler was able to experiment with new art forms, but US artists at the time also benefited generally from the large physical and geographical scale of their country. In post-war New York and other US cities, old factory buildings, lofts and spacious apartments were in good supply and relatively affordable – in stark contrast to the limited living and working spaces in war-ravaged Europe. At that moment in time, studios became experimental playgrounds for art; generous architectural spaces that could replace palettes, easels, frames and brushes.

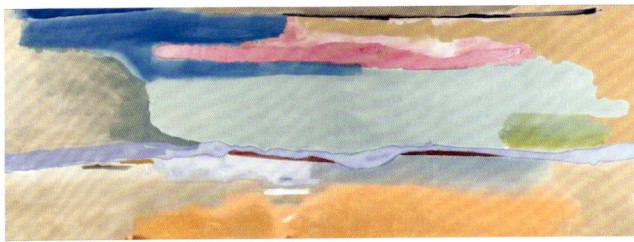

C.

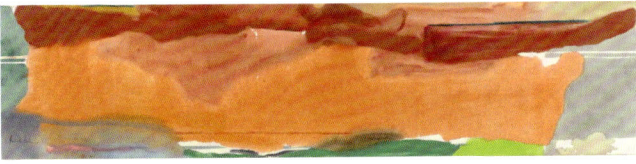

D.

A.　Helen Frankenthaler in her studio, New York, USA, photograph Gordon Parks, *c.* 1957
B.　Helen Frankenthaler tips the contents of a can of paint onto a canvas on the floor, New York, USA, photograph by Ernst Haas, 1969
C.　*April Mood*, Helen Frankenthaler, 1974, acrylic on canvas, 152 × 434 cm (59 ⅞ × 170 ⅞ in.)
D.　*Under April Mood*, Helen Frankenthaler, 1974, acrylic on canvas, 104.1 × 445.8 cm (41 × 175 ½ in.)

FRANCIS BACON 1909–1992

A palette on a plate

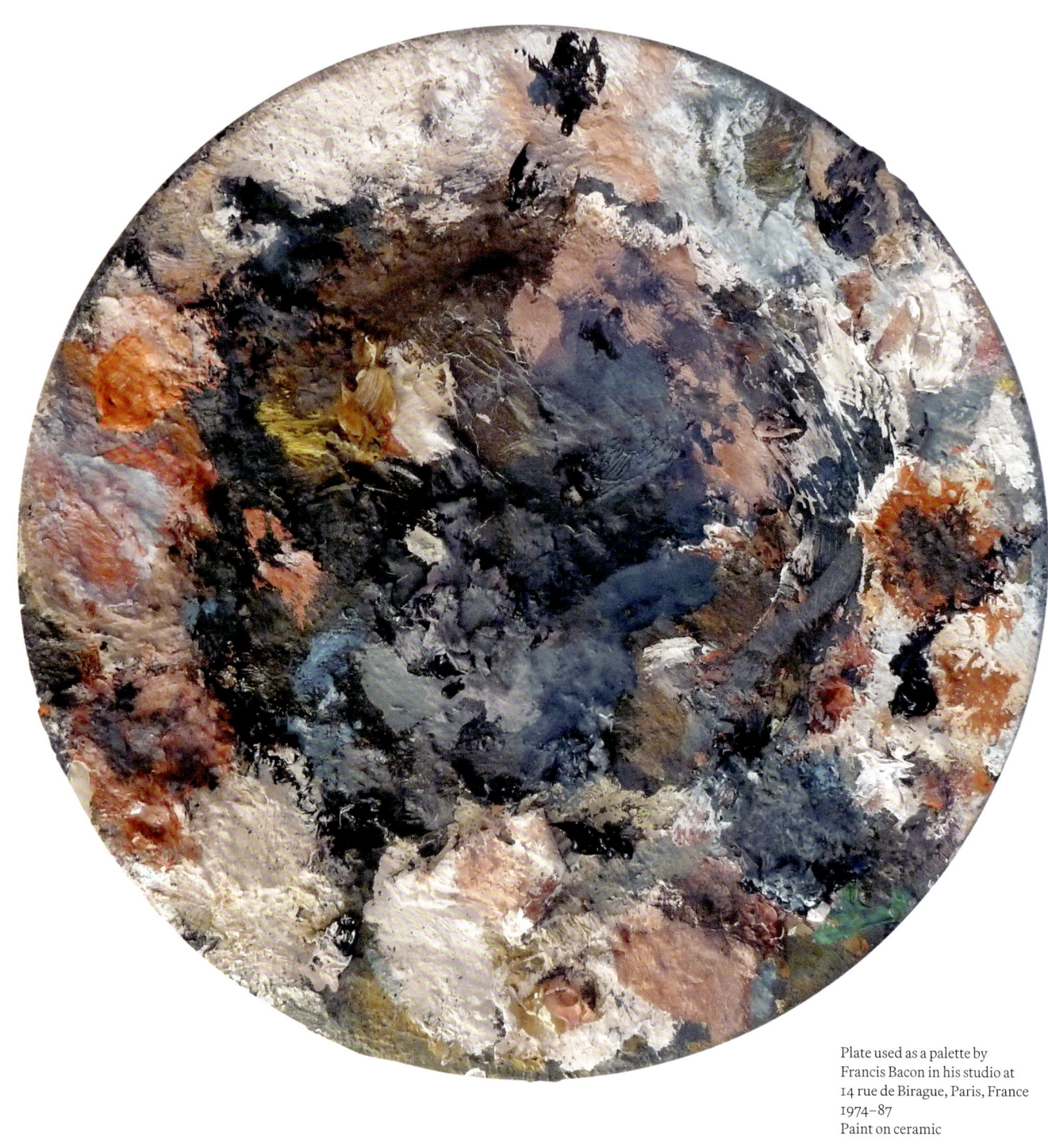

Plate used as a palette by
Francis Bacon in his studio at
14 rue de Birague, Paris, France
1974–87
Paint on ceramic

Portrait of Michel Leiris
Francis Bacon
1976
Oil on canvas
34 × 29 cm
(13 ½ × 11 ½ in.)

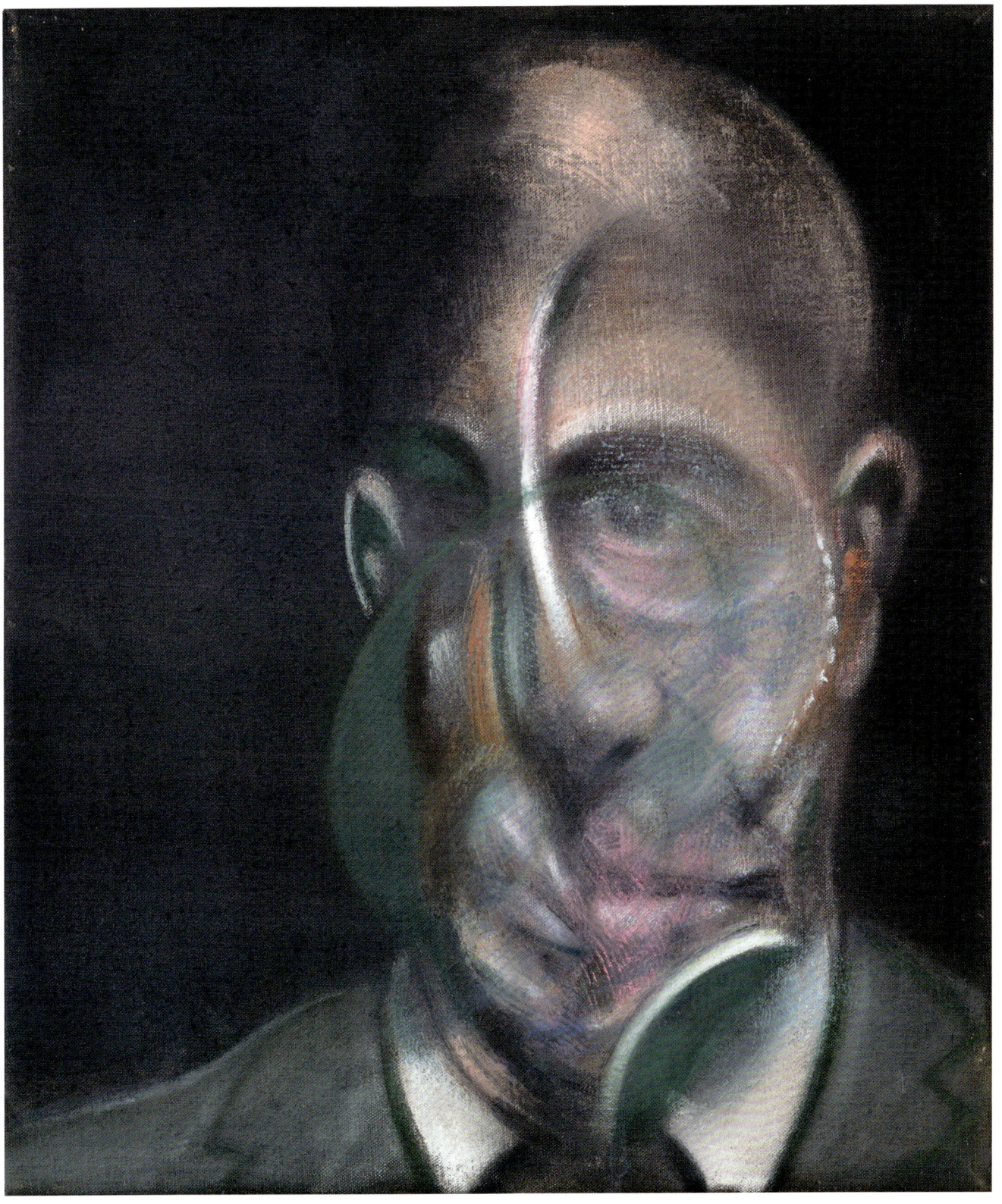

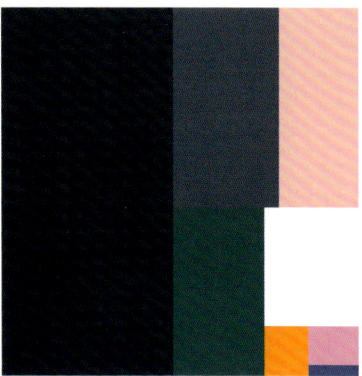

Proportional breakdown of colours used by Francis Bacon in *Portrait of Michel Leiris*, 1976, displayed on the previous page.

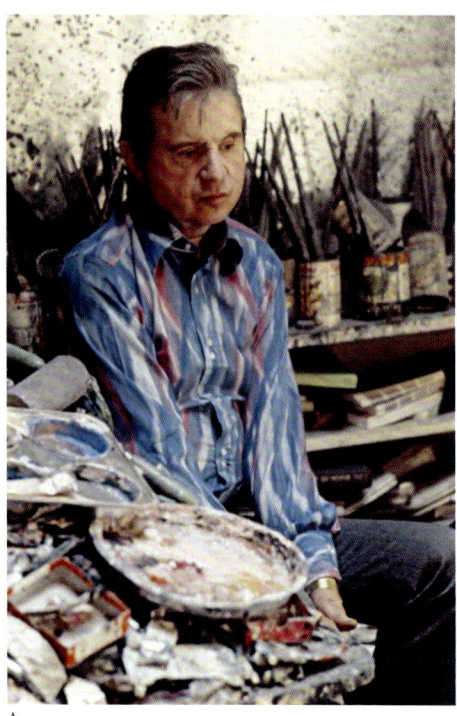

A.

TO LOOK AT ONE PHYSICAL PALETTE by Francis Bacon in isolation seems unnatural, even futile, considering the chaotic, crammed studio in which he worked for most of his life, but it may serve here as a metonymic object that encapsulates the way Bacon used colour, artists' tools and studio spaces. What we see here is not a traditional palette you would find in an art supplier's catalogue. It is a simple ceramic plate, probably grabbed from a nearby kitchen and used as surface on which to try out and mix paints. It is completely covered in paint and was probably cast aside as a disposable object that did not warrant cleaning. Bacon was not the first or only one using dinner plates as cheap alternatives to professional palettes but seen in the greater visual and spatial context of his studios, it becomes a fascinating reflection of his artistic persona.

This plate-palette from Bacon's studio in the Marais district of Paris, which he used intermittently from 1974 to 1987, tells a small part of the story of how Bacon painted. There is no direct link between this palette and a specific painting, but during his stays in Paris he almost exclusively painted small portraits, among them the one of Michel Leiris shown on the previous page. The palette shows how Bacon used a relatively reduced range of colours to create the sombre, ghostly appearance of the portraits. Yet, there are also bright and colourful areas on both the palette and in the painting. Bacon's preferred white was flake white and is present here in copious quantities. There are also subtle pinks, saturated blues, as well as small areas of yellow and orange.

Bacon was fond of highly saturated yellows and oranges. When John Edward visited him in his London studio in 1976, he noted that 'everything was covered with a fine orange and pink dust [...] a pigment [Bacon] liked so much, but which, because he was asthmatic, was so damaging to his health.'[1] The pigment in question was most likely cadmium orange. Importantly, this recollection tells us that Bacon did indeed use raw pigments, along with most other media and types of colour available, including household emulsion paints, oil and acrylic paints, spray cans, pastels and many more.

The yellow seen here is likely a cadmium lemon yellow or yellow-orange, and the blue perhaps a cobalt blue. Both were pigments purchased by Bacon from Winsor & Newton at some stage. Bacon used glaring yellows and oranges throughout his career to great effect, utilising its high spectral visibility as well as its association with warning or danger. They feature, for example, as the monochrome walls in several studies of fellow artist Lucian Freud (see pages 228–31) in the 1960s. Bacon may have associated yellows, oranges and blues with Vincent van Gogh (see pages 102–7),

A. Francis Bacon in his studio, London, photograph by Michael Holtz, 1974
B. *Three Studies for Figures at the Base of a Crucifixion*, Francis Bacon, 1944, oil paint on three boards, each: 94 × 73.7 cm (37 ⅛ × 29 ⅛ in.)

'I'm greedy for life; and I am greedy as an artist.'

FRANCIS BACON IN AN INTERVIEW WITH
RICHARD CORK, BROADCAST ON BBC RADIO 4'S
KALEIDOSCOPE, 17 AUGUST 1991

an artist he considered 'the greatest' and whom he painted in 1957.[2] Yellow also shrieks synaesthetically in many versions and studies of Bacon's 'Screaming Pope' series, in the form of grainy streaks against deep black, juxtaposed with its complementary purple.

For a more complete picture of Bacon's working methods, we also need to look at images of his studio in Kensington, London (as shown overleaf), which he occupied from 1961 until the end of his life. It was a tall, narrow space on the upper floor of a mews building, astonishingly small considering the size of many of his canvases and, metaphorically speaking, the enormity of his visions. Many visitors commented on the incomprehensible chaos and clutter in the space, and it became the setting for some of the most evocative photographic portraits of the artist. Here, he used much more than just dinner plates as palettes: doors, walls, the floor and many other surfaces became testing and mixing grounds for his colours and paints. Lucian Freud

recalled that Bacon even used his own forearm as a palette, and occasionally had allergic reactions to the paint.[3] A mottled circular mirror, probably dating from the 1930s, when Bacon was briefly an interior designer, was a sort of focal point, and may have influenced him in using the circle frequently as a compositional element in his art. Over the years, almost every inch of surface in the studio was splattered and covered with paint, and never wiped clean. These surfaces, or architectural makeshift palettes, form a fascinating insight into the life and work of Bacon. The incongruence between Bacon's success as an artist and the chaotic, humble architectural nature of his studio never seized to intrigue people, and it formed an almost theatrical background for many photography and interview sessions.

After Bacon's death, the Kensington studio was carefully dismantled, catalogued, and transported to Dublin, where Bacon was born in 1909. There, the architectural space of the studio was recreated and the contents and wall surfaces preserved at the Hugh Lane Gallery, donated in its entirety by Bacon's heir, John Edward. The studio, in all its glorious messiness, has become a museum, a shrine of sorts, perhaps a work of art in its own right, but it is also an invaluable inventory of Bacon's materials, preferences and techniques. Considered and thorough research is now being carried out into the many different types of pigments and paints he used, which brands he preferred, which binders he used. The palimpsests of Bacon's many palettes are now slowly being unpicked. This is how we know, for example, that the pigment that had such an adverse effect on his lungs was cadmium orange.

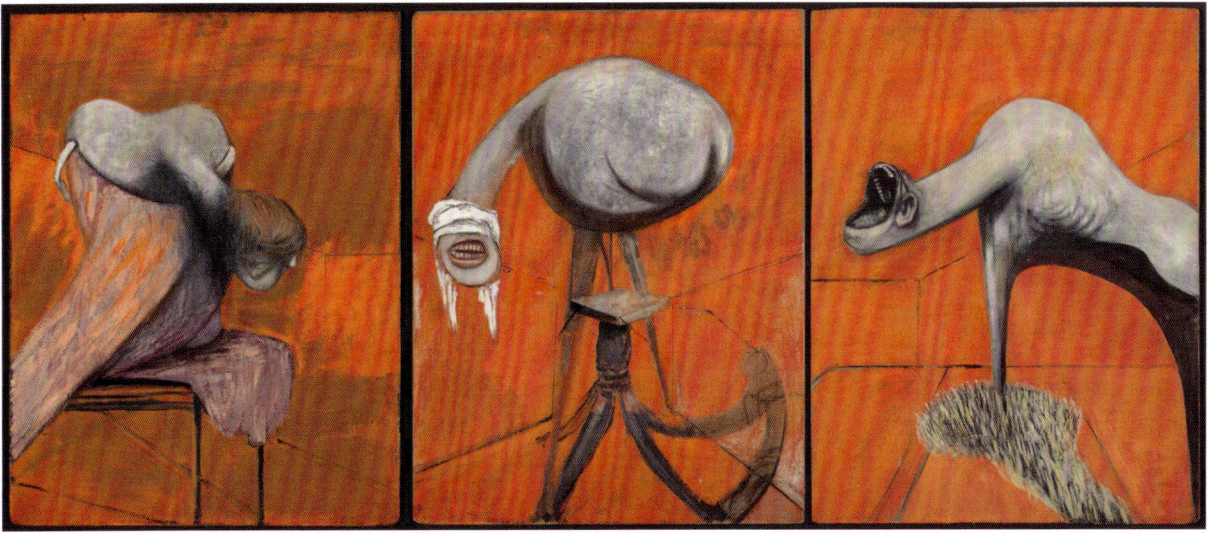

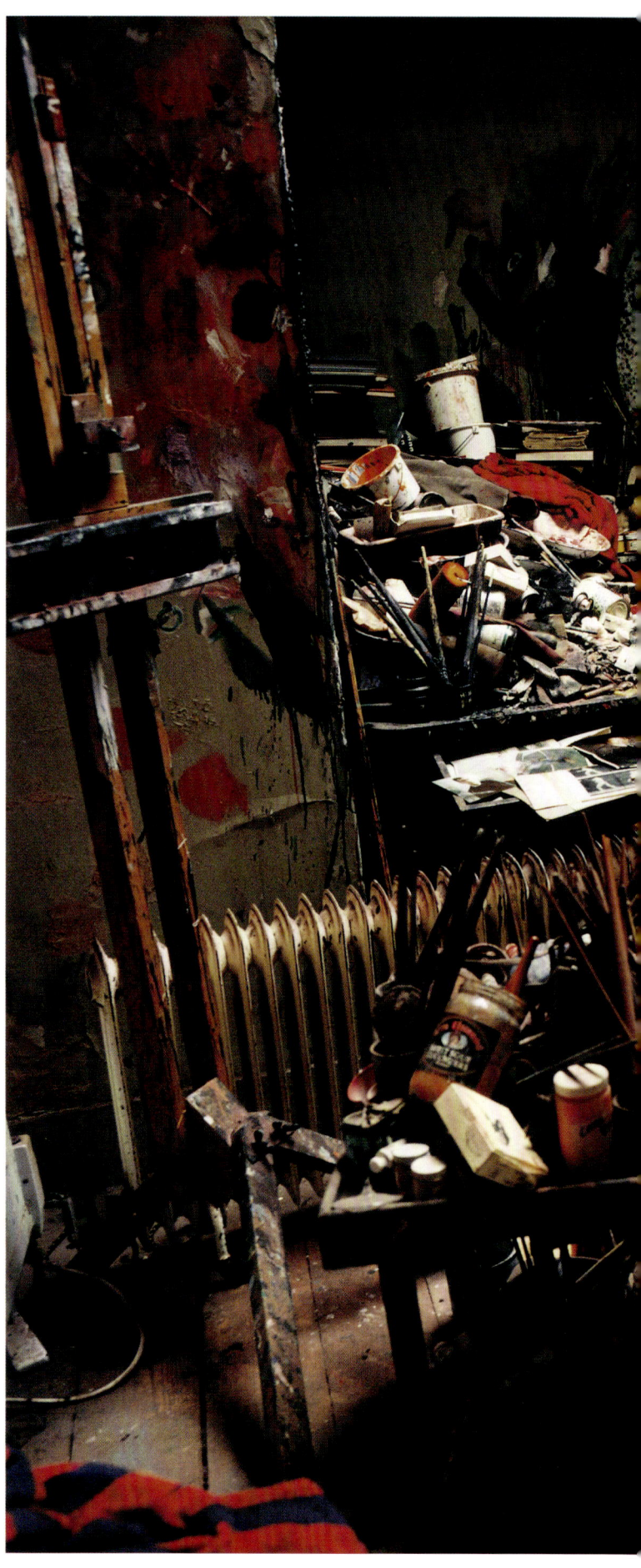

Francis Bacon's studio at
7 Reece Mews, London, England
Photograph by Perry Ogden
1998

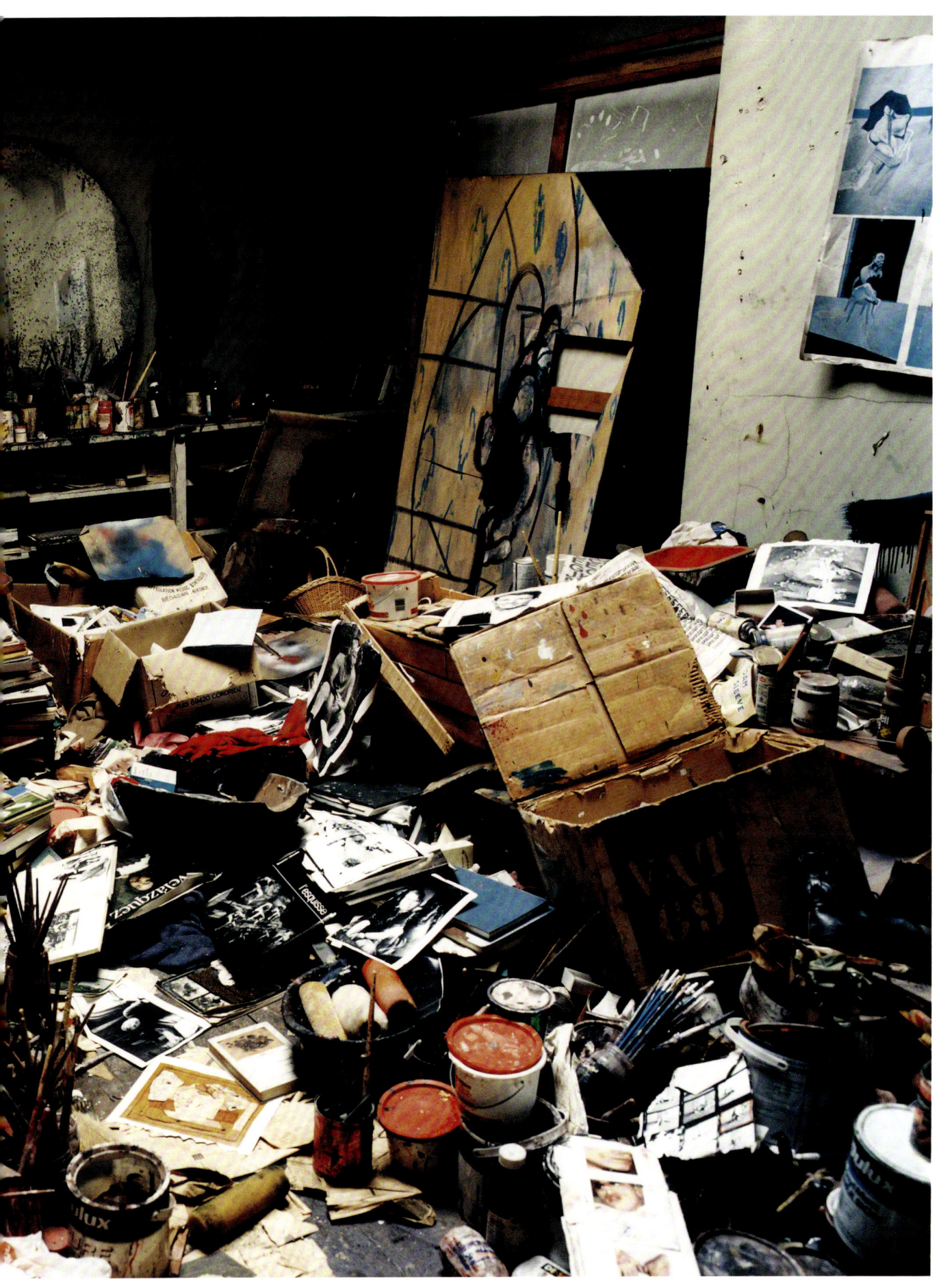

LUCIAN FREUD 1922–2011

A wild, fleshy palette

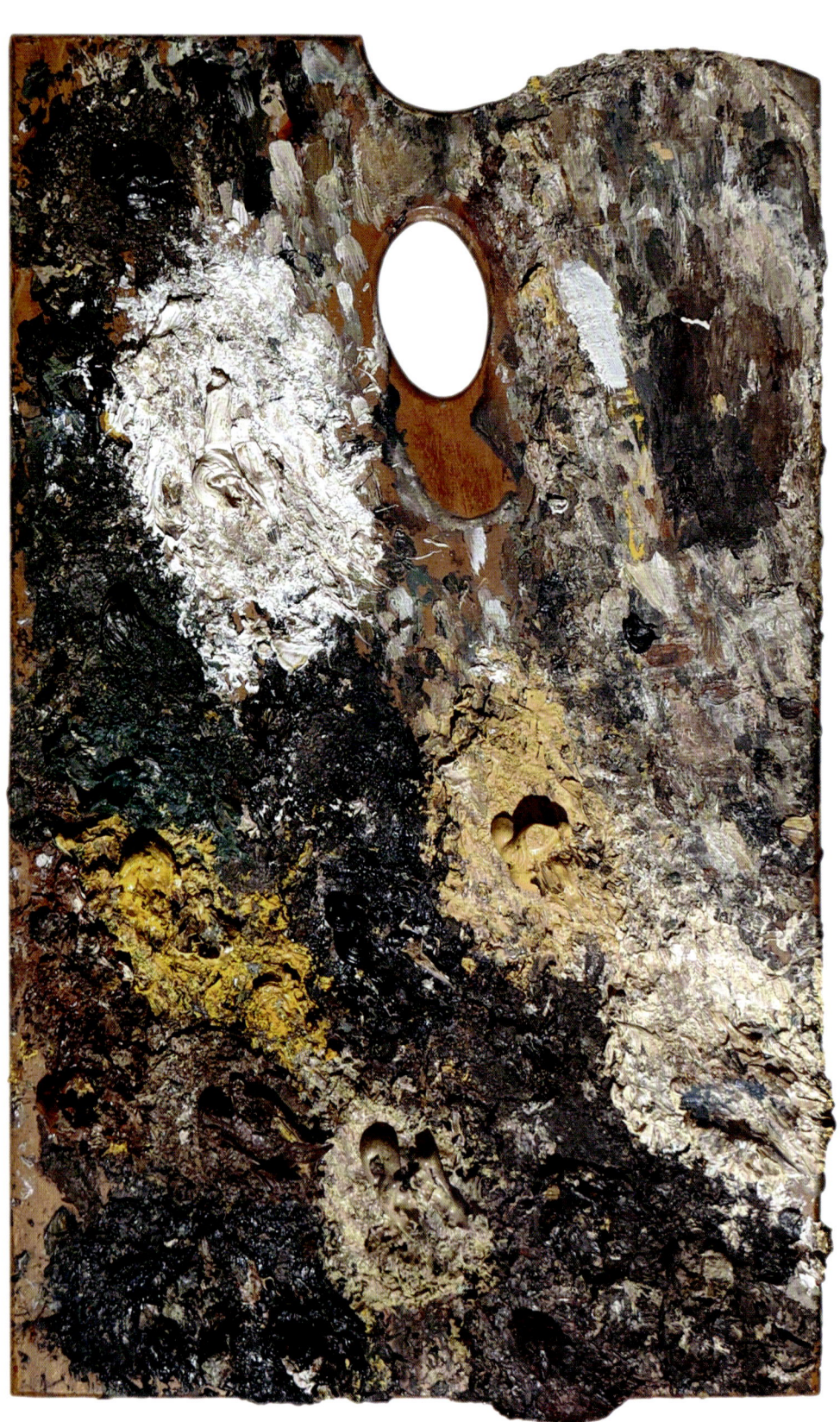

Lucian Freud's palette,
gifted to Nicola Bowery
after the completion
of *And the Bridegroom*
1993
Oil on wood
41 × 25 cm
(16 ¼ × 9 ⅞ in.)

And the Bridegroom
Lucian Freud
1993
Oil on canvas
232 × 196 cm
(91 ⅜ × 77 ¼ in.)

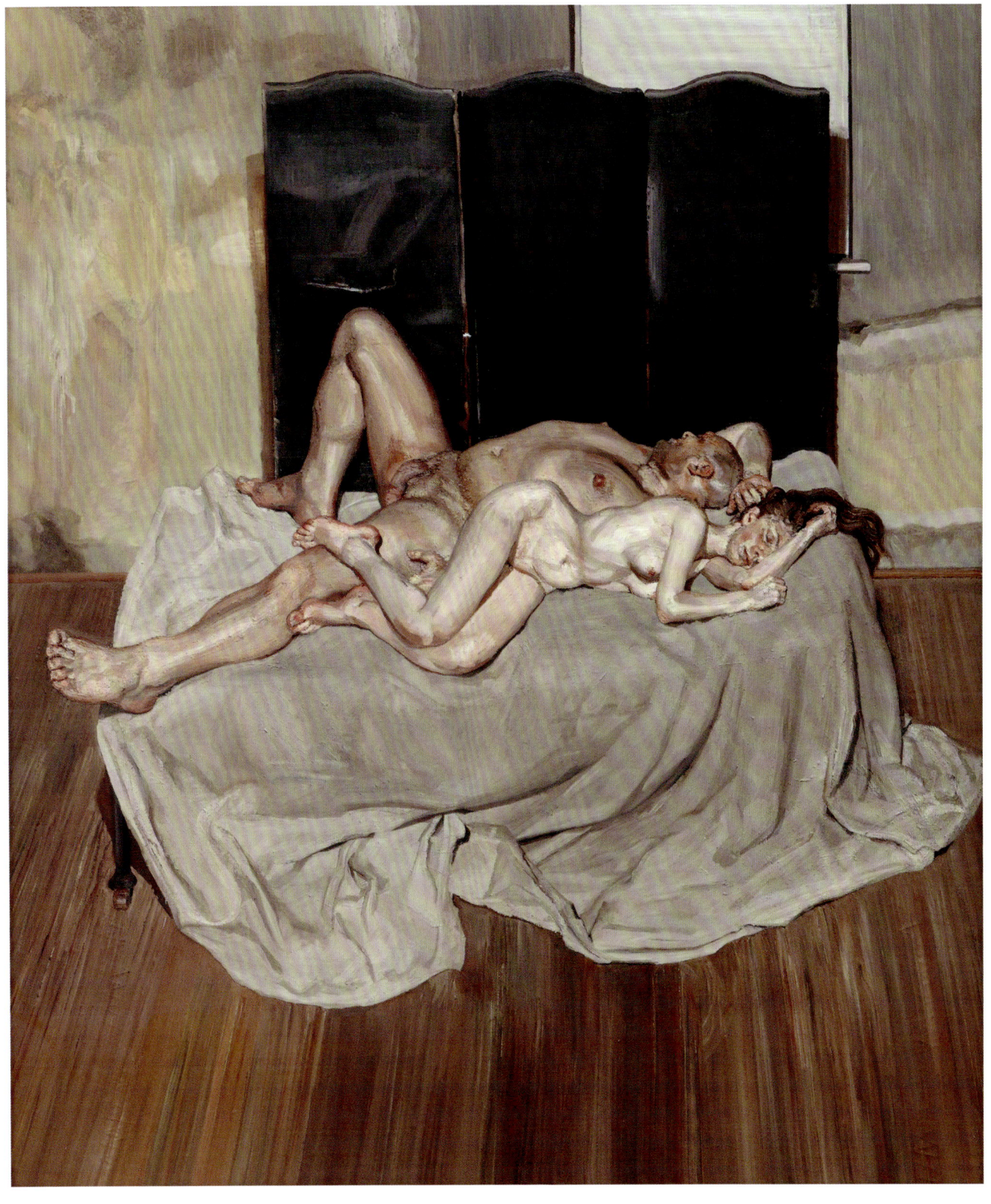

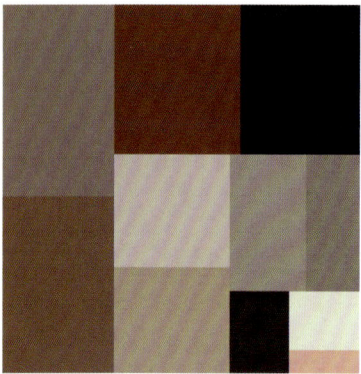

Proportional breakdown of colours used by Lucian
Freud in *And the Bridegroom*, 1993, displayed on the
previous page.

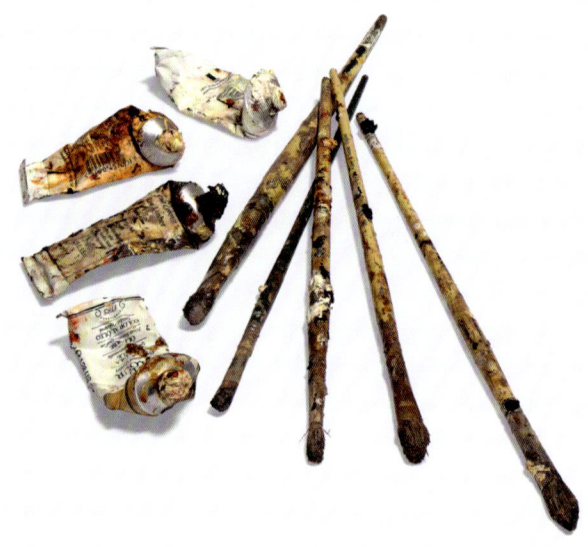

A.

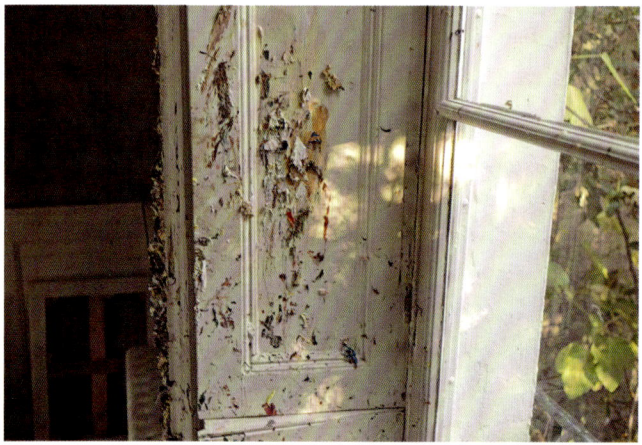

B.

THIS SIMPLE, SQUARE WOODEN PALETTE, made
by Daler-Rowney, was used in 1993 by Lucian Freud
for a nude double portrait of the performance artist
Leigh Bowery and his wife Nicola Bowery, titled
And the Bridegroom. After the painting was completed,
Freud gave the palette to Nicola. It is covered almost
completely with oil paint except for where Freud's
thumb held it. There is also paint on the reverse and
in some places it has spilled over the edge of the palette,
as if it were a living organism. A few other palettes of
Freud's later period survive, also covered with unruly,
wild remains of paint in similar colours.

Freud was fascinated by the flesh, muscle, hair
and skin of both humans and animals, and the colours
of his often unnerving, unflinchingly realistic and
seemingly unflattering depictions of the physical body
are reflected in his palette. Here there are colours that
are necessary to create a wide range of skin tones
through precise mixing: at least two types of yellow
ochre, a brighter artificial yellow (possibly a Naples
or cadmium yellow), a large amount of lead white
and an abundance of darker paints, some the result
of mixing on the palette, others squeezed from a tube.
The combination of earth pigments and a brighter
colour may be surprising, but this was deliberate and
not uncommon for Freud. David Hockney recalls him
searching for a specific tube of cerulean blue to paint
part of his portrait. The thick texture of the paint of the
palette resembles Freud's coarse, cratered paint surfaces
of this period, but below the thumbhole there is also
an area of thin paint surface where delicate mixing has
been carried out and the paint has been swept up by
flat brushes.

The physicality of Freud's art found a reflection not
only in his palette, but in his entire studio environment
and his personal appearance. The earthy, muted
tonality of much of his work was based on a very limited
range of achromatic colours, comprising blacks, greys,
ochres, browns, beiges and whites. His friend Martin
Gayford, who kept a diary of sitting for Freud for several
months in 2003 and 2004, reported him calling these
'the colours of life', colours that are not expressive in
themselves, but allowed him to concentrate on the
honest depiction of skin.[1] Gayford noticed that he
had a highly developed sense of colour and noticed
the slightest variations of tone.[2]

This palette cannot be considered without the
greater context of the studio Freud used from the late
1970s until the end of his life. He had divided one floor
of a large 18th-century house in Kensington, London,
into a naturally lit daytime studio and an artificially
lit night-time studio. The walls were painted so as not
to reflect light, and the space was scattered with select

*'I would wish my portraits to be of people, not like them.
Not having a look of the setter, being them.... As far as
I am concerned the paint is the person. I want it to work
for me just as flesh does.'*

LUCIAN FREUD, QUOTED IN MARTIN GAYFORD'S *MAN WITH A BLUE SCARF*, 2010

pieces of antique furniture that frequently appear in his compositions. Billowing piles of hospital sheets and discarded rags were strewn on the floor and often used as compositional elements in paintings, including in *And the Bridegroom*.

Freud would often wander around the studio naked or semi-naked, and the colouring of his clothing was similar to that of his art. He was, by all accounts, an intense and highly libidinous person, who constantly blurred the boundaries art and life, as well as painting and sex. Each painting, whether small or large, would take many sittings, often amounting to hundreds of hours of work, during which he would flick oil paint scraped from his palette onto the walls, doors and window frames of the studio. Over time, these surfaces became encrusted with paint, looking like an abstract version of the figurative realism on his canvases. Freud also scribbled notes on the walls, some about colours and pigments, such as rose madder (probably also used for skin tones). Unlike that of his contemporary and friend Francis Bacon (see pages 222–27), Freud's studio was dismantled after his death and never recreated.

The physicality of paint must have excited him, as his studio walls were never cleaned and his clothes were often speckled with oil paint. Yet, as his friend Geordie Greig noted, he would often have several baths a day and kept his hands scrupulously clean.[3] He had a great interest in the materiality of pigments, and a reckless penchant for the heaviest, most toxic lead white, Cremnitz white, which suited the granular appearance of his paint surfaces.[4] In some photographs taken during sittings, he looks like a wizard or a contorted figure in a painting by Caravaggio. He was as honest and uncompromising about the depiction of the human body in his self-portraits as in his portraits of others. In one (image C.) he stands naked but for a pair of shoes, arms outstretched, holding in one hand a palette similar in tone and appearance to this one, like an extension of his naked body, a self-referential symbol of his life and art.

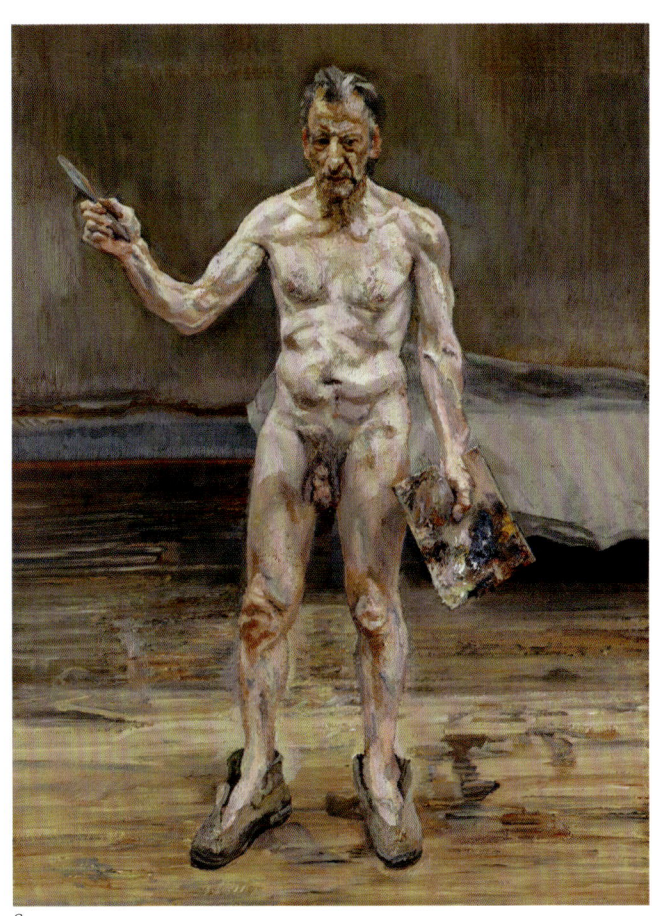

c.

A. Lucian Freud's brushes and empty tubes of paint
B. Paint on the window shutters of Lucian Freud's studio, London,
    England, photograph by David Dawson, 2011
C. *Painter Working, Reflection*, Lucian Freud, 1993, oil on canvas,
    101.2 × 81.7 cm (39 ⅞ × 32 ¼ in.)

BRIDGET RILEY

B. 1931

A geometric palette of colour, shape and mind

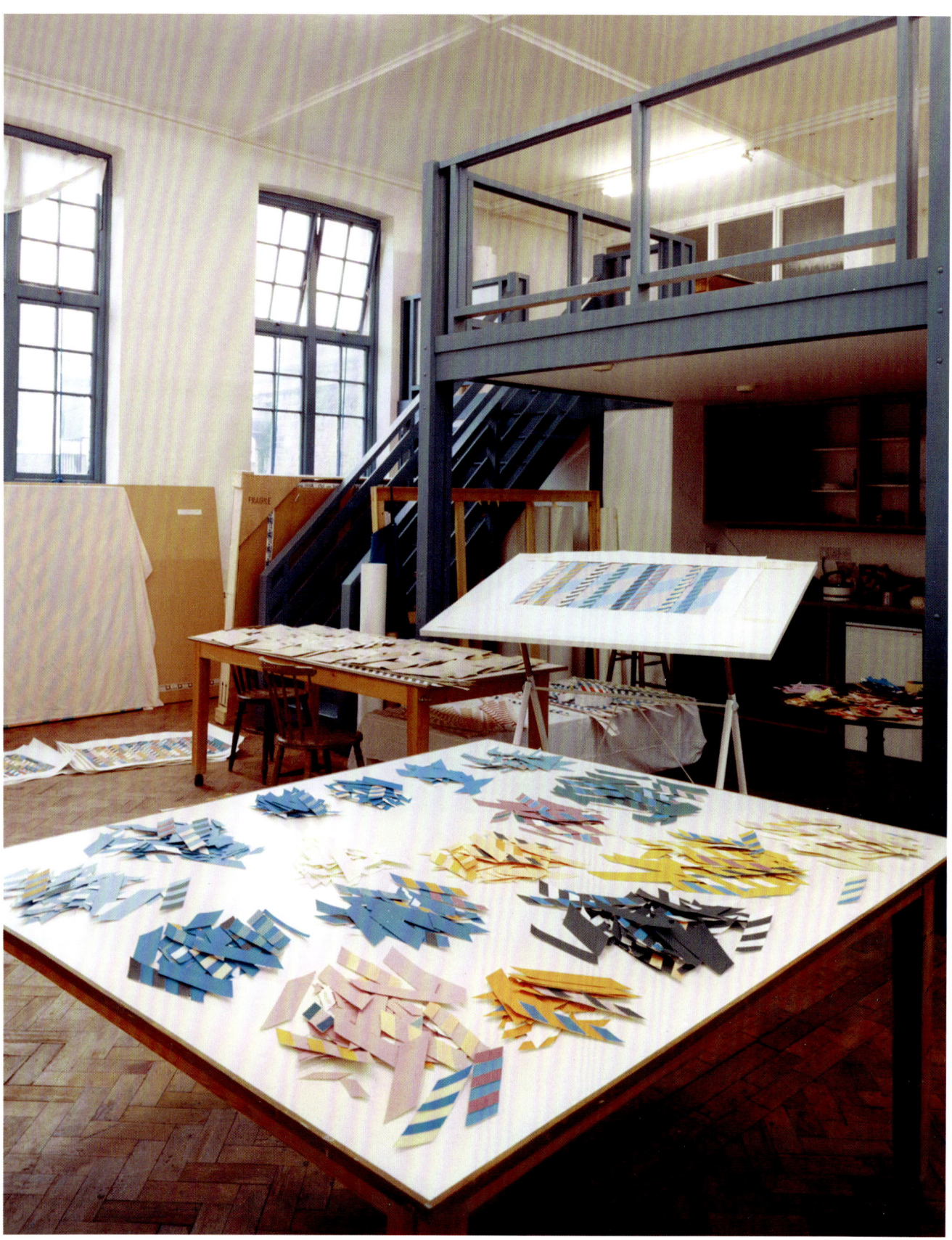

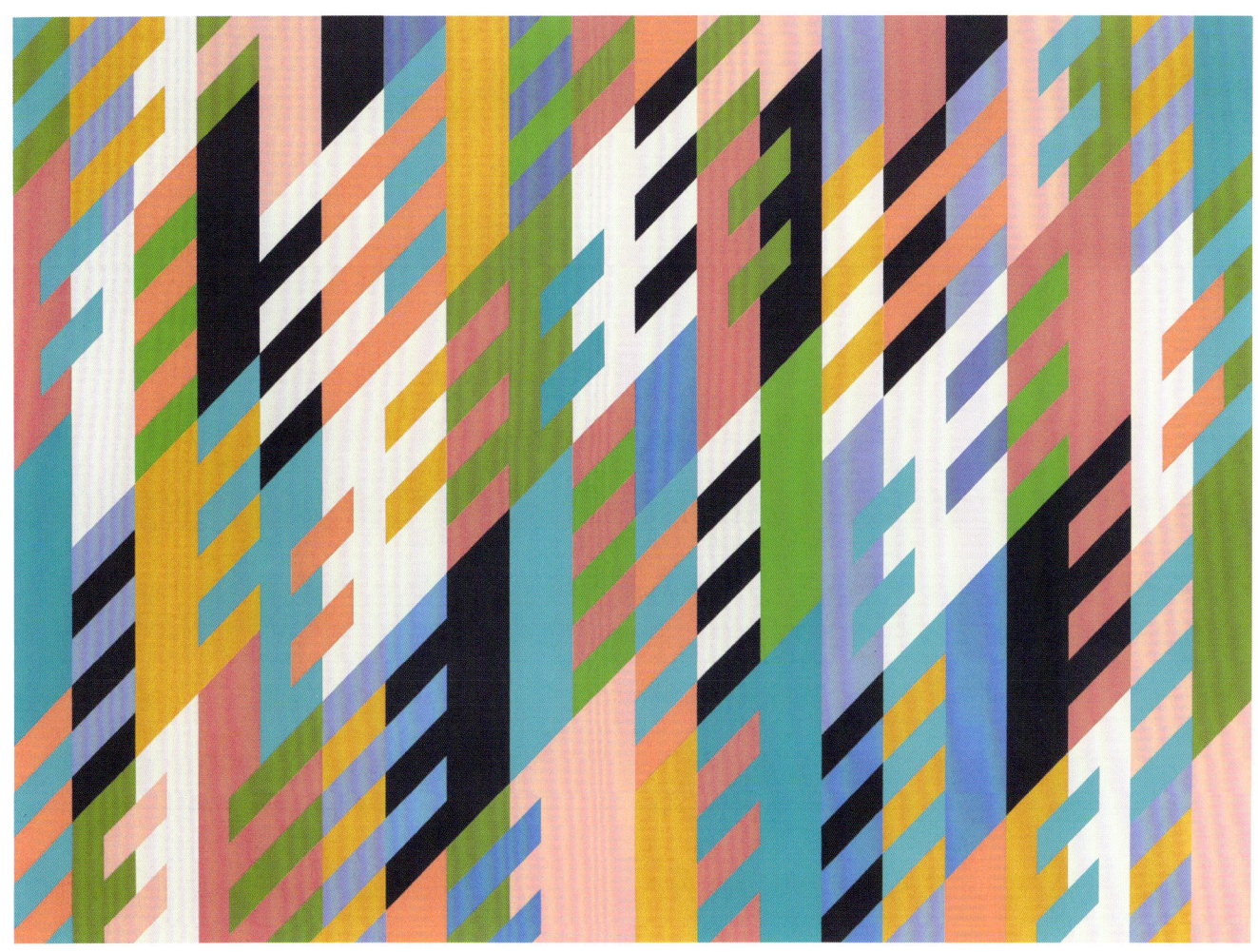

Bridget Riley's east
London studio, England
Photograph by
Terry Buchanan
Undated

New Day
Bridget Riley
1988
Oil on canvas
160 × 226 cm
(63 × 89 in.)

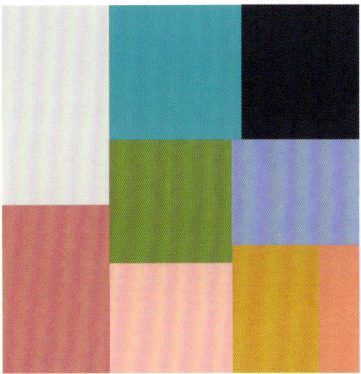

Proportional breakdown of colours used by Bridget Riley in *New Day*, 1988, displayed on the previous page.

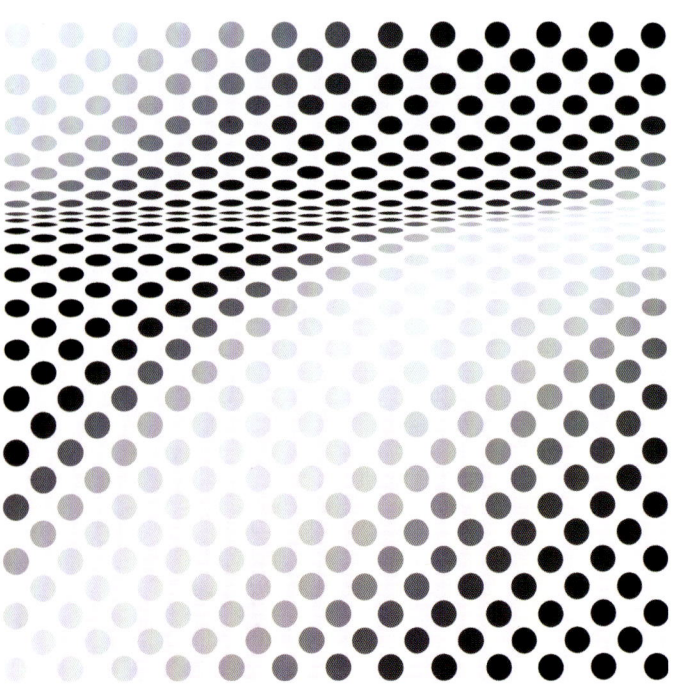

A.

BRIDGET RILEY IS AN ARTIST who works using a wide range of materials and media, including oil, emulsion and acrylic paint, gouache and pencil on paper, card, linen, canvas and board. Some of her work is very large in scale, but she also embraces smaller formats. Her completely abstract work focuses on the relationship between colours and between colour and form, and on how we perceive colour. Riley avoids traditional painters' palettes as a space for preparation. She works out carefully balanced colour relationships in advance and often uses the greater physical context of the studio like a palette. Her working style is both methodical and experimental – her colour schemes may develop through trial and error over many months but are always directed by Riley's creative impulse.[1] Although she involves studio assistants in the 'bulking up' of her colours, she mixes paint herself in gouache, acrylic and oil, avoiding prescriptive recipes, instead adjusting mixtures in groups of colour visually and instinctively.[2]

On page 232 we see a large white table in her studio that represents an enlarged version of a palette. On it are dozens of rhombic shapes cut from paper or thin card, painted with gouache and arranged in groups by colour and pattern. These are then used to create a 'cartoon' layout for one of her rhomboid paintings, the first of which she created in 1986. Riley is using colours here in specifically chosen tonal groups, treating them as geometric units in her chromatic jigsaw. This method is reminiscent of the late collage phase of Matisse, in which he metaphorically painted with scissors. Riley has been thinking about and using colour in this radically abstract and reduced way for decades, developing, as Paul Moorhouse has put it, 'a simple, restricted vocabulary of abstract shapes'.[3]

Riley's interest in the relationship between colours has its roots in the late 1950s, when she first became interested in Georges Seurat (see pages 126–29) and divisionism. After she had copied a Seurat painting and created divisionist work herself, she abandoned colour completely for several years, focusing instead on abstract, achromatic compositions in black and white and exploring the optical effects of greyscales. She returned to colour in 1967, choosing extreme geometric shapes and formats, such as long stripes of colour placed close together in vertiginous vertical or very long horizontal compositions. Since then, Riley has expanded, changed and broken up these shapes into curvilinear designs, diagonals, wavy lines, dots and circles. At the heart of this exploration of colour is always the optical quality of colour arrangements, and how the human eye and mind respond to them.

Riley works to a significant degree conceptually and intellectually. In an interview with Robert Kudielka

'The fusion of harmonies and the evocation of complementaries; this is the framework within which I articulate the colour event of the painting.'

BRIDGET RILEY, *THE EYE'S MIND*, 2009

in 1978, she explained how she groups colours: 'For several years I only used three colours in each painting, though more recently I have used five – and with those colours, say, yellow, pink, violet, blue and green, I build up a structure.'[4] Since first engaging with Seurat, Riley has developed a deep understanding of the laws of colour contrast and colour theory in general. Seurat and his contemporaries were influenced by the writings of Michel-Eugène Chevreul, Charles Blanc, Ogden Rood and other colour theorists and scientists. Although critical of the theoretical nature of these concepts, Riley acknowledges the geometric diagrams that underpin some of them: 'All five colours...relate to each other in such a way that, if one assembles them as they would be in a colour circle, they describe the shape of a pentagon.'[5] Riley's profound understanding of the relationship between colour, colour perception and materiality makes her one of the greatest colour theorists of the 20th century, albeit it one who did not see a practical value of theory for artists. Her colour wheel was the studio, and she replaced theory with physical engagement in colour shapes, paint and light. In 1993 she gave a lecture on colour for painters at Darwin College, Cambridge, which she began with a statement as clear, sharp and precise as her geometric colour shapes:

> We usually see colour as the colour of something –
> it is not a natural thing to see colour simply as itself
> alone, unless, of course, we happen also to be painters.
> For painters, colour is not only all those things which
> we all see, but also, most extraordinarily, the pigments
> spread out on the palette, and there, quite uniquely,
> they are simply and solely colour. This is the first
> important fact of the painter's art to be grasped.[6]

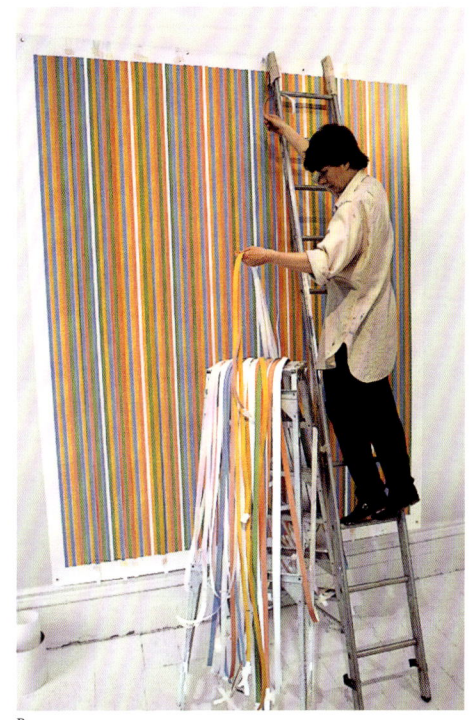

B.

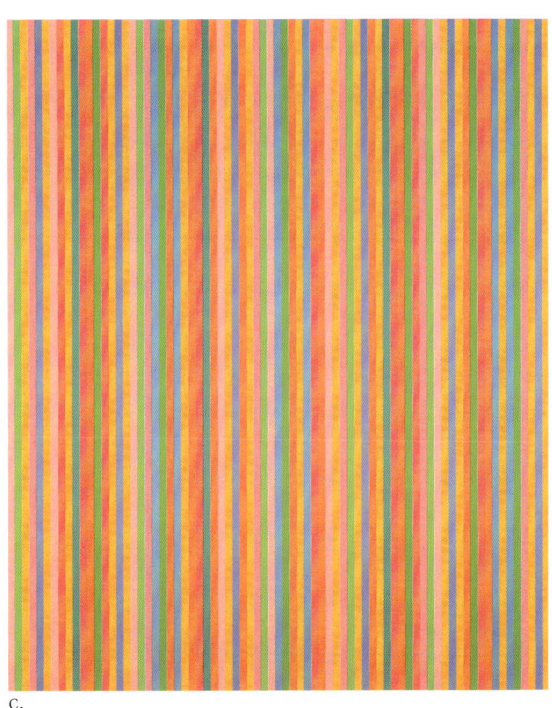

A. *Hesitate*, Bridget Riley, 1964, emulsion on board, 106.7 × 112.4 cm
    (42 ⅛ × 44 ⅜ in.)
B. Bridget Riley working on paper 'cartoons' in her west London
    studio, England, photograph by Bill Warhurst, 1983
C. *Rose Return*, Bridget Riley, 1985, oil on linen, 163 × 143 cm
    (64 ¼ × 56 ⅜ in.)

C.

KEITH HARING 1958–1990

A political palette for everyone

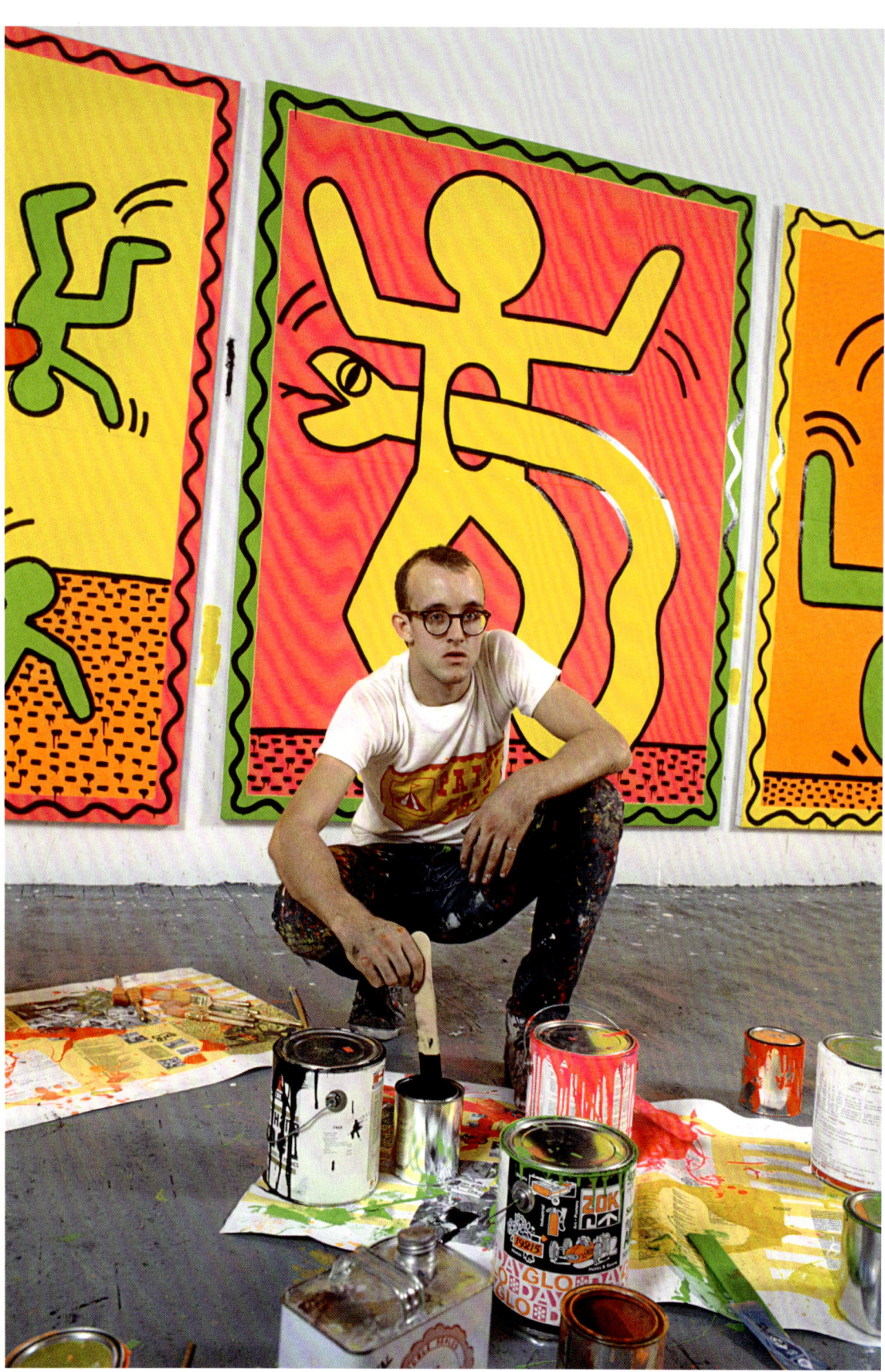

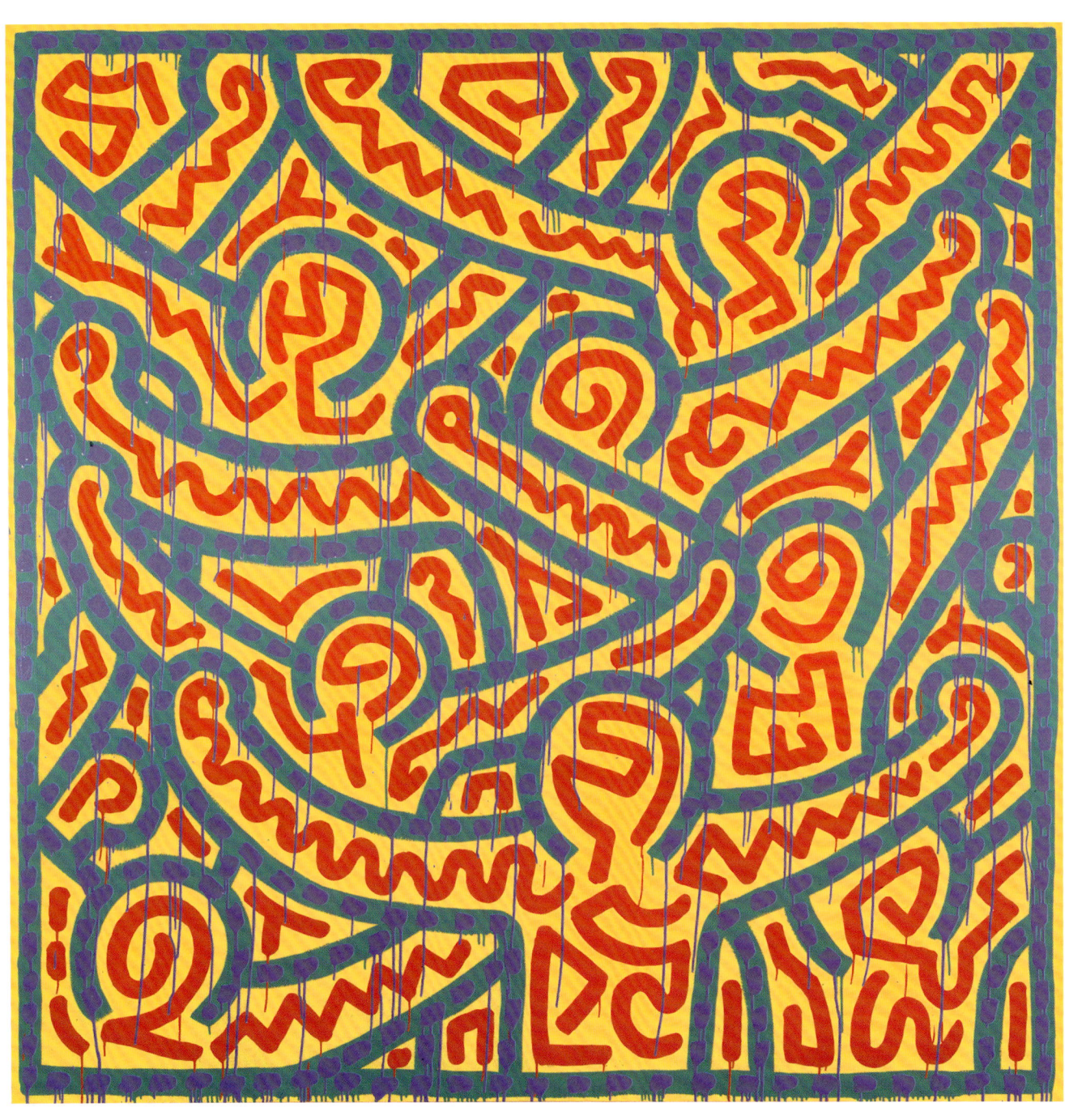

Keith Haring at
work in his studio,
New York, USA
Photograph by
Allan Tannenbaum
28 October 1982

Untitled
Keith Haring
1989
Enamel and acrylic
on canvas
182.8 × 182.8 cm
(72 × 72 in.)

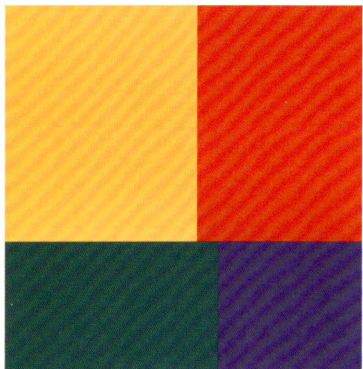

Proportional breakdown of colours used by Keith Haring in *Untitled*, 1989, displayed on the previous page.

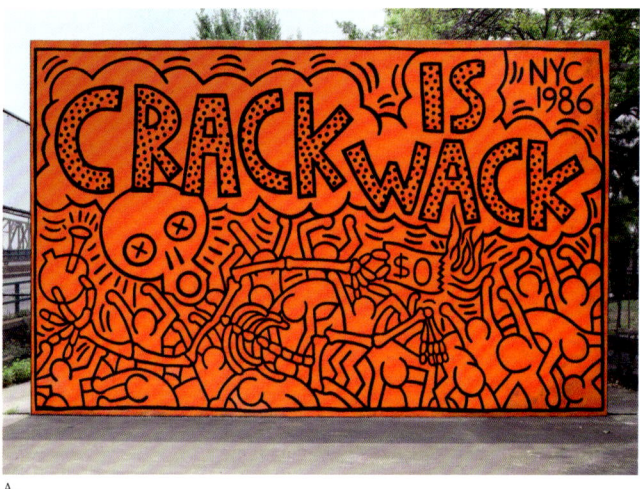

A.

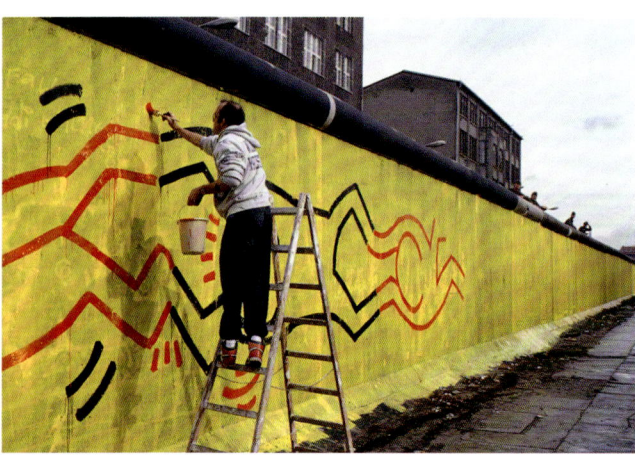

B.

IT IS UNLIKELY THAT KEITH HARING ever used a traditional painter's palette. He worked mostly, but not exclusively, in large formats in public spaces, on many surfaces, using a wide range of media, and at times abandoned material paint and surfaces altogether. He was inspired by emerging new technologies, such as computers, Xerox, and video cameras. Had he lived longer, he would undoubtedly have embraced the full possibilities of digital art. His 1980s Apple computer became a recurring motif in his iconography, and he even produced some early computer-generated artworks. His palette was – metaphorically and physically – the urban and public environment, his canvas a multitude of experimental spaces and surfaces, including buildings, floors, tarpaulin, fibreglass vases, surfboards, cars and even the human body, including at one point his own.

Haring's techniques, tools and methods were more complex and varied than they might at first appear. In the early 1980s, he drew in white chalk on empty black advertising spaces in the New York subway, for which he was sometimes arrested and fined. He had to work quickly on these occasions and there was no room for mistakes, but he produced his trademark emblems and designs, including 'cookie cutter' figures, the 'Radiant Baby' and barking dogs with great precision. These early drawings in public spaces were characteristic of several aspects of his work: the calculated element of performance and speed as part of an artwork, as well as its inherent ephemerality; and his interest in the relationship between line and colour, which has its roots in the intellectual conflict between *disegno* (drawing) and *colore* (colour) of the Italian Renaissance.[1]

Haring would move on to much larger formats, including around forty-five monumental murals, many of them outdoors and now lost to time and decay. His colours were vibrant but warm, comprising mostly unmixed, ready-made primaries and secondaries, with figures, icons and patterns sharply outlined in black. Unlike graffiti artists, he would almost never use spray paint. The colour surface was unmodulated, in an almost completely flat, cartoon-like appearance. Haring knew that he needed this flatness and the combination of pure colours in order to maximize the visibility and impact of his work.

Haring kept extensive notes and journals from 1977. His diaries reveal how he sourced his materials, and how he was involved with them at every step, taking delight in shopping locally for huge amounts of paint and other tools, including brushes and rollers. He enjoyed the physicality of working very publicly and at great speed, grappling with the challenges of each location and surface. He had a particular fondness for Japanese and Chinese brushes and ink.

'Nothing is important...
so, everything is important.'

KEITH HARING, JOURNAL ENTRY, 25 JUNE 1986

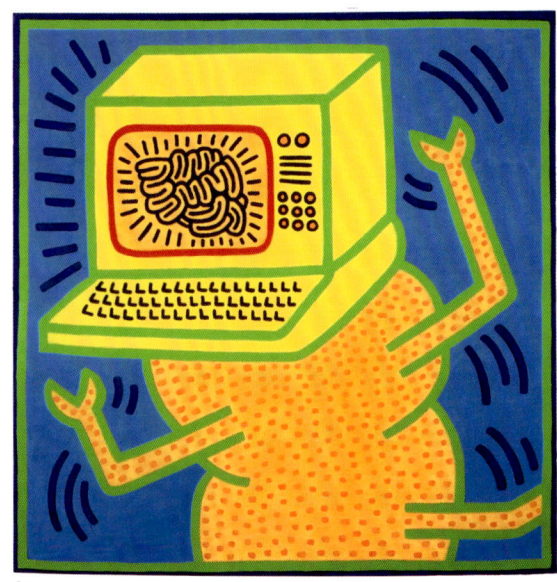

c.

His art was always meant to be for the greater good of everyone. It was political in the sense that he wanted to subvert the way art was seen, consumed, bought, sold and collected. Essentially, he believed in the value of the public space, and the positive power of immersive, tangible, accessible art: 'For me, the most effective public sculpture would function as visual and physical entertainment. I think public art (unless there is a specific political or ideological message) should make people comfortable, and brighten their environment.'[2]

In October 1986, commissioned by the director of the Mauermuseum (Haus am Checkpoint Charlie), Haring painted a stretch of approximately 100 metres (300 feet) of the west side of the Berlin Wall, one of the first artists to do so. This was not without danger as the wall itself and a strip of ground immediately in front of it was inside the East German border, and he could have been shot or arrested by armed guards. Haring chose as a ground the most visible colour possible, a bright yellow, onto which he painted a series of horizontal interlocking human figures in red and black. This was about more than visibility: these colours also had symbolic value, as they mirrored the colours of the flags of West and East Germany. It took him less than six hours to paint it (the yellow ground had been applied in advance). Within a few days his mural, itself having superseded work by other artists, was painted and sprayed over by protesters and graffiti artists, and by the end of 1989, the Iron Curtain and the Berlin Wall itself had crumbled. Nothing of Haring's physical mural survives, but this would not have bothered him. He believed in the psychological and visual attack he had carried out against the wall, and knew the work would live on in film, photography and people's memories.

In 1987 many of Haring's friends were dying of AIDS and he realized that it was likely he too would succumb to the virus. This added even more urgency, passion and empathy to his work. Vowing to do 'as much as possible as quickly as possible', he remarked that 'work is all I have and art is more important than life.'[3]

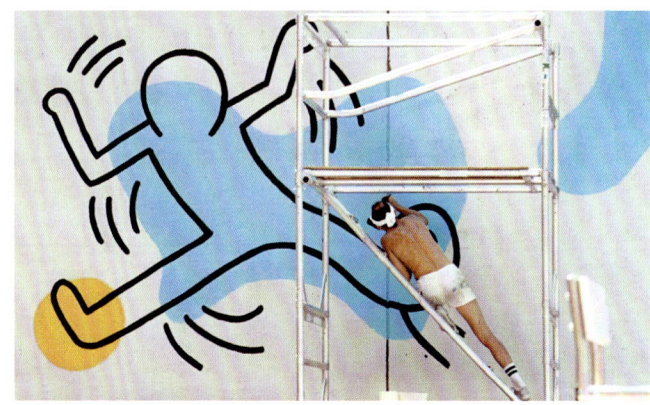

D.

A. *Crack is Wack* mural, located on handball court at 128th Street and 2nd Avenue, New York, USA, Keith Haring, 1986
B. Keith Haring paints the Berlin Wall, October 1986
C. *Untitled*, Keith Haring, 1984, acrylic on canvas, 152 × 152 cm (60 × 60 in.)
D. Keith Haring paints a mural on a 55.7 m (150 ft) wall at Clarkson Street and Seventh Avenue, New York, USA, 20 August 1987

PAULA REGO 1935–2022

A subversive, technicolour palette

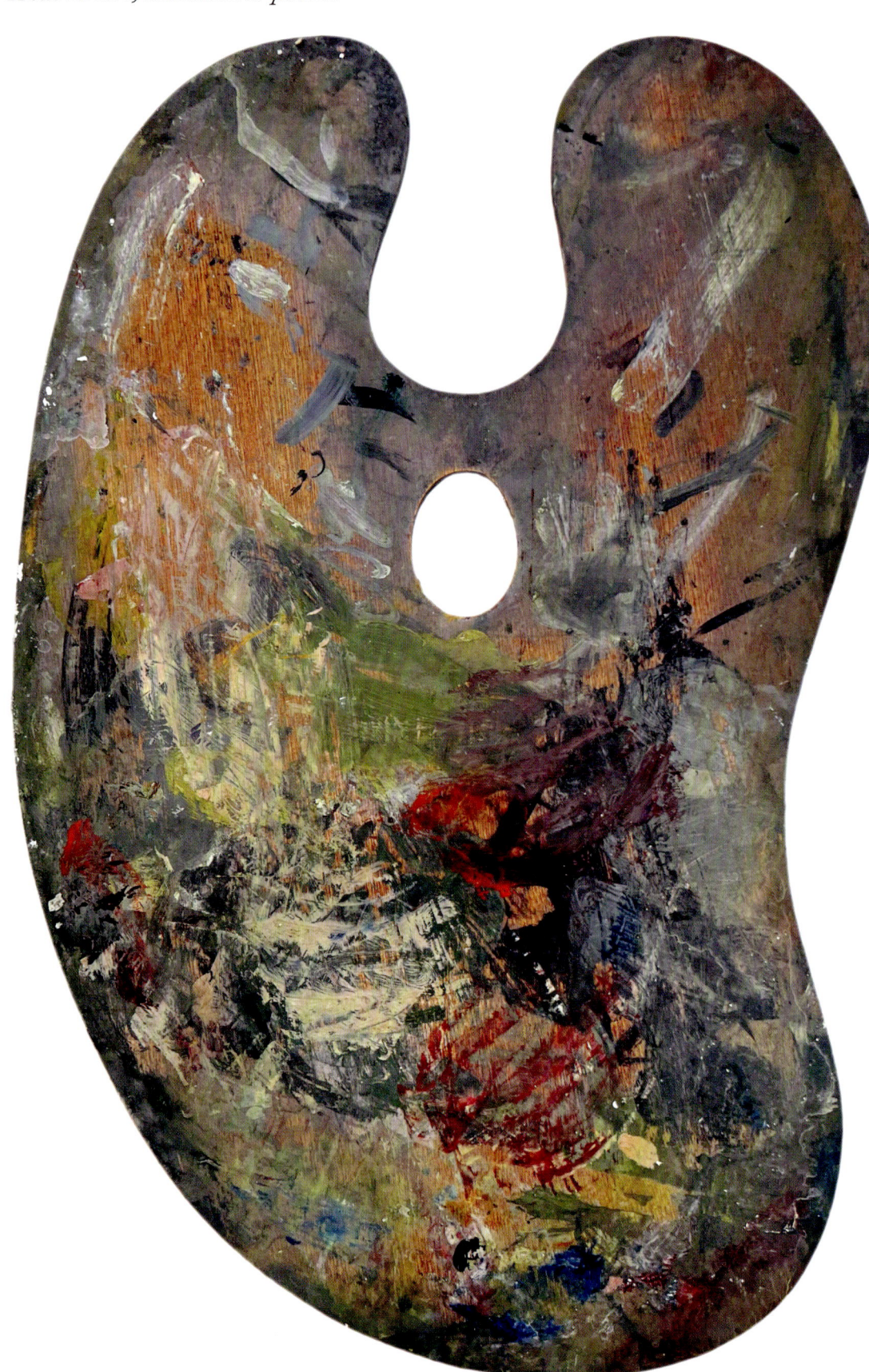

Paula Rego's palette
Undated
Paint on wood

The Artist in Her Studio
Paula Rego
1993
Acrylic on canvas
180 × 130 cm
(70 ⅞ × 51 ¼ in.)

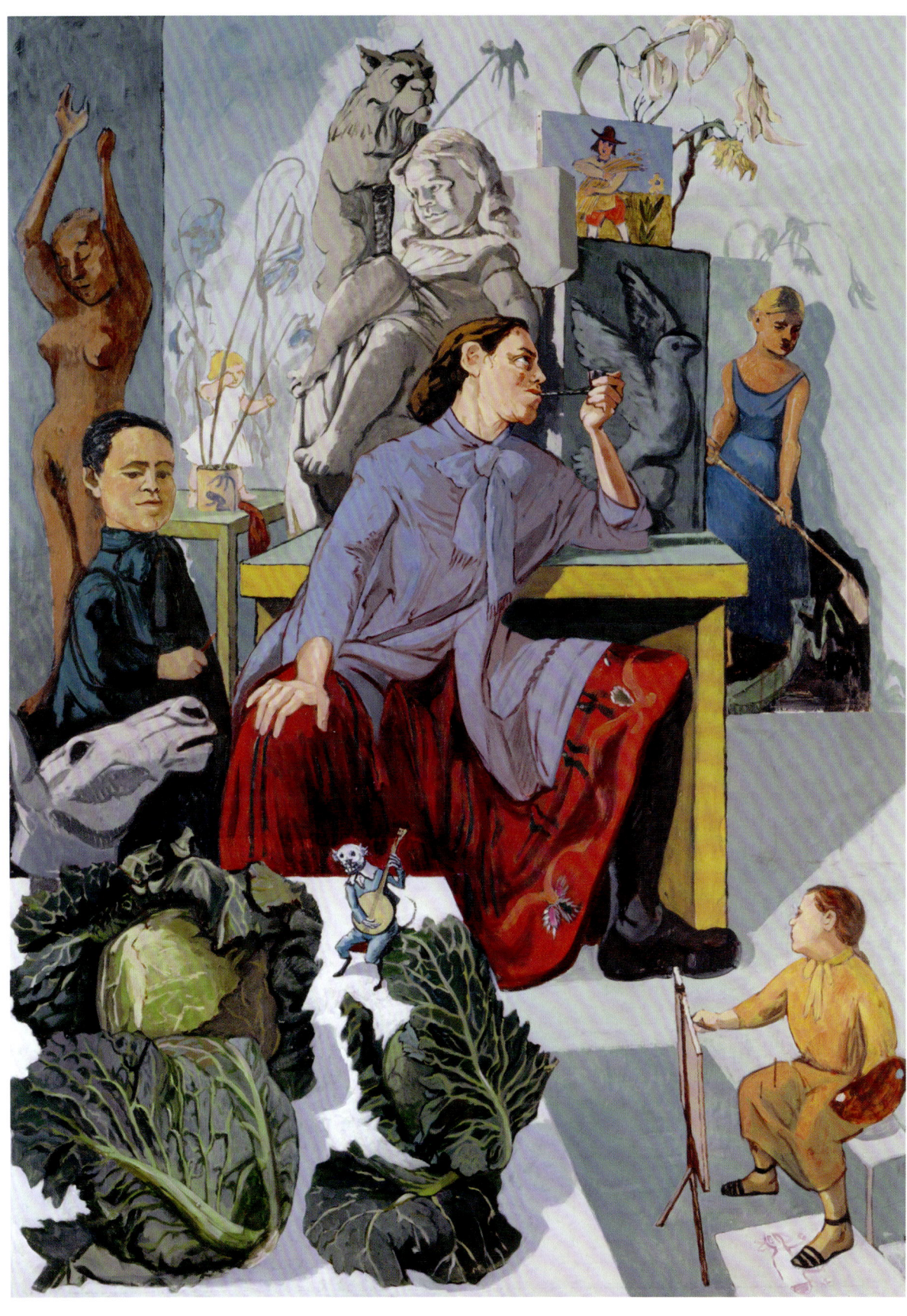

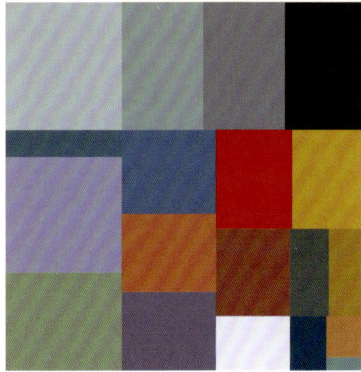

Proportional breakdown of colours used by Paula Rego in *The Artist in Her Studio*, 1993, displayed on the previous page.

THIS PALETTE BY PAULA REGO is deceptively traditional in appearance, and without context could easily be mistaken for having belonged to an impressionist or post-impressionist artist painting outdoors. Yet it is a rare object that gives us a glimpse of Rego, a subversive and daring artist who pushed the boundaries of representational art and artists' materials, focusing on the creation of one of her emotionally raw and often disturbing paintings.

This is a classic, kidney-shaped arm palette, suggesting that Rego used it for a larger canvas. It is undated, but chromatically close to *The Artist in Her Studio* (1993), shown on the preceding page. The medium is probably acrylic (although oil is also a possibility), which Rego embraced early in her career and continued to use throughout. Water-borne acrylic paints are fast-drying polymer emulsions that became commercially available as artists' and household paint in the mid 1950s. They can resemble oil paint, but are non-odorous, and thus allow artists to work in smaller studio spaces. For Rego, their appeal lay probably in the general ease of use, allowing her to work at her typical frantic speed.

There is no obvious methodical layout to the palette, but it shows signs of heavy and repeated use. Considerable patina has accumulated around the edges, whereas areas above and below the thumbhole appear to have been wiped clean. The paint traces include neutral whites and mixed greys and blues, as well as saturated reds and a mixed violet, the latter two similar to the skirt and smock-like top worn by the dominant seated figure in the centre of *The Artist in Her Studio*. A variety of vibrant greens have also been mixed, as used for the cabbages in the foreground of the painting. Rego's brushwork has left distinct marks on the palette, giving an impression of fast, intuitive mixing and painting.

Rego worked mostly with large formats and in various media, with a frenzy and energy that in her early work involved the deliberate corruption and cutting up of her drawings. These she reassembled as collages, packed with detail and ambiguous visual metaphors, against a flat background without perspective, showing the influence of art brut, with strong hints of cubist aesthetics.

From the 1980s onwards, her work became more focused and representational, comprising sculptural, strong figures commanding the pictorial space, with Rego zooming in on disturbing, often harrowing, events and on physical and emotional pain and violence. Out-of-scale human and animal figures, some gigantic, some diminutive, such as the titular

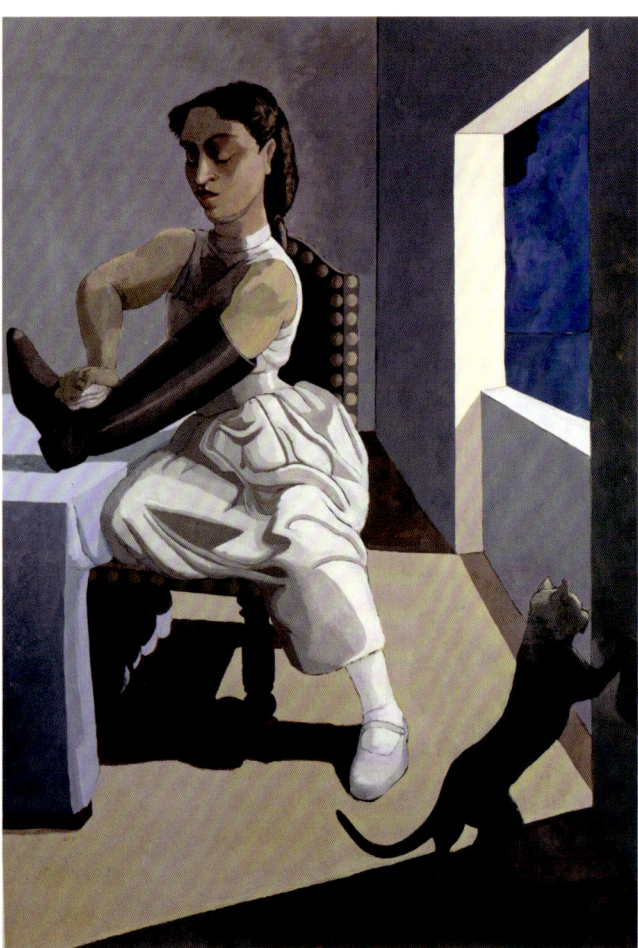

A.

*'All my work is to do with metamorphosis.
It comes about in the actual physical
making of the picture; the trial and
error of working.'*

PAULA REGO, QUOTED IN JOHN McEWEN'S *PAULA REGO*, 1992

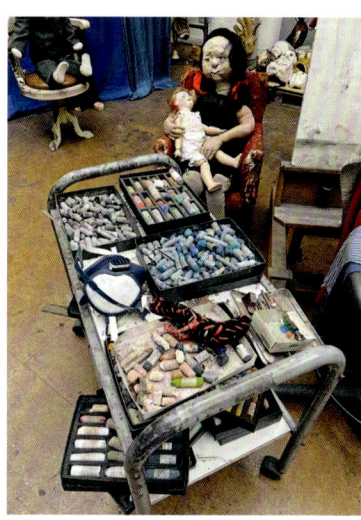

B.

artist in the bottom right corner in this painting,
occupy these later easel paintings, as if having emerged
from Alice's Wonderland.

Iconographically, her work was hugely influenced
by storytelling in the broadest sense, with inspiration
from fairy tales, folklore, mythology, even psychoanalytic
sessions. Chromatically, a shift occurred when Rego
started painting shadows, which she does here with
great skill. Note the hard, coloured shadows that fall
diagonally upwards, suggestive of theatrical lighting,
adding to the eerie and surreal feel of the composition.
Some of the bluish mixtures seen on this palette
may have been used to paint shadows. With all its
narrative and figural content, it is easy to overlook
how brilliantly Rego mastered colour and used it to
structure compositions, create atmosphere and express
the psychological and physical state of her figures.
Rego's son Nick Willing, a film director, once said:
'She paints in technicolour; and the lighting is cinematic.
The atmosphere is cinematic.'[1]

Despite or perhaps because of her hyper-creative
spirit and fast working style, Rego also embraced
pastels, a medium that requires the painter to paint
with a different pace and rhythm. Pastels consist of
finely ground pigments mixed with white fillers, such
as calcium carbonate or chalk, with only small amounts
of binder, and they are manufactured as small, rolled
sticks or in pencils. It is a brittle, powdery medium that
cannot be mixed on palettes, so artists need a multitude
of pastel sticks, or to rely on optical mixing. If handled
well, pastels produce the most brilliant colour schemes.
They are predominantly associated with subtle 18th-
century society portraits and Degas's diaphanous ballet
dancers, but Rego used them with the same powerful
results as her acrylics, creating large-scale, glowing
pictures with highly saturated colour schemes, such
as her magnificent painting *Angel* (1998, image C.),
which is quite possibly a self-portrait in disguise.

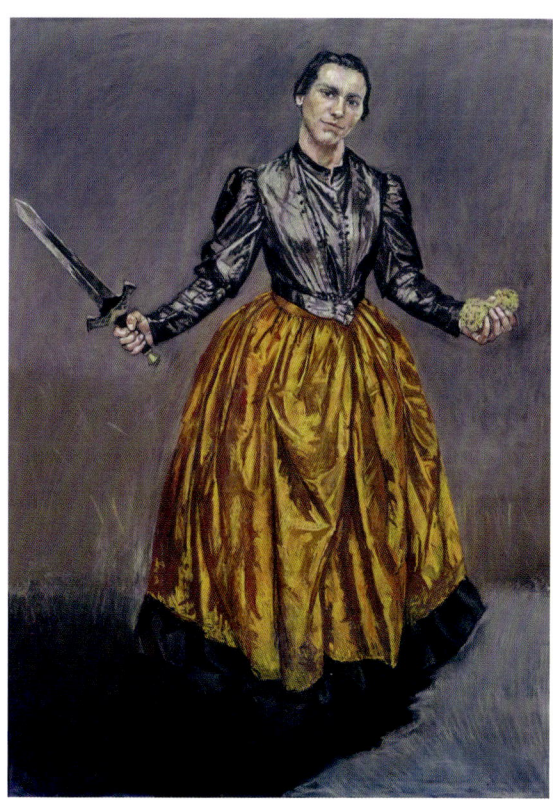

C.

A. *The Policeman's Daughter*, Paula Rego, 1987, acrylic on
     paper on canvas, 213.4 × 152.4 cm (84 ⅛ × 60 in.)
B. Paula Rego's pastel trolley in her studio
C. *Angel*, Paula Rego, 1998, pastel on paper on aluminium,
     180 × 130 cm (70 ⅞ × 51 ¼ in.)

KERRY JAMES MARSHALL B. 1955

How black and white is your palette?

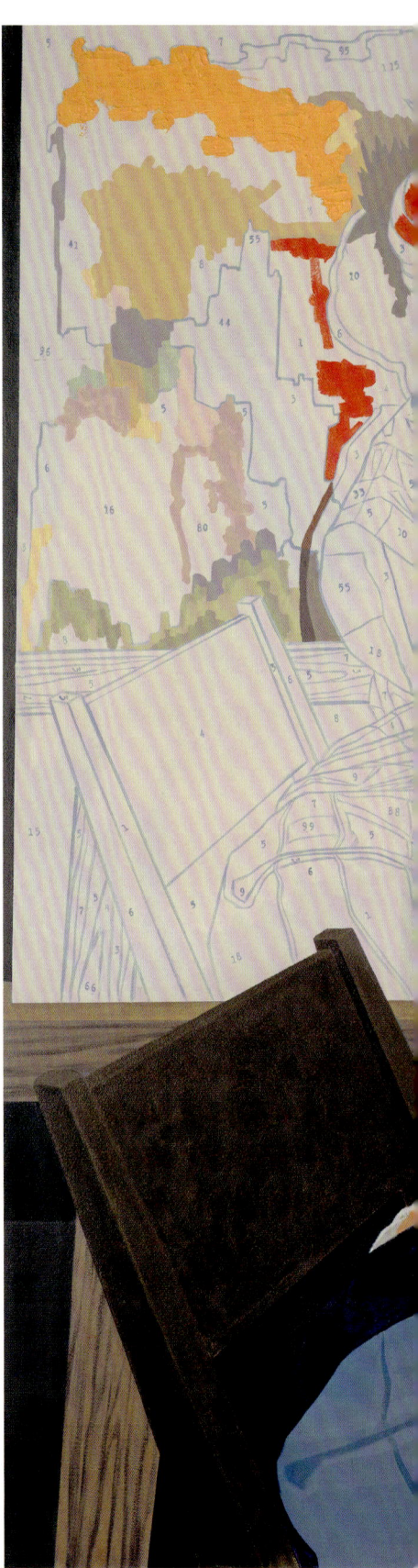

Untitled
Kerry James Marshall
2009
Acrylic on PVC panel
155.2 × 185.1 × 9.8 cm
(61 ⅛ × 72 ⅞ × 3 ⅞ in.)

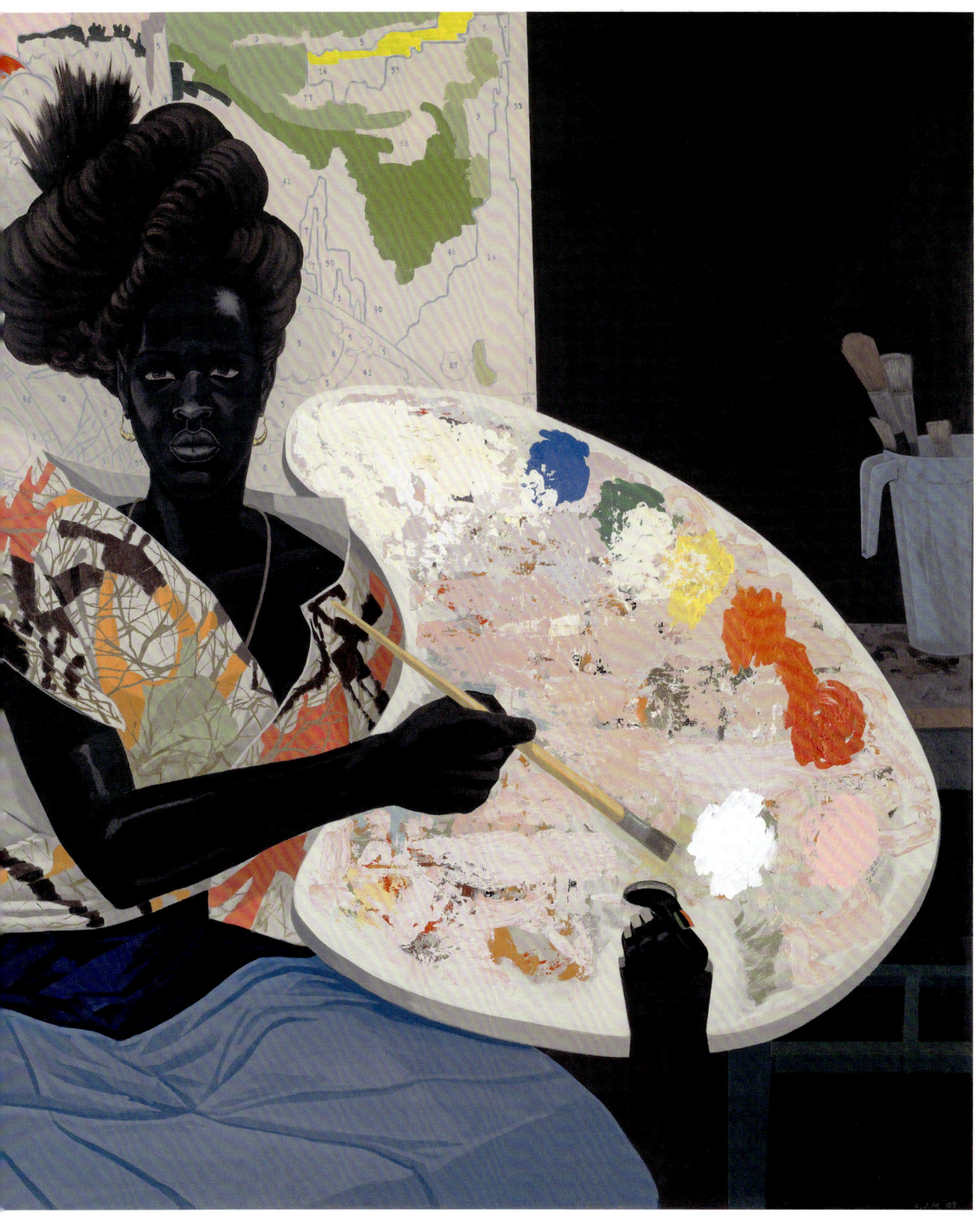

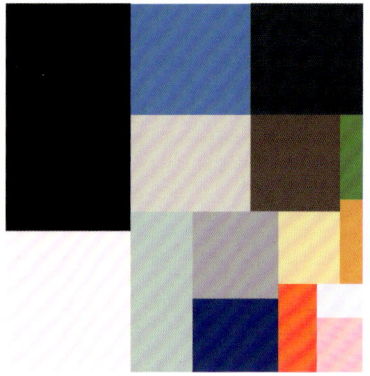

Proportional breakdown of colours used by Kerry
James Marshall in *Untitled*, 2009, displayed on the
previous page.

IN THE LATE 2000S, Kerry James Marshall painted
a series of works in which he addressed the themes of
colour, paint and portraiture. In these large pictures
of painters, including the ones shown here, palettes
serve as hugely symbolic objects. His signature Black
figures hold ridiculously oversized palettes that almost
wrap themselves around them, commanding much
of the pictorial space. The compositions follow the
traditional Western format of the artist facing the
viewer, proudly and assuredly posing with the tools of
their trade. They could be considered allegorical figures
of Painting, but Marshall also uses colour theory to
highlight issues concerning Black identity and history.

Marshall's outsized painted palettes are achingly
pristine, white or off-white surfaces, on which he places
predominantly pure, bright colours. The palettes
represent both the stage on which the history of colour
and art plays out and the blank slate on which history
will be rewritten or repainted. The female Black artist
in *Untitled* (shown on the preceding pages) is about to
dip her brush into the zinc-white blot of paint near the
thumbhole (in other paintings in the series the chosen
colour is black) and has already used some of the other
colours (blue, green, yellow, orange and red), mixing
them with white. Much of the space of the palette is
covered in a mixed pale pink, suggestive of the white
Western tradition of attempting to create white skin
colour in painting.

The storytelling and social commentary through
colour and colouring continue in the background of
the painting. The canvas behind the figure is marked
out with the outline of a self-portrait, an exact copy
of what we see in the foreground, with colour spaces
identified by numbers. The first colours the artist
has applied to her dark hair in the picture are entirely
non-realistic reds and oranges. In a seemingly joyful
style, here Marshall addresses significant and difficult
issues relating to Black history and Western art:
whose colours are on this magnified, symbolic palette?
Is painting in colour reduced to a flat, formulaic,
painting-by-numbers style? Where is the nuance?
And, perhaps most importantly, where is black, and
Blackness, on the historical palette of art history
and figurative representation?

Kerry James Marshall was born in 1955 in
Alabama, coming of age during the civil rights era in
the United States. At this time, state-sanctioned racial
segregation and violence against Black communities
were widespread. He moved to Los Angeles as a young
boy, where he witnessed first-hand the social unrest
erupting in the Watts riots of 1965. He was also deeply
inspired by the work of Charles White, a Black painter
and printmaker, born in Chicago in 1918, whose

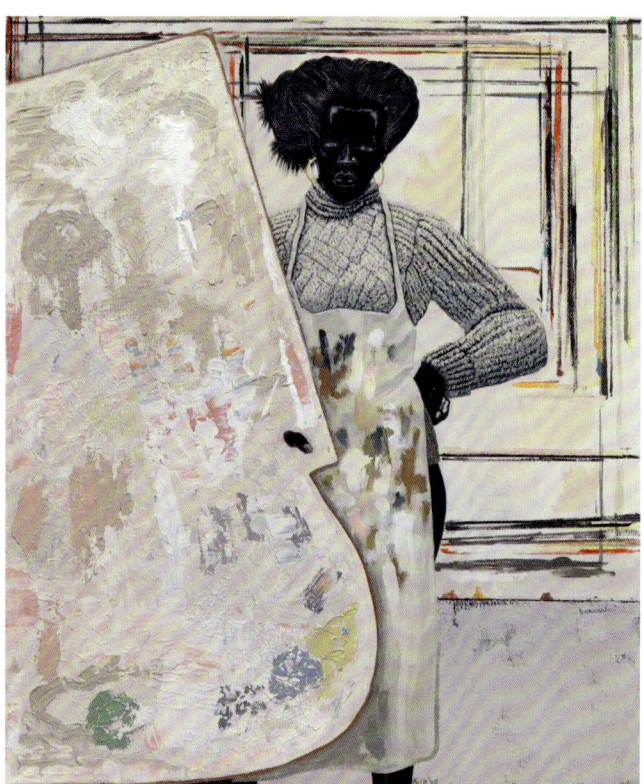

A.

'If you looked at the palette I was using you'd think, "Well, that's black, black and black next to each other."... But when I use them in a painting next to each other, the differences become more apparent. Because the iron oxide black is inherently red.... Or I'll mix in cobalt blue, a chrome oxide green, an earth tone like raw umber or yellow umber. What I'm doing is changing the temperature, from cool to warm and warm to cool.'

KERRY JAMES MARSHALL IN AN INTERVIEW WITH GABRIEL COXHEAD, 'WHEN YOU PUT BLACK PEOPLE IN A PICTURE, WHAT SHOULD THEY BE DOING?', *APOLLO*, MARCH 2019

unapologetically political work addressed the struggle of African-American people in the 20th century. Black, and being Black, became the dominant theme in Marshall's art, which is both epic and whimsical, peppered with hints of pop art aesthetics.

He has studied the canon of Western art history thoroughly, displaying a deep understanding of the overwhelmingly white traditions, styles and tropes of (self-)representation. He draws on techniques from Renaissance artists, such as Cennino Cennini, in order to expand his artistic tools, including the palette and colours, and to establish his own iconography and visual language to express what it means to be Black. To create his ultra-black colours, he combines the most common pigments commercially available, ivory black, carbon black and Mars black, while achieving nuance by adding cobalt blues, chrome greens or dioxazine violets.

Marshall plays with and utilizes colour contrasts, in both optical and metaphorical terms. From early in his career, he visualized the socially constructed invisibility of Black people by white society, often combining the comical with the grotesque. Ultra-black figures, whose features only appear after looking closer at the finer details of his large paintings, became a prominent motif in Marshall's art, subverting racist tropes of Black invisibility while also celebrating Black resilience and presence.

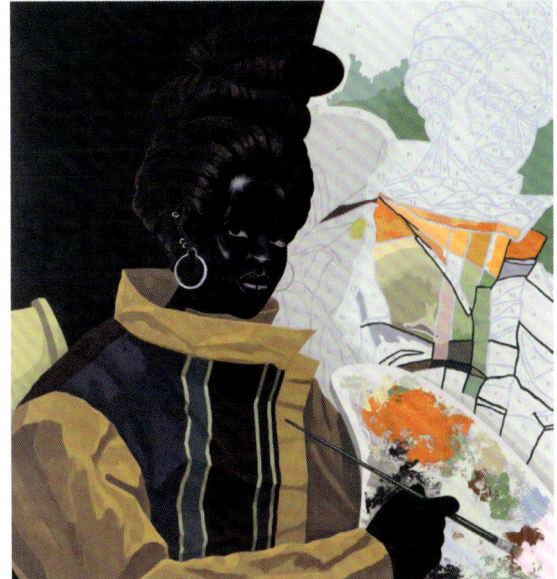

B.

A. *Untitled (Painter)*, Kerry James Marshall, 2008, acrylic on PVC panel, 73 × 62.9 cm (28 ¾ × 24 ¾ in.)
B. *Untitled (Painter)*, Kerry James Marshall, 2009, acrylic on PVC panel, 113.4 × 109.5 × 9.8 cm (44 ⅝ × 43 ⅛ × 3 ⅞ in.)
C. *Untitled (Studio)*, Kerry James Marshall, 2014, acrylic on PVC panels, 2.1 × 3 m (6 ft 11 ⅜ in. × 9 ft 11 ¼ in.)

C.

— INTRODUCTION (PP. 10–23)
1 Kandinsky, W. and Bill, M. (ed.) *Über das Geistige in der Kunst*. Benteli Verlag. 1952 [1912], pp. 59–61. [Author's translation]
2 Bate, J. *The Mysteries of Nature and Art*. Ralph Mabb. 1635, p. 211.
3 Fielding, T. H. *On Painting in Oil and Water Colours*. Ackermann & Co. 1839.
4 Cawse, J. *The Art of Painting Portraits, Landscapes, Animals, Draperies, Satins, &c. in Oil Colours*. Rudolph Ackermann. 1840 [1822].
5 For an overview of Kiefer's use of the palette in his iconography, see: Arasse, D. *Anselm Kiefer*. Thames & Hudson. 2014, pp. 98–117.
6 Vanderpoel, E. N. *Color Problems: A Practical Manual for the Lay Student of Color*. Longmans, Green & Co. 1902, p. 109.
7 Arasse, D. 2014, p. 101.
— CATERINA VAN HEMESSEN (PP. 26–29)
1 It has been suggested that Hemessen's palette set-up may follow Cennino Cennini's traditional medieval painting and mixing technique. See: Talon, C. 'Catharina Van Hemessen's Self-Portrait: The Woman Who Took Saint Luke's Palette'. In: Sutton, E. (ed.) *Women Artists and Patrons in the Netherlands, 1500–1700*. Amsterdam University Press. 2019, pp. 27–51.
2 Higgie, J. *The Mirror and the Palette*. Pegasus Books. 2021, p. 26.
— ARTEMISIA GENTILESCHI (PP. 30–33)
1 Keith, L. et al. 'Self Portrait as Saint Catherine of Alexandria'. In: *National Gallery Technical Bulletin*. Vol. 40 (2019), pp. 4–17.
— REMBRANDT (PP. 34–37)
1 Hall, M. B. *The Power of Colour: Five Centuries of European Painting*. Yale University Press. 2019, p. 111.
2 For a good overview of Rembrandt's pigments and techniques, see Bomford, D., Brown, C. and Roy, A. *Art in the Making: Rembrandt*. The National Gallery, London. 1988. For an in-depth technical examination of a late Rembrandt painting, see: Hermens, E. 'The Passion in Paint: A Technical Examination'. In: Black, P. *Rembrandt and the Passion*. Prestel. 2012, pp. 101–129.
— ANGELICA KAUFFMAN (PP. 38–41)
1 Holubec, I. M. 'Angelika Kauffman and the Neoclassical picture: Material, technology and painting progress'. In: Baumgärtel, B. (ed.) *Angelika Kauffman*. Exhibition catalogue. Hirmer. 2020, pp. 30–35.
— ÉLISABETH LOUISE VIGÉE LE BRUN (PP. 42–45)
1 Baillio, J., Baetjer, K. and Lang, P. *Vigée Le Brun*. Exhibition catalogue. The Metropolitan Museum of Art, New York. 2016, p. 21.
— JOHN CONSTABLE (PP. 46–49)
1 Beckett, R. B. (ed.) *John Constable's Correspondence*. Vol. VI: The Fishers. Boydell Press. 1968, p. 189.
2 *Ibid.*, p. 78.
— EUGÈNE DELACROIX (PP. 50–53)
1 For an extensive interpretation, translation and identification of pigments mentioned and used by Delacroix, see: Khandekar, N., Kianovsky, S. and Eremin, K. 'Delacroix's "Bacchus and Ariadne"'. In: *The Burlington Magazine*. Vol. 157, No. 1345: Art in France (April 2015), pp. 255–58.
2 Quoted in: Hannoosh, M. *Painting & the Journal of Eugene Delacroix*. Princeton University Press. 1995, p. 188.
— J. M. W. TURNER (PP. 54–57)
1 Most of the surviving sketchbooks are in the Turner Bequest at Tate. They have been meticulously catalogued and digitized. An excellent overview of the sketchbooks can be found in: Warrell, I. *Turner's Sketchbooks*. Tate Publishing. 2014.
2 Townsend, J. H. *How Turner Painted: Materials & Techniques*. Thames & Hudson. 2019, pp. 100–102.
3 Townsend has published extensively on Turner's painting methods. For the most comprehensive overview, see: *ibid.*
— GUSTAVE COURBET (PP. 58–61)
1 Herding, K. 'Color and Worldview'. In: *Courbet: To Venture Independence*. Yale University Press. 1991, pp. 111–34.
2 *Ibid.*, p. 114.
3 Hall, J. *The Artist's Studio: A Cultural History*. Thames & Hudson. 2022, p. 252.
4 Quoted in: Chu, P. T. D. 'Showing Making in Courbet's The Painter's Studio'. In: Esner, R., Kisters, S. and Lehmann, A. (eds) *Hiding Making, Showing Creation: The Studio from Turner to Tacita Dean*. Amsterdam University Press. 2013, pp. 62–72.
— JAMES ABBOTT MCNEILL WHISTLER (PP. 68–73)
1 See: Townsend, J. H. 'Whistler's Oil Painting Materials'. In: *The Burlington Magazine*. Vol. 136, No. 1099 (1994), pp. 690–95.
2 The exchange and subsequent libel court case are widely recorded, but here quoted in: Curry, D. P. *James McNeill Whistler: Uneasy Pieces*. Virginia Museum of Fine Arts/The Quantuck Lane Press. 2004, p. 15.
3 *Ibid.*, p. 184.
4 Quoted in: *ibid.*, p. 150.
5 Whistler, J. A. M. Letter to George Du Maurier, February 1862. In: Du Maurier, D. (ed.) *The Young George du Maurier: A Selection of his Letters, 1860–67*. Peter Davies. 1951, p. 105.
6 Whistler, J. A. M. Letter to the Editor, 1 July 1862. 'Our Weekly Gossip'. *The Athenaeum*. No. 1810 (5 July 1862), p. 23. In: Thorp, N. (ed.), *Whistler on Art: Selected Letters and Writings 1849–1903 of James McNeill Whistler*. Fyfield Books. 1994, p. 12.
— HENRI FANTIN-LATOUR (PP. 74–77)
1 Gibson, F. *The Art of Henry Fantin-Latour: His Life and Work*. Drane's Ltd. 1924, p. 129.
2 Druick, D. W. and Hoog, M. *Fantin-Latour*. National Museums of Canada. 1983, pp. 56–59.
3 Cited in: *ibid.* p. 57.
4 Bracewell, M. 'Peter Saville: Estate redux'. In: *Extracts from the exhibition catalogue published by Manchester Art Gallery and Manchester International Festival on the occasion of True Faith*. Manchester Art Gallery. 2017, pp. 1–16.
— ROSA BONHEUR (PP. 78–81)
1 Klumpke, A. *Rosa Bonheur: The Artist's (Auto)biography*. Trans. van Slyke, G. The University of Michigan Press. 2003, p. 219.
— PAUL CÉZANNE (PP. 86–89)
1 de Montifaud, M. *L'artiste*, 1 May 1874. Quoted in: Verdi, R. *Cézanne*. Thames & Hudson. 1997. pp. 66–67.
2 Callen, A. *Techniques of the Impressionists*. Orbis Publishing. 1982, p. 74.
3 Fry, R. *Cezanne: A Study of his Development*. The Hogarth Press. 1952, p. 52.
4 Bernard, É. *Souvenirs*. 1905. In: Doran, P. M. *Conversations avec Cézanne*. Macula. 1978, pp. 72–73.
5 Rilke, R. M. *Briefe über Cézanne*. Ed. Rilke, C. Insel Verlag. 1952, p. 40. [Author's translation]
— EDGAR DEGAS (PP. 90–93)
1 See: Dunstan, B. *Painting Methods of the Impressionists*. Watson-Guptill Publications/Pitman Publishing. 1976, p. 78.
2 Hall, M. B. 2019, p. 215.
3 Quoted in: Denvir, B. *The Impressionists at First Hand*. Thames & Hudson. 1987, p. 167.
— PIERRE-AUGUSTE RENOIR (PP. 98–101)
1 Quoted in: Hayes, C. *Renoir*. Spring Books. 1961, p. 49.
2 Quoted in: Fosca, F. *Renoir. His Life and Work*. Thames & Hudson. 1969, p. 194.
3 Renoir, J. *Renoir, My Father*. Collins. 1962, p. 341.
4 Quoted in: Muehsam, G. (ed.) *French Painters and Paintings from the Fourteenth Century to Post-Impressionism: A Library of Art Criticism*. Frederick Ungar Publishing. 1970, p. 511.
5 Chang, K. 'How This Renoir Used to Look'. In: *The New York Times*. 22 April 2014, Section D, p. 2.
— VINCENT VAN GOGH (PP. 102–7)
1 Letter to Theo van Gogh, 28 June 1890. Letter no. 893. In: *Vincent van Gogh: The Letters*. Volume 5: Saint-Remy – Auvers 1889–1890. Eds Jansen, L., Luijten, H. and Bakker, N. Thames & Hudson. 2009, p. 277.
2 Letter to Theo van Gogh, 5 August 1882. Letter no. 253. In: *Vincent van Gogh: The Letters*. Volume 2: The Hague 1881–1883. 2009, p. 125.
— JOHN SINGER SARGENT (PP. 114–17)
1 Townsend, J. H. and Rayner, G. 'Sargent's Painting Materials: New Discoveries and Their Implications'. In: *Visual Culture in Britain*. Vol. 19, Issue 1 (2018), pp. 89–111.
2 Quoted in: Ormond, R. and Kilmurry, E. *Sargent: Portraits of Artists and Friends*. Exhibition catalogue. National Portrait Gallery, London. 2015, pp. 92–93.
— PAUL GAUGUIN (PP. 118–21)
1 Jirat-Wasiutynski, V. and Travers Newton, H., Jr. *Technique and Meaning in the Paintings of Paul Gauguin*. Cambridge University Press. 2000, pp. 205–6.
2 Ashby, C. *Colours of Art*. Frances Lincoln. 2022, p. 136.
3 Quoted in: Thomson, B. *Gauguin*. Thames & Hudson. 1987, p. 172.
— CAMILLE PISSARRO (PP. 122–25)
1 *Camille Pissarro: Letters to his Son Lucien*. Ed. Rewald, J. Routledge and Kegan. 1980, p. 100.
— GEORGES SEURAT (PP. 126–29)
1 Gage, J. *Colour and Meaning* (1999), p. 214. The number of colours has been interpreted differently by others. For example, both W. I. Homer in *Seurat and the Science of Painting* (1964), pp. 146–51, and A. Dunstan in *Painting Methods of the Impressionists* (1976), p. 131, identify 11 instead of 9.
— JAMES ENSOR (PP. 130–33)
1 Quoted in: Lesko, D. *James Ensor: The Creative Years*. Princeton University Press. 1985, pp. 52–53.
2 Quoted in: Haesaerts, P. *James Ensor*. Harry N. Abrams. 1959, p. 108.
— WINSLOW HOMER (PP. 134–37)
1 Robertson, B. *Reckoning with Winslow Homer: His Late Paintings and their Influence*. Cleveland Museum of Art/ Indiana University Press. 1990, p. 25.
— VILHELM HAMMERSHØI (PP. 138–41)
1 Quoted in: Krämer, F., Sato, N. and Fonsmark, A. B. *Hammershøi*. Exhibition catalogue. Royal Academy of Arts, London. 2008, p. 21.
2 *Ibid.*
3 The ViHDA will make its findings available to the public over the next few years: www.smk.dk/en/article/the-vilhelm-hammershoei-digital-archive-vihda/ [accessed November 2023]. I am indebted to Loa Ludvigson from the SMK for some of the information about Hammershøi's pigments and techniques.
— EDVARD MUNCH (PP. 144–47)
1 In 2017, the National Gallery of Art in Washington staged an exhibition that focused on Munch and spiritualist colour theories: *Edvard Munch: Color in Context* (3 September 2017–28 January 2018).
— PAULA MODERSOHN-BECKER (PP. 148–51)
1 Modersohn-Becker, P. *Eine Künstlerin. Paula Becker-Modersohn. Briefe und Tagebuchblätter*. Ed. Gallwitz, S. D. Kestner-Gesellschaft. 1920, p. 19. [Author's translation]
2 *Ibid.*, p. 94.
3 Rilke, R. M. *Requiem. Für eine Freundin*. Niehans & Rokitansky. 1949. [Author's translation]
— CLAUDE MONET (PP. 152–55)
1 Proust, M. 'Les Éblouissements'. *Le Figaro*. Literary Supplement. 15 June 1907, p. 1.
2 Monet to the colour dealer George Durand-Ruel in July 1905. Cited from: *Monet by Himself*. Ed. Kendall, R. Little Brown & Company. 2000, p. 196.
3 For a complete list, see: House, J. *Monet: Nature into Art*. Yale University Press. 1986, p. 239.
4 Roy, A. 'Monet's Palette in the Twentieth Century: "Water-Lilies" and "Irises"'. In: *National Gallery Technical Bulletin*. Vol. 28 (2007), pp. 58–68.
5 Muir, K. and Sutherland, K. 'Color, Chemistry, and Creativity in Monet's Water Lilies'. Art Institute of Chicago. 2021. www.artic.edu/articles/862/color-chemistry-and-creativity-in-monets-water-lilies [accessed November 2023].
6 Quoted in: *ibid.*
— PIERRE BONNARD (PP. 156–59)
1 Quoted in: Amory, D. (ed.) *Pierre Bonnard: The Late Still Lifes and Interiors*. Metropolitan Museum of Art, New York. 2009, p. 3.
2 Quoted in: Wilkin, K. 'Radical Bonnard'. In: *The Hudson Review*. Vol. 51, No. 2 (Summer 1998), pp. 393–400, p. 396.
3 Quoted in: Watkins, N. *Bonnard*. Phaidon. 1994, p. 25.
— HENRI MATISSE (PP. 160–63)
1 Liberman, A. *The Artist in his Studio*. Thames & Hudson. 1969, p. 83.
2 Quoted in: Escholier, R. *Matisse from the Life*. Faber & Faber. 1960, p. 81.
3 Quoted in: *Matisse on Art*. Ed. Flam, J. D. Phaidon. 1978, p. 99.
4 Reproduced in: Escholier, R. 1960, p. 90.
5 Liberman, A. 1969, p. 57.
— GABRIELE MÜNTER (PP. 170–73)
1 Hille, K. *Gabriele Münter: Die Künstlerin mit der Zauberhand*. DuMont. 2012, p. 62. [Author's translation]
2 Quoted in: *Gabriele Münter 1877–1962*. Exhibition catalogue. Galerie Orangerie Reinz, Cologne. 1981, p. 95.
3 *Ibid.*, p. 3.
— EGON SCHIELE (PP. 174–77)
1 See: Smith, K. A. *Between Ruin and Renewal: Egon Schiele's Landscapes*. Yale University Press. 2004, p. 162.
2 *Briefe und Prosa von Egon Schiele*. Ed. Roessler, A. Lányi. 1921.
3 Quoted in: Whitford, F. *Egon Schiele*. Thames & Hudson. 1981, p. 45.
— GEORGIA O'KEEFFE (PP. 178–81)
1 For more information on Stieglitz's portraits of O'Keeffe, see: Peters, S. W. *Becoming O'Keeffe: The Early Years*. 1991. pp. 147–81.
2 Paul Rosenfeld in 1922. Quoted in: *ibid.*, p. 171.
3 For Dow's influence on O'Keeffe, see: *ibid.*, p. 81–100.
— EDWARD HOPPER (PP. 182–87)
1 In 2023, the palette was undergoing technical analysis at the University

of Delaware, along with some of Hopper's other painting materials.
2 Hopper, E. and Morse, J. D. 'Oral history interview with Edward Hopper'. 17 June 1959. Sound recording. Archives of American Art, New York. 1959.
3 Hopper, E. 'Notes on Painting'. In: *Edward Hopper, Retrospective Exhibition: November 1–December 7, 1933*. Exhibition catalogue. The Museum of Modern Art, New York. 1933, pp. 17–18.
4 Barter, J. A. 'Nighthawks: Transcending Reality'. In Troyen, C. et al. *Edward Hopper*. Exhibition catalogue. Thames & Hudson. 2007, pp. 194–209, p. 208.
5 *Ibid*.
— JOAN MIRÓ (PP. 190–93)
1 Miró, J. and Taillandier, Y. Interview, 1959. Quoted in: *Joan Miró: Selected Writings and Interviews*. Ed. Rowell, M. Thames & Hudson. 1986, p. 251.
2 Miró, J. Working notes, 1941–42. Quoted in: *ibid*., pp. 193–94.
3 Lobon, M. G. et al. 'A study of cadmium yellow paints from Joan Miró's paintings and studio materials preserved at the Fundació Miró Mallorca'. In: *Heritage Science*. Vol. 11, Article no. 145 (2023).
4 Miró, J. and Taillandier, Y., Interview, 1959. Quoted in: *Joan Miró*. 1986, p. 251.
— GEORGES BRAQUE (PP. 194–97)
1 Hope, H. R. *Georges Braque*. Exhibition catalogue. The Museum of Modern Art, New York/Simon & Schuster. 1949, p. 150–51.
2 *Ibid*., pp. 152–54.
— PIET MONDRIAN (PP. 198–201)
1 Mondrian, P. 'The New Plastic in Painting'. 1917. In: *The New Art, the New Life: The Collected Writings of Piet Mondrian*. Eds Holtzman, H. and James, M. S. Thames & Hudson. 1987, p. 36.
2 Mondrian, P. 'Toward the True Vision of Reality'. 1941. In: *ibid*., p. 339.
3 See: Blotkamp, C. *Mondrian: The Art of Destruction*. Reaktion Books. 2001, pp. 102–6.
4 Quoted in: Henkels, H. *Mondrian: From Figuration to Abstraction*. Thames & Hudson. 1988, p. 184.
— PABLO PICASSO (PP. 202–5)
1 In 2020, the Royal Academy in London staged a major exhibition, *Picasso and Paper*, drawing attention to his use of the medium. It included a paper and card collage for *Guernica*, measuring nearly 5 m (16 ft 4 ⅞ in.) in length.
2 FitzGerald, M. *Picasso: The Artist's Studio*. Wadsworth Atheneum Museum of Art/Yale University Press. 2001, pp. 46–49; 138–41.
— MARC CHAGALL (PP. 206–9)
1 Liberman, A. 1969, p. 252.
— WINIFRED NICHOLSON (PP. 210–13)
1 Nicholson, W. 'Unweave a Rainbow'. Foreword for exhibition catalogue at the Crane Kalman Gallery, London in March 1981. Quoted in: *Unknown Colour: Paintings, Letters, Writings by Winifred Nicholson*. Ed. Nicholson, A. Faber & Faber. 1987, p. 259.
2 Nicholson, W. 'Unknown Colour'. 1937. In: Martin, J. L., Nicholson, B. and Gabo, N. (eds) *Circle: International Survey of Constructive Art*. Faber & Faber. 1937, pp. 57–60. Nicholson's essay was also reprinted in *Unknown Colour*, an anthology compiled by Nicholson, A. in 1987, pp. 99–103.
3 Nicholson, W. 'Liberation of Colour'. In: *World Review*. December 1944. pp. 29–40. Also reprinted in *Unknown Colour* (1987), pp. 124–29, and in Nicholson, W. and Ede, J. *Winifred Nicholson: Music of Colour*. Ed. Fisher, E. Exhibition catalogue. Kettle's Yard, University of Cambridge. 2022. pp. 54–66.
4 The diagram follows Newton's sequence of seven rainbow colours, but they could only be shown in the three printing colours available for the original publication.
5 Quoted in: *Unknown Colour*. 1987, p. 101.
6 Nicholson, D. *Painting with my Grandmother Winifred Nicholson*. Unpublished recollections (September 2020) and in conversation with Alexandra Loske (3 December 2023).
7 Gilbert, R. *Recollections of Bankshead [Winifred Nicholson]*. Unpublished memoir. January 2023.
— SALVADOR DALÍ (PP. 214–17)
1 *Salvador Dalí's Forgotten Horizon*. Tate Conservation project, led by Patricia Smithen. www.tate.org.uk/about-us/projects/salvador-dalis-forgotten-horizon [accessed November 2023].
2 Ades, D. *Dalí*. Thames & Hudson. 1995, p. 60 and p. 83.
3 He was not the first or last artist to do so, of course. Picasso and other cubists had used sand and grit in their work, some of Turner's and van Gogh's outdoor paintings show accidental inclusions of other matter, while Francis Bacon sometimes added dust and dirt from his studio to his palette.
4 Bosquet, A. and Dalí, S. *Conversations with Dalí*. Trans. Neugroschel, J. E. P. Dutton & Co. 1969, pp. 74–75.
5 *Ibid*., p. 23.
6 *Ibid*., p. 71.
— FRANCIS BACON (PP. 222–27)
1 Edwards, J. and Ogden, P. *7 Reece Mews: Francis Bacon's Studio*. Thames & Hudson. 2001, p. 10.
2 Bacon, F. and Archimbaud, M. *Francis Bacon in Conversation with Michel Archimbaud*. Phaidon. 1993, p. 42.
3 Gayford, M. *Man with a Blue Scarf: On Sitting for a Portrait by Lucian Freud*. Thames & Hudson. 2012, p. 111.
— LUCIAN FREUD (PP. 228–31)
1 Gayford, M. 2012, p. 91.
2 *Ibid*., p. 161.
3 Greig, G. *Breakfast with Julian: Portrait of an Artist*. Jonathan Cape. 2013, p. 133.
4 Gayford, M. 2012, p. 111.
— BRIDGET RILEY (PP. 232–35)
1 Kudielka, R.; Naish, N. and Tommasini, A. *Bridget Riley: The Complete Paintings*. Thames & Hudson. 2018, p. 1684.
2 *Ibid*., p. 1692.
3 Moorhouse, P. *Bridget Riley*. Exhibition catalogue. Tate Publishing. 2003, p. 11.
4 *The Eye's Mind: Bridget Riley, Collected Writings 1965–2009*. Ed. Kudielka, R. Thames & Hudson. 2009, p. 111.
5 *Ibid*., p. 122–23.
6 First published in: Lamb, T. and Bourriau, J. *Colour: Art and Science*. Cambridge University Press. 1995. Here quoted from: *The Eye's Mind*. 2009, p. 222.
— KEITH HARING (PP. 236–39)
1 For a detailed study on this, see: Gehring, U. '*Disegno e Colore*: The Reconciliation of Two Rivals in the Art of Keith Haring'. *The Keith Haring Foundation: Selected writings*. www.haring.com/!/selected_writing/disegno-e-colore-the-reconciliation-of-two-rivals-in-the-art-of-keith-haring [accessed November 2023].
2 Haring, H. Journal entry, April 1986. In: *Keith Haring Journals*, p. 95.
3 Haring, H. Journal entry, 20 March 1987. In: *Ibid*., pp. 122–23.
— PAULA REGO (PP. 240–43)
1 McEwen, J. *Paula Rego*. Phaidon Press. 1992, p. 188.

11 Quoted in: 'Een zeldzaam palet'. *Algemeen Handelsblad*. 10 March 1893 (evening edition). [Author's translation]
27 Signature of van Hemessen, C. *Self-Portrait at the Easel*. 1548. [Author's translation]
31 Quoted in: Treves, Le. (ed.) *Artemisia*. Exhibition catalogue. The National Gallery, London. 2020.
35 Schama, S. *Rembrandt's Eyes*. Allen Lane. 1999, pp. 654–55.
39 Kauffman, A. *Mir träumte vor ein paar Nächten, ich hätte Briefe von Ihnen empfangen': Gesammelte Briefe in den Originalsprachen*. Ed. Maierhofer, W. Libelle. 2001, p. 190. [Author's translation]
43 *Memoirs of Madame Vigée Lebrun*. Trans. Strachey, L. Doubleday, Page & Co. 1903 [1835], p. 32.
49 Quoted in: Leslie, C. R. *Memoirs of the Life of Constable*. Phaidon Press. 1951, p. 307.
53 Quoted in: 'Palette once belonging to Delacroix'. Musée National Eugène Delacroix. www.musee-delacroix.fr/en/collection/masterpieces/palette-once-belonging-to-delacroix [accessed April 2024].
57 Quoted in: Killik, W. E. *A Short History of Winsor & Newton*. 1925. MSS in Winsor & Newton Archives, Harrow.
61 Quoted in: Lindsay, J. *Gustave Courbet: His Life and Art*. Harper & Row. 1973, p. 171.
65 Quoted in: Pavey, D. and Osborne, R. *Colour Concepts, Palettes & Pigments*. Micro Academy. 2015, p. 134.
71 Whistler, J. A. M. 'The Red Rag'. In: 'Celebrities at Home (No. XCII): Mr Whistler at Cheyne-Walk'. *The World*. 22 May 1878, pp. 4–5.
77 Gibson, F. *The Art of Henri Fantin-Latour: His Life and Work*. Drane's Ltd. 1924, p. 129.
81 Quoted in: Klumpke, A. *Rosa Bonheur: The Artist's (Auto)biography*. Trans. van Slyke, G. The University of Michigan Press. 2003, p. 219.
89 Quoted in: Gasquet, J. *Cézanne: a Memoir with Conversations (1897–1906)*. Thames & Hudson. 1991, p. 148.
93 Quoted in: Herbert, R. L. *Impressionism: Art, Leisure & Parisian Society*. Yale University Press. 1988, p. 45.
97 Quoted in: *Berthe Morisot: Shaping Impressionism*. Exhibition catalogue. Dulwich Picture Gallery and Musée Marmottan Monet. 2023, p. 62.
101 Quoted in: Pach, W. 'Pierre Auguste Renoir'. *Scribner's Magazine*, May 1912, p. 610.
105 Letter no. 801. *Vincent van Gogh: The Letters*. Van Gogh Museum. www.vangoghletters.org/vg/letters/let801/letter.html [accessed April 2024].
111 Quoted in: Schiff, B. 'The Many Faces of Gustave Moreau'. *Smithsonian Magazine*. 31 July 1999.
117 Quoted in: Charteris, E. *John Singer Sargent*. William Heinemann. 1927, p. 77.
121 Gauguin, P. *The Writings of a Savage*. Ed. Guérin, D. Viking Press. 1978, p. 128.
125 Quoted in: E. Protter, *Painters on Painting*. Dover. 1997, p. 124.
129 Quoted in: Herbert, R. (ed.) *Georges Seurat, 1859–1891*. Exhibition catalogue. The Metropolitan Museum of Art, New York/Harry N. Abrams, Inc. 1991, appendix K, p. 381.
133 Quoted in: E. Protter, *Painters on Painting*. Dover. 1997, p. 168.
137 Quoted in: Cross, W. R. *Winslow Homer: American Passage*. Farrar, Straus and Giroux. 2022.
141 Quoted in: Krämer, F. 'Vilhelm Hammershøi: The Poetry of Silence'. In: Krämer, F., Sato, N. and Fonsmark, A. B. *Hammershøi*. Exhibition catalogue. Royal Academy of Arts, London. 2008, p. 23.
147 Quoted in: S. Prideaux. *Edvard Munch: Behind the Scream*. Yale University Press. 2007, pp. 83–84.
151 Modersohn-Becker, P. and Jahn, B. (ed.) *Briefe und Aufzeichnungen*. Gustav Kiepenheuer Verlag. 1982, p. 181. [Author's translation]
155 *Monet by Himself*. Ed. Kendall, R. Little Brown & Company. 2000, p. 262.
159 Quoted in: Wilkin, K. 'Radical Bonnard'. In: *The Hudson Review*. Vol. 51, No. 2 (1998), pp. 393–400, p. 396.
163 Quoted in: *Matisse on Art*. Ed. Flam, J. D. Phaidon. 1978, p. 99.
167 Kandinsky, W. and Bill, M. (ed.) *Über das Geistige in der Kunst*. Benteli Verlag. 1952 [1912], p. 64. [Author's translation]
173 Quoted in: Schury, G. *Ich Weltkind: Gabriele Münter. Die Biographie*. Augbau Verlag. 2012, p. 238. [Author's translation]
177 *Egon Schiele: Letters and Poems 1910–1912 from the Leopold Collection*. Ed. Leopold, E. Leopold Museum/Prestel. 2008.
181 O'Keeffe, G. 'To MSS. and its 33 Subscribers'. *Mss*. No. 4 (December 1922). Quoted in: Barson, T. (ed.) *Georgia O'Keeffe*. Exhibition catalogue. Tate Publishing. 2016, p. 98.
185 Quoted in: Goodrich, L. *Edward Hopper*. Abradale Press, Harry N. Abrams. 1993, p. 11.
193 *Joan Miró: Selected Writings and Interviews*. Ed. Rowell, M. Thames & Hudson. 1986, p. 86.
197 Quoted in: Hope, H. R. *Georges Braque*. Exhibition catalogue. The Museum of Modern Art, New York/Simon & Schuster. 1949, p. 145.
201 *The New Art, the New Life: The Collected Writings of Piet Mondrian*. Eds and trans. Holtzman, H. and James, M. S. Thames & Hudson. 1987, p. 338.
205 Quoted in: E. Protter, *Painters on Painting*. Dover. 1997, p. 203.
209 *Chagall by Chagall*. Ed. Sorlier, C. and trans. Shepley, J. Harrison House. 1982 [1979], p. 195.
213 *Unknown Colour: Paintings, Letters, Writings by Winifred Nicholson*. Ed. Nicholson, A. Faber & Faber. 1987, p. 255.
217 Bosquet, A. and Dalí, S. *Conversations with Dalí*. Trans. Neugroschel, J. E. P. Dutton & Co. 1969.
221 Frankenthaler, H. and Geldzahler, H. 'An Interview with Helen Frankenthaler'. *ArtForum*. Vol. 4, No. 2 (October 1965), p. 37.
225 Transcribed in: Bacon, F. and Cork, R. 'An Interview with Francis Bacon'. Audio excerpt. *Kaleidoscope*. BBC Radio 4. 17 August 1991. www.bbc.co.uk/archive/kaleidoscope--francis-bacon/zk4y2sg [accessed April 2024].
231 Quoted in: Gayford, M. *Man with a Blue Scarf: On Sitting for a Portrait by Lucian Freud*. Thames & Hudson. 2010, p. 112.
235 *The Eye's Mind: Bridget Riley, Collected Writings 1965–2009*. Ed. Kudielka, R. Thames & Hudson. 2009, p. 123.
239 *Keith Haring Journals*. Penguin Books. 2010, p. 128.
243 Quoted in: McEwen, J. *Paula Rego*. Rizzoli. 1992, p. 111.
247 Marshall, K. J. and Coxhead, G. 'When you put black people in a picture, what should they be doing? – an Interview with Kerry James Marshall'. *Apollo*. March 2019.

Ades, D. *Dalí*. Thames & Hudson. 1995.

Adler, K. and Garb, T. *Berthe Morisot*. Phaidon Press. 2010.

Alexander, W., Harris, C. I. and Powell, R. *Kerry James Marshall: Mementos*. Exhibition catalogue. Renaissance Society, University of Chicago. 1998.

Amory, D. (ed.) *Pierre Bonnard: The Late Still Lifes and Interiors*. Metropolitan Museum of Art, New York. 2009.

[Anon.] 'Een zeldzaam palet.' *Algemeen Handelsblad*, 10 March 1893 (evening edition).

Aragon, L. *Henri Matisse: A Novel*. Harcourt Brace Jovanovich. 1972.

Arasse, D. *Anselm Kiefer*. Thames & Hudson. 2014.

Ashby, C. *Colours of Art*. Frances Lincoln. 2022.

Ayres, J. *The Artist's Craft: A History of Tools, Techniques and Materials*. Guild Publishing. 1985.

Bacon, F. and Archimbaud, M. *Francis Bacon in Conversation with Michel Archimbaud*. Phaidon. 1993.

Baillio, J., Baetjer, K. and Lang, P. *Vigée Le Brun*. Exhibition catalogue. The Metropolitan Museum of Art, New York. 2016.

Bal, M. (ed.) *The Artemisia Files. Artemisia Gentileschi for Feminists and Other Thinking People*. The University of Chicago Press. 2005.

Barnett, V. E., Derouet, C. et al. *Kandinsky in Paris: 1934–1944*. Solomon R. Guggenheim Museum, New York. 1985.

Barson, T. (ed.) et al. *Georgia O'Keeffe*. Tate Modern, Kunstforum Wien, Art Gallery of Ontario. 2016.

Barter, J. A. 'Nighthawks: Transcending Reality', in Troyen, C. et al. *Edward Hopper*. Exhibition catalogue. Thames & Hudson. 2007, pp. 194–209.

Bate, J. *The Mysteries of Nature and Art. In Foure Severall Parts. The first of water works. The second of fire works. The third of drawing, washing, limming, painting, and engraving. The fourth of sundry experiments*. 2nd edition. Ralph Mabb. 1635.

Baumgärtel, B. (ed.) *Angelika Kauffman 1741–1807 Retrospektive*. Exhibition catalogue. Hatje Verlag. 1998.

Beckett, R. B. (ed.) *John Constable's Correspondence*. Vol. VI: The Fishers. Boydell Press. 1968.

Bell, J. *Bonnard*. Phaidon. 1994.

Bell, J. *Van Gogh: A Power Seething*. New Harvest/Houghton Mifflin Harcourt. 2015.

Blashfield, E. H. 'John Singer Sargent: Recollections'. In: *North American Review*. Vol. 221 (June 1925), pp. 643–44.

Blotkamp, C. *Mondrian: The Art of Destruction*. Reaktion Books. 2001.

Bomford, D., Brown, C. and Roy, A. *Art in the Making: Rembrandt*. The National Gallery, London. 1988.

Borzello, F. *Seeing Ourselves: Women's Self-Portraits*. Thames & Hudson. 1998.

Bosquet, A. and Dalí, S. *Conversations with Dalí*. Trans. Neugroschel, J. E.P. Dutton & Co. 1969.

Bracewell, M. 'Peter Saville: Estate redux'. In: *Extracts from the exhibition catalogue published by Manchester Art Gallery and Manchester International Festival on the occasion of True Faith*. Manchester Art Gallery. 2017, pp. 1–16.

Broude, N. *Seurat in Perspective*. Prentice Hall. 1978.

Brown, C. (ed.) *James Ensor, 1860–1949: Theatre of Masks*. Lund Humphries. 1997.

Brown, D. B. 'Project Overview'. December 2012. In: Brown, D. B. (ed.) *J. M. W. Turner: Sketchbooks, Drawings and Watercolours*. Tate Research Publication. December 2012. www.tate.org.uk/art/research-publications/jmw-turner/project-overview-r1109225 [accessed 11 October 2023].

Callen, A. *Techniques of the Impressionists*. Orbis Publishing. 1982.

Callen, A. *The Art of Impressionism: Painting Technique & the Making of Modernity*. Yale University Press. 2000.

Carlyle, L. *The Artist's Assistant: Oil Painting Instruction Manuals and Handbooks in Britain 1800–1900*. Archetype Publications. 2001.

Carmean, E. A. *Helen Frankenthaler: A Paintings Retrospective*. Exhibition Catalogue. Museum of Modern Art, New York. 1989.

Cavé, M. E. *La Couleur*. Henri Plon. 3rd edition. 1863 [*c*. 1851].

Cawse, J. *The Art of Painting Portraits, Landscapes, Animals, Draperies, Satins, &c. in Oil Colours*. Rudolph Ackermann. 1840 [1822].

Chang, K. 'How This Renoir Used to Look'. In: *The New York Times*. 22 April 2014, Section D, p. 2.

Charteris, E. *John Singer Sargent*. William Heinemann. 1927.

Christiansen, K. and Mann, J. W. et al. *Orazio and Artemisia Gentileschi*. Exhibition Catalogue. Metropolitan Museum of Art, New York. 2001.

Chu, P. T. D. 'Showing Making in Courbet's The Painter's Studio'. In: Esner, R., Kisters, S. and Lehmann, A. (eds) *Hiding Making, Showing Creation: The Studio from Turner to Tacita Dean*. Amsterdam University Press. 2013, pp. 62–72.

Compton, S. P. (ed.) *Chagall*. Exhibition catalogue. Royal Academy of Arts, London/Wiedenfeld & Nicolson. 1985.

Constable, W. G. *The Painter's Workshop*. Oxford University Press. 1954.

Curry, D. P. *James McNeill Whistler: Uneasy Pieces*. Virginia Museum of Fine Arts/The Quantuck Lane Press. 2004.

Dabrowski, M. and Leopold, R. *Egon Schiele: the Leopold Collection, Vienna*. Exhibition catalogue. The Museum of Modern Art, New York/DuMont. 1997.

Dacre [Nicholson], W. 'Liberation of Colour'. In: *World Review*. December 1944. pp. 29–40.

Dacre [Nicholson], W. 'Unknown Colour'. In: Martin, J. L., Nicholson, B. and Gabo, N. (eds) *Circle: International Survey of Constructive Art*. Faber & Faber. 1937, pp. 57–60.

Dalí, S. *50 Secrets Magiques*. Edita Denoel. 1974.

Davey, R., Soriano, K. and Weikop, C. *Anselm Kiefer*. Exhibition catalogue. Royal Academy of Arts, London. 2014.

Denvir, B. *The Impressionists at First Hand*. Thames & Hudson. 1987.

Doran, P. M. *Conversations avec Cézanne*. Macula. 1978.

Droz-Emmert, M. *Catharina van Hemessen Malerin der Renaissance*. Schwabe. 2004.

Druick, D. W. and Hoog, M. *Fantin-Latour*. National Museums of Canada. 1983.

Dunstan, B. *Painting Methods of the Impressionists*. Watson-Guptill Publications/Pitman Publishing. 1976.

Edwards, J. and Ogden, P. *7 Reece Mews. Francis Bacon's Studio*. Thames & Hudson. 2001.

Escholier, R. *Matisse from the Life*. Faber & Faber. 1960.

Esner, R., Kisters, S., and Lehmann, A. (eds) *Hiding Making, Showing Creation: The Studio from Turner to Tacita Dean*. Amsterdam University Press. 2013.

Evans, M. et al. *John Constable: Oil Sketches from the Victoria and Albert Museum*. V&A Publishing. 2011.

Evans, M. et al. *John Constable: The Making of a Master*. Exhibition catalogue. V&A Publishing. 2014.

Farson, D. *The Gilded Gutter Life of Francis Bacon*. Century. 1993.

Fielding, T. H. *On Painting in Oil and Water Colours*. Ackermann & Co. 1839.

Fischer, M. *The Permanent Palette*. National Publishing Society. 1930.

FitzGerald, M. *Picasso: The Artist's Studio*. Wadsworth Atheneum Museum of Art/Yale University Press. 2001.

FitzHugh, E. W., Leona, M., and Shibayama, N. 'Pigments in a Paint Box Belonging to Whistler in the Library of Congress'. In: *Studies in Conservation*. Vol. 56, No. 2 (2011), pp. 115–24.

Fosca, F. *Renoir: His Life and Work*. Thames & Hudson. 1969.

Fry, R. *Cézanne: A Study of his Development*. The Hogarth Press. 1952.

Gabriele Münter 1877–1962. Exhibition catalogue. Galerie Orangerie Reinz, Cologne. 1981.

Gage, J. *Colour and Culture: Practice and Meaning from Antiquity to Abstraction*. Thames & Hudson. 1993.

Gage, J. *Colour and Meaning: Art, Science and Symbolism*. Thames & Hudson. 1999.

Garrard, M. D. *Artemisia Gentileschi: The Image of the Female Hero in Italian Baroque Art*. Princeton University Press. 1989.

Gasquet, J. *Cézanne: A Memoir with Conversations (1897–1906)*. Thames & Hudson. 1991.

Gauguin, P. *The Writings of a Savage*. Ed. Guérin D. Viking Press. 1978.

Gayford, M. *Man with a Blue Scarf. On Sitting for a Portrait by Lucian Freud*. Thames & Hudson. 2010.

Gehring, U. 'Disegno e Colore: The Reconciliation of Two Rivals in the Art of Keith Haring'. *The Keith Haring Foundation: Selected Writing*. No date. www.haring.com/!/selected_writing/disegno-e-colore-the-reconciliation-of-two-rivals-in-the-art-of-keith-haring [accessed November 2023].

Geldzahler, H. 'An Interview with Helen Frankenthaler'. *ArtForum*. Vol. 4, No. 2 (October 1965), pp. 36–38.

Gettens, R. J. and Stout, G. L. *Painting Materials. A Short Encyclopaedia*. Dover Publications. 1966.

Gibson, F. *The Art of Henry Fantin-Latour: His Life and Work*. Drane's Ltd. 1924.

Gilbert, R. *Recollections of Bankshead [Winifred Nicholson]*. Unpublished memoir. January 2023.

Goodrich, L. *Edward Hopper*. Abradale Press, Harry N. Abrams. 1993.

Goodrich, L. *Winslow Homer*. George Brazillier. 1959.

Greig, G. *Breakfast with Lucian: A Portrait of the Artist*. Jonathan Cape. 2013.

Haack Christensen, A., Ortiz Miranda, A. S.

et al. *The narrative of Vilhelm Hammershøi revised. Investigating the artist's use of cobalt blue, chromium-based green and cadmium yellow*. Conference paper. SMK Statens Museum for Kunst. 2023. https://pure.kb.dk/en/publications/the-narrative-of-vilhelm-hammersh%C3%B8i-revised-investigating-the-art [accessed 8 November 2023].

Haesaerts, P. *James Ensor*. Harry N. Abrams. 1959.

Hall, J. *The Artist's Studio: A Cultural History*. Thames & Hudson. 2022.

Hall, M. B. *The Power of Colour: Five Centuries of European Painting*. Yale University Press. 2019.

Hammer, M. *Francis Bacon*. Phaidon. 2013.

Hannoosh, M. *Painting & The Journal of Eugene Delacroix*. Princeton University Press. 1995.

Haring, K. *Keith Haring Journals*. Fourth Estate. 1996.

Hayes, C. *Renoir*. Spring Books. 1961.

Henkels, H. *Mondrian: From Figuration to Abstraction*. Thames & Hudson. 1988.

Herding, K. *Courbet: To Venture Independence*. Yale University Press. 1991.

Herdrich, S. L. and Yount, A. *Winslow Homer: Crosscurrents*. Yale University Press. 2022.

Hermens, E. 'The Passion in Paint: A Technical Examination'. In: Black, P. *Rembrandt and the Passion*. Prestel. 2012, pp. 101–29.

Higgie, J. *The Mirror and the Palette*. Pegasus Books. 2021.

Hiler, H. *Notes on the Technique of Painting*. Faber & Faber. 1934.

Hille, K. *Gabriele Münter: Die Künstlerin mit der Zauberhand*. DuMont. 2012.

Hodge, S. *Art in Detail*. Thames & Hudson. 2016.

Hodin, J. P. *Edvard Munch*. Thames & Hudson. 1972.

Holubec, I. M. 'Angelika Kauffman and the Neoclassical picture. Material, technology and painting progress'. In: Baumgärtel, B. (ed.) *Angelika Kauffman*. Exhibition catalogue. Hirmer. 2020, pp. 30–35.

Homer, W. I. *Seurat and the Science of Painting*. MIT Press. 1964

Hope, H. R. *Georges Braque*. Exhibition catalogue. The Museum of Modern Art, New York/Simon & Schuster. 1949.

Hopper, E. 'Notes on Painting.' In: *Edward Hopper, Retrospective Exhibition: November 1–December 7, 1933*. The Museum of Modern Art, New York. 1933, pp. 17–18.

Hopper, E. and Morse, J. D. 'Oral history interview with Edward Hopper'. 17 June 1959. Sound recording. Archives of American Art, New York. 1959.

House, J. *Monet: Nature into Art*. Yale University Press. 1986.

Howgate, S., Hockney, D. and Gayford, M. *Lucian Freud: Painting People*. National Portrait Gallery, London. 2012.

Hubbard, H. *Materia Pictoria: An Encyclopaedia of Methods and Materials in Painting and the Graphic Arts*. Vol. 1: Oil Painting. 1939.

Ives, H. E. 'Thomas Young and the simplification of the artist's palette'. In: *Proceedings of the Physical Society*. Vol. 46, No. 1 (1934), pp. 16–34.

Jirat-Wasiutynski, V. and Travers Newton, H., Jr. *Technique and Meaning in the Paintings of Paul Gauguin*. Cambridge University Press. 2000.

Joffe, C. and Behr, S. *Making Modernism:*

Paula Modersohn-Becker, Käthe Kollwitz, Gabriele Münter and Marianne Werefkin. Exhibition catalogue. Royal Academy of Arts, London. 2022.

Kahn, G. *Fantin-Latour*. John Lane, the Bodley Head Ltd. 1927.

Kandinksy, W. *Complete Writings on Art*. Ed. and trans. Lindsay, K. and Vergo, P. Faber & Faber. 1982.

Kandinsky, W. *Die gesammelten Schriften*. Ed. Roethel, H. and Hahl-Koch, J. Benteli Verlag. 1980.

Kandinsky, W. *Über das Geistige in der Kunst*. Ed. Bill, M. Benteli Verlag. 1952 [1912].

Kauffman, A. *'Mir träumte vor ein paar Nächten, ich hätte Briefe von Ihnen empfangen': Gesammelte Briefe in den Originalsprachen*. Ed. Maierhofer, W. Libelle. 2001.

Keith, L. et al. 'Self Portrait as Saint Catherine of Alexandria'. In: *National Gallery Technical Bulletin*. Vol. 40 (2019), pp. 4–17.

Khandekar, N., Kianovsky, S. and Eremin, K. 'Delacroix's "Bacchus and Ariadne"'. In: *The Burlington Magazine*. Vol. 157, No. 1345: Art in France (April 2015), pp. 255–58.

Kirby, J. *A Closer Look: Techniques in Painting*. The National Gallery, London. 2011.

Klumpke, A. *Rosa Bonheur: Sa vie, son oeuvre*. Ernest Flammarion. 1908.

Klumpke, A. *Rosa Bonheur: The Artist's (Auto)biography*. Trans. van Slyke, G. The University of Michigan Press. 1997.

Krämer, F., Sato, N. and Fonsmark, A. B. *Hammershøi*. Royal Academy of Arts, London. 2008.

Krämer, F., Sato, N. and Fonsmark, A. B. *Vilhelm Hammershøi*. Exhibition catalogue. Hamburger Kunsthalle. 2003.

Lacambre, G. *Gustave Moreau: Magic and Symbols*. Harry N. Abrams. 1999.

Lamb, T. and Bourriau, J. *Colour: Art and Science*. Cambridge University Press. 1995.

Lampe, A. and Chéroux, C. *Edvard Munch, the Modern Eye*. Tate Publishing 2012.

La Nasa, J. et al. 'A chemical study of organic materials in three murals by Keith Haring: A comparison of painting techniques'. In: *Microchemical Journal*. Vol. 124 (2016), pp. 940–48.

Leadbeater, C. W. *Man Visible and Invisible: Examples of Different Types of Men as Seen by Means of Trained Clairvoyance*. Theosophical Society. 1902.

Lesko, D. *James Ensor: The Creative Years*. Princeton University Press. 1985.

Leslie, C. R. *Memoirs of the Life of John Constable*. Phaidon. 1951.

Levin, G. *Edward Hopper: The Art and the Artist*. W. W. Norton & Company/ Whitney Museum of American Art. 1980.

Liberman, A. *The Artist in his Studio*. Thames & Hudson. 1969.

Lisle, L. *Portrait of an Artist: A Biography of Georgia O'Keeffe*. Washington Square Press. Revised edition. 1997.

Lobon, M. G. et al. 'A study of cadmium yellow paints from Joan Miró's paintings and studio materials preserved at the Fundació Miró Mallorca'. In: *Heritage Science*. Vol. 11, Article No. 145 (2023).

Loske, A. *Colour: A Visual History*. Ilex. 2019.

Loske, A. (ed.) *The Book of Colour Concepts*. Taschen. 2024.

Lowengard, S. *The Creation of Color in Eighteenth-Century Europe*. Columbia University Press. 2006.

Marshall, K. J. and Coxhead G. 'When you put black people in a picture, what should they be doing? – an Interview with Kerry James Marshall'. *Apollo*. March 2019, pp. 118–24.

Marshall, K. J. and Rowell, C. H. 'An Interview with Kerry James Marshall'. *Callaloo*. Vol. 21, No. 1 (1998), p. 263–72.

Martin, J. L., Nicholson, B. and Gabo N. (eds) *Circle: International Survey of Constructive Art*. Faber & Faber. 1937.

Matisse, H. *Matisse on Art*. Ed. Flam, J. D. Phaidon. 1978.

McBreen, E. and Burnham, H. *Matisse in the Studio*. Museum of Fine Arts, Houston. 2017.

McEwen, J. *Paula Rego Behind the Scenes*. Phaidon. 2008.

Miró, J. *Joan Miró: Selected Writings and Interviews*. Ed. Rowell, M. Thames & Hudson. 1986.

Modersohn-Becker, P. *Eine Künstlerin. Paula Becker-Modersohn. Briefe und Tagebuchblätter*. Ed. Gallwitz, S. D. Kestner-Gesellschaft. 1920.

Modersohn-Becker, P. *Letters and Journals of Paula Modersohn-Becker*. Ed. and trans. Radycki, D. J. Scarecrow Press/ Methuen. 1980.

Mondrian, P. *The New Art, the New Life: The Collected Writings of Piet Mondrian*. Eds Holtzman, H. and James, M. S. Thames & Hudson. 1987.

Monet, C. *Monet by Himself*. Ed. Kendall, R. Little Brown & Company. 2000

Monrad, K. *Hammershøi und Europa*. Statens Museum/Prestel Verlag. 2012.

Moorhouse, P. *Bridget Riley*. Exhibition catalogue. Tate Publishing. 2003.

Morisot, B. *The correspondence of Berthe Morisot, with her family and friends: Manet, Puvis de Chavannes, Degas, Monet, Renoir and Mallarmé*. Ed. Rouart, D. Trans. Hubbard, B. W. Intro. and notes Adler, K. and Garb, T. Camden Press. 1986.

Muehsam, G. (ed.) *French Painters and Paintings from the Fourteenth Century to Post-Impressionism: A Library of Art Criticism*. Frederick Ungar Publishing. 1970.

Muir, K. and Sutherland, K. 'Color, Chemistry, and Creativity in Monet's Water Lilies'. Art Institute of Chicago. 2021. www.artic.edu/articles/862/ color-chemistry-and-creativity-in-monets-water-lilies [accessed November 2023]

Nicholson, D. *Painting with my grandmother Winifred Nicholson*. Unpublished recollections (September 2020) and in conversation with Alexandra Loske (3 December 2023).

Nicholson, J. *Winifred Nicholson: Liberation of Colour*. Philip Wilson Publishers. 2016.

Nicholson, W. and Ede, J. *Winifred Nicholson: Music of Colour*. Ed. Fisher, E. Exhibition catalogue. Kettle's Yard, University of Cambridge. 2022.

Nicholson, W. *Unknown Colour: Paintings, Letters, Writings by Winifred Nicholson*. Ed. Nicholson, A. Faber and Faber. 1987.

Nicolson, B. *Courbet: The Studio of the Painter*. Allen Lane. 1973.

Ormond, R. and Kilmurry, E. *Sargent. Portraits of Artists and Friends*. Exhibition catalogue. National Portrait Gallery, London. 2015.

Pavey, D. and Osborne, R. *Colour Concepts, Palettes & Pigments*. Micro Academy. 2015.

Perry, G. *Paula Modersohn-Becker: Her Life and Work*. The Women's Press. 1979.

Peters, S. W. *Becoming O'Keeffe: The Early Years*. Abbeville Press. 1991.

Pih, D. (ed.) *Keith Haring*. Tate. 2019.

Piot, R. *Les palettes de Delacroix*. Librairie de France. 1931.

Pissarro, C. *Camille Pissarro: Letters to his Son Lucien*. Ed. Rewald, J. Routledge and Kegan. 1980.

Prettejohn, E. *Interpreting Sargent*. Tate Publishing. 1998.

Prideaux, S. *Edvard Munch: Behind the Scream*. Yale University Press. 2007.

Protter, E. *Painters on Painting*. Dover. 1997.

Proust, M. 'Les Éblouissements'. *Le Figaro*. Literary Supplement. 15 June 1907, p. 1.

Railing, P. (ed.) *Colour Palettes*. Series. Artists Bookworks. From 2015.

Renoir, J. *Renoir. My Father*. Collins. 1962.

Riley, B., Moorhouse, P. and Kudielka, R. *The Curve Paintings 1961–2014*. Exhibition catalogue. Ridinghouse/ De La Warr Pavilion. 2015.

Riley, B. *The Eye's Mind: Bridget Riley, Collected Writings 1965–2009*. Ed. Kudielka, R. Thames & Hudson. 2009.

Rilke, R. M. *Briefe über Cézanne*. Ed. Rilke, C. Insel Verlag. 1952.

Rilke, R. M. *Requiem. Für eine Freundin*. Niehans & Rokitansky. 1949.

Robertson, B. *Reckoning with Winslow Homer: His Late Paintings and their Influence*. Cleveland Museum of Art/ Indiana University Press. 1990.

Rosenblum, R. *Jean-Auguste-Dominique Ingres, 1780–1867*. Harry N. Abrams. 1967.

Roy, A. 'Monet's Palette in the Twentieth Century: "Water-Lilies" and "Irises"'. In: *National Gallery Technical Bulletin*. Vol. 28 (2007), pp. 58–68.

Rubin, J. H. *Monet: World of Art*. Thames & Hudson. 2020.

Russell, J. E. et al. 'Investigation of the materials found in the studio of Francis Bacon (1909–1992)'. *Studies in Conservation*. Vol. 57, No. 4 (October 2012), pp. 195–206.

Salvador Dali's Forgotten Horizon. TATE Conservation project, led by Patricia Smithen. No date. www.tate.org.uk/about-us/projects/ salvador-dalis-forgotten-horizon [accessed November 2023]

Schama, S. *Rembrandt's Eyes*. Allen Lane. 1999.

Schiele, E. *Briefe und Prosa von Egon Schiele*. Ed. Roessler, A. Lányi. 1921.

Schiele, E. *Egon Schiele: Letters and Poems 1910–1912 from the Leopold Collection*. Ed. Leopold, E. Leopold Museum/ Prestel. 2008.

Schmid, F. 'Some Observations on Artists' Palettes'. In: *The Art Bulletin*. Vol. 40, No. 4 (December 1958), pp. 334–36.

Schmid, F. 'The Painter's Implements in Eighteenth-Century Art'. In: *The Burlington Magazine*. Vol. 108, No. 763 (October 1966), pp. 519–21.

Schmid, F. *The Practice of Painting*. Faber. 1948.

Schury, G. *Ich Weltkind: Gabriele Münter. Die Biographie*. Aufbau Verlag. 2012.

Sexton, P. and Follin, F. *Seurat to Riley: The Art of Perception*. Compton Verney Art Gallery. 2017.

Sjåstad, Ø. *A Theory of the Tache in Nineteenth-Century Painting*. Routledge. 2019.

Smith, K. A. *Between Ruin and Renewal: Egon Schiele's Landscapes*. Yale University Press. 2004

Smith, P. *Seurat and the Avant-garde*. Yale University Press. 1997.

Solomon, S. J. *The Practice of Oil Painting and of Drawing as Associated with it*. Seeley and Co. 1910.

Spate, V. *The Colour of Time: Claude Monet*. Thames & Hudson. 1992.

Stoner, J. H. 'America's Colourmen: Bocour, Levison, Gamblin and Golden'. In: *Studies in Conservation*. Vol. 49, No. 2 (Septmber 2004), pp. 189–93.

Talon, C. 'Catharina Van Hemessen's Self-Portrait: The Woman Who Took Saint Luke's Palette'. In: Sutton, E. (ed.) *Women Artists and Patrons in the Netherlands, 1500–1700*. Amsterdam University Press. 2019, pp. 27–51.

Thomson, B. *Gauguin*. Thames & Hudson. 1987.

Tomkins, C. 'The Epic Style of Kerry James Marshall'. *The New Yorker*. 9 August 2021.

Townsend, J. H. and Rayner, G. 'Sargent's Painting Materials: New Discoveries and Their Implications'. In: *Visual Culture in Britain*. Vol. 19, No. 1: New Perspectives on the Works of John Singer Sargent (2018), pp. 89–111.

Townsend, J. H. *How Turner Painted: Materials & Techniques*. Thames & Hudson. 2019.

Townsend, J. H. 'The Materials of J. M. W. Turner: Pigments'. In: *Studies in Conservation*. Vol. 38, No. 4 (November 1993), pp. 231–54.

Townsend, J. H. *Turner's Painting Techniques*. Tate Publishing. 1993.

Townsend, J. H. 'Whistler's Oil Painting Materials'. In: *The Burlington Magazine*. Vol. 136, No. 1099 (1994), pp. 690–95.

Treves, Le. (ed.) *Artemisia*. Exhibition catalogue. The National Gallery, London. 2020.

Troyen, C. et al. *Edward Hopper*. Exhibition catalogue. Thames & Hudson. 2007.

Vad, P. *Vilhelm Hammershøi and Danish Art at the Turn of the Century*. Yale University Press. 1992.

Vanderpoel, E. N. *Color Problems: A Practical Manual for the Lay Student of Color*. Longmans, Green & Co. 1902.

van Druten, T. 'Making and Creating: The Painted Palette in Late Nineteenth-Century Dutch Painting'. In: Esner, R., Kisters, S. and Lehmann, A. (eds) *Hiding Making, Showing Creation: The Studio from Turner to Tacita Dean*. Amsterdam University Press. 2013, pp. 73–85.

van Gogh, V. *Vincent van Gogh: The Letters*. Eds Jansen, L., Luijten, H. and Bakker, N. Thames & Hudson. 2009.

Verdi, R. *Cézanne*. Thames & Hudson. 1997.

Warrell, I. *Turner's Sketchbooks*. Tate Publishing. 2014.

Watkins, N. *Bonnard*. Phaidon. 1994.

Watkins, N. *Bonnard: Colour and Light*. Tate Publishing. 1998.

Whitford, F. *Egon Schiele*. Thames & Hudson. 1981.

Wilkin, K. 'Radical Bonnard'. In: *The Hudson Review*. Vol. 51, No. 2 (Summer 1998), pp. 393–400.

Sources of Illustrations

Every effort has been made to locate and credit copyright holders of the material reproduced in this book. The author and publisher apologize for any omissions or errors, which can be corrected in future editions.

The palettes reproduced on pages 4–5 and details of palettes on pages 24, 84, 142 and 188 are all reproduced elsewhere in the book.

On the front cover:
Photo Centre Pompidou, MNAM-CCI, Dist. RMN-Grand Palais/Georges Meguerditchian

On the back cover:
Top row (left to right): Photo Leemage/Corbis via Getty Images; Photo © François Fernandez; Photo RMN-Grand Palais (musée d'Orsay)/ Tony Querrec
Middle row (left to right): Photo Bridgeman Images; Photo courtesy Worpswede Tourist Information Center. Photo Rüdiger Lubricht; © Paula Rego. All rights reserved 2024/ Bridgeman Images
Bottom row (left to right): Photo The Metropolitan Museum of Art/Art Resource/ Scala, Florence; Photo © Tate; Courtesy Francis Bacon MB Art Foundation, Monaco

2 *On Painting in Oil and Water Colours*, by T. H. Fielding, published by Ackermann and Co., London, 1839 **6–7** Minneapolis Institute of Art. The William Hood Dunwoody Fund. Acc. No: 52.15 **10** Private Collection. Photo Fine Art Images/Heritage Images/Alamy **13 A–D** Bibliothèque nationale de France, Paris. Département des Manuscrits. Français 12420 **14 A–F** *The Art of Painting: Portraits, Landscapes, Animals, Draperies, Satins, etc. in Oil Colours*, by John Cawse, published by R. Ackermann, London, 1840 **17 A** Yale Center for British Art, Paul Mellon Collection, New Haven. Acc. No: B1977.14.17541 **17 B** Private Collection **18 A–D** *The Theory and Practice of Painting in Oil and Water Colours for Landscape and Portraits*, by T. H. Fielding, published by D. Bogue, London, 1854 **21 A–F** *Color Problems: A Practical Manual for the Lay Student of Color*, by Emily Noyes Vanderpoel, published by Longmans, Green, and Co., London, 1902 **22 A** Courtesy White Cube, London. Photo Theo Christelis. © Anselm Kiefer **23 B** Tate, London. Acc. No: AR00613. Photo Tate. © Anselm Kiefer **26** Kunstmuseum Basel. Gift from the Prof. J. J. Bachofen-Burckhardt Foundation, 2015 **28 A** Collection City of Antwerp, MAS – Museum aan de Stroom, Antwerp. Acc. No: AV.1145 **29 B** Private Collection **30** Royal Collection Trust, London. Acc. No: RCIN 405551 **32 A** The Metropolitan Museum of Art, New York. The Elisha Whittelsey Collection, The Elisha Whittelsey Fund, 1949. Acc. No: 49.95.12 **32 B** The British Museum, London. Purchased from Rev. Dr Charles Sloman, 1835. Acc. No: Nn,7.51.3 **33 C** Schloss Weissenstein, Pommersfelden. Acc. No: 191 **34** Musée du Louvre, Paris. Former Royal/Crown collection. Acc. No: 1747 ; MR 936 **36 A** Photo Alberto Paredes/Alamy **36 B** Ashmolean Museum, University of Oxford. Presented by Chambers Hall, 1855. Acc. No: WA1855.8 **37 C** The Kremer Collection, Amsterdam. Photo Vidimages/ Alamy **37 D** Museum of Fine Arts, Boston. Zoe Oliver Sherman Collection given in memory of Lillie Oliver Poor. Acc. No: 38.1838 **38** Galleria degli Uffizi, Firenze. Acc. No: 4444-1890. Photo Gabinetto Fotografico delle Gallerie degli Uffizi **40 A** Yale Center for British Art, Paul Mellon Collection, New Haven. Acc. No: B1975.3.1237 **41 B** National Trust, Nostell Priory, West Yorkshire. Acc. No: 960079 **41 C** Royal Academy of Arts, London. Acc. No: 03/1130. Photo John Hammond/Royal Academy of Arts, London **42** The National Gallery, London. Bought, 1897. Acc. No: NG1653 **44 A** The Metropolitan Museum of Art, New York. Bequest of Mrs Charles Wrightsman, 2019. Acc. No: 2019.141.23 **44 B** The National Gallery, London. Bought, 1871. Acc. No: NG852 **45 C** Hessische Hausstiftung, Kronberg **46** Tate Archive, London. Acc. No: TGA 8135/6. Photo © Tate **47** National Galleries of Scotland, Edinburgh. Purchased with the aid of The Cowan Smith Bequest and Art Fund, 1944. Acc. No: NG 2016 **48 A** National Portrait Gallery, London. Purchased, 1907. Acc. No: NPG 1458 **48 B** Royal Academy of Arts, London. Acc. No: 03/1390. Photo John Hammond/Royal Academy of Arts, London **49 C** Victoria and Albert Museum, London. Given by Isabel Constable. Acc. No: 328-1888 **49 D** Clark Art Institute, Williamstown, MA. Gift of the Manton Art Foundation in memory of Sir Edwin and Lady Manton. Acc. No: 2007.8.57 **50** Musée national Eugène Delacroix, Paris. Acc. No: MD 2002-257. Photo RMN-Grand Palais (musée du Louvre)/Hervé Lewandowski **51** Musée du Louvre, Paris. Acc. No: 3820; L 3837 **52 A** Musée national Eugène Delacroix, Paris. Acc. No: MD 2002-264. Photo RMN-Grand Palais (musée du Louvre)/ Gérard Blot **52 B** *L'Illustration: Journal Universel*, Paris, 25 September 1852 **53 C** Musée national Eugène Delacroix, Paris. Acc. No: RF 2058 **53 D** Musée du Louvre, Paris. Acc. No: RF 10570. Photo RMN-Grand Palais (musée du Louvre)/Michel Urtado **54** Royal Academy of Arts, London. Acc. No: 03/7070. Photo Prudence Cuming Associates Limited/Royal Academy of Arts, London **55** Tate, London. Acc. No: D24640. Photo Tate **56 A** Royal Academy of Arts, London. Acc. No: 03/7072. Photo Royal Academy of Arts, London **56 B** National Portrait Gallery, London. Acquired, 1973. Acc. No: NPG D6996 **57 C** Royal Academy of Arts, London. Acc. No: 03/7071. Photo Royal Academy of Arts, London **57 D** Tate, London. Acc. No: D17149 and D17150. Photo Tate **58** Musée départemental Gustave Courbet, Ornans. Donated by the Friends of Gustave Courbet Association, 1976. Acc. No: 1976.1.94. Photo Aurélia Channaux **59** Private Collection **60 A** Petit Palais, Paris. Gift of Juliette Courbet, 1909. Acc. No: PPP734 **61 B** Musée d'Orsay, Paris. Purchased with the help of a public offering and the Société des Amis du Louvre, 1920. Acc. No: RF 2257 **61 C** Musée Carnavalet, Paris. Acc. No: PH4142-91 **62** Musée Ingres Bourdelle, Montauban. Acc. No: MI.2023.0.94. Photo © Musée Ingres Bourdelle/J. J. Ader **63** The Metropolitan Museum of Art, New York. Robert Lehman Collection, 1975. Acc. No: 1975.1.186 **64 A** Musée Ingres Bourdelle, Montauban. Acc. No: MI.2004.3.1 **65 B** Musée Ingres Bourdelle, Montauban. Acc. No: MI.867.4528. Photo © Musée Ingres Bourdelle/Guy Roumagnac **65 C** Musée Ingres Bourdelle, Montauban. Acc. No: MI 50.545 **66–67** Musée du Louvre, Paris. Purchase, 1899. Acc. No: RF 1158 **68** Colby College Museum of Art, The Lunder Collection, Waterville, Maine. Acc. No: 2013.404 **69** National Museum of Asian Art, Freer Gallery of Art Collection, Washington, DC. Gift of Charles Lang Freer. Acc. No: F1903.91a–b **70 A** Detroit Institute of Arts. Gift of Dexter M. Ferry, Jr. Acc. No: 46.309 **71 B** National Gallery of Art, Washington, DC. Harris Whittemore Collection. Acc. No: 1943.6.2 **71 C** Library of Congress, Pennell Collection of Whistleriana, Washington, DC. Acc. No: LOT 15190, no.1 **72–73** Library of Congress, Pennell Collection of Whistleriana, Washington, DC. Acc. No: LOT 15190, no.1 **74** Baltimore Museum of Art. The George A. Lucas Collection, purchased with funds from the State of Maryland, Laurence and Stella Bendann Fund, and contributions from individuals, foundations and corporations throughout the Baltimore community. Acc. No: BMA 1996.45.326. Photo Mitro Hood **75** The Metropolitan Museum of Art, New York. Purchase, Mr and Mrs Richard J. Bernhard Gift, by exchange, 1980. Acc. No: 1980.3 **76 A** Emil Bührle Collection, Zurich. Given by the heirs of Emil Bührle to the Foundation E. G. Bührle Collection Zurich, 1960. Inv. 44 **76 B** Musée des Beaux-Arts de Tournai. Bequest of Henri Van Cutsem, 1904 **77 C** Musée Carnavalet, Paris. Acc. No: PH8831 **76 D** © Peter Saville/New Order **78** Courtesy of Château de Rosa Bonheur, By-Thomery **79** Los Angeles County Museum of Art. Gift of Jane and Justin Dart. Acc. No: M.78.37 **80 A** Château de Rosa Bonheur, By-Thomery. Photo Patrick Escudero/Hemis/Alamy **81 B** Minneapolis Institute of Art. Gift of the Thomas Barlow Walker Foundation. Acc. No: 92.74 **81 C** The Metropolitan Museum of Art, New York. Gift of the artist, in memory of Rosa Bonheur, 1922. Acc. No: 22.222 **82–83** Courtesy of Château de Rosa Bonheur, By-Thomery **86** Musée d'Orsay, Paris. Acc. No: OD 21. Photo RMN-Grand Palais (musée d'Orsay)/ image RMN-GP **87** Musée d'Orsay, Paris. Acc. No: RF 1951 31. Photo RMN-Grand Palais (musée d'Orsay)/Hervé Lewandowski **88 A** Photo Alain Benainous/Gamma-Rapho via Getty Images **89 B** The Metropolitan Museum of Art, New York. The Walter H. and Leonore Annenberg Collection, Gift of Walter H. and Leonore Annenberg, 1997, Bequest of Walter H. Annenberg, 2002. Acc. No: 1997.60.1 **89 C** Emil Bührle Collection, Zurich. Given by the heirs of Emil Bührle to the Foundation E. G. Bührle Collection Zurich, 1960. Inv. 17 **90** Musée d'Orsay, Paris. Acc. No: ODO 1994 3. Photo RMN-Grand Palais (musée d'Orsay)/ Hervé Lewandowski **91** Harvard Art Museums/ Fogg Museum, Cambridge, MA. Bequest from the Collection of Maurice Wertheim, Class of 1906. Acc. No: 1951.47 **92 A** Musée d'Orsay, Paris. Acc. No: OD 91. Photo RMN-Grand Palais (musée d'Orsay)/Hervé Lewandowski **92 B** The Metropolitan Museum of Art, New York. Purchase, The Horace W. Goldsmith Foundation Gift, through Joyce and Robert Menschel and Rogers Fund, 2004. Acc. No: 2004.335 **93 C** Harvard Art Museums/Fogg Museum, Cambridge, MA. Bequest from the Collection of Maurice Wertheim, Class of 1906. Acc. No: 1951.68 **93 D** The Art Institute of Chicago. Bequest of Clara Margaret Lynch in memory of John A. Lynch. Acc. No: 1955.738 **94** Private Collection. Photo © Christie's Images Ltd 2023 **95** Wallraf-Richartz Museum, Cologne. Acc. No: WRM Dep. FC 614. Photo SuperStock/Christie's Images Ltd **96 A, B, 97 C** Private Collections **97 D** Musée Marmottan Monet, Paris. Annie Rouart's bequest, 1993. Acc. No: 6022 **98** Musée d'Orsay, Paris. Gift of Jean Renoir, 1954. Acc. No: RF 1954 30. Photo Gianni Dagli Orti/Shutterstock **99** The Art Institute of Chicago. Mr and Mrs Lewis Larned Coburn Memorial Collection. Acc. No: 1933.455 **100 A** Private Collection **101 B** Musée d'Orsay, Paris. Gift of Jean Renoir, 1954. Acc. No: RF1955-30. Photo RMN-Grand Palais (musée d'Orsay)/Gérard Blot **101 C** The Barnes Foundation, Philadelphia. Acc. No. BF475 **102** Musée d'Orsay, Paris. Gift of Paul Gachet, 1951. Acc. No: OD 30. Photo Leemage/Corbis via Getty Images **103** Kunstmuseum, Basel. Purchased in 1934. Acc. No: 1635 **104 A** The National Gallery of Art, Washington, DC. Collection of Mr and Mrs John Hay Whitney. Acc. No: 1998.74.5 **104 B** Musée d'Orsay, Paris. Acc. No: ODO31. Photo RMN-Grand Palais (musée d'Orsay)/ image GrandPalaisRmn **105 C** Musée Rodin, Paris. Acc. No: P.07302 **105 D** Van Gogh Museum, Amsterdam (Vincent van Gogh Foundation). Acc. No: b0244V1962v **106–107** Van Gogh Museum, Amsterdam (Vincent van Gogh Foundation). Acc. No: b515 V/1962 **108** Musée Gustave Moreau, Paris. Acc. No: 16257-51-1. Photo RMN-Grand Palais/ René-Gabriel Ojeda **109** Harvard Art Museums/ Fogg Museum, Cambridge, MA. Bequest of Grenville L. Winthrop. Acc. No: 1943.392 **110 A, B** Musée Gustave Moreau, Paris. Photo RMN-Grand Palais/Franck Raux **111 C** Private Collection **112–113** Musée Gustave Moreau, Paris. Photo RMN-Grand Palais/Franck Raux **114** Harvard Art Museums/Fogg Museum, Cambridge, MA. Gift of Miss Emily Sargent and Mrs Francis Ormond in memory of their brother, John Singer Sargent (through Thomas A. Fox, Esq.). Photo President and Fellows of Harvard College. Acc. No: 1933.49 **115** The Metropolitan Museum of Art, New York. Arthur Hoppock Hearn Fund, 1916. Acc. No: 16.53 **116 A** Harvard Art Museums/Fogg Museum, Cambridge, MA **116 B** Private Collection **117 C** Harvard Art Museums/ Fogg Museum, Cambridge, MA. Gift of Mrs Francis Ormond. Acc. No: 1937.7.27.1.A **117 D** Tate, London. Acc. No: N01615. Photo Tate **118** Musée d'Orsay, Paris. Acc. No: RF 1952 30. Photo RMN-Grand Palais (musée d'Orsay)/Hervé Lewandowski **119** National Gallery of Art, Washington, DC. Gift of Sam A. Lewisohn. Acc. No: 1951.5.1 **120 A** Kimbell Art Museum, Fort Worth. Acc. No: AP 1997.03 **120 B** Photo Albert Harlingue/Roger-Viollet/ Topfoto **121 C** Private Collection **121 D** National Gallery of Art, Washington, DC. Collection of Mr and Mrs Paul Mellon. Acc. No: 1983.1.19 **122** (above) Clark Art Institute, Williamstown, MA. Acquired by Sterling and Francine Clark before 1955. Acc. No: 1955.827 **122** (below) Private Collection **123** Staatsgalerie Stuttgart. Photo BPK, Berlin, Dist. RMN-Grand Palais/ image Staatsgalerie Stuttgart **124 A** The Metropolitan Museum of Art, New York. Gift of Katrin S. Vietor, in loving memory of Ernest G. Vietor, 1960. Acc. No: 60.174 **124 B** The National Gallery, London. Bought, Courtauld Fund, 1925. Acc. No: NG4119 **125 C** Dallas Museum of Art. The Wendy and Emery Reves Collection. Acc. No: 1985.R.44 **125 D** Ashmolean Museum, Oxford. Photo Heritage Image/ Alamy **126** Musée d'Orsay, Paris. Acc. No: OD 107. Photo RMN-Grand Palais (musée d'Orsay)/Tony Querrec **127** Musée d'Orsay, Paris. Bequest of John Quinn, 1927. Acc. No: RF 2511 **128 A** *Grammaire des arts du dessin*, by Charles Blanc, published by Jules Renouard, Paris, 1867 **128 B** *Cercle Chromatique*, by Charles Henry, published by Charles Verdin, Paris, 1888–89 **129 C** The National Gallery, London. Presented by Heinz Berggruen, 1995. Acc. No: NG6555 **129 D** The National Gallery, London. Bought, Courtauld Fund, 1924. Acc. No: NG3908 **130** James Ensor House/Mu.ZEE Collection, Oostende. Courtesy Collection City of Ostend. Photo Steven Decroos **131** Royal Museum of Fine Arts Antwerp (KMSKA). Acc. No: 3112. Photo Rik Klein Gotink **132 A** Museum of Fine Arts Ghent.

Acc. No: 2017-MT **133 B** Private Collection **133 C** Kimbell Art Museum, Fort Worth. Acc. No: AP 1981.20 **134** Bowdoin College Museum of Art, Brunswick, ME. Gift of the Homer Family. Acc. No: 1964.69.192.1 **135** Musée d'Orsay, Paris. Bought from Winslow Homer, 1900. Acc. No: RF 1977 427 Cleveland Museum of Art. Gift of J. H. Wade. Acc. No: 1924.195 **136 A** *Des Couleurs et de leurs applications aux arts industriels, à l'aide des cercles chromatiques*, by Eugène Chevreul, published by J. B. Baillière et Fils, Paris, 1864 **136 B** Bowdoin College Museum of Art, Brunswick, ME. Gift of the Homer Family. Acc. No: 1964.69.153.5 **137 C, D** Bowdoin College Museum of Art, Brunswick, ME. Gift of the Homer Family. Acc. No: 1964.69.192.1-2 and 1964.69.191 **137 E** National Gallery of Art, Washington, DC. John Davis Hatch Collection. Acc. No: 1979.20.57 **138** The Hirschsprung Collection, Copenhagen. Photo © The Hirschsprung Collection **139, 140 A, 141 B** Private Collections **141 C** The National Gallery of Denmark (SMK), Copenhagen. Acc. No: KMS7444 **144** Munch Museum, Oslo. Acc. No: MM.I.00994. Photo courtesy Munchmuseet **145** The National Museum, Oslo. Gift from Olaf Schou 1909. Acc. No: NG.M.00844 **146 A** Private Collection **146 B** The Rasmus Meyer Collection, The Bergen Art Museum **147 C** Munch Museum, Oslo. Photo courtesy Munchmuseet **147 D** *Man Visible and Invisible*, by C. W. Leadbeater, published by John Lane, The Bodley Head, New York, 1903 **148** Kindly loaned by Freunde Worpswedes, Käseglocke Collection. Courtesy Worpswede Tourist Information Center. Photo Rüdiger Lubricht **149, 150 A, B** Private Collections **151 C** Paula Modersohn-Becker Foundation, Bremen **151 D** Private Collection **152** Musée Marmottan Monet, Paris. Photo Bridgeman Images **153** The Art Institute of Chicago. Gift of Mrs Harvey Kaplan. Acc. No: 1982.825 **154 A, B** Private Collections **155 C** The Barnes Foundation, Philadelphia. Acc. No: BF730 **155 D** Tate, London. Acc. No: N04103. Photo Tate **156** Petit Palais, Musée des Beaux-Arts de la Ville de Paris. Acc. No: PPO3342. Photo RMN-Grand Palais/Agence Bulloz **157** Musée d'Orsay, Paris. Donation subject to usufruct, 2010. Acc. No: RF 2011 23 **158 A** Private Collection **159 B** Photo © IMEC, Fonds MCC, Dist. RMN-Grand Palais/Gisèle Freund **159 C** Kunstmuseum Bern. Legat von Eugen Loeb, Muri bei Bern, 1960 **160** Musée Matisse, Nice. Donated by Henri Matisse's heirs, 1960. Photo © François Fernandez **161** The Pushkin State Museum of Fine Arts, Moscow. Acc. No: 3299. © Succession H. Matisse/DACS 2024 **162 A** Photo Keystone-France/Gamma-Keystone via Getty Images © Succession H. Matisse/DACS 2024 **163 B** The Pushkin State Museum of Fine Arts, Moscow. Acc. No: 3295. © Succession H. Matisse/DACS 2024 **163 C** Musée Matisse, Nice. Gift of Henri Matisse's heirs, 1960. Photo © François Fernandez **164** Centre Pompidou, Paris. Bequest of Nina Kandinsky, 1981. Photo Centre Pompidou, MNAM-CCI, Dist. RMN-Grand Palais/Georges Meguerditchian **165** (above) Private Collection **165** (below) Lenbachhaus, Munich. Donation, 1957. Acc. No: GMS 446 **166 A** Centre Pompidou, Paris. Bequest of Nina Kandinsky, 1981. Photo Centre Pompidou, MNAM-CCI, Dist. RMN-Grand Palais/ Bertrand Prévost **166 B** Centre Pompidou, Paris. Bequest of Nina Kandinsky, 1981. Acc. No: AM 81-65-1282 **167 C** Courtesy Stockholms Auktionsverk **167 D** Photo Boris Lipnitzki/Roger-Viollet via Getty Images **168** Centre Pompidou, Paris. Photo Centre Pompidou, MNAM-CCI Bibliothèque Kandinsky, Paris, Dist. RMN-Grand Palais/ Fonds Kandinsky **169** Centre Pompidou, Paris. Bequest of Nina Kandinsky, 1981. Photo Centre Pompidou, MNAM-CCI, Dist. RMN-Grand Palais/Bertrand Prévost **170** Gabriele Münter and Johannes Eichner Foundation, Munich. Acc. No: D 63 **171** National Museum of Women in the Arts, Washington, DC. Gift of Wallace and Wilhelmina Holladay. Münter © DACS 2024 **172 A** Private Collection. Münter © DACS 2024 **172 B** Lenbachhaus, Munich. Donation, 1957. Acc. No: GMS 14 **173 C** Private Collection. Münter © DACS 2024 **174** Private Collection. Courtesy Ressler Kunst Auktionen, Vienna. Photo Klaus-Dieter Weber/ studio-weber.at **175** Neue Galerie Graz, Universalmuseum Joanneum. Acc. No: I/466 **176 A** Private Collection **176 B** The Belvedere, Vienna. Purchased by Robert Rieger, New York, 1950. Acc. No: 4438 **177 C** Leopold Museum, Vienna. Acc. No: 462 **177 D** Private Collection **177 E** The Belvedere, Vienna. Acc. No: 3917 **178** (above) The Georgia O'Keeffe Museum, Santa Fe. Gift of Juan and Anna Marie Hamilton. Acc. No: 2020.6.1. Photo © Georgia O'Keeffe Museum **178** (below) Private Collection **179** (above) Georgia O'Keeffe Museum, Santa Fe. Gift of The Burnett Foundation. Acc. No: 2007.1.6. © Georgia O'Keeffe Museum/DACS 2024 **179** (below) McNay Art Museum, San Antonio. Bequest of Helen Miller Jones. Acc. No: 1989.36. © Georgia O'Keeffe Museum/DACS 2024 **180 A** Photo © Todd Webb Archive. Painting © Georgia O'Keeffe Museum/DACS 2024 **180 B** The Georgia O'Keeffe Museum, Sante Fe. Gift of Juan and Anna Marie Hamilton. Acc. No: 2020.6.11. Photo © Georgia O'Keeffe Museum **181 C** Whitney Museum of American Art, New York. 50th Anniversary Gift of Sandra Payson. Acc. No: 85.47 **181 D** Photo Tony Vaccaro/Getty Images. Painting © Georgia O'Keeffe Museum/DACS 2024 **182** Edward Hopper House Museum & Study Center, Nyack. The Sanborn-Hopper Family Archive. Photo Dan Swindel **183** Private Collection **184 A** Whitney Museum of American Art, New York. Josephine N. Hopper Bequest. Acc. No: 70.1650. © Heirs of Josephine Hopper/ Licensed by Artists Rights Society (ARS) NY/ DACS, London 2024 **184 B** Edward Hopper House Museum & Study Center, Nyack. The Sanborn-Hopper Family Archive. Photo Paul Mutino **185 C** National Gallery of Art, Washington, DC. Gift of Herbert A. Goldstone. Acc. No: 1996.130.2 **185 D** Whitney Museum of American Art, New York. Gift of Lloyd Goodrich. 96.208. Photo Whitney Museum of American Art/Licensed by Scala. © Heirs of Josephine Hopper/ Licensed by Artists Rights Society (ARS) NY/DACS, London 2024 **186–187** Art Institute of Chicago. Friends of American Art Collection. Acc. No: 1942.51 **190** Fundació Miró Mallorca. Photo Estate of Evelyn Hofer/Getty Images **191** Kimbell Art Museum, Fort Worth. Acquired with the generous assistance of a grant from Mr and Mrs Perry R. Bass. © Successió Miró/ADAGP, Paris and DACS London 2024 **192 A** The Menil Collection, Houston. Acc. No: 1978-158 E. © Successió Miró/ADAGP, Paris and DACS London 2024 **192 B** Fundació Miró Mallorca. Photo Estate of Evelyn Hofer/Getty Images. © Successió Miró/ADAGP, Paris and DACS London 2024 **193 C** Fundació Joan Miró, Barcelona. Acc. No: FJM 7383. Photo Fundació Joan Miró, Barcelona. © Successió Miró/ ADAGP, Paris and DACS London 2024 **193 D** Fundació Miró Mallorca. Photo Estate of Evelyn Hofer/Getty Images. © Successió Miró/ ADAGP, Paris and DACS London 2024 **194** Musée des Beaux-Arts, Rouen. Inv. AG.1975.4.5598. Photo Y. Deslandes/Réunion des Musées Métropolitains Rouen Normandie **195** The Menil Collection, Houston. Acc. No: V 304. © ADAGP, Paris and DACS, London 2024 **196 A** Photo Pictorial Press Ltd/Alamy. Braque © ADAGP, Paris and DACS, London 2024 **196 B** Tate, London. Acc. No: P77198. Photo Tate. Braque © ADAGP, Paris and DACS, London 2024 **197 C** Kreeger Museum, Washington, DC. Braque © ADAGP, Paris and DACS, London 2024 **197 D** Photo Boris Lipnitzki/Roger Viollet via Getty Images. Braque © ADAGP, Paris and DACS, London 2024 **198** Courtesy Kunstmuseum Den Haag **199** Tate, London. Acc. No: T00648. Photo Tate **200 A** Museum Boijmans Van Beuningen, Rotterdam. Gift A. P. van Hoey Smith, 1928. Acc. No: 1543 (MK). Photo Studio Tromp **200 B** Private Collection. Photo Rogi André **201 C** The Art Institute of Chicago. Gift of Dorothy Braude Edinburg to the Harry B. and Bessie K. Braude Memorial Collection. Acc. No2013.984 **201 D** Museum of Modern Art, New York. Gift of Mr and Mrs William A. M. Burden. Acc. No: 510.1964 **202** Private Collection. Photo akg-images **203** Museum Ludwig, Cologne. Acc. No: ML 01587. Photo Rheinisches Bildarchiv, Cologne. Picasso © Succession Picasso/DACS, London 2024 **204 A** Philadelphia Museum of Art. A. E. Gallatin Collection, 1950. Acc. No: 1950-1-1. Picasso © Succession Picasso/DACS, London 2024 **204 B** The National Museum of Modern Art, Kyoto. Acc. No: O00101. Picasso © Succession Picasso/DACS, London 2024 **205 C, D** Musée national Picasso, Paris. Acc. No: MP1990-115 and MP3671. Photo RMN-Grand Palais/Mathieu Rabeau. Picasso © Succession Picasso/DACS, London 2024 **206** The Metropolitan Museum of Art, New York. The Pierre and Maria-Gaetana Matisse Collection, 2002. Acc. No: 2002.456.129. Photo The Metropolitan Museum of Art/ Art Resource/Scala, Florence **207** Private Collection. Chagall © ADAGP, Paris and DACS, London 2024 **208 A** Photo Bildarchiv Pisarek/akg-images **208 B** Private Collection. Chagall © ADAGP, Paris and DACS, London 2024 **209 C** Private Collection. Chagall © ADAGP, Paris and DACS, London 2024 **209 D** Private Collection. Photo SuperStock/ Christie's Images Ltd. Chagall © ADAGP, Paris and DACS, London 2024 **210** Private Collection. Photo © Trustees of Winifred Nicholson **211** Private Collection. Photo SuperStock/Christie's Images Ltd. © Trustees of Winifred Nicholson **212 A, B** Private Collections. © Trustees of Winifred Nicholson **213 C, D** Private Collections. © Trustees of Winifred Nicholson **214** Photo © Fundació Gala-Salvador Dalí, Figueres **215** The Dalí Museum, St. Petersburg, FL. Gift of A. Reynolds & Eleanor Morse. Acc. No: 2007.10. © Salvador Dalí, Fundació Gala-Salvador Dalí, DACS 2024 **216 A** Private Collection. Photo akg-images/François Guénet. © Salvador Dalí, Fundació Gala-Salvador Dalí, DACS 2024 **216 B** The Solomon R. Guggenheim Foundation Peggy Guggenheim Collection, Venice, 1976. Acc. No: 76.2553.100. © Salvador Dalí, Fundació Gala-Salvador Dalí, DACS 2024 **217 C** Photo Philippe Halsman/Toronto Star via Getty Images. © Fundació Gala-Salvador Dalí, Figueres **217 D** Photo Michael Ochs Archives/Getty Images. Paintings © Salvador Dalí, Fundació Gala-Salvador Dalí, DACS 2024 **218–219** Photo Alexander Liberman © J. Paul Getty Trust, Getty Research Institute, Los Angeles. Acc. No: 2000.R.19. Painting © Helen Frankenthaler Foundation, Inc./ARS, NY and DACS, London 2024 **220 A** Photo Gordon Parks/The LIFE Picture Collection/ Shutterstock. Paintings © Helen Frankenthaler Foundation, Inc./ARS, NY and DACS, London 2024 **221 B** Photo Ernst Haas/Hulton Archive/ Getty Images **221 C** ASOM Collection, Liechtenstein. © Helen Frankenthaler Foundation, Inc./ARS, NY and DACS, London 2024 **221 D** Private Collection. © Helen Frankenthaler Foundation, Inc./ARS, NY and DACS, London 2024 **222** Courtesy Francis Bacon MB Art Foundation, Monaco **223** Centre Pompidou, Paris. Donation Louise and Michel Leiris, 1984. Acc. No: AM 1984-487. © The Estate of Francis Bacon. All rights reserved. DACS 2024 **224 A** Photo Michael Holtz/ Photo 12/Alamy **225 B** Tate, London. Acc. No: N06171. Photo Tate. © The Estate of Francis Bacon. All rights reserved. DACS 2024 **226–227** Hugh Lane Gallery, Dublin. © The Estate of Francis Bacon. All rights reserved, DACS/Artimage 2024. Photo Perry Ogden **228** Private Collection. Photo courtesy Evan Bowman **229** Private Collection. © The Lucian Freud Archive. All Rights Reserved 2024/Bridgeman Images **230 A** Private Collection. Photo Christie's Images/Bridgeman Images **230 B** Photo © David Dawson. All rights reserved 2024/Bridgeman Images **231 C** Private Collection. © The Lucian Freud Archive. All Rights Reserved 2024/Bridgeman Images **232** Courtesy Bridget Riley Studio, photo Terry Buchanan. Painting © Bridget Riley **233** Private Collection. © Bridget Riley **234 A** Tate, London. Acc. No: T04132. Photo courtesy Bridget Riley Studio. © Bridget Riley **235 B** Courtesy Bridget Riley Studio, photo Bill Warhurst. Painting © Bridget Riley **235 C** Maclaurin Art Gallery, Rozelle House, Ayr. Acc. No: AYRAG:001270 © Bridget Riley **236** Photo Allan Tannenbaum/Polaris/eyevine. © Keith Haring Foundation **237** Private Collection. © Keith Haring Foundation **238 A** Photo James Leynse/Corbis via Getty Images. © Keith Haring Foundation **238 B** Photo Patrick Piel/Gamma-Rapho via Getty Images. © Keith Haring Foundation **239 C** Private Collection. © Keith Haring Foundation **239 D** Photo Mark Hinjosa/Newsday LLC via Getty Images. © Keith Haring Foundation **240** Private Collection. Photo © Paula Rego. All rights reserved 2024/ Bridgeman Images **241** Leeds Art Gallery. Acc. No: LEEAG.PA.1994.0012. © Paula Rego. All rights reserved 2024/Bridgeman Images **242 A** Private Collection. © Paula Rego. All rights reserved 2024/Bridgeman Images **243 B, C** Private Collections. © Paula Rego. All rights reserved 2024/Bridgeman Images **244–245** Yale University Art Gallery, New Haven. Purchased with the Janet and Simeon Braguin Fund and a gift from Jacqueline L. Bradley, B.A. 1979. 2009.161.1. Courtesy the artist and David Zwirner, London. © Kerry James Marshall **246 A** Private Collection. Collection of Charlotte and Herbert S. Wagner III. Courtesy the artist and David Zwirner, London. © Kerry James Marshall **247 B** Museum of Contemporary Art Chicago. Gift of Katherine S. Schamberg by exchange. Acc. No: 2009.15. Courtesy the artist and David Zwirner, London. © Kerry James Marshall **247 C** The Metropolitan Museum of Art, New York. Purchase, The Jacques and Natasha Gelman Foundation Gift, Acquisitions Fund and The Metropolitan Museum of Art Multicultural Audience Development Initiative Gift, 2015. Acc. No: 2015.366. Courtesy the artist and David Zwirner, London. © Kerry James Marshall

Acknowledgments

Thank you, Julian Bell, for gifting me a book that was yet unwritten, by introducing me to Jane Laing, Commissioning Editor at Thames & Hudson. Without Jane's calm and professional guidance, I would not have been able to write *The Artist's Palette*. Special thanks go to Assistant Editor Florence Allard and Picture Researcher Lise Seguin, who worked tirelessly to make this book happen, and to Creative Director Tristan de Lancey for his vision and passion. I have never worked with a nicer and more supportive editorial team. I must apologize to Jeremy Page and Flora Loske-Page for spending so many weekends and nights on yet another book. Thank you for indulging, feeding and watering me. I began writing this in a beautiful villa in Dresden I had last visited as a child. Thank you, Matthias Simmank, for inviting me to stay there again. As the book developed, I kept thinking of Eva Bodinet, a true artist, and a constant source of inspiration to me. This is for you, Eva.

About the Author

Alexandra Loske is a British–German art historian, writer, and museum curator. Originally from the Rhineland, she now lives in East Sussex, England, and is the Curator of the Royal Pavilion in Brighton. She read English and Linguistics at Humboldt University, Berlin, and Art History at the University of Sussex, UK, where she also received her DPhil in Art History. Loske has authored, edited, and co-authored many books and articles on colour and other subjects, including *Colour: A Visual History*, *The Book of Colour Concepts*, and *A Cultural History of Color in the Age of Industry*. She is a Research Associate at the School of Media, Arts and Humanities at the University of Sussex, where she is researching the role of women in the history of colour.

FRONT COVER Wassily Kandinsky's palette, 1933–44, paint on wood (also on page 164)

BACK COVER
Top left: Vincent van Gogh's palette, *c.* 1890, paint on wood, 35 × 27 cm (13 ⅞ × 10 ¾ in.) (also on page 102)
Top centre: Henri Matisse's palette, undated, oil on wood (walnut), 48.5 × 38 cm (19 ⅛ × 15 in.) (also on page 160)
Top right: Georges Seurat's palette, undated, oil on wood, 27 × 36 cm (10 ¾ × 14 ¼ in.) (also on page 126)
Middle left: Claude Monet's palette, undated, paint on wood, 32.5 × 51 cm (12 ⅞ × 20 ⅛ in.) (also on page 152)
Middle centre: Paula Modersohn-Becker's last palette, 1907, paint on wood and metal (also on page 148)
Middle right: Paula Rego's palette, undated, paint on wood (also on page 240)
Bottom left: Marc Chagall's palette, 1974, paint on wood, 37.5 × 48 cm (14 ¾ × 18 ⅞ in.) (also on page 206)
Bottom centre: John Constable's palette, undated, paint on wood, 40.5 × 24.5 cm (16 × 9 ¾ in.) (also on page 46)

Bottom right: Plate used as a palette by Francis Bacon in his studio at 14 rue de Birague, Paris, France, 1974–87, paint on ceramic (also on page 222)

PAGE 2 Frontispiece of T. H. Fielding, *On Painting in Oil and Water Colours*, 1839

PAGES 6–7 Jean-Baptiste-Siméon Chardin, *The Attributes of the Arts and the Rewards Which Are Accorded Them*, 1766, oil on canvas, 113 × 145.4 cm (44 ½ × 57 ¼ in.)

PAGE 24 John Constable's palette (detail), undated, paint on wood, 40.5 × 24.5 cm (16 × 9 ¾ in.)

PAGE 84 Georges Seurat's palette (detail), undated, oil on wood, 27 × 36 cm (10 ¾ × 14 ¼ in.)

PAGE 142 Henri Matisse's palette (detail), undated, oil on wood (walnut), 48.5 × 38 cm (19 ⅛ × 15 in.)

PAGE 188 Pablo Picasso's palette (detail), 17 June 1961, oil on card, 29 × 37.8 cm (11 ½ × 15 in.)

First published in the United States of America and Canada in 2024 by Princeton University Press
41 William Street, Princeton, New Jersey 08540
press.princeton.edu

Published by arrangement with Thames & Hudson Ltd, London

First published in the United Kingdom in 2024 by Thames & Hudson Ltd, 181A High Holborn, London WC1V 7QX

The Artist's Palette © 2024 by Thames & Hudson Ltd, London

Text © 2024 by Alexandra Loske

For image copyright information see pages 252–53

Designed by Daniel Streat, Visual Fields

Library of Congress Control Number 2024931585

ISBN 978-0-691-26396-0

Printed and bound in China by C&C Offset Printing Co. Ltd

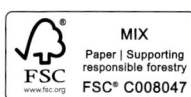

10 9 8 7 6 5 4 3 2 1

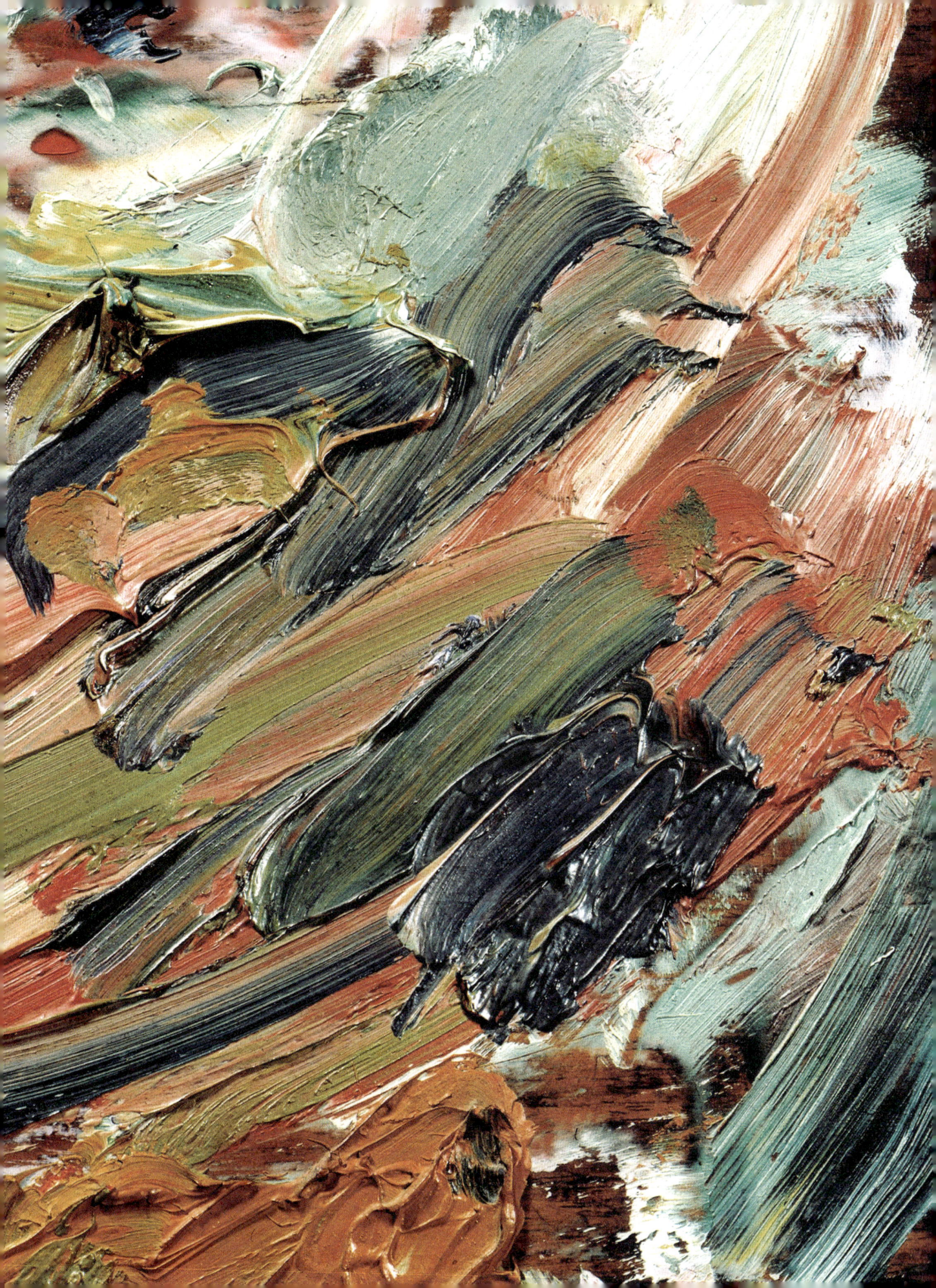

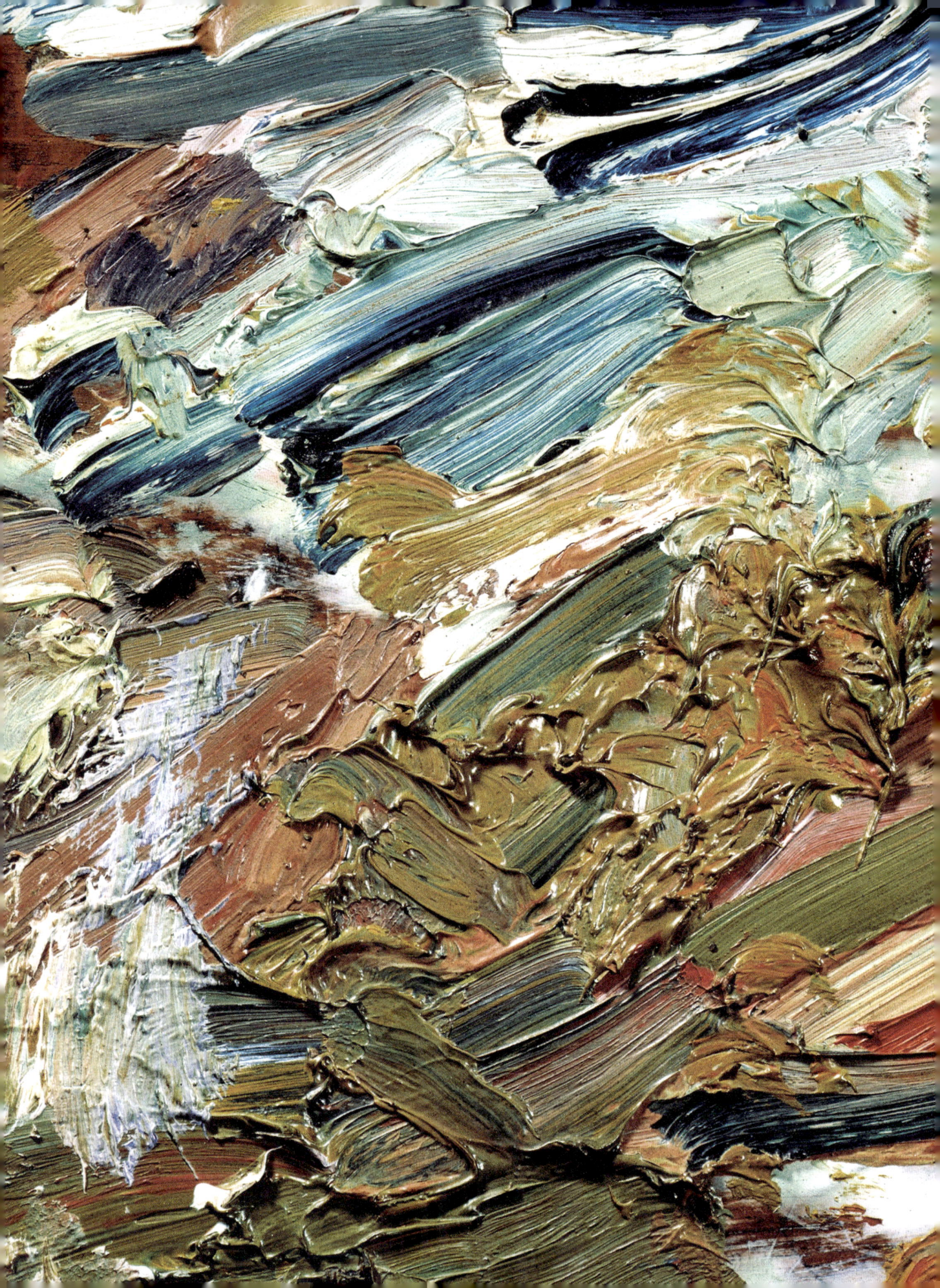